lonely planet

Washington, Oregon & the Pacific Northwest

Vancouver, Whistler &
Vancouver Island
p370

Northwestern Washington
& the San Juan Islands
p94

Seattle
p62

Olympic Peninsula &
Washington Coast
p121

Washington
Cascades
p152

Central
& Eastern
Washington
p185

Portland
p214

Columbia
River Gorge
p262

The Willamette
Valley & Wine
Country
p243

Central
Oregon &
the Oregon
Cascades
p275

Eastern
Oregon
p346

Oregon
Coast
p293

Ashland &
Southern Oregon
p325

THIS EDITION WRITTEN AND RESEARCHED BY

Sandra Bao,
Celeste Brash, John Lee, Brendan Sainsbury

Contents

MT RAINIER NATIONAL PARK P172

SPACE NEEDLE P71

ALAN MAJCHROWICZ/GETTY IMAGES ©

GLENN VAN DER KNIJFF/GETTY IMAGES ©

Contents

SPECIAL FEATURES

Welcome to the Pacific Northwest

Lush forests, a pristine coastline, awesome food, frothy microbrews, and music and art galore – Pacific Northwesterners have it good and they don't mind sharing.

Outdoor Adventures

You can't escape nature here. Even the big cities are punctuated by looming, snowy peaks: Seattle's Mt Rainier, Portland's Mt Hood and Vancouver's North Shore Mountains. Not to mention the raging rivers, rolling deserts, dense old-growth forests and glorious public beaches that are never far from any urban landscape.

The region offers endless outdoor opportunities: camping, hiking, cycling, skiing and mountaineering. And all that rain translates into a perfect storm of water sports; raft white water, kayak lake and sea, and kiteboard through ripping winds.

Foodies & Locavores

Seattle, Portland and Vancouver are all rich in gourmet restaurants, as well as a wide range of ethnic foods. Seattle boasts a long-established history of Northwest cuisine, while Portland's affordability has made it a relatively recent magnet for hot chefs. Vancouver offers some of the best Chinese food outside, well, China.

There's an abundance of locally grown food, from berries and hazelnuts to wild mushrooms, seafood, cheese and grass-fed beef. Locavores abound, getting their fix in the many specialty groceries, farmers markets and community gardens.

Beer, Wine & Coffee

In these parts, beverages are big. The nation's gourmet-coffee scene may have started in Seattle, but dozens of artisan microroasters across the Northwest now produce some of the best espresso in the world. In some coffee shops, pouring a latte is practically an art form.

Microbrewing also became famous here, within a stone's throw of the nation's highest concentration of hop farms. Today, craft brewers pump out fragrant India Pale Ales (IPAs) and more. Grapevines cover many hills, producing a harvest of intriguing reds and whites.

Art & Culture

There's no shortage of urban entertainment and culture: indie garage bands, world-class symphonies, jazz bars and an abundance of public art. Offbeat film houses and art galleries are tucked into even the smallest towns.

Seattle, Portland and Vancouver all support symphonies, operas, dance troupes and theater companies. Galleries and museums display pieces by Native American artists, ceramicists and painters, and glassmakers inspired by Tacoma's Dale Chihuly. You'll always have more than enough to appreciate in this highly creative part of the world.

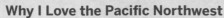

Why I Love the Pacific Northwest

By Sandra Bao, Author

Even after a decade of living in the Pacific Northwest, I'm still in awe of its vibrant beauty and uniqueness. Verdant forests cover every mountain, gorgeous snowcapped volcanoes dot the Cascades and the coastline is simply spectacular. The big cities offer everything that any visitor could want: cutting-edge museums, fine entertainment and some of the best food (and drink) in the world. People are pretty friendly, fiercely opinionated and ultimately very proud to belong to this amazing region – as I am.

For more about our authors, see page 488

Washington, Oregon & the Pacific Northwest

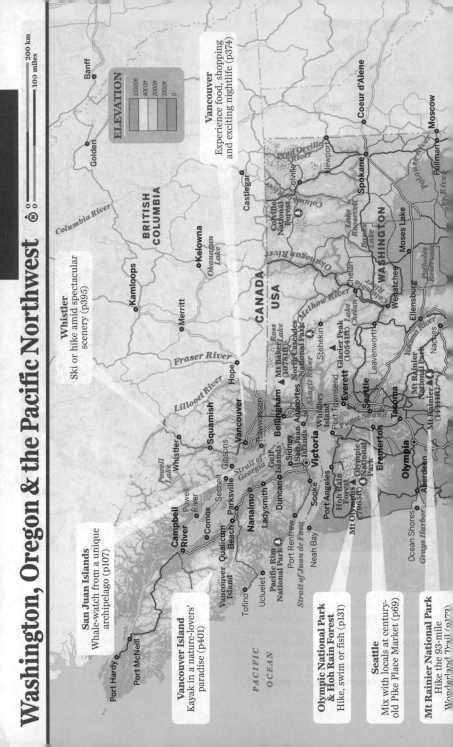

San Juan Islands
Whale-watch from a unique archipelago (p107)

Vancouver Island
Kayak in a nature-lovers' paradise (p401)

Olympic National Park & Hoh Rain Forest
Hike, swim or fish (p131)

Seattle
Mix with locals at century-old Pike Place Market (p69)

Mt Rainier National Park
Hike the 93-mile Wonderland Trail (p172)

Whistler
Ski or hike amid spectacular scenery (p395)

Vancouver
Experience food, shopping and exciting nightlife (p374)

ELEVATION

10000ft
4000ft
2000ft
1000ft
0

100 miles
200 km

BRITISH COLUMBIA

CANADA
USA

WASHINGTON

PACIFIC OCEAN

Banff
Golden
Columbia River
Kamloops
Merritt
Kelowna
Okanagan Lake
Castlegar
Colville
Colville National Forest
Newport
Pend Oreille River
Spokane
Lake Roosevelt
Columbia River
Moscow
Pullman
Palouse River
Snake River
Coeur d'Alene
Moses Lake
Potholes Reservoir
Banks Lake
Wenatchee
Ellensburg
Leavenworth
Chelan
Lake Chelan
Methow River
Glacier Peak (10541ft)
Stehekin
North Cascades National Park
Mt Baker (10781ft)
Ross Lake
Skagit River
Hope
Fraser River
Lillooet River
Squamish
Whistler
Powell Lake
Gibsons
Sechelt
Powell River
Campbell River
Comox
Qualicum Beach
Parksville
Nanaimo
Ladysmith
Duncan
Gulf Islands
Sidney
San Juan Islands
Anacortes
Bellingham
Tsawwassen
Vancouver
Strait of Georgia
Port Hardy
Port McNeill
Vancouver Island
Tofino
Ucluelet
Pacific Rim National Park
Port Renfrew
Strait of Juan de Fuca
Neah Bay
Sooke
Victoria
Port Angeles
Port Townsend
Whidbey Island
Everett
Seattle
Puget Sound
Bremerton
Tacoma
Olympia
Aberdeen
Grays Harbor
Ocean Shores
Hoh Rain Forest
Mt Olympus (7965ft)
Olympic National Park
Mt Rainier National Park
Mt Rainier (14410ft)
Naches
Yakima River

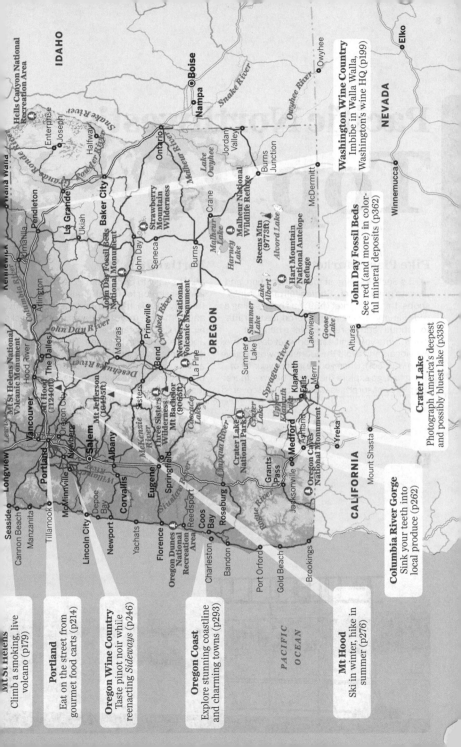

Mt St Helens
Climb a smoking, live volcano (p179)

Portland
Eat on the street from gourmet food carts (p214)

Oregon Wine Country
Taste pinot noir while reenacting *Sideways* (p246)

Oregon Coast
Explore stunning coastline and charming towns (p293)

Mt Hood
Ski in winter; hike in summer (p276)

Columbia River Gorge
Sink your teeth into local produce (p262)

Crater Lake
Photograph America's deepest and possibly bluest lake (p338)

John Day Fossil Beds
See red (and more) in colorful mineral deposits (p362)

Washington Wine Country
Imbibe in Walla Walla, Washington's wine HQ (p199)

IDAHO

NEVADA

OREGON

CALIFORNIA

PACIFIC OCEAN

Hells Canyon National Recreation Area

Boise

Nampa

Elko

Winnemucca

Owyhee

McDermitt

Burns Junction

Jordan Valley

Ontario

Snake River

Owyhee River

Lake Owyhee

Malheur River

Enterprise

Joseph

Halfway

Pendleton

La Grande

Baker City

Ukiah

Umatilla

Grande Ronde River

Powder River

Walla Walla

Columbia River

Arlington

Hood River

The Dalles

Vancouver

Portland

Longview

Seaside

Cannon Beach

Manzanita

Tillamook

McMinnville

Newberg

Oregon City

Salem

Albany

Corvallis

Eugene

Springfield

Lincoln City

Depoe Bay

Newport

Yachats

Florence

Reedsport

Coos Bay

Charleston

Bandon

Port Orford

Gold Beach

Brookings

Madras

Prineville

Bend

Sisters

La Pine

Roseburg

Grants Pass

Jacksonville

Medford

Ashland

Yreka

Mount Shasta

Klamath Falls

Merrill

Lakeview

Alturas

Summer Lake

Burns

John Day

Seneca

Crane

Steens Mtn (9775ft)

Alvord Lake

Harney Lake

Malheur Lake

Lake Albert

Summer Lake

Goose Lake

Upper Klamath Lake

Crater Lake National Park

Oregon Caves National Monument

Newberry National Volcanic Monument

Crater Lake

Mt Bachelor (9065ft)

Three Sisters Wilderness

Mt Jefferson (10495ft)

Mt Hood (12240ft)

Mt St Helens National Volcanic Monument

John Day Fossil Beds National Monument

Strawberry Mountain Wilderness

Malheur National Wildlife Refuge

Hart Mountain National Antelope Refuge

Oregon Dunes National Recreation Area

John Day River

Deschutes River

Crooked River

McKenzie River

Willamette River

Umpqua River

Rogue River

Siuslaw River

Sprague River

Cascade Lake

Lewis River

Columbia River

Snake River

Lake

John Day River

PACIFIC OCEAN

Pacific Northwest's
Top 25

Pike Place Market

 It's Seattle's biggest tourist attraction, and with great reason. Stuffed full of fun, funky shops, this old market (p69) has been selling a wide variety of wares – from produce to crafts to antiques and more – for over a hundred years. Time your visit early on weekdays to mix with locals and avoid the tourist crowds (you've been warned!). Once you've gotten your fill of flying fish, go explore the mazes below – there are plenty of surprises waiting to be discovered.

Portland

2 It's easy to brag about PDX, but no one w hassle you for it – after all, everyone love this city (p214). It's as friendly as a big town and home to a mix of students, artists, cyclis hipsters, young families, old hippies, ecofrea and everything in between. There's great foo awesome music and plenty of culture, plus it as sustainable as you can get. Come and visi but be careful: like everyone else, you might just want to pack up and move here.

Vancouver, BC

3 As big cities go, it's hard to get more sophisticated, international or beautiful than Vancouver (p374). Host of the 2010 Winter Olympics, this metropolis has it all: awesome food, trendy shopping, cool neighborhoods and exciting nightlife. There's so much to do – from visiting museums and art galleries to cycling and kayaking – that it'll make your head spin. And it's all framed by glorious mountains, forests and waterways, so there's always beauty in the background.

Washington Wine Country

4 Washington is the second-largest wine producing US state. Although its vines are relatively young, the terroir (environmental qualities) of Walla Walla (p199) is excellent, with rich layers of sediment from the long-ago Missoula floods. It's Washington's equivalent of California's Napa Valley, with a historic downtown and upscale tourist services. For a less primped-up wine destination, head out to the Yakima Valley (p193 or Spokane (p204), making sure to try the specialty reds of cabernet sauvignon, syrah and merlot.

MICHAEL DEFREITAS/GETTY IMAGES ©

BRUCE FORSTER/GETTY IMAGES ©

San Juan Islands

5 For something completely different, hop on a ferry to the San Juan Islands (p107)...and go back in time. Out of more than 450 'islands' (most are only rocky promontories), about 60 are inhabited, and just four are regularly served by ferries. Nature is the main influence in this archipelago and each island has its own personality, both geographic and cultural. What can you do here? Start with cycling, kayaking and spotting orcas – then just sit back and relax. Lime Kiln Lighthouse (p109)

Oregon Coast

6 Cruising along Oregon's stunning coast (p293) is an unforgettable experience at any time of year. Lofty headlands reach out to the ocean, offering spectacular views, while steep mountains of rock jut offshore like giant sentinels. There are beaches to walk on, dunes to explore and charming small towns to check out. And if you like camping, tide-pooling or whale-watching, you'll be in heaven. Just remember to bring your camera...and a sense of adventure.
Haystack Rock (p301), Cannon Beach

Microbreweries

7 Love beer? Welcome to paradise. The Pacific Northwest has some of the best microbrew in the world, and plenty of it (p447). In fact, Portland (aka 'Beervana') holds the distinguished record of 'most microbreweries of any city in the world.' And it shows – you can hardly cycle down any trendy street and not pedal past a bar serving the stuff. Seattle and Vancouver are no slouches, either: you'll find plenty of great choices there. So raise a pint and toast to 'buying local' – and feel good in more ways than one.

Portland Food Carts

8 Eat at a Portland food cart (p231)! They're good, cheap and locally owned, and the choices are endless: sandwiches, soups, pizza, pasta, waffles, pies, crepes. And they're international: Indian, Japanese, Peruvian, Thai, Cuban, Czech, Hawaiian...there are even Paleo-diet and gluten-free carts. Don't think you'll be getting run-of-the-mill grub – expect creations such as duck-confit sandwiches, beef goulash, chicken-coconut curry, vegan barbecue, kimchi quesadillas and fried risotto balls. Keep an eye out for these mobile trailers, and stop by for a bite.

Whistler

9 Love to ski? Then you'll be crazy abou Whistler (p395), a top-notch resort adored by celebrities and the jet set. This Canadian hot spot hosted a good chunk of the 2010 Winter Olympics, including the heart-stopping alpine-skiing events. Boasting 200 runs, it's one of North America's largest ski areas (the slopes are oper from November to June). But the mountains here aren't just for snow sports. In summer you can hike, mountain bike, raft and rock climb among some of the most spectacular scenery in Canada.

Oregon Wine Country

10 Pinot noir was Oregon's specialty grape long before the film *Sideways* pushed it into the limelight. Cruise the roads around the towns of Newberg, Dundee and McMinnville, at the heart of Oregon's wine country (p247), and sample chardonnay, riesling and pinot gris, along with the star grape. If you'd like to stay longer than a day there are plenty of B&Bs, along with some gourmet restaurants – all of which offer even more opportunities to sample the Dionysian nectar.

Live Music

11 Pacific Northwesterners love their live music (p442). This was, after all, the birthplace of grunge, and indie bands are a dime a dozen. Bluegrass and old-time music thrive in Portland, while Seattle has a happening rock and jazz scene, and Vancouver's highly diverse ethnic population means that anything goes. Outdoor concerts abound: don't miss Seattle's Bumbershoot, Portland's Waterfront Blues Festival and Vancouver's Folk Music Festival.
Crowd at Bumbershoot festival (p77)

Hot Springs

12 With its volcanic geography, you'd expect the Pacific Northwest to have some good hot springs – and you'd be right. There are springs in BC, and Washington has its popular Sol Duc resort (p133), with decent services and family-friendly pools. Oregon, however, has many more popular hot springs. Try Bagby (p252) or Umpqua (p337) for rustic soaks; Breitenbush (p252), Belknap (p260) or Crystal Crane (p366) for more services without being too fancy; and Bonneville Hot Springs Resort & Spa (p267) for the ultimate in luxury. And don't forget your rubber ducky.

Space Needle

13 Many visitors can't leave Seattle without heading to the top of the needle (p71), the city's most distinctive symbol and landmark. Why? From more than 500ft up you'll get views of everything, from downtown to Puget Sound to the Cascades and Mt Rainier. You can even break the bank at the rotating restaurant up top, but don't fool yourself – the best thing here is that 'I'm at the top of the world' feeling you get as the city seems to slowly spin around you.

Olympic National Park & Hoh Rain Forest

14 One of Washington state's premier tourist attractions, Olympic National Park (p131) takes up a huge chunk of the Olympic Peninsula and boasts its own mini-rainforest (p136). Hike through old-growth forests draped with moss, waltz through meadows filled with wildflowers, swim in pure mountain lakes or try to summit Mt Olympus. You can even go trout fishing, beachcombing, hot-springs soaking and cross-country skiing, all within the park's official boundaries, which include a thin strip along the Pacific Ocean.

Mt Rainier National Park

15 When the skies are clear, Mt Rainier looms high over Seattle, creating an amazing backdrop to the Emerald City. Still a live volcano, the 14,411ft peak is the shining centerpiece of this national park (p172), which offers a rare inland temperate rainforest, hikes through alpine wildflower meadows and the famous 93-mile Wonderland Trail. If you're fit and adventurous enough, attempt to climb the peak itself; just be ready to traverse some of the largest glaciers outside Alaska.

Orcas

16 Spotting a pod of majestic killer whales, also known as orcas, can make your day! And there's hardly a better place to do it than around Washington's Puget Sound. Take a boat tour from Friday Harbor (p108), on San Juan Island, where resident pods (totaling about 90 whales) frolic and hunt for salmon. Here, sightings are nearly guaranteed in summer. Or plant yourself at Lime Kiln Point State Park (p109) and get lucky from the shoreline. On Vancouver Island, Telegraph Cove (p423) is another exceptional jumping-off point from which to spot these great beasts.

15

16

Mt Hood

17 Oregon's highest peak, Mt Hood (11,240ft; p276) is a recreational wonderland. In winter there's skiing at four resorts (including one with the longest year-round season in North America), while in summer glorious hiking trails and campgrounds abound. Or test your climbing mettle and head to the top – Mt Hood is the second-most-climbed peak over 10,000ft in the world. Whatever you do, stop in for a drink or meal at Timberline Lodge (p280), whose facade was the star of the movie *The Shining*.

John Day Fossil Beds

18 It's hard to believe that hillsides can be so colorful, until you visit this amazing site (p362). Kaleidoscopic layers of red, gold, orange and brown mineral deposits decorate the landscape, and the hues can change dramatically. There are fossils, too – the bones of small horses, rhinos, primates and sabertooth-like cats have been (and are still being) uncovered. It's like an eerie moon surface, all created by volcanic eruptions and erosion over millions of years, and named after a man famous for getting robbed and stripped naked by Native Americans.

Columbia River Gorge

19 Carved out by the mighty Columbia as the Cascades uplifted, the Columbia River Gorge (p262) is a geologic marvel. With Washington state on its north side and Oregon to its south, the state-dividing gorge offers countless waterfalls and spectacular hikes, as well as agricultural bounties of apples, pears and cherries. And if you're into windsurfing or kiteboarding, then head straight to the sporty town of Hood River (p267), ground zero for these extreme sports. Whether you're a hiker, fruit-lover or adrenaline junkie, the gorge delivers.

Oregon Shakespeare Festival

20 The Shakespearean plays at this famous festival (p329) run from February to October, but this doesn't mean you shouldn't hurry to snag a ticket – performances sell out weeks in advance. There are three venues, but try for a play at the outdoor Elizabethan Theatre, which has to be the most dramatic setting in town; it's a replica of London's 17th-century Fortune Theatre. You might just feel like the Bard himself is nearby, overseeing the actors performing his masterpieces.

Coffee

21 You're unlikely to find better coffee (p448) anywhere in the world than in the Pacific Northwest. A huge number of coffee shops brew up rich espressos, creamy lattes, frothy cappuccinos and chocolaty mochas. But it's the specialty roasters you shouldn't miss – be sure to try Stumptown Coffee in Portland. And do hang out in some coffee shops; it's the perfect Pacific Northwesterly thing to do, whether you're sitting at a sunny sidewalk table or keeping warm inside when the rain pours down.

22

23

ML HARRIS/GETTY IMAGES ©

Native American Culture

22 Evidence of once-thriving Native American groups can be seen throughout the Pacific Northwest, but some of the best-known sites are Seattle's Pioneer Square (p66) and Vancouver's Stanley Park (including the iconic totem poles; p375). For exceptional exhibits, check out Vancouver's UBC Museum of Anthropology; Seattle's Burke Museum; Spokane's Northwest Museum of Arts & Culture; Eugene's University of Oregon Museum of Natural & Cultural History; and the Warm Springs Museum in Central Oregon. Totem pole

Crater Lake National Park

23 Beautiful doesn't begin to describe Crater Lake (p338). It's serene, sublime, transcendent – in other words, it might just blow your mind. A 6-mile-wide caldera created when Mt Mazama erupted nearly 8000 years ago, this amazingly blue lake is filled with some of the purest water you can imagine. It's also America's deepest lake at nearly 2000ft, and so clear you can easily peer a hundred feet down. Camp, ski or hike in the surrounding old-growth forests while enjoying unforgettable, jaw-dropping views. Crater Lake

Vancouver Island

24 The largest populated landmass off North America's west coast, Vancouver Island (p401) is ready-made for nature-lovers. Its diverse ecosystems include mountains, rivers, lakes, rainforests, marshes and beaches – a paradise to the island's many wildlife species, both on land and in water. Fish for salmon, go bird- or whale-watching or just explore the many nature reserves and parks. And when you get tired of all that green, stop off in lovely Victoria, where the historic architecture might just make you believe you're in Europe. Parliament Buildings (p404), Victoria

Mt St Helens

25 Having recently celebrated the 30th anniversary of its 1980 eruption, Mt St Helens (8366ft; p179) still occasionally billows out plumes of smoke. But this recent activity is nothing like the catastrophic event that killed 57 people, flattened 230 sq miles of forest and blew nearly 1300ft off its top. Today, you can hike to the edge and peer down into the mile-wide caldera, but if you're against strenuous exercise (and believe us, it's not easy) then just drop by one of the visitor centers for some history, and a faraway look at this amazing volcano.

SUNSET AVENUE PRODUCTIONS/GETTY IMAGES ©

Need to Know

For more information, see Survival Guide (p462)

Currency
US dollars ($)
Canadian dollars ($)

Language
English

Visas
Requirements vary widely for entry to the US and Canada. Check http://travel.state.gov/visa/visa_1750.html (USA) and www.cic.gc.ca/english/visit (Canada).

Money
ATMs widely available. Credit cards accepted at most hotels, restaurants and shops.

Cell Phones
The US and Canada use GSM-850 and GSM-1900 bands. SIM cards are relatively easy to obtain in both countries.

Time
Oregon (except most of Malheur County, near the Idaho border), Washington, and Vancouver, BC, are in the Pacific zone (GMT minus seven hours in summer, minus eight in winter).

When to Go

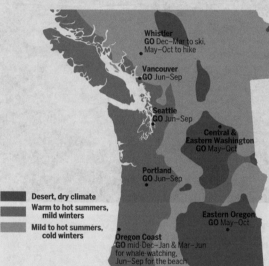

Whistler
GO Dec–Mar to ski, May–Oct to hike

Vancouver
GO Jun–Sep

Seattle
GO Jun–Sep

Central & Eastern Washington
GO May–Oct

Portland
GO Jun–Sep

Eastern Oregon
GO May–Oct

Oregon Coast
GO mid-Dec–Jan & Mar–Jun for whale-watching, Jun–Sep for the beach

- Desert, dry climate
- Warm to hot summers, mild winters
- Mild to hot summers, cold winters

High Season
(Jun–Sep)

➡ Sunny, warm days throughout the region.

➡ More crowds and higher prices for accommodations and sights.

➡ For ski resorts, busiest times are December to March.

Shoulder
(Apr–May & Oct)

➡ Crowds and prices drop off.

➡ Temperatures remain mild.

➡ Services are more limited, but there's less competition for them.

Low Season
(Nov–Mar)

➡ Colder days, less sunlight, more rain.

➡ Some services may close along the coast, and high passes can be blocked by snow.

➡ Indoor activities such as theater and music are at their best!

Useful Websites

Lonely Planet (www.lonelyplanet.com/usa/pacific-northwest)

Seattle Tourism (www.seattle.gov) The city's official website.

Washington State Tourism (www.experiencewa.com) Washington State Tourism's official website.

Travel Portland (www.travelportland.com) Portland info.

Oregon Tourism Commission (www.traveloregon.com) Travel-planning site.

Tourism British Columbia (www.hellobc.com) Official tourism website of British Colombia.

Important Numbers

The following numbers apply to both the USA and Canada.

Country code	☎1
International access code	☎011
Ambulance, fire and police	☎911
Local directory assistance	☎411

Exchange Rates

Australia	A$1	96¢
Canada	$1	96¢
Europe	€1	$1.39
Japan	¥100	$1.03
New Zealand	NZ$1	84¢
UK	UK£1	$1.62

For current exchange rates see www.xe.com.

Daily Costs

Budget: less than $100

➡ Inexpensive motel room/dorm bed: $75/25

➡ There are many supermarkets for self-caterers, or look for food carts in larger cities

➡ Some sights have free-admission days

Midrange: $100–200

➡ Good hotel room: $125 a night

➡ Meal in a good restaurant: $15–20

Top End: more than $200

➡ Upscale hotel room: $175

➡ Fine-dining meal: $25–30

Opening Hours

The following are very general hours and will vary depending on the business and sometimes the season.

Restaurants Breakfast 7am to 11:30am, lunch 11:30am to 2:30pm, dinner 5pm to 9pm

Shops 9am to 5pm (malls till 9pm) Monday to Friday, sometimes more limited on weekends

Supermarkets 8am to 10pm, sometimes 24 hours

Arriving in the Pacific Northwest

For rental cars, it's best to reserve online and pick up at the airport.

Seattle-Tacoma International Airport Link Light Rail connects to downtown Seattle in 30 minutes; Metro buses stop outside baggage claim; there are frequent shuttle services from $18 one way; taxis take 25 minutes to run to downtown, fare is $45.

Portland International Airport Max Light Rail connects to downtown Portland in 40 minutes; there are frequent shuttle services from $14 one way; taxis take around 20 minutes to run to downtown, fare is $35.

Vancouver International Airport SkyTrain connects to downtown Vancouver in 25 minutes; taxis take around 30 minutes to run to downtown, fare is $35.

Getting Around

Car The USA and Canada are very car-oriented societies. Getting around this region is much, much easier with a private vehicle, and car rentals (and gasoline) are affordable. In larger cities, car-share programs are available.

Public transportation Buses, trains and ferries have networks in the region, though services can be limited.

Bicycle Within the big cities of Seattle, Portland and Vancouver, BC, bicycling is a common method of transport. These are very bike-friendly places, with many bike lanes and bike paths. Drivers also have a general awareness of sharing the road with cyclists.

For much more on **getting around**, see p470.

What's New

Chihuly Garden & Glass

Providing yet another reason to visit the eclectic Seattle Center is this spectacular homage to Dale Chihuly, a master of blown-glass art. This museum of sorts captures an astounding array of his greatest work, most prominently displayed inside a peaked atrium and outside in lovely gardens. You'll never look at glass in quite the same way again. (p71)

Seattle Great Wheel

With Ferris wheels now gracing the skylines of numerous cities around the globe, Seattle has jumped on the bandwagon with its own lofty Great Wheel, designed to lure visitors toward the city's waterfront. (p69)

Evergreen Wings & Waves Waterpark

Part of the Evergreen Aviation & Space Museum in McMinnville, OR, this amazing water park is located in a building with a retired Boeing 747 airplane perched on its rooftop! Inside there are 10 slides (four start from inside the 747) and a large wave pool. (p248)

Grand Coulee Dam Light Show

Held nightly between Memorial Day weekend and the end of September, this free, 36-minute light show has recently undergone a $1.6-million upgrade – making it more spectacular than ever. (p210)

Robert Bateman Centre

Located in Victoria, BC, this new exhibition gallery highlights the greatest works by one of the world's most renowned wildlife artists. Over 160 of Bateman's original drawings and paintings are on display. (p404)

FlyOver Canada

A major new attraction at Canada Place in Vancouver, BC. Incorporating state-of-the-art technology, this 'ride' has guests suspended in front of a huge spherical screen while wind, mist and scents wash over them. (p374)

Alaskan Way Viaduct

Digging for a new tunnel to redirect noisy SR99 underground began in summer 2013. When it's finished the ugly Alaskan Way Viaduct will be demolished, leaving Seattle's waterfront a quieter and more salubrious place.

Pacific Maritime & Heritage Center

The center is the newest attraction in Newport, OR, featuring maritime-related exhibits – as well as art such as paintings – to educate and entertain visitors, and create a sense of community for locals. (p309)

New Wing at the Maryhill Museum of Art

Oddly located on a scenic bluff at the eastern end of the Columbia River Gorge is this excellent museum. Its $10-million new wing offers exciting new exhibits, a fine cafe – and spectacular gorge views from the terrace. (p266)

For more recommendations and reviews, see lonelyplanet.com

If You Like...

Wildlife

Lions and tigers and bears, oh my – well, maybe not the tigers. And the lions are the mountain kind. But if you're looking for wild critters, there are plenty of them here in the Northwest. Gray whales, seals and orcas frolic in the ocean, while Roosevelt elk, pronghorn antelope and black bears scamper over land. And raptors, such as bald eagles, often soar overhead, along with sandhill cranes, downy woodpeckers and many corvid family species.

San Juan Islands Ground zero for spotting orcas; several pods live here year-round. (p109)

Oregon Coast In winter and spring, gray whales migrate from Mexico to Alaska – and back. (p47)

Hart Mountain National Antelope Refuge Pronghorn central, but keep a sharp eye out – they're the world's second-fastest land mammals. (p369)

Klamath Basin National Wildlife Refuge You're nearly guaranteed a bald-eagle sighting; up to a thousand gather here in winter. (p344)

Hiking

In the Pacific Northwest, it's hard to throw a rock without hitting a hiking trail. Stomp around the volcanic cones, including Mt Rainier, Mt St Helens or Mt Hood; explore the far reaches of the Wallowas, the Columbia River Gorge or Olympic National Park; and go crazy figuring out which of British Columbia's trails are the most gorgeous.

Wonderland Trail Circumnavigate lofty Mt Rainier – it's 93 miles of spectacular nature. (p175)

West Coast Trail British Columbia's famous 47-mile ribbon of adventure is for those truly serious about their outdoors. (p417)

Oregon's Coast Neahkahnie Mountain, Cape Lookout, Saddle Mountain – whether you're after wildflower meadows or stunning views of the Pacific Ocean, you won't be disappointed.

Columbia River Gorge Tread up the easy Eagle Creek Trail (p263) for a waterfall wonderland, or sweat up Dog Mountain (p267) for unbeatable vistas.

Beaches

What says 'vacation' more than a day at the beach? Head to Oregon's coast for 360 miles of fun, while Washington has a beautiful shoreline within a national park. The Pacific Northwest has plenty of beaches to check out, whether you want to party at a resort or just be alone.

La Push Come here for beauty and adventure – the beaches offer kayaking, surfing, hiking and sublime scenery. (p141)

Long Beach Miles and miles of beachcombing, awesome breakers and even an old-growth forest to explore. (p416)

Cannon Beach With photogenic Haystack Rock looming just off shore, Cannon Beach is about as scenic as it gets. (p300)

Oregon Dunes Explore this National Recreation Area on foot or in a dune buggy; the sandy mountains tower up to 500ft and spread 3 miles inland. (p315)

IF YOU LIKE...GARDENS

Sniff flowers from Victoria's Butchart Gardens (p411) to Portland's International Rose Test Gardens (p218) – with plenty of others in between.

Microbrews

If you appreciate the rich, complex flavors of a lovingly microbrewed beer, then you'll find nirvana here. And while the Pacific Northwest didn't actually invent the stuff, it certainly raised the fermentation of hops to a fine art.

Fish Tale Brew Pub Olympia's oldest brewpub pours 14 hand-crafted brews, including organic beer and fruit ciders. (p125)

Green Dragon A huge variety of microbrews, with over 60 eclectic beers on tap from all around the country. (p236)

Belmont Station Both a bar and large beer store, this spot boasts more than 1200 local and international brews. (p236)

Alibi Room This tavern has 50 diverse taps, with a rotation of local selections; try the beer flights. (p390)

Wine

Pinot-noir lovers, unite! It's Oregon's most famous grape, finicky as a superstar and the foundation for some very exceptional wine. But Washington produces more wine than nearly any other state, and it's of a very high quality too. Just head to the Walla Walla Valley for a taste of cabernet or syrah, and you'll be tipping your glass in agreement.

Walla Walla Washington's hot wine-growing region, with its namesake town as a very pretty centerpiece. (p199)

Yakima Valley More than 50 wineries, most of them family-run, highlight this backbone of Washington's wine industry. (p198)

McMinnville The heart of Oregon's grape land; base yourself

Top: Butchart Gardens (p411)
Bottom: Pulled-pork sandwich with fries

here and your pinot noir glass will never run dry. (p248)

Cowichan Valley If you can't make it to British Columbia's prime Okanagan Valley, Vancouver Island's boutique vineyards are a worthwhile alternative. (p412)

Shopping

Love to shop? How does zero sales tax sound? That's Oregon for you. But there's plenty of fabulous shopping in Washington and British Columbia as well, from funky bohemian shops to fancy boutiques to farmers markets galore.

Pike Place Market Seattle's famous market boasts fruit, vegetable and seafood stalls above, while everything else lies in the maze below. (p69)

Portland's 23rd Ave Also called 'trendy-third' for its hip boutiques and upscale chains such as Gap, Banana Republic and Restoration Hardware. (p240)

Vancouver's Main St, south of 18th Ave The heart of the city's indie shopping scene, with cool record shops, bookstores and lots of local-designed fashion boutiques. (p392)

Granville Island Public Market More than just a covered farmers market, this Vancouver destination also hosts gourmet food shops and arts and crafts stalls. (p379)

Great Food

From Portland's farm-to-table movement to Seattle's award-winning restaurants to Vancouver's international-class Chinese food, this region boasts enough eating options to make your stomach spin – but in a good way.

IF YOU LIKE...FUNKY PUBLIC SCULPTURE

Seattle's bohemian Fremont neighborhood (aka 'Center of the Universe') is famous for its concrete bridge troll – and more. (p75)

Granville Island Public Market British Columbia's Granville Island has a tasty bite for everyone, from luscious pastry treats to a top international food court. (p379)

Pike Place Market Seattle's grand old market sells ripe fruit, fresh vegetables and gleaming fish – among many other things. (p69)

Portland's Food Carts Trendy, diverse and oh-so delicious, Portland has turned the lowly food mobile to a cutting-edge movable feast. (p231)

FareStart Restaurant Seattle restaurant with great food, good value and an even better cause; definitely one of a kind. (p82)

Jaw-Dropping Landscapes

This region is pretty much made up of amazing landscapes, from scenic shorelines to snow-dusted volcanic mountain ranges to desolate but beautiful desert panoramas. Lofty Cascade peaks can even be seen from the big cities of Seattle, Portland and Vancouver, making great natural backdrops to the urban bustle.

North Cascades National Park Stark Washington landscapes highlighted by formidable mountaintops, all in a national park known for its isolation. (p158)

John Day Fossil Beds An almost unbelievable palette of colors layer the sedimentary hills of

Oregon's geological wonder. (p362)

Three Sisters Wilderness A string of Oregon peaks with striking character, from Broken Top's jagged edges to South Sister's dimpled dome. (p284)

Cape Scott Provincial Park This part of British Columbia has some of the most rugged and wild coastline you'll ever see or experience. (p423)

Live Music

Portland, Seattle and Vancouver claim some of the hottest new bands on the indie circuit, though small towns such as Olympia have their own talent. Venues run from intimate rooms to quirky spaces with floating floors to large, loud clubs.

Doug Fir A hip haven with an impressive sound system, attracting cutting-edge talent for near-nightly shows. (p238)

Mississippi Studios A recording studio turned 300-seat venue with great atmosphere and up-and-coming bands. (p238)

Crocodile Seattle's historic music venue, which first saw grunge emerge from the shadows. Everyone from Cheap Trick to Yoko Ono has rocked here. (p87)

Commodore Ballroom Vancouver institution with art-deco atmosphere, unique dance floor and famous (or soon-to-be famous) local bands. (p391)

North Cascades National Park (p158)

Skiing

Strap on those skis – there are some great downhill slopes here. With plenty of precipitation, the snow pack can really add up to create some exceptionally deep powder. And, for some, the cross-country skiing is even better; there are endless scenic trails winding through lovely hills and forests.

Whistler The mother of all ski resorts, or close to it; a huge area with plenty of powder. (p396)

Mt Hood Availability is this mountain's appeal – you can ski here every month of the year. (p49)

Crystal Mountain Located on the flanks of Mt Rainier, this is Washington's largest ski resort, with over 50 named runs. (p179)

Methow Valley A cross-country skier's paradise, boasting more than 120 miles of groomed trails. (p163)

Hot Springs

If you're looking for a therapeutic mineral soak, there's lots to choose from in this volcanic region: lonely desert water holes, rustic, unpretentious springs and luxury resorts. Nudity is – unsurprisingly – de rigueur at the more remote and free locations.

Sol Duc Well-established springs with good services and family-friendly appeal. (p135)

Breitenbush Near the forest, with vegetarian food, yoga and accommodations. (p252)

Bagby Free but surprisingly developed, with hollowed-out tubs and even private 'rooms'. (p252)

Umpqua Free springs with an unbeatable location on a cliff above the Umpqua River. (p337)

Month by Month

TOP EVENTS

Oregon Shakespeare Festival, February

Whale-watching, March–June

Celebration of Light, July

Bumbershoot, September

Pendleton Round Up, September

January

One of the quieter, greener months in the lowlands and on the coast, where the rains fall. Mountain resorts bustle with skiers and boarders taking advantage of the white stuff, especially around New Year.

🏃 Truffle Hunting in the Cascade Mountains

The Northwest's best native edible truffles are ripe for the picking this month; Eugene becomes a hub with its Oregon Truffle Festival. (p450)

🏃 Polar Bear Swim

Hundreds of shivering, brave souls plunge into the icy waters of English Bay Beach in Vancouver, BC, on January 1 to celebrate the New Year.

February

A good time to visit the three metro areas, which become the territory of locals during these gray days. Book ahead for snow-related activities, though; resorts and mountain cabins fill up quickly.

🎎 Chinese New Year

Vancouver's large Chinese population celebrates with parades, cultural activities, dragon dances, traditional art and – of course – plenty of great Chinese food. (p382)

🎎 Oregon Shakespeare Festival

In Ashland, tens of thousands of theater fans party with the Bard at this nine-month-long festival (that's right!) highlighted by world-class plays and Elizabethan drama. (p329)

March

Early blooms are harbingers of the region's long spring and upcoming fruit bounty. Major destinations on the coast and in the mountains become crowded with local families during spring break; book early.

🏃 Spring Whale-Watching Week

Spot the gray whales' spring migration anywhere along the Pacific Coast. Around Oregon's Depoe Bay it's semiorganized, with docents and special viewpoints. The northward migration happens through June.

🎎 Moisture Festival

Seattle embraces its humidity with comedy, circus and burlesque acts that appeal to the whole family.

🎎 Victorian Festival

Port Townsend, Washington's Victorian jewel, dresses up in frilly costumes. Tours of period homes, fashion shows and ball dances offer fun. (p128)

April

Even though the rains continue, warmer temperatures and spots of sun inspire more outdoor activities, especially in the drier, eastern part of the region. Easter weekend can be crowded everywhere.

⚜️ Skagit County Tulip Festival

Acres of red, purple, yellow and orange tulips bob in the breeze as visitors partake in wine tastings, art shows and bike rides near the expansive fields surrounding La Conner, WA. (p103)

⚜️ Hood River Valley Blossom Festival

Celebrates the fruit bounty of Oregon's fertile Hood River Valley, with food, wine, crafts and a 35-mile agricultural tour route known as the Fruit Loop. (p269)

⚜️ Spring Arts Walk

Olympia, WA, celebrates the coming of spring with visual arts and performances. The highlight is a 'Procession of the Species' parade, which honors Earth Day and involves creative and colorful plant and animal costumes.

May

Spring has sprung, but don't leave the rain gear at home. Memorial Day weekend can be busy at campgrounds and parks despite the occasional drizzle.

⚜️ Northwest Folklife Festival

This Seattle festival is celebrated with hundreds of musicians, artists and performers from all over the world. (p77)

⚜️ Victoria Day

Originally honoring Queen Victoria's birthday, this Canadian holiday now celebrates the current sovereign's birthday (and the unofficial start of the summer season) with parades and fireworks.

June

Blooming roses and outdoor celebrations mark the beginning of summer. Hotels fill up fast in the cities and on the coast.

⚜️ Portland Rose Festival

Music concerts, floral parades, children's events, carnival rides, dragon-boat races, milk-carton boat races, fireworks and a half-million spectators. (p228)

⚜️ Britt Festival

An outdoor summer music celebration in Jacksonville, OR, featuring world-class jazz, blues, folk, pop, country and classical-music artists – including some mighty big names. (p332)

☆ Bard on the Beach

A season of four Shakespeare-related plays takes place in the Vanier Park tents in Vancouver, BC. Runs through September. (p383)

⚜️ Sandcastle Day

Cannon Beach becomes ground zero for art created with...sand. Expect stunning creativity and execution – these aren't your typical sand-bucket castles. (p301)

July

Soak up the sun during the region's summer peak.

Farmers markets are going strong this month, and the coast and mountains (and everywhere in between) are flooded with visitors.

⚜️ Oregon Brewers Festival

Enjoy Portland's summer weather at this fun beer festival, where 80,000 microbrew lovers eat, drink and whoop it up on the banks of the Willamette River. (p228)

⚜️ Seattle's Seafair

Three-week party that includes live music, a torchlight parade, hydroplane races, air shows and even pirates. (p77)

⚜️ Da Vinci Days

Kinetic sculpture and home-built electric-car races happen in this funky arts-and-science celebration in Corvallis, OR. (p254)

⚜️ Celebration of Light

What could be a bigger bang than an international fireworks festival? Head to Vancouver for this explosive event, and prepare for three nights of the best fireworks you've ever seen. (p383)

August

While the greener parts of the region may brown a bit this month, it's still a great time to be outdoors. Book early in the major cities, on the coast or at campgrounds.

☆ Pacific National Exhibition

Seventeen-day summer fair with family-friendly

shows, music, concerts and a fairground in Vancouver, BC. (p383)

✪ Washington State International Kite Festival

Huge kite festival on the sand at Long Beach, WA. Look for new world records, including the largest kite flown and the most kites aloft at one time.

✪ Garlic Festival

Chehalis, WA, celebrates this aromatic bulb with crafts, music and tons of garlic-laden food (of course).

September

Cool nights but reliably sunny days make this one of the best months to visit. Kids are back in school, and fall harvests begin for wine grapes, mushrooms and more.

☆ Pendleton Round Up

Country music, dances, art shows, a Native American powwow, bronco-breaking and Western pageantry preside here, at one of the country's most famous rodeos. (p347)

✪ Bumbershoot

Seattle's biggest arts and cultural event boasts two-dozen stages and hundreds of musicians, artists and theater troupes, attracting over 100,000 spectators. (p77)

✪ Vancouver International Fringe Festival

Wild and wacky theatricals at both mainstream and unconventional Granville Island venues. (p383)

October

Even though the weather begins to get wet this month, hearty Northwesterners still head outdoors for bike races, coast visits and beer fests.

✪ Vancouver International Film Festival

Highly regarded film festival screens some 380 international films and documentaries from around 75 countries. (p383)

✪ Fresh Hop Beer Festivals

The year's fresh hop beers are ready and the festivals begin. Look for the biggest ones in Yakima, Hood River and Portland.

🏃 Cross Crusade Race Series

Competitors ride intense laps through mud and over barriers in the largest cyclo-cross race series in the US, which occurs in Portland and surrounding areas. Spectating is fun too, involving beer and cowbells.

November

Book early for Thanksgiving weekend lodging. The most avid skiers and boarders will

take to the slopes for early snows, while city shoppers hit the streets.

✪ Eastside Culture Crawl

An open-studio art event, which takes place over three days in Vancouver, BC.

✪ Wine Country Thanksgiving

Nearly 200 wineries in Oregon's Willamette Valley open their doors for three special days. Hit some of the small, family-owned wineries usually closed to visitors.

December

The holidays mean larger crowds at mountain resorts and in cities. Find solitude on the coast and in rural areas.

✪ Victorian Christmas

A Christmas past; witness a community tree lighting, Father Christmas parade, vintage-dressed carolers and roasting chestnuts in Jacksonville, OR.

☆ New Year's Eve in Seattle

Washington's ground zero for the new year is the Space Needle, where revelers dress up, count down and drink champagne as fireworks go off.

Itineraries

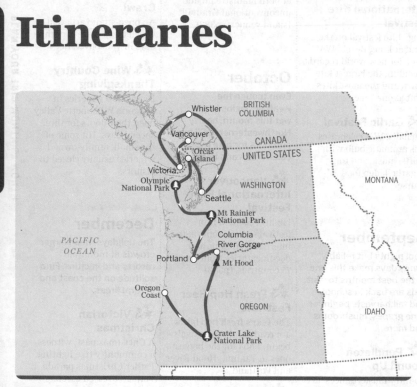

(4 WEEKS) Pacific Northwest Grand Tour

Just want to hit the highlights? **Vancouver** (p371) boasts wonderful parks, ethnic attractions and cool neighborhoods. Further south, on Vancouver Island, is charming and picture-perfect **Victoria** (p401). If it's winter, hit the world-class slopes of **Whistler** (p395).

Bustling **Seattle** (p62) offers myriad attractions, a unique skyline and great cuisine. Now head north to the beautiful San Juan Islands, such as woodsy **Orcas Island** (p114) – you can bike around or just relax. Back on the mainland, **Olympic National Park** (p131) is the jewel of the Olympic Peninsula, boasting a unique rainforest ecosystem. For more of the state's gorgeous landscapes, **Mt Rainier National Park** (p172) is a must.

There's no escaping the attractions in **Portland** (p214) – from its landmark Powell's bookstore to its many microbreweries to tax-free (and hip) shopping. Just east are the grand vistas, hiking trails and waterfalls of the **Columbia River Gorge** (p262). Nearby **Mt Hood** (p276) is unbeatable for camping, hiking and skiing. Much further south, **Crater Lake National Park** (p338) is a geologic wonder with supreme scenery. Finally, if you have time left over, there's the grandeur (and seafood cuisine) of the beautiful **Oregon Coast** (p293).

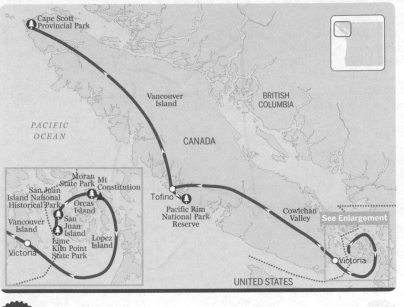

 **Island Hop**

Washington's San Juans are an archipelago of hundreds of islands covering some 750 sq miles. Only about 60 are inhabited, and just four are accessible by public ferry. Three of these islands bring thousands of vacationers every year, but each has managed to keep a serene atmosphere and distinct character.

San Juan Island (p108) has the best tourist facilities, along with the archipelago's only sizable town, Friday Harbor. **Lime Kiln Point State Park** (p109) has prime whale-watching; in June, keep a lookout for killer or minke whales feasting on salmon runs. To the north is **San Juan Island National Historical Park** (p109), with old British military facilities and earthwork fortifications and – on clear days – great mountain views.

The largest of the islands, **Orcas Island** (p114) is probably the most beautiful – and the poshest. It's dotted with fancy homes, and the lack of a central town gives it an exclusive neighborhood feel. Check out **Moran State Park** (p114), which offers camping, fishing, hiking and mountain biking. **Mt Constitution**, the archipelago's highest point, is also here, featuring some of the finest views in Washington.

Lopez Island (p118) is the most peaceful island, with friendly locals and pastoral charm. Don't expect too many tourist services – agriculture and farming are the main focus. The mostly flat island is made for cycling, and there's little vehicular traffic.

A much larger island to explore is BC's **Vancouver Island** (p401). Start in lovely **Victoria** (p401), a cosmopolitan city with a variety of ethnic cultures, along with a touch of old Britain. Can't-miss attractions include the world-famous Butchart Gardens and high tea at the grand Empress Hotel. Wine lovers and foodies should head to the **Cowichan Valley** (p412), home to boutique wineries and organic farms. Further west is the coastal town of **Tofino** (p418), where you can go kayaking and spot marine life including gray whales. Nearby is **Pacific Rim National Park Reserve** (p416), with rainforest, crashing surf, islands to explore and amazing hiking. Finally, head to land's end at **Cape Scott Provincial Park** (p423) to explore pristine beaches; outdoor lovers have miles of challenging trails and backcountry camping opportunities.

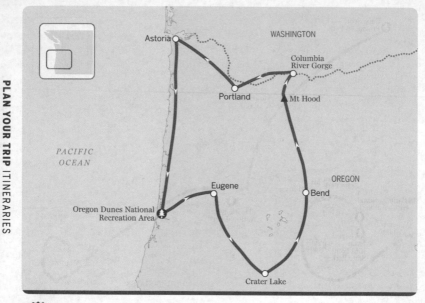

2 WEEKS Portland & Oregon Loop

Start your Oregon adventure in **Portland** (p214), well known for its roses, bridges, beer and progressive politics. Be sure to visit downtown's landmarks and the Pearl District's boutiques; Powell's City of Books is one of the world's largest independent bookstores. Over on the east side of the Willamette River are several distinct and fun neighborhoods including Hawthorne, Mississippi and Alberta. Take frequent breaks in the city's excellent coffee shops or microbreweries.

Now drive west towards the coast to **Astoria** (p294), the first permanent US settlement in the west. Today it's a pleasant port city with a restored downtown, historic museums and Victorian houses. Further south are plenty of beach resorts, fishing towns, state parks and scenic promontories that jut out to sea. If it's summer and you like to camp, there are endless opportunities along the Oregon coast. Just south of Florence is the **Oregon Dunes National Recreation Area** (p315), the largest expanse of coastal sand dunes in the US.

Heading inland, you'll soon hit **Eugene** (p255), a liberal and fun-loving city famous for founding Nike and putting out track-and-field champions. Drive further south on mountainous Rte 58 to **Crater Lake** (p338), Oregon's only national park, offering supreme views of an old volcanic caldera; the water here – fed only by rain and snow – is some of the clearest and purest in the world. Going north on Rte 97 will bring you to **Bend** (p285), a city tailor-made for outdoor lovers. Nearby you can go hiking, skiing, fishing, golfing, biking, kayaking, rafting and rock climbing.

Driving north you'll branch off onto Rte 26, ending at **Mt Hood** (p276), the state's highest peak at 11,240ft. While summiting the volcanic cone is only for hardy mountaineers, there are countless beautiful hikes on Mt Hood's flanks, along with plenty of campsites. Be sure to stop in for a drink (or meal) at the historic Timberline Lodge. Now head north again on Rte 35 and you'll come to the **Columbia River Gorge** (p262). Cruise through this amazing geologic feature, stopping for lovely waterfalls and hikes along the way, and you'll eventually finish your loop back where you started – Portland.

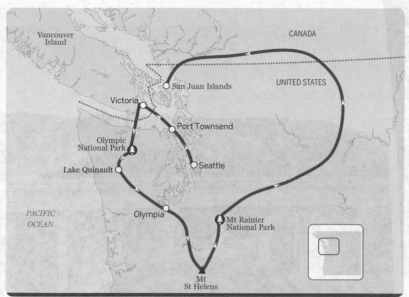

2 WEEKS: Seattle & Washington

The Pacific Northwest's largest city, **Seattle** (p62) has plenty going for it – a great location on Puget Sound, myriad dynamic neighborhoods, interesting sights and attractions, lots of first-rate coffee and beer, and – looming over it all – the lofty peak of majestic Mt Rainier. Must-sees include Pioneer Square, Pike Place Market, the Seattle Aquarium and the Space Needle, but there's plenty more to keep you busy.

Get out of town by hopping on a ferry to Bainbridge Island, then heading north to **Port Townsend** (p126). With its Victorian architecture and location on the Strait of Juan de Fuca, this picturesque little town is a magnet for artists and eclectic personalities. From here you can take a bicycle on a ferry to the San Juan Islands, though if you want to drive you'll have to access them via Anacortes (more on this later). Work your way east along the Olympic Peninsula, perhaps stopping in Port Angeles for a quick day trip to Vancouver Island's pretty capital, **Victoria** (p401).

Olympic National Park (p131) can't be missed. Its coastal strip includes 57 miles of remote beaches with pounding waves and wild scenery; visit Rialto Beach for amazing views. Inland, the Hoh Rain Forest is a prime destination with its famous Hall of Moss Trail. Now head further south to **Lake Quinault** (p136), a gorgeous glacier-fed lake boasting a historic grand lodge. This is the place to go fishing, boating or swimming. Then pack it up and drive to **Olympia** (p122), Washington's lively capital that's full of music culture.

If you like volcanoes, **Mt St Helens** (p179) should be on your itinerary; she blew her top in 1980, losing 1314ft of elevation. Not to be outclassed, Mt Rainier is another can't-miss geologic landmark. Hope for good weather and go hiking among glaciers, alpine meadows and old-growth forests in **Mt Rainier National Park** (p172).

Looping back to I-5, drive up to Anacortes and take a ferry to the beautiful **San Juan Islands** (p107). There are three distinct main islands to explore. San Juan Island has undulating hills and a scenic west coast where you can spot whales; upscale Orcas Island claims the area's highest peak; and Lopez Island is flat, laid-back and great for cycling.

Columbia River Gorge (p2█

Columbia River Gorge (p2█

Plan Your Trip

Pacific Northwest Road Trips

The Pacific Northwest offers an endless list of gorgeous panoramas, from stunning ocean coastlines to verdant forests dotted with pristine lakes to snowy volcanoes silhouetted against blue skies. And it's all accessible with your own four wheels, so fill up the gas tank and get ready for some unforgettable drives.

Planning

Top Tips

On some of these trips (like the Washington or Oregon Cascades) gas stations are sporadic, so top up whenever you can. Leave yourself extra time to explore unexpected sights along the way. Pack a bag in case you fall in love with a place and decide to stay overnight!

What to Bring

Ensure you take your swimsuit, good walking shoes, rain gear and other layers, and sun protection.

Best Experiences

Whale-watching and beachcombing along the Oregon coast, counting volcanoes in the Washington Cascades, hiking inside ancient forests at Olympic National Park, and taking in spectacular views along British Columbia's Sea to Sky Hwy.

Highway 101 Oregon Coast

Oregon's scenic, two-lane Hwy 101 follows hundreds of miles of shoreline punctuated by charming seaside towns, exhilarating hikes and ocean views. Everyone from nature-lovers to families can find their dream vacation along this exceptional coastal route.

Why Go

From the California border to Gold Beach (renowned for its Rogue River fishing) is

some of Oregon's most magnificent coastal scenery. Heading north, the quaint hamlet of Port Orford offers stunning state parks, including Cape Blanco, home to Oregon's oldest lighthouse and some exhilarating views.

Further north, Bandon has a picturesque downtown harbor and beautiful rock formations just offshore. Oregon Dunes National Recreation Area boasts the largest expanse of oceanfront sand dunes in the US, and they're hugely popular with hikers and dune buggies (but not in the same place!). The little town of Yachats offers great walks along its gorgeous coastline and nearby in Cape Perpetua.

In Newport, don't miss the first-rate Oregon Coast Aquarium. Just north is Yaquina Head Outstanding Natural Area, with amazing tide pools. If it's the season, take a whale-watching excursion at Depoe Bay, which claims to be the 'world's whale-watching capital.'

Keep heading north, stopping at the Tillamook Cheese visitor center for some free samples. Pacific Seafood, nearby in Bay City, is the place for the fastest oyster shucking you'll ever see. Meanwhile, small and upscale Manzanita offers a relaxing, laid-back atmosphere.

Exclusive Cannon Beach is great for people-watching, boutique shopping and fine dining. Finally, cute, family-friendly Astoria has plenty of services and great historical attractions to keep you busy.

When to Go

The best time to travel Oregon's coast is June through September. You'll get the warmest weather and most services, though accommodation will be at its scarcest and priciest.

The Route

Don't expect to drive fast on this direct US 101 route. Most of this highway is two lanes, with occasional slow trucks and RVs, and it goes through many small towns (or larger cities with stoplights).

Worthy Detour

Three Capes Scenic Drive is a worthwhile and beautiful 35-mile detour off Hwy 101. It passes Cape Meares, Cape Lookout and Cape Kiwanda, all with great walks and panoramic ocean views.

ALAN KEARNEY/GETTY IMAGES ©

Olympic National Park (p131)

Time & Mileage

Oregon boasts 363 miles of coastline, all publicly accessible. Expect your adventure to take at least one to two weeks, depending on stops.

Oregon Cascades Scenic Byway

This trip epitomizes Oregon's outdoors aesthetic. It's perfect for the road-tripper who wants to hike for hours, find hidden waterfalls, swim in crystal-clear lakes, see endless miles of forest – and, at the end of the day, strip down to soak in a natural hot spring.

Why Go

The Oregon Cascades are a nonstop parade of forests, lakes, mountains and waterfalls. Start in Bend, the most outdoor-focused city in the state. Now head north to cute Sisters, with its mild Wild West atmosphere.

You'll climb to Dee Wright Observatory, a unique viewpoint that looks over lava

fields and to mountain peaks. Not far away is pretty Proxy Falls, an easy 1.3-mile hike. Further on, highly developed Belknap Hot Springs makes a great stop to soak away road sores.

McKenzie Bridge is a magnet for fishers, but there's great hiking and white-water rafting too. Just south lies scenic Terwilliger Hot Springs, a much more rustic alternative to Belknap. To the south is Oakridge, Oregon's mountain-biking mecca, with hundreds of miles of glorious single-track trails. Beyond is another soaker, McCredie Hot Springs, along with Salt Creek Falls, Oregon's second-highest waterfall (after Multnomah Falls) at 286ft.

Now come the lakes – Waldo, Odell, Crescent, Davis, Lava, Elk, Sparks – and reservoirs like Wickiup and Crane Prairie. If you like to fish, swim, boat and camp, this region is your paradise. Finally, loop back to Bend and back to civilization.

When to Go

Go June through September for the best weather and to avoid seasonal road closures.

The Route

From Bend you'll head north to Sisters, then climb up Hwy 242 through the Cascades toward McKenzie Bridge and Oakridge. The loop then heads southeast via various lakes and reservoirs toward Mt Bachelor, then back to Bend.

Worthy Detour

Best known for its glorious, 500ft welded-tuff cliffs that attract rock climbers from all over the world, Smith Rock State Park also offers stunning scenery and hiking trails. It's just 25 miles north of Bend.

Time & Mileage

This loop is 240 miles; expect to be on the road about three to four days.

Columbia River Gorge & Mt Hood

Few places symbolize the grandeur of the Pacific Northwest like the Columbia River

Pacific Northwest Road Trips

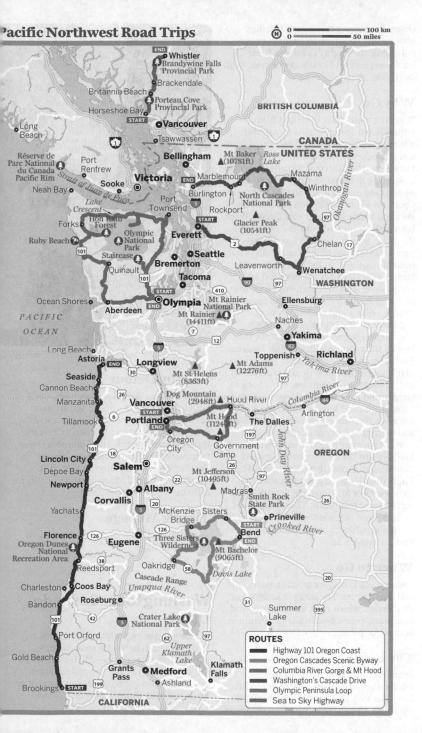

0 —————— 100 km
0 —————— 50 miles

ROUTES
- Highway 101 Oregon Coast
- Oregon Cascades Scenic Byway
- Columbia River Gorge & Mt Hood
- Washington's Cascade Drive
- Olympic Peninsula Loop
- Sea to Sky Highway

Gorge. Start along this massive cleft of 4000ft cliffs and drive by countless waterfalls, while the mighty Columbia River follows along and Mt Hood lurks behind, in all its 11,250ft glory.

Why Go

Towering waterfalls, excellent hiking, unparalleled scenery, fruit farms and wineries – what else could you want from a long weekend? Add snowcapped Mt Hood, and the diversity becomes surreal.

Starting in Portland, drive east on US 84 and take exit 22 to US 30 (the Historic Columbia River Hwy). Soon you'll hit the Portland Women's Forum and Crown Point, both with absolutely stunning views over the gorge. Staying on US 30, you'll pass various waterfalls; Multnomah Falls is the most famous. Just to the east, Bonneville Dam & Fish Hatchery are both fun and educational. And to stretch your legs, the beautiful Eagle Creek Trail is the gorge's most popular – and moderately easy.

Now cross the Bridge of the Gods to Washington, where you can visit the Columbia Gorge Interpretive Center Museum. Further east, Dog Mountain is another popular hike, but strenuous – and with amazing views. At White Salmon, cross back to Oregon and stop at Hood River, a mecca for windsurfing and kiteboarding. Its downtown is a pleasant place to explore as well, and there are plenty of places to sleep.

Point your car inland now; you'll follow US 35 to US 26, then head west. At Government Camp, drive up the road to Timberline Lodge, a great place for awesome views of Mt Hood, along with food services and trailheads. There's plenty of camping and other hikes in the area, so fill up on the outdoors before heading back to Portland via US 26.

When to Go

Early spring is best for gushing waterfalls and wildflowers. The gorge is known for its cherries, which peak in early July, and apples and pears, best in the fall. Summer is great for hiking.

The Route

From Portland your drive goes east on US 84, then onto the Historic Columbia River Hwy. Back on US 84, you'll head inland via US 35, then back to Portland via US 26.

Rock climbing, Smith Rock State Park (p286

Worthy Detour

At Hood River, keep heading east. You'll notice an abrupt change in the scenery as the western gorge's forests turn to dry mountainsides. Stop at Rowena Crest for mind-blowing vistas, and Columbia Gorge Discovery Center for the area's history. Further, on the Washington side, is the excellent Maryhill Museum of Art – and a full-size replica of Stonehenge.

Time & Mileage

This loop is around 175 miles; expect to it to take two days.

Washington's Cascade Drive

In Washington's Cascades, high-altitude roads succumb to winter snow storms, and the names of peaks – Mt Terror, Mt Fury, Forbidden Peak – are intimidating. But there's also gorgeous scenery, amazing white water and small esoteric towns in

Trillium Lake and Mt Hood (p276)

this region, so fill up the tank and prepare for one of the best road trips of your life.

Why Go

Rugged and inaccessible for half the year, this brawny mountain drive is etched with a monumental, Alaskan-style beauty that once inspired Jack Kerouac.

Start in Everett, 30 miles north of Seattle, then head eastward on US 2. You'll climb to Steven's Pass at 4045ft, then down to Leavenworth, a beautifully located Bavarian-themed village where you can get German sausages, beer and cheese. Continuing south 22 miles, the scenery changes abruptly around Wenatchee, self-proclaimed 'world's apple capital.'

Now head north towards Chelan, home to a long lake of the same name that's very popular with boaters – you can camp and play on the beach at pretty Lake Chelan State Park. Next up is Winthrop, another themed town – but with a defined Wild West atmosphere that might bring out the cowboy in you. Further north, the outpost of Mazama is the place to stock up before hitting the desolate North Cascades.

Your gears will work hard on the engineering feat that is US 20, and the scenery will be spectacular. Stop at Washington Pass and Rainy Pass for stunning views of nearby peaks. If you feel like hiking, consider the 6.2-mile Maple Pass Loop Trail or the 7.4-mile trudge up to Easy Pass.

Hike, boat or just enjoy the wild scenery at Ross and Diablo Lakes. Heading west, the Skagit River Valley opens up as you drive through Marblemount and Rockport. Your road trip ends at Burlington.

When to Go

The summer months of June through September are the best times, when all roads are snow free and passable.

The Route

From Everett climb southeast towards Stevens Pass, then down to Leavenworth and Wenatchee. Go north through Chelan and Winthrop to the outpost of Mazama, then climb up US 20 through the spectacular Washington Cascades. The road opens to a valley at Marblemount, then down to foothills and your drive's end at Burlington.

Tunnel Island, Quinault Indian Reservation (p136), Olympic Peninsul

Worthy Detour

North of Burlington about 20 miles is historic Fairhaven, where you can start a beautiful Puget Sound tour that takes you south along Chuckanut Dr (p101) and through Whidbey Island to end at Langley, an endearing seafront community.

Time & Mileage

This loop is around 350 miles; expect to be on the road at least four days.

Olympic Peninsula Loop

Thick forests collide with an end-of-the-continent coastline that hasn't changed much since Juan de Fuca sailed by in 1592. Bring hiking boots and an umbrella – you'll need them as you explore this wild peninsula, replete with ancient rainforests and countless hiking, camping and adventurous exploration opportunities.

Why Go

Freakishly wet and fantastically green, the Olympic Peninsula makes a great loop through lush forests that inspired Stephanie Meyer's *Twilight* series.

Start at Washington's capital, Olympia, a progressive city known not only for its bureaucrats but also for its music, arts and outdoor-loving population. Now go west on US 101 to SR 8, which turns into US 12 and then meets back up with US 101, where you'll turn north. Lake Quinault is a deep-blue glacial relic where you can stay at a historic lodge and explore nearby hiking trails.

To the north is ethereally beautiful Ruby Beach, dotted with offshore rock sentinels. A bit further up on a side road lies the surreal Hoh Rain Forest, home to the Hall of Moss Trail – a place taken out of a Tolkien novel, with old-man's beard moss and ferns covering ancient trees.

Keeping on track, you'll pass Forks – the town made famous for *Twilight* vampires. Further east is Lake Crescent, where you can hike, fish and stay at another celebrated lodge. Not far away are Olympic Hot Springs and Sol Duc Hot Springs Resort. Now take another side road to Hurricane Ridge, a wind-lashed and high-altitude ridge with breathtaking views.

Next up is Port Townsend, a darling Victorian-esque seaside town with historic buildings and art galleries. To the south on yet another offshoot, Staircase is a drier section of Olympic National Park where you can camp on Lake Cushman and take in some glorious hikes. Finally, you'll end back where you started, at Olympia.

When to Go

There's less rain during the summer months from June to September.

The Route

From Olympia, head west on US 101 and eventually veer north toward Lake Quinault. Pass through Ruby Beach and (after a side trip to the Hoh Rain Forest) turn east past Lake Crescent, then take detours to Hurricane Ridge and Port Townsend. Finally turn south to close your loop.

Time & Mileage

Expect to log around 435 miles over four days on this peninsula.

Sea to Sky Highway

This short drive reveals the essence of British Columbia's coast, with majestic sea and mountain views, opportunities to get active or watch wildlife, and a peek into rich Native American cultures and pioneer history.

Why Go

The coastal scenery here is magnificent, as are the deep forests, crashing waterfalls and lofty mountains. You can see it all in a day, making this trip nearly too good to be true.

Green-forested hillsides tumble down around the village of Horseshoe Bay, which has a pleasant small-town vibe. Grab some organic coffee and head up on Hwy 99 north to Porteau Cove Provincial Park, once a Native American fishing site and now a haven for divers and beachcombers.

Next up is Britannia Beach, an old copper-mine site where you can visit the Britannia Mine Museum and take a mine tour. Just north, Shannon Falls torpedoes 1100ft down, and Brackendale is home to the largest population of wintering bald eagles in North America. Nearby, Alice and Brohm Lakes offer hiking and swimming.

Further north is Tantalus Lookout, a viewpoint that looks across the Tantalus Mountain Range and Squamish peoples' old hunting grounds. Now go 14 miles to Brandywine Falls Provincial Park, where a dramatic waterfall plunges 230ft into a pool. Your last stop is gorgeous Whistler, famous for skiing in winter and hiking and mountain biking in summer – along with plenty of upscale shopping and restaurants.

When to Go

Visit from June to September for hikes, or November to March for snow.

The Route

It's a straight shot from Horseshoe Bay to Whistler, along Howe Sound's coastline and up Hwy 99 through mountainous forests.

Time & Mileage

You'll go 82 miles over one or two days on this route.

Plan Your Trip

Pacific Northwest Outdoors

Armed with kayaks, crampons, fly rods, mountain bikes and full racks of climbing gear, adventure-loving people who migrate to the Pacific Northwest come to experience its world-famous great outdoors. There's a huge diversity of landscapes, and it's all reasonably accessible from the nearest town or city; within a day you can be on a river, coast, mountain, alpine lake, lava field, or in a high-desert canyon, rainforest or wetland.

Best Times to Go

December, February and March These months have the finest powder for skiing.

February to May Waterfalls are at their fullest after the winter rains.

November to June Whale-watchers can bark 'Thar she blows!'.

July to September The summer months are the best for hiking, camping or cycling.

Best Experiences

Hiking The West Coast Trail in Pacific Rim National Park and the forests around Mt Rainier and Mt Hood are all super.

Skiing Whistler-Blackcomb boasts world-class facilities.

Rock climbing Smith Rock State Park is stunning, for both its routes and vistas.

Cycling For road trips, Washington's San Juan Islands are prime. Oakridge, outside Eugene, has top-drawer mountain biking.

In this diverse landscape, you can carve fresh tracks in the champagne powder of world-class ski resorts or cling to your kiteboard as you hurl across the water at ferocious speeds. You can spin around 360 degrees on the summit of Mt Rainier or pedal your heart out going up and over the breathtaking Cascades. And if it's solitude you crave, set off with a backpack into the wilds – the hardest part will be choosing where to go. The Pacific Northwest is paradise for those who worship Mother Nature. If you're one of her followers, let the area unroll her carpet of snowy mountains, desert panoramas and wildflower meadows – and welcome you to her world.

Hiking & Mountaineering

The Pacific Northwest is blessed with some of the most sublime hiking landscapes and terrain imaginable. Summer sees crowds at their peaks, but the warming spring is the perfect time to witness gushing rivers, while fall is a splendor of foliage colors with temperatures remaining perfectly mild. In winter you'll practically be by yourself.

Ranger stations and visitor centers are excellent resources for permits, fees, safety and trail conditions.

The Cascade volcanoes and jutting spires in Oregon, Washington and British Columbia present climbers with an unprecedented number of choices, from easier day-long up-and-backs to multiday technical challenges.

Inexperienced climbers should seek out guide services, as bagging these peaks can be a hazardous proposition. Professional guide companies include American Alpine Institute (p97) in Washington, Timberline Mountain Guides (p278) in Oregon and **Canada West Mountain School** (☎888-892-2266, 604-878-7007; www.themountainschool. com; 47 W Broadway; ☐9) in British Columbia.

Oregon's Mazamas (p227) is a nonprofit mountaineering organization that offers hikes and climbs for both members and nonmembers. In British Columbia, the **BC Mountaineering Club** (www.bcmc.ca) also offers climbs, courses and programs for members and nonmembers.

Washington

In the Olympic Mountains you can hike deep canyons and alpine meadows, and the glacier-carved valleys and towering ridges of Washington's North Cascade Mountain Range offer dramatic and unforgettable landscapes. For spectacular views of glaciers and peaks head up 3.7 miles to Cascade Pass, and either return by the same route or continue 19.3 miles on to High Bridge, where a shuttle bus runs to Stehekin (a tiny settlement at the head of Lake Chelan with no road links to the rest of the state). There are many other wonderful hikes in North Cascades National Park.

In the Southern Cascades, you can explore the foothills of Mt Adams, or trudge up the steep trail to smoldering Mt St Helens. To leave the crowds behind, try isolated Glacier Peak, which offers a sparkly lake and alpine goodness to satiate your inner hiker. The classic Wonderland Trail circumnavigates the snowcapped behemoth Mt Rainier, but it takes a commitment: it's a seven- to 10-day hike.

For climbers, the peaks to tackle include:

➡ **Mt Rainier** – the imperial landmark of the region

➡ **Mt St Helens** – noted for being one of the more geologically interesting climbs; sometimes blows smoke from its newly forming crater

➡ **Mt Adams, Mt Baker, Mt Olympus** and **Glacier Peak** – other popular climbing destinations in the state.

Oregon

The Oregon coast's windswept beaches and rocky bluffs offer rugged and grandiose beauty. Check them out from the tip of Cape Falcon or from the top of Neahkahnie Mountain – both in Oswald West State Park. The challenging hike up Saddle Mountain also offers unbeatable views. Further south, Cape Lookout has a magnificent coastal panorama.

Just east of Portland, you can hike in the Columbia River Gorge among lush fir forests and dramatic waterfalls. Multnomah Falls is the hallmark, but there are other knockout hikes nearby, such as the Eagle Creek Trail or Dog Mountain (which is actually in Washington). South of the gorge, the popular 40-mile Timberline Trail Loop circumnavigates Mt Hood through alpine forests, and offers outstanding views. Ramona Falls is another awesome area hike.

In the Cascades, the challenging South Sister hike offers spectacular views from Oregon's third-highest peak. For exceptionally lofty views of Crater Lake – that turquoise phenomenon – hike up Mt Scott, high above the rim. In remote northeastern Oregon, the Wallowa Mountains, Eagle Cap Wilderness and Hells Canyon are other outdoor paradises.

Peaks to bag:

➡ **Mt Hood** – Oregon's highest mountain and one of the most climbed peaks in the world

➡ **Three Sisters** – just west of Bend; each is over 10,000ft; hard-core climbers do all three in one day (the 'Three Sisters Marathon')

➡ **Mt Bachelor, Broken Top, Mt Jefferson** and **Three-Fingered Jack** – other lofty peaks.

British Columbia

British Columbia has hundreds of out-of-this-world parks and innumerable trails. On Vancouver Island, trails such as the 47-mile West Coast Trail in Pacific Rim National Park wind through ancient rainforests and gorgeous shorelines. Or take one of Whistler's gondolas and enjoy wandering on high alpine trails without making the high alpine climb. For a stellar coastal hike, you can do an extensive trip or a day hike on the Juan de Fuca Marine Trail.

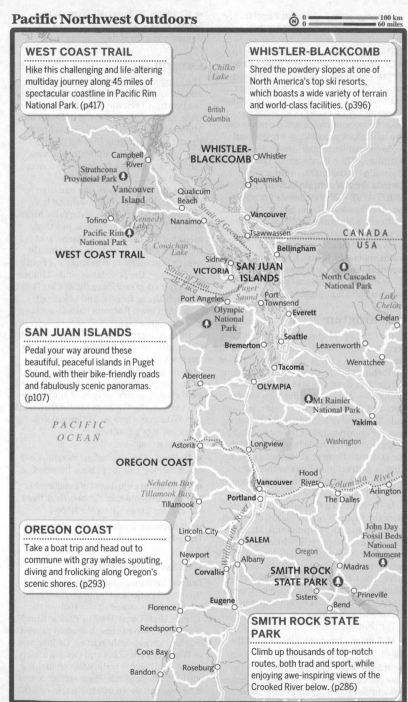

WEST COAST TRAIL

Hike this challenging and life-altering multiday journey along 45 miles of spectacular coastline in Pacific Rim National Park. (p417)

WHISTLER-BLACKCOMB

Shred the powdery slopes at one of North America's top ski resorts, which boasts a wide variety of terrain and world-class facilities. (p396)

SAN JUAN ISLANDS

Pedal your way around these beautiful, peaceful islands in Puget Sound, with their bike-friendly roads and fabulously scenic panoramas. (p107)

OREGON COAST

Take a boat trip and head out to commune with gray whales spouting, diving and frolicking along Oregon's scenic shores. (p293)

SMITH ROCK STATE PARK

Climb up thousands of top-notch routes, both trad and sport, while enjoying awe-inspiring views of the Crooked River below. (p286)

Cycling & Mountain Biking

A cyclist could hardly ask for more than the Pacific Northwest has to offer. Big cities including Seattle, Portland and Vancouver are some of the most bike-friendly on earth, offering safe bike lanes, a supportive bike network and endless shops for parts and advice. Even smaller cities such as Olympia, Eugene and Victoria (which even has a cycling festival) are well known for their bike culture.

Outside the urban centers there are diverse and spectacular cycling opportunities on the coast, in high deserts, through lush rainforest and up alpine mountains. Many ski resorts turn into mountain-biking destinations in summer; Whistler has an especially amazing trail system. And the bike-touring possibilities in the region are nearly limitless.

Local shops are great resources for route and back-road suggestions, while www.dbmechanic.com/biking has trail and bike-path info and links.

Washington

You can have an unparalleled multi-day cycling experience in the San Juan Islands that incorporates kayaking and hiking. Lopez Island is known for its flat terrain and bike friendliness, but all the islands are worth a pedal. If you're cycling with kids, head to Bainbridge or Vashon Islands. For a challenge, cycle the scenic loop around Mt Rainier.

The Yakima Valley offers picturesque wine country, while Lake Chelan also has vineyards – but is more of a mountain-biking spot. In eastern Washington, go to Moses Lake for the loop around Potholes Reservoir.

Near Mt St Helens, the Plains of Abraham/Ape Canyon Trail and the Lewis River Trail provide top-notch mountain biking in staggering Cascade scenery. The Wenatchee Lake and Leavenworth areas also attract riders; here you'll find Devil's

---

BIKE TOURS

A good way to start planning your tour is by deciding your vacation objectives and then building an itinerary around them. Go kayaking in the San Juans and have high tea in Victoria, but arrive by bicycle. Visit the Rose Garden in Portland then windsurf in the Gorge, but transport yourself by cycling the gorgeous landscape in between. The advantages are many: intimate experiences with the environment, staying in shape, rubbing elbows with the locals and traveling in an ecofriendly way. Maybe it seems intimidating, but once you get the hang of it, it's surprisingly pleasant and often addictive. You can choose to go fully loaded with camping equipment, or take it 'easy' and pedal from hotel to hotel.

Check www.bicycletouring101.com and www.bikingbis.com for more. *Cycling Sojourner: A Guide to the Best Multi-day Tours in Oregon* (www.cycletouringoregon. com) by Ellee Thalheimer is another recommended resource. (A similar book about bicycle touring in Washington is currently in the works and should be out in 2014.) Don't want to deal with the logistics? Try a tour company.

Adventure Cycling Association (www.adventurecycling.org) Guides supported and self-contained tours. It also sells good cyclist-specific maps for extensive touring.

Bicycle Adventures (www.bicycleadventures.com) Runs tours in Oregon, Washington and British Columbia, among other places.

Cascade Huts (www.cascadehuts.com) Offers mountain bikers hut-hopping, self-guided, multiday trips in Mt Hood National Forest.

Randonnée (www.randonneetours.com) Self-guided tours in BC's Gulf Islands.

Smith & Miller Productions (www.rollingpubcrawl.com) Tours Oregon by day and microbreweries by night.

Womantours (www.womantours.com) All-women company featuring an epic Northwest tour that circles half of Oregon.

Gulch, which boasts the smoothest, fastest single track in the state.

Closer to Seattle is easy Rattlesnake Lake, along with more challenging trails such as Black Diamond Coal Mine and Tiger Mountain's Poo Poo Point. Expert mountain-bike riders should head to Galbraith Mountain and Phillip Arnold Park.

Oregon

The Historic Columbia River Hwy and mellow Sauvie Island loop are two classic rides near Portland. Around the Cascade Range there are magnificent cycling destinations: the Cascade Lakes Hwy (Hwy 46) is stunningly beautiful, as is the Diamond Lake to Crater Lake challenge. On the

coast, Three Capes Dr near Tillamook has brilliant scenery and burly climbs. In the remote northeast, Hells Canyon Scenic Byway weaves more than 200 miles through dramatic landscape, and you can take side trips along Snake River.

For mountain biking near Portland there's Forest Park's Leif Erikson Dr, Powell Butte and Hagg Lake. Mt Hood's Surveyor's Ridge Trail has tremendous scenery (and makes you work for it), while Sandy Ridge is a relatively new and amazing trail system. Post Canyon (near Hood River) has gnarly free riding with big jumps and extensive wood features.

Oakridge, east of Eugene, has premier mountain biking. **Mountain Bike Oregon**

THE REGION'S BEST NATIONAL & PROVINCIAL PARKS

PARK	LOCATION	FEATURES	ACTIVITIES	BEST TIME TO VISIT
Crater Lake	Oregon	ancient volcano, deepest lake in North America	sightseeing, hiking, cross-country skiing	Jul-Sep
John Day Fossil Beds	Oregon	technicolor landscape of prehistoric ash flows, one of the world's foremost fossil sites	sightseeing, walking	year-round
Mt Rainier	Washington	alpine peaks, wildflowers; black bear, mountain goat, elk	hiking, climbing	Jul-Sep
Mt St Helens	Washington	spectacular volcano; elk, black bear, deer	hiking, sightseeing	Jun-Oct
North Cascades	Washington	alpine peaks, remote wilderness; mountain goat, grizzly bear, wolf	backpacking, climbing, fishing	Jul-Sep
Olympic	Washington	alpine peaks, lush rain forests, wild coasts; black bear, elk, spotted owl	backpacking, climbing, fishing	Jul-Sep
Oregon Dunes	Oregon	vast dune fields, remote coastlines, osprey	off-road vehicles, walking, horseback riding, canoeing, swimming, sandboarding	year-round
Pacific Rim	British Columbia	wild coast, giant rainforest trees, world-famous Coast Trail; bald eagle, black bear, cougar	hiking, kayaking	Jun-Sep
Strathcona	British Columbia	remote wilderness, solitude, highest Canadian waterfall; wolf, black-tailed deer, elk	backcountry hiking & adventure	Jul-Sep

(www.mtbikeoregon.com) is a well-known, three-day mountain-biking festival that happens twice in summer. Also relatively nearby, the McKenzie River Trail is some of the best single-track trail in Oregon; it takes you past scenic lakes, streams, waterfalls and lava fields.

Bend is the unofficial mountain-bike capital of the state, with ecosystems such as alpine forests and high desert canyons. Fine trails here include the Deschutes River, Phil's and Riverside.

British Columbia

This whole region is full of roads begging to be cycled. Vancouver Island's Saanich Peninsula is definitely a highlight, as are the rolling hills and pastoral scenery of the Cowichan Valley wine country. For short island rides with picturesque seascapes, take a couple of days and hop around the Gulf Islands. Right in Vancouver, both tourists and local cyclists frequent the beautiful 1000-acre Stanley Park – especially its 5.5-mile Seawall Trail.

Mountain biking is everywhere in British Columbia, both free riding and cross country. Rossland has some of the best technical rides in the region. Whistler, Squamish and Nelson are famous for their diverse, world-class mountain trails, while North Vancouver, Sun Peaks and the Sunshine Coast have extensive trail systems.

Whale-Watching

The Pacific Northwest is one of the world's premier spots for whale-watching. Since the shoreline is so long, if you want to see whales at their peak, pick a particular coastal spot – then find out when most whales will be passing through.

Washington

You can spot gray and humpback whales from Washington's coastline, especially from Long Beach (near the Oregon border), Westport and Ozette. The most famous kind of whale in this state, however, is the killer whale or orca.

About 90 resident orcas in several pods live year-round in the Puget Sound and San Juan Islands area, feeding on fish. The San Juan Islands in particular are the best place for spotting orcas, since they often swim close to shore. You can take boat tours from the islands or spot them from land – Lime Kiln Point State Park on San

---

WHALE-WATCHING IN OREGON

The high capes and headlands of the Oregon coast are excellent vantage points to watch for gray whales. Gray and humpback whales have the longest migrations of any mammal in the world: more than 5000 miles from the Arctic to Mexico, and back again. There are both spring and fall migrations; the springtime journey, which peaks in late March, brings the whales closer to shore, while the winter peak is in late December. Favorite whale-watching spots include Cape Arago, Cape Blanco, Cape Perpetua, Cape Meares, Cape Lookout, Ecola State Park, Shore Acres State Park and Yaquina Head Outstanding Natural Area.

Depoe Bay and Newport are especially dedicated to the activity, though, and here you'll find several tour-boat companies willing to take you out. An organization called **Whale Watching Spoken Here** (www.whalespoken.org) rallies hundreds of trained volunteers to assist visitors in spotting whales at various sites all along the Oregon Coast. Check the website for details. And be sure to drop into the **Whale Watching Center** (Depoe Bay), offering exhibits and sea views.

Although whales can be seen with the naked eye, it's best to have a good pair of binoculars. After seeing a blow, watch for glimpses of the whale's head, knuckled back and flukes (tail). A whale's rhythmic breathing and diving usually follows a pattern of three to five short, shallow dives spread a minute or two apart, followed by one deep dive (called a 'sounding') lasting five minutes or more. A tail that breaks the surface usually indicates a sounding – the whale should reappear 300yd to 400yd from where it was last sighted. If you're lucky, you might even witness a breach, where the whale propels nearly its whole body out of the water!

Juan Island is an especially good place. And while you're here, be sure to visit the Whale Museum (p108) in Friday Harbor.

The best time to spot orcas is from April to September; numerous charter companies run cruises from the San Juans, Puget Sound and Seattle. You might be able to spot orcas from a ferry too.

Out on the coast, any orcas you might see are part of transient pods that can roam from Alaska to California. These killer whales don't interact with resident pods, and their diet includes seals, sea lions and even small whales.

British Columbia

Every March, Tofino and Ucluelet – the communities surrounding Pacific Rim National Park Reserve on Vancouver Island – put on the **Pacific Rim Whale Festival** (www. pacificrimwhalefestival.com), celebrating the northbound travels of the gray whale during its spring migration. With an estimated 20,000 whales passing through, you're likely to spot a few blowholes around here from March to May.

Another good place on land to try spotting whales is Telegraph Cove, where orcas can often be seen; visit the Whale Interpretive Centre (p423) here. If you'd rather go for a super close-up, however, there are several boat-tour companies in Victoria.

Skiing & Snowboarding

A legion of mountainsides dusted with prime powder translates into top-drawer skiing or snowboarding in the Northwest. Add a down-to-earth, casual and family-friendly regional vibe – without the pretensions of many uberfancy resorts (except for perhaps Whistler) – and you're sure to have a great, laid-back time on the slopes.

The peak season runs from about December to March, with shoulder seasons offering fewer crowds and the possibility of discount tickets. On Mt Hood you can ski any month of the year; it's the only resort in the US that offers year-round skiing (though it's closed for maintenance for two weeks around Labor Day in September). If you want to avoid waiting in long lines, go midweek.

Backcountry skiing is very popular in the Pacific Northwest. Obviously, you will need to be skilled in backcountry travel, know how to ski out of an avalanche and be trained in wilderness first aid (and carry a kit). A couple of books with great information are *Backcountry Ski! Oregon* by Christopher Van Tilburg and *Backcountry Ski! Washington* by Seabury Blair Jr. Local mountain shops should have recommendations on where to go, based on the latest weather conditions.

If you're willing to take the financial plunge, there's also heli-skiing/boarding. The North Cascade mountains are the place to go in Washington. In British Columbia there's a wide variety. Check out www. heliskiguide.com.

Cross-Country Skiing & Snowshoeing

In the Pacific Northwest, snowy winters make for a diversity of wonderlands to explore on cross-country skis or snowshoes. And these sports are easy, accessible and appealing to almost anyone. Renting equipment is affordable but not always available on-site, so you may need to snag your gear before reaching your destination. Mountain-sport shops and ranger stations are a great source of local information.

Washington

Washington's premier destination is the Methow Valley, the second-largest cross-country skiing area in the USA, which boasts around 120 miles of groomed trails. You can also break trail through alpine meadows and evergreens in Olympic National Park. The Mt Baker area also offers many spectacular jaunts, with especially good trails around Silver Fir campground and at Heather Meadows. Meanwhile, Wenatchee National Forest holds some prime trails with mountain vistas, ice caves, ancient forests and solitude.

Oregon

Oregon's Mt Hood area has fantastic spots including Teacup Lake, Trillium Lake and White River Canyon, all with great views of the mountain. Around Bend there's Mt Bachelor, a world-class Nordic center with extensive groomed trails, and Dutchman

Flat, offering panoramas of the surrounding peaks. Further south you can ski around serene Odell Lake and through pristine snow along the rim of Crater Lake, which is gorgeous in winter – and devoid of crowds. And in eastern Oregon, near Baker City, is the Anthony Lakes Mountain Resort.

British Columbia

In BC, cross-country skiing and snowshoeing are hugely popular, and there are endless possibilities all over the region. Vancouver has three ski areas less than 30 minutes from downtown, with Grouse Mountain especially popular. Ski resorts such as Big White and Whistler have tremendous trail systems.

TOP SKI RESORTS
••

Washington

Crystal Mountain (☎360-663-2265; www.crystalmountainresort.com; 33914 Crystal Mountain Blvd, Hwy 410) Just off the eastern flank of Mt Rainier National Park, this majestic ski area offers unparalleled views of Mt Rainier and some of the best skiing on the West Coast. Located 80 miles from Seattle, Crystal is the largest of the ski areas with the most accessible peak skiing, a wide variety of terrain and a reputation for powder. It is consistently rated by ski magazines as a top North American ski destination.

Mt Baker (☎360-734-6771; www.mtbaker.us; Hwy 542) Mt Baker boasts the highest annual snowfall of any ski resort in the world (640in), and as such holds the world record for most snow in a season (1140in during the 1998–99 season). Rightly famous for its powder, expert runs and backcountry, Baker is also home to the **Legendary Banked Slalom** every February. The slalom started in 1985 and is considered to be the first organized snowboarding competition in the world. Situated east of Bellingham, Mt Baker is about three hours' drive from Seattle.

Stevens Pass (☎206-812-4510; www.stevenspass.com; Summit Stevens Pass, 9331 US Hwy 2) Stevens Pass is some 80 miles east, and slightly north, of Seattle. The resort averages 450in of annual snowfall and is known for its wide variety of terrain. It has everything from glades to bowls to bumps to an elaborate terrain park, making it good for groups and families that vary in skill level. There's also a huge lift-accessible 'backside' area that gives an awesome backcountry experience, and to top it all off it's 100% run by wind power.

Oregon

Cat Ski Mt Bailey (☎800-733-7593, ext 754; www.catskimtbailey.com) Backcountry tours only. Acclaimed powder is accessed via snow cats that seat up to 12. Very close to Crater Lake.

Mt Bachelor (☎800-829-2442; www.mtbachelor.com) Very boarder friendly, with colder, drier snow. Located just outside Bend.

Mt Hood (☎503-337-2222; www.skihood.com) Consists of three main resort areas: Meadows, the biggest and most renowned; Timberline, with year-round skiing; and Ski Bowl, the largest night-ski area in the US.

British Columbia

Big White Ski Resort (☎800-663-2772; www.bigwhite.com) Deep, dry powder combined with terrain that pleases both skiers and snowboarders. Plenty of backcountry options.

Cypress Mountain (☎604-419-7669; www.cypressmountain.com) Home to the freestyle snowboarding park of the 2010 Winter Olympics, with great night skiing.

Whistler-Blackcomb (☎866-218-9690; www.whistlerblackcomb.com) Gigantic, powder-laden resort that hosted the alpine events of the 2010 Winter Olympics. A new gondola (over 4km long) connects the peaks of Whistler and Blackcomb Mountains.

SEA & LAKE KAYAKING

To a kayaker, the Pacific Northwest is an oasis. It offers intricate and protected waterways, abundant marine life, coastal splendor, campsite access, alpine lakes and plentiful public parks. Sea or lake kayaking is more relaxed than white-water kayaking, inspiring quiet exploration of the natural world rather than rampaging through it with a big dose of adrenaline.

On a calm lake or estuary you can usually paddle around knowing just the basic safety fundamentals, but paddling on the ocean requires some technical knowledge and close attention to tides and currents. In temperate regions sea kayaking can be a year-round activity, but summer is really when sea kayakers luxuriate in their sport.

In Washington there is world-class kayaking on the Olympic Peninsula, in the San Juan Islands and in Puget Sound; avid sea kayakers shouldn't miss the stunning Cascadia Marine Trail. In British Columbia, the Pacific Rim National Park Reserve's Broken Group Islands are kayaking heaven, but there are also great spots in the Southern Gulf Islands and around Victoria and Tofino. Oregon has plenty of coastal bays and inland lakes to explore, along with excellent rivers including the McKenzie, Deschutes and North Umpqua.

Nearly all outdoor towns and cities near large bodies of water have kayaking outfitters; tours and renting gear are both possible.

Rock Climbing

With its wide variety of geology – think high granite cliffs and colorful volcanic rock – there's some world-class sport and trad climbing in the Pacific Northwest. Anyone from beginner to expert should find excellent, fun routes, many with views of surrounding mountains, forests or even bodies of water.

Washington

Washington's climbing mecca is Leavenworth, which refers to both the Bavarian-themed tourist town and its surrounding climbing area. You'll have hundreds of single and multipitch routes to choose from among the highly featured granite crags, and there's some great bouldering as well. Climbing here is best in spring or fall, as summertime can be very hot.

Just an hour's drive northeast of Seattle are the thin, clean cracks of Index Town Wall. The granite faces here rise up to 500ft from a verdant forest below. As most routes are 5.8 or higher, this area is best for advanced climbers. And close to the Oregon border is Beacon Rock, offering technically demanding multipitches. Other good destinations in Washington include Darrington, Mt Erie, North Bend and Vantage. For more information see www.climbingwashington.com.

Oregon

Smith Rock State Park is Oregon's premier rock-climbing destination – and a gorgeous place to visit even if you don't climb. Eroded from an old volcanic vent, the high canyon walls here are home to more than 1000 sport and traditional routes of all levels. The views are spectacular, especially from multipitch routes, and bouldering is also possible. As with Leavenworth, spring and fall are the best times to climb, as summertime sees high temperatures.

Other hot Oregon climbing spots are French's Dome near Mt Hood, Broughton Bluff near Troutdale and Horsethief Butte in the Columbia River Gorge. Also note that Beacon Rock is very close to Portland.

British Columbia

British Columbia spoils its climbing community with places such as Squamish, located about 40 miles north of Vancouver. Featuring high-quality granite often compared with Yosemite's, this destination boasts more than 200 diverse routes including the Chief, a 2000ft-high granite dome with world-class multipitches.

Fleming Beach, Mt Wells, Mt MacDonald, East Sooke Park and Strathcona Provincial Park are all good climbing destinations on Vancouver Island.

White-Water Kayaking & Rafting

Water gushes down from ice-capped volcanoes and spires in the Pacific Northwest, creating a play-land for white-water enthusiasts. The region's diversity of world-class river landscapes is amazing; there's high desert, steep canyons or old-growth forest. White-water crazies run rivers year-round, but most people come out from May until September.

Washington

Washington's rivers are prime time. The Upper Skagit River has great rafting opportunities, along with a chance to spot bald eagles. The Klickitat flows through remote wilderness canyons, while the Tieton boasts

BUT WAIT, THERE'S MORE...

ACTIVITY	WHERE?	WHAT?	MORE INFORMATION PLEASE
Diving	east coast of Vancouver Island, BC	wolf eels, octopuses, navy ships	www.divenanaimo.travel
	Puget Sound, WA	famously clear water, diverse marine life (giant octopuses!)	www.underwatersports.com, www.pugetsound-divecharters.com
Horseback riding	Long Beach, WA	guided rides on beach & dunes	www.longbeachhorse rides.com
	Methow Valley, WA	day rides with cowboy barbecue	www.sunmountainlodge.com
	Pasayten Wilderness, WA	multiday llama trekking	www.delillama.com
	Washington Cascades, WA	reasonably priced day rides out of Easton	www.happytrailsateas-tonwa.com
	Florence, OR	romantic beach rides	www.oregonhorseback-riding.com
	Oregon Cascades, OR	lava flows, lakes & forests	www.lhranch.com
	Vancouver Island, BC	panoramic island scenery	www.woodgatestables.com
Paragliding & hang gliding	Lake Chelan, WA	soar nearly endlessly; 100-mile flights are not uncommon	www.chelanflyers.com
	Lakeview, OR	warm thermals, towering cliffs & conditions for all levels	www.lakecountychamber.org/hang, www.cascadeparaglidingclub.org/pages/lakeview.php
	Fraser Valley, BC	wide rivers, rolling farmland & verdant valleys	www.flybc.org, www.westcoastsoaringclub.com
Surfing	Westhaven State Park, Half Moon Bay & the Groins, all near Westport, WA	extreme tides & rugged surfing conditions – especially outside summer	www.steepwatersurf-shop.com, www.surfwa.org
	short sands near Oswald West State Park, OR	friendlier than most, good for all levels, great scenery	www.oregonstateparks.org/park_195.php, www.oregonsurf.com
	Otter Rock near Depoe Bay, OR	great for beginners & longboarders	http://magicseaweed.com/Otter-Rock-Surf-Report/317
	Tofino, BC	dramatic waves & long, sandy beaches	www.coastalbc.com

the state's fastest white water. The White Salmon River is known for its smorgasbord of rapids and for hosting competitions for the extreme white-water elite. And let's not forget the Wenatchee and the Skykomish – both roaring, popular rivers – while the Hoh and Elwha offer milder, scenic adventures.

Portland

There are worthy rivers relatively close to Portland, such as the Clackamas and North Santiam (a locally known jewel). The Deschutes is another river very popular with Portlanders, and often boasts sunny, warm weather. The Rogue is a classic – a premier run protected by Congress and offering beauty, wildlife, history and amazing rapids. Other excellent rafting rivers include the North Umpqua (great forest scenery), John Day (longest free-flowing river in Oregon), McKenzie (with great hot springs and fishing nearby) and the Owyhee (in a remote but stunningly beautiful canyon).

British Columbia

On Vancouver Island, you can live it up rafting the varied waters of the Campbell, Cowichan, Nimpkish and Gold Rivers. Conveniently located near Vancouver is the Capilano, or travel about 1½ hours away for the Chilliwack River.

Windsurfing & Kiteboarding

The Columbia River Gorge is the gusty superstar of wind sports in the Pacific Northwest. Unlike any other river in the US, here you can windsurf or kiteboard with the eastbound winds and float back on the westbound current. People pilgrimage to Hood River (ground zero for these activities) from all over the world to take on the gorge's famously strong and consistent winds. Check them at http://thegorgeismygym.com.

Oregon

There are other first-class wind-sport sites, especially on the Oregon Coast. These include the South Jetty at Fort Stevens State Park (in Astoria), Floras Lake (outside Port Orford) and Pistol River State Park (between Gold Beach and Brookings); the last hosts the Pistol River Wave Bash, a competition that takes place in June. Sauvie Island, near Portland, is a great place to learn.

Washington

In Washington, Jetty Island in the Seattle area has world-class kiteboarding and is one of the top places for beginners, as is Lake Washington. Other outstanding places are Lake Wenatchee and Bellingham Bay.

British Columbia

The beaches of Kitsilano in Vancouver are popular launching points for urban windsurfers, while breezy Squamish Spit, 40 miles north, is BC's favorite spot to catch some kiteboarding wind. Tofino, on Vancouver Island's west coast, is the province's surf central, with dozens of operators (best for advanced kiteboarders).

Fishing

The waterways of the Olympic Peninsula, such as the Hoh, Queets and Elwha, are regarded as some of the best salmon rivers in the world. North of Seattle, the Sauk and Skagit Rivers are famous for winter steelhead. Saltwater fishing in Westport, Ilwaco and Puget Sound is revered by anglers.

The Deschutes River near Bend is famous for its trout and steelhead. Close to Roseburg, the North Umpqua – with 33 miles of river set aside for fishing – is touted for summer steelhead and small-mouth bass, along with its fall salmon runs. Other steelhead rivers are the Rogue, Sandy and Clackamas, while the McKenzie is home to trout and salmon. The John Day is great for small-mouth and large-mouth bass, and the mighty Columbia is hard to beat for its salmon and sturgeon.

On the coast, Tillamook Bay is a prime spot for salmon because several large runs converge here. Up and down the coast, however, are opportunities to hook some albacore tuna, rockfish and halibut.

The Thompson and Skeena Rivers have made names for themselves with their plentiful salmon and steelhead. Near Vancouver, the Pitt River is known for its trout varieties. Over on the Sunshine Coast, the fruitful lakes and inlets are popular with anglers.

For state information see www.dfw. state.or.us, wdfw.wa.gov and www.env.gov. bc.ca/fw.

Plan Your Trip

Travel with Children

From aquariums teeming with sea life to cowboys riding bucking broncos, the Pacific Northwest will spark any child's imagination. Whether you head to the coast, the mountains or rolling farmland, you'll be greeted with kindness and patience – this is a culture that loves kids and knows how to treat families right, whether they're giving wee ones a glimpse of rural life (who doesn't like to milk goats?) or showing them public art that was designed to be scaled by the younger set.

Pacific Northwest for Kids

From the sun, sand and surf along the coast to the snow-covered slopes further inland, the Pacific Northwest is a fun and exciting destination for families. Kids will love exploring the many child-oriented museums, amusement parks, zoos and animal safaris. National and state parks often organize family-friendly exhibitions or activities, and whale-watching can be a big hit. There are also plenty of kid-friendly hotels, restaurants, shops, playgrounds and even skateboard parks in the region. Finding things to do with your kids won't be a problem, but dragging them away from all that fun might be.

For general information, advice and anecdotes, read Lonely Planet's *Travel with Children*.

Best Regions for Kids

Seattle

Kids will love the Pacific Science Center, Children's Museum, Seattle Aquarium, Woodland Park Zoo and Pike Place Market. Nearby, Tacoma's Point Defiance Zoo & Aquarium boasts sharks *and* elephants.

Portland

Frolicking fountains, the world-class Oregon Zoo, and hands-on museums, including the Children's Museum and World Forestry Center.

Oregon Coast

Miles of beaches, plus the Oregon Coast Aquarium in Newport, the less flashy Seaside Aquarium, and Port Orford's dinosaur-filled Prehistoric Gardens.

Vancouver, Whistler & Vancouver Island

Vancouver highlights are Stanley Park, the Vancouver Aquarium and Granville Island's Kids Market. And what could be better than British Columbia's Victoria Bug Zoo, home to millipedes and tarantulas?

Children's Highlights

Theme Parks

➡ Riverfront Park in Spokane, WA. (p204)

➡ Oaks Amusement Park in Portland, OR. (p223)

➡ Enchanted Forest near Salem, OR. (p253)

➡ **Playland at the PNE** (www.pne.ca/playland; Hastings Park; day pass adult/child $33/24; ◷10am-6pm, variable by date, May-late Sep) in Vancouver, BC.

Sun, Sand & Sea

➡ Long Beach (p146) and La Push (p141; teenagers and *Twilight* connection!) in Washington.

➡ Newport's Oregon Coast Aquarium and Seaside's boardwalk in Oregon. (p308)

Historical Places

➡ San Juan Island National Historical Park (p109) and Fort Vancouver (p150) in Washington.

➡ Lewis & Clark National Historical Park (p294) and Champoeg State Heritage Area (p246) in Oregon.

➡ Fort Langley (p381) and **Britannia Mine Museum** (www.britanniaminemuseum.ca; adult/child $21.50/13.50; ◷9am-5pm) in Vancouver.

Science Museums

➡ Seattle's Pacific Science Center (p72) and Spokane's Mobius Children's Museum in Washington.

➡ Olympia's Hands On Children's Museum in Washington. (p122)

➡ Eugene's Science Factory (p257), Ashland's Scienceworks (p326) and Portland's Oregon Museum of Science & Industry (p223) in Oregon.

➡ Science World in Vancouver. (p378)

Snow Sports

➡ Crystal Mountain (p49) and Stevens Pass (p49) in Washington.

➡ Mts Hood and Bachelor in Oregon. (p49)

➡ Grouse Mountain (p381) and Whistler-Blackcomb (p49) in Vancouver.

Watery Antics

➡ Wings & Waves Waterpark in McMinnville, OR. (p248)

➡ Slidewaters Water Park at Lake Chelan, WA. (p170)

➡ **Granville Island Water Park** (◷10am-6pm mid-May–early Sep) FREE in Vancouver, BC.

Fun Food Frolics

➡ Portland's Saturday Market (p218), Seattle's Pike Place Market (p69) and Vancouver's Granville Island Public Market (p379).

➡ Baked goods, produce and cheese samples from any of the region's hundreds of farmers markets.

Watching Wildlife

➡ Whale-watching all down the Pacific Northwest coast, from November to June. (p47)

➡ Tide pools! Check out the best ones on p456.

➡ Sea Lion Caves on the Oregon Coast. (p312)

Planning

Kids often get discounts on motel stays, museum admission and restaurant meals; the definition of child, however, can vary from age zero to 18 years.

Supermarkets have a great choice of baby food, infant formula, soy and cow's milk, disposable diapers (nappies) and other necessities. In urban areas you'll find all manner of organic and dietary-restricted kids food in restaurants and natural markets. If you don't want to lug gear around for your whole trip, head to a baby-equipment rental company, such as http://new.happylittletraveler. com in Seattle, www.katelynscloset.com in Portland or www.weetravel.ca in Vancouver. Diaper-changing stations can be found in many public toilets, including ones inside the multitude of rest areas along highways and interstates. Online services including www.sittercity.com and www.care.com can help you find a babysitter.

When crossing the border from the US into Canada, be sure to bring birth certificates or passports for each child; if a child enters the country with only one parent, she or he must have a letter from the other parent saying it's OK for the child to enter Canada. Very family-friendly destinations are marked with a ⛑ icon.

Sweet Dreams

Most hotels accept children; a few offer babysitting services. Motels are even more family friendly, sometimes boasting pool, playground and/or kitchenettes. Larger campgrounds often cater to families; yurts in state parks are a great way for families to camp in some luxury.

Places that aren't as good for kids are youth hostels and B&Bs, which often don't take children under a certain age. Consider asking some questions when booking. Do kids stay for free? Do you offer playpens, cribs or roll-away beds? How far to the nearest park or playground?

BEST PLACES TO STAY
··

Check out (and into) these places if you have young ones along:

➜ Kennedy School (p230) in Portland, OR. It's a former elementary school, but there's no homework – just rooms in old classrooms and a theater in the old gym (showing 'Mommy Matinees'!)

➜ Out 'n' About Treesort (p335) near Oregon Caves National Monument, OR. Ever stay in a treehouse? Here's your chance! Zip lines, tree climbs and horseback rides are also available.

➜ Stehekin Valley Ranch (p168) in Stehekin, WA. Stay in various types of cabins, set in the beautiful North Cascades. Activities include hikes, horseback riding, mountain biking and kayaking.

➜ Seabrook Cottage Rentals (p143) in Pacific Beach, WA. Vacation rentals on lovely Pacific Beach. Fly kites, ride bikes, watch birds, go clam digging, build sand castles, collect seashells...

➜ Ocean Village (p419) in Tofino, BC. A cabin beach resort that supplies families with beach toys, boogie boards, campfires, games, crafts, kids' programs and a 50ft indoor saltwater pool.

Dining Out

In general, restaurants welcome children of all ages and have high chairs and booster seats. Many have children's menus and some even supply crayons. If you're planning a special, high-end meal, especially one that requires reservations, ask if children are welcome.

While most eateries in Seattle qualify as kid friendly, some excel at welcoming little ones, including Twirl Cafe and Molly Moon's. Portland is also considered particularly kid friendly, and some restaurants – such as Old Wives' Tales – have a playroom. Even a few brewpubs here welcome children, such as the Laurelwood Public House. In Vancouver, families love Little Nest.

Group Play

Parks with water features, coffeehouses with playrooms and a variety of classes are all ways that parents and kids can meet new people. Seek out activities through websites such as www.urbanmamas.com, which has a calendar of events in Portland as well as weekly summer camps (a good way to entertain kids during longer stays). Similar websites in Seattle and Vancouver are www.redtri.com/seattle-kids and www.bcparent.ca.

Driving Safely

Child-restraint laws vary state by state and are subject to change, so always double check before traveling.

In Oregon, Washington and Vancouver, BC, child passengers under 40lb must be restrained in an approved child safety seat. Children over 40lb (or who are at the maximum weight limit of their car seat's harness system) must use a booster seat until they are 4ft9in (145cm) or eight years of age (nine in Vancouver).

A child over 4ft9in or eight years of age (nine in Vancouver) must properly use the vehicle's seat belt. Infants under one year of age and under 20lb must ride in a rear-facing child safety seat away from air bags.

Most car-rental agencies rent safety seats for infants and older children. Reserve in advance.

In Washington and Oregon, there are reasonably spaced rest areas along I-5.

Regions at a Glance

The Pacific Northwest boasts everything from crashing surf along its spectacular coastline to the gorgeous, scenic peaks of Mt Rainier and Mt Hood, creating a varied outdoor playground for hikers, climbers, campers and skiers. And its rich agricultural lands offer a diverse array of year-round seasonal produce that has inspired chefs, winemakers and beer brewers throughout the region.

The major urban centers of Seattle, Portland and Vancouver are also shaped by the natural world, with parks and outdoor sculpture gardens. But indoor culture rivals any outdoor fun, especially during the gray days of winter; think coffee bars, brewpubs, art museums, theater, music and great restaurants.

Seattle

Nightlife
Food
Art

Bars & Pubs

Find a mixture of cocktail bars, dance clubs and live music on Capitol Hill. From funky to upscale, these watering holes serve up local craft brews and fruity cocktails to the perennially thirsty. And the city that was home to grunge won't disappoint live-music lovers.

Seafood

Few cities are so intertwined with the ocean's bounty. If Seattle's waterfront isn't proof enough, head to Pike Place Market for its slippery 'flying' fish show. Then pick a nearby restaurant to taste the seasonal oysters and catch of the day.

Visual Expression

Begin to understand the city's fascination with art at Olympic Sculpture Park, then visit the Seattle Art Museum, the Asian Art Museum and the absolutely stunning Chihuly Garden & Glass exhibit.

p62

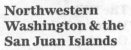

Northwestern Washington & the San Juan Islands

Whales
Cycling
Landscapes

Thar She Blows

Whales frequently populate waters near the coastline and around the islands of this verdant region. From Lime Kiln Point State Park, scan the horizon for signs of that telltale blow – or pop into the Whale Museum in Friday Harbor to learn more about orcas.

Pedal Power

Bicycles rule the landscape of the San Juans. Island-hop with your two-wheeler to enjoy rolling paved roads that reveal stunning vistas overlooking the sea. Don't forget to detour at coffee shops and juice bars for fuel.

Sweet Scenery

Heavy rains make this a lush place, with fir-covered islands and green mountain foothills. But the sparkling sea provides the most impressive backdrop, especially on the jewel-like San Juan Islands.

p94

Olympic Peninsula & Washington Coast

Forests
Beaches
Lodges

Olympic National Park

Declared a national park in 1938, the 1406-sq-mile Olympic National Park holds some of the country's most pristine forests. Hikers, cyclists, fishers and campers flock here to see wildlife and enjoy trails, rivers and lakes.

Kites & Oysters

Washington's coastline stretches from Ocean Shores to the edge of the Columbia River, offering hundreds of miles of smooth kite-flying areas, sandy dunes and crashing surf. Don't miss local oyster farms, which can supply a feast on the half shell.

Waterside Lodges

After a full day of outdoor exploring, settle into a bed at Lake Crescent Lodge or Lake Quinault Lodge – both are historic national-park lodges full of character. And don't forget Kalaloch Lodge, spectacularly located on a bluff overlooking the Pacific.

p121

Washington Cascades

Volcanoes
Scenic Drives
Mountain Treks

Explosive Geology

Five potentially lethal volcanoes punctuate the Washington Cascades – and showed their potential in May 1980, when Mt St Helens erupted with devastating consequences. Visit the trails or crevasse-covered glaciers traversing their flanks.

Glacier & Mountain Views

Roads here wind between wilderness areas and two national parks, creating the ideal conditions for a road trip. Enjoy the views of glacier-draped peaks and the rolling ridges of the Cascades, making scenic memories that will last a lifetime.

Peak Bagging

All levels of mountaineers bag peaks in these parts, although Mt Rainier rules as the most challenging summit. Even so, beginners can hire experienced guides and make the ascent during the wee hours of the morning.

p152

Central & Eastern Washington

Wine
Culture
Outdoors

Tasting Rooms

The parched desert hills of southeastern Washington are producing some stellar grapes, the prima donnas of the state's burgeoning wine industry. Head to Walla Walla for a high concentration of tasting rooms, wineries and wine-friendly restaurants.

Bavarian Transplant

Dust off your lederhosen and belt out a German drinking song in Leavenworth, Washington's very own Bavarian village. The quirky theme town sits within easy reach of the picturesque North Cascade peaks, a good place to take a picnic of brats and gingerbread.

Natural Solitude

Don't cross this remote area off your list for outdoor recreating. National forests, tiny ski areas and pockets of alpine splendor offer quiet, off-the-beaten-path spots for great outdoor fun.

p185

Portland

Food
Cycling
Drinking

Locavore Nation

What happens when young, expressive chefs collide with some of the nation's best locally grown produce and meats? Portland's food scene. Even the food carts here have become outlets for culinary expression, as the city's top restaurants take Northwest cuisine to new heights.

Celebrating the Bike

With the highest percentage of bicycle commuters in the US, this town celebrates all things bikey through costume theme rides, races, the Zoobomb, handcrafted-bike shows and a slew of bike-delivery businesses.

Brewpubs, Wine Bars & Cafes

Countless breweries and brewpubs offer craft beers, while just as many wine bars pour their own wares – and even more coffee shops serve the country's best java! And did we mention the distillery movement?

p214

The Willamette Valley & Wine Country

Wine
Hot Springs
B&Bs

Pinot Production

The valley's mild summers and long, wet winters foster the delicate, thin-skinned pinot-noir grape, the variety that's become famous in these parts. Try various vintages at winery tasting rooms, B&Bs and wine bars, which are popping up even in small towns.

Steaming Soaks

One of Oregon's best free soaks, Bagby Hot Springs, is a few hours' drive east of Salem. Climb into hollowed-log tubs here or head down the road to the Breitenbush Hot Springs Resort, a rustic, laid-back experience with yoga, massage and vegetarian food.

Small-Scale Lodging

As wine country grows, so do its lodging options, and tiny, well-run B&Bs provide the perfect base for navigating the vines. Look for historic inns, working farms and vineyard homes with tasting areas and cozy rooms for guests.

p243

Columbia River Gorge

Waterfalls
Hiking
Fruit

Raging Waters

The massive Columbia River is fed by hundreds of waterfalls, many of which flow year-round. Hike to and around some roaring giants that soak the surrounding mossy forests with a perpetual sprinkling.

The Gorge for All

The gorge is a prime destination for hikers and backpackers, especially those who like to gain vertical. But well-maintained trails usually come with a gentle crisscross of switchbacks, making any gorge trail doable at the right speed. Look for spring wildflowers and fall foliage.

Fruit Loop Drive

Just outside Hood River, a 35-mile driving loop takes you through dozens of orchards and farms selling everything from lavender and pumpkins to pears and cherries – depending on the season. There are even a few wineries on the way, and many orchards offer U-pick opportunities.

p262

Central Oregon & the Oregon Cascades

Mountains
Water
Beer

Winter Fun

Starting with the glaciers of Mt Hood and stretching down through the Three Sisters Wilderness, some of Oregon's steepest slopes translate to prime skiing, snowboarding and mountain biking. Resorts outside Bend generally offer fluffier powder than their Mt Hood counterparts.

Lakes & Rivers

While Crater Lake – down south toward Ashland – is the best-known lake in the Cascades, you can't ignore other serene waters. Visit Waldo and Cascade Lakes, and waterways such as the Deschutes and Metolius Rivers – prime spots for white-water rafting, kayaking and fishing.

Bend's Craft Brews

Bend's brewing scene has exploded. Today, 14 breweries (and counting) pump out exceptional beers; stop by the tasting rooms (and maybe 'hop' on a tour!) to sample the sudsy creations.

p275

Oregon Coast

Beaches
Cycling
Weather

Public Access

Thanks to some serious forward thinking, every inch of Oregon's 363 coastal miles is public land. Since the early 1900s the state has created more than 80 parks and recreation areas along this exceptionally beautiful shoreline.

Riding 101

Cyclists everywhere dream of riding this stretch of Hwy 101, a windy road that rises and falls between bluffs and cliffside overlooks. It can get busy with cars and RVs, so nerves of steel are a must. But those who've made the journey know it's worth sharing the road.

Storm-Watching

The coast can be a dramatic place, defined by brilliant sunbursts followed by pounding hailstorms, rainbows or lightning. Delight in the drama, especially during the winter months when empty beaches create the chance to commune with the boastful weather gods.

p293

Ashland & Southern Oregon

Wine
Theater
Lodging

Rising Vines

A warmer, sunnier climate has helped create some of Oregon's fledgling wine regions. Grapes in the Umpqua and Applegate Valleys, and around Jacksonville, Grants Pass and Medford, are transformed into big reds and oakey whites.

Shakespeare

Any festival that runs for nine months of the year shouldn't be ignored, but Ashland's Oregon Shakespeare Festival will grab your attention more for quality than quantity. Topnotch productions, including plays, readings and concerts, honor the Bard and his vast body of work.

Sweet Sleeps

Maybe it's the nearby Shakespeare Festival that inspires such charm, but this region boasts exceptional lodgings, including the landmark Crater Lake Lodge, Wolf Creek Inn (near Grant's Pass) and Ashland's Country Willows B&B.

p325

Eastern Oregon

Wilderness
Hiking
Geology

Desert Solitude

If you think wilderness is defined by how many people you don't see on any given day, this region is pure bliss. Hard to reach and bare of national parks or huge attractions, this is the place to slip into forests, mountains and especially deserts – and find peace.

Twisting Trails

Hikers can find amazingly scenic trails here. Backpackers should spend multiple days in the Eagle Cap Wilderness, while day hikers will find plenty of scenic options in the Wallowa Mountains. Or walk the mellow trails in the colorful John Day Fossil Beds National Monument.

Fossils

Discovered in the 1860s, the John Day Fossil Beds were laid down between six and 50 million years ago – a span that's captured everything from dungbeetle balls to the bones of pint-sized horses and sabertoothed, felinelike animals.

p346

Vancouver, Whistler & Vancouver Island

Skiing
Coastline
Food

Olympic Action

In 2010, snow-sports fans gathered at Whistler-Blackcomb to witness awe-inspiring feats. Sports lovers can take advantage of excellent snowfalls and a long resort season (November to June) by skiing and boarding famous Olympic race runs and half-pipes.

Waterways

The geography here is defined by water – abundant rivers, miles of island inlets and dramatic coastline. Stroll the seawall at Stanley Park or kayak the Sunshine Coast. Then there's Vancouver Island's Pacific shoreline, wild and rugged, with a wonderfully primordial feel.

Authentic Asian

Rub shoulders with Asian-language students, immigrants and fanatical foodies who flock to Vancouver's Asian restaurants. Dim sum, sushi bars and creative Asian fusion: prepare your taste buds for a spicy adventure.

p370

On the Road

Seattle

POP 634,535

Best Places to Eat

➡ Sitka & Spruce (p84)

➡ Cascina Spinasse (p84)

➡ Serious Pie (p82)

➡ Wild Ginger (p79)

➡ Top Pot Hand-Forged Doughnuts (p81)

Best Places to Stay

➡ Hotel Five (p78)

➡ Maxwell Hotel (p78)

➡ Moore Hotel (p78)

➡ Edgewater (p78)

➡ Alexis Hotel (p77)

Why Go?

Combine the brains of Portland with the beauty of Vancouver and you'll get something approximating Seattle. It's hard to believe that the Pacific Northwest's largest metropolis was considered a 'secondary' US city until the 1980s, when a combination of bold innovation and unabashed individualism turned it into one of the dot-com era's biggest trendsetters, spearheaded by an unlikely alliance of coffee-supping computer geeks and navel-gazing musicians. Reinvention is the buzzword these days in a city where alt-rock still resonates and grassroots microbusinesses compete with global brands. Surprisingly elegant in places and coolly edgy in others, Seattle is notable for its strong neighborhoods, locavore food, outlandish public art and proactive city mayors who harbor green credentials. Lording over it all is Mt Rainier, Seattle's unifying symbol, a 14,411ft mass of rock and ice that acts as a perennial reminder to the city's huddled masses that raw wilderness is never far away.

When to Go
Seattle

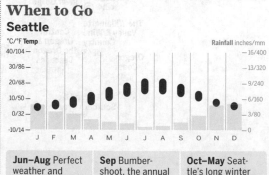

Jun–Aug Perfect weather and some of Seattle's best festivals – book ahead.

Sep Bumbershoot, the annual music, arts and culture festival, is a big draw.

Oct–May Seattle's long winter adds to the appeal of its many coffee shops and good pubs.

Advance Planning

One month before your trip, start looking at options for car rental, accommodations, tours and train tickets. If you're hoping to see a particular performance or game, whether it's the Mariners or the opera, it's wise to buy tickets a couple of weeks in advance. A day or two before you arrive, book popular restaurants and search the *Stranger* and the *Seattle Times* for upcoming art and entertainment listings.

TRANSPORTATION

Public transportation in Seattle has improved exponentially over the last five years with big investment in infrastructure. Light-rail and streetcar extensions are still in the works.

Light Rail

Link Light Rail is operated by **Sound Transit** (www.soundtransit.org). The first and, as yet, only Seattle line, 'Central Link', runs from Sea-Tac Airport to Westlake station downtown and opened in 2009. There are 13 stations, including stops in SoDo, the International District and Pioneer Square. Fares within the city limits are $2.25. From downtown to the airport costs $2.75. Trains run between 5am and 12:30am.

Bus

Buses are a major form of public transportation; they are operated by **Metro Transit** (www.metro.kingcounty.gov). The website prints schedules and maps and has a trip planner. To make things simple all bus fares within Seattle city limits are a flat $2.50 at peak hours (6am to 9am and 3pm to 6pm Monday to Friday). Off-peak rates are $2.25. Those aged six to 18 pay $1.25; kids under six are free; seniors and disabled travellers pay 75¢.

Streetcar

The **Seattle Streetcar** (www.seattlestreetcar.org) opened in 2007 with the the 2.6-mile South Lake Union line that runs between the Westlake Center and Lake Union. There are 11 stops and fares are $2.50/1.25 per adult/child. Streetcars breeze by every 15 minutes from 6am to 9pm (slightly later on Friday and Saturday). A second 10-stop line will open in 2014, running from Pioneer Square via the International District and First Hill to Capitol Hill.

What's New

➡ Chihuly Garden & Glass (p71)

➡ Seattle Great Wheel (p69)

➡ Bill & Melinda Gates Foundation Visitor Center (p72)

➡ Pioneer Square–Capitol Hill streetcar

FOR KIDS

Top picks are the Pacific Science Center (p72), the Children's Museum (p72) and the Aquarium (p69). Seattle boasts numerous parks; Gas Works (p74) is particularly good for flying kites. Also check out the Pinball Museum (p68), the zoo (p74) and Pike Place Market (p69).

Sports Teams

➡ **Seattle Storm** (☎206-217-9622; www.wnba.com/storm; single game tickets $20-200; Ⓜ Seattle Center) Basketball.

➡ **Seattle Seahawks** (www.seahawks.com; tickets $42-95) Football.

➡ **Seattle Sounders** (☎206-622-3415; www.seattlesounders.net; tickets from $37) Soccer.

Fast Facts

➡ **Nickname** Emerald City

➡ **Famous for** Grunge, Starbucks, *Frasier*, Amazon, Boeing

Resources

➡ **Stranger** (www.thestranger.com) Best entertainment listings; and it's free.

➡ **Not for Tourists** (www.notfortourists.com/seattle.aspx) Irreverent reviews.

➡ **Lonely Planet** (www.lonelyplanet.com/usa/seattle) Succinct summaries on traveling, and the Thorn Tree bulletin board.

History

Seattle was named for Chief Sealth, leader of the Duwamish tribe of Native Americans that inhabited the Lake Washington area when David Denny led the first group of European settlers here in 1851. The railway came through in 1893, linking Seattle with the rest of the country. For a decade, prospectors headed for the Yukon gold territory would stop in Seattle to stock up on provisions.

The boom continued through WWI, when Northwest lumber was in great demand and the Puget Sound area prospered as a shipbuilding center. In 1916 William Boeing founded the aircraft-manufacturing business that would become one of the largest employers in Seattle, attracting tens of thousands of newcomers to the region during WWII.

The city has spawned some major business success stories and international brands – Microsoft and Starbucks are loved and loathed in equal measure. Boeing has relocated its headquarters to Chicago, though it's still a major presence in Seattle.

The city is about to be reshaped yet again. The Alaskan Way Viaduct – which takes Hwy 99 along the waterfront and is generally considered to be structurally unsound as well as an eyesore – is being replaced with a bored-out tunnel alternative. Meanwhile, light-rail and streetcar transit have expanded to serve the airport as well as a hub of biotech companies and residences in South Lake Union. Seattle anticipates a 40% population growth in the next two decades.

◉ Sights

Most of Seattle's attractions are concentrated in a compact central area that includes downtown, historic Pioneer Square (the original downtown), the waterfront, touristy but *real* Pike Place Market and the adjacent nightlife strip of Belltown. As long as you account for the hilly terrain, it's easy enough to walk back and forth among all of these areas. Public transportation serves the outlying neighborhoods.

◉ Downtown & First Hill

What most people mean by 'downtown' is the collection of office buildings, hotels and retail shops between 2nd and 7th Aves. It's home to much of the city's most important architecture. The jungle of high-rises teetering on the steep streets makes for an impos-

ing skyline, though the core is quite compact and walkable.

Seattle Art Museum   MUSEUM
(SAM; Map p66; www.seattleartmuseum.org; 1300 1st Ave; adult/child $17/11; ⊙ 10am-5pm Tue, Wed, Sat & Sun, to 9pm Thu & Fri; ⊠ University St) While not comparable with the big guns in New York and Chicago, Seattle Art Museum is no slouch and is constantly updating. Over the last decade it has added over 100,000 sq ft to its gallery space and acquired about $1 billion worth of new art, including works by Zurbarán and Murillo. The museum is known for its extensive Native American artifacts and work from the local Northwest school, in particular by Mark Tobey (1890–1976). Modern American art is also well represented.

Seattle Public Library   LIBRARY
(Map p66; ☑ 206-386-4636; www.spl.org; 1000 4th Ave; ⊙ 10am-8pm Mon-Thu, 10am-6pm Fri & Sat, noon-6pm Sun; ℗ ; ⊠ Pioneer Sq) FREE There's not much chance you'll miss glimpsing the Seattle Public Library, but it's worth going inside for a closer look. Conceived by Rem Koolhaas and LMN Architects, the $165.5-million sculpture of glass and steel was designed to serve as a community gathering space, a tech center, a reading room and, of course, a massive book-storage facility. The main room, on level 3, has especially high ceilings, a teen center, a small gift shop and a coffee stand.

Frye Art Museum   MUSEUM
(Map p66; ☑ 206-622-9250; www.fryemuseum.org; 704 Terry Ave; ⊙ 11am-5pm Tue-Sun, to 7pm Thu; ℗ ; ⊠ First Hill South) FREE This small museum on First Hill preserves the collection of Charles and Emma Frye. The Fryes collected more than 1000 paintings, mostly 19th- and early-20th-century European and American pieces, and a few Alaskan and Russian artworks.

If this inspires a stifled yawn, think again. Since its 1997 expansion, the Frye has gained a hipness that it once lacked with fresh ways of presenting its artwork, music performances, poetry readings and interesting rotating exhibits from traveling painters to local printmakers.

Benaroya Concert Hall   CONCERT HALL
(Map p66; ☑ 206-215-9494; 200 University St; ⊠ University St) With a hefty bill of almost $120 million in construction costs, it's no wonder that Benaroya Concert Hall, Seattle Symphony's primary venue, oozes luxury. From

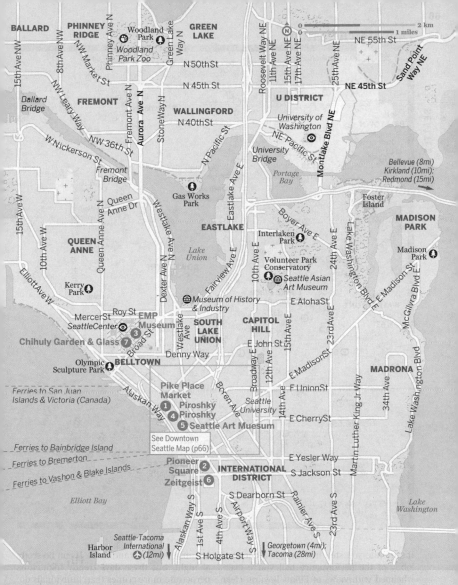

Seattle Highlights

① Wandering the maze of shops and restaurants in historic **Pike Place Market** (p69).

② Soaking up the old-town atmosphere in **Pioneer Square** (p66), then exploring the tunnels below.

③ Riding the monorail to a rock-and-roll adventure at the

EMP Museum (p71), where you can kneel at the altar of Hendrix and Cobain.

④ Joining the line for a cheap, take-out pastry at Pike Place Market phenomenon **Piroshky Piroshky** (p81).

⑤ Seeing how nine suspended cars can become

spectacular modern art at **Seattle Art Museum** (p64).

⑥ Enjoying a damned fine cup of coffee at **Zeitgeist** (p86).

⑦ Pondering the shimmering art that sprang from the creative mind of Dale Chihuly in **Chihuly Garden & Glass** (p71).

Downtown Seattle

the minute you step into the glass-enclosed lobby of the performance hall you're overwhelmed with views of Elliott Bay; on clear days you might be lucky enough to see the snowy peaks of the Olympic Range far in the distance.

◉ Pioneer Square

This enclave of redbrick buildings, the oldest part of Seattle, languished for years and was almost razed to build parking lots until a wave of public support led to Historic Register status followed by an influx of art galler-

ies, antique shops and cafes. It can be seedy at night, but these days trendy nightclubs perpetrate more crimes than individuals do.

Pioneer Square Park   SQUARE
(cnr Cherry St & 1st Ave S) The original Pioneer Square is a cobbled triangular plaza where Henry Yesler's sawmill cut the giant trees that marked Seattle's first industry. Known officially as Pioneer Square Park, the plaza features a **bust of Chief Seattle** (Sealth, in the original language), an ornate pergola and a **totem pole**.

waiting for the cable car that went up and down Yesler Way. The reportedly elaborate restroom eventually closed due to serious plumbing problems at high tide. In January 2001 the pergola was leveled by a wayward truck, but it was restored and put back where it belonged the following year, looking as good as new.

Klondike Gold Rush National Historical Park   MUSEUM
(www.nps.gov/klse; 117 S Main St; ⊙9am-5pm; ⊠International District/Chinatown) **FREE** This is a shockingly good museum eloquently run by the US National Park Service with exhibits, photos and news clippings from the 1897 Klondike gold rush, when a Seattle-on-steroids acted as a fueling depot for prospectors bound for the Yukon in Canada. It would cost $10 anywhere else; in Seattle it's free!

The best aspect of the museum is its clever use of storytelling. At the outset you are introduced to five local characters who became stampeders (Klondike prospectors) in the 1890s and you are invited to follow their varying fortunes and experiences periodically throughout the rest of the museum. Sound effects and interactive exhibits are used to good effect.

Smith Tower   LANDMARK
(cnr 2nd Ave S & Yesler Way; observation deck adult/child $7.50/5; ⊙10am-dusk) A mere dwarf amid Seattle's impressive modern stash of skyscrapers, the 42-storey neoclassical Smith Tower was, for half a century after its construction in 1914, the tallest building west of Chicago. The beaux-arts-inspired lobby is onyx- and marble-paneled, while the brass-and-copper elevator is still manually operated by a uniformed attendant. The public can access the 35th-floor Chinese Room decorated with a hand-carved ceiling and similarly sculpted Chinese furniture.

Milepost 31   MUSEUM
(211 1st Ave S; ⊙11am-5pm Tue-Sat; ⊠Pioneer Sq) **FREE** A project as comprehensive and long-winded as the Alaskan Viaduct Replacement Program (the viaduct is currently being demolished in favor of a new tunnel) requires an explanatory museum and this small but concise exhibit in Pioneer Square does a fine job of relaying the facts – plus there are some fascinating nuggets of incidental Seattle history thrown in for good measure.

Numerous old photos and a scale model of the drilling machine encourage lingering.

Some wayward early Seattleites, so the story goes, stole the **totem pole** from the Tlingit natives in southeastern Alaska in 1890. An arsonist lit the pole aflame in 1938, burning it to the ground. When asked if they could carve a replacement pole, the Tlingit took the money offered, thanking the city for payment for the first totem, and said it would cost $5000 to carve another one. The city coughed up, and the Tlingit obliged with the pole you see today.

The decorative **pergola** was built in the early 1900s to serve as an entryway to an underground lavatory and to shelter those

The exhibit will remain open as long as the program lasts – until 2016 at least.

Occidental Park
PARK

(btwn S Washington & S Main Sts; 🚇 Pioneer Sq) Notable in this cobblestone plaza are the **totem poles** carved by Duane Pasco, a nationally respected Chinookan carver and artist from Poulsbo on the Kitsap Peninsula. The totems depict the welcoming spirit of Kwakiutl, a totem bear, the tall Sun and Raven, and a man riding on the tail of a whale.

Also eye-catching is the **Firefighters' Memorial**, featuring life-size bronze sculptures of firefighters in action.

⊙ International District

A lively part of town that's home to various Asian cultures, 'the ID' has all of the trappings of a multiethnic neighborhood, from bustling markets to fun import shops to amazing places to eat.

Wing Luke Asian Museum
MUSEUM

(www.wingluke.org; 719 S King St; adult/child $12.95/8.95; ⊙10am-5pm Tue-Sun; 🚇 Chinatown/ International District E) Relocated and refurbished in 2008, the Wing Luke examines Asian and Pacific American culture, focusing on prickly issues such as Chinese settlement in the 1880s and Japanese internment camps in WWII. There are also art exhibits and a preserved immigrant apartment. Guided tours are available and recommended.

Seattle Pinball Museum
MUSEUM, GAMES

(508 Maynard Ave S; ⊙11am-5pm Sun & Mon, 6-9pm Thu, 2-10pm Fri, 1-10pm Sat; 🖈; 🚇 Chinatown/International District E) Got kids? Got kidlike tendencies? Love the buzzers and bells of good old-fashioned games machines? Lay aside your iPad apps and become a pinball wizard for the day in this fantastic games room in the ID with antique machines from the 1960s onwards. A mere $10 buys you unlimited games time.

Downtown Seattle

◉ Pike Place Market & Waterfront

The first stop for many visitors to Seattle, this area of town rewards early birds. It's particularly important to get to the market early if you want to avoid that cattle-truck feeling. Weekdays and before 10am on weekends are best. The Waterfront is more weather-dependent – it will be swarming with people on a sunny weekend afternoon, while on a misty weekday morning you'll have the place pretty much to yourself.

★ **Pike Place Market**   MARKET
(Map p66; www.pikeplacemarket.org; btwn Virginia St, Union St, 1st Ave & Western Ave; ⊙9am-6pm Mon-Sat, to 5pm Sun; 🚊Westlake) 🍴 Take a bunch of small-time businesses and sprinkle them liberally around a spatially challenged waterside strip amid crowds of old-school bohemians, new-wave restaurateurs, tree huggers, bolshie students, artists, urban buskers and artisans. The result: Pike Place Market, a cavalcade of noise, smells, personalities, banter and urban theater that's almost London-like in its cosmopolitanism. In operation since 1907, Pike Place is Seattle in a bottle, a wonderfully local experience that highlights the city for what it really is: all-embracing, eclectic and proudly singular.

Seattle Aquarium   AQUARIUM
(Map p66; www.seattleaquarium.org; 1483 Alaskan Way, at Pier 59; adult/child $19/12; ⊙9:30am-5pm; ♿; 🚊University St) While not comparable to Seattle's nationally lauded Woodland Park Zoo, the aquarium is probably the most interesting site on the waterfront, and a handy distraction for visiting families with itchy-footed kids.

While there are no large sea mammals such as whales and dolphins, the aquarium does have harbor seals and resident sea and river otters. An underwater dome on the lower level gives a pretty realistic glimpse of the kind of fish that inhabit the waters of Puget Sound, and the daily 'diver show' here is probably the best of the aquarium's live events.

Seattle Great Wheel   FERRIS WHEEL
(Map p66; www.seattlegreatwheel.com; 1301 Alaskan Way; adult/child $13/8.50; ⊙11am-10pm Mon-Thu, to midnight Fri & Sat, 10am-10pm Sun; 🚊University St) With the Alaskan Way Viaduct soon to be confined to the 'ugly post-

war architecture' chapter of the history books, Seattle has started work on beautifying its often neglected waterfront. Leading the way is this 175ft Ferris wheel – called the Seattle Great Wheel – that was installed in June 2012 with 42 gondolas, each capable of carrying eight people on a 12-minute ($13!) ride.

Victor Steinbrueck Park   PARK
(Map p66; cnr Western Ave & Virginia St; 🚊Westlake) When you've had enough of the market and its crowds, wander out the end of the North Arcade and cross Western Ave to Victor Steinbrueck Park, a small grassy area designed in 1982 by Steinbrueck and Richard Haag.

◉ Belltown

North of Pike Place Market is Belltown, famous as one of the breeding grounds of grunge music. A few of the original clubs are still here, but the area shifted upscale, with fancy restaurants and designer boutiques alongside the rowdy bars and noodle shops. It's one of the best parts of town for nightlife, and the Olympic Sculpture Park provides an anchor for daytime visits.

Olympic Sculpture Park   PARK, SCULPTURE
(2901 Western Ave; ⊙sunrise-sunset; 🚌13) **FREE**
Hovering over train tracks, in an unlikely oasis between the water and busy Elliott Ave, is the 8.5-acre, $85-million Olympic Sculpture Park. Worth a visit just for its views of the Olympic Mountains over Elliott Bay, the park has begun to grow into its long-range plan.

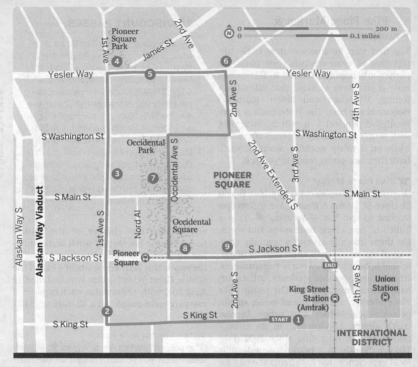

City Walk
Historical Pioneer Square Circuit

START/END KING STREET STATION
LENGTH 1 MILE; ONE HOUR

Start off at ❶ **King Street Station** (p90), recently returned to its opulent 'gilded age' glory. Before the advent of the motor car this was most people's first impression of Seattle. Exiting via the side door, walk west along King St in the shadow of Safeco Field; the bars and restaurants here are packed with baseball supporters on match days. Turn right onto redbrick ❷ **1st Avenue South**, little altered since it rose in the aftermath of the 1889 fire. Galleries and antique shops will catch your eye, but be sure to descend, as President Obama recently did, to the ❸ **Grand Central Baking Co** (p80) in the eponymous arcade for cakes and sandwiches. Further north, the small, triangular ❹ **Pioneer Square Park** (p66) – usually awash with tourists and local characters selling the newspaper *Real Change* – sports an Eiffel-esque iron pergola and the Richardsonian Romanesque Pioneer Building. Leading east, ❺ **Yesler Way** (p71) holds the dubious distinction of being the nation's original 'Skid Row'. The ugly appearance of the concrete car park on the fork with James St (the site of the old Seattle Hotel) sparked 1960s activists into saving the rest of Pioneer Square from falling to the same fate. You can divert on the corner with 2nd Ave for a quick glance at the neoclassical ❻ **Smith Tower** (p67), erected by LC Smith, a man who built his fortune on typewriters (Smith-Corona) and guns (Smith & Wesson). Go right on S Washington St and ❼ **Occidental Park** (p68), with its ivy-covered edifices, quickly opens out on your left. Cross Main St into Occidental Sq before heading left on ❽ **S Jackson Street**, the western terminus of Seattle's newest streetcar. In the 1890s S Jackson's stores outfitted prospectors heading for the Klondike, Canada. Fill in your historical blind spots at the ❾ **Klondike Gold Rush National Historical Park** (p67) before pacing one block back to King Street Station.

Among the highlights is *The Eagle,* Alexander Calder's 39ft-tall red-steel creation from 1971, which crouches along the horizon of the park. The thing probably weighs about a ton, but from where it's positioned, it looks like it's about to launch itself off the top of the hill and into the distant mountains.

The glass building at the top of the park contains a small cafe, restrooms, a gift shop and visitor information.

Seattle Glassblowing Studio GLASSBLOWING
(Map p66; www.seattleglassblowing.com; 2227 5th Ave; ⊙9am-6pm Mon-Fri, 10am-6pm Sat & Sun; ▣13) If Dale Chihuly's decadent chandeliers have inspired you, try creating your own modest glass art at this blow-your-own glass studio a few blocks from the master's museum. One-off sessions cost $85 to $125, or there are four-hour group or private lessons most days. Alternatively, you can just watch the fascinating process as a spectator (there's a cafe with a viewing window overlooking the workshop).

◉ Seattle Center

In 1962 Seattle hosted a summer-long World's Fair, an exhibition that enticed nearly 10 million visitors to view the future, Seattle-style. The vestiges, which 45 years later look simultaneously futuristic and retro, are on view at the Seattle Center.

Space Needle LANDMARK
(www.spaceneedle.com; 400 Broad St; adult/child $19/12; ⊙10am-11pm Mon-Thu, 9:30am-11:30pm Fri & Sat, 9:30am-11pm Sun; Ⓜ Seattle Center) You might be from Alabama or Timbuktu, but your abiding image of Seattle will probably be of the Space Needle, a streamlined, modern-before-its-time tower built for the 1962 World's Fair that has been the city's defining symbol for over 50 years. The needle anchors the World's Fair site, now called the Seattle Center, and, despite its rather steep admission fee, still persuades over one million annual visitors to ascend to its flying-saucer-like observation deck.

EMP Museum MUSEUM
(www.empsfm.org; 325 5th Ave N; adult/child $20/14; ⊙10am-7pm Jun–mid-Sep, to 5pm mid-Sep–May; Ⓜ Seattle Center) Recently rebranded as the EMP Museum, this dramatic marriage of supermodern architecture and rock and roll history was inaugurated as the Experience Music Project (EMP) in 2000. Founded by Microsoft cocreator Paul Allen, it was inspired by the music of Seattle-born guitar icon Jimi Hendrix and was initially intended as a tribute to Hendrix alone, although the collection has since morphed.

The main exhibits are housed on the 2nd floor and are anchored by the *If VI Was IX* sculpture, a tower of 700 instruments designed by German-born artist Trimpin. Many of the permanent exhibits center on Hendrix, including the Fender Stratocaster guitar that he played at Woodstock in 1969. Other collections are more ephemeral, although you'll always find interesting paraphernalia on grunge, guitar history and facts pertaining to bands from the Pacific Northwest. Dominating proceedings is the Sky Church, a huge screen that displays various musical and sci-fi films.

Chihuly Garden & Glass MUSEUM
(✆ 206-753-3527; www.chihulygardenandglass.com; 305 W Harrison St; adult/child $19/12; ⊙11am-7pm Sun-Thu, to 8pm Fri & Sat; Ⓜ Seattle Center) Opened in May 2012 and reinforcing Seattle's position as the Venice of North America, this exquisite exhibition of the life and work of artist Dale Chihuly requires a sharp intake of breath on first viewing. It has quickly become a top city icon to rival the neighboring Space Needle.

The masterpieces are split between an eight-room exhibition hall, a Glasshouse filled with natural light and an outdoor Garden. Between them they showcase the full gamut of Chihuly's Pacific Northwest influences, most notably Native American art, Puget Sound sea life and wooden boats.

THE ORIGINAL 'SKID ROW'

In Seattle's early days, loggers in a camp above town would send logs skidding down Yesler Way to Henry Yesler's pierside mill. With the slump in the timber industry and the resulting decline of the area, the street became a haven for the homeless. The nickname Skid Rd (or 'Skid Row') eventually came to mean the opposite of 'Easy St' in cities across the US.

LOCAL KNOWLEDGE

HIGHER THAN THE SPACE NEEDLE

Everyone makes a rush for the iconic Space Needle, but it's neither the tallest nor the cheapest of Seattle's glittering viewpoints. That honor goes to the sleek, tinted-windowed **Columbia Center** (Map p66; 701 5th Ave; adult/concession $9/6; ⊙8:30am-4:30pm Mon-Fri), built between 1982 and 1985, which at 932ft high is the loftiest building in the Pacific Northwest. The tower sports 76 floors. An elevator in the lobby takes you up to the free-access 40th floor, where there's a Starbucks. From here you must take another elevator to the plush observation deck on the 73rd floor, from where you can look down on ferries, cars, islands, roofs and – ha, ha – the Space Needle!

Children's Museum
MUSEUM

(☑206-441-1768; www.thechildrensmuseum.org; 305 W Harrison St; adult & child/grandparent $8.25/7.25; ⊙10am-5pm Mon-Fri, to 6pm Sat & Sun; ⊞; ⊡Seattle Center) In the basement of Center House near the monorail stop, the Children's Museum is an anachronistic learning center that offers activities and displays seemingly imported from an earlier time; it's a museum that might itself belong in a museum. But it's all very charming, if lacking in modern-day bells and whistles.

Bill & Melinda Gates Foundation Visitor Center
VISITOR CENTER

(440 5th Ave N; ⊙10am-5pm Tue-Sat; ⊡Seattle Center) ✔ **FREE** The world's most unselfish billionaire's generous actions are eloquently displayed at this suitably high-tech visitor center (part of the larger foundation building), which opened opposite the Space Needle in February 2012.

Spread over five rooms with highly interactive exhibits, the center lays out the Gates' bios and shows examples of their work around the world (including fighting malaria in Africa and notable philanthropic activities inside the US). It also offers scope for plenty of visitor involvement. Various screens and notepads invite visitors to jot down ideas, help solve tricky problems and lend their own brainpower to the foundation's 'intellectual bank.'

Pacific Science Center
MUSEUM

(www.pacsci.org; 200 2nd Ave N; adult/child exhibits only $18/13, with Imax $22/17; ⊙10am-5pm Mon-Fri, to 6pm Sat & Sun; ⊞; ⊡Seattle Center) This interactive museum of science and industry once housed the science pavilion of the World's Fair. Today the center features virtual-reality exhibits, a tropical butterfly house, laser shows, holograms and other wonders of science, many with hands-on demonstrations. Also on the premises is the vaulted-screen **Imax Theater**, a laserium and a planetarium.

◉ Lake Union & Queen Anne

Salubrious Queen Anne, high on its eponymous hill, hoards old money in beautiful fin de siècle mansions. In the melee down below, Lake Union's southern shores are changing quicker than the fresh-faced influx of techies can tweet about them, with celebrity chefs, a traffic-lightening streetcar and the sprawling new offices of Amazon.com.

Museum of History & Industry
MUSEUM

(MOHAI; ☑206-324-1126; www.mohai.org; 860 Terry Ave N; adult/child under 14yr $14/free; ⊙10am-5pm, to 8pm Thu; ⊞; ⊡Lake Union Park) Almost everything you need to know about Seattle is crammed into the refurbished Museum of History and Industry, which in December 2012 relocated to new digs in the emerging South Lake Union neighborhood. In operation since the early 1950s, and with an astounding archive of over four million objects to draw upon, MOHAI displays its rich stash of historical booty in an impressively repurposed naval armory building. If only school history lessons could've been this riveting.

Kerry Park
PARK

(211 W Highland Dr; ⊞; ⊡2) Amid the glittering Beverly Hills–like mansions of Highland Dr, mere commoners can enjoy eagle's-eye views of downtown Seattle and Elliott Bay (and Mt Rainier should it take its cloudy hat off) from this spectacular lookout.

Binoculars (50¢) are provided, so you can look back at the people at the top of the Space Needle looking over at you. The park is set on a steep incline of Queen Anne Hill (looking south) and is split in two, with a stairway linking to a popular children's playground below. This is a favorite spot to end a romantic date night – or make a proposal!

Center for Wooden Boats MUSEUM

(☑206-382-2628; www.cwb.org; 1010 Valley St; sailboat/rowboat rental per hour $30/25, beginner sailing course $375; ☺12:30pm-dusk Sat & Sun & by appointment Oct-Apr, 12:30pm-dusk Tue-Sun May-Sep; 🚇Lake Union Park) If you have an interest in the history and craft of wooden boats, then you'll definitely want to visit the Center for Wooden Boats. This museum and enthusiast's center features vintage and replica boats, and offers sailing lessons, including an excellent beginner course that gives you as many lessons as it offers in a four-month period (usually eight to 12 lessons).

The center also offers free boat rides every Sunday afternoon.

◎ Capitol Hill

This stylish, irreverent part of town displays all the panache and vitality you'd expect from Seattle's primary gay-and-lesbian neighborhood. The junction of Broadway and E John St is the core of activity, with restaurants, bars, shops and plenty of interesting characters to watch.

Capitol Hill is about 1.5 miles northeast of downtown. Take bus 7 or 10 and get off at Broadway. Continue north to find stately Volunteer Park, on E Prospect St, which was originally Seattle's main cemetery.

Seattle Asian Art Museum MUSEUM

(www.seattleartmuseum.org; 1400 E Prospect St; adult/child $7/5, 1st Thu & Sat of month free; ☺10am-5pm Wed-Sun, to 9pm Thu; 🅿; 🚌10) In stately Volunteer Park, this outpost of the Seattle Art Museum houses the extensive art collection of Dr Richard Fuller, who donated this late art-deco gallery (a fine example of Streamline Moderne architecture) to the city in 1932.

Spread over one floor and beautifully presented in uncluttered, minimalist rooms, the collection is notable for its Japanese hanging scrolls, some of which date from the 1300s and have been skilfully restored (the restoration process is detailed along with the art). Also of interest are the Indian stone sculptures in the foyer and some remarkably intricate Chinese bronzes dating from around 1600 BC.

Jimi Hendrix Statue MONUMENT

(Map p66; 1600 Broadway E; 🚇Pike-Pine) Psychedelic guitar genius of the late 1960s and Seattle's favorite son, Jimi Hendrix is captured sunk to his knees in eternal rock-star pose in this 1987 bronze sculpture by local artist Daryl Smith. The sculpture is located close to the intersection of Broadway and E Pine St.

Hendrix fans often leave flowers and candles at the statue's base, and it's not unusual to find a half-burnt cigarette stuck between his lips.

LOCAL KNOWLEDGE

STARBUCKS – IT STARTED HERE (ALMOST)

It's practically impossible to walk through the door of **Starbucks** (Map p66; 1912 Pike Pl; ☺6am-9pm) in Pike Place Market without appearing in someone's Facebook photo, so dense is the tourist traffic. But, while this hallowed business might be the world's oldest surviving Starbucks store, it is not – as many assume – the world's first Starbucks location, nor is it Seattle's oldest espresso bar. The original Starbucks opened in 1971 at 2000 Western Ave (at the northern end of Western Ave). It moved to its current location, a block away, in 1976. The honor of Seattle's oldest continuously running coffee bar goes to Café Allegro in the U District, which opened in 1975. Until the early 1980s Starbucks operated purely as a retail store that sold coffee beans and equipment (plus the odd taster cup). The company didn't open up its first espresso bar until 1984, after CEO Howard Shultz returned from an epiphanic trip to Italy. The Pike Place cafe is unique in that, in keeping with the traditional unbranded ethos of the market, it doesn't sell food or baked goods – just coffee.

Other interesting Starbucks facilities in Seattle include the cafe on the 40th floor of the Columbia Center (Seattle's tallest building); the company's first Leadership in Energy & Environmental Design–certified cafe, which opened downtown on the corner of Pike St and 1st Ave in 2009 and sports the original brown logo, and Roy Street Coffee & Tea in Capitol Hill. The latter is sometimes known as a 'Stealth Starbucks' as, despite being run by the company, it goes under a different name and is used as a testing ground for new ideas and products.

⊙ U District

U Dub, a neighborhood of young, studious out-of-towners, places the beautiful, leafy University of Washington campus next to the shabbier 'Ave,' an eclectic strip of cheap boutiques, dive bars and ethnic restaurants.

Burke Museum MUSEUM
(www.burkemuseum.org; cnr 17th Ave NE & NE 45th St; adult/child $10/7.50; ⊙10am-5pm; ☐70) The best museum of natural history in the Northwest is situated near the junction of NE 45th St and 16th Ave. The main collection has an impressive stash of fossils, including a 20,000-year-old sabre-toothed cat. The Burke's other tour de force is its focus on 17 different Native American cultures.

Of note is the Pacific Northwest basketry collection, but tribes from all around the Pacific Rim are represented, including groups from Asia and Micronesia.

Henry Art Gallery MUSEUM
(www.henryart.org; cnr 15th Ave NE & NE 41st St; adult/child $10/6, Thu free; ⊙11am-4pm Wed, Sat & Sun, to 8pm Thu & Fri; ☐70) This sophisticated space centers on a remarkable permanent exhibit by light-manipulating sculptor James Turrell, featuring various temporary and touring collections. Expos here are modern, provocative and occasionally head-scratching. Think of replayed black-and-white home movies, twittering bird noises and loose piles of bricks.

Suzzallo Library LANDMARK
Those architecturally minded will be interested in the University of Washington's Suzzallo Library. Designed by Carl Gould around 1926, this bibliophile's dream was inspired by Henry Suzzallo, UW's president at the time. Suzzallo wanted the building to look like a cathedral, because 'the library is the soul of the university.' Unfortunately for him, his bosses disagreed; on reviewing the building, they deemed it too expensive and fired Suzzallo for his extravagance.

However, the dream was partially realized in the grand neogothic entrance lobby and the truly beguiling **reading room** with its massive cathedral-like windows that, on fine days, cast filtered sunlight onto the long reading pews.

⊙ Fremont, Wallingford & Green Lake

These three residential neighborhoods are all fun to explore for a sense of everyday Seattle life. Green Lake is centered on a lake-filled park circumnavigated daily by hundreds of walkers, bladers, cyclists and strollers. Wallingford is a quiet little neighborhood that branches out from NE 45th St. And Fremont, about 2 miles north of Seattle Center, is known for its lefty vibe, farmers market and wacky public sculpture, including a rocket sticking out of a building and a statue of Lenin shipped over from Slovakia.

Gas Works Park PARK
(Meridian Ave, at N Northlake Way; ♿; ☐26) FREE
Urban reclamation has no greater monument in Seattle than Gas Works Park. The former power station here produced gas for heating and lighting from 1906 to 1956, but the works were thereafter considered an eyesore and an environmental menace. However, the beautiful location – with stellar views of downtown over Lake Union, sailboats and yachts sliding to and from the shipping canal – induced the city government to convert the site into a park in 1975.

Rather than tear down the factory, landscape architects preserved much of the old plant. Painted black and now highlighted with rather joyful graffiti, it looks like some odd remnant from a former civilization. It also makes a great location for shooting rock album covers and music videos. Be sure to climb the small hill in order to see the sundial at the top.

Woodland Park Zoo ZOO
(☏206-684-4800; www.zoo.org; 5500 Phinney Ave N; adult/child Oct-Apr $12.50/8.75, May-Sep $18.75/11.75; ⊙9:30am-4pm Oct-Apr, to 6pm May-Sep; ♿; ☐5) In Woodland Park, up the hill from Green Lake Park, Woodland Park Zoo is one of Seattle's greatest tourist attractions, consistently rated as one of the top 10 zoos in the country. It was one of the first in the nation to free animals from their restrictive cages in favor of ecosystem enclosures, where animals from similar environments share large spaces designed to replicate their natural surroundings.

Feature exhibits include a tropical rainforest, two gorilla exhibits, an African savanna and an Asian elephant forest.

Fremont Troll   MONUMENT

(cnr N 36th St & Troll Ave) The Fremont Troll lurks beneath the northern end of the Aurora Bridge at N 36th St. The troll's creators – artists Steve Badanes, Will Martin, Donna Walter and Ross Whitehead – won a competition sponsored by the Fremont Arts Council in 1990. The 18ft-high cement figure snacking on a Volkswagen Beetle is now a favorite place for late-night beer drinking.

Waiting for the Interurban   MONUMENT

(cnr N 34th St & Fremont Ave N) Seattle's most popular piece of public art, the recycled-aluminum *Waiting for the Interurban*, depicts six people waiting for a train that never comes. The train that once passed through Fremont stopped running in the 1930s, and the people of Seattle have been waiting for a new train – the Interurban – ever since (a new train connecting Seattle with Everett opened in 2003, but it doesn't stop in Fremont).

The sculpture is prone to regular 'art attacks,' when locals lovingly decorate the people in outfits corresponding to a special event, the weather, someone's birthday, a Mariners win – whatever. Rarely do you see the sculpture 'undressed'. Take a look at the human-faced dog peeking out from between the legs of the people. That face belongs to Armen Stepanian, one of the founders of today's Fremont and its excellent recycling system. Sculptor Richard Beyer and Stepanian had a disagreement about the design of the piece, which resulted in Beyer's spiteful yet humorous design of the dog's face.

Theo Chocolate Factory   CHOCOLATE FACTORY

(☑206-632-5100; www.theochocolate.com; 3400 Phinney Ave N; tours $5; ☉10am-6pm, tours 1pm & 3pm daily plus 11am Sat; ☐28) Adding a bit of Willy Wonka to Fremont's atypical street life is this chocolate factory on the site of the old Redhood Brewery (now moved to Woodinville). The micro-chocolate producer makes organic chocolate, producing an aroma that permeates half the neighborhood. Follow the smell to the small store, where you can put your name down for a factory tour.

◉ Ballard & Discovery Park

Ballard, despite its hip veneer, still has the feel of an old Scandinavian fishing village – especially around the locks, the marina and the Nordic Heritage Museum. The old town is a nightlife hot spot, but even in the day-time its historic buildings and cobblestone streets make it a pleasure to wander through.

Nordic Heritage Museum   MUSEUM

(☑206-789-5707; www.nordicmuseum.org; 3014 NW 67th St; adult/child $6/4; ☉10am-4pm Tue-Sat, noon-4pm Sun; ☐17) This museum preserves the history of the northern Europeans who settled in Ballard and the Pacific Northwest, as well as bringing in special exhibits of new work by contemporary Scandinavian artists. It's the only museum in the USA that commemorates the history of settlers from all five Scandinavian countries.

A permanent exhibit, with one room for each country, features costumes, photographs and maritime equipment, while a second gallery is devoted to changing exhibitions. The museum also offers Scandinavian-language instruction, lectures and films.

Hiram M Chittenden Locks   LOCK

(3015 NW 54th St; ☉locks 24hr, ladder & gardens 7am-9pm, visitor center 10am-6pm May-Sep; ☐62) Seattle shimmers like an Impressionist painting on sunny days at the Hiram M Chittenden Locks. Here, the freshwater of Lake Washington and Lake Union that flows through the 8-mile-long Lake Washington Ship Canal drops 22ft into salt-water Puget Sound. Construction of the canal and locks began in 1911; today 100,000 boats a year pass through them. They are situated a half-mile west of Ballard, off NW Market St, and act as a bridge across the canal for pedestrians.

On the southern side of the Locks, the **fish ladder** was built in 1976 to allow salmon to fight their way to spawning grounds in the Cascade headwaters of the Sammamish River, which feeds Lake Washington. Visitors can watch the fish from underwater glass-sided tanks or from above (there are nets to keep salmon from overleaping and stranding themselves on the pavement). Sea lions munch on the salmon while the fish attempt to negotiate the ladder. The best time to visit is during spawning season, from mid-June to September.

On the northern entrance to the lock area is the **Carl English Jr Botanical Gardens**, a charming arboretum and specimen garden. Trails wind through gardens filled with flowers and mature trees, each labeled. Flanking the gardens is a small museum and visitor center documenting the history of the locks.

WORTH A TRIP

GEORGETOWN & THE MUSEUM OF FLIGHT

Even people with absolutely no interest in aviation have been known to blink in quiet astonishment at the remarkable **Museum of Flight** (☎206-764-5720; www.museumof-flight.org; 9404 E Marginal Way S, Boeing Field; adult/child $18/10, 5-9pm 1st Thu each month free; ☺10am-5pm Fri-Wed, to 9pm Thu; ☲124), which tells the tale of how humankind got from the Wright Brothers to the first moon landing in fewer than 66 years. Not surprisingly, the city that spawned Boeing does a grand job of relating the full flying story in this sprawling but impressive museum, using flight simulators, a decommissioned Concorde and a full fuselage trainer of the Space Shuttle.

The museum is situated 9 miles south of downtown Seattle at the old Boeing Field Airport and visitors can combine the trip with a dip into the city's up-and-coming Georgetown neighborhood, a place with a scrappy yet independent artistic sensibility that's recently been deemed cool. Clustered largely on one street (Airport Way S) a couple of miles north of the Museum of Flight, Georgetown's venerable redbrick buildings are replete with pubs, funky shops and art galleries.

Metro buses 106 and 124 run frequently from downtown to Georgetown. The 124 carries on to the Museum of Flight.

🏃 Activities

Seattle's location lends itself to hiking, cycling and all kinds of activities on the water. Cyclists shouldn't miss the 16.5-mile **Burke-Gilman Trail**, meandering from Ballard to Seattle's Eastside via Fremont, Wallingford and the U District.

Dutch Bike Co   CYCLING
(☎206-789-1678; www.dutchbikeseattle.com; 4741 Ballard Ave NW; ☺11am-7pm; ☲17) Perfectly positioned at the western end of the Burke-Gilman intra-urban trail, this is one of the few bike-rental places within shouting distance of the trail itself. You'll pay $12 an hour or $60 per day for a sturdy bike. There's also a cafe on-site – ideal for a pre- or post-ride coffee or a glass of wine.

Recycled Cycles   CYCLING
(www.recycledcycles.com; 1007 NE Boat St; rentals per 6/24hr $20/40; ☺10am-8pm Mon-Fri, to 6pm Sat & Sun; 🚲; ☲66) A friendly U District shop, this place also rents out chariots and trail-a-bike attachments for kids.

Agua Verde Paddle Club   KAYAKING
(☎206-545-8570; 1303 NE Boat St; single/double kayaks per hour $17/22; ☺10am-dusk Mon-Sat, to 6pm Sun Mar-Oct; ☲72) On Portage Bay, near the university, you can rent kayaks from this friendly place right at the edge of the water. Stand-up paddleboards are also available (one/two hours $20/34). When you get back from your paddle, be sure to visit the cafe upstairs to eat fish tacos on the covered deck.

Northwest Outdoor Center Inc   KAYAKING
(www.nwoc.com; 2100 Westlake Ave N; kayaks per hour $14-22; ☲62) On Lake Union; rents kayaks and offers tours and instruction in sea and white-water kayaking.

UW Waterfront Activities Center   CANOEING
(☎206-543-9433; canoes & rowboats per hour weekday/weekend $9/11; ☺10am-7pm, closed Nov-Jan; ☲43) Another good way to explore the waters surrounding the Arboretum is to rent a canoe or rowboat from the University of Washington's facility. You need a current driver's license or passport. The center is in the southeast corner of the Husky Stadium parking lot.

👉 Tours

**Bill Speidel's Underground
Tour**   TOUR
(Map p66; ☎206-682-4646; www.underground-tour.com; 608 1st Ave; adult/child/senior $17/9/14; ☺departs every 30min 11am-4pm Oct-Mar, to 6pm Apr-Sep) Seattle's famous 'underground' tour, which takes you through the tunnels and sidewalks hidden beneath the streets of Pioneer Square, might get a little corny at times, but it delivers the goods on historic Seattle as a rough and rowdy industrial town. The tour starts at Doc Maynard's Public House. No reservations are accepted, so try to arrive half an hour early if you want to be sure you get in.

Seattle by Foot   WALKING TOUR
(☎206-508-7017; www.seattlebyfoot.com; tours $20-25) This company runs a handful of

tours including the practically essential Coffee Crawl ($25), which will ply you liberally with caffeine while explaining the nuances of latte art and Starbucks, and a unique Seattle Kids Tour – two hours of educational fun involving art, music and chocolate.

Savor Seattle TOUR
(2 206-209-5485; www.savorseattletours.com) These guys lead a handful of gastronomic tours, the standout being the two-hour Booze-n-Bites that runs daily at 4pm from the corner of Western Ave and Virginia St and costs $59.99.

⚡ Festivals & Events

Northwest Folklife Festival MUSIC
(www.nwfolklife.org) International music, dance, crafts, food and family activities held at the Seattle Center on the Memorial Day weekend in May.

Seafair WATER
(www.seafair.com; ⊙ Jul/Aug) Huge crowds attend this festival held on the water, with hydroplane races, a torchlight parade, an air show, music and a carnival.

Bumbershoot MUSIC, LITERATURE
(www.bumbershoot.com; ⊙ Sep) A major arts and cultural event at Seattle Center on the Labor Day weekend in September, with live music, author readings and lots of unclassifiable fun.

⌂ Sleeping

Many downtown hotels participate in **Seattle Super Saver Packages** (2 800-535-7071; www.seattlesupersaver.com), a program run by the Convention & Visitors Bureau. Room prices are generally 50% off the rack rates from November through March, with substantial discounts all year, and the program includes a coupon book that offers savings on dining, shopping and attractions.

⌂ Downtown & First Hill

★ **Alexis Hotel** HOTEL $$$
(Map p66; 2 206-624-4844; www.alexishotel.com; 1007 1st Ave; r/ste from $280/310; ▣❋◉❤❄; ▣ University St) Run by the Kimpton Hotel group, the Alexis is a boutique hotel that is positively lavish, with huge rooms, thick carpets, gleaming bathrooms and some luxury extras – a steam room and fitness center, for instance. The hotel's pet-friendly moniker is taken seriously; visiting dogs get bowls of distilled water on arrival.

Thick double-glazed windows keep out the cacophony of downtown just outside the front door.

Sorrento Hotel HOTEL $$$
(Map p66; 2 206-622-6400; www.hotelsorrento. com; 900 Madison St; d from $269; ▣❋◉❤❄; ▣64) William Howard Taft, 27th US president, was the first registered guest at the Sorrento, an imposing Italianate hotel known since its birth in 1909 as the jewel of Seattle. The combination of luxurious appointments, over-the-top service and a pervasive sense of class add up to a perfect blend of decadence and restraint.

The hotel's restaurant, the Hunt Club, is worth a stop whether you're staying here or not. Continental breakfast ($11) and a shuttle to the airport ($65) are among the extras on offer.

Hotel Monaco BOUTIQUE HOTEL $$$
(Map p66; 2 206-621-1770; www.monaco-seattle. com; 1101 4th Ave; d/ste $339/399; ▣◉❤❄; ▣ University St) ✔ Whimsical, with dashes of European elegance, the downtown Monaco is worthy of all four of its illustrious stars. Bed down amid the stripy wallpaper and heavy drapes.

⌂ Pioneer Square

Best Western Pioneer Square Hotel HOTEL $$
(2 206-340-1234; www.pioneersquare.com; 77 Yesler Way; r from $159; ▣◉❄; ▣ Pioneer Sq) Rooms and common areas at this historical hotel feature period decor and a comfortable atmosphere. The only hotel in the historical heart of Seattle, it can't be beaten for location – as long as you don't mind some of the saltier characters who populate the square in the off hours. Nightlife, restaurants and shopping are just steps from the door.

⌂ Pike Place Market & Waterfront

Green Tortoise Hostel HOSTEL $
(Map p66; 2 206-340-1222; www.greentortoise. net; 105 Pike St; 8-/6-/4-bed dm incl breakfast $32/34/36; ◉; ▣ Westlake) Seattle's backpacker central – and what a location right across the street from Pike Place Market! Once pretty crusty, the Tortoise moved to the Elliot Hotel Building a few years back and now offers 30 bunk rooms and 16 European-style

rooms (shared bath and shower). Breakfast includes waffles and eggs.

The hostel offers a free dinner three nights a week and there are weekly events such as open-mic nights.

Pensione Nichols   B&B $$
(Map p66; ☑206-441-7125; www.pensionenichols. com; 1923 1st Ave; r from $130; @☎; ☒Westlake) In a town with few cheap hotels and hardly any B&Bs right downtown, Pensione Nichols is a treat. Right in the urban thick of things between Pike Place Market and Belltown, this charmingly remodeled European-style pensione has 10 rooms that share four retro-cool bathrooms, two large suites and a spacious common area that overlooks the market.

★**Edgewater**   HOTEL $$$
(☑206-728-7000; www.edgewaterhotel.com; Pier 67, 2411 Alaskan Way; r 420-750; ☐❄@☎; ☐13) Fame and notoriety have stalked the Edgewater. Perched over the water on a pier, it was once the hotel of choice for every rock band that mattered, including the Beatles, the Rolling Stones and, most infamously, Led Zeppelin, who took the 'you can fish from the hotel window' advertising jingle a little too seriously and filled their suite with sharks.

These days, the fishing – and Led Zeppelin – is prohibited, but the rooms are still deluxe with a capital 'D.'

🛏 Belltown

★**Moore Hotel**   HOTEL $
(Map p66; ☑206-448-4851; www.moorehotel. com; 1926 2nd Ave; s/d with shared bath $68/80, with private bath $85/97; ☎; ☒Westlake) Old world and allegedly haunted, the Moore nonetheless has a friendly front desk and a prime location. If that doesn't swing you, the price should. There's a cute little cafe on the premises and the dive-y Nitelite Lounge next door. You can practically hold your breath and walk to Pike Place Market from here.

City Hostel Seattle   HOSTEL $
(☑206-706-3255; www.hostelseattle.com; 2327 2nd Ave; 6-/4-bed dm $28/32, d $73, all incl breakfast; @☎; ☒Rapid Ride D-Line) ✐ Sleep in an art gallery for peanuts – in Belltown, no less. That's the reality in this new 'art hostel,' which will make your parents' hostelling days seem positively spartan by comparison. Aside from arty dorms, expect a common

room, hot tub, in-house movie theater (with free DVDs) and all-you-can-eat breakfast.

★**Hotel Five**   BOUTIQUE HOTEL $$
(Map p66; ☑206-441-9785; www.hotelfiveseattle. com; 2200 5th Ave; r from $165; ☐❄☎; ☒13) This wonderful reincarnation of the old Ramada Inn mixes retro-'70s furniture and sharp color accents to produce something that is dazzlingly modern. And it's functional too. The ultracomfortable beds could be nominated as a valid cure for insomnia, while the large reception area invites lingering, especially when they lay out the complimentary cupcakes and coffee in the late afternoon.

There's an on-site gym and a decent restaurant.

Ace Hotel   HOTEL $$
(☑206-448-4721; www.acehotel.com; 2423 1st Ave; r with shared/private bath $109/199; ☐☎; ☒13) Emulating (almost) its hip Portland cousin, the Ace sports minimal, futuristic decor (everything's white or stainless steel, even the TV), antique French army blankets, condoms instead of pillow mints and a copy of the *Kama Sutra* instead of the Bible. Parking costs $15.

Hotel Andra   BOUTIQUE HOTEL $$$
(Map p66; ☑206-448-8600; www.hotelandra. com; 2000 4th Ave; r from $289; ☐❄☎; ☒Westlake) It's in Belltown (so it's trendy), and it's Scandinavian-influenced (so it has lashings of minimalist style), plus the Andra's fine location is complemented by leopard-skin fabrics, color accents, well-stocked bookcases, fluffy bathrobes, Egyptian-cotton bed linen and a complimentary shoe-shine. The Lola restaurant next door does room service. Say no more.

🛏 Seattle Center & Queen Anne

★**Maxwell Hotel**   BOUTIQUE HOTEL $$
(☑206-286-0629; www.themaxwellhotel.com; 300 Roy St; r from $179; ☐❄@☎❄; ☒Rapid Ride D-Line) Another gorgeous boutique hotel that has recently graced Lower Queen Anne, the Maxwell's huge designer-chic lobby is enough to make anyone dust off their credit card – and it's not too pricey either (if you look out for periodic offers online).

Rooms look like they've just won an HGTV design competition, plus there's a small pool, a gym and free bikes if you're a Seattle outdoor type.

Mediterranean Inn
HOTEL **$$**

(☑206-428-4700; www.mediterranean-inn.com; 425 Queen Anne Ave N; r from $159; P✳@; ☐Rapid Ride D-Line) There's something about the surprisingly un-Mediterranean Med Inn that just clicks. Maybe it's the handy cusp-of-Belltown location, or the genuinely friendly staff, or the kitchenettes in every room, or the small downstairs gym, or the surgical cleanliness in every room. Don't try to define it – just go there and soak it up.

MarQueen Hotel
HOTEL **$$**

(☑206-282-7407; www.marqueen.com; 600 Queen Anne Ave N; r from $175; P✳@☎; ☐Rapid Ride D-Line) A classic old-school apartment building (built in 1918), the MarQueen has hardwood floors throughout and a variety of rooms, all with kitchenettes. The neighborhood is an under-visited gem, handy to various attractions. If hill walking isn't your thing, there is a courtesy van to take you to nearby sights.

☲ Capitol Hill

Gaslight Inn B&B
B&B **$$**

(☑206-325-3654; www.gaslight-inn.com; 1727 15th Ave; s $98-128, d $108-168; @☎☲; ☐10) In two neighboring homes, the Gaslight Inn has 15 rooms, 12 of which have private bathrooms. In summer it's refreshing to dive into the outdoor pool or just hang out on the sun deck. No pets: the B&B already has a cat and a dog.

11th Avenue Inn
B&B **$$**

(☑206-720-7161; www.11thAvenueInn.com; 121 11th Ave E; r $139-199; @☎; ☐Capitol Hill) Formerly a boarding house and a dance studio, this 1906 home has been a B&B since 2003. Its facade is not the grandest of Seattle's B&Bs, but you know what they say about judging a book by its cover.

The inn has eight rooms, each with eclectic Victorian furnishings, Oriental rugs, handsome headboards and hand-pressed Egyptian-cotton sheets. You won't go hungry here: breakfast is a full-course sit-down affair in the Victorian dining room, and you're invited to help yourself to snacks and drinks throughout the day.

☲ U District

College Inn
HOTEL **$**

(☑206-633-4441; www.collegeinnseattle.com; 4000 University Way NE; s/d incl breakfast from $65/75; @☎; ☐70) This pretty half-timbered building in the U District, left over from the 1909 Alaska-Yukon-Pacific Exposition, has 25 European-style guest rooms with sinks and shared baths. There's no elevator.

★ University Inn
HOTEL **$$**

(☑206-632-5055; www.universityinnseattle.com; 4140 Roosevelt Way NE; r incl breakfast from $189; P✳@☎☲; ☐66) What pushes this spotless, modern, well-located place over the edge into greatness is, believe it or not, the waffles served at breakfast. They're amazing. The hotel is three blocks from campus, and its 102 rooms come in three levels of plushness.

All of them offer such basics as a coffeemaker, a hair dryer and wi-fi; some have balconies, sofas and CD players. There's a Jacuzzi, an outdoor pool, laundry facilities and a guest computer in the lobby.

Chambered Nautilus B&B Inn
B&B **$$**

(☑206-522-2536; www.chamberednautilus.com; 5005 22nd Ave NE; d $109-194; ✳@☎; ☐74) The 1915 Georgian-style Chambered Nautilus has six guest rooms that are decorated with authentic British antiques, as well as an annex with one- and two-bedroom suites. All B&B rooms here come with private bathrooms, down comforters, handmade soaps and a teddy bear. The communal living room has a welcoming fireplace, and the full gourmet breakfast is reason enough to stay.

Across the street it offers four kid-friendly, pet-friendly suites with kitchenettes ($124 to $214).

✗ Eating

Possibly the most fun way to assemble a meal in Seattle is by foraging in Pike Place Market for fresh produce, baked goods, deli items and take-out ethnic foods. But Seattle has an embarrassment of riches when it comes to restaurants – without much effort, you can find everything from an Argentinean steak to a vegan cupcake.

✗ Downtown & First Hill

Aside from old-fashioned oyster bars and cavernous steakhouses, downtown is home to two places that seem particularly characteristic of Seattle.

★ Wild Ginger
ASIAN **$$**

(Map p66; www.wildginger.net; 1401 3rd Ave; mains $15-28; ⊙11am-3pm & 5-11pm Mon-Sat, 4-9pm Sun; ☐University St) All around the Pacific Rim, via China, Indonesia, Malaysia, Vietnam – and Seattle, of course – is the wide-ranging theme at this highly popular downtown fusion restaurant. The signature fragrant duck goes down nicely with a glass of riesling. The restaurant also provides food for the swanky **Triple Door** (Map p66; ☑206-838-4333; www.thetripledoor.net; 216 Union St; ☒University St) club downstairs.

Taste Restaurant   NORTHWESTERN **$$**
(Map p66; ☑206-903-5291; www.tastesam.com; 1300 1st Ave; mains $15-25; ☺11am-close, to 5pm Tue & Sun; ☒University St) Inside the Seattle Art Museum, Taste offers a menu that changes to honor the gallery's various temporary exhibitions. British bangers and mash were doffing a cap to Gainsborough at last visit. The venue is popular among city workers for its 3pm-to-6pm happy hour, when red-eyed bankers wash down oysters with cocktails. Aside from the rather chic sit-down space there's also a take-out counter.

🍴 Pioneer Square

The historic core of the city has a surprising number of good budget-friendly dining options scattered amid its atmospheric old saloons and steak houses.

★**Salumi**   SANDWICHES **$**
(www.salumicuredmeats.com; 309 3rd Ave S; sandwiches $7-10; ☺11am-4pm Tue-Fri; ☒International District/Chinatown) The queue outside Salumi has long been part of the sidewalk furniture. It's even formed its own community of chatterers, food bloggers, tweeters and gourmet-sandwich aficionados comparing notes. Being owned by the father of celebrity chef Mario Batali probably helps.

When you make it inside the sinuous, three's-a-crowd shop, the sandwiches come with any of a dozen types of Italian-style cured meat and fresh cheese. Great for a picnic!

Grand Central Baking Co   SOUP, SANDWICHES **$**
(☑206-622-3644; Grand Central Arcade, 214 1st Ave S; sandwiches $4-10; ☺7am-5pm Mon-Fri, 8am-4pm Sat; ☒Pioneer Sq) Already well established by the time President Obama popped in in 2011 and asked for a turkey-chutney sandwich, Grand Central (located in the eponymous arcade) is considered one of the best bakeries in Seattle. Its artisan breads can be bought whole or sliced up for sandwiches in its cafe. Beware the lunchtime queues.

Delicatus   DELI, SANDWICHES **$$**
(☑206-623-3780; www.delicatusseattle.com; 103 1st Ave S; sandwiches $9-12; ☺11am-9pm Mon-Thu, to 10pm Fri & Sat, to 4pm Sun; ☒Pioneer Sq) It's a testament to a good eating joint when it is cited as an excuse to visit a whole neighborhood – and newly established Delicatus is certainly luring people to Pioneer Square. The reason is as simple as a sandwich and Delicatus' are well stuffed and enlivened with interesting relishes. Go at lunchtime for the best atmosphere.

★**Bar Sajor**   MEDITERRANEAN **$$**
(☑206-682-1117; www.sitkaandspruce.com; 323 Occidental Ave; plates $10-25; ☺11am-8pm Mon, to late Tue-Fri; ☒Pioneer Sq) ✐ Resembling a bright, open-plan French country kitchen and claiming to serve Portuguese-inspired food created from the raw ingredients of Seattle's hinterland, Bar Sajor is another project from Matt Dillon, owner of Capitol Hill's hugely popular (and sustainable) Sitka & Spruce.

Both the atmosphere and the food (homemade bread, cheese and salami selections, and genuinely delicious vegetable plates) will have you living vicariously like a European without ever having to abandon your locavore instincts.

🍴 International District

The International District is a great neighborhood for cheap eats, or you can go all-out on a multifarious eight-course dinner banquet. Don't miss a chance for a dim sum brunch – or dinner, or midday snack – if you're in the area.

★**Green Leaf**   VIETNAMESE **$**
(☑206-340-1388; www.greenleaft··· com; 418 8th Ave S; pho $7·· ·· _c c_   ·lam-10pm; ☒Chinatow··   As sinuous as a   crowded as a pub f   rs, Green Leaf shoot   from its tiny kitchen   s. People shout about   tional or vegetarian ph   a swoon-inducing versi·· · or ·u··· ·wco – sort of a cross between a pancake and an omelet.

Purple Dot Café   CHINESE **$**
(☑206-622-0288; 515 Maynard Ave S; mains $7-14; ☺9am-1am Sun-Thu, to 3:30am Fri & Sat; ☒Chinatown/International District E) The Purple Dot looks like the inside of an '80s video game (it is actually purple) and draws a late-night

drunken-disco crowd on weekends, but most of the time it's a calm, quiet place to get dim sum and Macao-style specialties (meaning you can feast on baked spaghetti and French toast along with your Hong Kong favorites).

House of Hong CHINESE $$
(206-622-7997; 408 8th Ave S; dim sum $2-3 per item, mains $12-15; 9am-11pm; ; Chinatown/International District E) This huge mainstay of the neighborhood serves dim sum from 10am until 4:30pm every day – handy if your craving hits in the middle of the day.

Pike Place Market & Waterfront

Explore the market on an empty stomach and commit to a few hours of snacking – you'll be full by the time you leave, and it doesn't have to cost much. If you're looking for serious dining, you can find that here too – some of Seattle's favorite restaurants are tucked into mysterious corners of the market.

★Piroshky Piroshky BAKERY $
(Map p66; www.piroshkybakery.com; 1908 Pike Pl; snacks $2-7; 8am-6:30pm Oct-Apr, from 7:30am May-Sep; Westlake) Proof that not all insanely popular Pike Place holes-in-the-wall go global (à la Starbucks), Piroshky is still knocking out its delectable mix of sweet and savory Russian pies and pastries in a space barely big enough to swing a small kitten. Join the crush and order one 'to go.'

Beecher's Handmade Cheese SNACKS $
(Map p66; www.beechershandmadecheese.com; 1600 Pike Pl; snacks $3-5; 9am-6pm; Westlake) Artisan beer, artisan coffee...next up, Seattle brings ~~~ ~2 of ~se and it's made as you ~~~~ ~s-crowded Pike Place no ~~~~ y all kinds of cheese-rel ~~~~ s for that long, snakin; ~~~ queue – that's people ~~~ vonderful homemade mac 'n' cheese that comes in two different-size tubs and is simply divine.

Ivar's Acres of Clams SEAFOOD $
(Map p66; 206-624-6852; www.ivars.com; 1001 Alaskan Way, Pier 54; fish & chips $8-9; 11am-10pm Sun-Thu, to 11pm Fri & Sat; ; University St) Ivar Haglund was a beloved local character famous for silly promotional slogans ('Keep clam!'), but he sure knew how to fry up fish and chips. Ivar's is a Seattle institution that started in 1938, and its founder

still stands sentinel at the door (albeit as a statue).

Forgo the dining room for the outdoor lunch counter; the chaotic ordering system involves a lot of yelling, but it seems to work, and then you can enjoy your clam strips or fish and chips outdoors on the pier. The tradition at Ivar's is to feed chips to the seagulls, who'll swoop down and take them out of your hand.

Lowells DINER $
(Map p66; www.eatatlowells.com; 1519 Pike Pl; mains $6-9; 7am-6pm; Westlake) 'Fish and chips' is a simple meal often done badly – but not here. Slam down your order for Alaskan cod at the front entry and take it up to the top floor for delicious views over Puget Sound. It also serves corned-beef hash and an excellent clam chowder.

Pink Door Ristorante ITALIAN $$
(Map p66; 206-443-3241; 1919 Post Alley; mains $16-24; 11:30am-10pm Mon-Thu, to 11pm Fri & Sat, 4-10pm Sun; Westlake) A restaurant like no other, the Pink Door is probably the only place in the US (the world?) where you can enjoy fabulous *linguine alla vongole* (pasta with clams and pancetta) and other Italian favorites while watching live jazz, burlesque caberet or – we kid you not – a trapeze artist swinging from the 20ft ceiling.

Steelhead Diner SEAFOOD $$
(Map p66; 206-625-0129; www.steelheaddiner. com; 95 Pine St; sandwiches $9-13, mains $15-33; 11am-10pm Tue-Sat, 10am-3pm Sun; Westlake) Homey favorites such as fish and chips, grilled salmon or braised short ribs and grits become fine cuisine when they're made with the best of what Pike Place Market has to offer.

Belltown

A hodgepodge of dining options, Belltown has everything from chic to sushi, with plenty of casual noodle houses, pizza joints and cafes thrown into the mix.

★Top Pot Hand-Forged Doughnuts CAFE $
(Map p66; www.toppotdoughnuts.com; 2124 5th Ave; doughnuts from $1.50; 6am-7pm; 13) Top Pot is to doughnuts what champagne is to wine – a different class. And its cafes – especially this one in an old car showroom with floor-to-ceiling library shelves and art-deco signage – are equally legendary. The coffee's pretty potent too.

Macrina
BAKERY $

(206-448-4032; 2408 1st Ave; pastries $2-3.75; 7am-7pm; 13) That snaking queue's there for a reason – damned good artisan bread (you can watch the experts roll out the dough through the window). There are two options and two lines at Macrina. One's for the fantastic take-out bakery (possibly the best in Seattle); the other's for the sit-down cafe with its so-good-it-could-be-Paris sandwiches, soups and other such snacks. Join the pilgrimage.

★ Serious Pie
PIZZERIA $$

(Map p66; www.tomdouglas.com; 316 Virginia St; pizzas $16-18; 11am-11pm; Westlake) It's an audacious move to take the down-to-earth Italian pizza and give it a gourmet spin, but local culinary phenomenon Tom Douglas pulls off the trick with casual aplomb. In the crowded confines of Serious Pie, you can enjoy beautifully blistered pizza bases topped by such unconventional ingredients as clams, kale, potato, apples, pistachio and more. It's seriously good!

FareStart Restaurant
NORTHWESTERN $$

(Map p66; 206-443-1233; www.farestart.org; 700 Virginia St; 3-course dinner $25; 11am-2pm Mon-Fri, 5:30-8pm Thu; Westlake & 7th) 🖋 FareStart serves substantial meals that benefit the community. All proceeds from lunch and the popular Thursday-night Guest Chef dinners – when FareStart students work with a famous local chef to produce outstanding meals – go to support the FareStart program, which provides intensive job training, housing assistance and job placement for disadvantaged and homeless people.

Palace Kitchen
NORTHWESTERN $$

(Map p66; 206-448-2001; www.tomdouglas. com; 2030 5th Ave; starters $9-15, mains $15-26; 4:30pm-1am; Westlake) Owned by Tom Douglas, the Palace is a see-and-be-seen hot spot that really picks up for the late-night cocktail scene. Daily dinner specials present such wonders as spaetzle-stuffed pumpkin or traditional pork loin.

Snack on appetizers – including a smoked-salmon-and-blue-cheese terrine or a sampler plate of regional cheeses – or go for the whole shebang with grilled trout, leg of lamb or roast chicken with blackberries and nectarines. There's a late-night happy hour starting at 11pm that includes barbecued short ribs and other awesome deals ($4 to $5), plus drink specials.

Black Bottle
MODERN AMERICAN $$

(www.blackbottleseattle.com; 2600 1st Ave; plates $8-12; 4:30pm-2am; 13) This trendy minimalist bar-restaurant showcases the new Belltown of smart condo dwellers and well-coiffed wine quaffers. The food is mainly appetizers, but with menu items such as grilled lamb and sumac hummus, and braised artichoke heart and greens, even the nostalgic grunge groupies of yore will find it hard to resist.

Dahlia Lounge
NORTHWESTERN $$$

(Map p66; 206-682-4142; www.tomdouglas.com; 2001 4th Ave; lunch $10-22, dinner starters $9-15, mains $22-38; 11:30am-2:30pm & 5-10pm Mon-Fri, 9am-2pm & 5-11pm Sat & Sun; Westlake) Owner Tom Douglas started fusing flavors at this Seattle institution in the late 1980s and singlehandedly made Seattleites more sophisticated; his empire has grown a lot since then, but the flagship restaurant remains a local favorite. There's a bakery next door where you can pick up one of the Dahlia's fabulous desserts to go. Reservations are recommended.

Shiro's Sushi Restaurant
JAPANESE $$$

(www.shiros.com; 2401 2nd Ave; mains $26.75; 5:30-9:45pm; 13) There's barely room for all the awards and kudos that cram the window in this sleek Japanese joint. Grab a pew behind the glass food case and watch the experts concoct delicate and delicious Seattle sushi.

🍴 Seattle Center & Queen Anne

Queen Anne is a favorite spot for a casual, homey meal. Lower Queen Anne – or 'uptown' as it's sometimes known – is locally renowned for its eclectic mix of restaurants, most of which are quick, casual and, above all, easy on the wallet.

★ Toulouse Petit
CAJUN $$

(206-432-9069; 601 Queen Anne Ave N; mains $13-17; 8am-2am; 13) Something of a Seattle phenomenon, Toulouse Petit is hailed for its generous happy hours, cheap brunches and rollicking atmosphere – it's perennially (and boisterously) busy. Somewhere underneath all this cacophony is the specialty food, which pays more than a passing nod to the 'Big Easy' (aka New Orleans). Soak up your cocktails with plates of gumbo, po'boys, catfish and the like.

LOCAL KNOWLEDGE

SEATTLE'S GASTRONOMY DISSECTED

Surrounded by water, Seattle is an obvious powerhouse of fresh seafood – and they know exactly how to prepare it. Local favorites include Dungeness crab, salmon, halibut, various types of oyster, spot prawns and clams. Although it's not one of the US' most cosmopolitan cities, Seattle has a sizable Chinese population and a strong selection of dim sum restaurants in the International District. The ID also harbors a good cluster of Vietnamese restaurants in its 'Little Saigon' quarter. Seattle's Italian restaurants are often highly progressive, many of them specializing in regional Italian food such as Roman or Piedmontese. Chef Ethan Stowell has successfully married Italian cuisine with Northwestern traditions and popularized the use of homemade pasta. Other genres in which Seattle excels are bakeries (a by-product of its coffee-shop culture), Japanese food (the sushi is unwaveringly good) and – perhaps surprisingly – spicy Ethiopian food; the bulk of the East African restaurants are in the Central District (CD). Many visitors from the south comment on the dearth of Mexican restaurants (though there are a handful of good 'uns) and, while the Indian fare can't compete with the likes of Vancouver to the north, the appearance of Canada's Vikram Vij's Shanik restaurant has upped the ante somewhat. In common with most American cities, Seattle loves a good steak – especially one that's led a happy, grass-fed life on a farm just outside of town. The city's latest food fashion is crusty sweet or savory pies, with several new restaurants dedicating themselves exclusively to the genre.

How to Cook a Wolf   ITALIAN $$
(☑206-838-8090; www.ethanstowellrestaurants. com; 2208 Queen Anne Ave N; pasta $16-18; ☺5-11pm; ☐13) ✆ Despite its scary name, the Ethan Stowell–run HTCAW has nothing to do with roasting wild fauna over your campfire. Rather, the name is poached from a book written by MFK Fisher during wartime rationing about how to make the most of limited ingredients. Though times have changed, Stowell embraces the same philosophy.

The food is simple but creative Italian nosh listed on a single sheet of paper and served in a small denlike restaurant. If they ever invent a culinary genre called 'Pacific Northwest Italian' HTCAW will be its archetype.

Shanik   INDIAN, FUSION $$$
(☑206-486-6884; www.shanikrestaurant.com; 500 Terry Ave N; mains $16-27; ☺11:30am-2pm & 5:30pm-late Mon-Fri, 5:30pm-late Sat; ☐Terry & Mercer) Vancouver culinary institution Vikram Vij brought his internationally lauded Indian-fusion food south in 2012, saving countless driving miles for the loyal stream of Seattleites who regularly used to head north to Canada in order to taste his famous spice-encrusted lamb popsicles (yes, they are *that* good).

Shanik is run by Vij's wife, Meeru, and promises more of the same clever crossover cuisine that marries the flavors of the subcontinent with Western style and presentation. It'll stay etched in your memory for months.

✗ Capitol Hill

The scene on Capitol Hill is almost as much about style as food. It's no use enjoying a fabulous dinner if no one can see how chic you look while you're eating it. Then again, ambience hardly detracts from a fine dining experience, so who's complaining?

Molly Moon's   ICE CREAM $
(Map p66; ☑206-708-7947; www.mollymoon-icecream.com; 917 E Pine St; ice creams $3-5; ☺noon-11pm; ☐Pike-Pine) ✆ So what flavor will it be today? The chamomile blossom with 'vegan cold' topping, the Stumptown coffee or the salt licorice? Choices can be confusing at Molly Moon's, where lines stretch out the door and the whole place smells enticingly of waffles. Nursing locavore sensibilities, Molly's cream comes from hormone-free Washington dairy cows. The store's original location is in Wallingford.

Bimbo's Cantina   MEXICAN $
(☑206-329-9978; www.bimboscantina.com; 1013 E Pike St; burritos $5.50-7.50; ☺noon-2am; ☐Pike-Pine) Bimbo's slings fat tacos, giant burritos and juicy quesadillas until late. The space is bordello kitsch with velvet matador portraits, oil paintings with neon elements and a hut-style thatched awning. The best feature of the restaurant is its subterranean bar, the Cha-Cha Lounge.

Oddfellows Cafe MODERN AMERICAN $$

(Map p66; 206-325-0807; www.oddfellowscafe. com; 1525 10th Ave; mains $14-18; 8am-late; Pike-Pine) A trendy dude dressed in '70s retro gear welcomes you at the door and puts your name on the list. The wait's 10 minutes, long enough to take in the decor (historic meeting hall reborn as rustic-meets-urban restaurant) and the clientele (dressed mostly like the guy at the door).

The food, when it comes, is just what your taste buds were craving, especially the brunch, a smorgasbord of flaky biscuits, fluffy eggs and well-dressed salads.

Coastal Kitchen NORTHWESTERN $$

(206-322-1145; www.coastalkitchenseattle.com; 429 15th Ave E; mains $9-19; 8am-midnight; 10) This longtime favorite turns out some of the best food in the neighborhood – it has an eclectic mix of Cajun, Mayan and Mexican inspirations, and an Italian-language instruction tape running in the bathroom, if that gives you a clue about influences. Menus rotate by theme, but constant favorites include roast chicken, pork chops and all-day breakfast.

Fish dishes are startlingly fresh and always interesting. The pasta lunch specials are also highly recommended.

★**Sitka & Spruce** NORTHWESTERN $$$

(Map p66; 206-324-0662; www.sitkaand-spruce. com; 1531 Melrose Ave E; small plates $8-24; 11:30am-2pm & 5:30-10pm; 10) Now in a new location in the Capitol Hill 'hood, this small-plates fine diner has won acclaim for its casual vibe, constantly changing menu, good wine selection and involved chef-owner (he'll be the guy who brings bread to your table). All the ingredients are obtained from local producers, and the idea is to assemble a meal out of a bunch of different taster-size dishes.

Only a few reservations are accepted each night, and the wait can be long, so grab yourself a beer and spend some time studying the chalkboard menu until it's your turn.

★**Cascina Spinasse** ITALIAN $$$

(206-251-7673; www.spinasse.com; 1531 14th Ave; 2-course meals $40; 5-10pm Sun-Thu, to 11pm Fri & Sat; 11) Behind the rather fussy lace curtains hides what is possibly the finest new restaurant in Seattle. Spinasse specializes in cuisine of the Piedmont region of northern Italy. This means delicately prepared ravioli, buttery risottos (enhanced with stinging nettles, no less), rabbit meatballs and roasted artichokes. The impressive wine menu is dominated by fine Piedmontese reds including Barolo, available by the glass.

U District

This is one of the best neighborhoods for authentic, inexpensive ethnic food and inventive vegan menus. Don't be put off by unappetizing-looking storefronts – some of the most interesting food comes from places that have the outward appearance of run-down five-and-dime stores. The adventurous will be rewarded.

Thai Tom THAI $

(206-548-9548; 4543 University Way NE; mains $7-10; 11:30am-9:30pm; 72) About as wide as a train carriage, with permanently steamed-up windows, an open-kitchen lunch counter and flames leaping up from beneath the constantly busy pans on the stoves, Thai Tom feels like some backstreet-Bangkok hole-in-the-wall. Yet, many hail its simple Thai food as the best in the city.

Push in among the elephant heads, dark-brown walls and elbow-to-elbow crowds to find out. Cash only.

Flowers VEGETARIAN, CAFE $

(206-633-1903; 4247 University Way NE; lunch buffet $8, mains $7-15; 11am-2am; ; 72) One of the most stylish places in the U District, Flowers has a vegetarian buffet served until 5pm, and dinners include meat choices. The lunch menu includes 20 sandwiches, each around $5. After hours it becomes an inviting place to sip a cocktail, munch on an appetizer and 'do homework' with a promising study partner.

★**Portage Bay Cafe** NORTHWESTERN, BRUNCH $$

(206-547-8230; www.portagebaycafe.com; 4130 Roosevelt Way NE; brunch $10-13; 7:30am-2:30pm; 66) Hugely popular brunch spot, and for good reason. Aside from the usual suspects (eggs, bacon, pancakes), there's a help-yourself breakfast bar loaded up with fresh fruit, cream, syrup, nuts and the like (all local, of course) waiting to be spread on your doorstep-thick slices of French toast. Arrive early or after 1pm at weekends to avoid the rush.

Cedars Restaurant INDIAN, MIDDLE EASTERN $$
(✆206-527-5247; 4759 Brooklyn Ave NE; mains
$8-15; ⊙11:30am-10pm Mon-Sat, 1-9pm Sun; ✐;
▣72) Cedars serves enormous curries and
vindaloos so smooth and creamy you want
to dive into them. Eat here just once and
you will dream about it later. There's also a
great selection of Mediterranean specialties
like shish kebabs, falafel and gyros, much of
which is vegetarian. The covered wooden
patio is a cool hangout in nice weather.

✗ Fremont, Wallingford & Green Lake

These residential neighborhoods have a
number of well-loved restaurants, old and
new.

★Pie PIES $
(✆206-436-8590; www.sweetandsavorypie.com;
3515 Fremont Ave N; pies $5.95; ⊙9am-9pm Mon-
Thu, to 2am Fri & Sat, 10am-6pm Sun; ▣26) ✐
It's as simple as P-I-E. Bake fresh pies daily
on-site, stuff them with homemade fillings
(sweet and savory) and serve them in a cool,
bold-colored Fremont cafe. The pies are ide-
al for a snack lunch or you can double up
and get a sweet one for dessert too. Broccoli
cheddar and peanut butter cream go down
a treat.

Paseo CUBAN $
(www.paseoseattle.com; 4225 Fremont Ave N; sand-
wiches $6-9; ⊙11am-9pm Tue-Fri, to 8pm Sat; ▣5)
Proof that most Seattleites aren't posh (or
pretentious) is the local legend known as Pa-
seo, a Cuban-style hole-in-the-wall located in
a nondescript part of Fremont which people
alter their commute drive to visit. The fuss
centers on the sandwiches; in particular
the Midnight Cuban Press, with pork, ham,
cheese and banana peppers, and the Cuban
Roast, with slow-roasted, marinated pork.
Grab plenty of napkins.

Homegrown SANDWICHES $
(✆206-453-5232; www.eathomegrown.com; 3416
Fremont Ave N; half/full sandwiches $7/12; ⊙8am-
8pm; ▣26) ✐ Slavishly sustainable, this
newish sandwich bar proves that green
doesn't have to be tasteless. Bread is baked
daily in-house and filled with unique ingre-
dients such as split-pea pesto and pork loin
rubbed in Stumptown coffee that's been
laced with cayenne. Now, that's what you
call creative.

✗ Ballard & Discovery Park

Ballard has an ever-changing restaurant
scene, so don't hesitate to ask around and
check local papers for the latest recom-
mended places.

★Cafe Besalu BAKERY, CAFE $
(✆206-789-1463; www.cafebesalu.com; 5909 24th
Ave NW; pastries from $2.30; ⊙7am-3pm Wed-
Sun; ▣40) Once off the itinerary of Ballard's
weekend visitors, who traditionally stick to
Ballard Ave, Besalu has started to cause a
stir from its isolated perch on 24th Ave with
its French-style baked goods (in particular
the croissants and quiches), which some
bloggers have hailed as 'better than Paris.'

La Carta de Oaxaca MEXICAN $
(✆206-782-8722; www.lacartadeoaxaca.com; 5431
Ballard Ave NW; mains $7-12; ⊙11:30am-3pm &
5-11pm Tue-Sat, 5-11pm Mon; ▣17) Mexican res-
taurants are often duds in Seattle, but then
you walk into this place, which almost feels
like Oaxaca, the Mexican city famous for its
black mole sauces – try the *mole negro Oax-
aqueno*, a house specialty. You can sample
the same stuff on tamales or go for a combi-
nation of various small plates.

Seating is mostly picnic-style, and there's
a full bar – handy considering that there's
usually a wait for a table.

★Bastille Cafe & Bar FRENCH $$
(www.bastilleseattle.com; 5307 Ballard Ave NW;
mains $17-24; ⊙4:30pm-midnight, to 1am Fri & Sat,
brunch 10am-3pm Sun; ▣17) ✐ French but not
at all faux, Bastille could easily pass for a
genuine Parisian bistro if it weren't for the
surfeit of American accents. First there's the
decor: beautiful white tiles juxtaposed with
black wood, mirrors and chandeliers. Then
there's the menu: *moules* (mussels), *frites*
(real french fries), rabbit paté, oysters and
steak (all sourced locally).

♟ Drinking

You'll find cocktail bars, dance clubs and
live music on Capitol Hill. The main drag in
Ballard has brick taverns old and new, filled
with the hard-drinking older set in daytime
and indie rockers at night. Belltown has
gone from grungy to fratty but has the advantage of many drinking holes neatly lined
up in rows. And, this being Seattle, you can't
walk two blocks without hitting a killer coffee shop.

Zeitgeist
CAFE

(www.zeitgeistcoffee.com; 171 S Jackson St; ⏲6am-7pm Mon-Fri, from 8am Sat & Sun; 📶; 🚇Pioneer Sq) Listen: the comforting buzz of conversation! People actually talk in the attractive exposed-brick confines of Zeitgeist – they're not all glued to their laptops. Bolstered by tongue-loosening doses of caffeine, you can join them discussing the beautiful smoothness of your *doppio macchiato* or the sweet intensity of your to-die-for almond croissant in what could very well be Seattle's best indie coffee bar.

★ Shorty's
DIVE BAR

(Map p66; www.shortydog.com; 2222 2nd Ave; ⏲noon-2am; 🚇13) Shorty's is all about beer, pinball and music, which is punk and metal mostly. A remnant of Belltown's grungier days that refuses to become an anachronism, it keeps the lights low (to cover the grime?) and the music loud. Pinball machines are built into every table and very basic snacks (hot dogs, nachos) soak up the beer.

★ Pike Pub & Brewery
BREWPUB

(Map p66; www.pikebrewing.com; 1415 1st Ave; ⏲11am-midnight; 🚇University St) Leading the way in the microbrewery revolution, this brewpub was an early starter, opening in 1989 underneath Pike Place Market. Today it continues to serve high-palate pub food and hop-heavy beers in a neo-industrial multilevel space that's a beer nerd's heaven. The brewery runs free tours daily at 2pm.

Zig Zag Café
COCKTAIL BAR

(Map p66; 📞206-625-1146; www.zigzagseattle.com; 1501 Western Ave; cocktails from $8; ⏲5pm-2am; 🚇University St) For serious cocktails, this is the unmissable destination in town. Classic and inventive drinks are made with precision by handsome and nattily attired alchemists – including some of the best bartenders in Seattle. These folks know how to sling a bottle of chartreuse; sitting at the bar on a quiet night and watching them command the stage is a treat.

★ Fremont Brewing
BREWPUB

(www.fremontbrewing.com; 3409 Woodland Park Ave N; ⏲11am-7pm Mon-Wed, to 8pm Thu-Sat, to 6pm Sun; 🚇26) No conventional bar (this, after all, is Fremont!), this new brewery inaugurated in 2008 has what is called an Urban Beer Garden: you sit at a couple of communal tables in the brewery and enjoy samples of what are quickly being hailed as some of the finest microbrews in the city.

Pets and kids are welcome and you can bring your own food.

★ Noble Fir
BAR

(📞206-420-7425; www.thenoblefir.com; 5316 Ballard Ave NW; ⏲4-11pm Mon-Wed, to 1am Thu-Sat, noon-11pm Sun; 🚇17) Possibly the first bar devoted to the theme of wilderness hiking, the Noble Fir is a bright, shiny new Ballard spot with an epic beer list that might just make you want to abandon all your plans for outdoor adventure. Should your resolve begin to flag, head to the back corner, where there's a library of activity guides and maps that will reinspire you.

Blue Moon
DIVE BAR

(712 NE 45th St; ⏲2pm-late; 🚇66) A legendary counterculture dive near the university that first opened in 1934 to celebrate the repeal of the Prohibition laws, the Blue Moon makes much of its former literary patrons: doyens Dylan Thomas, Allen Ginsberg and Tom Robbins get mentioned a lot.

These days it's unlikely you'll meet anyone quite so erudite, though it's still good for impromptu poetry recitations, jaw-harp performances and inspired rants.

★ Espresso Vivace at Brix
CAFE

(www.espressovivace.com; 532 Broadway E; ⏲6am-11pm; 🚇60) Loved in equal measure for its no-nonsense walk-up stand (also on Broadway) and this newer cafe (a large retro place with a beautiful Streamline Moderne counter), Vivace is known to have produced some of the Picassos of latte art. But it doesn't just offer pretty toppings. Many of Seattle's coffee experts rate its espresso shots as the best in the city.

Re-Bar
GAY

(Map p66; www.rebarseattle.com; 1114 Howell St; 🚇70) Storied dance club where many of Seattle's defining cultural events happened (such as Nirvana album releases). Welcomes gay, straight, bi or undecided revelers to its lively dance floor. It's in the Denny Triangle.

Owl & Thistle
IRISH PUB

(Map p66; 📞206-621-7777; www.owlnthistle.com; 808 Post Ave; ⏲11am-2am; 🚇Pioneer Sq) One of the best Irish pubs in the city, the dark, cavernous Owl & Thistle is located slap-bang downtown but misses most of the tourist traffic (who home in on the more 'themed' Fado) because it's hidden in Post Ave.

Aside from Celtic folk bands or acoustic singer-songwriters who make pleasant noises here most evenings, it serves excellent beer and possibly the cheapest fish and chips in the city (less than $4 during happy hour). Most importantly, it's run by an Irishman (and his wife).

Panama Hotel Tea & Coffee House CAFE
(607 S Main St; ⊙8am-7pm Mon-Sat, from 9am Sun; ⓖChinatown/International District W) The Panama, a historic 1910 building containing the only remaining Japanese bathhouse in the US, doubles as a memorial to the neighborhood's Japanese residents forced into internment camps during WWII. The beautifully relaxed cafe has a wide selection of teas and is one of the few places in Seattle to sell Lavazza Italian coffee. Board games and old photos encourage lingering.

Neighbours GAY
(Map p66; www.neighboursnightclub.com; 1509 Broadway Ave E; ⓖPike-Pine) Check out the always-packed dance factory for the gay club scene and its attendant glittery straight girls.

Hale's Ales Brewery BREWPUB
(www.halesbrewery.com; 4301 Leary Way NW; ⊙11:30am-11pm; ⓖ40) Hale's makes fantastic beer, notably its ambrosial Cream Ale. Its flagship brewpub in Fremont feels like a business hotel lobby, but it's worth a stop. There is a self-guided tour leaving near the entrance.

R Place GAY
(Map p66; ☎206-322-8828; www.rplaceseattle.com; 619 E Pine St; ⊙4pm-2am Mon-Fri, 2pm-2am Sat & Sun; ⓖPike-Pine) Weekend cabaret performances, amateur strip shows, go-go boys and DJs – there's something entertaining going on every night of the week at this welcoming gay bar. Relax with a beer on the deck or dance your ass off.

☆ Entertainment

Live music is still a huge draw in Seattle; clubs come and go, but the scene thrives. Consult the *Stranger* and *Seattle Weekly* for listings.

Cinephiles shouldn't miss the **Seattle International Film Festival** (SIFF; www.siff.net; tickets $13-30; ⊙mid-May). The festival has a new dedicated cinema in the Seattle Center next to the **Seattle Repertory Theater** (☎206-443-2222; www.seattlerep.org; 155 Mercer St; ⊙box office 10am-6pm Tue-Fri; ⓂSeattle Center). It also uses the **Uptown Cinema** (☎206-285-1022; 511 Queen Anne Ave N; ⓖ13) in nearby Lower Queen Anne.

FIRST THURSDAY ART WALK

Art walks are two a penny in US cities these days, but they were pretty much an unknown quantity when the pioneering artists of Pioneer Square instituted their first amble around the local galleries in 1981. The neighborhood's **First Thursday Art Walk** (www.firstthursdayseattle.com) claims to be the oldest in the nation and a creative pathfinder for all that followed (and there have been many). Aside from gluing together Pioneer Square's network of 50-plus galleries (only a few of which can be listed in this book), the walk is a good excuse to admire creative public sculpture, sip decent coffee (many cafes serve as de facto galleries), browse an array of stalls set up in Occidental Park, and get to know the neighborhood and its people. The Art Walk is self-guided, but you can pick up a map from the information booth in Occidental Park.

★**Crocodile** LIVE MUSIC
(Map p66; www.thecrocodile.com; 2200 2nd Ave; ⓖ13) Nearly old enough to be called a Seattle institution, the Crocodile is a clamorous 560-capacity music venue that first opened in 1991, just in time to grab the coattails of the grunge explosion. Everyone who's anyone in Seattle's alt-music scene has since played here, including a famous occasion in 1992 when Nirvana appeared unannounced, supporting Mudhoney.

Despite changing ownership in 2009 and undergoing a grunge-cleansing refurbishment, the Croc remains plugged into the Seattle scene, though these days aspiring stage-divers are more likely to get kicked out than crowd-surfed on the arms of an adoring audience. There's a full bar, a mezzanine floor and a no-frills pizza restaurant on site. Shows kick off around 10pm.

Neumo's LIVE MUSIC
(Map p66; www.neumos.com; 925 E Pike St; ⓖPike-Pine) A punk, hip-hop and alternative-music venue that counts Radiohead and Bill Clinton (not together) among its former guests, Neumo's (formerly known as Moe's) fills the big shoes of its original namesake. Yes, it can get hot, and yes, midshow it's a long walk to the toilets, but that's rock and roll.

The club's latest addition is the Barboza Lounge, a more intimate downstairs music venue.

Chop Suey
LIVE MUSIC

(www.chopsuey.com; 1325 E Madison St; 🚇12) Chop Suey is a dark, high-ceilinged space with a ramshackle faux-Chinese motif and eclectic bookings – indie, hip-hop and rock are staples, although its Jai Ho nights with Bollywood-Bhangra dancing led by Mumbai native and DJ Prashant have become riotously popular.

Tractor Tavern
LIVE MUSIC

(☑206-789-3599; www.tractortavern.com; 5213 Ballard Ave NW; 🚇17) The premier venue for folk and acoustic music, the elegant Tractor Tavern also books local songwriters and regional bands such as Richmond Fontaine, plus touring acts like John Doe and Wayne Hancock. It's a gorgeous room, usually with top sound quality.

Cinerama
CINEMA

(Map p66; www.cinerama.com; 2100 4th Ave; 🚇13) Possibly Seattle's most popular theater, Cinerama is one of only three of its type left in the world (with a giant, curved three-panel screen) and has a fun, sci-fi feel. Regular renovations, the last of them in 2010, have kept it up-to-date. It presents a good mix of new releases and 70mm classics.

Northwest Film Forum
CINEMA

(www.nwfilmforum.org; 1515 12th Ave; 🚇Pike-Pine) A film-arts organization with a two-screen cinema that offers impeccable programming, from restored classics to cutting-edge independent and international films. It's in Capitol Hill, of course!

★A Contemporary Theatre
THEATER

(ACT; Map p66; www.acttheatre.org; 700 Union St; 🚇University St) One of the three big companies in the city, the theater fills its $30-million home at Kreielsheimer Place with performances by Seattle's best thespians and occasional big-name actors. Terraced seating surrounds a central stage and the interior has gorgeous architectural embellishments.

Intiman Theater Company
THEATER

(☑206-269-1900; www.intiman.org; 201 Mercer St; ⊙ticket office noon-5pm Tue-Sun; Ⓜ Seattle Center) In a shocking move, Seattle's Tony Award–winning Intiman Theater abruptly closed in April 2011, a victim of the financial crisis, cancelling its whole planned summer season in the process. But city icons aren't allowed to die. Emergency resuscitation was administered and the Intiman raised the $1 million necessary for a heroic reopening in 2012.

With a new artistic director (Andrew Russell) in place, the Intiman is back doing what it does best: magnificent stagings of Shakespeare and Ibsen. Time for another Tony?

BEST NEIGHBORHOODS FOR ENTERTAINMENT

Downtown Classical music, contemporary theater plus an eclectic and always entertaining assortment of buskers in Pike Place Market.

Pioneer Square Seattle's best comedy club, sports crowds, plus a few tough pubs peddling punk and metal.

Belltown & Seattle Center Alt-rock and jazz venues raise the pulse in Belltown; opera, ballet and theater enliven the Seattle Center.

Queen Anne & Lake Union Fringe theater, a festival-hosting cinema and a few hallowed old-school rock venues.

Capitol Hill Everything outside the mainstream, including alt-rock and electronica, along with some art-house cinemas and spontaneous street theater.

U District Small pubs showcase guitar strummers and stand-up comics. Larger music venues and art-house cinemas punctuate 'the Ave'.

Fremont Intimate live venues and neighborhood pubs book small-name up-and-coming live acts.

Ballard Pubs and clubs plus the iconic Tractor Tavern cement a good self-contained live-music scene.

Seattle Opera   CLASSICAL MUSIC
(www.seattleopera.org; M Seattle Center) Features a program of four or five full-scale operas every season at McCaw Hall, including a Wagner's *Ring* cycle that draws sellout crowds in summer.

Seattle Symphony   CLASSICAL MUSIC
(Map p66; www.seattlesymphony.org; R University St) A major regional ensemble. It plays at the Benaroya Concert Hall, which you'll find downtown at 2nd Ave and University St.

Pacific Northwest Ballet   DANCE
(www.pnb.org; M Seattle Center) The foremost dance company in the Northwest puts on more than 100 shows a season from September through June at Seattle Center's McCaw Hall.

Richard Hugo House   COMMUNITY CENTER
(☏ 206-322-7030; www.hugohouse.org; 1634 11th Ave; ◷ house noon-6pm Mon-Fri, to 5pm Sat, zine archive 4-8pm Wed, 1-5pm Thu & Sat; ⛴ Pike-Pine) Established in honor of famed Northwest poet Richard Hugo, and the nexus of Seattle's literary community, the 1902 Hugo House (a former mortuary) hosts readings, classes and workshops, as well as offering various events around town. Writers-in-residence keep office hours, during which they're available for free consultations about writing projects.

The extensive zine library invites all-day lingering, and there's also a library, a conference room, a theater and a cafe with a small stage.

🔒 Shopping

Downtown dominates Seattle's retail scene with big-name shopping malls. But take a look in the corners of Pioneer Square for art and antique shops, or in the many nooks and crannies of Pike Place Market for everything from embroidered tea towels to lollypop condoms. Make the waterfront your stop for obligatory souvenirs. For fashion or novelties, browse on Capitol Hill.

Note: a 9.5% sales tax is added to all purchases except food to be prepared for consumption (ie groceries). Unlike the European VAT or Canadian GST, the sales tax is not refundable to tourists.

★ Easy Street Records & Café   MUSIC
(☏ 206-938-3279; 4559 California Ave SW; ⛴ RapidRide C-Line) This place has everything: rock and roll, coffee, beer, food...and an open, airy place to hang out while enjoying all of the above. Any place where you can shop for new-import records, have a beer and then kick back on the couch for a while is bound to attract attention, and you might have to elbow some hipsters out of your way to grab that coveted album – just try not to spill.

Elliott Bay Book Company   BOOKS
(Map p66; www.elliottbaybook.com; 1521 10th Ave; ◷ 10am-10pm Mon-Fri, to 11pm Sat, 11am-9pm Sun; ⛴ Pike-Pine) Perish the day when ebooks render bookstores obsolete. What will happen to the Saturday-afternoon joy of Elliott Bay books, where 150,000 titles inspire author readings, discussions, reviews and hours of serendipitous browsing?

Pure Food Fish   FOOD
(Map p66; ☏ 206-622-5765; www.freshseafood.com; 1511 Pike Pl; ◷ 9am-5pm; R Westlake) Perhaps the gift that says 'I heart Seattle' the most is a whole salmon or other fresh seafood from the fish markets. All the markets will prepare fish for transportation on the plane ride home, or you can just call and have them take care of the overnight shipping; Pure Food Fish has the best reputation locally for quality and value.

Babeland   ADULT
(Map p66; www.babeland.com; 707 E Pike St; ◷ 11am-10pm Mon-Sat, noon-7pm Sun; ⛴ Pike-Pine) Remember those pink furry handcuffs and that glass dildo you needed? Well, look no further.

Red Light   CLOTHING
(☏ 206-329-2200; www.redlightvintage.com; 312 Broadway E; ◷ 11am-8pm Sun-Thu, to 9pm Fri & Sat; ⛴ Capitol Hill) Red Light carries stylish, painstakingly selected vintage clothing, organized by decade or sometimes by color. It's a cool shop...maybe too cool. Rest assured: you will be judged by your purchases. There's also a branch in the **U District** (☏ 206-545-4044; 4560 University Way NE).

Hardwick's Hardware Store   JUNK
(☏ 206-632-1203; 4214 Roosevelt Way NE; ◷ 8am-6pm Mon-Fri, 9am-6pm Sat, later hours in summer; ⛴ 66) Locals in the know come to Hardwick's to explore the rows and rows of buckets filled with bizarre little gadgets and gizmos. Some people probably know what these objects are for, but most shoppers are looking for things to use in their art projects. It's a hive of a place that's fun just to explore.

Uwajimaya
FOOD, GIFTS

(☎206-624-6248; 600 5th Ave S; ⊙9am-10pm Mon-Sat, to 9pm Sun; ⬛Chinatown/International District W) Dried squid? Yes. Sheets of seaweed? Absolutely. Dumpling steamers, teapots, chopsticks? All of the above. The enormous Asian grocery and supply store Uwajimaya, anchoring an eponymous shopping center, has everything you need to prepare Thai, Japanese, Chinese and just about any other type of Asian specialties.

ℹ Information

EMERGENCY & MEDICAL SERVICES

45th Street Community Clinic (☎206-633-3350; 1629 N 45th St) Medical and dental services.

Harborview Medical Center (☎206-731-3000; 325 9th Ave) Full medical care, with emergency room.

Seattle Police (☎206-625-5011)

Washington State Patrol (☎425-649-4370)

INTERNET ACCESS

Practically every bar and coffee shop in Seattle has free wi-fi, as do most hotels.

MEDIA

Radio stations include KEXP 90.3FM, a legendary independent-music and community station, and KUOW 94.9FM, with NPR news.

Seattle Gay News (SGN; www.sgn.org) Covers the gay and lesbian scene.

Seattle Times (www.seattletimes.com) The state's largest daily paper.

Seattle Weekly (www.seattleweekly.com) Free weekly with news and entertainment listings.

Stranger (www.thestranger.com) Irreverent weekly edited by Dan Savage of 'Savage Love' fame.

MONEY

American Express (Amex; 600 Stewart St; ⊙8:30am-5:30pm Mon-Fri)

Travelex-Thomas Cook Currency Services (400 Pine St, Level 3; ⊙9:30am-6pm Mon-Sat, 11am-5pm Sun) There's also a booth at the main airport terminal, behind the Delta Airlines counter.

POST

Post Office (Map p66; 301 Union St; ⊙8:30am-5:30pm Mon-Fri)

TOURIST INFORMATION

Seattle Visitor Center & Concierge Services (Map p66; ☎206-461-5840; www.visitseattle. org; Washington State Convention Center, E Pike St & 7th Ave; ⊙9am-5pm)

ℹ Getting There & Away

AIR

Seattle-Tacoma International Airport (SEA; www.portseattle.org/Sea-Tac), 13 miles south of Seattle on the I-5, has daily services to Europe, Asia, Mexico and points throughout the USA and Canada, with frequent flights to and from Portland and Vancouver, BC.

BOAT

Victoria Clipper (www.clippervacations.com) operates several high-speed passenger ferries to Victoria, BC (from one to three daily), and to the San Juan Islands. It also organizes package tours, which can be booked through the website.

The **Washington State Ferries** (www.wsdot. wa.gov/ferries) website has maps, prices, schedules, trip planners, weather updates and other news, as well as estimated waiting times for popular routes. Fares depend on the route, size of the vehicle and duration of the trip, and are collected either for round-trip or one-way travel, depending on the departure terminal.

BUS

Greyhound (Map p66; www.greyhound.com; 811 Stewart St; ⊙6am-midnight) connects Seattle with cities all over the country, including Chicago ($228 one way, two days, two daily), Spokane ($51, eight hours, three daily), San Francisco ($129, 20 hours, three daily) and Vancouver, BC ($32, four hours, five daily).

The fast, efficient **Quick Shuttle** (www.quick-coach.com; ☎), with five to six daily buses to Vancouver ($43; with free on-board wi-fi), picks up at the Best Western Executive Inn on Taylor Ave N near the Seattle Center. Grab the monorail or walk to downtown.

The **Bellair Airporter Shuttle** (Map p66; www. airporter.com) runs buses to Yakima, Bellingham and Anacortes and stops at King Street Station (for Yakima) and the Downtown Convention Center (for Bellingham and Anacortes).

TRAIN

Amtrak (www.amtrak.com) serves Seattle's **King Street Station** (303 S Jackson St; ⊙6am-10:30pm, ticket counter 6:15am-8pm). Three main routes run through town: the *Cascades* (connecting with Vancouver, BC, Portland, OR, and Eugene, OR), the *Coast Starlight* (connecting with Oakland, CA, and Los Angeles, CA) and the *Empire Builder* (connecting with Spokane, WA, Fargo, ND, and Chicago, IL).

Sample one-way fares include Seattle–Chicago ($227, 46 hours, daily), Seattle–Portland ($25, three to four hours, five daily) and Seattle–Vancouver, BC ($30, three to four hours, five daily).

ⓘ Getting Around

TO/FROM THE AIRPORT

Sea-Tac International Airport is one of the top 20 airports in the US, with numerous domestic flights. The options for making the 13-mile trek from the airport to downtown Seattle improved drastically with the completion of the airport light-rail line in 2009. It's fast and cheap and takes you directly to the heart of downtown, as well as a handful of other stops along the way. **Shuttle Express** (☑ 800-487-7433; www.shuttleexpress.com) has a pickup and drop-off point on the 3rd floor of the airport garage; it charges approximately $18 and is handy if you have a lot of luggage. Taxis are available at the parking garage on the 3rd floor. The average fare to downtown is $42.

CAR & MOTORCYCLE

Seattle traffic is disproportionately heavy and chaotic for a city of its size, and parking is scarce and expensive. Add to that the city's bizarrely cobbled-together mishmash of skewed grids, the hilly terrain and the preponderance of one-way streets and it's easy to see why driving downtown is best avoided if at all possible. If you are traveling with a car, consider stashing it at your hotel and using public transportation to get around within the city center.

PUBLIC TRANSPORTATION

Seattle's public transportation is wide-ranging and improving. Buses are ubiquitous. A new streetcar line opens in 2014 and an extension of the existing Link Light Rail should be in place by 2016.

TAXI

You can hail a cab from the street, but it's a safer bet to call and order one. All Seattle taxis operate at the same rate, which at the time of writing was $2.50 at meter drop, then $2.70 per mile. There may be an extra charge for extra passengers and baggage.
Orange Cab Co (☑ 206-444-0409; www.orangecab.net)
Yellow Cab (☑ 206-622-6500; www.yellowtaxi.net)

AROUND SEATTLE

Blake Island

An easy way to get from Seattle onto the Puget Sound is with **Tillicum Village Tours** (Map p66; ☑ 206-443-1244; Pier 55, Seattle; tours adult/child $79.95/30; ☉ daily summer, Sat & Sun only Oct-Mar). The four-hour visit to Blake Island, the birthplace of Seattle's namesake Chief Sealth, includes a salmon bake, a native dance and a movie at an old Duwamish Native American village.

Bainbridge Island

The island is a popular destination with locals and visitors alike. It's the quickest and easiest way to get out on the water from Seattle, and the ferry ride provides stunning views of both Seattle and the Sound. Prepare to stroll around lazily, tour some waterfront cafes, taste unique wines at the **Bainbridge Island Winery** (☑ 206-842-9463; ☉ tastings 11am-5pm Fri-Sun), 4 miles north of Winslow on Hwy 305, and maybe rent a bike and cycle around the invitingly flat countryside.

Washington State Ferries (☑ 206-464-6400, ferry traffic info 551, in Washington 888-808-7977; www.wsdot.wa.gov/ferries) run several times a day from Pier 52 (adult/car and driver $7.85/13.55, bicycle surcharge $1).

Vashon Island

More rural and countercultural than Bainbridge, Vashon Island has resisted suburbanization – a rare accomplishment in the Puget Sound area. Much of Vashon is covered with farms and gardens; the small community centers double as commercial hubs and artists' enclaves. Cascade views are great, with unencumbered vistas of Mt Rainier and north to Baker.

Vashon is a good island to explore by bicycle or car, lazily stopping to pick berries or fruit at a 'U-pick' garden or orchard. There's also the option to plan a hike in one of the county parks.

From Pier 50 in Seattle, a passenger-only ferry leaves six times each weekday for Vashon Island ($5, 25 minutes). However, the ferry deposits you far from the centers of Vashon commerce and culture, so you'll need to bring a bike ($1 extra charge) or have a lift arranged. From Fauntleroy in West Seattle, a car ferry leaves over 30 times daily for Vashon (passenger/car and driver $5.10/17.25, 15 minutes). Fares are collected only on the journey to the island.

Bremerton

Seattle's other ferry destination is Bremerton, the largest town on the Kitsap Peninsula and Puget Sound's principal naval base.

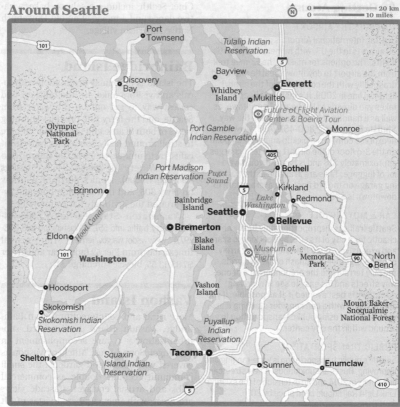

The main attractions here are the **Puget Sound Navy Museum** (☎ 360-479-7447; www.pugetsoundnavymuseum.org; 251 First St; ⊙ 10am-4pm Mon-Thu & Sat, 1-4pm Sun) **FREE** and the historic destroyer **USS Turner Joy**, right next to the ferry terminal.

The car ferry to Bremerton makes frequent daily trips from the terminal at Pier 52 (passenger/car and driver $7.85/13.55, one hour). Passengers are charged only on the westbound journey; those with vehicles pay both ways.

Boeing Factory & Everett

One of the Seattle area's most worthwhile outlying sights is the **Future of Flight Aviation Center & Boeing Tour** (☎ 1-800-464-1476; www.futureofflight.org; 8415 Paine Field Blvd; adult/child $18/12; ⊙ 8:30am-5:30pm) in the city of Everett, 25 miles north of Seattle. Serving as a good complement to Georgetown's

Museum of Flight, the center, aside from its museum, offers something different: a tour of the real working Boeing factory where the famous airplanes are made. The huge complex is the world's most voluminous building, meaning that the 90-minute tours involve plenty of traveling around, some of it by bus. Getting to the center without a car can be a pain, but you can save time by partaking in an organized tour with **Tours Northwest** (☎ 206-768-1234; www.toursnorthwest.com), which picks up from downtown hotels. It charges $65/49 per adult/child, including admission. No cameras are allowed.

Bellevue, Kirkland & Redmond

Bellevue, on the eastern shores of Lake Washington, is an upscale burg with high-income housing, attractive parks and some interesting shops and boutiques. Civic and social life centers on Bellevue Sq, at Bellevue Way NE and NE 8th St, the shopping mall that sets the tone for downtown and the surrounding communities. Across from the mall is the **Bellevue Art Museum** (☑425-519-0770; www.bellvuearts.org; 510 Bellevue Way NE; adult/reduced $10/7, 1st Fri of month free; ⊘11am-5pm Tue-Sun), featuring changing exhibits of contemporary Northwest art.

To reach Bellevue from downtown Seattle, take I-90 east and exit on I-405 northbound. By bus, take 550 from Convention Pl or any of the 3rd Ave tunnel stations ($2.25).

North of Bellevue on I-405 is Kirkland, known for its lakefront business district, marinas and antique shopping malls. Some of the best public access to Lake Washington is along Lake Ave W. Lots of waterfront restaurants are found here, some with docks for their boat-transported customers. East of Kirkland is Redmond, a sprawling suburb and the center of Seattle's high-tech industry. To reach Kirkland and Redmond from central Seattle, take Hwy 520 over the Evergreen Point Bridge or catch bus 251 along 4th Ave.

Northwestern Washingto & the San Juan Islands

Best Places to Eat

➡ Seeds Bistro & Bar (p104)

➡ Pepper Sisters (p98)

➡ Mijita's (p117)

➡ Adrift (p102)

Best Places to Stay

➡ Willows Inn (p100)

➡ Wild Iris Inn (p103)

➡ Rosario Resort & Spa (p116)

➡ Hotel Bellwether (p98)

Why Go?

Between Seattle, the Cascade Mountains and Canada lies Washington's most archetypal region, a 'greatest hits' of the Pacific Northwest. There's the skyline-hogging volcano (Mt Baker); the wilderness-flecked natural parks (everywhere); the liberal, collegiate city (Bellingham); the antiresort ski 'resort' (Baker, again); innumerable islands (the San Juan archipelago); and even a stash of credible vineyards.

The Northwest's urban hub is laid-back Bellingham, while its rural highlight could be any one of the 200-plus islands that speckle the northern reaches of Puget Sound. Cultural life tends to be influenced by Vancouver and Seattle, ensuring that the music's electric, the microbreweries abundant and the coffee aromatic. And wherever you go you'll be sure to find an abundance of Northwestern cuisine featuring locally sourced ingredients, from wild-caught salmon to the world's sweetest blackberries.

When to Go
Bellingham

Mar & Apr Vibrant flower displays at the Skagit County Tulip Festival.

Jun Dutch-inspired Holland Days Festival in Lynden.

Sep & Oct Avoid summer crowds and enjoy fall colors in the San Juan Islands.

NORTHWEST COAST

Bellingham

POP 81.862

Imagine a slightly less-eccentric slice of Portland, OR, broken off and towed 250 miles to the north. Welcome to laid-back Bellingham, a green, liberal and famously livable settlement that has taken the libertine, nothing-is-too-weird ethos of Oregon's 'City of Roses' and given it a peculiarly Washingtonian twist. Mild in both manners and weather, the 'city of subdued excitement,' as a local mayor once dubbed it, is an unlikely alliance of espresso-supping students, venerable retirees, all-weather triathletes and placard-waving peaceniks. Publications such as *Outside Magazine* have consistently lauded Bellingham for its abundant outdoor opportunities, while adventure organizations such as the American Alpine Institute call it home base.

Historically, Bellingham was four different towns – Fairhaven, Sehome, Whatcom and Bellingham – that amalgamated into a single metro area in the late 19th century. Despite vestiges of an ugly industrial past along the waterfront, and a flirtation with out-of-town 1980s mall development directed mainly toward bargain-hunting Canadians, Bellingham's downtown has been revitalized in recent years with intra-urban trails, independent food co-ops, tasty brunch spots and – in genteel Fairhaven – a rejuvenated historic district.

Bellingham is 18 miles south of the Canadian border crossing at Blaine and 89 miles north of Seattle on I-5. The current city center is west of I-5; exit 253 leads to Holly St, a major downtown artery and one of the few streets to cut through the area without getting caught up in conflicting street grids.

◎ Sights

Whatcom Museum of
History & Art   MUSEUM
(www.whatcommuseum.org; 121 Prospect St; adult/child $10/8; ☉noon-5pm Tue-Sun) 🖋 This revamped museum is spread over three buildings: historic Whatcom City Hall (built in 1892), the adjacent Syre Education Center, and the innovative new Lightcatcher building. The last incorporates a spectacular 37ft glass wall and is Leadership in Energy and Environmental Design–certified. A rich array of exhibits includes historical material, Northwest art and Native American basket weaving.

There's also a small shop and a special Family Interactive Gallery with exhibits and art for kids.

The Whatcom Museum has formulated an Old Town Bellingham Walking Tour that starts close to the museum and incorporates 20 sites in and around West Holly St. Pick up a map and leaflet when you visit the museum.

SPARK Museum of Electrical
Invention   MUSEUM
(www.amre.us; 1312 Bay St; adult/child $6/3; ☉11am-4pm Wed-Sat, noon-4pm Sun) This museum showcases more than 2000 exhibits relating to the early days of electricity and the golden age of radio. It houses the largest collection of its kind in the US.

Western Washington University   GALLERY
Founded in 1893 as a teacher training institute, WWU was redesignated as a university in 1977. Environmental Studies is a popular specialty here. The **WWU Visitors Information Center** (☉7am-5pm Mon-Fri) at the end of South College Dr can provide details of a self-guided tour of the campus' two dozen outdoor sculptures, and you can also pop into the **Western Gallery** (www.westerngallery.wwu.edu; ☉10am-4pm Mon-Fri, to 8pm Wed, noon-4pm Sat) to view the art exhibits. The gallery is closed for summer recess.

Whatcom Falls Park   PARK
🖋 You might feel you have wandered unwittingly into the North Cascades. Bellingham's eastern suburbs are bisected by a wild region that stretches from Lake Whatcom down to Bellingham Bay. The change in elevation is marked by four sets of waterfalls, including **Whirlpool Falls**, a popular summer swimming hole. There are numerous trails in the park as well as picnic tables and recreational facilities.

🏃 Activities

Wedged precariously between mountains and sea, Bellingham offers outdoor activities by the truckload. Lakes Whatcom, Samish and Padden, all within a few minutes of town, make for great picnicking and boating, while walkers and hikers can trace the well-paved trail through Fairhaven to Larrabee State Park.

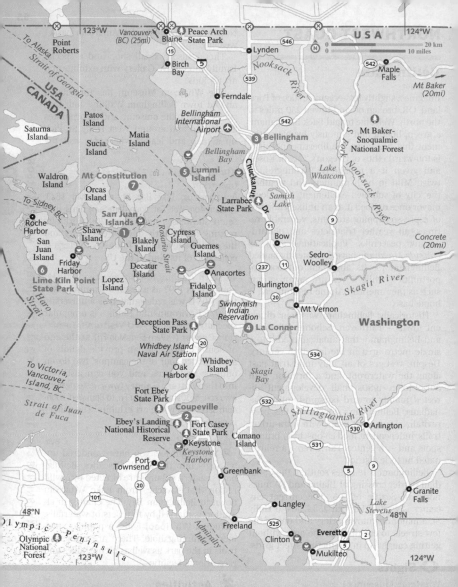

Northwestern Washington & the San Juan Islands Highlights

1 Propelling yourself by human-powered transport around the **San Juan Islands** (p116).

2 Eating mussels in **Coupeville** (p105) on Whidbey Island.

3 Browsing Bellingham's historic neighborhoods while licking a **Mallard** (p98) ice cream cone.

4 Staying in a La Conner B&B during the **Skagit County Tulip Festival** (p103).

5 Hiking lush Baker Mountain on **Lummi Island** (p100).

6 Whale-watching from **Lime Kiln Point State Park** (p109) on San Juan Island.

7 Taking in the view from the top of **Mt Constitution** on Orcas Island (p114).

Climbing

Bellingham is a mini Kathmandu for the ever-active Northwest climbing community and home to the highly regarded **American Alpine Institute** (www.aai.cc; 1515 12th St), which organizes everything from Everest ascents to guided trips up Mt Baker and a slew of other North Cascade peaks.

Cruises

Bellingham offers a number of scenic and wildlife cruises; shop the options at the visitors center or the Bellingham Cruise Terminal.

San Juan Cruises   CRUISE
(www.whales.com; 355 Harris Ave) Runs cruises around Bellingham Bay (maximum 149 persons) with beer or wine tasting ($35), whale-watching around the San Juan Islands (from $99) and more.

Northwest Navigation   CRUISE
(☎877-670-7863; www.northwestnavigation.com; 2-day cruise per person from $795) For an intimate, boutique cruise experience (maximum six passengers), Northwest Navigation runs exceptional multiday cruises on a beautifully refurbished 1929 tow boat. Expect to experience the natural world at its finest and dine on exquisite fresh food. Most tours take in the San Juan Islands, but the boat goes as far afield as Alaska via the Inside Passage.

Other Activities

Moondance Sea Kayak
Adventures   KAYAKING
(www.moondancekayak.com; ☺Apr-Sep) If you're interested in renting kayaks, try Moondance Sea Kayak Adventures, which runs a full-day trip in Chuckanut Bay, launching from Larrabee State Park ($95).

Fairhaven Bike & Mountain Sports   CYCLING
(www.fairhavenbike.com; 1103 11th St) Fairhaven Bike & Mountain Sports rents bikes from $40 a day and has all the info and maps on local routes. This is one of the most bike-friendly cities in the Northwest, with a well-maintained intra-urban trail going as far south as Larrabee State Park. Also rents out cross-country skis and snowshoes in the winter.

🛏 Sleeping

Guesthouse Inn   MOTEL $
(☎360-671-9600; www.bellinghamvaluinn.com; 805 Lakeway Dr; r from $95; ❉🐾) The clean, personable Guesthouse Inn is just off I-5 and an easy 15-minute walk from downtown Bellingham. The Vancouver–Seattle Bellair Shuttle stops here, making it an ideal base for overnighters who want to explore the Bellingham area.

Larrabee State Park   CAMPGROUND $
(☎360-676-2093; Chuckanut Dr; tent/RV sites $23/30) Seven miles south of Bellingham, along scenic Chuckanut Dr, these campsites sit among Douglas firs and cedars with access to Chuckanut Bay and 12 miles of hiking and biking trails.

Birch Bay Hostel   HOSTEL $
(☎360-371-2180; www.birchbayhostel.org; 7467 Gemini St off Alderson Rd; dm/d $30/50; ☺May-Sep) If you're on your way to or from the British Columbia (BC)/Washington border, you can stay at this HI hostel at Bay Horizon County Park in Blaine, just south of the 49th parallel. Clean dormitory beds and private rooms for up to four are housed in old military barracks with a cozy social space. Nearby are the beach, waterfront restaurants and Canada.

THE GREAT SKI TO SEA RACE

If one event sums up the essence of modern Bellingham it's the annual **Ski to Sea Race** (www.skitosea.com), held in late May. This seven-leg team relay from the top of Mt Baker 93.5 miles down to Fairhaven Marine Park on Puget Sound enshrines the eccentric combination of magic and madness that make this great city tick. The seven relay disciplines are cross-country skiing, downhill skiing, running, cycling, canoeing, mountain biking and kayaking, and around 4000 participants give it their all. Anyone not racing is supporting the competitors with cheers at the finish line. This event has consumed the town since 1911.

And the race isn't just a time for getting down that hill. Before the competition there's a massive block party on Railroad Ave with live music, plenty of adult beverages and food. There's also a kids parade and junior ski to sea a few days before the race and a 'Grande' parade through town the day before. If you're in town at this time, prepare yourself to party (and book far in advance if you need a hotel room).

★ Hotel Bellwether
BOUTIQUE HOTEL $$$

(☎ 360-392-3100; www.hotelbellwether.com; 1 Bellwether Way; r $165-284, lighthouse from $398; ❋ 🛜 ❋) Bellingham's finest and most charismatic hotel is positioned on a redeveloped part of the waterfront and offers views over toward the whalelike hump of Lummi Island. Billing itself as a European hotel on the basis of its Italian furniture and Hungarian down duvets, the Bellwether advertises 66 luxury rooms, none of which are exactly the same.

Its crowning glory is the celebrated 900-sq-ft lighthouse condominium, an old converted three-story lighthouse with a wonderful private lookout.

Fairhaven Village Inn
HOTEL $$$

(☎ 360-733-1311; www.fairhavenvillageinn.com; 1200 10th St; r with bay/park view $199/209; ❋ 🛜) Downtown Bellingham lacks a decent number of well-appointed independent hotels, but one good alternative option is this prime place in genteel Fairhaven. Well in keeping with the vintage tone of the historic district, the Village Inn is a class above the standard motel fare, with prices to match. In this instance, they're probably justified.

✕ Eating

Strict vegans, visiting Californians and parents sick of stuffing their kids with hot dogs will all find solace in Bellingham, where the reverence for good food has an almost San Francisco–like aura. Railroad Ave is a good place to start looking.

Old Town Cafe
CAFE $

(316 W Holly St; mains $6-9; ⊙ 6.30am-3pm) This is a classic bohemian breakfast haunt where you can get to know the locals over fresh pastries, espresso and an excellent huevos rancheros. Wandering musicians sometimes drop by to enhance the happy-go-lucky atmosphere.

Swan Cafe
CAFE $

(www.communityfood.coop; 220 N Forest St; dishes $5-9; ⊙ 8am-9pm; 🖭) 🍴 Swan Cafe is pure Bellingham: a community food co-op with an on-site cafe-deli that sells fresh, organic, fair-trade and guilt-free food. It's also a vegetarian and vegan's heaven, offering vegan muffins, organic beer and a delicious daily selection of fresh, interesting salads. Take out or eat on-site in a bright, airy seating area.

Mallard
ICE CREAM $

(www.mallardicecream.com; 1323 Railroad Ave; ⊙ 10am-11pm Sun-Thu, 11am-11pm Fri & Sat) 🍴 Bellingham's date-night central is a lurid 1950s-style ice-cream parlor with a zillion different flavors – many of them weirdly exotic. Come here before or after a show and sample the vanilla-and-pepper or green-tea varieties – all organic, of course!

★ Pepper Sisters
MODERN AMERICAN $$

(www.peppersisters.com; 1055 N State St; mains $9-16; ⊙ from 5pm Tue-Sun; 🖭) People travel from far and wide to visit this cult restaurant with its bright turquoise booths. The food is hard to categorize; let's call it Mexican cuisine with a Northwestern twist. Try the cilantro-and-pesto quesadillas, blue corn rellenos and potato-garlic burritos. There's even a chicken-strip-free kids' menu.

Bayou on Bay
SOUTHERN $$

(1300 Bay St; mains $10-23; ⊙ 11am-10pm Tue-Fri, 10am-10pm Sat & Sun) A Bellingham favorite, especially when the sun comes out and the dining area spills out onto the sidewalk. Start with breaded okra or an alligator skewer, move on to anything from smoked pork ribs to a vegan jambalaya and wash it down with a Bayou Margarita or Cajun coffee. The ambience is as fun and lively as the food.

D'Anna's Café Italiano
ITALIAN $$

(www.dannascafeitaliano.com; 1317 N State St; mains $12-25) Bellingham does a fine job in transporting you gastronomically to other parts of the world. For D'Anna's read Sicily, meaning fresh homemade pasta, authentic chicken marsala and a Mt Etna–like portion of linguini and clams. The wine list mixes Italian favorites with some up-and-coming Washington cab savs.

Mount Bakery
BRUNCH $$

(www.mountbakery.com; 309 West Champion St; brunch $6-14; ⊙ 8am-3:30pm) 🍴 This is where you go on Sunday mornings with a Douglas fir–sized copy of the *New York Times* for Belgian waffles, crepes and organic eggs done any way you like.

Dirty Dan Harris
STEAKHOUSE $$

(www.dirtydanharris.com; 1211 11th St, Fairhaven; mains $16-24) Named after Fairhaven's notoriously unhygienic founder, Dirty Dan's has been knocking out excellent steaks, ribs and seafood from this historic Victorian tenement for more than 35 years.

🍷 Drinking

Boundary Bay Brewery & Bistro   BREWPUB
(www.bbaybrewery.com; 1107 Railroad Ave) Perennially popular Boundary Bay crafts its own ales and serves excellent, hearty Northwest-influenced fare for lunch and dinner. The smoked-salmon chowder hits the spot on a rainy night.

Copper Hog Gastro-Pub   PUB
(www.thecopperhog.com; 1327 N State St) A downtown pub with a strong food bias, the Copper Hog styles itself as 'European,' meaning you get a dozen ales (including IPA) and soccer on the big screen.

☆ Entertainment

Pickford Cinema   CINEMA
(www.pickfordcinema.org; 1318 Bay St) If you can't face getting in the car to catch the latest blockbuster at a satellite mall, check out the latest art-house movie at the 88-seat Pickford, run by the Whatcom Film Association.

Mt Baker Theatre   THEATER
(www.mountbakertheatre.com; 106 N Commercial St) With its minaret-like tower and elaborately designed interior, this grand old historic theater, built in 1925, has become one of Bellingham's signature buildings. Showcasing everything from live music to dance to plays, the theater regularly draws in top-name acts.

WWU Performing Arts Center   THEATER
(www.pacseries.wwu.edu; 516 High St) WWU's performing arts center usually features an intriguing lineup of international music and dance figures. See the website for the current program.

Wild Buffalo   LIVE MUSIC
(www.wildbuffalo.net; 208 W Holly St) Bellingham's 'house of music' is hidden in this inviting century-old building and is bereft of the traditional pub foibles of games machines and unsubtly positioned TV sets. Come here to enjoy local and national acts play jazz, blues, funk, salsa, rock and roll, and much more. Microbrew ales are served and dancing is de rigueur.

🔒 Shopping

Bellingham is a genuine readers' haven, with at least a dozen great bookstores. Music collectors will be equally enamored by a clutch of offbeat record stores, many of which stock old vinyl.

Village Books   BOOKS
(www.villagebooks.com; 1210 11th St) This is a real community resource in Fairhaven, with lots of literary activities, to say nothing of being the home of the popular Colophon Cafe.

EM Everyday Music   MUSIC
(www.everydaymusic.com; 115 E Magnolia St; ⊙9am-midnight) Late-night vinyl browsing available until midnight 365 days a year. Plenty of time to search for that rare New Order 12-inch.

ℹ Information

There's a downtown **Visitor Info Station** (www.downtownbellingham.com; 1304 Cornwall St; ⊙9am-6pm) and another **office** (905 Potter St; ⊙8:30am-5:30pm) close to I-5.

ℹ Getting There & Away

AIR
Bellingham International Airport is northwest of town off I 5 exit 258 and is served by **Alaska Airlines** (www.alaskaair.com) and **Allegiant Air** (www.allegiantair.com), with regular flights to Seattle, Las Vegas and Hawaii. **San Juan Airlines** (www.sanjuanairlines.com) flies daily from Bellingham to the San Juan Islands and BC.

BOAT
Bellingham is the terminal for the **Alaska Marine Hwy Ferries** (AMHS; www.dot.state.ak.us/amhs; 355 Harris Ave), which travel once a week up the Inside Passage to Juneau, Skagway and other southeast Alaskan ports. Passenger fares to Skagway start at $363; add a small car (up to 15ft) for $820. Cabins for the three-day trip cost an additional amount and can be hard to come by, so reserve well in advance.

At the time of writing there were no regular passenger ferry services from Bellingham to Victoria, BC or to the San Juan Islands, but this could change so check online or at the Alaska Ferries terminal.

BUS
Greyhound buses serve Bellingham on the Seattle–Vancouver run, with three heading north to Vancouver ($20, two hours) and another three going south to Seattle ($14, 2½ hours). The **depot** (Harris Ave) is in the same building as the Amtrak station in Fairhaven.

The **Bellair Shuttle** (www.airporter.com) runs around the clock to Sea-Tac airport ($34) and Anacortes ($11). You can also reserve Ferndale and Blaine pickups/drop-offs. It stops at the Guesthouse Inn, just off I-5 exit 253; and at

Bellingham airport. **Quick Shuttle** (www.quick-coach.com) runs comfortable buses with free onboard wi-fi between downtown Vancouver and Bellingham airport five times a day (one way/round-trip $28/49).

TRAIN

Daily **Amtrak** (www.amtrak.com) trains from Vancouver, BC (from $15, one hour 50 minutes), and Seattle (from $30, two hours 25 minutes) stop at the train depot at the end of Harris Ave, near the ferry terminal.

🛈 Getting Around

The city has a fairly extensive local bus system run by **Whatcom Transportation Authority** (www.ridewta.com). Bus 15 connects downtown Bellingham with the Bellis Fair shopping mall, buses 105 and 401 run to Fairhaven and the Alaska ferry terminal, and bus 50 runs out to Gooseberry Point and the ferry embarkation for Lummi Island. Fares start at $1 for local trips.

Around Bellingham

Lynden

'Welkom to Lynden,' reads the greeting on a shop wall in Front St. Here in the state's dyke-fortified, tulip-embellished north-west corner this unconventional spelling is the proud expression of the region's Dutch culture. Yet Lynden, a small town of 9000 people 5 miles south of the Canadian border, wears its Low Countries credentials with understatement.

First settled in the 1850s, Lynden received its first wave of Dutch settlers in the early 1900s – a steady trickle of Calvinist farmers who arrived from the Netherlands via brief stopovers in the Midwest. United by raspberries (the town produces 60% of the US crop), they formed a Christian Reform Church and set up mixed farms on the kind of flat pastoral fields that would have had Van Gogh grasping for his paint palette.

Don't show up here on a Sunday: Christian Lynden's shops are all closed for the day and even the main drag is like a ghost town.

As well as competing for the prize of 'cleanest town in the US,' Lynden also excels in historical preservation. Handsome Front St includes a 72ft windmill, a mall with a canal, various Dutch eateries and the inspired **Lynden Pioneer Museum** (www.lynden-pioneermuseum.com; 217 Front St; admission $7; ⊙10am-4pm Mon-Sat). For real Dutch immer-

sion, come to Lynden in early June for the ecstatic **Holland Days Festival**.

Rumor has it that people from as far away as California plan pie sorties to **Lynden Dutch Bakery** (421 Front St; ⊙7am-4pm Mon-Thu, 7am-5pm Fri & Sat) in an old-time shop on Front St. Accommodations can be found in the tall windmill that doubles as the **Dutch Village Inn** (☑360-354-4440; www.dutchvillageinnandgiftwinkle.com; 655 Front St; r from $79). Rooms are comfy B&B-style if a little dated. The check-in is in the adjacent gift shop.

Lummi Island

POP 822

Not technically one of the San Juan Islands, but with them in spirit, Lummi is a five-minute ferry ride (passenger/car $7/13 round-trip) from the mainland at Gooseberry Point (10.5 miles off I-5 exit 260). A slender green finger of land measuring approximately 9 miles long by 2 miles wide and supporting a population of just under 1000, this tranquil dose of rural realism is home to the world's only reef-net salmon-fishing operation, a pioneering agritourism project, and an unhurried tempo of life best epitomized by the island maximum speed limit – a tortoiselike 25mph. Often described as a state of mind rather than a physical entity, Lummi is sprinkled with enough simple diversions to consume a weekend of quiet serendipity. Pencil in cycling around the 7-mile road loop, hiking 1664ft Baker Mountain (the second-highest point in offshore Washington), picking up composting tips at organic **Nettles Farm** (☑360-758-7616; www.nettlesfarm.com; Matia View Rd), and counting whales in nearby Rosario Strait. Many of the roads and beaches are private, however, so exploration is limited and takes a little time.

The uphill slog to the top of **Baker Mountain** starts at the tiny Baker Reserve parking lot just south of the junction of Suncrest Dr and Sunrise Rd and traverses a protected preserve managed by the Lummi Island Trust. The beautiful hike through shady fern forest is steep for the first 15 minutes and then flattens out for peek-a-boo views of the San Juan Islands from an elongated ridge.

★**Willows Inn** (☑360-758-2620; www.willows-inn.com; 2579 West Shore Dr; r from $175; ❋ 🛜) is a 100-year-old inn with a variety of compact but cozy rooms poised above the Rosario Strait. It also has a creative, upscale restaurant where pretty much all the ingredients are plucked from nearby farms or the island's unique reef-net fishing operation (the owner is an experienced reef-net fisherman).

Anacortes

POP 15,941

Travelers striking out for the San Juan Islands have been known to thank the odd summer ferry delay. Without it they would never have uncovered the latent joys of ferry port Anacortes. Linger in town for an hour or three and you'll find a main street embellished by arty murals, an expansive waterfront park, a yacht-filled marina, and good-enough-to-write-home-about seafood (check out the crab cakes and oysters in particular). What the heck, there goes another ferry!

Anacortes is on Fidalgo Island, separated from the mainland by a narrow channel, 17 miles west of I-5 on Hwy 20. The downtown harbor skirts the edge of the business district, giving the town a detectable maritime air.

◉ Sights & Activities

Anacortes History Museum MUSEUM
(8th St & M Ave; ⊙11am-5pm Jun-Aug, Sat & Sun only Apr, May, Sep & Oct) FREE Has photo exhibitions showcasing the area's maritime history.

Snagboat Heritage Center MUSEUM
(713 R Ave; admission $3) Contains the restored hulk of the *WT Preston* snagboat that operated on Puget Sound between 1929 and 1981, removing navigational hazards from the waterways.

Washington Park PARK
For prime picnic spots and attractive oceanside hiking and biking trails make your way over to Washington Park just west of the ferry terminal.

🛏 Sleeping

Islands Inn MOTEL $
(☑360-293-4644; www.islandsinn.com; 3401 Commercial Ave; r $79-99; ▒ ⛫ ▒) The coziest of the cluster of motels on Commercial Ave, this well-equipped inn is meticulously run by a Dutch couple and offers a wide variety of spacious rooms, some with whirlpool tubs. Petite Wine Bar, which serves gourmet, European-inspired light meals and of course wine, is also on-site.

Majestic Inn & Spa HOTEL $$
(☑360-299-1400; www.majesticinnandspa.com; 419 Commercial Ave; r $169-299; ▒ ⛫) Once home of the oldest store (1890) in Skagit County, the Majestic was restored as a hotel after a fire in 2005. Its plush modern amenities offer the best of both worlds and add character to this significant building. Expect bathrobes in your closet and whirlpool tubs in your bathroom. The in-house spa heals outdoor-activity-induced aches and pains.

✖ Eating

Rockfish Grill/Anacortes Brewery SEAFOOD $
(320 Commercial Ave; fish & chips $8) If you're in the area, this place is worth a visit in its own right on two counts: first, the locally brewed beer, and second, the hearty pub grub. Try the halibut and chips washed down with a pilsner, or plump for the Aviator Doppelbock,

---

ROAD TRIP: CHUCKANUT DRIVE

Chuckanut Dr (SR11) is one of the West Coast's most spectacular and historic coastal back roads, a thin ribbon of winding asphalt that provides a refreshing alternative to the cars speeding along busy I-5. Running 21 miles from Old Fairhaven in Bellingham down to Burlington in Skagit County, the route takes in the craggy coastline overlooking the San Juan Islands, protecting hidden beaches and a 2500-acre state park, and offering such myriad diversions as hiking, cycling, beachcombing and fine dining along the way.

Defying steep oceanside terrain, the 'drive' was first laid out in 1896 to link Whatcom County with Mt Vernon and Seattle to the south. In 1912 a railcar was added on the northern part of the route and in 1915 local entrepreneur Charles Larrabee donated 20 acres of Chuckanut Mountain to make Washington's first state park. But in the 1920s, as traffic demands between Seattle and Vancouver exploded, Hwy 99 (now I-5) was constructed further east to ply an easier route through the coastal lowlands, leaving Chuckanut as something of a rural road relic.

If you're ambling by, be sure to pull over at the spectacularly located **Oyster Bar** (2578 Chuckanut Dr; ⊙11:30am-10pm) for a laid-back lunch.

in which case you'll probably want to skip lunch.

★ **Adrift** INTERNATIONAL $$
(506 Commercial Ave; mains $15-30; ☺8am-9pm Mon-Thu, to 10pm Fri & Sat) Warm service and high-class food will satisfy all levels of taste at the nautical-cozy Adrift, where you can get everything from a delicious hearty soup to a fancy fish meal. The interesting decor features a small library, chairs on wheels and a classic long bar with high stools. There are regular art exhibitions, and music some evenings.

❶ Information

Visitor Information Center (www.anacorteschamber.com; 819 Commercial Ave; ☺9am-5pm Mon-Fri, 10am-3pm Sat & Sun)

❶ Getting There & Away

The Bellair Shuttle (p99) offers eight runs a day from Burlington to Anacortes and the San Juan ferries (one way/round-trip $6/10). The shuttle picks up passengers from the ferry terminal and the Texaco station on 14th St and Commercial Ave (no reservations required). Connections can be made in Burlington to Bellingham and Sea-Tac airport.

Skagit Transit (www.skat.org) bus 410 travels hourly between Anacortes (10th St and Commercial Ave) and the San Juan ferry terminal. Bus 513 connects Anacortes with Mt Vernon's Skagit station four times a day. Standard fare is $1.

Lower Skagit River Valley

Exiled Hollanders from Amsterdam and Utrecht have been known to do a double-take in the Lower Skagit, a flat, fertile river delta backed by the imposing Cascade Mountains, where hardworking second-, third- and fourth-generation farmers (many of them with Dutch ancestry) grow daffodils, tulips and copious amounts of vegetables, including 100% of the nation's parsnips and Brussels sprouts.

Mt Vernon

POP 32,070

A former and rather unlikely winner of the 'Best Small City in America' prize, Mt Vernon is a place that most people only see the back end of as they race through on their way to Seattle or Vancouver on I-5. And, despite its prominence as a local agricultural nexus and headquarters for Skagit County's annual tulip festival, they're not missing much. Aside from a summer farmers market and a rather quaint theater (the Lincoln), Mt Vernon's attractions are limited. Far more alluring are La Conner to the west or Mt Baker to the east.

For an inexpensive stopover try the **Tulip Inn** (☎360-428-5969; www.tulipinn.net; 2200 Freeway Dr; r from $69; ❋❀), a comfortable motel just off I-5. For a potent tipple check

---

OFF THE BEATEN TRACK

GUEMES ISLAND

Spend an hour skimming pebbles across the bay on Guemes Island (population 700) and you'll quickly realize things are a little different in this corner of the state. Situated five minutes by ferry from Anacortes, this 3-sq-mile slice of bucolic bliss is the San Juans' resident contrarian. Shunning tourist celebrity, Guemes has only one store – the dependable **Anderson's** (☺10am-7pm Mon-Thu, 8am-8pm Fri & Sat, 9am-7pm Sun) – along with bevies of munching sheep and cows, and a tourist infrastructure that begins and ends at the rustic and decidedly unresortlike **Guemes Island Resort** (☎360-293-6643; www.guemesislandresort.com; 4268 Guemes Island Rd; yurts/d cabins from $88/190; ❋) right in the water.

Most travelers bound for the San Juan Islands don't even know Guemes exists (it uses a different hard-to-find ferry dock in Anacortes). Indeed, part of its innate attraction is the fact that it isn't really an attraction at all. Guemes visitors can't whale-watch or hunt for antiques like other San Juan vacationers; but they *can* go crabbing, circumnavigate the island by kayak, contemplate life without an iPhone, or sit on the deck outside Anderson's with a glass of Anacortes beer listening to the local folk band serenade the sunset.

The 22-car **Guemes Island Ferry** (500 I Ave, Anacortes; ☺half-hourly btwn 6:30am & 7pm, hourly until 11pm) costs $7 round-trip. The crossing from Anacortes takes seven minutes.

out the **Skagit River Brewery** (www.skagit-brew.com; 404 S 3rd St), an atmospheric pub that sells its own home brew beers including Dutch Girl lager, IPAs and the famous Trumpeter stout. You can also load up on fine pizza here.

La Conner

POP 901

Celebrated for its tulips, wild turkeys, erudite writers' colony, and (among other culinary treats) enormous doorstop-sized cinnamon buns; La Conner's myriad attractions verge on the esoteric. Abstract writer Tom Robbins lives here if that's any measuring stick, along with about 900 other creative souls, many of whom devote much of their time and energy to tourism. Jammed with gift shops, classy B&Bs and – in April, at least – long lines of cars, once-decrepit La Conner has undergone a post-1970s renaissance, transforming itself from forgotten Northwest port into out-of-the-box artists' community.

The zenith of La Conner's cultural calendar is the annual tulip festival. This is either the best or worst time to visit, depending on your traffic tolerance levels.

◉ Sights & Activities

La Conner's three small yet interesting museums are highly informative and well maintained.

Roozengaarde Display Garden   GARDENS
(www.tulips.com; 15867 Beaver Marsh Rd, Mt Vernon; admission $6; ⊙9am-6pm Mon-Sat, 11am-4pm Sun) Halfway between La Conner and Mt Vernon, this renowned 3-acre garden plants 250,000 tulip bulbs annually and, with Mt Baker and a Dutch-inspired windmill glimmering in the background, photo opportunities abound. Bring a camera!

Museum of Northwest Art   MUSEUM
(www.museumofnwart.org; 121 S 1st St; admission $8; ⊙10am-5pm Tue-Sun) This art gallery endeavors to portray the 'special Northwest vision' through the works of representative artists. The ground floor is dedicated to changing shows by regional artists, while the upstairs space houses pieces from the permanent collection.

Skagit County Historical Museum MUSEUM
(501 S 4th St; adult/child $5/4; ⊙11am-5pm Tue-Sun) Perched atop a hill that affords impressive views of Skagit Bay and the surrounding farmlands, this place presents indigenous crafts, dolls, vintage kitchen implements and other paraphernalia utilized by the region's early inhabitants.

La Conner Quilt Museum   MUSEUM
(☑360-466-4288; 703 S 2nd St; admission $7; ⊙10am-4pm Wed-Sat, noon-4pm Sun) Of more specialized interest, the quilt museum displays examples of quilt art from several generations. The museum is housed in the old Gaches mansion, which has stood here since 1891.

☆ Festivals & Events

Skagit County Tulip Festival   FLOWERS
(www.tulipfestival.org) La Conner finds its pulse when the annual Skagit County Tulip Festival lights up the surrounding countryside with shades of red, purple, yellow and orange. Events include wine tasting, bike tours and bird's-eye helicopter rides over the expansive fields, which are embellished with a colorful carpet of daffodils (March), tulips (April) and irises (May).

⛏ Sleeping

★ **Wild Iris Inn**   B&B $$
(☑360-466-1400; www.wildiris.com; 121 Maple Ave; r $119-179; 🛜) La Conner's B&Bs have the swank of boutique hotels and the homeyness of your gran's house. As a consequence, you'll never feel like you're kipping in someone else's property. Take the Wild Iris for instance, where you can sit back and enjoy fluffy bathrobes, a crackling fireplace, Jacuzzi baths, a stellar breakfast and complimentary homemade cookies.

La Conner Country Inn   HOTEL $$
(☑360-466-1500; 205 N 1st St; r from $99; ❄🛜) Though of recent vintage, this handsome luxury lodge does its best to look in keeping with the rest of old La Conner. Large and airy rooms have fireplaces and decks facing the channel and a polished grand piano adorns the lounge. A few hundred yards away, **La Conner Channel Inn** (☑360-466-3101; 107 S 2nd St; r $149-289), run by the same company, offers similar facilities and prices.

Hotel Planter   HOTEL $$
(☑800-488-5409, 360-466-4710; www.hotelplanter.com; 715 S 1st St; d $99-169; 🛜) This refurbished national historic hotel offers a decent blend of c 1907 charm and modern amenities, including a covered hot tub in the courtyard. The downtown location is hard to beat.

NORTHWESTERN WASHINGTON & THE SAN JUAN ISLANDS LOWER SKAGIT RIVER VALLEY

✕ Eating & Drinking

Calico Cupboard   BAKERY $

(www.calicocupboardcafe.com; 720 S 1st St; ⊙7:30am-4pm Mon-Fri, to 5pm Sat & Sun) The size of the cinnamon buns here beggar belief, and their quality (there are four specialist flavors) is equally good. Factor in a 10-mile run through the tulip fields before you tackle one and you should manage to stave off instant diabetes. The rest of the goods are also highly addictive. Try the bread pudding, flans, omelettes or light lunches.

There's another branch in Anacortes.

★ Seeds Bistro & Bar   MODERN AMERICAN $$$

(☑360-466-3280; www.seedsbistro.com; 623 Morris St; mains $18-25) Situated in the old Tillinghurst Seed building, Seeds Bistro offers that rare combo of classy food and brunch-cafe-style friendliness. The key lies in harnessing the fresh flavors of the surrounding farmland and mixing it with equally fresh fish. The result: unparalleled ling cod, off-the-ratings-scale crab cakes, and a raspberry and white chocolate bread pudding you'll be talking about months later.

The best time to visit is happy hour (3pm to 6pm daily) when you can sample several $8 to $10 plates of the restaurant's specialties.

La Conner Brewing Co   BREWPUB

(117 S 1st St; pizzas $8-11, sandwiches $7-9; ⊙11:30am-10pm, until 11pm Fri & Sat) A polished pine pub that manages to combine the relaxed atmosphere of a cafe with the quality beers (including IPA and stout) of an English drinking house. Bonuses include wood-fired pizzas, fresh salads and eight homebrews on tap.

ℹ Information

La Conner Chamber of Commerce (www.laconnerchamber.com; Morris St) Pick up helpful maps to orientate yourself.

Whidbey Island

Whidbey Island is an idyllic emerald escape beloved of stressed-out Seattleites. While not as detached or nonconformist as the San Juans (there's a bridge connecting it to adjacent Fidalgo Island at its northernmost point), life is certainly slower, quieter and more pastoral here. Having six state parks is a bonus, along with a plethora of B&Bs, two historic fishing villages (Langley and Coupeville),

famously good mussels and a thriving artists' community. Of less interest to travelers is the US Naval Air Station that dominates Oak Harbor. At 41 miles long, Whidbey is the longest island on the US West Coast. A free weekday bus service provides a useful way of getting around (see the box below).

ℹ Getting There & Around

BOAT

Services from Washington State Ferries run between Clinton and Mukilteo (car and driver/passenger $8.60/3.95, 20 minutes) and between Keystone and Port Townsend ($11.15/2.60, 30 minutes).

BUS

Seatac Shuttles (☑877-679-4003; www.seatacshuttle.com) offers frequent bus service to nine locations on Whidbey Island from Sea-Tac (one way/round-trip $37/66). Prepaid reservations are required to ensure a seat.

Deception Pass State Park

Captain George Vancouver originally supposed Whidbey Island to be a peninsula. Eventually Joseph Whidbey – who set off in a small boat to explore and map Puget Sound – found this narrow cliff-lined crevasse churned by rushing water and Whidbey's insularity was confirmed. Deceived no more, the spectacular narrow passage gained a name – though even today it remains a challenge to navigate with a motorized boat.

Emerging from the flat pastures of Fidalgo Island, Deception Pass leaps out like a mini Grand Canyon, its precipitous cliffs overlooked by a famous bridge made all the more dramatic by the sight of the churning, angry water below. The bridge consists of two steel arches that span Canoe

---

ℹ ISLAND TRANSIT

Island Transit (www.islandtransit.org) is a community-financed scheme offering the ultimate encouragement for people to get out of their cars and onto the buses. Buses run the length of Whidbey daily except Sunday, from the Clinton ferry dock to Greenbank, Coupeville, Oak Harbor and Deception Pass. Other routes reach the Keystone ferry dock and Langley on weekdays. Service is hourly and free – yes – free!

Pass and Deception Pass, with a central support on Pass Island between the two. Visitors to the 5.5-sq-mile park (☑360-675-2417; 41229 N State Hwy 20) usually introduce themselves to the spectacular land and seascape by parking at the shoulders on either end and walking across the bridge. Built during the 1930s by the Civilian Conservation Corps (CCC), the bridge was considered an engineering feat in its day. The park also spans the channel, with facilities – including campgrounds – on both the north and south flanks of the passage.

More than 3.5 million visitors per year visit Deception Pass, which makes it Washington's most popular state park. Besides the dramatic bridge overviews, the park's attractions include more than 15 miles of saltwater shoreline, seven nearby islands, three freshwater lakes, boat docks, hundreds of picnic sites and 27 miles of forest trails. Scuba divers and sea kayakers can explore the area's reefs and cliff-edge shores. For organized kayaking (per person from $39) contact Anacortes Kayak Tours (☑800-992-1801; www.anacorteskayaktours.com).

The park sports three campgrounds (☑888-226-7688; tent/RV sites $23/30) with more than 300 spaces nestled in the forests located beside a lake and a saltwater bay. Facilities include running water, flush toilets, hot showers and snack concessions. The best sites are the few along the water at Bowman Bay. Reserve well ahead for summer weekends, as competition can be fierce.

Oak Harbor

POP 22,239

There are two main distinctions between the San Juan Islands and Whidbey Island. First, Whidbey has a mainland bridge connection (via Deception Pass) and second, it has Oak Harbor, a modern mishmash of boxlike chain stores and recent urban development that looks rather like a Seattle suburb. Dominated by Naval Air Station Whidbey Island, completed in 1942, Oak Harbor is a military town with a distinguished Irish and Dutch heritage dating back to the late 19th century. Today it accommodates the island's largest marina, a notable playhouse and – surprise, surprise – plenty of indigenous Garry oak trees.

Ever keen to shake off its lackluster image, Oak Harbor has embarked upon a major charm offensive in recent years, with a redevelopment plan emphasizing its nautical heritage and waterfront amenities. Holland Happenings is held during the last week in April when the tulips are still in bloom.

Oak Harbor's most 'culturally distinctive' and great-value lodging is the Auld Holland Inn (☑360-675-2288; www.auld-holland. com; 33575 State Rte 20; r $59-114; 🐕🐾🅿), a nod at the town's Dutch heritage that dominates SR-20 with its towering old-fashioned windmill. Run by a family from the Netherlands, the rooms and service here live up to their European promise, and extra bonuses include an outdoor swimming pool, a gym, a children's playground and a gift shop that sells clogs. The hotel also has a good on-site restaurant.

The helpful Oak Harbor Visitor Center (32630 State Rte 20; ⊙10am-5pm Mon-Fri), situated on the main drag through town, should be able to put you straight on the town's not-so-obvious attractions.

Coupeville

POP 1842

This picturesque fishing community is what the island is all about: an antique pier, fresh mussels and clams, old-world B&Bs, historic clapboard shopfronts and instant access to a National Historic Reserve (the village actually sits on the eastern edge of Ebey's Landing National Historical Reserve). For those who thought Whidbey Island began and ended at Deception Pass (and there are quite a few), think again!

◉ Sights & Activities

Island County Historical Society Museum
MUSEUM

(908 NW Alexander St; admission $3; ⊙10am-5pm May-Sep, to 4pm Fri-Mon Oct-Apr) The island's most comprehensive museum has plenty of local historical testimonies showcased in meticulous and well-presented display cases. Also on offer are self-guided walking-tour maps of Coupeville's vintage homes. The helpful staff can also enlighten you on the highlights of Ebey's Landing National Historical Reserve.

Whidbey's Greenbank Berry Farm
FARM

(www.greenbankfarm.com; Hwy 525, off Wonn Rd; ⊙10am-5pm) Go 10 miles south of Coupeville to find the world's largest producer of loganberries, a sweet, blackish berry rather like a black raspberry. The winery-style farm is open daily for touring, tasting and picnicking.

🛏 Sleeping

★ Captain Whidbey Inn   INN $$
(☑360-678-4097; www.captainwhidbey.com; 2072 W Captain Whidbey Inn Rd; r with shared bath from $103, cabins from $210; 🛜) The beautifully forest-clad Captain Whidbey is a 1907 inn built entirely out of madrone (arbutus) wood. With its low ceilings, creaky floors and cozy lounge strewn with faded copies of *National Geographic*, it feels more like something out of a medieval forest than a 21st-century tourist island.

Lodging is in 12 sea-galleon-style guest rooms in the main lodge, as well as wood-heated cottages and a more modern building with verandahs facing a lagoon.

Anchorage Inn   B&B $$
(☑360-678-5581; www.anchorage-inn.com; 807 N Main St; r $99-159; 🛜) Continuing the Northwestern penchant for Victorian-style B&Bs, this place comes up trumps with plenty of lace curtains, patterned wallpaper and old-fashioned upright chairs. Seven rooms with private baths are encased in a turreted house overlooking Penn Cove; the owners even run a course on inn-keeping. With so much fine china on display, children under 10 aren't permitted.

Coupeville Inn   MOTEL $$
(☑800-247-6162; www.thecoupevilleinn.com; 200 Coveland St; r with/without balcony incl breakfast $150/110; ✳🛜) It bills itself as a motel, but with its French architecture, oak furniture and rather plush interior this is far from your standard highway sleepover. Situated close to Coupeville's tiny town center, this plush place is a bargain, given its fancy furnishings and substantial complimentary breakfast.

🍴 Eating

Christopher's   SEAFOOD $$
(☑360-678-5480; www.christophersonwhidbey.com; 103 NW Coveland St; mains $15-23; ⊙11:30am-2pm Mon-Fri, noon-2:30pm Sat & Sun, nightly from 5pm) The mussels and clams are the best in town (no mean feat in Coupeville) and the seafood alfredo pasta is wonderfully rich.

Toby's Tavern   PUB $$
(www.tobysuds.com; 8 Front St; mains $15-20; ⊙lunch & dinner) A quintessential Coupeville pub housed in a vintage mercantile building dating from the 1890s; even the polished back bar was originally shipped here around Cape Horn in 1900. These days the

attention to detail is no less fastidious, with home-produced microbrews and a menu spearheaded by local classics like fantastic mussels, clam strips, and halibut and chips.

ℹ Information

Visitor Information Center (☑360-678-5434; www.centralwhidbeychamber.com; 23 NW Front St; ⊙10am-5pm) Right in town.

Ebey's Landing National Historical Reserve

This National Historical Reserve was the first of its kind in the nation when it was created in 1978 in order to preserve Whidbey Island's historical heritage from the encroaching urbanization that had already partly engulfed Oak Harbor. Ninety per cent privately owned, Ebey's Landing (www.nps.gov/ebla; ⊙8am-5pm mid-Oct–Mar, 6:30am-10pm Apr–mid-Oct) FREE comprises 17,400 acres encompassing working farms, four historic blockhouses, two state parks and the town of Coupeville itself. A series of interpretive boards shows visitors how the patterns of croplands, woods (or the lack of them) and even roads reflect the activities of those who have peopled this scenic landscape, from its earliest indigenous inhabitants to 19th-century settlers.

At the reserve's southern end is **Fort Casey State Park**, with facilities for camping and picnicking. Fort Casey was part of the early 1900s military defense system that once guarded the entrance to Puget Sound. Visitors can investigate the old cement batteries and underground tunnels that line the coast. Other recreational activities here include scuba diving, boating and bird-watching – best along Keystone Spit on the southwestern tip of Crockett Lake. **Admiralty Head Lighthouse**, built in 1861, houses the park's interpretive center. From here, it's a 4-mile walk north along the beach to **Fort Ebey State Park**, a wonderfully secluded spot with eroded cliffs and old WWII-era coast defenses, where further trails meander off into the surrounding woodland.

The Island County Historical Society Museum in Coupeville distributes a brochure on suggested driving and cycling tours through the reserve. Highly recommended is the 3.6-mile **Bluff Trail** that starts from a small parking area at the end of Ebey Rd. The energetic can walk or cycle here from

Coupeville (approximately 2.5 miles along a quiet road), thus crossing the island at one of its narrowest points.

Fort Casey State Park offers 38 campsites (tent sites $12–26, serviced sites $30–37) overlooking Keystone Harbor, and Fort Ebey has 53 sites ($21) plus four with RV hookups ($28). Facilities include flush toilets and running water.

An unusual lodging option is **Fort Casey Inn** (360-678-8792; www.fortcaseyinn.com; 1124 S Engle Rd; r $85-190). The inn consists of a series of five c 1909 houses that served as WWI officers' quarters and are now rented as overnight accommodations (the rooms sleep up to four guests). Perched on a bluff overlooking the lighthouse at Fort Casey, the houses have restful porches with oak armchairs.

Langley

POP 1041

Langley is a tiny seafront community that has changed little since the late 19th century and is arguably even cuter than Coupeville. Encased in an attractive historic center are small cafes, antique furniture shops, funky clothing boutiques and a couple of decent B&Bs. While there's little to do here activity-wise, Langley provides a perfect seaside escape from the modern world.

Langley is 8 miles north of Clinton and the ferry service from Mukilteo, making this the closest of the Whidbey Island communities to the urban areas of northern Seattle.

🛏 Sleeping & Eating

Stroll along Langley's 1st St for several more very good dining options.

Eagles Nest Inn   B&B $$
(360-221-5331; www.eaglesnestinn.com; 4680 E Saratoga Rd; r $150-180;) In an octagonal house on a forested hill, Eagles Nest Inn is a B&B gem even by Whidbey Island's high standards. Four lovingly furnished rooms blend perfectly with their natural surroundings, while extras such as locally roasted coffee, aromatherapy shampoos, private lounge (with piano) and well-stocked cookie jar add a memorable touch. The property is adjoined by 400 acres of public trails.

Inn at Langley   INN $$$
(360-221-3033; www.innatlangley.com; 400 1st St; r incl breakfast $175-595;) This contemporary, condo-esque inn is the trend-setter in style and expense. The 26 beautifully furnished waterfront rooms have large windows, whirlpool tubs and fireplaces. A full-service spa provides Swedish massage and seaweed body masks, plus there's a fine-dining restaurant serving six-course meals.

Cafe Langley   MEDITERRANEAN $$
(www.cafelangley.com; 113 1st St; lunch around $10, dinner $11-23; 11:30am-2:30pm & 5-8:30pm Mon & Wed-Sat, to 3pm Sun) Mediterranean cuisine, with a few deft Northwestern seafood infusions (eg mussels) thrown in for good measure.

SAN JUAN ISLANDS

POP 15,844

Leafy hedgerows, soporific settlements and winding lanes jammed with more cyclists than cars. Where the heck are you? Not in continental America, surely. The answer is both 'yes' and 'no.' The San Juan Islands, a nebulous archipelago of approximately 172 landfalls, islets and eagle perches that lie splayed between the mouth of Puget Sound and Vancouver Island, conjure up images of a sleepy American throwback where the clock last chimed in the 1970s, '60s or even '50s, depending on where you dock. Sharing a jagged watery border with Canada, it's also where the 'special relationship' between Britain and the US got distinctly tetchy in 1858 over a ridiculously overblown dispute about a dead pig (the two countries nearly went to war). These days peace, not war, is the archipelago's greatest hallmark in communities where cars are left unlocked, motorists offer salutary waves, and shopping malls remain a ghostly mainland apparition. Don't come for the Starbucks and casinos (there aren't any); come instead for the fishing, whale-watching, beachcombing, sailing, hiking, cycling, paddling, crabbing, clamming, philosophizing and memorable, psychedelic sunsets.

ℹ Information

For general information about the San Juans, contact the **San Juan Islands Visitors Bureau** (www.guidetosanjuans.com; Technology Center, Bldg A, Suite 210/215, 640 Mullis St, San Juan Island; 10am-2pm Mon-Fri). Its website provides links to numerous San Juan businesses and organizations. In addition, the chambers of commerce of San Juan, Orcas and Lopez Islands maintain their own visitor walk-in information centers.

❶ Getting There & Away

AIR

Two airlines fly from the mainland to the San Juans. **Kenmore Air** (www.kenmoreair.com) flies from Lake Union and Lake Washington to Lopez, Orcas and San Juan Islands daily on three- to 10-person seaplanes. Fares start at $130 one way. **San Juan Airlines** (www.sanjuanairlines.com) flies from Anacortes and Bellingham to the three main islands (one way/return $64/138).

BOAT

The majority of people who visit the San Juans arrive on **Washington State Ferries** (WSF; www.wsdot.wa.gov/ferries), which runs a fleet of comfortable and efficient car ferries. The main port on the mainland is Anacortes; ferries for the four principal islands of Lopez, Shaw, Orcas and San Juan depart from here. From April to December, two Washington State Ferries a day continue on to Sidney, near Victoria on Vancouver Island, before returning in the opposite direction. There is no US–Canada service from January to March.

You can pick up an easy-to-decipher WSF timetable at any ferry outlet or access it on the website. The timetable varies depending on the season, but follows a standard route of Anacortes–Lopez (45 minutes), then Shaw (one hour), Orcas (70 minutes), Friday Harbor (80 minutes) and Sidney (three hours). Four or five ferries a day are interisland, in that they don't call at either Sidney or Anacortes.

Fares are collected on westbound ferries only. They are $12.45 for foot passengers to any destination except Sidney, which is $18. Car and driver fares range from $32.25 (Lopez) to $47.75 (Sidney). Bike passengers pay a $4 surcharge. Foot passengers and cyclists can ride interisland ferries for free in either direction.

You can only reserve tickets for the Sidney sailing. All other ferries operate on a first-come, first-served basis. In winter drivers are advised to arrive 45 minutes before sailing; in summer arrive two hours early.

There are three additional privately owned passenger-only ferries (no cars) that travel to the San Juans:

Puget Sound Express (www.pugetsoundexpress.com) Runs from Port Townsend to Friday Harbor from March to September.

Victoria Clipper (www.victoriaclipper.com) A Seattle–Friday Harbor link, with service on to Victoria, BC. It only runs from late June to late September.

Victoria San Juan Cruises (www.whales.com; 355 Harris Ave, Suite 104, Bellingham) Operates between Bellingham, San Juan Island, Orcas and Victoria from May to September.

San Juan Island

POP 6894

The most exciting aspects of the archipelago's history have been preserved on San Juan Island (how does a near war between Britain and the US grab you?) in a couple of old military camps. It is also the island with the 'biggest' town; compact Friday Harbor acts as the archipelago's unofficial capital. Other San Juan Island highlights include sheltered Roche Harbor and blustery Lime Kiln Point State Park, where you can whale-watch from the shoreline overlooking deep Haro Strait.

The ferry terminal is at Friday Harbor, on the eastern side of the island. The main route south from here is Cattle Point Rd, while Beaverton Valley Rd heads to the west coast. To get to Roche Harbor, take 2nd St to Guard St, then turn right on Tucker Ave; from there it's a 10-mile drive to the resort.

⊙ Sights

With a population of 2000, **Friday Harbor** is San Juan's only town, with a grid of wide paved streets lined with restaurants, shops and a couple of interesting museums. In all it provides enough diversions to fill a good morning's exploration. In recent years a growing contingent of realty offices has added disquiet. But Friday Harbor is still a low-key, pedestrian-friendly kind of place where the worst kind of hassle you're likely to face is an uneven paving stone.

Whale Museum　MUSEUM
(www.whale-museum.org; 62 1st St, Friday Harbor; adult/child $6/3; ⊙10am-5pm) If you have time for only one sight, be sure to pop into the Whale Museum, a small but cleverly arranged display space dedicated to the life of the orca (killer whale), which has become something of a San Juan Island mascot. Among whale skeletons and life-size models of orcas, there are eloquent DVD presentations, interactive maps and details of local research projects, all of which will teach you everything you need to know about these magnificent but cruelly misunderstood sea mammals.

San Juan Historical Museum　MUSEUM
(www.sjmuseum.org; 405 Price St, Friday Harbor; adult/child $5/3; ⊙10am-4pm Thu-Sat, 1-4pm Sun May-Sep) In an 1890s farmhouse on the outskirts of Friday Harbor, the San Juan Historical Museum commemorates early pioneer

life on San Juan Island. While the building itself is interesting for its vernacular architecture, the displays of kitchen and parlor furnishings – like the pump organ and massive wood range – are also worth checking out. Open afternoons only in the winter.

San Juan Island National Historical Park
HISTORIC SITE
(www.nps.gov/sajh; ⊘8:30am-4pm, visitor center 8:30am-4:30pm Thu-Sun, daily Jun-Sep) 🅿 **FREE**
More known for their scenery than their history, the San Juans nonetheless hide one of the 19th century's oddest political confrontations, the so-called 'Pig War' between the USA and Britain. This curious standoff is showcased in two separate historical parks on either end of the island that once housed opposing American and English military encampments.

On the southern flank of the island, the **American Camp** hosts a small **visitors center** and is a good place to start your historical excursion. Among the remnants of an old fort are the officers' quarters and a laundress' house, while a series of interpretive trails lead to earthwork fortifications, a British farm from the dispute era and desolate South Beach. The 1.8-mile hike along the ridge of Mt Finlayson makes for a pleasant hike with splendid views and unlimited bird-watching potential.

At the opposite end of the island, **English Camp**, 9 miles northwest of Friday Harbor, contains the remains of British military facilities dating from the 1860s. A path from the parking area leads down to a handful of restored buildings that lie in an attractive setting overlooking Garrison Bay. Hikes from here lead to an old British cemetery and the top of 650ft Young Hill.

Lime Kiln Point State Park
PARK
(⊘8am-5pm mid-Oct–Mar, 6:30am-10pm Apr–mid-Oct) 🅿 Clinging to the island's rocky west coast, this beautiful park overlooks the deep Haro Strait and is, reputedly, one of the best places in the world to view whales from the shoreline – word is out, however, so the view areas are often packed with hopeful picnickers. There is a small **interpretive center** (☏360-378-2044) in the park open from Memorial Day (last Monday in May) to Labor Day (first Monday in September), along with trails, a restored lime kiln and the landmark Lime Kiln lighthouse, built in 1919. Offering exceptional views of Vancouver Island and the Olympic Mountains, the park is best enjoyed at sunset.

🏃 Activities

San Juan Vineyards
WINE TASTING
(www.sanjuanvineyards.com; 3136 Roche Harbor Rd; tastings per glass $1; ⊘11am-5pm) This unlikely but frequently award-winning winery has a tasting room in an old schoolhouse built in 1896. Open-minded tasters should try the Siegerrebe and Madeleine Angevine varieties which are the only estate-grown grapes – other varieties come from the warmer climes of the Yakima Valley. Make sure to at least glance at the camel across the road.

Trophy Charters
FISHING
(www.fishthesanjuans.com) Fishing trips for black bass and tiger rockfish can be arranged through Trophy Charters, which does half-day fishing tours aboard a 29ft sport fisher from $95 per person.

Western Prince Cruises
WHALE-WATCHING
(www.orcawhalewatch.com; 1 Spaing St, Friday Harbor) 🅿 Western Prince Cruises is the San Juan Islands' oldest whale-watching tour company and its year-round ecofriendly excursions keep an eye out for eagles, seals and porpoises as well as the formidable orcas. Tours on the *Western Prince*, which accommodates up to 30 people, depart daily from June to August (adult/child $85/56), less often and less expensively in spring and fall. You can make reservations via its website or visit the office right next to the ferry dock in Friday Harbor.

ORCAS FROM THE SHORE

The best way to view orcas with the least environmental impact is from the shore. This sounds unlikely, but the Salish Sea surrounding the San Juans boasts some of the best whale- and orca-viewing shore locations in the world. Peak season is May through July. We suggest packing a picnic and binoculars to the following locations:

➡ **San Juan County Park** San Juan Island.

➡ **Lime Kiln Point State Park** (p109) San Juan Island.

➡ **American Camp** (p109) San Juan Island.

➡ **Cattle Point** South San Juan Island.

➡ **Lopez Island** West side.

San Juan Islands

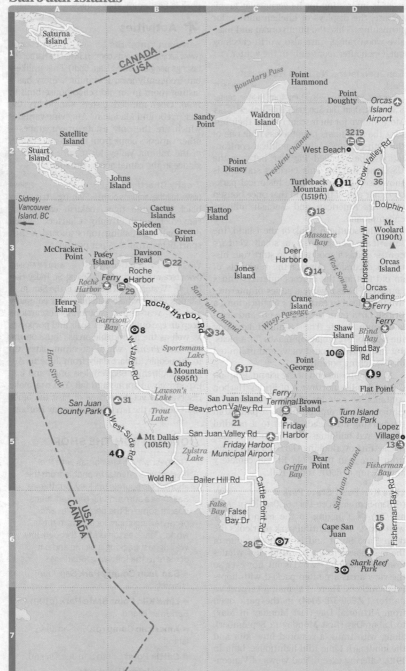

NORTHWESTERN WASHINGTON & THE SAN JUAN ISLANDS SAN JUAN ISLAND

🛏 Sleeping

San Juan County Park Campground   CAMPGROUND $

(☎360-378-1842; 380 West Side Rd; hiker/cyclist sites per person $10, campsites $32) San Juan's best campground is beautifully located in a county park on the scenic western shoreline. The site includes a beach and boat launch, along with 20 pitches, flush toilets and picnic tables. At night the lights of Victoria, BC, flicker theatrically from across the Haro Strait. Reservations are mandatory during peak season.

Wayfarer's Rest   HOSTEL $

(☎360-378-6428; 35 Malcolm St, Friday Harbor; dm $35, r $65-80; 🖥) The island's only backpackers hostel is a short hike from the ferry terminal. Budget travelers will love its comfortable dorms and cheap private rooms but beware – it gets busy.

Roche Harbor Resort   RESORT $$

(☎800-451-8910; www.rocheharbor.com; Roche Harbor; r with shared bath $149, 1- to 3-bedroom condos $275-450, 2-bedroom townhouses $499; ❄🖥🏊🛗) Located on the site of the former lime kiln and estate of limestone king John McMillin, this seaside 'village' is a great getaway. The centerpiece is the old Hotel de Haro, where the pokey rooms are enlivened by the fact that John Wayne once brushed his teeth here. Town houses are up behind the harbor, and modern condominiums are tucked behind trees.

Waterfront restaurants, a 377-berth marina with boat rentals, a new spa and an old dockside general store make the place quite self-contained. It can feel a bit contrived and overly gentrified – lovers of back-to-nature type lodgings should stay elsewhere.

Earthbox Motel & Spa   MOTEL $$

(☎360-378-4000; www.earthboxmotel.com; 410 Spring St, Friday Harbor; r from $182; 🖥🏊🐾) Earthbox is a hybrid of simplicity and sophistication as a former motor inn embellished with features more commonly associated with a deluxe hotel. The result: a variety of funky, cleverly designed rooms with comfy beds and colorful yet minimalist undercurrents. Other bonuses include a pool, spa, fitness room, bike rental and fine gardens.

Juniper Lane Guest House   INN $$

(☎360-378-7761; www.juniperlaneguesthouse.com; 1312 Beaverton Valley Rd; r $85-135; 🖥) 🌿 The handful of wood paneled rooms here

San Juan Islands

are decorated with a colorful and eclectic assortment of art and furnishings, much of it refurbished or recycled. The result is a sublimely cozy and livable hybrid of an upscale backpackers and a hip inn. Chill on the couch in the common area and meet other guests cooking in the common kitchen.

It's 1.3 miles from the ferry dock.

Lonesome Cove　　　　　　　　CABIN $$
(☏ 360-378-4477; www.lonesomecove.com; cabins from $180) Not much has changed since this collection of cabins, tucked into a magnificent cove, was a 1940s-era salmon-fishing camp. It's got a bit of Hemingway-esque salt-of-the-earth romance, a lot of isolation and a very silly black labrador to keep tails wagging. All this makes it popular, so it can be booked up to a year in advance in July and August.

Olympic Lights B&B　　　　　　B&B $$
(☏ 360-378-3186; www.olympiclights.com; 146 Starlight Way; r $155-165) Once the centerpiece of a 320-acre estate, this splendidly restored 1895 farmhouse now hosts an equally formidable B&B that stands on an open bluff facing the snow-coated Olympic Mountains. The four rooms are imaginatively named Garden, Ra, Heart and Olympic; sunflowers adorn the garden and the hearty breakfasts include homemade buttermilk biscuits.

Friday Harbor House　　　　　HOTEL $$$
(☏ 360-378-8455; www.fridayharborhouse.com; 130 West St, Friday Harbor; r with/without view $309/269; ❉ ⦿) Friday Harbor's most exclusive lodging is a modern boutique hotel with great views over the harbor. All 20 rooms have a fireplace, open-plan bathroom/Jacuzzi tub and other upscale niceties, and the whole place exudes a surgical level of cleanliness.

✕ Eating

Market Chef　　　　　　　　　　DELI $
(225 A St, Friday Harbor; ⦿ 10am-6pm) 𝄃 Welcome to a San Juan Island legend. Eat-in or take-out options such as sandwiches, salads and tacos are rustled up rapidly and come with unusual infusions. All are made with local ingredients. You might have to fight for a place to sit – it's that popular.

Lime Kiln Cafe　　　　　　　　DINER $
(Roche Harbor; mains $6-15; ⦿ 8am-2pm) Perched on the end of the Roche Harbor marina wharf, this simple but pleasurable establishment serves up mouthwatering American breakfasts that feature organic

eggs in a hearty San Juan scramble with avocado and sour cream. The lunch menu offers deli sandwiches. Even better, fresh home-cooked doughnuts are served all day.

Doctor's Office
CAFE $

(www.do-cafe.com; 85 Front St, Friday Harbor; ⊙4:30am-10pm; @ 🕾) Break up the boredom of a long ferry lineup in the portside Doctor's Office, where the best 'prescriptions' are locally roasted coffee, hot soups, sandwiches and homemade ice cream. And where else opens at 4:30am 365 days a year?

Duck Soup Inn
FUSION $$$

(☑360-378-4878; www.ducksoupinn.com; 50 Duck Soup Lane; mains $29-35; ⊙Apr-Oct) 🍴 It ain't cheap, but it's really good. Situated 4 miles northwest of Friday Harbor amid woods and water, Duck Soup offers the best island fine dining using its own herb garden to enhance menu items such as oysters, scallops and – best of all – blueberry habanero chicken. The extensive wine list includes island-produced chardonnay.

McMillin's
SEAFOOD $$$

(☑360-378-5757; Roche Harbor; mains $26-30; ⊙5-10pm) 🍴 Set in the former house of lime and cement entrepreneur John McMillin, this intimate dining room offers the best of Pacific Rim cooking. Favorites include hazelnut-crusted halibut, local spot prawns and Dungeness crab ravioli.

🍷 Drinking

Front Street Ale House & San Juan Brewing Company
BREWPUB

(1 Front St, Friday Harbor; mains $10-19; ⊙11am-11pm Mon-Thu, to midnight Fri & Sat) The island's only brewery serves up British-style beers, including Royal Marine IPA, in a real spit-and-sawdust-style pub. Traditional pub grub features shepherd's pie and bangers and mash, and it ain't 'arf bad (as they say in London).

ℹ Information

Chamber of Commerce (www.sanjuanisland.org; 135 Spring St, Friday Harbor; ⊙10am-5pm Mon-Fri, to 4pm Sat & Sun) Inside a small arcade; a good place to pick up free maps and other information.

ℹ Getting Around

From May to October, **San Juan Transit** (www.sanjuantransit.com) shuttles visitors from the ferry landing to Roche Harbor, plus points along the West Coast, including Lime Kiln Point State Park and the English Camp. Buses run hourly between 10am and 6pm (round-trip $10, day pass $15). Otherwise, call **San Juan Taxi** (☑360-378-8294).

Susie's Mopeds (125 Nichols St, Friday Harbor), just up from the ferry dock, rents electric bicycles or mopeds for $30/70 per hour/day, 'scoot coupes' (a sort of miniature buggy-moped hybrid for two people) for $70/150 per hour/day, or Geo Tracker jeeps from $96 a day.

CASCADIA MARINE TRAIL

On paper it sounds like an oxymoron (unless you've mastered the art of walking on water), but in practice it's one of the USA's long-distance odysseys.

The Cascadia Marine Trail (CMT) is a 160-mile saltwater sailing/paddling route starting in Olympia and finishing at the Canadian–US border that links more than 50 specially designated campsites and 30 or more waterside inns in a spectacular aquatic journey through Washington's sheltered inland seas. Conceived in 1993 by the Washington Water Trails Association (WWTA), a group of avid kayakers from the Seattle area, the trail is designed to be used by wind- or human-powered water craft making use of myriad campsites en route, spaced approximately 5 to 8 miles apart.

The San Juan Islands make up one of the most popular segments of the trail, with many of the archipelago's outlying state parks sporting rustic CMT campsites (maximum capacity 16 people) equipped with landing areas, picnic tables, toilets (usually 'compost-style') and official CMT signs (the sites are checked regularly by volunteer stewards). Other popular stop-offs are Whidbey Island, Port Townsend and Blake Island near Seattle.

For a comprehensive trail guidebook you'll need to become a member of WWTA (www.wwta.org).

In 2000 the CMT was chosen by the White House as one of only 16 'National Millennium Trails' reflecting 'defining aspects of America's history and culture.'

Orcas Island

POP 5387

Orcas is a special island. More rugged than Lopez yet less crowded than San Juan Island, it has struck a delicate balance between friendliness and frostiness, development and preservation, tourist dollars and priceless privacy – for the time being at least.

Lying in the dry rain shadow of the storm-lashed Olympic Mountains, the island was once an important trading post for the North Straits Salish Native Americans, who maintained a permanent settlement in present-day West Sound. The first European homesteaders arrived in the 1860s and within a couple of years they had set about clearing the old-growth rainforest for crops and fruit orchards. Another early industrial project was lime production, and by the early 20th century 35 lime kilns dotted the island, burning huge amounts of local wood.

The growth of tourism is a distinctly modern development and an inevitable consequence of Orcas' refreshing get-away-from-it-all location. Former Seattle mayor Robert Moran opened the doors to the deluge in the early 1900s when he constructed a Xanadu-like mansion, the Rosario (now a hotel), overlooking the shimmering waters of East Sound.

⊙ Sights & Activities

For kayaking and biking options see the box on p116.

★ Moran State Park   PARK

(⏰6:30am-dusk Apr-Sep, from 8am Oct-Mar) In 1911, Robert Moran donated 7 sq miles of his property to create this park on the island's eastern saddlebag. The park, which has enough attractions to consume the best part of a day, is dominated by 2409ft **Mt Constitution**, the archipelago's highest point and a mountain with the grandeur of a peak twice its size. To say that the view from the summit is jaw-dropping would be an understatement. On a clear day you can see Mt Rainier, Mt Baker, Vancouver's north shore and a patchwork of tree-carpeted islands floating like emerald jewels on a blue crystalline ocean. To see above the lofty firs a 53ft **observation tower** was erected in 1936 by the Civilian Conservation Corp.

For drivers, the mountain has a paved road to the summit, though the view is infinitely better if you earn it via a 4.3-mile hike up from Cascade Lake's North End Campground or a 5-mile cycle that begins just past Cascade Lake. Beginners beware: the grade is a persistent 7% (7ft vertical rise for every horizontal 100ft) with frequent hairpin turns.

The park's two major bodies of water, **Cascade Lake** and **Mountain Lake**, offer campgrounds, good trout fishing, rentable paddle boats and rowboats, picnic areas and swimming beaches. The lakes are also ringed by hiking trails and linked via a pleasant wooded ramble that passes the spectacular 100ft-high **Cascade Falls**.

Of the more than 30 miles of trails, about half are open seasonally for mountain biking and one or two for horses. Get a trail map from the park headquarters at the southern end of Cascade Lake.

Rosario Mansion Museum   MUSEUM

(Rosario Resort; ⏰9am-8pm) **FREE** Set in the eponymous resort, these rooms around the hotel's lobby tell the life and times of former Seattle mayor, shipbuilder and groundbreaking environmentalist Robert Moran, who lived here from 1906 until 1938. Look out for the ship memorabilia and the huge custom-made organ.

Turtleback Mountain Preserve   PARK

🌿 Saved from possible development when it was bought for $18.5 million as public land in 2007, Orcas' second mountain (rising to 1519ft) was in private hands for so long that most people had forgotten what was there. The answer: fragile wetlands, Garry oak savannah, spectacular overlooks, wild orchids and acres of solitude. It now has trails open to hikers (daily) and bikers/horseback riders (alternate days). There are two trailheads; one is on Crow Valley Rd, while the other (best) one is Wild Rose Lane near Deer Harbor and has a steep 1.3-mile trail that leads to Ship's Peak and a view that rivals the one from Mt Constitution.

Horse-trail riding on the mountain is run out of nearby **Turtlehead Farm** (www. turtleheadfarm.com; 231 Lime Quarry Rd) for $60 an hour.

Orcas Island Historical Museum   MUSEUM

(www.orcasmuseum.org; 181 North Beach Rd, Eastsound; admission $5; ⏰10am-4pm Tue-Sun late May-late Sep) Housed in a series of six original homesteader cabins dating from the 1880s, this island museum relates the pioneer and local history of Orcas and the San Juan Islands. Besides the usual collection of household goods, tools, weapons and photographs, there's a history of the lime-kiln industry and a focus on Orcas' first residents, the North Straits Salish.

Deer Harbor Charters WHALE-WATCHING
(Deer Harbor Resort; www.deerharborcharters.com) Deer Harbor Charters offers year-round whale-watching trips departing from either Deer Harbor or the Rosario Resort. Its boats run on biodiesel. It guarantees sightings; trips cost from $99.

Outer Island Whale Watching WHALE-WATCHING
(360-376-3711; www.outerislandx.com; Eastsound) From Eastsound, Outer Island Whale Watching is an excellent choice. Also guarantees sightings and costs from $99.

Kruger Escapes SAILING
(360-298-1023; www.krugerescapes.com; Deer Harbor; 3hr sails for up to 6 people from $300) For day sailing charters try the recommended Kruger Escapes.

🛏 Sleeping

Fear not. An Orcas 'resort' is a quiet, modest place; nothing like the beachside all-inclusives of Cancun or Puerto Vallarta. There are also numerous private rentals available – see www.orcasislandchamber.com for details. Book well ahead in July and August when the island is insanely popular.

Doe Bay Village Resort & Retreat HOSTEL, RESORT $
(360-376-2291; www.doebay.com; dm $55, cabin d from $90, yurts from $120; 🐾) Doe Bay, on the island's easternmost shore, is as lovely a spot as any on Orcas. By far the least expensive resort in the San Juans, Doe Bay has the atmosphere of an artists' commune cum hippie retreat. Accommodations include sea-view campsites, a small hostel with dormitory and private rooms, and various cabins and yurts, most with views of the water.

There's also a natural-foods store, a cafe, yoga classes ($10), an organic garden and special discounts for guests who arrive by bike. The sauna and clothing-optional hot tub are set apart on one side of a creek.

Golden Tree Hostel HOSTEL $
(360-317-8693; www.goldentreehostel.com; 1159 North Beach Rd, Eastsound; dm/d with shared bath $38/88; @🌐) Take an 1890s-era heritage mansion, give it a hip remodel that retains the building's old charm then add plenty of fireside, couch-filled communal areas and a well-equipped kitchen. Oh and there's a hot tub and sauna out back. Whether you choose to stay in the immaculate six-bed single-sex dorms or bright private rooms with shared bath, you'll be in hostel heaven.

Bikes can be rented for a bargain $15 and shuttles from the ferry are $3.

Orcas Hotel HOTEL $
(360-376-4300; www.orcashotel.com; Orcas Landing; r with shared/private bath from $89/160; 🌐) Built in 1904 and refurbished in the 1990s, the rather pokey interior and small rooms of the Orcas Hotel are like something from the pages of a stiff Jane Austen novel, with narrow corridors, patterned wallpaper and a manicured garden. Perched on a bluff above the ferry terminal, it's not in the luxury bracket but has a certain old world vitality.

Moran State Park CAMPGROUND $
(360-376-2326; campsites $23) The largest camping area in the San Juans has more than 150 campsites (no hookups) at four lakeside locations: one at Mountain Lake and three at Cascade Lake. Reservations are a must in summer.

Outlook Inn HOTEL $$
(360-376-2200; www.outlookinn.com; 171 Main St, Eastsound; r with shared/private bath from $79/119; 🌐) Eastsound's oldest and most eye-catching building, the Outlook Inn (1888) is an island institution that has kept up with the times by expanding into a majestic, white (but still quite small) bayside complex. All rooms are bright with a timeless style but the cheapest have shared bathrooms, while rooms in the motel-style east building have en suites.

The positively luxurious bay-view suites boast Jacuzzi tubs. Also on-site is the fancy New Leaf Cafe.

Beach Haven CABIN $$
(360-376-2288; www.beach-haven.com; West Beach; apt $125, cabins $150-300; 🌐📶) Log cabins in an assortment of sizes line a quiet and private gray-pebble beach. The tall trees throughout the whole property give the resort a magical feel of being both in the forest and on the seashore at the same time. Apartments are in a lodge that's also on the beach and managment is exceptionally friendly.

THE SAN JUANS BY HUMAN-POWER

From 1-acre Posey Island to 57-sq-mile Orcas Island, the San Juans aren't large, meaning you don't need a 210HP V6 engine to get around. Instead, a leg-powered bicycle or an arm-powered kayak will easily do the job.

The biking is memorable on all three main islands (and Shaw if you're up for a short circuit). Lopez Island is the most popular with cyclists thanks to its flattish terrain and salutation-offering local motorists (there are bike racks outside almost every shop and business). San Juan Island's roads are a little busier but no less alluring, while hilly Orcas offers the biggest challenge for aspiring cyclists, with the 5-mile-long drag to the top of 2409ft Mt Constitution worthy of a miniature 'King of the Mountains' competition. All three islands have bike rentals that can deliver cycles to the ferry terminal during peak months. Hire fees are approximately $35 per day. Contact the following:

Island Bicycles (www.islandbicylces.com; 380 Argyle Ave, Friday Harbor) San Juan Island.

Lopez Bicycle Works (www.lopezbicycleworks.com; 2847 Fisherman Bay Rd; ⊙10am-6pm May-Sep) Lopez Island.

Wildlife Cycles (www.wildlifecycles.com; 350 North Beach Rd, Eastsound) Orcas Island.

Off-land the islands are navigable via the complicated web of sea channels that lie between them. Kayaking away from the coast can be challenging, with strong winds, riptides and ever-changing weather; join an organized trip or stick to the sheltered shorelines and coves if you're unsure. **Shearwater Adventures** (www.shearwaterkayaks.com; 138 North Beach Rd, Eastsound) on Orcas Island is considered one of the best kayaking schools in the state if you decide to take lessons. More experienced kayakers can progress along the Cascadia Marine Trail (see the boxed text, p113). Kayak rentals (from around $40 for four hours) and organized trips (three hours from $80) can be organized at the following:

Cascadia Kayak & Bike (www.cascadiakayakandbike.com; 135 Lopez Rd, Lopez Village) Lopez Island.

San Juan Kayak Expeditions (☑360-378-4436; www.sanjuankayak.com; Friday Harbor) San Juan Island.

Body, Boat & Blade (☑360-376-5388; www.bodyboatblade.com; Prune Alley, Eastsound) Orcas Island.

West Beach Resort　　　　CABIN $$
(☑1877-937-8224; www.westbeachresort.com; tent cabins $99, cottages from $165; 🔊📶🐾) Welcome to another rustic cabin-resort that feels like its own small village, with a shop, cafe and marina on a shimmering waterfront facing crimson Canadian sunsets. Besides the cabins there are deluxe fixed 'tent cabins' with wood floors but no electricity, and a few campsites ($33) in a grassy clearing a few hundred feet from the shore.

★ Rosario Resort & Spa　　RESORT $$$
(☑360-376-2222; www.rosario-resort.com; 1400 Rosario Rd, Eastsound; r $149-400; 🏧❄🐾📶) This magnificent seafront mansion built by former shipbuilding magnate Robert Moran in 1904 is now the centerpiece of an upscale resort, and the setting oozes F Scott Fitzgerald–style romance. The 180 modern rooms sprawl across the grounds surrounding the old mansion, and the complex includes tennis courts, a swimming pool, a marina and a spa.

🍴 Eating

You'll find a surprising variety of good eating places in the small settlement of Eastsound. Elsewhere there are restaurants and cafes in Doe Bay, Olga, Rosario, Deer Harbor and Orcas Village.

Rose's Bakery & Cafe　　　　CAFE $
(382 Prune Alley, Eastsound; breakfast $4-13; ⊙8:30am-6pm Mon-Sat) Go where the locals go for fresh baked goods and French-influenced dishes like baked eggs with Gruyère, *pain perdu* (French toast) or a thick slab of homemade wholewheat bread with gouda cheese and sliced apples. There's plenty of seating in the bright restaurant or

get baked goods and sandwiches to go at the attached deli and shop.

Cafe Olga
CAFE $
(11 Point Lawrence Rd, Olga; mains $9-12; ⊙9am-6pm Mon-Fri, lo 8pm Sat & Sun, closed Wed Mar-Apr) The definitive Orcas hangout is this quiet and isolated cafe-art gallery in the three-building settlement of Olga, on the island's secluded eastern saddlebag. Living up to the hype, the scones, cinnamon buns and pies here are stupendous – perfect if you've just busted a gut cycling up and down Mt Constitution.

Enzo's Italian Caffé
CAFE $
(365 North Beach Rd, Eastsound; sandwiches $6-8; @⊙) More popular with tourists than with locals, Enzo's is however a great stop for a good cup of joe or scoop of gelati. If you're just off the ferry, you can remind yourself that you're not too far from 'civilization' with a creamy crepe or a filling panini while tweeting all and sundry on your laptop (yes, the wi-fi's gratis).

Kitchen
FUSION $
(249 Prune Alley, Eastsound; salads & wraps $8-15; ⊙11am-7pm Mon-Sat; ☑) Given that the food here is only vaguely Asian and service slow, this cafe's tagline of 'Fast Asian,' deserves a giggle. The food, however – from pulled-pork wraps to Asian-influenced salads with tempeh or tofu – is worth the wait. The outdoor seating makes you feel like you're having a country picnic.

★Mijita's
MEXICAN $$
(310 A St, Eastsound; mains $13-22; ⊙4-9pm Wed-Sun) When the Oaxacan guy at the table next to you can't stop raving about the food, it's gotta be good. Even if Mexican isn't your *fuerte*, it's difficult to go wrong in this creative, outdoor-indoor restaurant with its rustic Mexican furnishings and fairy-lit garden slap-bang in the middle of Eastsound.

Ooh and aah over the Mexican chef's family recipes like slow-braised short ribs with blackberry mole or the vegetarian quinoa cakes with mushrooms, chevre, almonds and *pipian* – everything is even better on your plate than it sounds on the menu.

Doe Bay Café
NORTHWESTERN $$
(mains $14-26; ⊙breakfast, lunch & dinner Thu-Mon) ☑ Religiously sustainable, Doe Bay has its own organic garden, a tight network of trusted farm suppliers and a damned good chef. Few things on the planet are better than the pizza topped with locally 'foraged' mushrooms.

Inn at Ship Bay
SEAFOOD $$$
(☎877-276-7296; www.innatshipbay.com; 326 Olga Rd; mains $17-28; ⊙5:30-11pm Tue-Sat) ☑ Locals unanimously rate this place as the best fine dining experience on the island. The chefs work overtime preparing everything from scratch using the freshest island ingredients. Seafood is the specialty and it's served in an attractive 1860s orchard house a couple of miles south of Eastsound. There's also an on-site 11-room hotel (doubles $175 to $195).

New Leaf Cafe
MODERN AMERICAN $$$
(☎360-376-2200; Main St, Eastsound; mains $18-30; ⊙brunch Sat & Sun, lunch Mon-Fri, dinner Tue-Sun) Two words: crab cakes. Throw in some *dijonaise* sauce and pecans and you might want to think about postponing your ferry till next week. Complement those crab cakes with smoked-bacon-wrapped pork tenderloin and you'll probably find the financial investment worth it.

☕ Drinking

Island Hoppin' Brewery
BREWPUB
(www.islandhoppinbrewery.com; 33 Hope Lane, Eastsound; ⊙4-9pm Tue-Sun) The location just off Mt Baker Rd near the airport makes this new brewery hard to find but the locals sure know it's there – this is *the* place to go to enjoy six changeable brews on tap while making friends with those islanders who enjoy beer. There's often live music on weekends.

🔒 Shopping

No malls, but some interesting local crafts might leave you departing with more than you arrived with. Tiny Eastsound has a very browsable collection of shops from books to crafts and everything in between.

Crow Valley Pottery & Gallery
ARTS & CRAFTS
(www.crowvalley.com; Main St, Eastsound; ⊙10am-5pm) Crow Valley Pottery & Gallery sells jewelry to paintings, but its specialty is hand-painted pottery, all conceived and produced on the island. It also maintains a cabin (2274 Orcas Rd; ⊙10am-5pm May-Sep) exhibiting more pottery, glasswork and garden art.

❶ Information

Orcas Island Chamber of Commerce (www.orcasisland.org; 120 North Beach Rd, Eastsound; ⊘10am-3pm Mon-Sat)

❶ Getting Around

If you're not biking, the **Orcas Island Shuttle** (www.orcasislandshuttle.com) can meet most of your transport needs, arranging car rental (from $60), 24-hour taxis and a May-to-September public bus (one way $6).

Lopez Island

POP 2383

While some of the smaller San Juans are known for their standoffish 'No Trespassing' signs, Lopez – or *Slow-pez* as it's sometimes known – is the ultimate friendly isle where local motorists give strangers the 'Lopezian wave' (two to five fingers raised from the steering wheel) and you can leave your bike outside the village store and it'll still have both wheels when you return several hours later.

Though less well set-up for tourism than its two more populous neighbors, Lopez' tight-knit community and well-organized infrastructure offer a surprisingly varied selection of campgrounds and B&Bs. Lopez village is the island's centerpiece, a pinprick of a settlement that holds a weekly summer farmers market and boasts a couple of enterprising restaurants, while a couple of miles to the north, Lopez Island Vineyards showcases the island's local wine production.

Every April Lopez stages the ironically named **Tour de Lopez**, a laid-back noncompetitive cycle race where winning is incidental. The balloons are out again on July 4, when the island temporarily breaks out of its stupor to host what is, allegedly, the state's most electrifying **firework display**.

For maps and information go to the **Lopez Island Chamber of Commerce** (www.lopezisland.com; Lopez Rd, Lopez Village).

❍ Sights

★Spencer Spit State Park PARK
Spencer Spit State Park is one of only four state parks on the San Juan archipelago. Two sand spits have formed a marshy lagoon that is a prime spot for various species of waterfowl. It's a good place to kayak, fish, beachcomb and enjoy the stunning scenery. If you've got gear and a shellfish licence it's also a popular spot for foraging mollusks.

Watmough Head BEACH
This scenic area at the island's southeastern extremity holds three trails, the best being the under-a-quarter-mile stroll to Watmaugh Bay, a stunning arc of pebbly sand framed by a sheer rock cliff on its northern side. Young seals may pop their heads up at you from the water as you stroll the shore.

Lopez Island Historical Museum MUSEUM
(www.lopezmuseum.org; Lopez Village; ⊘noon-4pm May-Sep) This tiny museum exhibits antiquated farm machinery, early pioneer photos and various rotating exhibitions. What it lacks in scale it makes up for in charm.

Port Stanley Schoolhouse HISTORIC BUILDING
The restored 1917 schoolhouse is run by the local historical society and offers a good photo op. To get to the schoolhouse from Lopez Village, take the road east past Hummel Lake. Turn left at the T-junction and follow the road around.

🏃 Activities

Lopez Island Vineyards WINE TASTING
(www.lopezislandvineyards.com; Lopez Village; tastings from $5; ⊘noon-5pm Fri & Sat May-Sep) Lopez Island Vineyards has been making wines from grapes grown organically on the island since 1987. You can drop by the tasting room to sample its Madeleine Angevine and Siegerrebe varieties.

Harmony Charters FISHING, CRUISE
(www.harmonycharters.com; 973 Shark Reef Rd) Skippered day and overnight fishing trips are available from Harmony Charters which operates out of Fisherman Bay. Visitors select from a number of organized packages, or they can schedule individualized tours or cruises including a lunch cruise on a 63ft yacht or an overnight cruise with meals and chef (per person $375).

🛏 Sleeping

Odlin County Park Campground CAMPGROUND $
(☑360-378-1842; campsites $23) Handily situated 1 mile south of the ferry landing and 3 miles north of Lopez Village, this pleasant waterfront campground features a picnic area, vault toilets and mooring buoys. There is an adjacent sandy beach, and hiking trails disappear off into the surrounding woods. The nearest showers are in Lopez Village (coin operated).

Lopez Islander Resort   RESORT $$

(☏ 800-736-3434; www.lopezfun.com; Fisherman Bay Rd; r from $139; 🛜🏊♿) Equipped with a restaurant, swimming pool, Jacuzzi, gym and 'Tiki Lounge Bar,' this so-outdated-it's-kind-of-cool 'resort' sits alongside a 64-slip marina in Fisherman Bay, where eagles glide. What it lacks in intimacy it makes up for in amiability and good service. The resort offers free parking spots for guests at the Anacortes ferry terminal.

Edenwild Inn   B&B $$

(☏ 360-468-3238; www.edenwildinn.com; Lopez Rd, Lopez Village; r $170-195) Eden is the word at this Victorian-style mansion in Lopez Village with its lovely formal gardens, wide porch and meticulous attention to detail. Encased in what must be the island's most sumptuous setting are eight individually crafted rooms, all with private bathrooms. All of the island's low-key facilities are within shouting distance.

MacKaye Harbor Inn   B&B $$

(☏ 360-468-2253; www.mackayeharborinn.com; 949 MacKaye Harbor Rd; r $175-235; 🛜) Relatively isolated on Lopez' southern reaches, this 1927 farmhouse contains four bedrooms and one harbor-view suite and gets consistently fantastic reviews from guests. The cheap kayak rental and complimentary mountain bikes make it more of a deal than the price tag suggests.

THE OUTLYING ISLANDS

Stand on the clamorous ferry dock at Anacortes during the halcyon summer months and you'll quickly realize you're not the only one with designs on the San Juans' beauty. But don't get dragged down by the crowds. Ninety-nine per cent of these vociferous vacationers are heading to one of the big four – San Juan, Orcas, Lopez or Shaw. A quick bit of mental arithmetic will reveal that this leaves approximately 168 islands largely tourist free. Granted, many of the lesser San Juans are privately owned and/or hard to reach, but with a bit of furtive planning, genuine Robinson Crusoe experiences are possible, especially in the spring and fall. Here's a quick rundown of the options.

Other Inhabited Islands

The fourth-largest San Juan, **Cypress Island** (population 40) has a salmon hatchery, 25 miles of trails and is a popular kayaking destination, while **Waldron Island** (population 104) – perhaps the quirkiest island of all – is inhabited by a feisty contingent of back-to-the-landers who live without electricity or landline phones and are well known for their self-sufficiency. Two of the more visited 'populated' islands are **Stuart Island** (population 40) and **Sucia Island** (population 4). Stuart, the last landfall before Canada, has a schoolhouse, a light station, 3.5 miles of trails, 18 campsites and an unstaffed 'honesty store' where you can buy souvenir T-shirts. Sucia (whose name means 'dirty' in Spanish, though it's anything but) is easily accessed by a March-to-November private ferry from Orcas and has a large state park, 60 campsites, access to drinking water and 10 miles of hiking trails.

Uninhabited Islands & Marine State Parks

Remoter still are the uninhabited islands, many of which are designated state parks or earmarked as pit stops on the Cascadia Marine Trail. Recommended are:

Matia Island (145 acres) With six campsites and a short loop trail that between 1892 and 1921 was home to US Civil War veteran Elvin A Smith, aka the 'Hermit of Matia Island.'

Patos Island (207 acres) Seven campsites and a light station.

Jones Island (188 acres) Has 24 campsites and a herd of resident black-tail deer.

James Island (113 acres) Has 13 campsites, great for crabbing.

Posey Island (1 acre) Two campsites, renowned for its crimson sunsets and beautiful wildflowers.

Outlying Islands (☏ 360-376-3711; www.outerislandx.com) on Orcas Island can organize various trips and boat transfers to the outlying San Juans. Phone or check out the website. Alternatively, you can visit with your own boat/kayak. Campsites generally cost $23 per night.

✖ Eating & Drinking

In keeping with their salutary 'waves,' Lopezians are congenial and hospitable people who are always happy to engage visitors in casual chitchat. Hang around in one of the village's small cafes and you'll soon be on first-name terms with half the island. All of Lopez' eating places are on the main drag in tiny Lopez Village.

Holly B's Bakery   BAKERY $
(www.hollybsbakery.com; Lopez Rd; pastries around $3; ☉ Apr-Nov) Holly's heads the early-morning latte and pastry rush while harnessing the slow island vibe and thus remaining effortlessly low key. The seasonal fruit pastries are worthy of any swanky Seattle patisserie.

Bay Cafe   SEAFOOD $$
(☑ 360-468-3700; www.bay-cafe.com; 9 Old Post Rd; mains $14-30; ☉ 5-9pm Wed-Fri, noon-9pm Sat & Sun) 🍃 Lopez' one and only attempt at fine dining offers romantic sunset views right on the water, with classic fish dishes, including chowder and crab cakes. You could also go bolder with specialties like truffled mac 'n' cheese or rack of lamb paired with wine from the local vineyard.

Cafe La Boheme   CAFE $
(Lopez Rd; ☉ 7am-4pm) Puffed cushions and Middle Eastern–style sofas lure you into this tiny caffeine station, where you can listen to a cacophony of chatter – everything from local gossip to the merits of biodiesel versus gas – over coffee and cookies.

Isabel's Espresso   CAFE $
(Lopez Rd; ☉ 7:30am-5pm) A retro wood-paneled coffee bar that offers a fine selection of java coffee, herbal teas and fruit shakes, and features colorful furnishings and a small book collection. It's the most hippie-hip of the island's coffee-shop choices.

Vortex Juice Bar   JUICE BAR
(Lopez Rd S; lunch dishes $5-9; ☉ 10am-7pm Jun-Sep, to 6pm Oct-May) Fresh juices are Vortex's forte, made with whatever fruits and vegetables are on hand. Above-average salads and wraps are among its other healthy offerings.

ℹ Getting Around

Lopez is is one of the best of the San Juans for biking because of its relatively flat terrain, and also because it's your only option for getting around if you don't bring your car. Rent bikes in Lopez Village at **Village Cycles** (☑ 360-468-4013; www.villagecycles.net; 9 Old Post Rd; rentals per hour/day from $7/30; ☉ 10am-4pm Wed-Sun), which will drop bikes at the ferry for $5 and also leads two-hour, half-day and full-day island bike tours for $55, $75 and $105 respectively.

Shaw Island

The quietest and smallest of the four main San Juan Islands, tranquil Shaw is famous for its restrictive property laws and handsome Benedictine monastery. Here, enveloped in a pristine, tree-carpeted time warp, Catholic nuns tend to llamas, wild deer forage on deserted roadways and idyllic sandy beaches are sprinkled with rather foreboding 'no trespassing' signs.

Aware of rising property prices and the burgeoning resort development of their larger and swankier neighbors, Shaw islanders have steadfastly resisted the lure of the tourist dollar and chosen to remain private. That's not to say that travelers aren't welcome. Plenty of ferries arrive daily on Shaw, but with only one campsite offering just 11 overnight berths, opportunities to linger are limited.

For purists, that is what the island is all about. Shaw is fondly redolent of Orcas 30 years ago (and the rest of America 60 years ago), a close-knit rural community where neighbor still helps out neighbor and kids play happily in the countryside free from the paranoia of modern living. Until the early 2000s, the ferry wharf and the island's only store were managed by three Franciscan nuns who collected tickets and directed traffic in bright-yellow safety vests worn over their dark-brown habits. In 2004 the Franciscans moved on and today only the Benedictine and the Sisters of Mercy orders remain.

For the curious, Shaw is worth a slow spin on a mountain bike or an afternoon of quiet contemplation on a pebbly beach. History buffs can break the reverie at the Shaw Island Historical Museum (Blind Bay Rd), while perennial peace-seekers can find lazy solace on quiet South Beach in Shaw Island County Park (☑ 360-378-1842; Squaw Bay Rd; tent sites $14) with overnight room for 11 (note there are no shower facilities).

Olympic Peninsula & Washington Coast

Best Places to Eat

➡ Bella Italia (p131)

➡ Sweet Laurette Cafe &
Bistro (p129)

➡ OleBob's Seafood Market
(p150)

➡ Depot (p148)

Best Places to Stay

➡ Lake Quinault Lodge
(p138)

➡ Seabrook Cottage Rentals
(p143)

➡ Shelburne Country Inn
(p148)

Why Go?

The Olympic Peninsula is an unblemished wilderness of the highest order, with an interior redolent of a unicorn fantasy novel and an end-of-the-continent coastline that makes Big Sur look positively calm. Then there's the precipitation. While Seattleites whine about a little winter drizzle, the Hoh Rain Forest is drowning in up to 200in of rain a year. There's an upside to all this water, of course; it's green here, a thousand verdant shades of it if you stare hard enough. And it's virgin too. Untouched in over a millennium lie sapphire lakes, rarely climbed mountains, and ancient cedar and spruce trees older than most of Europe's medieval castles. It took a lucrative series of vampire novels to put the Olympic Peninsula on the world's radar, but *Twilight* is only 1% of what this wild, fog-shrouded landmass is about.

When to Go

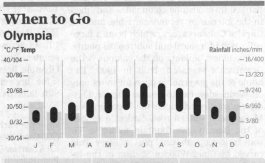

Olympia

Mar Port Townsend's unique Victorian Days festival.

Jul & Aug Best hiking opportunities and least chance of rain.

Aug Long Beach's International Kite Festival in the third week.

OLYMPIA

POP 47,266

Small in size but big in clout, state capital Olympia is a political, musical and outdoor powerhouse that punches well above its 47,000-strong population. Look no further than the streetside buskers on 4th Ave, the smartly attired bureaucrats marching across the lawns of the resplendent state legislature or the Gore-Tex–clad outdoor fiends overnighting before rugged sorties into the Olympic Mountains. Truth is, despite its Classical Greek–sounding name, creative, out-of-the-box Olympia is anything but ordinary. Progressive Evergreen college has long lent the place an artsy turn (creator of *The Simpsons* Matt Groening studied here), while the dive bars and secondhand guitar shops of downtown provided an original pulpit for riot-grrrl music and grunge.

◉ Sights & Activities

Washington State Capitol   LANDMARK
(⊙8am-4:30pm) FREE Looking like a huge Grecian temple, the Capitol complex dominates the town. Its beautiful setting, in a 30-acre park overlooking Capitol Lake with the Olympic Mountains glistening in the background, is a visitor favorite. The campus' crowning glory is the magnificent **Legislative Building**. Completed in 1927, it's a dazzling display of craning columns and polished marble, topped by a 287ft dome that is only slightly smaller than its namesake in Washington, DC.

As well as the Legislative Building, visitors are welcome to peek inside both the Supreme Court aka the **Temple of Justice**, flanked by sandstone colonnades and lined in the interior by yet more marble, and the **Capitol Conservatory**, which hosts a large collection of tropical and subtropical plants.

The oldest building on the campus is the **Governor's Mansion**, built in 1908. The home of the governor is open for tours only on Wednesday; call to reserve a space. Outdoor attractions include the Vietnam War Memorial, a sunken rose garden, a replica of the Roman-style fountain found in Tivoli Park, Copenhagen, plus a Story Pole carved by Chief William Shelton of the local Snohomish tribe in 1938. The manicured grounds are an attraction in themselves, and a well-marked path zigzags down to Capitol Lake where it connects with more trails.

State Capital Museum   MUSEUM
(211 W 21st Ave; admission $2; ⊙10am-4pm Tue-Fri, from noon Sat) This premier museum is housed in the 1920s Lord Mansion, a few blocks south of the campus, and preserves the general history of Washington State from the Nisqually tribe to the present day.

Hands On Children's Museum   MUSEUM
(114 Jefferson St NE; admission $9.95; ⊙10am-5pm Mon-Sat, noon-5pm Sun; ⛟) Recently remodeled and relocated at a cost of $9 million, this is the ne plus ultra of kid interactive fun. Highlights include an eagle's nest that can be scaled – a slide tumbles down from here to the Puget Sound interpretive area, where there's an underwater world and crane-lift port area. The **WET Science Center** next door is dedicated to water-reclamation education (and has an artificial creek to play in).

Percival Landing Park   PARK
When Olympia was founded, its narrow harbor was a mudflat during low tides, but after years of dredging, a decent harbor was established. This park is essentially a boardwalk that overlooks the assembled pleasure craft and provides informative display boards describing Olympia's past as a shipbuilding port and a center of the lumber and cannery trades.

Priest Point Park   PARK
(2600 East Bay Dr NE) Many Olympians cite this as their favorite park for the nature trails that lead to Bud Inlet on Puget Sound, the many shore birds, the rose garden and the playground with views of downtown and the Capitol Building.

Tumwater Falls Park   WATERFALL
(110 Deschutes Way SW, Tumwater; ⊙8am-8pm) FREE Paralleling I-5 near the turnoff to US 101, 15 acres of park trails follow the Deschutes River from the abandoned 1906 Olympic Brewery brick building up to the same brewery's midcentury location, the 82ft falls, fish ladders and a small salmon hatchery.

Olympia Farmers Market   MARKET
(700 Capitol Way N; ⊙10am-3pm Thu-Sun Apr-Oct, Sat & Sun Nov-Dec) ⌀ Second only to Seattle's Pike Place in size and character, Olympia's local market is a great place to shop for organic herbs, vegetables, flowers, baked goods and the famous specialty oysters.

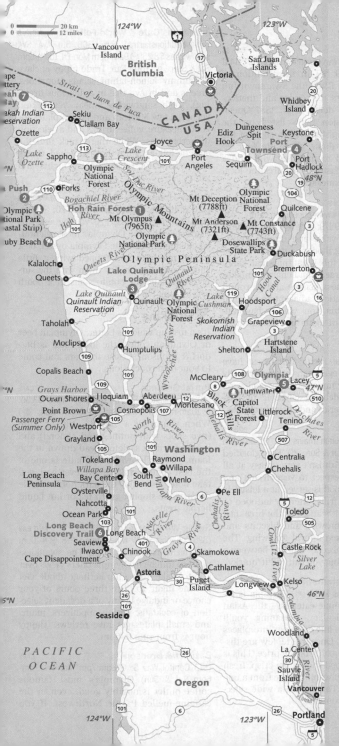

Olympic Peninsula & Washington Coast Highlights

1 Thinking you've uncovered a real-life hobbit in the moss-covered **Hoh Rain Forest** (p136).

2 Finding solitude, but no vampires, on a mist-enshrouded beach at **La Push** (p141).

3 Driving (or hiking) miles to enjoy Northwestern cuisine and a roaring fireplace at **Lake Quinault Lodge** (p138).

4 Debating whether to don kayaking gear or a Victorian bowler hat in nostalgia-obsessed **Port Townsend** (p126).

5 Drinking coffee that's good enough to wake a zombie in small but hip **Olympia** (p124).

6 Trying to evoke the sense of accomplishment felt by Lewis and Clark on the **Long Beach Discovery Trail** (p148).

7 Visiting one of the nation's best **Native American museums** (p139) in Neah Bay.

🛏 Sleeping

Swantown Inn   B&B $$

(☎ 360-753-9123; www.swantowninn.com; 1431 11th Ave; r $129-179; 🛜) In the tradition of Washington state B&Bs, the Swantown Inn features great personal service and meticulous attention to detail in an 1887 Queen Anne–style mansion that's listed on the state historical register. Within sight of the imposing capitol dome, there are four elegantly furnished rooms, plus wi-fi and a formidable breakfast that features the local specialty, ginger pancakes.

Phoenix Inn Suites   HOTEL $$

(☎ 360-570-0555; www.phoenixinn.com; 415 Capitol Way N; r $139-179; ❄🛜🏊) The modern Phoenix is good value and dazzles guests with its sparkling modern interior and indoor pool and hot tub. What this small chain hotel lacks in character and charm it makes up for in cleanliness, service and all-round comfort. The location, adjacent to Percival Landing, also puts you within baseball-pitching distance of sights and restaurants.

🍴 Eating

Few places in the Pacific Northwest have as many good vegetarian or veg-friendly restaurants as Olympia. The city is also renowned for its delicate Olympic oysters, myriad ethnic eateries and cheap brunches.

Darby's Café   DINER $

(211 5th Ave SE; lunch mains $7; ⊗ 7am-9pm Wed-Fri, 8am-9pm Sat & Sun; 🍴) This glorified greasy spoon on 5th isn't very greasy at all and pays equal respect to vegetarians and vegans. Unfussy food is served at a leisurely pace and without frills (often by tattooed or cross-dressing wait staff), but the breakfast scrambles, hash browns, and biscuits and gravy have garnered a loyal following. The decor is self-described as 'halfway between a diner and a dive,' but you can call it 'quirky'.

Lemon Grass Restaurant   THAI $

(212 4th Ave W; mains $8-10; 🍴) Olympia is renowned for its ethnic eateries – the Asian variants in particular – meaning you'll sometimes have to line up to get into places like Lemon Grass. Once inside, few are disappointed by the quality or the price. This is everything Thai food should be: crisp, fresh and as spicy as you want (choose from a one to a four rating). There's also a wide selection of vegetarian options.

Traditions Cafe & World Folk Art   AMERICAN $

(www.traditionsfairtrade.com; 300 5th Ave SW; sandwiches $8.25; ⊗ 9am-6pm Mon-Fri, 10am-5pm Sat & Sun; 🍴) Your Fair Trade hippy enclave of yummy lemon-tahini salads (tomatoes, greens and brown rice in a delicious dressing), fresh sandwiches (meat, veggie and vegan), a few Mexican and Italian plates for good measure, coffee drinks and a selection of herbal teas. While there, tuck into the eclectic folk-art store that's attached. Check the website for music, poetry nights and more.

Oyster House   SEAFOOD $$

(320 W 4th Ave; seafood dinners $15-20; ⊗ 11am-11pm, to midnight Fri & Sat) As you'd guess, this place specializes in Olympia's most celebrated cuisine, the delicate Olympia oyster, best served pan-fried and topped with a little cheese and spinach. Try them with the surprisingly delicious potato skins in a booth overlooking the placid harbor.

🍷 Drinking

It's a toss-up which is better: Olympian beer or Olympian coffee (the local roast is Batdorf & Bronson). Cruise the bars and come to your own conclusions.

Burial Grounds   CAFE

(406 Washington St SE; specialty lattes $3.50; ⊗ 10am-midnight Mon-Sat, to 10pm Sun; @) When you order a 'zombie attacker' latte (two shots with nutmeg and almond) and it comes with a skeleton head drawn in the foam, you smile; when said latte is one of the best coffee drinks you've ever had, you take note. Also enjoy the dark horror-movie decor while sipping green tea or hot liquid herbal treats.

Swing Wine Bar & Cafe   WINE BAR

(825 Columbia St SW; wine flights $8-18; ⊗ 4-10pm Mon-Thu, to midnight Fri & Sat) The swankiest place to imbibe in Olympia offers views over Capitol Lake from a hip heritage abode. Get a 'wine flight' to taste three pours of your choice or indulge in any of a decadent selection of cocktails. Fusion appetizers, mains and small plates get rave reviews. Happy hour is from 4pm to 6pm.

Batdorf & Bronson   CAFE

(513 Capitol Way S; ⊗ 6am-7pm Mon-Fri, 7am-6pm Sat & Sun) Olympia's most famous coffee outlet is notably good, even in the caffeine-fuelled Pacific Northwest. If you

like your morning brew fair trade, shade grown and certified organic, this is the place to come. For travelers with an insatiable caffeine addiction, head down to the company's new roasting house for expert banter.

Fish Tale Brew Pub BREWPUB
(515 Jefferson St) Fish has a classic selection of organic beers, hard ciders and India Pale Ales, making it one of Washington's best-known microbreweries. The company's cozy pub, just across the road from its famous brewery, is a must for all visiting beer aficionados. It also serves great oyster, lamb or grass-fed beef burgers.

☆ Entertainment

Long before Nirvana played their formative gigs here, Olympia was a breeding ground for indie, lo-fi and antifolk sounds, spearheaded by musical pioneers such as Calvin Johnson, member of the band Beat Happening and founder of K Records. To see music at its roguish best, look out for buskers on 4th Ave and read homemade posters on lampposts.

Washington Center for the Performing Arts THEATER
(☑360-753-8586; 512 Washington St) Comedy, art, ballet and plays – this is Olympia's primary venue for national touring shows and other cultural activities, and brings the city to center stage in Washington's surprisingly varied cultural life.

State Theater THEATER
(☑360-786-0151; 202 4th Ave E) Harlequin Productions stages an eclectic lineup of contemporary plays and classics in this recently restored theater. Expect everything from Shakespeare to little-known musicals.

Capitol Theatre THEATER
(☑360-754-6670; 206 E 5th Ave) Of 1924 vintage, the beaux-arts-inspired Capitol Theater is the headquarters of the Olympia film society and puts on everything from Fellini movies to Rick Steves travel presentations. There is a film festival every November and the occasional rock or rap concert.

ℹ Information

For news about the community, sports and events check out www.thurstontalk.com.
State Capitol Visitor Center (cnr 14th Ave & Capitol Way; ⊙10am-2pm Oct-Apr, to 4pm May-Sep) Offers information on the capitol campus, the Olympia area and Washington state. Note the limited opening hours.
USFS Office (1835 Black Lake Blvd) West of town; backcountry permits for wilderness camping in Olympic National Park can be obtained here.

ℹ Getting There & Away

BUS
Three Greyhound buses a day link Olympia to Seattle ($14.85, 1½ hours) and other I-5-corridor cities from its **station** (107 7th Ave E). **Grays Harbor Transportation Authority** (www.gh-transit.com) offers a bus service to Aberdeen on the Pacific Coast ($3, 1½ hours).

TRAIN
Amtrak (www.amtrak.com) *Cascade* and *Coast Starlight* trains stop at **Centennial Station** (6600 Yelm Hwy) in Lacey, the only volunteer-staffed train station in the world (apparently). Five trains a day link Olympia with Seattle ($17) and five with Portland ($25). Bus 64 goes between the station and downtown hourly 6:30am to 7:30pm, or it's a 3-mile walk.

ℹ Getting Around

The **Capital Aeroporter** (www.capair.com) has frequent service to Seattle-Tacoma International Airport, leaving from Phoenix Inn Suites at 415 Capitol Way N ($31, two hours). Reservations are suggested.
Olympia's free public-bus system is **Intercity Transit** (www.intercitytransit.com). The downtown transit center is at State Ave and Washington St.

OLYMPIA'S MUSIC SCENE

While Olympia's alternative-music scene has quietened down since the days of grunge and riot grrrl in the early 1990s, innovative local artists are in evidence in many of the city's bars, brewpubs and theaters. Dip into *Volcano*, the weekly South Puget Sound music paper distributed in local bars, restaurants and purple and green boxes on the street and found inside the *Ranger* and *Northwest Airlifter* newspapers (or online at www.northwestmilitary.com).

OLYMPIC PENINSULA

Cut off from the rest of the state by water on three sides, the remote Olympic Peninsula exhibits all the insular characteristics of a separate island. Dominated by the Olympic National Park, the region's main population centers are in the northeast and include Port Angeles, Port Townsend and the drier, balmier settlement of Sequim, now a budding retirement community. As the region's protected climatically by the Olympic Mountains, outdoor activities abound here.

Washington's coast north of Gray's Harbor is one of the most undisturbed slices of coastal wilderness in the US. Here tiny Native American towns list populations in the hundreds rather than the thousands and, bar a 15-mile stretch of US 101, there are few roads. Outside of small Native American reservations around Oil City, La Push and Ozette, 53 miles of this wild coast is protected as part of the Olympic National Park (added in 1953). Parts of it haven't changed since precolonial times.

Exempt from strict wilderness regulations, the area outside of the Olympic National Park is largely given over to the lumber industry.

History

Some of the peninsula's Native American history is well documented in the Ozette excavations that unearthed a 500-year-old Makah village in 1970. Other native groups included the Quileute and the Quinault.

European sailors were exploring the Northwest coast as early as 1592, but contact with the local people didn't occur until some two centuries later, when the land was claimed by the Spanish, who subsequently planted a colony at Neah Bay.

Port Townsend was established as the peninsula's premier settlement in 1851 and the first expanses of virgin forest began to fall to the saws in the 1880s when the mill towns of Aberdeen and Hoquiam sprang up in the south.

Early attempts to explore the interior were limited until the 1930s, when US 101 pushed through the deep forests, linking longtime coastal communities by road for the first time. Finally, in 1938, following a 40-year struggle among conservationists, industrialists and logging companies, the Olympic National Park was established in the heart of the peninsula.

Northeastern Olympic Peninsula

Hugging the protected coast of the Strait of Juan de Fuca, the northeastern corner of the Olympic Peninsula is the region's most populated enclave and provides a popular gateway to the national park. It's famous for its dry climate (courtesy of the Olympic rain shadow), and outdoor activities such as sea kayaking and whale-watching abound, while a rare historical treat awaits travelers in time-warped Port Townsend. Thanks to numerous ferry connections (Port Angeles to Victoria, Canada; Port Townsend to Whidbey Island; and Seattle to Bainbridge Island), the area is easily accessible from the population centers of Puget Sound.

Port Townsend

pop 8925

Inventive eateries, elegant fin de siècle hotels and an unusual stash of year-round festivals make Port Townsend an Olympic Peninsula rarity: a weekend vacation that doesn't require hiking boots. It's cut off from the rest of the area by eight bucolic miles off US 101, so don't come here to base yourself for national-park exploration unless you don't mind driving a lot. Instead, settle in and enjoy one of the prettiest towns in the state.

History

Back in the 1880s a number of nascent settlements were vying to become Washington's preeminent city (Walla Walla, Ellensburg and eventual winner Seattle to name but three). An early casualty in the battle for urban supremacy was Port Townsend, a speculation-fuelled boomtown at the nautical entrance to busy Puget Sound that went bust in the 'great panic of 1893.' Port Townsend's loss was a catastrophe for the local businessmen of the day, but the cloud had a long-term silver lining. After years of dire poverty when there wasn't even enough money to demolish the old unused buildings, Port Townsend experienced a flowery 1970s renaissance. The rebirth, based on urban rejuvenation and tourism, has endowed the Northwest with a frozen-in-time slice of redbrick Victorian architecture caught at its 1890s high watermark.

CENTRALIA STOPOVER

The overriding reason to make this rather mundane mining and lumber town a pit stop on the long drive (or train ride) north or south is to stay at a converted brothel, the **Olympic Club Hotel** (360-736-5164; 112 N Tower Ave; bunks/queens/kings with shared bath $40/60/70;), a 'venue hotel' where you can eat, sleep, drink, shoot billiards, listen to music and go to the cinema, all in the same evening and all without having to leave the hotel. The Olympic Club dates from 1908, when it opened as a 'gentlemen's resort' designed to satisfy the various drinking, gambling and sexual vices of transient miners and loggers. Portland's McMenamins has restored the brothel to its former glory, complete with creaking floorboards, art-deco murals, bar, billiard room, restaurant and small movie theater, where friendly wait staff bring in food orders during the movie as guests recline in sofas and armchairs. Upstairs, atmospheric bedrooms sport arty graffiti chronicling the misdemeanors of past guests.

If you're overnighting you can enjoy a hearty brunch at the acclaimed **Berry Fields** (201 S Pearl St; mains $10), situated in Centralia's biggest antique mall, where the cinnamon buns are the size of soccer balls.

◉ Sights

Port Townsend has a large stash of handsome Victorian buildings dating from the 1860s to about 1893 (when the economy collapsed). Styles run the gamut of Italian Renaissance, Queen Anne, Greek Revival and Gothic. The Victorian shop fronts of Water St were mostly built in a manic boom between 1886 and 1891.

Art galleries are another of the town's fortes and you can pick up a map of the best, all clustered within four blocks of the ferry dock, at the visitor center. Higher up on the bluff, be sure to stop and admire the 100ft clock tower of the **Jefferson County Courthouse** (1892) and also **Manresa Castle** (now a hotel).

Jefferson County Historical Society Museum   MUSEUM
(210 Madison St; adult/12yr & under $4/1; ⊙11am-4pm Mar-Dec) The local historic society runs this well-maintained exhibition area that includes mock-ups of an old courtroom and a jail cell, along with the full lowdown on the rise, fall and second coming of this captivating port town. The society also runs the **Rothschild House** (cnr Jefferson & Taylor Sts; admission $4; ⊙11am-4pm May-Oct) up on the bluff, with an atmospheric interior furnished in period fashion.

Fort Worden State Park   PARK
(www.parks.wa.gov/fortworden; 200 Battery Way; ⊙6:30am-dusk Apr-Oct, from 8am Nov-Mar) This attractive park located within Port Townsend's city limits is the remains of a large fortification system constructed in the 1890s to protect the strategically important Puget Sound area from outside attack – supposedly from the Spanish during the 1898 war.

The extensive grounds and historic buildings have been refurbished in recent years into a lodging, and nature and history park; sharp-eyed film buffs will recognize the setting as the backdrop for the movie *An Officer and a Gentleman*. The **Commanding Officer's Quarters** (admission $4; ⊙10am-5pm daily Jun-Aug, 1-4pm Sat & Sun Mar-May & Sep-Oct), a 12-bedroom mansion, is open for tours, and part of one of the barracks is now the **Puget Sound Coast Artillery Museum** (admission $2; ⊙11am-4pm Tue-Sun), which tells the story of early Pacific coastal fortifications.

Fort Worden offers a number of camping and lodging possibilities. Hikes lead along the headland to **Point Wilson Lighthouse Station** and some wonderful windswept beaches. On the park's fishing pier is the **Port Townsend Marine Science Center** (532 Battery Way; adult/child $5/3; ⊙noon-6pm Tue-Sun summer) featuring four touch tanks and daily interpretive programs.

♟ Activities

It's not all history. Port Townsend is the center for sea kayaking on Puget Sound and Fort Worden is a stop on the Cascadia Marine Trail. **PT Outdoors** (1017b Water St) rents single kayaks and stand-up paddle boards (SUP) from $25 an hour and offers guided tours from $60/45 per adult/child for two to three hours. **Puget Sound Express** (www.pugetsoundexpress.com; 431 Water St) offers four-hour whale-watching tours from May to October for $88/48 per adult/child, or an eight-hour excursion that includes a stopover in Friday Harbor on San Juan Island.

PT Cyclery (252 Tyler St; per hr/day $7/28) on a back lot on Tyler St, has mountain bikes and tandems for rent. It also provides local trail maps.

☞ Tours

Art walks leave on the first Saturday evening of every month. Ask at the visitor center for details.

Port Townsend Historical Society Walking Tours   WALKING TOUR
(adult/child $10/5) Guided walking tours around town from June through September. Inquire at the museum.

✺ Festivals & Events

Port Townsend has a busy calendar of annual events. Nonprofit arts foundation **Centrum** (www.centrum.org), based at Fort Worden State Park, sponsors an endless stream of arts and music festivals and seminars, many held at the fort. Among the most popular are the Festival of American Fiddle Tunes and Jazz Port Townsend, both in July. Contact Centrum for a schedule.

Victorian Days   HISTORY
(www.victorianfestival.org) In late March this unique festival offers an array of exhibits, walking tours and craft workshops. Horses and carriages are dusted off, refined manners are polished and half the town dons asphyxiating corsets or austere waistcoats to relive the days when lamb-chop whiskers and handlebar mustaches were the height of fashion.

⌓ Sleeping

Palace Hotel   HISTORIC HOTEL $
(☎360-385-0773; www.palacehotelpt.com; 1004 Water St; r $59-109; ❉ 🕾) Built in 1889, this beautiful Victorian building is a former brothel that was once run by the locally notorious Madame Marie, who did business out of the 2nd-floor corner suite. Each of the 15 rooms is named after the woman who used to occupy it. Reincarnated as an attractive period hotel with antique furnishings and old-fashioned claw-foot baths, the Palace's seediness is now a thing of the past.

Waterstreet Hotel   HOTEL $
(☎360-385-5467; www.waterstreethotelporttown send.com; 635 Water St; r $60-160; ❉ 🕾) Of Port Townsend's old dockside hotels, the easy-on-the-wallet Waterstreet has to be the best bargain in town. A multitude of rooms can accommodate between two and six people. Some have shared bathrooms.

Fort Worden State Park   CAMPGROUND $
(☎360-344-4400; www.parks.wa.gov/fortworden; 200 Battery Way; campsites $34 plus one-off reservation fee $8) A variety of 80 RV hookup sites, many of them beachfront, plus a handful of hiker-cyclist sites ($14). Amenities include kitchen shelters, flush toilets and hot showers.

Old Consulate Inn B&B   B&B $$
(☎360-385-6753; www.oldconsulateinn.com; 313 Walker St; r $110-220; 🕾🖧) Another Queen Anne masterpiece, this former residence of the German consul is a splendid eight-room B&B adorned with the kind of authentic 19th-century decor that will leave you thinking you've wandered into the pages of a Henry James novel. The only trouble is that you'll want to linger here all day, sampling the breakfast, shooting balls in the pool room or relaxing in a hot tub set rather romantically in an outdoor gazebo.

Manresa Castle   HISTORIC HOTEL $$
(☎360-385-5750; www.manresacastle.com; cnr 7th & Sheridan Sts; d & ste $109-229; 🕾) One of Port Townsend's signature buildings has been turned into a historic hotel-restaurant that's light on fancy gimmicks but heavy on period authenticity. This 40-room mansion castle, built by the town's first mayor, sits high on a bluff above the port and is one of the first buildings to catch your eye as you arrive by ferry. The vintage rooms may be a little spartan for some visitors, but in a setting this grandiose it's the all-pervading sense of history that counts. The most expensive room is in a turret.

Swan Hotel   HOTEL $$
(☎360-385-6122; www.theswanhotel.com; cnr Monroe & Water Sts; r from $140; 🕾🖧) Stay in rooms in an eye-catching three-story mansion with impressive wraparound porches, or in three well-decked-out one-story cabins close to the waterfront action. There's even a penthouse suite.

✗ Eating

Belmont Restaurant & Saloon   SEAFOOD $
(925 Water St; mains $7-13) Dine on seafood in a lace-shaded booth or on a dais overlooking the water in a one-time dockside saloon that once heaved with crowds of brokers, hustlers and merchant seamen.

El Sarape
MEXICAN $

(628 Water St; mains $6-13; 🖉) Decked out in traditional red, white and green, El Sarape is proudly Mexican, with plenty of seafood and vegetarian options for those who just can't face another chicken burrito.

★ Sweet Laurette Cafe & Bistro
FRENCH $$

(1029 Lawrence St; mains $12-28; ⊘8am-5pm Wed & Thu, to 9pm Fri & Sat, to 3pm Sun; 🖉) This adorable French shabby-chic cafe serves breakfast, lunch and dinner in the bistro and delicious coffee and pastries between mealtimes. The food is made with sustainable and mostly local ingredients – try a breakfast *croque madame* with honey-baked ham and gruyere on French bread for breakfast, a pork-loin, caramelized-onion and blue-cheese sandwich for lunch or Cape Cleare king salmon for dinner. Seating is in the colorful heritage building or outdoors on wrought-iron tables in a herb-filled garden. Plenty of vegetarian options are available.

Silverwater Café
FUSION $$

(237 Taylor St; mains lunch $6-12, dinner $10-22; ⊘11:30am-10pm, to 11pm Sat & Sun) The Silverwater provides a romantic atmosphere in the not-too-fancy setting of a classic Port Townsend Victorian-era building. Renowned for its creatively prepared local dishes such as ahi tuna and artichoke parmesan paté, the restaurant also rustles up more homely desserts such as the not-to-be-missed blackberry pie.

Waterfront Pizza
PIZZERIA $$

(951 Water St; large pizzas $11-21) This buy-by-the-slice outlet inspires huge local loyalty and will satisfy even the most querulous of Chicago-honed palates. Is the secret in the crisp sourdough crusts or the creative but not overstacked toppings? Who knows? Just don't leave town without trying it.

🍷 Drinking & Nightlife

Sirens
BAR

(832 Water St; mains $6-8) A dimly lit, romantic, yet unpretentiously hip upstairs bar with a balcony overlooking the port. This is the perfect spot to have a burger and a beer and wait for your ship.

☆ Entertainment

Rose Theatre
CINEMA

(235 Taylor St) A Northwest diamond and an architectural emblem for the city, this gorgeously renovated movie theater lay woefully abandoned for 37 years before being brought back to life in the 1990s as an art cinema. If only there were more like it.

🛍 Shopping

Downtown Water St has all kinds of independent shops housed in handsome Victorian buildings. Look out for Native American crafts, art galleries, antiques, books, gifts, handmade jewelry and clothing and outdoor apparel.

April Fool & Penny Too
ANTIQUES

(725 Water St; ⊘11am-6pm) One of the best of Water St's bric-a-brac antiques, jewelry and gift shops. It's housed in a feel-good heritage house.

Quimper Sound & the Analog Lounge
MUSIC

(230 Taylor St; ⊘10am-5pm Mon-Thu, 10am-6pm Fri & Sat, 11am-5pm Sun) To continue the time-warp effect of Port Townsend, peruse this record store that's remained pretty much the same since it opened in 1974 – save the installation of its on-site cafe.

ℹ Information

Port Townsend Visitor Center (www.ptch-amber.org; 440 12th St; ⊘9am-5pm Mon-Fri, 10am-4pm Sat, 11am-4pm Sun) Pick up a useful walking-tour map and guide to the downtown historic district here.

ℹ Getting There & Around

BOAT

Washington State Ferries (📞206-464-6400; www.wsdot.wa.gov/ferries) operates up to 15 trips daily (depending on the season) to Coupeville on Whidbey Island from the terminal in downtown (car and driver/passenger $10.20/3.10, 35 minutes).

Puget Sound Express (www.pugetsound-express.com; 431 Water St) boats depart to San Juan Island at 9am between May and October (one way/round-trip adult $56/89, child $42/48, bicycles and kayaks round-trip $15, 2½ hours).

BUS

Jefferson Transit (www.jeffersontransit.com; 1615 W Sims Way) serves Port Townsend and outlying areas in Jefferson County. Buses travel as far west as Sequim, where connections can be made to Port Angeles and points west on Clallam County's intercity transit system. To the south you can connect with Mason County transit in Brinnon. The basic fare is $1.50.

To reach Port Townsend from Seattle on weekdays, take the ferry from downtown Seattle to Bainbridge Island (35 minutes). At the ferry dock catch Kitsap Transit bus 90 to Poulsbo (20 minutes), then transfer to the Jefferson Transit bus 7 to Port Townsend (one hour).

For a more direct journey, **Olympic Bus Lines** (www.olympicbuslines.com) offers connections to and from its Port Angeles–Seattle run, by reservation. Shuttles arrive and depart from the Haines Place Park and Ride on E Sims Way. Fares are $39/49 to downtown Seattle/Seattle-Tacoma International Airport.

Port Angeles

POP 18,397

Despite the name, there's nothing Spanish or particularly angelic about Port Angeles, propped up by the lumber industry and backed by the steep-sided Olympic Mountains. People come here to catch a ferry for Victoria, Canada, or base themselves here for excursions into the northern parts of Olympic National Park. The town itself is not a draw.

Named Puerto de Nuestra Señora de los Angeles by Spanish explorer Francisco Eliza in 1791 (the name was later anglicized), Port Angeles entered history in 1862 when president Abraham Lincoln created a navy and military reserve around the natural harbor and made it only the second planned city in the US (after Washington, DC). Though the fishing industry has declined in recent years, Port Angeles has added dynamism to its cultural life with a fine-arts center and numerous public sculptures.

Sights & Activities

Clallam County Museum　MUSEUM

(cnr 1st & Oak Sts; 8:30am-4pm Mon-Fri, closed holidays) FREE Housed in the 1927 Federal Building, the museum retells the story of the community's growth. Two-hour **Heritage Tours** (www.portangelesheritagetours.com; adult/child $12/6) run twice daily Monday to Saturday at 10am and 2.30pm (10.30am and 2pm in winter). The tours include the town's 'lost' underground, buried when the downtown area was raised in the early 1900s.

Port Angeles Fine Arts Center　GALLERY

(1203 E Lauridsen St; 11am-5pm Tue-Sun) FREE Here you'll find the work of many of the professional artists who live on the peninsula. The gallery is high above the city amid a 5-acre sculpture garden with views over the strait.

Olympic Discovery Trail　HIKING, CYCLING

(www.olympicdiscoverytrail.com) The trail is an ongoing project that ultimately aims to link Port Townsend and Forks by means of an off-road hiking-biking trail. Fifty-three miles of the trail is already complete between Port Angeles and Sequim, starting at the end of **Ediz Hook**, the sand spit that loops around the bay before cutting east along the waterfront. You can pick up the trail at the base of the City Pier, site of the **Feiro Marine Life Center** (adult/child $2.50/1; 10am-6pm Tue-Sun Jun-Sep, noon-4pm Sat & Sun Oct-May;), where hands-on touch tanks are inhabited by the aquatic denizens of the strait.

Bikes for the Olympic Discovery Trail can be rented at **Sound Bikes & Kayaks** (www.soundbikekayaks.com; 120 Front St; bike rental per hour/day $9/30).

🛏 Sleeping

Downtown Hotel　HOTEL $

(360-565-1125; www.portangelesdowntownhotel.com; 101 E Front St; d with shared/private bath $60/95;) Nothing special on the outside but surprisingly elegant within, this family-run place down by the ferry launch is Port Angeles' secret bargain. Bright rooms are decked out in wicker and wood, while showers and communal hallways are kept surgically clean. The Corner House diner downstairs is an ideal place for breakfast.

Toadlily House　HOSTEL $

(360-797-3797; www.toadlilyhouse.com; 105 E 5th St; per person $25;) New, bright and clean hostel in a lime green heritage home, with three bunk rooms, an upstairs room for groups of up to seven people and a private room off the back garden. The bathroom and kitchen are shared, the layout is perfect for socializing and the owner is young, hip and friendly.

Olympic Lodge　HOTEL $$

(360-452-2993; www.olympiclodge.com; 140 Del Guzzi Dr; r from $119;) There are plenty of reasons to make this your Olympic National Park HQ, including a swimming pool, an on-site bistro, so-clean-they-seem-new rooms and complimentary cookies and milk. It's the most comfortable place in town – no contest.

Port Angeles Inn　MOTEL $$

(360-452-9285; www.portangelesinn.com; 111 E 2nd St; r incl breakfast $99-130;) A better-than-average family-run motel perched on the bluff above downtown and enjoying views over the harbor.

George Washington Inn   B&B $$$
(939 Finn Hall Rd; ste from $175; 🖥) 🌱 This striking modern replica of US President George Washington's Mount Vernon home sits on a lavender farm on a cliff overlooking a sublime stretch of the Juan de Fuca Strait. If the grand, spotless suites with colonial furniture, ocean and mountain views, gracious service and plush bathrooms weren't enough, you can sleep even better knowing the place is powered geothermically. Find it on a quiet road between Port Angeles and Sequim.

✖ Eating

★ Bella Italia   ITALIAN $$
(118 E 1st St; mains $12-20; ⊙from 4pm) Bella Italia has been around a lot longer than Bella, the heroine of the *Twilight* saga, but its mention in the book as the place where Bella and Edward Cullen go for their first date has turned what was already a popular restaurant into an icon. In the book Bella has mushroom ravioli and a Coke (now one of the most ordered menu items), but more discerning gastronomes might want to opt for the clam linguine, chicken marsala or smoked duck breast washed down with an outstanding wine from a list featuring 500 selections.

Alder Wood Bistro   FUSION $$
(☑ 683-4321; 139 W Alder St, Sequim; pizzas $9-18, mains $17-24 ; ⊙4:30-9pm Tue-Sat) 🌱 Organic, local and sustainably produced ingredients are used to create unique woodfired pizzas (try the lamb sausage and pumpkin) and delectable mains such as plank-grilled fish or polenta lasagna – all to pair with Washington wines or craft beers. If it's warm enough, sit and enjoy the garden, where some of your food was probably grown. It's a small place, so reservations are recommended.

Wildfire Woodfire Grill   AMERICAN $$$
(929 W 8th St; mains $18-30; ⊙4:30-8:30pm Tue-Thu, to 9pm Fri & Sat) The heritage building is filled with eclectic bric-a-brac, art and plants, while the grill fires up tasty seafood, meat and veggies. Dine indoors or near the outdoor fire pit. Anything involving the local Dungeness crab comes particularly recommended.

❶ Information

Adjacent to the ferry terminal you'll find the **Port Angeles Visitor Center** (www.portangeles.org; 121 E Railroad Ave; ⊙8am-8pm mid-May–mid-Oct, 10am-4pm mid-Oct–mid-May). Olympic National Park visitor center is 1 mile south of town, off Race St.

❶ Getting There & Around

AIR
Kenmore Air (☑ 866-435-9524; www.kenmoreair.com) has direct flights daily from Seattle to Fairchild International Airport, just west of Port Angeles.

BOAT
Black Ball Transport's **MV Coho ferry** (www.cohoferry.com) provides passenger and automobile service to Victoria (adult/child/car and driver $11.50/5.75/44 one way, 1½ hours), with three crossings a day from May to September. There are two crossings a day the rest of the year, although service is briefly halted during January for maintenance. The passenger-only **Victoria Express** (☑ 360-452-8088) runs three or four times a day from late May through September (adult/child $12.50/7, one hour); there's a $2 fee to transport a bicycle.

BUS
Olympic Bus Lines (www.olympicbuslines.com) runs two buses a day to and from Sequim (adult/child $8/4, 30 minutes), the Seattle Greyhound terminal (adult/child $39/20, 2½ hours) and Sea-Tac Airport (adult/child $49/25, 3½ hours). Buses arrive and depart from the transit terminal at Front and Oak Sts.

Clallam County's **The Bus** (www.clallamtransit.com) travels as far west as Neah Bay and La Push and as far east as Diamond Point. In Port Angeles, the main transfer center is at Oak and Front Sts, conveniently near the ferry dock and visitors center.

Olympic National Park

Declared a national monument in 1909 and a national park in 1938, the 1406-sq-mile Olympic National Park shelters a unique rainforest, copious glaciated mountain peaks and a 57-mile strip of Pacific coastal wilderness that was added to the park in 1953. One of North America's great wilderness areas, most of the park remains relatively untouched by human habitation, with 1000-year-old cedar trees juxtaposed with pristine alpine meadows, clear glacial lakes and a largely roadless interior.

Opportunities for independent exploration in this huge backcountry region abound, be it hiking, fishing, kayaking or skiing. The park's distinct and highly biodiverse ecosystem is rich in plant and animal life, much of it – such as the majestic Roosevelt elk – indigenous to the region. Boasting numerous large, car-accessible campgrounds and around 100 backcountry campgrounds, the park offers easy and rewarding overnight excursions.

Eastern Entrances

The eastern entrances to the Olympic National Park are less developed than the northern and western entrances but are handy for visitors traveling over the Hood Canal from Seattle and the 'mainland.'

◉ Sights & Activities

Dosewallips River Valley WILDERNESS VALLEY

This narrow valley (pronounced doe-sey-wal-ups) is surrounded by some of the highest mountains in the Olympics, including Mt Anderson and Mt Deception. The gravel Dosewallips River Rd terminates at the ranger station 15 miles from US 101, where hiking trails begin.

Staircase HIKING

Staircase is another favorite entrance for hikers, and is popular with families, anglers and boaters bound for nearby Lake Cushman State Park. The **Staircase Ranger Station** (☑360-877-5569; ⊘May-Sep) is just inside the park boundary, 16 miles from US 101 and the small town of Hoodsport.

The trail system here follows the drainage of the North Fork Skokomish River, which is flanked by some of the most rugged peaks in the Olympics. The principal long-distance trail is the **North Fork Skokomish Trail**, which leads up this heavily forested valley, eventually crossing into the Duckabush River valley to intercept other transpark trail systems. Ambitious day-hikers might consider following this trail 3.7 miles to the **Flapjack Lakes Trail**, an easy 4-mile climb up to several small lakes that shimmer beneath the crags of the Sawtooth peaks.

A popular short hike follows the south bank of the North Fork Skokomish River through lush old-growth forest along the **Staircase Rapids Loop Trail**. Continue up the trail a short distance to the Rapids Bridge, which crosses over to the North Fork

Skokomish Trail and makes for a nice 2-mile loop.

🛏 Sleeping

Dosewallips State Park CAMPGROUND $

(☑888-226-7688; tent/RV sites $23/32) Near Brinnon along US 101 is this 425-acre, year-round campground situated in an expanse of meadow, close to the mouth of the Dosewallips River and facing Hood Canal. There are 70 tent spaces, 55 utility spaces, a dump space and two showers.

Skokomish Park at Lake Cushman CAMPGROUND $

(Camp Cushman; ☑360-877-6770; 7211 N Lake Cushman Rd; tent/RV sites $25/32) Eight miles northwest of Hoodsport, this campground is centered on a large reservoir on the Skokomish River, popular with anglers, water-skiers and campers. There are 50 tent sites and 30 RV sites open from early Memorial Day (late May) to Labor Day (early September).

Northern Entrances

The most popular access to Olympic National Park is from the north. Port Angeles is the park's urban hub, and other good access points are Hurricane Ridge, the Elwha Valley and Lake Crescent, the park's largest lake.

South of Port Angeles the Olympic Mountains rise up to Hurricane Ridge, one of the park's most accessible viewing points and an active ski station in the winter. Starting in Race St, the 18-mile Hurricane Ridge Rd climbs 5300ft toward extensive wildflower meadows and expansive mountain vistas often visible above the clouds.

◉ Sights & Activities

Hurricane Ridge is a good base for many activities including cross-country and downhill skiing, and snowboarding from mid-December to March, weekends only.

Hurricane Ridge is also the takeoff point for a number of short hikes leading through meadows to vista points. Hurricane Hill Trail, which begins at the end of the road leading up, and the Meadow Loop Trails network, starting at the visitor center, are popular, moderately easy hikes. The first half-mile of these trails is wheelchair accessible.

From Hurricane Ridge you can drive a rough, white-knuckle 8-mile road to Obstruction Peak, laid out by the Civilian Conservation Corps (CCC) in the 1930s.

OLYMPIC PENINSULA & WASHINGTON COAST OLYMPIC NATIONAL PARK

Here, hikers looking for long-distance treks can pick up either the Grand Ridge Trail, which leads 7.5 miles to Deer Park, much of the way above the timberline, or the Wolf Creek Trail, an 8-mile downhill jaunt to Whiskey Bend, where it picks up the Elwha Trail.

Lake Crescent
LAKE

If you're heading anticlockwise on the Olympic loop from Port Angeles toward Forks, one of the first scenic surprises to leap out at you will be luminous Lake Crescent, a popular boating and fishing area and a departure point for a number of short national-park hikes. The area is also the site of Lake Crescent Lodge, the oldest of the park's trio of celebrated lodges (the others are the Quinault and the Kalaloch) that first opened in 1916.

The best stop-off point is in a parking lot to the right of US 101 near the **Storm King Information Station** (☎ 360-928-3380; ☺ May-Sep). A number of short hikes leave from here, including the Marymere Falls trail, a 2-mile round trip to a 90ft cascade that drops over a basalt cliff. For a more energetic hike, climb up the side of Mt Storm King, the peak that rises to the east of Lake Crescent. The steep, 1.7-mile ascent splits off the Barnes Creek Trail.

Trout fishing is good here – the lake is deep with steep shorelines – though only artificial lures are allowed. Rowboat rentals ($9/25 per hour/half day) are available at Lake Crescent Lodge in the summer months.

Elwha River Valley
HIKING

The Elwha, the largest river on the Olympic Peninsula, and Lake Mills (actually a reservoir) are popular **trout fishing** havens. Elwha River Rd turns south from US 101 about 8 miles west of Port Angeles. Follow it for 10 miles to the **Elwha Ranger Station** (480 Upper Elwha Rd). The road immediately forks. Turn west to reach the Olympic Hot Springs trailhead, or turn east toward Whiskey Bend to reach the Elwha River and other trailheads.

Commercially developed as a resort in the 1930s, the Olympic Hot Springs once featured cabins that have long since disappeared. In 1983, park supervisors closed the road out, and the area has largely returned to nature. The 2.2-mile hike along the old roadbed is well worth it – what's left of the old pools steam alongside the rushing Boulder Creek, all in a verdant deep-forest grove.

From Whiskey Bend, the Elwha Trail leads up the main branch of the Elwha River and is one of the primary cross-park long-distance hikes. Day-hikers may elect to follow the trail for 2 miles to Humes Ranch, the remains of a homestead-era ranch.

Hurricane Ridge Ski & Snowboard Area
SKIING

(www.hurricaneridge.com; ♿) Has two rope tows and a lift, and is one of only three national-park ski areas in the US.

Sol Duc River Valley
HOT SPRINGS, HIKING

The 14-mile interior road that leads off US 101 into the heart of the national park along the headwaters of the Sol Duc River is worth a turn for some great day hikes, a dip in a natural spa and a vivid glimpse of the amazing Olympic rainforest. Note how the trees along the roadside become taller and more majestic almost immediately.

As Native American legend tells it, the geological phenomenon at Sol Duc is the legacy of a battle between two lightning fish. When neither fish won the contest, each crawled beneath the earth and shed bitter tears, forming the heated mineral springs here. These springs have been diverted into three large tiled pools for health and recreation at Sol Duc Hot Springs Resort. Entry costs $12.25/9.25 per adult/child. There's also a standard swimming pool to cool off in, as well as a restaurant, a snack bar, a gift shop and overnight accommodations.

Olympic National Park

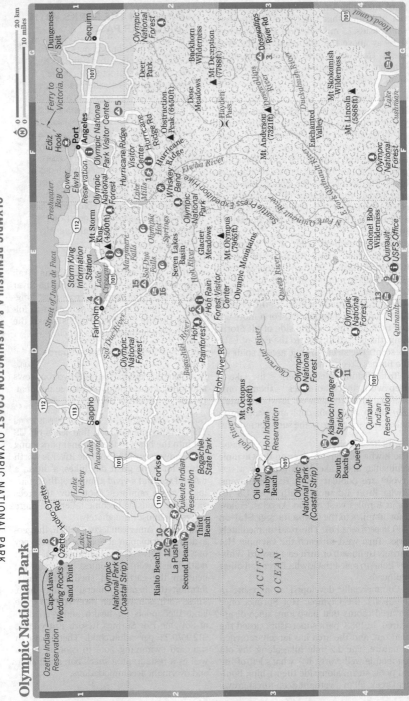

The road ends 1.5 miles past the resort, and this is where most of the trails start. The most popular hike is the 0.75-mile **Sol Duc Falls Trail**, where the river plummets 40ft into a narrow gorge. Other more strenuous hikes cross the bridge at the falls and climb the **Deer Lake Trail** along Canyon Creek. This sometimes steep, 8-mile round-trip trail reaches the tree-rimmed lake then joins the **High Divide Trail** before tracking back via the Seven Lakes Basin, a popular overnight destination. Another good leg-stretcher is the 2.5-mile **Mink Lake Trail**, departing from the resort. The marshy lake is noted for its bird-watching and wildlife-viewing.

🛏 Sleeping

Sol Duc Campground   CAMPGROUND **$**
(☑360-327-3534; campsites $14) This 80-site facility, with its tall fir and cedar trees and mossy undergrowth, offers a quintessential Olympic rainforest experience. It's also handy for both the local trails and the spa.

Fairholm Campground   CAMPGROUND **$**
(☑360-928-3380; campsites $12; ⊙year-round) The only national-park campground on Lake Crescent features 88 sites, a general store and boat rentals. It's at the lake's western end.

Heart o' the Hills
Campground   CAMPGROUND **$**
(☑360-452-2713; 876 Hurricane Ridge Rd; campsites $12) Five miles south of Port Angeles, this is the closest campground to Hurricane Ridge, with 105 sites.

Lake Crescent Lodge   LODGE **$$**
(☑360-928-3211; www.olympicnationalparks. com; 416 Lake Crescent Rd; lodge r $153, cottages $162-300; ⊙May-Oct; P❄🐾) This lodge is handsomely furnished in antiques and is surrounded by giant fir trees along the shores of Lake Crescent. There's a wide variety of lodging available, but the most popular (and the only ones open in winter) are the cozy, lakefront, kitchen-equipped Roosevelt fireplace cottages. Sumptuous Northwestern-style food is served in the lodge's ecofriendly restaurant.

Sol Duc Hot Springs Resort   RESORT **$$$**
(☑360-327-3583; www.northolympic.com/solduc; 12076 Sol Duc Hot Springs Rd, Port Angeles; RV sites $36, r $172-210; ⊙late Mar-Oct; ❄🐾) 🌿 While Sol Duc lacks the classic touches and style of the more luxurious and older park lodges, this well-known spa retreat packs a punch with its therapeutic waters and surrounding

forest. While it's self-contained – with mineral pools, a small store and a restaurant – there's still a tangible sense of being in a remote wilderness.

Thirty-two modern but basic cabins offer private bathrooms and, in some cases, a kitchenette. Aside from the steaming waters there's also a massage service available. Day-hikers and visitors are welcome at the Spring Restaurant or poolside deli. There are 17 RV sites for hire but no tent sites.

ℹ Information

Hurricane Ridge Visitor Center (⊙9:30am-5pm daily summer, Fri-Sun winter) Has a snack bar, gift shop, toilets, and ski and snowshoe rentals but no overnight accommodation or camping. The weather here can be fickle. Call ☑360-565-3131 for the latest conditions.

Western Entrances

The Pacific side of the Olympics is the most remote part of the park and home to the foggy, moss-draped temperate rainforests. It is also the wettest area, receiving 12ft of rain annually, and you can expect a soaking at any time.

US 101 is the only road that accesses this vast, heavily wooded area. Paved roads penetrate the interior at the Hoh Rain Forest and Lake Quinault but are sometimes washed out.

◉ Sights & Activities

Lake Quinault
LAKE

The enchanting Quinault River Valley is one of the park's least crowded corners. Clustered around the deep-blue glacial waters of Lake Quinault lie forested peaks, a historic lodge and some of the oldest (and tallest) Sitka spruce, Douglas fir and western red cedar trees in the world.

The lake itself offers plenty of activities such as fishing, boating and swimming, while upstream both the north and south branches of the Quinault River harbor a couple of important transpark trails.

The lake may be accessed from the north and the south. The south shore hosts the tiny village of Quinault, complete with the luscious Lake Quinault Lodge, a USFS office (☑360-288-2525; 353 S Shore Rd), restaurant, couple of stores, post office (S Shore Rd) and gas station. The North Shore Rd passes the Quinault Ranger Station (☑360-288-2444; ☺8:30am-4:30pm) before climbing up to the North Fork Quinault trailhead.

Lake Quinault is part of the Quinault Indian Reservation, and fishing is regulated by the tribe; check locally for tribal licenses and regulations. Boat rentals are available from Lake Quinault Lodge.

A number of short hiking trails begin just below Lake Quinault Lodge; pick up a free map from the USFS office. The shortest of these is the Quinault Rain Forest Nature Trail, a half-mile walk through 500-year-old Douglas firs. This short trail adjoins the 3-mile Quinault Loop Trail, which meanders through the rainforest before circling back to the lake. The Quinault region is renowned for its huge trees. Close to the village is a 191ft Sitka spruce tree (purported to be up to 1000 years old), and nearby are the world's largest red cedar, Douglas fir and mountain hemlock trees.

Beyond the lake, both N Shore Rd and S Shore Rd continue up the Quinault River Valley before merging at a bridge just past Bunch Falls. From here, more adventurous hikers can sally forth into backcountry. The area's sparkling highlight is the photogenic Enchanted Valley Trail, which climbs up to a large meadow (a former glacial lake bed) traversed by streams and springs, and resplendent with wildflowers and thickets of alders. To the north rise sheer cliff faces and peaks craning 2000ft from the valley floor; during spring snowmelt, the 3-mile precipice is drizzled by thousands of small waterfalls.

To hike the Enchanted Valley Trail, start at the Graves Creek Ranger Station at the end of S Shore Rd; note the hike is 13 miles each way. Long-distance hikers can continue from this trail up to Anderson Pass (19 miles from Graves Creek) and link up with the West Fork Dosewallips Trail to complete a popular transpark trek.

The classic Seattle Press Expedition hike passes through the North Fork Quinault River valley to join the lengthy Elwha River trail system further north.

★Hoh Rain Forest
HIKING

The most famous section of the Olympic rainforest, the Hoh River area offers a variety of hikes and an interpretive center. If you have room for only one stop on the western side, this should be it. The paved Upper Hoh Rd winds 19 miles from US 101 to the visitor center, passing a giant Sitka spruce tree along the way. This lord of the forest is 270ft high and over 500 years old.

At the end of Hoh River Rd, the Hoh Rain Forest Visitor Center (☑360-374-6925; campsites $12; ☺9am-6pm Jul & Aug, to 4:30pm Sep-Jun) offers displays on the ecology of the rainforest and the plants and animals that inhabit it, as well as a bookstore. Rangers lead free guided walks twice a day during summer.

Leading out from the visitor center are several excellent day hikes into virgin rainforest. The most popular is the Hall of Moss Trail, an easy 0.75-mile loop through the kind of weird, ethereal scenery that even Tolkien couldn't have invented. Epiphytic club moss, ferns and lichens completely overwhelm the massive trunks of maples and Sitka spruces. The 1.25-mile Spruce Nature Trail is another short interpretive loop leading out from the visitor center. There is also a short wheelchair-accessible nature trail through a rainforest marsh.

The Hoh River Trail is the major entry trail into the wide, glacier-carved Hoh River Valley. It is also the principal access route to Mt Olympus. The trail follows an easy grade for 12 miles, and day-hikers can use it as a pleasant out-and-back excursion.

Queets River Valley
HIKING

The Queets Corridor was added to the park in 1953 in an attempt to preserve one of the peninsula's river valleys all the way from its

BACKCOUNTRY HIKES IN OLYMPIC NATIONAL PARK

Many skirt the park's well-trampled edges on easily accessible 'touch the wilderness' hikes. Far fewer plunge into the Olympic's mossy, foggy, roadless interior. Here are a few ways in.

Seattle Press Expedition Hike

One of the most popular cross-park treks follows the pioneering route taken by James H Christie, a former Arctic explorer who answered the call of the *Seattle Press* newspaper in 1889 to 'acquire fame by unveiling the mystery which wraps the land encircled by the snow-capped Olympic range.' Starting at the Whiskey Bend trailhead on the Elwha River, the route tracks south and then southwest through the Elwha and Quinault River valleys to Lake Quinault, covering 44 moderately strenuous miles. Called the Seattle Press Expedition Hike, it commonly takes walkers five days to complete.

Pacific Coastal Hikes

There are two long-distance beach hikes along Washington's isolated coast. The most northerly is the 32.7-mile stretch between the Makah Shi Shi trailhead near Cape Flattery and Rialto Beach near La Push (a shorter 20.2-mile version runs from Ozette to Rialto Beach), which commonly makes up a moderate five-day, four-night trek. This hike stays faithfully close to the shoreline, meaning that a good understanding of tidal charts is imperative. There are 14 campgrounds en route, eight of which take reservations.

The more southerly hike runs from Third Beach just south of La Push to the Oil City trailhead at the mouth of the Hoh River. This 17.5-mile route is more precipitous and tougher than the northern route, with the trail ascending and descending over numerous headlands. As a consequence, fewer people do it. All seven campsites on this segment are first come, first served.

If you are contemplating a trek along the coast, request information from the **National Park Service** (www.nps.gov/olym), buy good maps, learn how to read tide tables and be prepared for bad weather year-round.

The Scenic Bits

Though the Seattle Press Expedition hike is the Olympics' best-known trek, it isn't necessarily the park's most scenic. Purists rave about the **Enchanted Valley**, which you can reach by trekking 13 miles beyond the Graves Creek trailhead northeast of Lake Quinault. After the late-June snowmelt it is possible to lengthen this hike by continuing over 4464ft Anderson Pass and descending to the Dosewallips Trailhead on the park's eastern side. Another favorite is a circular hike from the Deer Park trailhead southeast of Port Angeles. After a 4.3-mile walk out to the Three Forks backcountry campground you can trek up over **Cameron Pass** and **Gray Wolf Pass** for fantastic views of McCartney Peak (6728ft) and Mt Deception (7788ft).

For all of the above, hikers should first take stock of local weather conditions (June to September is the recommended walking window), wise up on wilderness rules and regulations, and pack all necessary camping equipment and supplies. Hikers will also need to acquire a wilderness camping permit ($5 per group plus an additional $2 per person) from the **Wilderness Information Center** (3002 Mt Angeles Rd, Port Angeles; ⊙7:30am-6pm Sun-Thu, to 8pm Fri & Sat May-Sep, 8am-4:30pm daily Oct-Apr), behind the Olympic National Park Visitor Center (p138), before commencing. For more information on this and other backcountry hikes, check out the national-park website: www.nps.gov/olym.

glacial beginnings to the coast. It is one of the park's least accessible areas.

The unpaved Queets River Rd leaves US 101 and almost immediately drops into the national park. The road then follows the river for 13 miles before ending at **Queets Ranger Station** (☑360-962-2283). From here, there is one popular day hike – the gentle 3-mile **Queets Campground Loop Trail**.

Experienced or adventurous hikers can elect to ford the Queets River in late summer or fall and explore the **Queets Trail**, which leads up the river for 15 miles before petering out in heavy old-growth rainforest.

🛏 Sleeping

Several holiday lodges can be found on the shores of Lake Quinault that cater to hikers, fishers and families.

Quinault River Inn   INN $
(☎360-288-2237; www.quinaultriverinn.com; 8 River Dr; r $79-119; ❋ 🏠) A sort of motel meets mountain lodge, the River Inn is handily positioned on US 101 next to the eating and gas facilities at Amanda Park. Its position on the Quinault River makes it popular with crack-of-dawn-waking fishers. Rooms are warm and well maintained, with decent-size beds and copious TV channels. Bonuses include a small gym, attractive cedar decor and extra-friendly service.

There are also some RV sites ($27).

Queets Campground   CAMPGROUND $
(☎360-962-2283; campsites $10) Located at the end of Queets River Rd (not recommended for RVs), this small campground with 20 primitive sites is tucked amid temperate rainforest.

Hoh Campground   CAMPGROUND $
(☎360-374-6925; campsites $12) Adjacent to the Hoh Rain Forest Visitor Center, the campground features 88 sites, most alongside the Hoh River.

★**Lake Quinault Lodge**   HISTORIC HOTEL $$$
(☎360-288-2900; www.olympicnationalparks.com; 345 S Shore Rd; r $202-305; ❋ 🏠 ⚊) Everything you could want in a historic national park lodge and more, the suspended-in-time 'Quinault' has a massive fireplace, peek-a-boo lake views, a manicured cricket-pitch-quality lawn, huge, comfy leather sofas, a regal reception area and a dignified lake-view (in daylight hours at least) restaurant serving upscale American cuisine. Trails into primeval forest leave from just outside the door.

In all it's a more posh and cozy version of the holiday lodge featured in *Dirty Dancing*. Built in 1926, the Quinault's warmth and character are no secret and reservations are recommended. Rates drop by about 40% in low season.

ⓘ Information

Olympic National Park Visitor Center (3002 Mt Angeles Rd, Port Angeles; ⊙9am-5pm) is about a mile south of Port Angeles and is the park's most comprehensive information center. Aside from giving out excellent free maps and leaflets, the center offers children's exhibits, a bookstore, a replica of a prehistoric Makah seal-hunting canoe and a 25-minute film. Pick up a (free) detailed park map along with an even more detailed 'Wilderness Trip Planner' with back-country trails and campgrounds marked.

USFS headquarters (www.fs.fed.us/r6/olympic; 1835 Black Lake Blvd SW; ⊙8am-4:30pm Mon-Fri) is outside Olympia and is the information font for everything on the Olympic National Forest, a 630,000-acre area that borders much of the park's perimeter. Alternatively, you can try the field offices in Hoodsport, Quilcene, Quinault and Forks. These offices distribute free back-country permits for wilderness camping in the park as well as Northwest Forest Passes ($5), required for parking at trailheads in the forest.

Park admission fees are $15 per vehicle and $5 per pedestrian/cyclist, and are valid for seven days for park entry and re-entry. An annual 'passport' for one year's unlimited entry costs $30. Fees are collected year-round at the Hoh and Heart o' the Hills entry points, and from May to October at Elwha, Sol Duc and Staircase entrances. (Payment is not mandatory where

---

CLIMBING MT OLYMPUS

Mt Olympus (7965ft) is the Olympic National Park's highest and most commonly climbed peak, though, due to extensive glaciers and fickle weather, ascents should not be undertaken lightly. There are injuries and deaths every year, usually due to falls into glacial crevasses or exposure during storms.

Access is via the Hoh Trail, which extends for 17 miles from the Hoh Rain Forest Visitor Center to Glacier Meadows. The campground here is frequently used as a base camp for ascents of the mountain. Much of the remaining climb is on glaciers and along craggy escarpments. Most people make the ascent between June and early September, although some begin as early as April. Guided climbs are available through various agencies. Try **Mountain Madness** (☎206-937-8389; www.mountainmadness.com), which is based out of Seattle and offers guided five-day summit attempts starting from $1050.

there is no entrance station or when an entrance station isn't open.)

Backpackers must register for overnight stays in backcountry areas. There's a $5 permit fee for groups of up to 12, valid for two weeks from purchase, plus a $2-per-person nightly fee for anyone over 16 years old. You can get permits from the Wilderness Information Center (p137), behind the visitor center. You can also get them from the Hoh visitor center or from ranger stations throughout the park.

Northwestern Olympic Peninsula

Despite not falling within the boundaries of the Olympic National Park, the northwest section of the Olympic Peninsula remains sparsely populated and remote. Logging is a primary industry here and, in the cultural sphere, four different Native American reservations offer plenty of local legends and history.

Forks is the area's only major settlement, though the fishing town of Neah Bay is reachable by public bus and boasts one of the finest museums of Native American history in the US. The beautiful coastline around La Push in the west provides another worthwhile diversion.

Neah Bay

POP 794

Isolated Neah Bay is a rather lackluster settlement that sits amid breathtaking coastal scenery at the end of Hwy 112 in North America's extreme northwestern corner. Hit hard by the decline in the salmon-fishing industry, this small town, characterized by its weather-beaten boats and craning totem poles, is the home of the Makah Indian Reservation.

◉ Sights & Activities

★**Cape Flattery**   VIEWPOINT
The dramatic promontory known as Cape Flattery is the most northwesterly point in the lower 48 states. From the four observation points atop the wild, wind-buffeted cape, cliffs fall 60ft to the raging Pacific and small forested islets jut out of the kelp-strewn blue waters. It's spectacular.

Just offshore is Tatoosh Island, with a lighthouse and Coast Guard station. The cape is frequented by 250 species of bird and is a good place to watch for whales during migration season. Users of the trail are

required to purchase a permit ($10) issued by the Makah Cultural Center (inside the Makah Museum) or at the marina.

From where the road turns left at the end of Neah Bay town, drive 7 miles till you reach a parking lot. From here a 0.5-mile boardwalk leads out to the promontory.

★**Makah Museum**   MUSEUM
(www.makah.com; 1880 Bayview Ave; admission $5; ⊙10am-5pm) Hosted by the Makah Reservation, this museum displays artifacts from one of North America's most significant archaeological finds and is reason enough to visit the town. Exposed by tidal erosion in 1970, the 500-year-old Makah village of Ozette proved to be a treasure trove of Native American history, containing whaling weapons, canoes, spears and combs. The museum's centerpiece is a mock-up of an old Ozette longhouse. Ask about the whale skeleton for a great story about the community.

⨳ Sleeping & Eating

Cape Motel   CABIN $
(☎360 645 2250; Neah Bay; r $45-75; ❄❆) Like most accommodations in Neah Bay, this place with simple new cabins (built in 2012) doesn't aspire to much beyond the regular fishing crowd, but having reached the end of the road in mainland America, what more could you want than four walls, a roof and a small kitchenette? There's also an RV park and tent spaces are available.

Warm House Restaurant   AMERICAN $$
(1471 Bayview Ave; mains from $10; ⊙breakfast, lunch & dinner) Enjoy simply cooked American fare like burgers or grilled fish surrounded by windows overlooking Neah Bay. There's a fireplace roaring in winter to help the place live up to its name.

Ozette

Former home of the Makah tribe, whose ancient cliffside village was destroyed in a mudslide in the early 18th century before being unearthed in the 1970s, Ozette is more than just a well-excavated archaeological pit. It is also one of the most accessible slices of isolated beach on the Olympic coastal strip.

The Hoko–Ozette road leaves Hwy 112 about 3 miles west of Sekiu and proceeds 21 miles to **Lake Ozette Ranger Station** (⊙8am-4:30pm), on Lake Ozette. There is no village here but, from the ranger station, two boardwalk trails lead out to one of two beaches at Cape Alava and Sand Point.

The 3.3-mile **Cape Alava Trail** leads north to the westernmost point of land in the continental US and is the site of the ancient Makah village, where archaeologists unearthed 55,000 artifacts, many of which are on display at the Makah Museum (p139) in Neah Bay. The southern **Sand Point Trail** from Lake Ozette Ranger Station leads 3 miles to beaches below a low bluff; whale watchers often come here in the migration season.

The two shorter Ozette trails can easily be linked as a long day hike by walking the 3 miles between Cape Alava and Sand Point along the beach (beware of the tides) or overland (although the trail is brushy and primitive).

The high point of this hike is the **Wedding Rocks**, the most significant group of petroglyphs on the Olympic Peninsula. Approximately a mile south of Cape Alava, the small outcropping contains carvings of whales, a European square-rigger and fertility figures. The site was traditionally used for Makah weddings and is still considered sacred.

The really hardcore can hike the 20 miles from Ozette to Rialto Beach near La Push. Note that this last hike is dependent on the tides and hikers often have to retreat into the wilderness, where there's no trail. All hikes require the $15 Olympic National Park fee. **Lake Ozette Campground** (☑360-963-2725; campsites $12) The 15 sites fill every day before noon at the small camp on Lake Ozette, a popular playground for boats and kayaks.

Forks

Forks, a small lumber town on US 101, was little more than a speck on the Washington state map when Stephenie Meyer set her now famous vampire novel *Twilight* here in 2003. Meyer had never been to Forks when she created the ghoulish legacy with the first of what has become a series of insanely popular 'tweenage' books. Since this time, Forks has seen an outlandish rise in tourism, the bulk of the visitors being vampire fans who are more than a little surprised to find Forks for what it really is – chillingly ordinary (and wet).

For those who haven't got a clue about *Twilight* (where have you been for the last 10 years?), Forks is actually a terrific spot to base yourself for forays into some of the highlights of the Olympic National Park: the Hoh Rainforest and the dramatic coastline around La Push.

◉ Sights & Activities

Aside from the *Twilight* kitsch, Forks is pretty sleepy.

Timber Museum   MUSEUM
(US 101; admission $3; ◷10am-4pm mid-Apr–Oct) Next door to the chamber of commerce, the Timber Museum commemorates the early settlers and loggers of the region. Included in the museum's collection is a steam donkey (used to transport logs), pioneer farming implements and a fire lookout tower.

Fishing Tours

You can organize fishing trips for steelhead and coho salmon from $275/330 for one/two people per day on the local rivers at the **Three Rivers Resort** (☑360-374-5300; 7764 La Push Rd), 8 miles west of Forks on Hwy 110. The lodge also rents surf and boogie boards for Pacific Coast adventurers.

⌂ Sleeping

There are plenty of motels along the main drag that are all quite similar in price and quality.

Bogachiel State Park   CAMPGROUND $
(☑360-374-6356; Hwy 101; tent/RV sites $17/24) The most convenient campground is 6 miles south of Forks, right on the Bogachiel River, with 37 sites, piped water and flush toilets.

Miller Tree Inn   B&B $$
(☑360-374-6806; www.millertreeinn.com; 654 E Division St; r $115-230; ☎❀) A note on the door from the Cullens (a fictional family in the *Twilight* books) tells you that they're away on vacation but the innkeepers will take care of you. While this 1916 farmhouse in a bucolic residential area has little in common with the deep-forest modern home of the vampire family in the films, it is still a lovely place to stay. Decor is country-cute and your hosts small-town friendly. Warm up your nights in the hot tub.

Huckleberry Lodge   CABIN $$
(☑360-374-4090; www.huckleberryforks.com; 1171 Big Pine Way; cabins $70-112; ☎) Tucked into the woods a few minutes off Hwy 101, this place feels miles away but is conveniently located very near the services of Forks. New-feeling cabins with sturdy wooden furniture

and country quilts have a range of kitchen facilities, and the biggest sleeps up to eight people. Note that the smallest cabin has an outdoor bathroom. There's a hot tub, a sauna and a fish-cleaning station too.

 Eating

In Place DINER $$

(320 S Forks Ave; sandwiches $5-8, mains around $16) Forks is no culinary Rome, meaning you'll probably have to settle for this mediocre but friendly home-style-cooking place on Hwy 101 opposite the Forks Motel. Burgers, serve-yourself salads and soups are offered in well-worn booths. Save the best till last – a slice of bumbleberry pie.

ⓘ Information

Get orientated with the extremely helpful and happy folks at the **Forks Chamber of Commerce** (www.forkswa.com), which shares digs with the Olympic National Park and the **USFS Recreation Information Station** (551 S Forks Ave) along the southern approach to Forks. The rec station is staffed by knowledgeable rangers, and is the place to get backcountry permits, maps, tide charts and animal-resistant containers for coastal camping.

ⓘ Getting There & Away

Clallam Transit (www.clallamtransit.com) offers three daily buses between Forks and Neah Bay (1¼ hours), and three between Forks and La Push (55 minutes). The Forks–Port Angeles bus (number 14) runs eight times daily (four on Saturday) and takes one hour and 20 minutes. Buses south from Forks to Lake Quinault (1½ hours) are operated by **Jefferson Transit** (www.jeffersontransit.com) and run three to four times daily. Note: no buses operate on Sunday.

La Push

La Push, 12 miles west of Forks on Hwy 110, is a small fishing village at the mouth of the Quillayute River and home of the Quileute Indian tribe, some of the peninsula's oldest inhabitants and the modern-day inspiration for the werewolves in the *Twilight* series.

Known for its raw, untamed beaches, La Push is popular with surfers and sea kayakers, who love to ride the dramatic Pacific waves, especially in January. Outside of this, the settlement is revered primarily for its remoteness and isolation (despite a recent influx of *Twilight* hunters). Tracking north along the Mora road will bring you to Rialto Beach and the start of a 20-mile coastal

hike north to Cape Alava. Just outside of La Push are the trailheads to rugged and beautiful Third and Second Beaches (1.4 miles and 0.8 miles, respectively). Third Beach is the starting point for a popular three-day beach hike to Oil City, 17 miles south, at the edge of the Hoh Indian Reservation.

🛏 Sleeping & Eating

Quileute Oceanside Resort RESORT $$

(⌨ 360-374-5267; www.quileuteoceanside.com; 330 Ocean Dr; tent/RV sites $15/25, motel r $63-105, cabins $85-280) Sitting above one of Washington's most beautiful beaches, the tribe-owned-and-operated resort has accommodations ranging from basic A-frame cabins with sleeping-bag loft and toilet (no shower) to deluxe oceanfront cottages with stone fireplaces and whirlpool tubs. Somewhere in the middle are newly remodeled motel rooms in two buildings with balconies and kitchenettes. No reservations are accepted for camping or RVs.

River's Edge Restaurant SEAFOOD $$

(⌨ 360-374-5777; 41 Main St; mains $8-25) One of the few restaurants on this stretch of coast. Stick to the freshly caught seafood options and look out for outdoor barbecues in the summer, when salmon is baked in the Quileute tradition. Located in an old boathouse, the restaurant is famous for its free ornithological shows, courtesy of the resident eagles and pelicans.

Ruby Beach to South Beach

This southernmost portion of the Olympic coastal strip, between the Hoh and Quinault Indian Reservations, is abutted by US 101, making it more accessible than the beaches further north. Your first stop here should be Ruby Beach, arguably the most scenic beach on the whole peninsula, where a short 0.2-mile path leads down to a large expanse of windswept sand embellished by polished black stones and wantonly strewn tree trunks. Heading south toward Kalaloch (*klay*-lock), other accessible beachfronts are unimaginatively named Beach Four through to Beach Six (Beaches One through Three are accessed from the road to La Push), all of which are popular with beachcombers. At low tide, rangers give talks on tidal-pool life at Beach Four and on the ecosystems of the Olympic coastal strip.

📖 Sleeping

Between May and September, advance reservations are required to stay at the designated campsites along the beach at Cape Alava and Sand Point. To make a reservation contact the Wilderness Information Center (p137) or reserve online. In addition, campers must obtain a wilderness permit.

Mora Campground   CAMPGROUND $
(📞 360-374-5460; campsites $12) Along the Quillayute River, 2 miles east of Rialto Beach, Mora offers 95 regular sites. Guided nature walks take off from here in the summer.

Kalaloch Lodge   HISTORIC HOTEL $$$
(📞 360-962-2271; www.thekalalochlodge.com; 157151 US 101; r incl breakfast $155-400; 🅿🅿🅿) 🍴 A little less grand than the Lake Quinault and Lake Crescent lodges, the Kalaloch (built in 1953) nonetheless enjoys an equally spectacular setting perched on a bluff overlooking the crashing Pacific. In addition to rooms in the old lodge, there are log cabins and motel-style units, and a family-friendly restaurant and store that offer incomparable ocean views. Trails lead down to the nearby beaches.

ℹ️ Information

For information about this area, contact the **Kalaloch Ranger Station** (📞 360-962-2283; ⏰ 9am-5pm May-Oct).

WASHINGTON COAST

The stretch of Washington coast from Ocean Shores down to Cape Disappointment at the mouth of the Columbia River, with its expansive beaches and locally run oyster farms, is the state's maritime playground. Free of the wild coves and stormy sea stacks common further north, this is where the whole of Washington (and beyond) comes to sail, fish, fly kites and hang out. It gets quieter just north of here heading up towards Moclips, where Hwy 109 hugs the evergreen-thick coast and small sandy beaches hide between rocky coves.

Though pockets of modern commercialism may have diluted the quaintness of places such as Long Beach and Ocean Shores, there are still enough state parks, wildlife refuges and lonesome stretches of

---

THE TWILIGHT ZONE

It would have been impossible to envisage back in the early 2000s: Forks, a depressed lumber town full of hard-nosed loggers, reborn as a pilgrimage site for girls following two fictional sweethearts named Bella and Edward. The reason for this weird metamorphosis is the *Twilight* saga, a four-part book series by US author Stephenie Meyer about love and vampires on the foggy Olympic Peninsula that in several short years has shifted well over 100 million books and spawned five Hollywood movies. With Forks acting as the book's main setting, the town has been catapulted to international stardom – now Bud-slugging lumberjacks in dive bars are juxtaposed with romance-hungry 15-year-olds shopping for kitschy vampire paraphernalia (of which there is plenty). Economic reasons have so far ensured that relations between the two camps have remained cordial. Forks' tourist numbers have reached the stratosphere since the 2008 release of the first *Twilight* movie, and the financial rewards in this isolated, boom-bust town have been felt by everyone.

Not much was actually filmed in Forks. Many film locations were in Oregon, including some Forks High School scenes, which were shot in Portland. You'll have better luck in nearby Port Angeles, where key scenes were shot (check out www.portangelesdowntown.com for specifics).

Dazzled by Twilight (www.dazzledbytwilight.com; 11 N Forks Ave; ⏰ 10am-6pm; 🚗) runs two *Twilight* merchandise shops in Forks (and another in Port Angeles) as well as the Forks **Twilight Lounge** (81 N Forks Ave). The lounge hosts a downstairs restaurant along with an upstairs music venue that showcases regular live bands and a blood-curdling 5pm to 8pm Saturday-night tween karaoke. The company also runs four daily **Twilight Tours** (adult/child $39/25; ⏰ tours 8am, 11:30am, 3pm & 6pm) visiting most of the places mentioned in Meyer's books.

In La Push itself, *Twilight* boat tours operated by the **Quileute Nation** (www.quileute-nation.org) sail out to Bella and Jacob's cliff (from which Bella jumps in *New Moon*). You'll probably see plenty of seabirds but no Taylor Lautner.

sand to hide an abundance of unheralded local secrets.

Further east the I-5 corridor cuts from Olympia down to Portland, whizzing past Centralia, Castle Rock (with access to Mt St Helens) and the US (and first) incarnation of Vancouver.

Moclips to Copalis Beach

This coastal strip south of the Quinault Indian Reservation is wild and forested, cut only by the small towns of Moclips, Pacific Beach, Seabrook and Copalis. Of these, surreal Seabrook, established in 2004 as a planned vacation hamlet, is the most noteworthy for its strangely endearing faux-Victorian homes and perfectly manicured community areas – it feels like something out of *The Stepford Wives* or *The Truman Show*. The surrounding area is perfect for explorations into Olympic National Park and enjoying the beautiful hidden beaches

Most of the over 200 single-family homes (and counting – the town was only two-thirds finished in 2013) are holiday rentals. There's a huge variety, from small, romantic cottages to huge party pads that can accommodate 22 people. Guests can enjoy the Seabrook community's swimming pool, shops, restaurants, spa and even a pottery studio. See Seabrook Cottage Rentals (☑360-276-0265; www.seabrookcottagerentals.com; Seabrook; houses $99-710; 🎧 ⛱ 🛏 🐾).

Grays Harbor Area

Once home to the Chehalis tribe, Grays Harbor was first charted by non-native explorers in 1792 when American Robert Gray arrived in the bay, which acts as an estuary for the Chehalis River. Farming, fishing and fur trading were the staple of the settlers in the 1840s and '50s, though this was quickly replaced by lumber in the 1880s. With most of the mills now closed, Grays Harbor has become a sleepy backwater, although the area is doing its best to lure in tourism with a variety of charter-fishing and beachcombing activities.

❶ Getting There & Away

BOAT

A passenger ferry crosses from Westport to Ocean Shores six times daily mid-June to Labor Day, and on weekends only May to mid-June and September ($6/10 one way/round-trip). Purchase tickets at Float 10. Call **Westport/Ocean Shores Ferry** (☑360-268-0047) for information.

BUS

Grays Harbor Transit (www.ghtransit.com) runs weekday buses from Aberdeen to Olympia (two hours, six daily), Lake Quinault (one hour, four daily), Ocean Shores (1½ hours, 10 daily), Westport (30 minutes, seven daily) and Centralia Amtrak station (1½ hours, one daily). There are connections to the Long Beach Peninsula with **Pacific Transit System** (www.pacifictransit.org). The downtown Aberdeen bus station is on Wishkah and G Sts, in Hoquiam at 7th and J Sts.

Ocean Shores

Washington state's most popular coastal resort is a manufactured beach haven known as Ocean Shores that was constructed in the 1960s on a scenic stretch of shoreline. While the settlement boasts its fair share of clichéd resort activities, including golf, dune-buggy riding and gambling at the Quinault Beach Resort and Casino, the area is far from spoiled, with kite flying, canoeing (there are over 20 miles of interconnecting canals) and razor clamming (digging in the sand for razor clams) also enduringly popular.

◎ Sights & Activities

You can rent boats to ply the region's ubiquitous canals at **Ocean Shores Electric Boat Company** (☑360-289-0487; www.oselectricboat.com; 952 Point Brown Ave SE). Beach horseback riding can be arranged through **Nan-Sea Stables** (☑360-289-0194; 255 SR 115). If the weather turns ugly (and it often does), check out the local history, wildlife and geology at **Ocean Shores Interpretive Center** (1013 Catala Ave SE; ◷10am-4pm Apr-Sep) FREE.

🍽 Sleeping & Eating

Ocean Shores is chock-full of soulless chain hotels and cheaper motels off the beach.

Collins Inn & Seaside Resort INN $$ (☑360-591-1130; www.collinsinn.com; 318 Marine View Dr SE; r $150-195, cottages $195-250; 🎧 🛏) Classy yet cozy, right on the beach and with friendly owners who go out of their way to ensure all their guests' needs are met: it's hard to do better than this in Seaside. Rooms in the inn are for adults only, but the family-friendly cottages sleep up to six people.

Nellie's Kitchen in the Elk Head Tap Room
PUB $

(No 5, 739 Point Brown Ave NW; mains from $8; ⊘ 3-7pm Thu, noon-7pm Fri & Sat, noon-4pm Sun) Small and rustic, with bar seating. Order one of Elk Head's excellent beers on tap, some hot nuts, and a meal (the menu changes regularly) crafted from locally sourced meats and more. You'll get to know a few locals and maybe enjoy a football game while you're at it. Under 21s not allowed.

ⓘ Information

Ocean Shores Chamber of Commerce (www.oceanshores.org; Catala Mall, 899 Point Brown Ave)

Aberdeen & Hoquiam

The tourist blurb likes to talk them up but, in reality, Olympic twins Aberdeen and Hoquiam comprise one pretty gritty city. Nonetheless, there's a rousing history hidden behind the boarded-up shops and general air of decay. Much of it can be told through the life stories of the famous locals. Despite (or perhaps *because of*) the apparent decrepitude, the cities have churned out enough noted citizens to fill a Hollywood Blvd–style Walk of Fame. Kurt Cobain of Nirvana was born in Aberdeen, Denver Broncos quarterback John Elway spent his childhood in Hoquiam, and aviation pioneer William Boeing made his first inroad into big business by buying up extensive tracts of timberland around Grays Harbor.

Aberdeen developed around a salmon-packing plant in the 1870s and Hoquiam's first lumber mill opened in 1882. By 1910 there were over 30 lumber mills ringing the harbor and the burgeoning twin towns had earned a reputation as the roughest places in the nation, replete with whorehouses, gambling dens and a sky-high murder rate. Following the Great Depression, when the lumber mills were reduced to less than a dozen, Grays Harbor hit a long decline, exacerbated by an equally catastrophic fall in Pacific salmon stocks. When a planned nuclear facility went bust in 1982 the unemployment rate doubled, and the gritty rough-around-the-edges feel can still be sensed today.

⊙ Sights & Activities

First impressions deceive. There's actually more to Aberdeen and Hoquiam than meets the eye.

Lady Washington
HISTORIC SHIP

For some interesting local history, check out this full-scale replica of one of the ships piloted by Captain Robert Gray when he first sailed into Grays Harbor. The ship is open for tours when moored at **Grays Harbor Historical Seaport** (www.ladywashington.org; 813 E Heron St, Aberdeen; adult/child $3/1; ⊘ 10am-5pm). It's still used as a working boat.

Hoquiam's Castle
HISTORIC BUILDING

(☎ 360-533-2005; www.hoquiamcastle.com; 515 Chenault Ave, Hoquiam; tours $5) Part museum, part local landmark, this ornate Victorian mansion was built in 1897 on a hill above Hoquiam by lumber tycoon Robert Lytle. The lavish furnishings and period details look like something out of a Scooby Doo cartoon and include lots of dark wood, delicate antiques and even a fully working Victorian bathroom. Tours leave most days at 3pm, but call in advance to be sure.

Arnold Polson Museum
MUSEUM

(1611 Riverside Ave, Hoquiam; adult/child $2/50¢; ⊘ 11am-4pm Wed-Sun Jun-Sep, noon-4pm Sat & Sun Oct-May) Built in 1924 by one of the timber barons of Hoquiam, this 26-room edifice is filled with period furniture, clothing, a doll collection and logging implements.

Aberdeen Museum of History
MUSEUM

(111 E Third St, Aberdeen; admission by donation; ⊘ 10am-5pm Tue-Sun) Aberdeen's archive plots the history of this tough mill town from its earliest days, with a strong focus on the lumber industry. You can also ask here about the self-guided **Kurt Cobain Tour** around some of the former houses and hangouts of the late Nirvana star.

🛏 Sleeping & Eating

Olympic Inn
MOTEL $

(☎ 360-532-8161; www.aberdeenolympicinn.com; 616 W Heron St, Aberdeen; r from $60; ✳ @ 🛜) Beware; the twin towns' motels can be gritty. The Olympic's standout features are that it's clean and recently upgraded and has Belgian waffles for breakfast. Not so gritty after all.

COME AS YOU ARE

'Yeah I was run out of town. They chased me up to the castle of Aberdeen with torches. Just like the Frankenstein monster. And I got away in a hot air balloon. And I came here to Seattle.' Kurt Cobain, *Monk Magazine*, 1992.

Aberdeen's biggest star, the late Kurt Cobain, front man of the 1990s band Nirvana and the oft-dubbed father of grunge, wasn't in a loving relationship with his hometown. He often criticized the logging outpost for being small-minded (among other things) and the tales from his youth, from dropping out of school to sleeping in cardboard boxes and becoming a janitor, do not speak of happy times. But today he can perhaps smile in his grave as everyone driving into Aberdeen is greeted with the sign 'Welcome to Aberdeen: Come as You Are' (a quote from the Nirvana song of the same title). The boy who once painted 'queer' on the sides of trucks to shake up the status quo, ended up making more of a mark than anyone expected. Still, some locals joke that little has changed and the sign out of town should read 'Leave as you were.'

Pick up a copy of the Kurt Cobain tour map at the Aberdeen Museum of History (or get less organized information off the website). Sites to see include a guitar statue dedicated to Cobain near the Young Street Bridge, where the artist used to hang out and drink Thunderbird with local homeless people; Seafirst Bank (now a Bank of America, 101 E Market St), where the singer was once arrested for vandalism; and Rosevear's Music Center (110 E Wishkah St), where an uncle bought Cobain a guitar for his 14th birthday.

A Harbor View Inn   B&B $$
(☑ 360-533-7996; www.aharborview.com; 111 W 11th St, Aberdeen; r $129-225) Aberdeen's Victorian masterpiece has five clean, quirky rooms that blow everything else in town out of the water.

Billy's Bar & Grill   PUB, STEAKHOUSE $$
(322 E Heron St, Aberdeen; burgers $8-11; ⊙ 8am-11pm Mon-Sat, to 9pm Sun) In the rootin' tootin' days of yore, this bar was haunted by Billy Gohl (better known as Billy Ghoul), a murderous fellow who robbed and killed drunken sailors and loggers. Billy and the era are both commemorated at this handsome old bar and restaurant with OK sandwiches, full dinners and regional microbrews. The local ambience is five star.

ℹ Information

Grays Harbor Chamber of Commerce (www.graysharbor.org; 506 Duffy St; ⊙ 9am-5pm Mon-Fri) Affords visitors a warm welcome. Pop by for free maps and plenty of informative leaflets.

Westport

Guarding the entrance to Gray's Harbor, stormy Westport is famous for its deep-sea fishing, rugged surfing and isolated beachcombing possibilities. Once the largest whaling port on the West Coast and the largest charter-fishing center in the Northwest, the town has suffered since restrictions were placed on salmon fishing in the last couple of decades. In a bid to reinvent itself as Washington's most happening coastal destination, Westport has invested heavily in a chain of restaurants, condos and golf courses. Still on offer are the ever-popular chartered fishing trips and whale-watching expeditions, though the backbone of the fishing industry disappeared years ago.

⊙ Sights

Westport Maritime Museum   MUSEUM
(2201 Westhaven Dr; adult/child $5/2; ⊙ 10am-4pm Memorial Day-Labor Day, noon-4pm Thu-Mon Sep-May) This former Coast Guard station was built in 1939 and boasts some great period photos and artifacts of seafaring days gone by. A separate building houses the 6-ton, 18ft-high **Fresnel lens**, manufactured in France in 1888, that beamed for over 70 years from the lighthouse of Destruction Island, 50 miles north of Westport.

Grays Harbor Lighthouse   LANDMARK
(1020 West Ocean Ave; admission $3; ⊙ 10am-4pm May-Sep, noon-3pm Oct-Apr) Westport's lighthouse used a French-made Fresnel lens until recently, when it was replaced by a simpler electronic device. To reach the lighthouse – the tallest in the state at 107ft – return to

uptown Westport and head west on Ocean Ave. You can also bike or hike there along the **Westport Maritime History Trail**, a 6.5-mile pedestrian pathway that passes the marina and treks along a dune trail into Westhaven State Park. Tours of the lighthouse are available through the maritime museum. Just beyond the lighthouse, **Westport Light State Park** has wind-screened picnic sites and access to a stretch of beach that's closed to motor vehicles in summer.

✦ Activities

Charter fishing is still a hot drawcard in Westport. The best fishing season runs from April through October (depending on the fish). Regular trips target black rockfish, ling cod, salmon, halibut and tuna, using live bait and conforming to set fishing limits. One-day licenses can be purchased with the excursion. Deckhands can fillet your fish for an extra fee and even arrange to have it vacuum-packed, smoked or stored. Prices start at around $120 per person per day for salmon fishing and up to about $230 for halibut, but shop around.

Most of these charter companies also run whale-watching excursions in the spring. Stroll along the marina and check the offerings. An hour-long excursion will generally cost around $38/28 per adult/child.

For more about charter fishing contact **Deep Sea Charters** (www.deepseacharters.net; 2319 Westhaven Dr, Westport), or procure a full list of operators at the visitor center.

🛏 Sleeping & Eating

Glenacres Inn B&B   B&B $$
(☑ 360-268-0958; 222 N Montesano St, Westport; d $50-125, cottages $160; 🛜) Westport's contribution to the vintage B&B scene is this large house on the hill where – legend has it – Bobby Kennedy once stayed the night (albeit 45 years ago). Having changed ownership in the last couple of years, the inn has undergone some renovations, though it still has an affordable midrange price tag.

Bathrooms are small, but there's wi-fi, morning coffee, and deer on the lawn. There's also a small cottage in the grounds for families or larger groups.

One-Eyed Crab   SEAFOOD $$$
(2309 Westhaven Dr; mains $20-30) A small, family-run place operated by people who know their crab. Aside from the obvious (Dungeness, of course), there's a decent seafood chowder, clams, prawns, scallops and crab legs – wait for it – deep-fried. Service can be a little tardy, but hey, this is low-key Westport, not Seattle.

ℹ Information

Westport-Grayland Chamber of Commerce & Visitors Center (www.westportcam.com; 2985 S Montesano St; ◷ 9am-5pm Mon-Fri, 10am-3pm Sat & Sun) Located at the turnoff from Hwy 105.

Long Beach Peninsula

The name's hardly original, but of the half a dozen or so Long Beaches in the US, the Washington version – a 28-mile-long sand spit that lies directly to the north of the Columbia River estuary – is unequivocally the longest (less proven is its claim to be the *world's* longest beach). The adjoining 28 miles of seaside development aren't quite as unique. There's nothing particularly eye-catching about the amusement arcades, cheap motels and trinket shops that characterize Hwy 103, though none of the half-dozen or so settlements are large or high-rise. Much of the beach itself is overrun with pickup trucks in peak season (as Washington state beaches are considered highways). Purists might prefer the Willapa Bay side of the peninsula, with its old towns, oyster beds and wildlife-viewing. The main settlements on the peninsula, running north to south, are Oysterville, Nahcotta, Ocean Park, Klipsan Beach, Long Beach, Seaview and Ilwaco.

Oysterville & Nahcotta

The charm of these old communities – the only ones on the bay side of the Long Beach Peninsula – derives not just from their history but also from their surrounds of mossy Douglas fir trees and bird-filled wetlands. Here, wildlife-viewing, oyster harvesting and gracious dining occupy residents and visitors alike. Oysterville stands largely unchanged since its heyday in the 1870s, when the oyster boom was at its peak.

◉ Sights & Activities

Oysterville   TOWN
Oysterville is filled with well-preserved Victorian homes including the 1863 **Red Cottage** (Territory Rd) near Clay St, which served as the first Pacific County courthouse, and

the **Big Red House** (cnr Division St & Territory Rd), the original home of Oysterville cofounder RH Espy, built in 1871. Other historic buildings include a one-room schoolhouse and the 1892 **Oysterville Church** (cnr Clay St & Territory Rd); pick up a walking-tour brochure here.

Leadbetter Point State Park Natural Area PARK
(Stackpole Rd) The 807-acre Leadbetter Point State Park Natural Area, 3 miles north of Oysterville, is a kind of buffer between the straggling developments of Long Beach Peninsula and a section of the Willapa National Wildlife Refuge, a band of dunes increasingly breached by Pacific waves. The narrow peninsula has four trails ranging from 1.1 to 2.9 miles that lead along the bayside wetlands or the coastal dune forest or out to the wild ocean beach. It's as good a place as any in the Northwest to watch for shorebirds.

🍴 Sleeping & Eating

Moby Dick Hotel & Oyster Farm HOTEL $$
(☎360-665-4543; www.mobydickhotel.com; 25814 Sandridge Rd, Nahcotta; d incl breakfast $90-150) 🐚 Get intimate with the whale vertebrae that furnish the patio in this 1929 structure that once served as a Coast Guard barracks. Other features include a sauna, three communal lounge rooms and a celebrated restaurant that serves up delicious oysters picked from the hotel's very own oyster beds. Bold colors and eclectic themes characterize the 10 rooms (two of which have private bathroom), and the substantial three-course breakfast should keep you going all day.

Bailey's Bakery & Café BAKERY, CAFE $
(www.baileysbakerycafe.com; 26910 Sandridge Rd, Nahcotta; snacks from $3; ⊙8am-3pm Thu-Sat & Mon, from 9am Sun) Sharing digs with Nahcotta post office, this small nook serves locally roasted Long Beach coffee and the lauded 'thunder buns': currants, pecans, honey-butter glaze and a whole lot of bun.

Long Beach & Seaview

Long Beach (population 1393) blends seamlessly into Seaview (population 516) to comprise the major population center on the peninsula. Both towns began as beach resorts in the late 1880s. A few old inns from this era have been beautifully restored, though the modern strip on Hwy 103 (aka Pacific Way) is lined with T-shirt shops, middle-

brow boutiques and bumper-car arenas. To the west, the beach is separated from the town by a wide swath of dunes and dwarf pines and remains pretty wild, especially along the 8.2-mile Discovery Trail.

Thousands of people descend on Long Beach during the third week of August for the **Washington State International Kite Festival**, billed as the largest such event in the western hemisphere. Festival-goers seek to gain new world records: the greatest number of kites in flight at one time, the largest kite flown, the longest time aloft and so on.

⦿ Sights & Activities

Several Long Beach outfitters offer horseback-riding tours (solo riding is discouraged); try **Back Country Wilderness Outfitters** (☎360-642-2576; 409 SW Sid Snyder Dr; beach rides per hour from $25). Biking along the boardwalk is another fun activity, with rentals around town from around $5 per hour.

★**Marsh's Free Museum** MUSEUM
(409 Pacific Ave S, Long Beach; ⊙9am-6pm) **FREE**
Half souvenir shop and half sideshow starring *Weekly World News* media stars like Jake the Alligator Boy (a freakish taxidermy that appears to be an alligator bottom stuck together with a real human upper half), an Amazon shrunken head, and a one-eyed lamb: if you love kitsch, don't miss this place. Bring change for the antique circus peep-show machines.

Beaches BEACH
Primary beach-access points in Long Beach are off 10th St SW and Bolstad Ave; a 0.25-mile boardwalk links the two entryways. In Seaview, take 38th Pl, just south of US 101. Cars and trucks aren't allowed on these busy beaches in summer, but the beach north of Bolstad Ave to Ocean Park is open to vehicles year-round.

Note that surf swimming here is dangerous due to strong waves and quickly changing tides. Instead of plunging into the water, you might hit the saddle and ride on horseback along the endless dunes.

World Kite Museum & Hall of Fame MUSEUM
(303 Sid Snyder Dr, Long Beach; adult/child $5/3; ⊙11am-5pm daily Jun-Aug, Fri-Mon Sep-May; ♿) If you think a museum devoted to the history and artistry of kites might be a bore, think again. Kites have been used for scientific research, aerial photography, mail delivery

WORTH A TRIP

THE HISTORIC LONG BEACH DISCOVERY TRAIL

For American history buffs, Long Beach and the adjacent hulk of Cape Disappointment are hallowed ground. In November 1805, William Clark of the Discovery Corps arrived here looking for his first close-up glimpse of the Pacific Ocean. One year after leaving St Louis, MO, on a journey to map and explore the barely known continent, Clark, along with fellow explorer Meriwether Lewis and three dozen others, had finally staggered into a sheltered cove on the Columbia River 2 miles west of the present-day Astoria Bridge and christened it 'Station Camp.' Adamant to find a better winter bivouac, Clark and several companions continued the hike west to Long Beach Peninsula, coming to a halt near present-day 26th St, where Clark dipped his toe in the Pacific and carved his name on a cedar tree for posterity. The route of this historic three-day trudge has been re-created in the **Long Beach Discovery Trail**, which runs from the small town of Ilwaco near the mouth of the Columbia River to Clark's 26th St turnaround. Officially inaugurated in September 2009, the trail has incorporated some dramatic life-size sculptures along its 8.2-mile length. One depicts a giant gray-whale skeleton, another recalls Clark's recorded sighting of a washed-up sea sturgeon, while a third re-creates in bronze the original cedar tree (long since uprooted by a Pacific storm).

and reconnaissance – as well as for amusement – for centuries. The whole story's here, along with the largest, smallest and wackiest kites.

🛏 Sleeping

Shelburne Country Inn   HOTEL $$
(☎360-642-4142; 4415 Pacific Way, Seaview; r $139-199; ☏) A Washington classic, the inn offers 17 elegant guest rooms at giveaway prices when you factor in the complimentary cookies, fresh flowers and gourmet breakfast.

Our Place at the Beach   MOTEL $$
(☎800-538-5107; www.ourplacelongbeach.weebly.com; 1309 Ocean Beach Blvd, Long Beach; r $74-187; ☏☒) Nothing fancy, but under new ownership and keen to please, this smallish motel offers good beach access (five minutes' walk through the dunes), a small gym, two hot tubs and comfortable if slightly dated rooms. It's an easy walk to all of Long Beach's downtown facilities.

✗ Eating

Cottage Bakery & Deli   BAKERY, CAFE $
(118 Pacific Way S, Long Beach; cakes from 85¢) Worth-getting-up-for cakes and pastries, or roll in for breakfasts of healthy porridge followed by a slightly less healthy old-fashioned glazed doughnut. Old signs on the walls advertise war bonds, but the high quality of the cakes never changes.

42nd Street Cafe   AMERICAN, FUSION $$
(☎360-642-2323; 4201 Pacific Hwy, Seaview; mains $12-28; ⊗8am-2pm & 4:30pm-close) The menu is small, but there's something for everyone here, from great burgers to grilled salmon and bouillabaisse. Classy country-style decor, an extensive wine and cocktail menu and service that makes you feel like a local by meal's end make this one of this area's coziest dining experiences. All ingredients are locally sourced.

Depot   FUSION $$$
(☎360-642-7880; 1208 38th Pl, Seaview; mains $22-30; ⊗dinner) Dine in Seaview's 1905 train station, where a Detroit-raised chef cooks up dishes inspired from his multi-ethnic youth. Mains and 'small plates' are created from local seafood, meats and veggies – there are dishes like Peruvian mango scallops, Moroccan osso buco and fig-glazed quail marsala. It's consistently rated the top dining option in town, so reservations are recommended.

Restaurant at Shelburne Country Inn   NORTHWESTERN $$$
(☎360-642-4142; 4415 Pacific Way, Seaview; mains pub $20-26, restaurant $22-33; ⊗from 5:30pm) Many consider the restaurant at the Shelburne Country Inn one of the showplaces of Northwest cuisine. The dining room, dominated by stained-glass windows salvaged from an English church, is certainly one of the most charming you'll find. Local seafood, fish, poultry and lamb are served with a consistently inventive flair. An English-style pub on the premises serves lighter fare.

ℹ Information

Long Beach Peninsula Visitors Bureau (www. funbeach.com; cnr US 101 & Pacific Hwy, Seaview; ◷9am-5pm Mon-Sat, 10am-4pm Sun) Can help you get reservations for the area's motels and lodgings. The website is an excellent information portal on the whole peninsula.

ℹ Getting There & Around

Pacific Transit System (www.pacifictransit. org) runs buses throughout Pacific County, from Aberdeen to towns along the Long Beach Peninsula via South Bend and Raymond, and as far south as Astoria, OR. Bus 20 runs approximately once an hour between Ilwaco and Oysterville from around 6am to 7pm weekdays (35¢, 40 minutes), less often on Saturday and not at all on Sunday. Bus 24 connects Ilwaco with Astoria (50¢, 30 minutes, Monday to Friday only). There are no connections east toward Longview and Kelso.

Ilwaco

POP 936

Blink-and-you'll-miss-it Ilwaco is known for its port that's crammed with fishing boats bringing in salmon, Dungeness crab, albacore tuna and other treats from the Pacific. What passes for downtown is a collection of wooden cabin-style homes overlooking a Popeye-worthy harbor. The early growth of the salmon-canning industry here was aided by the development of salmon traps, a method of catching the fish that was made illegal in the 1930s.

Unlike the rest of the Long Beach Peninsula, Ilwaco is hemmed in by rocky hills. West of town, on a rugged promontory above the mouth of the Columbia River in Cape Disappointment State Park, are the remains of Fort Canby, a Civil War–era bulwark designed to protect river shipping from Confederate interference. The hiking-biking Discovery Trail (p148) terminates here.

⊙ Sights

★**Cape Disappointment State Park**   PARK
(☑360-642-3078; Hwy 100; ◷dawn-dusk) Although little remains of the original Fort Canby that once stood in what is now 2 miles southwest of Ilwaco in Cape Disappointment State Park, the location is of considerable interest because of its interpretive center, wild beach and hiking trails (8 miles in total) to its two dramatic lighthouses.

Established in 1852, Fort Canby was heavily armed during the Civil War to prevent Confederate gunboats from entering the Columbia River. Upgraded dramatically during WWII, the fort stood as the principal defender of the river. Although no shots were fired from Fort Canby, a Japanese submarine did manage to penetrate close enough to the Oregon side to fire on Fort Stephens in 1942.

Lewis and Clark camped near here in November 1805 and visited the cape while searching for a winter camp. Their whole cross-continental journey is faithfully recounted at the sequentially laid-out **Lewis & Clark Interpretive Center** (Hwy 100; adult/child $5/2.50; ◷10am-5pm), on a high bluff inside the state park overlooking the point where the Columbia River meets the Pacific. There's a succinct 20-minute film recounting their journey.

From the interpretive center, a hiking trail leads half a mile to **Cape Disappointment Lighthouse**. Built in 1856, it's the oldest such structure still in use on the West Coast. On the other side of the park (accessible via a trail), the **North Head Lighthouse**, built in 1896, offers tours from $2.50. Call the park for more details.

Columbia Pacific Heritage Museum   MUSEUM
(115 SE Lake St; adult/child $5/3; Thu free; ◷10am-4pm Tue-Sat, noon-4pm Sun) Investigating ancient Chinook culture, along with the exploration and trade of successive Spanish, Russian, British and American explorers, is this fine museum. It also features the *Old Ilwaco,* a restored narrow-gauge passenger train also known as the *Nahcotta,* that ran along the peninsula railway.

🏃 Activities

Unsurprisingly, Ilwaco has plenty of charter fishing options, with expeditions sallying forth in search of salmon, sturgeon, halibut or bottom fish, depending on the season. Try **Sea Breeze Charters** (☑360-642-2300; www.seabreezecharters.net; trips per person from $105) for some of the best organized trips. The office is right on the harbor front.

🛏 Sleeping & Eating

Cape Disappointment State Park Campground   CAMPGROUND $
(☑360-642-3078; Hwy 100; tent/RV sites $23/32, yurts & cabins from $69) There are nearly 250 sites in two zones: by the beach and around a lake near the park entrance. Coin-operated

hot showers and flush toilets are within easy reach. Yurts, cabins (which each can accommodate up to six people) and three former lightkeeper's residences provide further unique accommodations options.

Inn at Harbor Village   HOTEL **$$**
(☑ 360-642-0087; www.innatharborvillage.com; 120 Williams Ave NE; r incl breakfast $115-185; 🛜) One of Washington's most improbable and creative accommodations is this recently refurbished 1928 Presbyterian church, with sloped ceilings and nine exquisite guest rooms. The parlor has an old grandfather clock, plus you can enjoy the delights of a complimentary breakfast and wine. The inn is set in woodland, an easy walk from Ilwaco port.

★**OleBob's Seafood Market**   SEAFOOD **$**
(151 Howerton Way; mains around $9; ⊙10am-5:30pm Thu-Mon; 🛜) Overlooking the marina, this salt-of-the-sea fish market and cafe serves up fresh-off-the-boat fish and chips, amazing fish tacos, clam chowder and the best crab cakes...ever.

Vancouver

POP 164,759

While the TV show *Portlandia*'s first episode sings about saving the planet and hot girls in glasses, the YouTube spoof *Vancouvria*, about Portland's neighbor across the bridge, waxes about coffee at McDonald's and hot dads wearing Old Navy. The town (even though it's the fourth-largest metropolis in Washington) is often seen as a glorified suburb of Portland and – maybe worse – is forever confused with its much more glamorous, Olympic-hosting namesake to the north (yes, the occasional BC-bound traveler still rolls in here assuming they've reached Canada). Recent efforts to rename it have been met with both enthusiasm and mirth (Fort Vancouver was the most popular choice), but the gutsy citizens have put on a brave face. Aside from a talent for self-deprecation, Vancouver, WA, offers pioneer history, a decent weekend farmers market, and the oldest surviving fort in the Pacific Northwest. Go on, give it a whirl.

◉ Sights & Activities

★**Vancouver National
Historic Reserve**   HISTORIC RESERVE
(www.fortvan.org) Situated within easy walking distance of the city center is Vancouver's – and one of Washington's – most important historical monuments. Comprising an archaeological site, the region's first military post, a waterfront trail and one of the nation's oldest operating airfields, the complex's highlight is the reconstructed **Fort Vancouver Historic Site** (www.nps.gov/fova; adult/family $3/5; ⊙9am-5pm).

At the reconstructed fort, resident rangers and actors in period costume skillfully summon up the era from 1825 to 1845, when the fort was under the sole administration of the British Hudson's Bay Company (the so-called Oregon Country was run jointly by the British and the Americans until 1846). Within the stockaded grounds, you can learn how the fort was once a center for the burgeoning Northwest fur trade and a bulwark in a shaky 40-year alliance between the Americans and the British. As historical presentations go, it's one of the most entertaining and educational walkabouts in the state. Tours generally leave on the hour.

Travelers should also pop into the **visitor center** (612 E Reserve St; ⊙9am-5pm) **FREE**, which boasts a small museum and a fascinating video on the Lewis and Clark expedition that wound up near here in November 1805 – and the nearby **Pearson Air Museum** (☑ 360-694-7026; 1115 E 5th St; adult/child $7/5; ⊙10am-5pm Wed-Sat), devoted to the colorful history of Northwest aviation.

Along the northern side of E Evergreen Blvd are the historic homes of **Officers Row**. Built between 1850 and 1906 for US Army officers and their families, they are currently rented out as offices and apartments. Three of the homes are open for self-guided tours. **Grant House** (1101 Officers Row; ⊙11am-9pm), built in 1850 from logs and later covered with clapboard, now houses a restaurant. **Marshall House** (⊙9am-5pm), home to General George Marshall in the 1930s, is a grand Queen Anne–style mansion. The **OO Howard House**, built in 1879, was a non-commissioned-officer's club during WWII and was restored in 1998. It now houses a small gift shop. Ask at the visitor center about guided walks. Elsewhere, the lovely open spaces of the historic reserve are great places to enjoy a picnic, fly a kite or take a stroll. A land bridge connects the reserve with the Columbia River waterfront.

🛏 Sleeping

Briar Rose Inn   B&B **$**
(☑ 360-694-5710; www.briarroseinn.com; 310 W 11th St; r with shared bath from $96; ✳🛜) A 1908 Craftsman-style home turned B&B with

antique-laden rooms, the Briar Rose is one of the few accommodations in the vicinity of downtown Vancouver. Venture further out and you're in big-chain hotel-motel land and a substantial hike from the downtown core.

Heathman Hotel   HOTEL $$
([phone] 360-254-3100; www.heathmanlodge.com; 7801 NE Greenwood Dr; r from $139; [amenities]) Calling yourself a mountain lodge when you're slap-bang in the middle of a metro area and next to a freeway might seem cheeky to some, but this place carries the moniker with an eye-catching lobby, beyond-the-call-of-duty service, sleep-invoking mattresses and several notebooks' worth of thoughtful extras.

✖ Eating

Farmers Market   MARKET $
(W 8th St, cnr Columbia St; ⊙ 10am-6pm Tue-Sun) One of the best and cheapest places to eat in Vancouver is at this daily indoor-outdoor farmers market in Esther Short Park. Inside you'll find German deli sandwiches, tasty pastries and excellent pad Thai noodles for as little as $5.

Beaches   SEAFOOD $$
(www.beaches.simplehelix.com; 1919 SE Columbia River Dr; mains from $12; ⊙ lunch & dinner; [icon]) An ebullient place right on the river, Beaches gets points for its atmosphere, happy hour and cheery service. The food is well-prepared American fare (pizzas, steak, fish and chips) with some nice surprises (steamed clams).

Add it all up and it's worth a detour from Portland.

Grant House Restaurant   NORTHWESTERN $$
([phone] 360-696-1727; 1101 Officers Row; dinner mains from $16; ⊙ breakfast & lunch Mon-Fri, dinner Tue-Sat, brunch Sun) Choose to dine on the garden patio or in the bright window-enclosed verandah of this lovely heritage building. Check the website for live music throughout the weekend and supper-club set menus every third Thursday of the month. While there, ask the staff to show you the exposed logs of the original log-cabin structure. Gluten-free menu available.

ⓘ Information

Southwest Washington Visitors & Convention Bureau ([phone] 360-750-1553; 101 E 8th St, Suite 240).

ⓘ Getting There & Away

BUS
Three Greyhound buses a day stop in Vancouver on their way between Portland and Seattle.

TRAIN
Amtrak (www.amtrak.com) runs a coastal service to Seattle in the north and Portland in the south.

The *Empire Builder* stops in Vancouver before heading west to Pasco, Spokane and, ultimately, Chicago, IL. **Tri-Met Transit** (www.trimet.org) offers frequent service between downtown Portland and Vancouver's 7th St transit center.

Washington Cascades

Includes →

Why Go?

Grafted onto one of the more temperamental segments of the Pacific Ring of Fire, the Washington Cascades are a rugged, spectacular mountain range capped by five potentially lethal volcanoes: Mt Baker, Glacier Peak, Mt Rainier, Mt Adams and – fieriest of all – Mt St Helens.

Renowned for their world-record–breaking precipitation and copious crevasse-covered glaciers, the highest Cascade peaks are vast stand-alone mountains that dominate almost every vista in the western state and create scrubby, almost desertlike conditions further east.

Protected within a string of overlapping wilderness areas and national parks, the mountains offer some of the most awe-inspiring backcountry adventures in the US. For the less outdoor-attuned, rarefied Cascadian beauty can be glimpsed through the windows of cars, buses and trains, or enjoyed in a handful of classic 'parkitecture' lodges.

Best Places to Eat

→ Sorrento's Ristorante (p170)

→ Graham's (p155)

→ Twisp River Pub (p166)

→ Copper Creek Inn (p176)

Best Places to Stay

→ Sun Mountain Lodge (p165)

→ Ross Lake Resort (p161)

→ Paradise Inn (p176)

→ Trout Lake Country Inn (p184)

When to Go
Mt Rainier National Park

Dec & Jan
Cascade ski areas get big dumpings of snow.

Feb The 'Mt Baker Legendary Banked Slalom' snowboarding extravaganza.

Jul–early Oct Higher elevations are snowfree from early July for a short, intense hiking season.

NORTH CASCADES

Dominated by Mt Baker and – to a lesser extent – the more remote Glacier Peak, the North Cascades is made up of a huge swath of protected forests, parks and wilderness areas that dwarf even the expansive Rainier and St Helens parks to the south. The crème de la crème is the North Cascades National Park, a primeval stash of old-growth rainforest, groaning glaciers and untainted ecosystems whose savage beauty is curiously missed by all but 2500 or so annual visitors who penetrate its rainy interior.

Geologically different to the South Cascades, these wild northern giants are peppered with sharp, jagged peaks, copious glaciers and a preponderance of complex metamorphic rock. This gives them their distinctive alpine feel and has helped create the kind of irregular, glacier-sculpted characteristics that have more in common with the mountains of Alaska than the 'rounder' ranges further south. Thanks to their virtual impregnability, the North Cascades were a mystery to humans until relatively recently. Steep peaks such as Liberty Bell weren't climbed until the late 1940s, the first road was built across the region in 1972 and, even today, it remains one of the Northwest's most isolated outposts.

Mt Baker Area

Of all Washington's snowcapped volcanoes, Baker is possibly the most majestic, a massive icy dome that towers over the US–Canada border and is clearly visible everywhere from Vancouver, BC, to Seattle. Legendary among snowboarders and hikers, Baker has been revered by the indigenous natives of Puget Sound for millennia. The Coast Salish called it Koma Kulshan (White Sentinel), while the mountain's modern name comes from Captain George Vancouver's third lieutenant, Joseph Baker, who was allegedly the first European to spot it in 1792. Though over 3000ft lower than Mt Rainier, Baker is a more volcanically active and snowier peak; the mountain actually holds the world record for snow in a single season (1140in in 1998–99).

Baker was first ascended by an Englishman, Edmund Coleman, in 1868. The modern route, though more straightforward than Rainier, requires travel across one of the mountain's 10 permanent glaciers.

🏃 Activities

Mt Baker Scenic Byway   SCENIC DRIVE

The 57-mile drive east along Hwy 542 from metropolitan Bellingham to the otherworldly **Artist Point** through moss-draped forests and past melodious creeks is one of the Northwest's most magic-invoking drives. Glacier, 33 miles in, is the last main settlement on the route. Seven miles further on, turn right on Wells Creek Rd and after half a mile you'll encounter **Nooksack Falls**, which drop 175ft into a deep gorge. This was the site of one of America's oldest hydropower facilities, built in 1906 and abandoned in 1997. Back on Hwy 542 the road begins to climb in earnest until you reach **Heather Meadows** at mile 56. The Mt Baker Ski Area is here, and just up the road is **Austin Pass**, a picnic area and the starting point of several hiking trails.

Climbing

The two principal routes up Mt Baker ascend **Coleman Glacier**, on the northwestern side of the mountain, and **Easton Glacier**, on the southern side. Both require two to three days, with a night spent camping at the base of the glacier. Technical equipment is highly recommended. The northern ascent begins at the Heliotrope Ridge trailhead and continues across Coleman and Roosevelt Glaciers for a final steep and icy climb up the North Ridge to the summit. Novice climbers should consider classes and guided climbs. Contact the American Alpine Institute (p97), which offers general training programs, along with guided climbs up Mt Baker for $640 (three days).

Hiking

While Mt Baker offers plenty of advanced hikes for experienced walkers, there are also a handful of easier options that leave from the Artist Point parking lot and are manageable for families. Most are snowfree by mid-July. The interpretive **Artist Ridge Trail** is an easy 1-mile loop through heather and berry fields with the craggy peaks of Mts Baker and Shuksan scowling in the background. Another option is the 0.5-mile **Fire & Ice Trail**, adjacent to the Heather Meadows Visitors Center, which explores a valley punctuated by undersized mountain hemlock. The 7.5-mile **Chain Lakes Loop** starts at the Artist Point parking lot before dropping down to pass a half-dozen icy lakes surrounded by huckleberry meadows.

WASHINGTON CASCADES MT BAKER AREA

Washington Cascades Highlights

1 Watching bald eagles soar above the **Upper Skagit River** during a frigid January float trip (p158).

2 Hiking cross country through the **North Cascades National Park** to the hidden village of Stehekin (p158).

3 Sitting in an alfresco hot tub outside the **Sun Mountain Lodge** (p165) trying to remember if you've ever enjoyed a more tranquil view.

4 Breaking trail with a pair of cross-country skis in the sunny **Methow Valley** (p163).

5 Being one of the lucky few to reach the top of **Mt Rainier** (p172) when the clouds clear.

6 Watching new life tentatively re-emerge on **Mt St Helens** (p179).

7 Following in the tracks of snowboarding legends at the **Mt Baker Ski Area** (p155).

Many of Mt Baker's best trails start lower down on Hwy 542 from a series of unpaved forest roads. The 7.4-mile out-and-back **Heliotrope Ridge Trail** begins 8 miles down unpaved USFS Rd 39, 1 mile east of Glacier, and takes hikers from thick old-growth forest to flower-filled meadows and, ultimately, a breathtaking Coleman Glacier overlook. At the 2-mile point the path for the Coleman Glacier ascent of Mt Baker branches to the left.

The 11-mile out-and-back **Skyline Divide Trail** is another spellbinding stroll through forests and meadows on the edge of the Mt Baker Wilderness, with views of the main mountain and countless other more distant peaks. Access is via USFS Rd 37, which branches off USFS 39 soon after Hwy 542 and runs for 12 miles to the 4400ft trailhead.

Access to the North Cascades National Park and an abundance of multiday backcountry hikes is via **Hannegan Pass**, 5 miles from the trailhead at the end of USFS Rd 32. Walk in through a beautiful roadless valley.

Skiing

Baker prides itself in being the classic 'non-resort' ski area and a rustic antidote to Whistler in Canada. While luxury facilities are thin on the ground, the fast, adrenaline-fueled terrain has garnered many dedicated admirers. It was also one of the first North American ski locations to accommodate and encourage snowboarders.

Situated at the end of Hwy 542, the **Mt Baker Ski Area** (www.mtbakerskiarea.com) receives record-breaking annual snowfall and enjoys one of the longest seasons in the US. Lift tickets cost from $49 to $54 per day. There are two day lodges, both equipped with ski shops and restaurant-cafeterias: the Cascadian-flavored **White Salmon Day Lodge** at milepost 52 and the **Heather Meadows Day Lodge** 4 miles higher up. The nearest overnight lodging is in Glacier, 25 miles away. Decent cross-country skiing is possible on the forest roads lower down Hwy 542.

White-Water Rafting

Rafters can put in just above the Douglas Fir Campground and ride down the North Fork Nooksack, a class III river, to Maple Falls, a total of 10 miles. For a guided raft trip, contact **River Riders** (www.riverrider.com); trips run June to August.

🎎 Festivals & Events

Mt Baker Legendary Banked Slalom SNOWBOARDING
(www.lbs.mtbaker.us) The iconic slalom is one of the world's premier snowboard events and has been won by the biggest names in the sport. Inaugurated inauspiciously in 1985, it takes place in a natural river gully doubling as a half-pipe in early February.

🛏 Sleeping

The Baker area doesn't have many private lodges or motel-hotels. However, there are plenty of cottages, chalets and cabins for short-term rent (minimum is usually two nights). For more information see www.mtbakerlodging.com. More varied options are available in the Upper Skagit River Valley on the drive up towards the mountain.

Douglas Fir Campground CAMPGROUND $
(☑360-599-2714; Mt Baker Hwy; campsites $18-20) An attractive USFS campground on scenic Hwy 542 and the North Fork Nooksack River. It's located 3 miles east of Glacier, making it handy for sorties to the village store and restaurant. Drinking water and pit toilets are on-site.

Silver Fir Campground CAMPGROUND $
(☑360-599-2714; Mt Baker Hwy; campsites $16) Ten miles up from the Douglas Fir Campground on Hwy 542, the Silver Fir is equally scenic though a little more remote from Glacier. There are pit toilets and drinking water.

Inn at Mt Baker INN $$
(☑360-599-1359; www.theinnatmtbaker.com; 8174 Mt Baker Hwy; r $155-165; ☜) When Mt Baker breaks through the clouds, the views from this attractive, well-run B&B are unsurpassable. It's situated 7 miles east of Maple Falls, and uncluttered rooms and ample skylights give it an airy feel. Breakfast is taken on a spectacular deck – weather permitting – in the summer.

When it gets stormy you can enjoy heated floors, comfortable rocking chairs and a cozy communal reading room. No kids.

🍴 Eating

⭐ **Graham's** DINER, PUB $
(9989 Mt Baker Hwy; mains $4-14; ☺dinner daily, breakfast & lunch Sat & Sun) Here's your perfect modern-day Western saloon with a clunky piano at the back, Willie Nelson on the stereo and old rusty tools on the walls for

decoration. The old-fashioned wooden bar serves up microbrews, but the surprise is the food: this is the last place you'd expect to order polenta cakes with grilled vegetables in a balsamic reduction and have it be outrageously good.

When the furniture gets pushed aside for live music expect a foot-stomping, raucous night.

Wake & Bakery BAKERY $

(6903 Forest St, Glacier; munchies from $4; ⊙7:30am-5pm) Even before pot went legal in Washington, you could safely 'get sconed' at this cozy bakery with – as you'd expect – exceptionally happy service. Take a hit of espresso and ease the munchies with breakfast burritos, sandwiches and way-better-than-a-Power-Bar nut and seed slabs (the perfect trail food).

Milano's Restaurant & Deli ITALIAN $$

(9990 Mt Baker Hwy; dinner $16-20) In common with much of the Mt Baker area, Milano's doesn't win any 'wows' for its fancy interior decor. But when the pasta's al dente, the bread's oven fresh and you've got an appetite that's been turned ravenous by successive bouts of white-knuckle snowboarding, who's complaining?

WASHINGTON'S SKI AREAS

Despite taunts from Rocky Mountain purists who compare Washington's snow to 'wet concrete,' the state maintains a dozen excellent downhill-skiing areas. Those with an aversion to crowds will be doubly impressed. Only one of the centers (Crystal Mountain) is classed as a resort, and it's tiny compared to Aspen or Whistler. Here's a quick precis of what's on offer.

➡ **Crystal Mountain** (p179) The largest ski area in Washington and the state's only destination 'resort' tops out at 7000ft. A huge variety of terrain and a small ski village are complemented by killer Mt Rainier views.

➡ **Summit at Snolquamie** (www.summitatsnolquamie.com; 1001 SR 906; day pass adult/youth $56/42; ⊙9am-10pm late Nov-Apr) The closest ski area to Seattle (read: busy) also boasts the largest floodlit ski network in the US.

➡ **49 Degrees North** (p212) Recent expansion has made this 2350-acre ski area in northeast Washington the state's second largest – yet it's still quiet. The accessible terrain gets big votes from families.

➡ **Mt Baker** (p155) Rugged, undone and legendary among snowboarders, Baker gets twice as much annual snow (650in) as other resorts. Its advanced terrain offers some white-knuckle backcountry options.

➡ **Mission Ridge** (p191) Situated 12 miles south of Wenatchee, Mission is celebrated for its light, fluffy powder and 300-plus days of annual sunshine.

➡ **Stevens Pass** (p49) Established in 1937, Stevens is a day ski area popular with Seattleites. Uniquely, its facilities are powered entirely by wind.

➡ **Loup Loup** (p211) Just east of Winthrop, this small 550-acre ski bowl is economical and safe and has almost no lines. Great for first-timers.

➡ **Hurricane Ridge** (p133) This tiny ski center (only three lifts) just inside the Olympic National Park is the westernmost in the lower 48.

➡ **Bluewood** (p201) Adrift from the Cascades in the southeast of the state, modern Bluewood runs on diesel generators and is lauded for its good tree skiing and dry snow.

➡ **White Pass** (p179) A laid back, less frenetic alternative to nearby Crystal Mountain that spawned the legendary Mahre brothers (gold and silver slalom medalists in the 1984 Winter Olympics).

➡ **Mt Spokane** (p206) Only 28 miles east of Spokane, this is the nearest ski area to a large population center. Learning to ski? Look no further.

➡ **Leavenworth Ski Hill** (p188) A tiny facility with two tow ropes that is renowned for its ski-jumping opportunities.

ⓘ Information

Jointly run by the national forest and park services, **Glacier Public Service Center** (1094 Mt Baker Hwy; ☺8am-4:30pm Memorial Day-Oct, 9am-3pm Sat & Sun Oct-Mar) is just east of Glacier. At this handsome stone lodge built by the Civilian Conservation Corps are a small bookstore, interpretive displays on the park and a ranger to answer questions. In summer there's also a staffed visitor center at **Heather Meadows** (mile 56, Mt Baker Hwy; ☺8am-4:30pm May-Sep).

For more information about the wilderness area, contact the **Mt Baker Ranger Station** (junction of Hwys 9 & 20, Sedro-Woolley).

ⓘ Getting There & Away

Mt Baker is accessed by Hwy 542 (Mt Baker Scenic Byway) from Bellingham via Kendall or by Baker Lake Rd, off Hwy 20 west of Concrete, which dead ends at the northern end of Baker Lake.

Public transportation is scant and many boarders hitchhike (the usual risks apply). When the ski area's open the **Baker Bus** (☎360-599-3115; www.bakerbus.org; to Mt Baker Ski Area from Kendall/Bellingham $9/14) runs daily from Kendall and on weekends from Bellingham to the top of the mountain with stops in between.

Upper Skagit River Valley

Tracking up through the foothills of the North Cascades, the youthful Skagit River becomes increasingly narrow and fast-flowing. Settlement here is thin on the ground. Blink and you'll miss the small roadside towns of Concrete (population 712), Rockport (population 109) and Marblemount (population 203) and, aside from a sprinkling of campgrounds and a couple of inns, your next decent accommodations will be in Mazama on the other side of the mountains.

◎ Sights

Baker Lake & Lake Shannon   SCENIC LAKES
Just north of Concrete are two reservoirs formed by a pair of dams on the Baker River. Washington's largest colony of nesting osprey is found at Lake Shannon. Baker Lake is a popular place to launch a boat and go fishing for kokanee salmon or rainbow trout. There are also several hiking trails.

Baker Lake Rd runs along the western side of the lake, passing several campgrounds and the **Shadow of the Sentinels**,

ⓘ HIGHWAY 20 CLOSURE

Hwy 20, the only road across the North Cascades, closes yearly between Marblemount and Mazama due to heavy winter snowfalls. As a rule, the road is blocked from late November to early or mid-April, though unseasonal snow has sometimes kept it closed until June. Call 888-766-4636 for road conditions.

a wheelchair-accessible trail through old-growth Douglas firs. Beyond the end of the road, the relatively flat **Baker River Trail** makes a good family hike, running 2.6 miles up the jade river past huge old cedars and beaver ponds.

To reach the lakes, turn north off Hwy 20 onto Baker Lake Rd, which is 6 miles west of Concrete.

★**Upper Skagit Bald Eagle Area**   WILDLIFE CENTER
The Bald Eagle area is essentially the 10-mile stretch of the Skagit River between Rockport and Marblemount. After salmon spawn, their spent carcasses become meals for the more than 600 eagles that winter here. January is the best time to view the eagles, which are present from November through early March.

Those who want to learn more about these illustrious raptors should visit the **Skagit River Bald Eagle Interpretive Center** (www.skagiteagle.org; 52809 Rockport Park Rd, Rockport; ☺10am-4pm Sat, Sun & holidays mid-Dec–mid-Feb) ✦. Guided walks around the eagle sanctuary leave from here, one block south of Hwy 20, at 1:30pm weekends and holidays.

☂Activities

Climbing

Since the washing out of the White Chuck River trail in 2003, **Glacier Peak**, Washington's oft-forgotten wilderness volcano, is usually tackled from the **North Fork Sauk River Trail**, which begins at a trailhead off the Mountain Loop Hwy. The push to the top takes you across the Sitkum Glacier, a relatively nontechnical but steep route to the 10,541ft summit. The 2003 storm also damaged this route. Check ahead. Seattle-based **Mountain Madness** (www.mountain-madness.com) offers guided trips and six-day ice-climbing courses in the area from $900 and $1395, respectively.

Rafting

One of the preferred ways of seeing the Skagit's abundant eagle population is on a winter float trip. **Alpine Adventures** ([J]360-863-6505; www.alpineadventures.com) runs these floats from early November to mid-February – bundle up! The cost is $74 for three hours. Whitewater rafting (class II and III) and kayak schools are available with the same company from May through August.

🛏 Sleeping

Buffalo Run Inn   MOTEL $
([J]360-873-2103; www.buffaloruninn.com; 58179 Hwy 20, Marblemount; r $49-109) Situated on a sharp bend on Hwy 20, the Buffalo doesn't look much from the outside. But within its wooden walls is a clean motel (kitchenettes, TVs and comfy beds) and backcountry cabin (kitschy bear and buffalo paraphernalia). Five of the 15 rooms share baths and a sitting area upstairs. There's an included microwaveable breakfast 'buffet' stuffed in a communal fridge.

Ovenell's Heritage Inn   B&B $$
([J]360-853-8494; 46276 Concrete Sauk Valley Rd; r $115-150, cabins $140-150; @🛜🐾) The B&B tag doesn't do Ovenell's justice. It's a 500-acre working cattle ranch abutting the Skagit River with various accommodations, namely four inn rooms (only one of which has a private bathroom), five rustic wooden cabins (sleeping up to four) and an eight-person guesthouse.

Breakfast is available for the inn guests to enjoy in a stunning rural setting with views of Mt Baker and ospreys and eagles overhead. The ranch is a couple of miles south of Concrete.

🍴 Eating & Drinking

Buffalo Run Restaurant   AMERICAN $$
(60084 Hwy 20, Marblemount; mains $10-34; ⏱lunch & dinner; 🛗) Thought you could only eat bull-calf testicles in the Rocky Mountains? Despair no more. Buffalo Run serves massive steamy bowls of 'Cascade mountain oysters.' Otherwise stick to the buffalo, kangaroo, ostrich or (yes!) beef burgers. Several decoratively draped animal skins and a huge buffalo head grace the walls. Surprisingly, a few good vegetarian options are also available.

The restaurant was for sale when we passed, so hopefully new management will continue serving these Wild West–worthy specialties.

Marblemount Diner   DINER $$
(60147 Hwy 20, Marblemount; mains $9-22; ⏱11am-8pm Mon, Thu & Fri, 8am-8pm Sat & Sun) A filling as-much-as-you-can-eat breakfast buffet (served 8am to 11am) at weekends is the highlight of this friendly diner with booths, tables and seating at the bar. Obey 'rule one' of all buffets: arrive early, before all the food is taken and/or dried out.

Cascadian Farms   JUICE BAR
(Hwy 20, mile 100; milkshakes $5; ⏱9am-7pm May-Oct) 🍃 The first of several organic snack huts on the Cascades Loop, this place 3 miles east of Rockport offers fresh injections of organic blueberry fruit shakes, ice cream or coffee. It's housed in an Indonesian-style Batak hut, and you can sup from your cup at an outdoor picnic table before taking a self-guided tour around the adjacent organic farm.

North Cascades National Park

Ordained in 1968, the North Cascades National Park is Alaska transplanted into the lower 48, a thousand square miles of dramatic, daunting wild country strafed with mountains, lakes, glaciers (over 300 of them) and wildlife, but with almost no trace of civilization. Schizophrenic weather, massive precipitation, thick rainforest and vertiginous cliffs have long ensured the remoteness of the park's mountains: steep, alpine behemoths furnished with names like Mt Terror, Mt Fury, Mt Despair and Forbidden Peak. Aspiring bushwhackers and free-climbers love the unique challenges offered by this eerie wilderness (most of the peaks weren't climbed until the 1930s). The less adrenaline-hungry stick close to arterial Hwy 20 and prepare for the drive of a lifetime.

For administrative reasons, the park is split into two sections – north and south – separated in the middle by the Ross Lake National Recreation Area, which encases a spectacular 20-mile section of the North Cascades Hwy (US 20). Bordering the park's southern border around Stehekin lies a third region, the Lake Chelan National Recreation Area, a 62,000-acre protected park that surrounds the fjordlike Lake Chelan. To avoid confusion, the three zones are managed as one contiguous area and overlaid by the Stephen Mather Wilderness, created in 1988.

It is possible to get a basic overview of this vast alpine wilderness by motoring through in a car on US 20 making use of the numerous pullouts and short interpretive hikes that are scattered along the route, but to taste the park's real gritty essence you'll need a tent, a decent knapsack and a gung-ho sense of adventure. Call in at the visitor center in tiny Newhalem and let the glimmering peaks seduce you.

◎ Sights

Ross Lake   SCENIC LAKE
(milepost 134) Ross Lake stretches north for 23 miles, all the way across the Canadian border, but – in keeping with the wild Cascades terrain – is accessible only by trail or water. Incorporated into the Ross Lake National Recreation Area, the lake was formed by the building between 1937 and 1949 of the Ross Dam, an ambitious hydroelectric project that was designed to generate much-needed electricity for the fast-growing Seattle area. You can hike down to the Ross Dam from a trailhead on Hwy 20. The trail descends for 1 mile and crosses over the dam. For an extra leg-stretch you can follow the west bank of Ross Lake another mile to Ross Lake Resort.

Diablo Lake   SCENIC LAKE
(supply ferries adult/child 1 way $10/5) Just below Ross Lake, Diablo Lake is held back by the similarly huge 389ft Diablo Dam. A pullout off Hwy 20 known as the Diablo Dam Overlook provides incredible views of the turquoise-green lake framed by glacier-capped peaks. Diablo was the world's highest arch-type dam at the time of its completion in 1930, and building it in such a hostile region with no road access was one of the greatest engineering feats of the interwar age.

Diablo Lake is popular with kayakers and canoeists (there's a launch site at Colonial Creek campground). The water's turquoise hue is a result of powdered rock ground down by glaciers.

North Cascades Environmental Learning Center (www.ncascades.org) 🌿, on the lake's northern banks, is operated by the North Cascades Institute in partnership with the National Park Service. The center offers a bevy of activities, many of them educationally oriented such as Lake Diablo Lake tours ($35) and Powerhouse tours ($40), as well as a variety of weekend retreats from

$245, including on-site food and accommodation. If you just want lodging, you can rent rooms from $125 per night. Note that many of the excursions and lodging sell out even before summer starts. See the website for more details.

🏃 Activities

Hiking

Free permits are required for backcountry camping in the park and must be obtained in person from the Wilderness Information Center (p162) or at a park ranger station.

One of the park's most challenging but rewarding day hikes is the strenuous **Sourdough Mountain Trail**, which gains a mile in height for the 5.5 miles (one way) traveled on the ground. Most concede the effort is worth it; the views of Cascadian peaks and turquoise Diablo Lake 5000-plus feet below are some of the best in the park.

The 3.7-mile hike to 5384ft **Cascade Pass** is the best loved in these mountains, and gets you very quickly up into a flower-carpeted, glacier-surrounded paradise that will leave you struggling for superlatives.

From the southern end of the Colonial Creek Campground (mile 130, Hwy 20), the long **Thunder Creek Trail** leads along a powerful glacier-fed river through old-growth forest and clumps of wildflowers flourishing in the dank forest. After 2.5 miles the **Fourth of July Trail** branches left to a pass of the same name and makes a good early-season hike (10 miles round-trip from the campground). Alternatively, you can continue along Thunder Creek to Park Creek Pass and, ultimately, Stehekin.

Just past the Ross Dam trailhead at mile 134.5, the easy and wheelchair-accessible **Happy Creek Forest Walk** (0.5 miles) gets you an up-close look at the forest on a raised boardwalk.

At Rainy Pass, the **Pacific Crest Trail** (PCT) crosses Hwy 20. To sample the trail, strike out north from here for 6800ft **Cutthroat Pass** (4 miles). Heading in the other direction down the PCT will bring you to Bridge Creek Campground, 12 miles away, where you can pick up the road to Stehekin. Several more leisurely hikes also start from Rainy Pass. Try the easy 4-mile out-and-back walk to cirque-cradled **Lake Ann**.

Just to the west of Washington Pass, between miles 161 and 162, the **Blue Lake Trail** is an ambling 2.2-mile climb through subalpine meadows to Blue Lake, at 6250ft.

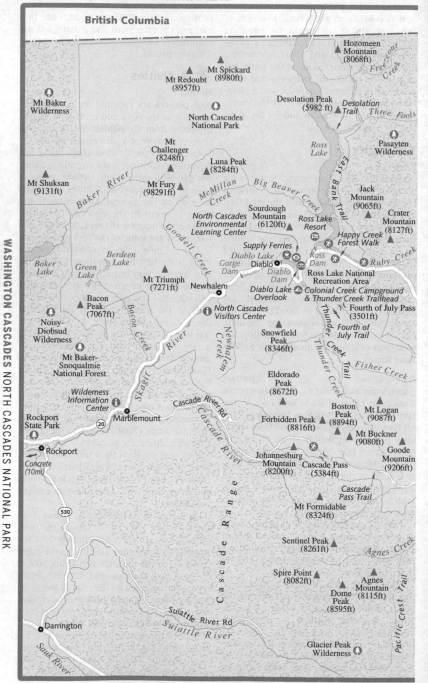

British Columbia

WASHINGTON CASCADES NORTH CASCADES NATIONAL PARK

Hozomeen
Mountain
(8068ft)

Free

Mt Spickard
(8980ft)

Mt Redoubt
(8957ft)

Desolation Peak
(5982 ft)

Desolation
Trail

Three Fools

Mt Baker
Wilderness

North Cascades
National Park

Ross
Lake

Pasayten
Wilderness

Mt
Challenger
(8248ft)

Luna Peak
(8284ft)

Jack
Mountain
(9065ft)

Crater
Mountain
(8127ft)

Mt Shuksan
(9131ft)

Mt Fury
(98291ft)

McMillan
Creek

Big Beaver Creek

East Bank Trail

Baker River

Goodell Creek

North Cascades
Environmental
Learning Center

Sourdough
Mountain
(6120ft)

Ross Lake
Resort

Happy Creek
Forest Walk

Supply Ferries

Ruby Creek

Berdeen
Lake

Diablo Lake

Ross
Dam

Baker
Lake

Green
Lake

Gorge
Dam

Diablo

Mt Triumph
(7271ft)

Newhalem

Diablo
Dam

Ross Lake National
Recreation Area

Bacon
Peak
(7067ft)

Diablo Lake
Overlook

Colonial Creek Campground
& Thunder Creek Trailhead

Noisy-
Diobsud
Wilderness

Bacon Creek

North Cascades
Visitors Center

Newhalem Creek

Fourth of July Pass
(3501ft)

Thunder Creek

Fourth of
July Trail

Mt Baker-
Snoqualmie
National Forest

Skagit River

Snowfield
Peak
(8346ft)

Thunder Creek Trail

Fisher Creek

Wilderness
Information
Center

Eldorado
Peak
(8672ft)

Rockport
State Park

Marblemount

Cascade River Rd

Boston
Peak
(8894ft)

Mt Logan
(9087ft)

Forbidden Peak
(8816ft)

Rockport

Cascade River

Johannesburg
Mountain
(8200ft)

Mt Buckner
(9080ft)

Goode
Mountain
(9206ft)

Concrete
(10mi)

Cascade Pass
(5384ft)

Cascade
Pass Trail

Cascade Range

Mt Formidable
(8324ft)

Sentinel Peak
(8261ft)

Agnes Creek

Spire Point
(8082ft)

Agnes
Mountain
(8115ft)

Darrington

Suiattle River Rd

Dome
Peak
(8595ft)

Pacific Crest Trail

Suiattle River

Sauk River

Glacier Peak
Wilderness

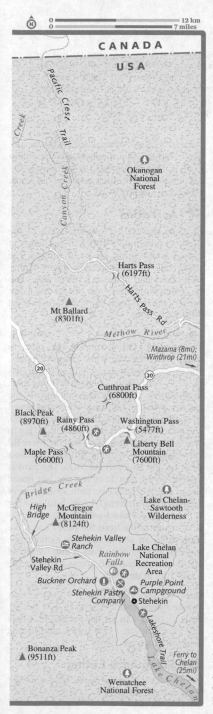

Rafting

Although it doesn't offer the heart-in-the-mouth white-water runs of less tamed waterways, the dam-controlled Upper Skagit makes for a good class II or III family trip through old-growth forest, offering plenty of opportunities for wildlife-watching. A number of companies offer excursions here, including **Alpine Adventures** (www.alpineadventures.com). Prices start at $69/59 per adult/child.

🛏 Sleeping & Eating

Newhalem Creek Campground
CAMPGROUND $

(☎877-444-6777; Hwy 20, mile 120; campsites $12, reserve sites $21) Handily situated near the North Cascades Visitors Center and surrounded by short interpretive trails, this 111-capacity campsite can accommodate large RVs. It's open year-round. If it's full try the smaller Goodall Creek campground 1 mile to the west on Hwy 20.

Colonial Creek Campground
CAMPGROUND $

(☎206-386-4495; Hwy 20, mile 130; campsites $12) These 142 campsites skirt the Thunder Arm of Diablo Lake on either side of the highway. On the southern side, several walk-in campsites among dense woods offer a chance to get away from the cars. There are toilets and water but no showers or hookups. In summer naturalist programs are given nightly in the amphitheater. Open year-round.

★ Ross Lake Resort
HISTORIC HOTEL $$

(☎206-386-4437; www.rosslakeresort.com; cabins $155-315; ⊗mid-Jun–Oct) The floating cabins at this secluded resort, on the lake's west side, were built in the 1930s for loggers working in the valley soon to be flooded by Ross Dam. There's no road in – either hike the 2-mile trail from Hwy 20 or take the resort's supply boat from the parking area near Diablo Dam. Cabins vary in size and facilities, but all feature electricity, plumbing and kitchenettes.

Bedding and kitchen supplies are provided, but guests should bring food. The resort rents canoes ($34 per day), kayaks ($44) and motorboats ($105), and operates a water-taxi service for hikers destined for trailheads around the lake ($2). If you need to pick up some food, stop by the Skagit General Store in Newhalem, which has sandwiches, fudge and hot coffee. Note that there's no internet or phone reception out here, so this is a complete getaway.

WASHINGTON CASCADES NORTH CASCADES NATIONAL PARK

LOCAL KNOWLEDGE

TAKING THE SUPPLY FERRY

The Ross Lake Resort (p161) runs twice-daily supply ferries ($10 one way) from the ferry dock situated on the right just after you cross the Diablo Dam. The first ferry leaves at 8.30am and turns round at the Ross Powerhouse dock at 9am. The second leaves Diablo at 3pm and turns round at 3.30pm. Visitors can take the ferry one way and hike back to the Diablo Dam on the moderate 3.8-mile **Diablo Lake Trail**.

ℹ Information

North Cascades Visitors Center (502 Newhalem St, Newhalem; ⊗9am-4:30pm mid-Apr–Oct, closed Mon-Fri Nov-Mar) An essential orientation point for visitors, even for those just sticking to Hwy 20 and not strictly entering the park itself. A walk-through exhibit mixes informative placards about the park's different ecosystems with nature videos. Expert rangers will enlighten you on everything from melting glaciers to the fickleness of the weather. Various short trails track the Skagit River and Newhalem Creek, the longest of which is the 1.8-mile River Loop Trail. Park rangers give interpretive talks in the vicinity in summer.

Wilderness Information Center (7280 Ranger Station Rd, Marblemount; ⊗7am-6pm Sun-Thu, to 8pm Fri & Sat May-Oct) Pick up backcountry permits here.

Methow Valley

After the white-knuckle drive across the North Cascades, the mellower Methow Valley, situated immediately to the east, offers a more tranquil and less terrifying antidote. Bucolic, surprisingly sunny and pleasantly isolated in winter when Hwy 20 shuts down due to snow blockage, this is where the sporty and the savvy come to hot-air balloon, horseback ride and mountain bike. Winter is, arguably, an even better time to visit. Resisting the economic lure of big-name ski resorts, the local nonprofit Methow Valley Sport Trails Association has pieced together the second-largest network of cross-country skiing trails in North America.

The US Forest Service maintains the **Methow Valley Visitors Center** (24 West Chewuch Rd; ⊗8am-5pm May-Oct) on Hwy 20 at the western end of Winthrop.

Mazama

The first settlement to the east of the North Cascades wilderness is little more than a pinprick on the map – albeit a very pleasant one – with broad mountain-backed vistas and a couple of excellent places to stay. Tiny Mazama (the name means 'mountain goat' in Spanish) marks the gateway to the Methow Valley (heading east) and the North Cascades (heading west).

🏃 Activities

Mazama marks the western extent of the Methow Community Trail and has plenty of cross-country skiing trails. In summer the same trails become routes for hikers, mountain bikers and horseback riders. Bikes can be rented at the Freestone Inn for $38 a day. Most of the best trails start on Harts Pass Rd (USFS Rd 5400).

Harts Pass SCENIC DRIVE
If you prefer white-knuckle car rides to white-water rafting trips, consider taking the single-lane gravel track up to Hart's Pass (6197ft), Washington's highest drivable road, and also its most vertigo-inducing. If the narrow, winding route and scary unguarded drop-offs don't knock the wind out of you, the panoramic views certainly will. To get to Harts Pass head northwest on Lost River Rd (also known as Mazama Rd) past Mazama Country Inn to USFS Rd 5400. The road is paved for the first 12 miles; the last dozen are gravel. At Harts Pass there's still more of a climb for the intrepid driver; head another 3 miles up to **Slate Peak** (7450ft), where – after a short hike from the road's end – the view from an abandoned fire lookout is... well, go and see. Slate Peak is also the site of the northernmost road access to the Pacific Crest Trail in the USA.

Early Winters Outfitting OUTDOORS
(www.earlywintersoutfitting.com; HCR 74 Box B6, Mazama; hiking trips per day from $220) Offers horseback riding, cattle drives, and fishing and hunting trips.

🛏 Sleeping & Eating

Both of the following places have excellent in-house restaurants.

Mazama Country Inn HOTEL $$

(☎509-996-2681; www.mazamacountryinn.com; 42 Lost River Rd, Mazama; lodge r $100-170, cabins $85-310; ☎☒) Welcome to a self-contained rustic oasis situated on the edge of the Pasayten Wilderness but also in the tiny town of Mazama. Aside from 18 simple but comfortable rooms, the inn lies at the nexus of countless outdoor activities, with numerous ski and bike trails starting from just outside the front door (rentals are available).

Other facilities include pool, gym, squash and tennis courts, sauna and restaurant. The inn also rents a number of self-contained cabins around Mazama.

Freestone Inn HOTEL $$$

(☎509-996-3906; www.freestoneinn.com; 17798 Hwy 20; cabins/r/ste/lodges from $135/155/235/435; ☎☒⊞) Located on an evergreen-clad ranch, rooms here are cabin chic with big pine beams and stone fireplaces. Even better are private, kitchen-equiped cabins tucked in the woods or massive 'lakeside lodges' that are two- to five-bedroom houses right on Freestone Lake. The on-site Jack's Hut adventure center organizes outdoor adventures from snowmobiling to heliskiing and balloon tours.

Winthrop & Around

Winthrop (population 397) is – along with Leavenworth – one of two themed towns on the popular Cascade Loop. Once a struggling mining community, it avoided 'ghost town' status in the 1960s when it was made over to look like a cowboy settlement out of the Wild West. Though on paper it sounds more Hollywood back lot than *Gunfight at the OK Corral,* the Gary Cooper touches are surprisingly authentic. Winthrop's *High Noon* shopfronts hide a genuine frontier

> **DON'T MISS**
>
> ### CROSS-COUNTRY SKIING IN THE METHOW
>
> Broad, beautiful and littered with trails, the Methow is to cross-country skiing what Aspen is to downhill, but with only a fraction of the fame. To devotees of the more environmentally congruous free-heel method, this is the primary draw: no crowds, no Gore-Tex fashion parade, and no beer-fueled après-ski – just you, miles of sugary powder and the Cascades.
>
> With 200km of groomed trails, the valley comprises the second-largest cross-country skiing area in the US (after California's Royal Gorge). But, unlike other ski areas, there's no resort pampering here. A bucolic mix of farmland, aspen groves, rivers and old barns, the Methow is a real-life rural community whose far-sighted residents have created a nonprofit organization, the **Methow Valley Sport Trails Association** (MVSTA; www.mvsta.com; 209 Castle Ave, Winthrop) ✦. When it's not fighting off profit-hungry ski-resort developers, the MVSTA promotes and protects a well-maintained trail system that enables skiers to meander at will between a handful of huts, cabins, lodges and small settlements.
>
> The network's 'aorta' is the 20-mile **Methow Community Trail** (MCT), a flat, central valley route groomed for classic and skate skiing that plies its way between strategically placed warming huts (with water and toilets), linking Winthrop with the even tinier settlement of Mazama. Higher up but equally comprehensive are the interconnecting Rendezvous and Sun Mountain Lodge trail systems.
>
> Between early December and late March you can ski door-to-door between various accommodations options, including Sun Mountain Lodge, Freestone Inn, Wolf Ridge Resort and Mazama Country Inn. For information on the Rendezvous huts (self-catering huts in scenic trail locations placed approximately 8km apart and sleeping up to eight people), check www.rendezvoushuts.com. Ski rental ($17 first day, $9 a day thereafter) and MVSTA trail passes ($22/57 for one/three days) are available at outlets in Sun Mountain Lodge, **Methow Cycle & Sport** (www.methowcyclesport.com; 29 Rte 20, Winthrop; ◷9:30am-6pm Mon-Sat, 10am-5pm Sun), and Mazama Junction in Mazama.
>
> The Methow Valley Ski School is based at Sun Mountain Lodge. Group lessons cost $25. One lesson is usually sufficient to get started.
>
> The valley's trails are all clearly marked on a free local map: green for easy, blue for intermediate, black for challenging. Distance markers follow the Nordic metric system (ie kilometers, not miles).

spirit (the road ends in winter not far beyond here) and some fantastic eating places and accommodations.

The area's first European settler was Harvard educated Guy Waring, who in 1891 built a trading post at the confluence of the Chewuch (*chee*-wok) and Methow Rivers. When the mining business dried up after 1915, Winthrop teetered catastrophically on the brink of extinction, until Robert Jorgenson, the architect who had redesigned Leavenworth, stepped forward with his false-fronted shops and cowboy memorabilia.

Winthrop's renaissance coincided with the opening in 1972 of the North Cascades Hwy, which brought in a flood of new visitors. When the highway closes in winter, Winthrop becomes the Methow's cross-country-skiing HQ.

◉ Sights

Winthrop's photogenic core is compact and cheery, with plenty of gift shops, coffee bars and a decent bookstore.

Shafer Museum   MUSEUM
(www.shafermuseum.com; 285 Castle Ave; admission by donation; ⊙10am-5pm Memorial Day-Labor Day) It's hard to differentiate the reconstructed buildings in the museum from the rest of Winthrop, such is the town's eerie authenticity. However, the museum does retain one original construction: a log cabin known as 'the Castle,' built by Winthrop founder Guy Waring in 1896 as a present to his wife.

North Cascade Smokejumper Base   MUSEUM
(23 Intercity Airport Rd; ⊙8am-5pm Jun-Oct) FREE Smokejumping is a method of firefighting that involves parachuting out of a plane into a rural area to tackle a forest fire before it gets out of control. It's hard to avoid feeling humbled by the heroic exploits of the people who have been trained to do it. The Methow Valley is often seen as the birthplace of modern smokejumping (which was pioneered in the 1930s); you can tour the base, halfway between Winthrop and Twisp.

⚐ Activities

The Winthrop area is famous for its cross-country ski trails, with the best network congregated around Sun Mountain Lodge 10 miles to the west. During the summer months the trails are given over to hiking, mountain biking and horseback riding. They range from the 2.5-mile **Sunnyside**

Loop, with jaw-dropping vistas of the North Cascades, to the more adventurous **Pete's Dragon**, with its white-knuckle twists and turns. Horseback riding around Beaver Pond and Patterson Lake is another popular summertime option. You can rent bikes ($15/25/35 per two hours/four hours/day) from Sun Mountain Lodge; helmets are included. Guided horseback treks go from $40 for 1½ hours or $85 for a half-day.

Fishing for steelhead trout and chinook salmon is popular in the Methow River, but anglers are required to use catch-and-release techniques for these endangered species. **Moccasin Lake**, a mile-long hike from Patterson Lake Rd, has very good fly-fishing, with rainbow trout averaging 3lb to 5lb.

Morning Glory Balloon Tours   HOT-AIR BALLOONING
(☑509-997-1700; www.balloonwinthrop.com; 960 Hwy 20, Winthrop; adult/child $225/175) Morning Glory operates serene early-morning balloon flights over the valley between March and November. Flights last one hour.

🛏 Sleeping

Hotel Rio Vista   HOTEL $
(☑509-996-3535; www.hotelriovista.com; 285 Riverside Ave; d $80-135; ❄🐾) It looks plain at first glance, but inside are big, comfy rooms with fine views over the fast-flowing Methow River, which races within pebble-skimming distance of each individual terrace. Enjoy a riverside hot tub and magnificent Methow sunsets.

Duck Brand Hotel   HOTEL $
(☑509-996-2192; www.methownet.com/duck; 248 Riverside Ave; s/d $69/79; ❄) An apparition from *The Good, the Bad and the Ugly*, the Wild West–ified Duck Brand is not short on character, offering old-fashioned, nearly tacky (floral bedspread, lace curtains etc) lodge rooms with balconies overlooking downtown. It's perched above a popular cantina slap-bang in the middle of the town.

Mt Gardener Inn   INN $$
(☑509-996-2000; www.mtgardenerinn.com; 611 Hwy 20; r $109-139; 🐾❄) A half-mile walk from downtown Winthrop, this friendly place has a big garden area with communal BBQs and a selection of spacious and exceptionally clean cabin-style rooms decorated in soothing light woods and muted earth tones. Excellent value.

KEROUAC IN THE CASCADES

'Hozomeen, Hozomeen; most beautiful mountain I've ever seen.'

Traveling in Washington without a car might seem a bit onerous; but a little over 50 years ago Jack Kerouac, beatnik writer and author of the seminal travel novel *On the Road*, traversed the lower 48's most northwesterly state with no more than an overnight bag and an upturned thumb. Unbeknownst to many, Kerouac never owned a car and only learned to drive – somewhat reluctantly – at the age of 34. His first adventurous foray into the Pacific Northwest, documented in the later chapters of the book *The Dharma Bums*, came about when he hitched from California up to the North Cascade Mountains to work as a fire lookout on isolated Desolation Peak in the summer of 1956.

Kerouac spent 63 solitary days atop Desolation Peak, passing his hours in a small hut with panoramic views of the surrounding wilderness. With so much time on his hands, he had plenty of opportunity to contemplate life, the universe and his ever-evolving Buddhist philosophy, as he gazed out over Ross Lake and the twin-peaked majesty of looming Hozomeen (8066ft), a mountain he referred to rather chillingly as 'the Void.'

It is undocumented how many fire alarms Kerouac raised during his time in the Cascades, though he did famously use his collected scribblings in *Desolation Angels*, published in 1965, a novel that provides a fascinating insight into both the mountain scenery and the writer's ongoing battle with his inner demons.

It is still possible to hike the **Desolation Trail** up to Desolation Peak (6102ft) and ponder the fire lookout – built in 1933 – where Kerouac passed so many hours. The hike is 6.8 miles one way and is pretty strenuous, although you'll be richly rewarded with the same stunning vistas that inspired the author. To complete the hike in a day you'll need to catch a water taxi from Ross Lake Resort (p161) to the trailhead on the upper eastern side of Ross Lake. Alternatively, the hike can be incorporated into a longer backcountry adventure.

★ Sun Mountain Lodge
LODGE **$$$**

(☎509-996-2211; www.sunmountainlodge.com; Box 1000, Winthrop; r $175-375, cabins $150-750; ☺closed 21 Oct-7 Dec; ❄ 🌐 ♿ 🐾) Without a doubt one of the best places to stay in Washington, Sun Mountain Lodge has an incomparable natural setting, perched like an eagle's nest high above the Methow Valley. The 360-degree views from its highly lauded restaurant are awe-inspiring, and people travel from miles around just to enjoy breakfast here.

Inside, the lodge (check out the taxidermy collection bought from an elderly local) and its assorted cabins manage to provide luxury without pretension, while the outdoor attractions that are based around its extensive network of lakes and trails could keep a hyperactive hiker, cyclist or skier occupied for weeks. Not surprisingly, the Sun Mountain is pricey, but if you have just one splurge in the Washington wilderness east of Seattle, this should be the place.

✕ Eating

East 20 Pizza
PIZZERIA **$**

(720 Hwy 20 S; pizzas from $6.50; ☺11:30am-9pm Jun-Sep, 3-8pm Oct-May) Who'd expect such fine, authentic pizzas way out here? After a day in the mountains you can't get much better than these thin-crusted, well-topped (everything from pepperoni to curried cashews and portabello mushrooms) pies to fill the belly. Pair them with cold draft beer and salads to enjoy on the outdoor patio. Gluten-free crusts are also available.

Sheri's
CAFE **$**

(201 Riverside Av) This delightful alfresco cafe and ice-cream parlor adjacent to Sheri's Sweet Shoppe is the best place to snatch an espresso and a hot, sticky cinnamon bun. In keeping with the surroundings, the bar stools are made out of horse saddles and behind the coffee cabin you can enjoy a quick round of crazy golf while they blast steam into your grande cappuccino.

Old Schoolhouse Brewing
PUB **$$**

(www.oldschoolhousebrewery.com; 155 Riverside Ave; mains $9-14; ☺4-8pm Mon-Thu, 4-10pm Fri, noon-10pm Sat, noon-8pm Sun) Carb-load on beer in this unusual pub that occupies a former little red schoolhouse on the main street. You can choose from an impressive range of homebrewed ales; aficionados opt for the light-bodied Black Canyon Porter or the heavier, darker Grampa Clem's Brown

Ale. Classic pub-grub highlights include outlaw chili, and fish and chips with a Japanese twist. There's live music and an open mic on Friday.

Arrowleaf Bistro
FUSION $$$

(☑509-996-3920; www.arrowleafbistro.com; 253 Riverside Ave; mains $15-27; ☉ lunch & dinner) Winthrop's poshest restaurant, with its starched white tablecloths and polished wine glasses, is a notable departure from the saloon-bar staples elsewhere. But the Arrowleaf works hard to justify its price tag with knowledgeable waiting staff, an excellent riverside setting, and a menu that contains such un-cowboy-like treats as pistachio-crusted halibut and maple-brined pork chops.

ℹ️ Information

Winthrop Chamber of Commerce (www.winthropwashington.com; 202 Riverside Ave) At the corner where Hwy 20 enters downtown.

Twisp
POP 926

The largest of the Methow Valley's three tiny settlements, Twisp is a stomping ground for fishers, bird-watchers (this is prime bald-eagle country) and appreciators of fine ale – it's the site of a rip-roaringly good brewpub. Contrary to its one-horse-town image, Twisp is also the crucible of a budding artists community, though outdoor activities have long been its raison d'être.

◉ Sights & Activities

Diminutive Twisp supports a small art gallery in the shape of the **Confluence Gallery & Art Center** (☑509-997-2787; www.confluencegallery.com; 104 Glover St; ☉10am-3pm Wed-Sat) **FREE** but, outside of this, the main attractions are outdoors related. Hikes in the area are popular, with a number of them fanning off the Twisp River Rd that proceeds west of town along the banks of the Twisp River. Try the 7-mile **Eagle Creek Trail** that starts from the trailhead on W Buttermilk Creek Rd (11 miles west of Twisp) or strike out further into the **Lake Chelan-Sawtooth Wilderness Area**.

If you don't mind a few snowmobiles, **cross-country skiing** is easy along the flat Twisp River Rd. Nearer to downtown, trails start at the Idle-a-While Motel and meander around Twisp and along the Methow River.

🛏️ Sleeping & Eating

Methow Valley Inn
INN $$

(☑509-997-2253; www.methowvalleyinn.com; 234 E 2nd St; r with shared bath $89, private bath $129-149) In a storybook-cute turn-of-the-century farmhouse, this inn has eight rooms decorated country-style with handmade wrought-iron beds, beautiful quilts and plenty of mountain light through the picture windows. Downtown Twisp is walking distance or you can just chill in the lush half-acre garden.

★ **Twisp River Pub**
PUB $

(www.methowbrewing.com; 201 Hwy 20; ☉11:30am-11pm Wed-Sun; 🛜) Twisp might look like the back of beyond, but inside this beer-fueled establishment there are enough food, music and ale variations to keep the most fidgety of travelers happy. Encircling the culinary world from Africa to Asia, the menu includes bratwurst, Thai peanut stir-fry, Greek salad and the good old steak sandwich.

Beers are brewed on the premises and music rocks the rafters at least twice a week.

★ **Cinnamon Twisp**
BAKERY $

(116 N Glover St; pastries around $2.50; ☉6am-3pm) Folks from all around the valley drive however far they have to for this homey place's fresh-baked breads, terrific sandwiches, smoothies, coffee and pastries, including the signature 'cinnamon twisp', an uber cinnamon roll – almost a sticky bun – that glistens in a butter and brown-sugar glaze.

ℹ️ Information

Twisp Ranger Station (502 Glover St; ☉7:45am-4:30pm Mon-Fri) On Twisp's main street; has information on trails and campgrounds in the Okanogan National Forest.

Twisp Visitor Information Center (www.twispinfo.com; 201 S Methow Way) Operates out of the Methow Valley Community Center.

Stehekin
POP 79

What, no road access? Cut off from the rest of Washington's highway network by craggy mountains, Stehekin is that rarest of modern American settlements: one that is unreachable by car. Visitors get here either by boat or seaplane across Lake Chelan, or by a trio of long-distance hikes through the wilderness-flecked North Cascades National Park to the north.

Such purposeful inaccessibility has worked wonders for the settlement's special beauty. Largely untouched by the foibles of 21st-century culture, Stehekin is within the boundaries of the Lake Chelan National Recreation Area (part of the North Cascades National Park). It has become a byword for solitude, and a magnificent obsession for backcountry adventure enthusiasts keen to break away from the pleasure cruisers and water-skiers who ply Lake Chelan further south.

Though Stehekin does have *one* road and a handful of cars (all of which have been ferried here from Chelan or elsewhere), its isolation is both unusual and refreshing. The vast majority of visitors arrive in the settlement as part of a 90-minute stopover on a day trip from Chelan on one of two passenger boats. Stick around after they've gone home and you'll feel more like Robinson Crusoe.

◉ Sights & Activities

Browse Stehekin-made crafts at the **House That Jack Built** and visit the Golden West Visitor Center (p169) next door.

Walking

Buckner Orchard is one of the Stehekin area's oldest homesteads and makes for a refreshing walk. Once there, you'll find a homestead cabin built in 1889, plenty of old farm equipment and hundred-year-old trees that keep on bearing apples. Head 3.4 miles up Stehekin Valley Rd, turn left at the far end of the Rainbow Creek bridge and look for a sign about 20yd off the road, marking the **Buckner Orchard Walk**, an easy 1-mile round trip to the apple orchards. Park rangers offer guided walks here at 2.15pm at weekends in the summer. From just past the bridge, there's also a short path leading to **Rainbow Falls**.

Boating

Stehekin Outfitters (p168) offers rafting trips on the Stehekin River in spring and summer, as well as two-hour kayaking trips on Lake Chelan (adult/child $35/20).

Cycling

You can rent bikes from **Discovery Bikes** (www.stehekindiscoverybikes.com; per hour/day $4/20), five minutes from the dock. Prices include helmets, racks and maps. Discovery Bikes can also shuttle cyclists and their bikes up the road to the Stehekin Valley Ranch,

which is just far enough to bike back down the valley in time to catch the 2pm boat back to Chelan.

Fishing

The lower Stehekin River is open for seasonal catch-and-release fishing, with cutthroat and rainbow trout living in the upper river. **Stehekin Fishing Adventures** (www.stehekinfishingadventures.com; guided trips per day from $295) offers all number of guided fishing trips on Lake Chelan. Cabin rental is also available.

Hiking

Backpackers planning an overnight stay will need a backcountry camping permit, which can be obtained at Golden West Visitor Center (p168) or from the Chelan Ranger Station.

The mile-long **Imus Loop Trail** and the quarter-mile-loop **McKeller Cabin Trail** are both near the Stehekin boat landing.

The easy **Lakeshore Trail** starts at the Golden West Visitor Center and heads south near Lake Chelan's shore. Lake and mountain vistas framed by Ponderosa pines are visible throughout. You can walk as long as you want then turn around and backtrack, or you can make this into a backpacking trip: between May 1 and October 15 the *Lady II* passenger boat can drop you off 17 miles south of Stehekin and you can hike the one to two days north (camping permits aren't required on this stretch). Watch out for rattlesnakes along the way.

Other treks include the 5-mile **Rainbow Loop Trail**, with great lake and valley views, and the **Purple Creek Trail** toward 6884ft Purple Pass, 7.5 miles away.

Horseback-Riding

From Stehekin Valley Ranch Cascade Corrals leads three-hour horseback rides to Coon Lake ($50 per person), as well as guided hikes into the mountains with gear carried on horseback. Make bookings for all these activities at the **Courtney Log Office** (☏ 509-682-4677; www.courtneycountry.com) 200yd from the dock.

☞ Tours

Bus Tour BUS TOUR
(adult/child $8/6) A narrated bus tour is coordinated with boat arrivals during summer months and goes to impressive, 312ft-high **Rainbow Falls**.

🛏 Sleeping

There are various cabins for rent in the river valley. Check www.stehekin.com for links and more information.

Golden West Visitor Center　　CAMPGROUND $
(☑ 360-854-7365, ext 14) Provides information and backcountry camping permits for the 11 National Park Service–maintained primitive campsites along the road up the valley. All camps have pit toilets, but only the Purple Point Campground provides potable water.

Stehekin Valley Ranch　　CABIN $$$
(☑ 509-682-4677; www.stehekinvalleyranch. com; tent/ranch cabins per person $100/120; 🐾) All number of activities go on at this well-organized place 9 miles upriver from the boat landing, including cycling, horseback riding, kayaking and hiking. Even better, the price for lodging in the ranch's rustic cabins includes all meals at one of Stehekin's few proper dining establishments, along with a bus to get there.

Tent cabins are simple, canvas-topped affairs, with screened windows and showers in a nearby building. Ranch cabins have private bathrooms.

North Cascades Lodge at Stehekin　　HOTEL $$$
(☑ 509-682-4494; www.lodgeatstekehin.com; r $162-202, kitchen units $182-222; @🐾) Located next to the ferry landing, the 28 varied rooms here have lush lake views. The location is enough to make staying here an amazing experience, but it's rustic for the price and service can be grumpy. There's a recreation room (with TV), restaurant, hot tub and the village's only tiny grocery store. Sit back and switch your brain off.

🍴 Eating

There are only three places to eat in Stehekin: the two listed here as well as the restaurant in the Stehekin Landing Resort.

THE WAY THROUGH

To Native Americans, Stehekin at the head of Lake Chelan was 'the way through,' a vital trade route that linked the rainy coast with the dry interior. For adventurous modern hikers nothing much has changed. Eschewing the motor car and most other 21st-century comforts, Stehekin is reachable only by boat or on foot. For hikers, there are three main entry points – all from the north.

The quickest and most popular is via spectacular 5392ft **Cascade Pass**, reached via a steep 3.7-mile path that starts at the parking lot at the end of the Cascade River Rd, 23 miles southeast of Marblemount. After ascending to the pass, the trail continues down the other side into the Stehekin River Valley, where it joins briefly with the Pacific Crest Trail before homing in on High Bridge. From here it's 11 miles along the Stehekin Rd to the ferry landing, or you can opt to catch the four-times-daily Stehekin shuttle (summer only). The total hiking distance is 32 miles (or 21 miles if you catch the bus).

Route two starts at Colonial Creek campground at mile 130 on Hwy 20. Follow the wondrous **Thunder Creek Trail** through old-growth forest and past vertiginous glaciers up to Park Creek Pass (6059ft) before descending on the **Park Creek Trail**, 8 miles to the junction with Stehekin Rd. From here follow the Stehekin River down to High Bridge where, once again, you can either walk or catch the shuttle to Stehekin (45 miles in total, or 34 miles if you use the bus).

The easiest route starts at Rainy Pass at mile 157 on Hwy 20 and follows the well-marked and flattish **Pacific Crest Trail** (PCT; www.pcta.org) along Bridge Creek into the Stehekin River Valley. The trail, once more, comes out at High Bridge: total distance 19 miles to High Bridge, or 30 miles to Stehekin.

All of the above trips are multiday hikes that take between two and four days depending on your speed. Numerous backcountry campsites are available en route. For greater comfort (and a lighter pack) you can take advantage of a tent-to-tent hiking service offered by **Stehekin Outfitters** (☑ 509-682-4494; www.stehekinoutfitters.com; day trips adult/child $50/40). The company maintains large outfitter tents at the Cottonwood and Bridge Creek campsites, equipped with stove, cots, kitchen utensils and food. The cost is $95 for two people and an extra $25 per person thereafter. Phone ahead to reserve.

★**Stehekin Pastry Company** CAFE, BAKERY $
(www.stehekinpastry.com; Stehekin Valley Rd; pastries $2-6) In a large city this improbable coffee and pastry shop would do a roaring trade. Out in the middle of a wilderness area it appears like a mirage and is guaranteed to give fresh ardor to even the most challenging of hikes. Two miles up the valley from the boat landing, this is where to come for espresso, cinnamon buns, pies and baked-from-scratch pastries. You can take the 'bakery special' shuttle service to get there.

Stehekin Valley Ranch TRADITIONAL $$
(☑509-682-4677; www.stehekinvalleyranch.com; mains breakfast & lunch $5-8, dinner $13-18; ☺breakfast, lunch & dinner ☑) Reservations are required here for the daily set dinner menu (there's a $3 shuttle service from the dock to the lodge at 5:30pm). Grill items like burgers (beef and veggie) and fish are also available.

❶ Information

Golden West Visitor Center (PO Box 7, Stehekin; ☺8:30am-5pm May-Oct, 12:30-2pm Oct-May) A short walk up the hill from the boat landing you'll find rangers, wilderness permits, summer naturalist programs, kids activities, a 10-minute video on the surrounding area and the Golden West Art Gallery.

❶ Getting There & Away

The seaplane and ferry company work together, so you can arrange to fly to Stehekin one way and take the ferry the other for $113.

Chelan Seaplanes (☑509-682-5555; www.chelanseaplanes.com; 1328 W Woodin Ave, Chelan) Provides seaplane service between Stehekin and Chelan for $89/178 one way/round-trip.

Lake Chelan Boat Company (www.ladyofthelake.com; 1418 W Woodin Ave, Chelan) Operates the 285-passenger *Lady of the Lake II* ferry (no cars) leaving from Chelan boat dock daily at 8:30am and arriving at Stehekin at 12:30pm. It makes a 90-minute stopover before returning at 2pm (arriving back in Chelan at 6pm). The round-trip cost is $40.50. Alternatively, you can travel on the faster *Lady Express,* which cuts the four-hour boat trip in half (leave Chelan 8:30am, arrive Stehekin 10:45am). The *Lady Express* lays over in Stehekin for one hour before heading back at 11:45am (arriving back in Chelan at 2:20pm). The round-trip cost is $61. Both boats stop on the way at Lucerne and a few other docks on request. From October 15 to May 1 only the *Lady Express* runs the trip.

❶ Getting Around

Although there are roads and cars *in* Stehekin, there are no roads *to* Stehekin. Courtesy transportation to and from the boat landing is included in most lodging prices.

Bicycles are the easiest way to get around. If you'd prefer to bring your own, the Lake Chelan Boat Company charges $24 round-trip for bike transportation.

From late May to early October, the National Park Service runs the **Stehekin Shuttle Bus** (☑360-856-5700) up and down Stehekin Valley Rd four times a day. The 11 miles from the boat landing to High Bridge, where the drivable road ends, costs $5/2.50/5 per adult/child/bike.

Chelan & Around

POP 3945

Chelan is an elongated natural lake (at 1486ft it's the third deepest in the US) that once provided a prime fishing ground for Native Americans. Today it is an outstanding recreation spot for anyone with a penchant for water sports. Surrounded by wineries, apple orchards, hotels and a slightly incongruous water park, the lake's southern shore is taken up by its eponymous town, while 55 miles to the north lies a get-away-from-it-all antidote: high, steep mountains and isolated Stehekin. Yin and yang – take your pick.

🏃 Activities

Lake Chelan shelters some of the nation's cleanest water and has consequently become one of Washington's premier water-recreation areas. Not surprisingly, the place is cheek by jowl in summer, with all number of speedboats, Jet Skis and power craft battling it out for their own private slice of water.

There are public beaches at Lakeside Park, near the western side of town, and at Lake Chelan State Park, 9 miles west on S Lakeshore Rd. Manson Bay Park, in the small lakeside community of Manson, 8 miles northwest of Chelan, has a swimming area that features several floating docks.

Fishing is popular in Lake Chelan, with lake trout, kokanee salmon, ling cod and smallmouth bass relatively abundant.

Mountain bikers should stop by the ranger station (p171) and pick up a map of USFS roads open to cycling. One popular trail follows the north fork of Twenty-Five Mile Creek, climbing steeply for 3 miles before leveling out through pine forest and eventually meeting the Devil's Backbone trailhead. At Echo Ridge near Manson, there are 35 miles of traffic-free trails ideal for mountain biking. In winter these are used for **cross-country skiing**.

Slidewaters Water Park   WATER PARK
(www.slidewaters.com; 102 Waterslide Dr; day pass adult/child $18/15; ⊙10am-7pm May-Sep; ⊛) If you have kids, don't even think they'll let you sneak past this park. It's off W Woodin Ave, on a hill above the *Lady of the Lake* boat dock.

Don Morse Memorial Park   WATER PARK
(Chelan; ⊙10am-10pm Memorial Day-Labor Day) **FREE** On the lake's northern shore is this water funland, with beach, boat launch, putting green, playground, skate park and much more.

**Darrell & Dad's Family Guide
Service**   FISHING
(www.darrellanddads.com; 231 Division, Manson; half-/full day for 2 people from $175/370) Guided fishing excursions.

Lake Rider Sports   KAYAK RENTAL
(www.lakeridersports.com; Lakeshore Waterfront Park; single/double kayaks per day $50/70) To avoid any high-speed collisions close to Chelan town, try renting a kayak, paddleboard or rowboat here and paddling up the lake to see some undiluted Cascadian nature firsthand.

Uncle Tim's Toys   EQUIPMENT RENTAL
(www.uncletimstoys.com; Lakeshore Marina & Park, Chelan; zip-lining per person from $39) Rents out bikes and ski equipment and offers four zip-line runs.

🛏 Sleeping

Midtowner Motel   MOTEL $
(☑509-682-4051; www.midtowner.com; 721 E Woodin Ave; r $65-120; ⊛@⊛⊛) This bargain is a healthy five blocks from the town center and lake, a small price to pay considering the reasonable fee, cleanliness and above-average motel facilities. These include coffee on tap, a Jacuzzi and an indoor-outdoor swimming pool.

Lake Chelan State Park   CAMPGROUND $
(☑509-687-3710; S Lakeshore Rd; tent/RV sites $23/32) A guarded swimming beach, picnic areas and a boat launch make this a busy summertime destination. Of the nearly 150 sites, there are some nice lakeside spots and 35 RV hookups. Reservations are necessary in summer.

Campbell's Resort   HOTEL $$$
(☑509-682-2561; www.campbellsresort.com; 104 W Woodin Ave; r/ste in summer from $152/225; ⊛⊛⊛⊛) The plushest place in town, Campbell's hogs the waterfront along Manson Hwy with its 170 guest rooms, marina, two swimming pools, restaurant, pub and 1200ft stretch of sandy beach. Modern rooms are spotless and have balconies, but

---

CHELAN WINE COUNTRY

In May 2009 Lake Chelan became Washington's 11th certified American Viticultural Area (AVA). There are currently 20 wineries in a region stretching from Chelan to just beyond Manson (find a winery map at www.lakechelanwinevalley.com). A mild lake effect adds distinctive features to the wine here.

Tsillan Cellars (www.tsillancellars.com; 3875 Hwy 97A; ⊙noon-5pm Sun-Thu, to 6pm Fri & Sat) has a stunning Tuscan-inspired chateau on a sloping shore over the lake and is a favorite spot for weddings and events. The award-winning wines, however, do not cower under the beautiful scenery – try the reserve syrah, then stay to dine at upscale, delicious and romantic **Sorrento's Ristorante** (☑509-682-5409; mains $16-34; ⊙5pm-late Wed-Fri, noon-late Sat, 10am-late Sun), the finest restaurant in the region.

Vin du Lac (www.vindulac.com; 105 Hwy 150; ⊙11am-7pm) wines are enjoyed in a pretty, family-friendly yellow tasting room surrounded by flowery patios and overlooking Lake Chelan. An old orchard now knocks out decent syrah and chardonnay. There's also an on-site bistro serving lunch, dinner and in-between gourmet snacks of charcuterie and imported cheeses.

Hard Row to Hoe (www.hardrow.com; 300 Ivan Morse Rd, Manson; ⊙noon-6pm) gets its name from its nefarious past as a brothel (which clients got to by row boat). All tongue in cheek aside, the 'Good in Bed' sparkling sangiovese and pinot noir blend is good in a glass too.

the privilege of staying here doesn't come cheap – especially in the summer, when rates triple.

Lakeside Lodge & Suites HOTEL **$$$**
(☑509-682-4396; www.lakesidelodgeandsuites.com; 2312 W Woodin Ave; d incl breakfast $197-270; ✱ 🛜 ☒ ♨) This is the best location in town, aside grassy Lakeside Park, which boasts Chelan's most idyllic municipal setting along with the town's best stretch of sand-and-shingle beach. There's a lovely pool, top lake views and suitably well-furnished rooms, though you may spend a lot of time dodging the plethora of passing convention delegates.

✖ Eating

Vogue CAFE **$**
(www.thevoguelounge.com; 117 E Woodin Ave; 🛜) Putting aside the ubiquitous chai lattes and blueberry muffins, this venerable and popular 'cafe' showcases everything from live music (at weekends) and local art to a selection of its own jams and vinaigrettes. It also acts as a popular tasting room for aspiring wine connoisseurs. There's alfresco seating out front and wi-fi access inside.

Bear Foods & Creperie CREPERIE **$**
(125 E Woodin Ave; crepes $6-8; ⏱10:30am-2:30pm) Inside the natural-food market are the locals' favorite quick bites: sweet and savory crepes (try the hummus, roast pepper and olive) and fresh soups and salads.

Sojourners PIZZERIA **$$**
(110 E Woodin Ave; pizzas from $18; ⏱11:30am-8pm Wed & Thu, to 8:30pm Fri & Sat) Bright and clean with bench seating, about the friendliest owners you may ever meet and good, basic pizza. Whether you order them or not your meal will probably start with garlic rolls fresh from the oven.

ℹ Information

Chelan USFS/NPS Ranger Station (428 W Woodin Ave; ⏱7:30am-4:30pm Mon-Fri) For a wealth of information on Wenatchee National Forest and other protected areas.
Lake Chelan Visitors Center (www.lakechelan.com; 102 E Johnson Ave) Tourist information.

ℹ Getting There & Around

Chelan Seaplanes (p169) operates a daily seaplane service to Stehekin from the airfield, 1 mile west of town on Alt US 97.

Lake Chelan Boat Company (p169) runs the *Lady of the Lake II* and the *Lady Express* daily for trips across Lake Chelan to Lucerne and Stehekin. The **dock** (www.ladyofthelake.com) is located on the south shore, just a mile west of downtown on Alt US 97.

Wenatchee-based **Link Transit** (www.linktransit.com) provides bus services between Manson and Wenatchee (1½ hours) via Chelan (15 minutes) on Rte 21. For those traveling to/from Chelan, buses stop on the south side of Johnson Ave, right next to the local visitor center.

SOUTH CASCADES

More rounded and less hemmed in than their sawtoothed cousins to the north, the South Cascades are nonetheless higher. Their pinnacle in more ways than one is 14,411ft Mt Rainier, the fifth-highest mountain in the lower 48 and arguably one of the most dramatic stand-alone mountains in the world. Further south, fiery Mt St Helens needs zero introduction, while unsung Adams glowers way off to the east like a sulking middle child.

Most of the South Cascades are protected by an interconnecting patchwork of national parks, forests and wilderness areas. The largest and most emblematic of these is Mt Rainier National Park, inaugurated in 1899, while the most unusual is the Mt St Helens National Volcanic Monument, formed in 1982, two years after the mountain's eruption.

While development inside the parks is refreshingly light, keen downhill skiers can find solace at Crystal Mountain, just outside the limits of Mt Rainier National Park. While it's no Whistler, it is the largest ski resort in Washington state.

Snoqualmie Valley

East of Seattle's Eastside, the Snoqualmie Valley has long been a photogenic backwater of dairy farms, lush orchards and produce gardens surrounded by steep alpine peaks. Although suburbs are quickly taking over the valley, there's still enough of a rural, small-town ambience to make for a beautiful drive or bike ride.

North Bend, on Hwy 202 just off I-90, is *Twin Peaks* country, the setting for David Lynch's surreal TV series from the early 1990s. The former Mar T's Café, now called **Twede's** (137 W North Bend Way; burgers from $11; ⏱6:30am-8pm Mon-Thu, to 9pm Fri & Sat, to 7pm

Sun), was the diner with the famous cherry pie (not so good nowadays) and cups of joe; a fire gutted it in 2000, but it has been rebuilt and is still a good place to try one of the 50 types of burger. The decor is so much as it was in the show – down to the waitstaff – that it's pleasantly eerie.

Continue along Hwy 202 to the little town of Snoqualmie, where you'll find antique shops and a store devoted to Northwest wines. Just north of town, Salish Lodge & Spa (☎425-888-2556, 800-826-6124; www.salishlodge.com; 6501 Railroad Ave; d from $229) is a beautiful resort that sits atop 268ft Snoqualmie Falls. *Twin Peaks* fans know the hotel as the Great Northern; the exterior of the lodge appeared in the opening credits, and an observation point near the parking lot offers the same view. Visitors can also see the falls from the lodge's dining room or hike to them along a winding trail.

Hwy 203 branches off from 202 at Fall City; follow it north to Carnation, where the Snoqualmie and Tolt Rivers meet at John McDonald Park. This is a great place for a riverside picnic, swim or hike. Carnation was once the center of the valley's dairy industry, and several farms here sell fruit and vegetables at roadside stands.

Duvall, about 25 miles north of North Bend along Hwys 202 and 203, has a rural small-town atmosphere despite its recent growth spurt. Wander Main St and check out the shops and nurseries. From here, head west on Woodinville–Duvall Rd for about 10 miles to reach Woodinville, home of several good wineries and the legendary, very, very upscale Herbfarm (14590 NE 145th St; dinner $180-200; ☉7pm Thu-Sat, 4:30pm Sun), where nine-course dinners are drawn from the gardens and farm itself, as well as small local growers, and matched with locally produced wines. There's a trail along the Sammamish River, if you fancy walking it off. From here it's a quick drive along I-405 back to Seattle.

Tacoma

Tacoma gets a bad rap as a beleaguered mill town known mostly for its distinctive 'Tacomaroma,' a product of the nearby paper mills. Its nickname, 'City of Destiny' – because it was Puget Sound's railroad terminus – once seemed like a grim joke. But destiny has started to come through for Tacoma. Renewed investment in the arts and significant downtown revitalization make it a worthy stop on the Portland–Seattle route.

Tacoma's tribute to native son Dale Chihuly, the Museum of Glass (☎866-468-7386; 1801 Dock St; admission $12; ☉10am-5pm Wed-Sat, noon-5pm Sun, 10am-8pm 3rd Thu each month), with its slanted tower called the Hot Shop Amphitheater, has art exhibits and glassblowing demonstrations. Chihuly's characteristically elaborate and colorful Bridge of Glass walkway connects the museum with the enormous copper-domed neobaroque 1911 Union Station. Some huge pieces by Chihuly greet visitors to the city's Federal Courthouse (1717 Pacific Ave). For smaller-scale work, don't miss Chihuly's permanent collection at the Tacoma Art Museum (☎253-272-4258; 1701 Pacific Ave; adult/student $9/8; ☉10am-5pm Wed-Sun, to 8pm 3rd Thu each month).

Take Ruston Way out to Point Defiance (☎253-591-5337; zoo adult/child $13.50/11.50; ☉9:30am-5pm), a 700-acre park complex with free-roaming bison and mountain goats, a logging museum, a zoo, an aquarium and miles of trails.

Mt Rainier National Park Area

Emblazoned on every Washington license plate and visible throughout much of the western state, Mt Rainier is the contiguous USA's fifth-highest peak and, in the eyes of many, its most awe-inspiring.

Close to Puget Sound's urban areas and unobstructed by any other peaks, the mountain's overwhelming presence, set off by its 26 glaciers, has long enraptured the millions of inhabitants who live in its shadow. Though it's an iconic peak to bag, climbing Rainier is no picnic; old hands liken it to running a marathon in thin air with crampons stuck to your shoes. Approximately 9000 people attempt it annually, but only half of them make it to the top.

Beneath Rainier's volatile exterior, even darker forces fester. As an active stratovolcano that recorded its last eruptive activity as recently as 1854, Rainier harnesses untold destructive powers that, if provoked, could threaten downtown Seattle with mudslides and cause tsunamis in Puget Sound. Not surprisingly, the mountain has long been imbued with myth.

The Native Americans called the mountain Tahoma or Tacoma, meaning the 'mother of waters'; George Vancouver named it Rainier in honor of his colleague and friend Rear Admiral Peter Rainier, while most Seattleites refer to it reverently as 'the Mountain' and forecast the weather by its visibility.

Encased in a 368-sq-mile national park (the US' fifth national park when it was inaugurated in 1899), the mountain's forest-covered foothills harbor numerous hiking trails and huge swaths of flower-carpeted meadows. When the clouds magically disappear during long, clear days in July and August, it becomes one of Washington's most paradisiacal playgrounds.

Nisqually Entrance

This southwestern corner of Mt Rainier National Park is its most developed (and hence most visited) corner. Here you'll find the park's only lodging, the only year-round road and the gateway settlements of Ashford and Copper Creek that offer plenty of useful park-related facilities and lodging.

Hwy 706 enters the park about an hour and a half's drive southeast of Seattle, just past Ashford and adjacent to the Nisqually River. After the entry tollbooth, a well-paved road continues east, offering the first good views of Mt Rainier – weather permitting – a few miles further on at Kautz Creek.

At the 7-mile mark you'll pass Longmire, the park's first orientation point, replete with lodging, food and hiking trailheads. From here the road climbs steeply for 12 miles, passing numerous hairpin turns and viewpoints until it emerges at the elevated alpine meadows of Paradise, where you'll find the area's biggest and best information center–museum.

◉ Sights

Longmire Hiker Information Center   VISITOR CENTER
(☑ 360-569-2211, ext 3317; ⊘ summer) FREE
Worth a stop to stretch your legs or gain an early glimpse of Rainier's mossy old-growth forest, Longmire was the brainchild of a certain James Longmire, who first came here in 1883 during a climbing trip when he noticed the hot mineral springs that bubbled up in a lovely meadow opposite the present-day National Park Inn. He and his family returned the following year and established Longmire's Medicinal Springs, and in 1890

he built the Longmire Springs Hotel. Since 1917 the National Park Inn has stood on this site – built in classic 'parkitecture' style – and is complemented by a small store, some park offices, the tiny **Longmire Museum** (☑ 360-569-2211, ext 3314; ⊘ 9am-6pm Jun-Sep. to 5pm Oct-May) FREE and a number of important trailheads.

★ Paradise   VISITOR CENTER
FREE 'Oh, what a paradise!' exclaimed the daughter of park pioneer James Longmire on visiting this spot for the first time in the 1880s. Suddenly, the high-mountain nirvana had a name, and a very apt one at that. One of the snowiest places on earth, 5400ft-high Paradise remains the park's most popular draw, with its famous flower meadows backed by dramatic Rainier views on the days (a clear minority annually) when the mountain decides to take its cloudy hat off. Aside from hiding numerous trailheads and being the starting point for most summit hikes, Paradise guards the iconic Paradise Inn (built in 1916 and refurbished in 2008) and the massive,

---

SOUTHERN CASCADES: UFO HOT SPOT

In 1947 search-and-rescue pilot Kenneth Arnold spotted nine cylindrical disks that he timed flying between Mt Rainier and Mt Adams in 102 seconds – which would make their speed twice that of sound and significantly faster than any known aircraft. That same day there were numerous similar reports across Washington and Oregon. Although the US Air Force deemed these mysterious sightings a mirage, Arnold's descriptions of the pan-shaped objects coined the phrase 'flying saucer.'

Over on the east side of Mt Adams, the Yakima people have reported seeing white lights moving low in the sky for over a hundred years. Meanwhile, James Gilliland, author of several UFO books and owner of the website **Enlightened Contact with Extraterrestrial Intelligence** (ECETI; www. eceti.org) runs the Satvva Sanctuary in Trout Lake, where you can apply for UFO-viewing privileges from the ranch. Pretty much everyone who goes sees something; naysayers have their explanations, while believers have very different ones.

Mt Rainier National Park

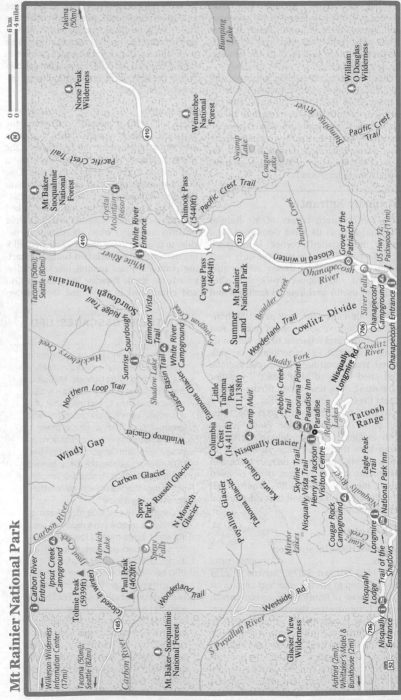

informative Henry M Jackson Visitor Center (p177), that holds a cutting-edge museum with hands-on exhibits on everything from flora to glacier formation and shows a must-see 21-minute film entitled *Mount Rainier: Restless Giant*. Park naturalists lead free interpretive hikes from the visitor center daily in summer, and snowshoe walks on winter weekends.

🏃 Activities

Climbing

Mt Rainier was first climbed in 1870 by Hazard Stevens and PB Van Trump. The most popular route starts at Paradise and involves a brief night's rest at Camp Muir before rising between midnight and 2am to don crampons and ropes for the climb over Disappointment Cleaver and the Ingraham Glacier to the summit. All climbers going higher than Camp Muir must register at the Paradise Ranger Station next to the Henry M Jackson Visitors Center. Excellent four-day guided ascents ($991) are led by **Rainier Mountaineering Inc** (www.rmiguides.com; 30027 SR706 E, Ashford; 4-day ascent $991).

Cross-Country Skiing

During the winter the road is generally plowed as far as Paradise, and people take to the trails on cross-country skis and snowshoes. The **Longmire Ski Touring Center** (⊙8am-6pm Sat & Sun Thanksgiving-Apr), in the Longmire General Store, has trail information, lessons and cross-country ski and snowshoe rentals.

Hiking

Rainier's textbook long-distance hike is the 93-mile **Wonderland Trail** that completely circumnavigates the mountain with a cumulative elevation gain of 21,400ft. Longmire is its most popular starting point, with the majority of hikers tackling the route over 10 to 12 days in a clockwise direction in July or August. There are 18 backcountry campsites en route.

For a shorter hike from Longmire you can test your mettle on the precipitous **Eagle Peak Trail**, a steep 7.2-mile out-and-back hike. A more laid-back look at some old-growth forest and pastoral meadows is available on the signposted **Trail of the Shadows** loop, a 0.8-mile trail that begins across the road from the museum and is wheelchair accessible for the first 0.4 miles.

Paradise, situated at 5400ft, has a much shorter hiking season than Longmire (snow can persist into late June), but its wildflower pastiche, which includes avalanche lilies, western anemones, lupines, mountain bog gentians and paintbrushes, makes the experience spectacular.

The Paradise area is crisscrossed with trails of all types and standards, some good for a short stroll (with the kids), others the realm of more serious hikers. To get a close-up of the Nisqually Glacier follow the 1.2-mile **Nisqually Vista Trail**. For something more substantial like the 5-mile **Skyline Trail**, starting behind the Paradise Inn and climbing approximately 1600ft to **Panorama Point**, with good views of Mt Rainier and the neighboring Tatoosh Range.

Intrepid day-hikers can continue up the mountain from Panorama Point via the **Pebble Creek Trail** to the permanent snowfield track that leads to **Camp Muir**, the main overnight bivouac spot for climbing parties. At 10,000ft, this hike is not to be undertaken lightly. Take sufficient clothing and load up with a good supply of food and water.

👉 Tours

EverGreen Escapes   BUS TOUR
(www.evergreenescapes.com; 10hr tour $195) Biodiesel Mercedes minivans make this the most luxe and eco tour option. It offers tours year-round, so expect to strap on snowshoes (included) in winter months. Tours also include a gourmet lunch and morning and afternoon tea with snacks.

Tours Northwest   BUS TOUR
(📞888-293-1404; www.toursnorthwest.com; 10hr tours $119; ⊙Apr-Nov) Twenty-four-passenger 'mini coaches' head out from Seattle and up to Paradise and back, stopping at all the sights and leaving time for short hikes.

🛏 Sleeping & Eating

Beyond what we've listed here there are numerous sleeping options between Elbe and Copper Creek, close to the park entrance. A great option is one of the many cabin rentals. Try www.visitrainier.com for options.

Whittaker's Motel & Bunkhouse   HOSTEL $
(📞360-569-2439; www.whittakersbunkhouse.com; 30205 SR 706 E; dm/d $35/90; 🕸) Part of Rainier's 'furniture,' Whittaker's is the home base of legendary Northwestern climber Lou Whittaker, who first summited the mountain at the age of 19 and has guided countless adventurers to the top in the years since. Down-to-earth and comfortable, this

> ### ℹ PARK INFORMATION
>
> For information on the park check out the National Park Service website at www.nps.gov/mora, which includes downloadable maps and descriptions of 50 park trails.
>
> Park entrance fees are $15 per car and $5 for pedestrians and cyclists (those under 17 are admitted free), and are valid for seven days from purchase. A $30 annual pass admits the passholder and accompanying passengers for 12 months from date of purchase.
>
> The driving loop around the mountain is 147 miles (driving time is about five hours without stops) and the main roads are usually open mid-May through October.

place has a good old-fashioned youth-hostel feel, with cheap sleeps available in six-bed dorms.

The alluring on-site **Whittaker's Café & Espresso** (☉7am-9pm) is a fine place to hunker down for breakfast – no cling-wrapped day-old muffins here. It's open weekends only in winter.

Nisqually Lodge　　　　　　　　MOTEL $
(☑360-569-8804; http://nisqually.whitepasstravel.com; 31609 SR 706 E; r $78-98; ❉🐾) With an expansive lobby complete with crackling fireplace and huge well-stocked rooms, this lodge is far plusher than an average motel. The outdoor Jacuzzi and easy access to the park pretty much seal the deal in this price bracket.

Cougar Rock Campground　　CAMPGROUND $
(☑360-569-2211; campsites late Jun-Labor Day $15, rest of season $12; ☉late May–mid-Oct) Cougar Rock, 2.3 miles north of Longmire on the way to Paradise, has 173 individual campsites and flush toilets. Rangers lead campfire talks on summer evenings.

★**Paradise Inn**　　　　　HISTORIC HOTEL $$
(☑360-569-2275; www.mtrainierguestservices.com; r with shared/private bath from $69/114; ☉May-Oct) The historic Paradise was constructed in 1916. Designed to blend in with the environment and constructed almost entirely of local materials, including exposed cedar logs in the Great Room, the hotel was

an early blueprint for National Park-rustic-style architecture countrywide.

Reopening in 2008 after a two-year, $30-million, earthquake-withstanding revamp, the smallish rooms (some with shared bath) retain their close-to-the-wilderness essence, while the communal areas are nothing short of regal.

National Park Inn　　　　　HISTORIC INN $$
(☑360-569-2275; www.guestservices.com/rainier; r with shared/private bath $116/164, units $244; 🅿❉) The National Park Inn, parts of which date from 1917, goes out of its way to be rustic, with no TVs or telephones and small yet cozy facilities. But who needs HBO and the Discovery Channel when you've got fine service, fantastic surroundings and delectable complimentary afternoon tea and scones served in the comfortable dining room? The inn's the pride of Longmire. Book ahead in the summer.

✗ Eating

Aside from the two historic inns, the only eating in the park is in the cafeteria of the Henry M Jackson Visitor Center (p177). The Ashford area, just outside the Nisqually entrance, has half a dozen options, spearheaded by the Copper Creek Inn.

★**Copper Creek Inn**　　　　　AMERICAN $$
(www.coppercreekinn.com; 35707 SR 706 E, Ashford; breakfast from $7, burgers $10, dinner mains $12-27; ☉7am-9pm) Forget the historic inns. This is one of the state's great rural restaurants, and breakfast is an absolute must if you're heading off for a lengthy hike inside the park. Situated just outside the Nisqually entrance, the Copper Creek has been knocking out pancakes, wild blackberry pie and its own home-roasted coffee since 1946.

National Park Inn　　　　　HOMESTYLE $$
(mains $16-19; ☉lunch & dinner) Hearty hiking fare is served at this homely inn-restaurant and – in the absence of any real competition – it's surprisingly good. Try the pot roast or the chicken with honey glaze, and make sure not to miss the huge blackberry cobbler with ice cream that will require a good 2-mile hike along the Wonderland Trail (which starts just outside the door) to work off.

Paradise Inn　　　　　　　HOMESTYLE $$
(brunch $24, dinner mains $16-23; ☉breakfast, lunch & dinner Jun-Sep) The huge stone fireplace is the highlight of this dining room

and it easily overshadows the food. Buffalo meatloaf and crab mac 'n' cheese are the most enticing options.

❶ Information

In Longmire, the museum (p173) can field basic questions, but the information center in Paradise is the best place to get answers.

Henry M Jackson Visitor Center (☑360-569-2211, ext 2328; Paradise; ⊙10am-7pm daily Jun-Oct, to 5pm Sat & Sun Oct-Dec)

Ashford Visitors Center (30027 SR 706; ⊙9am-8pm May-Oct, to 5pm Nov-Apr) The best source of information outside the park, the center is located 6 miles before the Nisqually entrance. Has a shop, maps, leaflets and helpful staff.

Ohanapecosh Entrance

Ohanapecosh (o-*ha*-nuh-peh-*kosh*) in the park's southeastern corner is accessed by the small settlement of Packwood, 12 miles to the southwest on US 12. Packwood harbors a small number of eating and sleeping options. Shoehorned between Mt Rainier and its two southern neighbors, Mt St Helens and Mt Adams, this is a good base for travelers wanting to visit two or more of the mountains. It's linked to Paradise by Hwy 706, but Ohanapecosh's roads are generally closed in the winter months due to adverse weather, making it less accessible than Nisqually.

🏃 Activities

Starting just north of the Ohanapecosh Visitors Center, the 1.5-mile **Grove of the Patriarchs Trail** is one of the park's most popular short hikes and explores a small island (the grove) in the Ohanapecosh River replete with craning Douglas fir, cedar and hemlock trees, some of which are over 1000 years old.

🛏 Sleeping & Eating

Packwood is the closest settlement outside the park and holds a bevy of sleeping options.

Hotel Packwood HOTEL **$**
(☑360-494-5431; 104 Main St, Packwood; tw/d with shared bath $38/42, d $54; 🕾) A frontier-style hotel with a wraparound verandah, the Packwood ain't fancy, but it's authentic – and at this price, who can argue? There are nine varied rooms in the renovated 1912 establishment, two of which can accommodate four people. Chuck in free wi-fi, free coffee and

the odd elk roaming the grounds and you're laughing.

Ohanapecosh Campground CAMPGROUND **$**
(☑360-494-2229; Hwy 123; campsites May, Jun, Sep & Oct $12, late Jun-Labor Day $15; ⊙closed Nov-Apr) Near the visitor center, this NPS facility has 188 campsites and flush toilets. Rangers lead campfire talks on summer evenings.

Cowlitz River Lodge MOTEL **$$**
(☑360-494-4444; www.escapetothemountains. com; Hwy 12, at Skate Creek Rd, Packwood; r incl breakfast $78-98; ❉🕾) Probably the most convenient accommodations for both Mt Rainier and Mt St Helens, the Cowlitz is the sister motel to Ashford's Nisqually Lodge and offers 32 above-average motel rooms along with the obligatory outdoor Jacuzzi.

Butter Butte CAFE, BAKERY **$**
(105 E Main St, Packwood; ⊙7am-5pm) While cops eat doughnuts, park rangers seem to prefer muffins. Stop in at this cozy morning spot for the best coffee in town (staff roast their own beans), baked goods and perhaps an informative chat with a friendly, khaki-clad officer.

❶ Information

Destination Packwood (www.destinationpackwood.com; 12990 US Hwy 12, www.destinationpackwood.com; ⊙8.30am-5pm Mon-Fri) A good source of information for the White Pass area.

Ohanapecosh Visitors Center (⊙9am-5pm May–mid-Oct) At the park's southeastern corner on Hwy 123. The displays here focus on tree identification and the local old-growth forest. Rangers also offer information on hiking trails.

White River Entrance

Rainier's main eastern entrance is the gateway to Sunrise, which at 6400ft marks the park's highest road. Thanks to the superior elevation here, the summer season is particularly short and snow can linger well into July. It is also noticeably drier than Paradise, resulting in an interesting variety of subalpine vegetation, including masses of wildflowers.

The views from Sunrise are famously spectacular and – aside from stunning close-ups of Mt Rainier itself – you can also, quite literally, watch the weather roll in over the distant peaks of Mts Baker and Adams. Similarly impressive is the glistening Emmons

Glacier, which, at 4 sq miles in size, is the largest glacier in the contiguous USA.

🏃 Activities

Day hikes from Sunrise offer dramatic scenery and rewarding mountain vistas, and while the crowds here can be thick in the summer, the lack of tour buses makes it substantially quieter than Paradise.

A trailhead directly across the parking lot from the Sunrise Lodge Cafeteria provides access to the **Emmons Vista**, with good views of Mt Rainier, Little Tahoma and the Emmons Glacier. Nearby, the 1-mile **Sourdough Ridge Trail** takes you out into pristine subalpine meadows for stunning views over the Washington giants of Mt Rainier, Mt Baker, Glacier Peak and Mt Adams.

To get to **Emmons Glacier**, you'll need to set off from the White River Campground, 13 miles by road from Sunrise. Look out for both mountain goats and mountain climbers ascending the Inter Glacier as you track west along the **Glacier Basin Trail**. The official overlook is about 1 mile from the campground along a spur path to the left.

🛏️ Sleeping & Eating

White River Campground CAMPGROUND **$**
(☎360-663-2273; campsites $12; ⊘late Jun–mid-Sep) This 112-site campground is 10 road miles or 3.5 steep trail miles downhill from Sunrise. Facilities include flush toilets, drinking water and crowded, though not unpleasant, camping spaces.

Sunrise Lodge Cafeteria CAFETERIA **$**
(☎360-569-2425; snacks $5-7; ⊘10am-7pm Jun 30-Sep 16) As the only eating joint in a 30-mile radius, Sunrise's posthike chili can look deceptively appetizing. There's not a lot else here apart from the ubiquitous hot dogs and hamburgers, and there's no overnight accommodation.

ℹ️ Information

Sunrise Visitors Center (⊘10am-6pm early Jul-early Sep)
Wilderness Information Center (⊘7.30am-4.30pm) At the White River entrance; dispenses backcountry permits and hiking information.

Carbon River Entrance

The park's northwestern entrance is its most isolated and undeveloped corner, with two unpaved (and unconnected) roads and little in the way of facilities, save a lone ranger station and the very basic Ipsut Creek Campground. But while the tourist traffic might be thin on the ground, the landscape lacks nothing in magnificence or serendipity.

Named for its coal deposits, Carbon River is the park's wettest region and protects one of the few remaining examples of inland temperate rainforest in the contiguous USA. Dense, green and cloaked in moss, this verdant wilderness can be penetrated by a handful of interpretive trails that fan off the Carbon River Rd.

For close-up mountain views head for Mowich Lake on a separate road which branches off a few miles outside the park entrance. This is Rainier's largest and deepest lake and a starting point for various wilderness hikes. In close proximity to Mowich is the Carbon Glacier, the nation's lowest glacier; its snout touches an elevation of 3520ft.

🏃 Activities

To experience the rare thrill of walking inside a thick canopied temperate rainforest, venture out on the 0.3-mile **Rainforest Trail**, just inside the park entrance. The trail loops via a raised boardwalk past huge-leafed ferns and giant dripping trees.

The 3520ft snout of the **Carbon Glacier** can be accessed via a trail from the Ipsut Creek Campground, which proceeds southeast for 3.5 miles to a constructed overlook. Hikers are warned not to approach the glacier, as rockfall from its surface is unpredictable and dangerous. This hike is technically part of the longer Wonderland Trail.

From Mowich Lake, one extremely popular trail heads south and passes **Spray Falls** on its way to **Spray Park**, flush with wildflowers late in the summer. It's almost 3 miles to Spray Park, but with numerous steep switchbacks above the falls the trail is far from easy.

🛏️ Sleeping

Ipsut Creek Campground CAMPGROUND **$**
(☎360-829-5127; campsites with wilderness camping permit free; ⊘year-round, weather permitting) This free campground is at the end of the Carbon River Rd and has 12 campsites and one group site. There are pit toilets but no drinking water. Ipsut currently has no road access; walk-ins only.

ℹ Information

Carbon River Ranger Station & Wilderness Information Center (⊘8:30am-4pm May-Nov, 7:30am-7:30pm Jun-Aug) Come here to pick up permits for backcountry camping and for north-side climbs. Note that, after closure since 2006, Carbon River will not reopen to vehicles and will be maintained as a foot and mountain-bike trail.

Crystal Mountain

Just outside the northeastern corner of Mt Rainier National park lies **Crystal Mountain Resort** (www.skicrystal.com; 🖫), Washington's largest ski area, 39 miles east of Enumclaw off Hwy 410. This is the state's only ski 'resort' with various overnight accommodations at the base. However, in reality, Crystal still functions primarily as a day-use area due to its relative proximity to Seattle and Tacoma. The mountain's 2600 acres, first opened in 1962, have an incredible array of terrain including some wonderful backcountry. In winter 2010 it opened the state's first gondola. Daily lift passes are $78/67 per adult/child (with gondola).

🛏 Sleeping & Eating

A variety of condos are available at the mountain base from **Crystal Mountain Lodging** (www.crystalmountainlodging.com; condos $200-275). Aside from the resort eating options, there are a couple of restaurants on the mountain itself.

Alpine Inn   HOTEL **$$**
(☑360-663-2262; www.crystalhotels.com; r $85-190; 🖥) Run by Crystal Mountain Hotels, this Bavarian-style inn looks as if it's been dragged across from kitschy Leavenworth on the other side of the Wenatchee National Forest. Cozy, comfortable and playing deftly on its European image, the inn boasts restaurant, rathskeller, deli, bar and ski-snowboard shop.

Alta Crystal Resort   SUITES **$$$**
(☑360-663-2500; www.altacrystalresort.com; 2-6 person ste from $190; 🖥🖂🛏) This resort is popular year-round thanks to its proximity to the ski resort (winter) and Mt Rainier National Park's Sunrise Lodge Cafeteria and trailheads (summer). It's one of the area's plushest accommodations (though it's technically outside the park). Encased in 22 wooded acres and bisected by Deep Creek, it consists of 24 suites surrounding a pool and Jacuzzi.

One-bedroom suites sleep up to four and loft suites accommodate up to six. All have kitchenettes and wood stoves or fireplaces.

ℹ Getting There & Away

On weekends and holidays from December to March a **shuttle bus** (☑206-626-5200; www.crystalsnowbus.com; round-trip $35) transports skiers to/from Seattle.

WHITE PASS

Long considered the smaller, quieter sibling of Crystal Mountain, **White Pass** (www.skiwhitepass.com) ski area, 50 miles west of Yakima on US 12, was expanded in 2010, doubling in size to 1500 acres and incorporating a new midmountain **lodge** (☑509-672-3131; www.whitepassvillageinn.com; 38933 US 12; studios $130, 1-bed condos $176; 🖥🖂). During the ski season **South West Washington Charter Tours** (www.swwashingtonchartertours.com) runs a ski shuttle to White Pass from Centralia/Olympia for $25/30.

Mt St Helens

What it lacks in height (it's now 8366ft) Mt St Helens makes up for in fiery infamy; 57 people perished on the mountain when it erupted on May 18, 1980, in an explosion bigger than 1500 atomic bombs. The cataclysm began with an earthquake of 5.1 on the Richter scale that sparked the biggest landslide in recorded history and buried 230 sq miles of forest under millions of tonnes of volcanic rock and ash.

When the smoke finally lifted, Mt St Helens sported a new mile-wide crater on its northern side and had lost 1300ft in height. Resolving to leave nature to its own devices, the Reagan administration created the 172-sq-mile Mt St Helens National Volcanic Monument in 1982. A visit here today will demonstrate how, over three decades on, nature has restored much life to the mountain, although the devastation wreaked by the explosion is still hauntingly evident.

Westside Entrance

◉ Sights

The plethora of Mt St Helens visitor centers on this side of the mountain can be a little confusing on paper, but they line up nicely on the road. Here we list the sights in order from west to east as you'll come upon them on Rte 504. You'll also come across several magnificent viewpoints which are well worth pulling over for, especially on a clear day.

Mt St Helens Silver Lake Visitor Center   INTERPRETIVE CENTER
(3029 Spirit Lake Hwy; admission $5; ⊙ 9am-5pm; 📷) 🖉 Situated 5 miles east of Castle Rock, the Silver Lake is the best introduction to the monument. There's a classic film and various exhibits, including a mock-up of the volcano where you can duck beneath the cone for displays on the subterranean workings of the mountain. Outside is the 1-mile **Silver Lake Wetlands Trail**.

Hoffstadt Bluffs Visitors Center   INTERPRETIVE CENTER
(www.hoffstadtbluffs.com; 15000 Spirit Lake Hwy; ⊙ 9am-6pm) **FREE** At mile 27 on Hwy 504, this impressive post-and-beam structure has a good restaurant – the Fire Mountain Grill – and panoramic views of the Toutle River Valley. Exhibits focus on St Helens' ecology pre-blast. This is where you can organize helicopter tours (per person $179) over the crater.

Charles W Bingham Forest Learning Center   INTERPRETIVE CENTER
(17000 Spirit Lake Memorial Hwy; ⊙ 10am-4pm Fri-Sun mid-May–Oct) **FREE** Situated at mile 33 on Hwy 504, the learning center is basically a showcase for the lumber industry, though it does run another interesting film about the eruption. There are restrooms and a gift shop on site.

Coldwater Lake   LAKE
Coldwater Lake, 43 miles east of Castle Rock, was created in 1980 when water backed up behind a dam caused by debris was brought down by the eruption. The recreation area here (restrooms, phone, boat launch) is the starting point of the 0.6-mile **Birth of a Lake Trail**, a paved interpretive hike that seeks to demonstrate the regrowth of vegetation in the area.

★ **Johnston Ridge Observatory**   LOOKOUT
(⊙ 10am-6pm mid-May–late Oct) Situated at the end of Hwy 504 and looking directly into the mouth of the crater, the observatory has exhibits that take a more scientific angle than the Silver Lake center, depicting the geologic events surrounding the 1980 blast and how they advanced the science of volcano forecasting and monitoring. The paved 1-mile round-trip **Eruption Trail** offers once-in-a-lifetime views toward the crater.

🏃 Activities

Ask a ranger at the Silver Lake Visitor Center to direct you to the best trail for the weather and distance you want to tackle – they'll also provide basic trail maps. Suggested hikes include a circumnavigation of Coldwater Lake on the 9-mile **Lakes Trail/Coldwater Trail** (hikes 211 and 230), through an area of forest blow-down and developing shrubs (with 2500ft of ascent, the trail is graded 'difficult'), and the **Truman Trail** (hike 207; named after the unfortunate Harry Truman, who perished in the eruption), which leads from the Windy Ridge viewpoint through pumice fields and wildflower fields for 5.7 miles. The 2.5-mile **Hummocks Trail** (hike 229) is a good choice when the upper areas haven't yet opened for summer, and loops around mounds of volcanic debris (called hummocks) as well as along the Toutle River for spectacular views of the mountain.

Mt St Helens' version of Mt Rainier's Wonderland trail is the 30-mile **Loowit Trail** (hike 216) that circumnavigates the volcano, crossing numerous ecosystems. Since the destructive storms that wracked the whole Pacific Northwest area in November 2006 the trail quality has been patchy; inquire at Silver Lake Visitor Center before setting out.

☞ Tours

Eco Tours of Oregon   TOUR
(www.ecotours-of-orgeon.com; 3127 SE 23rd Ave, Portland; $59.50) Runs a Mt St Helens volcano tour from mid-June to late September. The eight-hour tour ($59.50 plus $8 park entry fee) leaves from Portland's hotels at 9am and visits Silver Lake Visitor Center, the Coldwater Lake recreation area and Johnston Ridge Observatory.

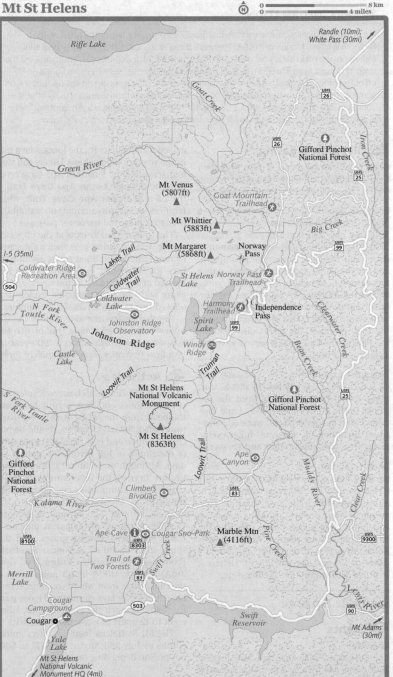

N

0 — 8 km
0 — 4 miles

Riffe Lake

Randle (10mi);
White Pass (30mi)

Goat Creek

USFS 26

USFS 26

Gifford Pinchot
National Forest

Iron Creek

USFS 25

Green River

Mt Venus
(5807ft)

Goat Mountain
Trailhead

Big Creek

USFS 99

I-5 (35mi)

Mt Whittier
(5883ft)

Mt Margaret
(5868ft)

Norway
Pass

Lakes Trail

Coldwater Ridge
Recreation Area

St Helens
Lake

Norway Pass
Trailhead

USFS 504

Coldwater
Trail

N Fork
Toutle River

Coldwater
Lake

Harmony
Trailhead

Independence
Pass

Cleariwater Creek

Johnston Ridge
Observatory

Spirit
Lake

USFS 99

Johnston Ridge

Windy
Ridge

Bean Creek

Castle
Lake

Loowit Trail

Truman
Trail

S Fork Toutle
River

Mt St Helens
National Volcanic
Monument

Gifford Pinchot
National Forest

USFS 25

Muddy River

Mt St Helens
(8363ft)

Ape
Canyon

Clear Creek

Gifford
Pinchot
National
Forest

Loowit Trail

Katama River

Climbers
Bivouac

USFS 83

USFS 9300

USFS 8100

Ape Cave

Cougar Sno-Park

Marble Mtn
(4116ft)

Pine Creek

USFS 8303

Trail of
Two Forests

Swift Creek

Merrill
Lake

USFS 83

Lewis River

Cougar
Campground

USFS 90

503

Swift
Reservoir

Cougar

Mt Adams
(30mi)

Yale
Lake

Mt St Helens
National Volcanic
Monument HQ (4mi)

❶ PARK INFORMATION

For information online visit www.fs.fed.us/gpnf. The entrance fee for the Mt St Helens National Volcanic Monument is $8. There are three entrances to this uniquely beautiful mountain: the main 'westside' via Castle Rock on Rte 504, a well-trodden 'southside' via the town of Cougar from Rte 503 to Forest Rd 83 and the remote 'eastside' from Forest Rd 99 off of Forest Rd 25. Note that while the southside and eastside entrances link up (but only in summer months when the passes are open), the westside entrance ends shortly after the Johnston Ridge Observatory, so it's impossible to drive a loop around the mountain. There is also no public transportation to Mt St Helens unless you take an organised tour.

🛏 Sleeping & Eating

Good chow can be found at Fire Mountain Grill in the Hoffstadt Bluffs Visitor Center and the Backwoods Café at the Eco Park Resort.

Eco Park Resort   CAMPGROUND, CABIN $
(☑ 360-274-6542; www.ecoparkresort.com; 14000 Spirit Lake Hwy; campsites $20, yurts $75, cabins $100-110) The closest full-service accommodations to the blast zone offers campsites and RV hookups, basic cabins and rather incongruous Genghis Khan–style yurts. Shared bathrooms are known as 'wilderness comfort stations.' Owned by the family whose Spirit Lake Lodge was swept away by the 1980 eruption, the resort also features the Backwoods Café, which serves anything as long as it's beef.

Seaquest State Park   CAMPGROUND $
(☑ 206-274-8633; Hwy 504; tent/RV sites $23/32; ☺ year-round) Directly across from the entrance to the Mt St Helens Silver Lake Visitors Center, Seaquest has 90 wooded campsites, including a separate hiker/cyclist camp area, with flush toilets and showers.

Blue Heron Inn   INN $$
(☑ 360-274-9595; www.blueheroninn.com; Hwy 504; d/ste $169/235; 🛜) A welcome B&B in an accommodation-lite area, the Blue Heron offers seven rooms, including a Jacuzzi suite, in a large house almost opposite the Silver Lake Visitor Center on Hwy 504. Rooms are clean if unspectacular, but the views of Silver Lake and Mt St Helens – weather permitting – are spellbinding.

Southside Entrance

◉ Sights

Ape Cave   NATURAL SITE
Ape Cave is a 2-mile-long lava tube formed 2000 years ago by a lava flow that followed a deep watercourse. It's the longest lava tube in the western hemisphere. Hikers can walk and scramble the length of Ape Cave on either the 0.8-mile **Lower Ape Cave Trail** or the 1.5-mile **Upper Ape Cave Trail**, which requires a certain amount of scrambling over rock piles and narrower passages.

The trail eventually exits at the upper entrance. You can bring your own light source or rent lanterns for $5 at **Apes' Headquarters** (8303 Forest Rd; ☺ 10:30am-5pm Jun-Sep), located at the entrance to the caves, and tag along with the free ranger-led explorations offered several times a day in the summer.

Another interesting side trail is the 0.6-mile wheelchair-accessible Trail of Two Forests, on a boardwalk across a 1900-year-old lava flow that once buried an ancient forest.

🏃 Activities

Due to Mt St Helens' delicate volcanic state, climbers must obtain a permit to ascend the peak from the **Mt St Helens Institute** (www.mshinstitute.org). Permits should be purchased online and cost $22 April to October (a maximum of 100 permits are issued per day). Although no technical climbing abilities are needed, the hike is no walk in the park; many summit-seekers camp by the trailhead at Climbers Bivouac the night before climbing. The bivouac is situated 14 miles northeast of Cougar at the end of USFS Rd 830 (a narrow gravel road that spurs off USFS Rd 83 at Cougar Sno-Park). From here, the **Monitor Ridge Trail** (hike 216A) ascends 1100ft in 2.3 miles to reach the timberline, from where you must scramble 5 miles over lava chunks and loose pumice fields to reach the summit cliffs. Allow eight to 12 hours to make the round-trip.

The Mt St Helens Institute offers guided climbs in July and August for $175 to $300 per person depending on the route.

MAY 18, 1980

Where were you on May 18, 1980, when Mt St Helens blew its top? Pacific Northwesterners remember it as an unusually clear spring day, quickly extinguished by a humungous black cloud. But first there was a loud bang. One of St Helens' most perplexing riddles was the noise – or lack of it. People in the mountain's vicinity (the so-called 'quiet zone') claim they heard nothing, whereas people as far away as Vancouver, Canada, jumped out of their seats. Another curiosity was the dust fallout. Due to prevailing winds from the west, the major population centers of Seattle and Portland avoided any choking smog. Instead, the huge volcanic cloud drifted east, cloaking Yakima in 5in of dust and bringing darkness at noon to Spokane. Later on, dust was reported as far away as Minnesota and within two weeks it had circled the globe.

Though scientists had known an eruption on St Helens was imminent, few had predicted its magnitude. The loss of comparatively few lives (57) was partly down to luck. First, the eruption happened on a Sunday, when the mountain's logging parties were on weekend vacation. Second, it happened at 8:32am, 90 minutes before an army of homeowners was due to be let into the restricted 'red zone' to pick up their possessions (the area had been evacuated two weeks earlier in anticipation of an imminent eruption). In fact, only four people were inside the restricted zone at the time of the explosion: Harry Truman, the stubborn 83-year-old proprietor of the Spirit Lake Lodge; David Johnston, a US Geographical Survey volcanologist; and two further amateur volcanologists. All perished. The blast and subsequent landslide also claimed 7000 animals, 40,000 salmon, 47 bridges and over 185 miles of highway. The federal government was left with a bill for over $2.7 billion in today's prices. President Jimmy Carter, after flying over the smoldering volcano, is reported to have said: 'Someone said the area looked like a moonscape. But the moon looks more like a golf course compared to what's up here'.

ⓘ Information

Mt St Helens National Volcanic Monument Headquarters (42218 NE Yale Bridge Rd, Amboy; ⊘8am-5pm Mon-Fri Oct-May, to 5pm Mon-Sat Jun-Sep) On Hwy 503, 16 miles southeast of Cougar on the mountain's south side.

Eastside Entrance

More remote, but less crowded than Johnston Ridge at the westside entrance, is the harder-to-reach **Windy Ridge viewpoint** on this less developed side of the mountain. Here visitors get a palpable, if eerie, sense of the destruction that the blast wrought with felled forests, desolate mountain slopes and the rather surreal sight of lifeless **Spirit Lake**, once one of the premier resorts in the South Cascades. There are toilets and a snack bar at the viewpoint parking lot, which is often closed until June. Steps ascend the hillside for close-up views of the crater. A few miles down the road you can descend 600ft on the 1-mile-long **Harmony Trail** (hike 224) to Spirit Lake.

Mt Adams

Adams is the state's forgotten peak, the second tallest of Washington's Cascades but a mountain that has long been overshadowed by Rainier's height and St Helens' explosive power. Nonetheless, Adams remains an impressive mountain; the lack of a major glacier on its south side allows for a comparatively easy, nontechnical ascent for aspiring peakbaggers. On its lower slopes Adams is renowned for the juicy huckleberries and pretty wildflowers that fill its grassy alpine meadows during a short but intense summer season.

Protected in the 66-sq-mile Mt Adams Wilderness, Adams sports plenty of picturesque hikes, including the much-loved **Bird Creek Meadow Trail**, a 3-mile loop that showcases the best of the mountain's meadows, wildflowers and waterfalls.

While most climbs are nontechnical slogs up a glacier, even these require basic climbing gear. The easiest approach (grade II) is from the south, via Cold Springs Campground, and up the South Spur to the summit. The climb is best between May and August. Climbers should sign in and out at the USFS ranger station at either Trout Lake or Randle. For guided hikes contact Seattle-based Mountain Madness (p157).

🛏 Sleeping

★**Trout Lake Country Inn**   HISTORIC HOTEL **$**
(☎509-395-3667; www.troutlakecountryinn.net; 15 Guler Rd, Trout Lake; r $50) It calls itself a true honky tonk and that's exactly what this Wild West, bluegrass-band-playing, creaky-wood-floor-stomping, roast-chicken-with-a-side-of-pataters inn and restaurant is. It's rare to find this much fun and American character so far out in the woods – with a view of Mt Adams, no less! Don't expect luxury, but do expect to dance, imbibe, then crash under a homemade quilt.

Takhlakh Lake Campground   CAMPGROUND **$**
(☎509-395-3400; campsites $15) Fifty-four campsites with running water and pit toilets are situated here, 25 miles north of Trout Lake on USFS Rd 23.

Trout Lake Cozy Cabins   CABIN **$$**
(☎509-395-2068; www.troutlakecozycabins.com; 2291 Hwy 141; cabins $89-129; 🐾) A mile south of Trout Lake on Hwy 141 are four beautifully presented cabins in the woods, in the shadow of snow-sprinkled Mt Adams. Wonderfully landscaped and amply equipped with kitchen, bathroom, wood stove and Jacuzzi, they make you let out a deep 'aaah.' Dining is also available.

ℹ Information

Mt Adams Ranger District USFS Office (2455 Hwy 141; ⊙8am-4:30pm Mon-Sat Oct-May, daily Jun-Sep) For huckleberry permits and information on hiking and climbing; in Trout Lake village.

ℹ Getting There & Away

The easiest access to Mt Adams is from the Columbia River Gorge near Hood River, OR. From here Hwy 141 proceeds north for 25 miles to the tiny community of Trout Lake. Access from the north is from Randle on US 12 and is only passable in the summer.

Central & Eastern Washington

Best Places to Eat

➡ Saffron Mediterranean Kitchen (p202)

➡ Mizuna (p208)

➡ Birchfield Manor Restaurant (p197)

➡ Graze (p201)

Best Places to Stay

➡ Davenport Hotel (p207)

➡ Hotel Pension Anna (p188)

➡ Inn at Abeja (p201)

➡ Marcus Whitman Hotel (p201)

Why Go?

If states were delineated purely by geography, Washington east of the Cascade Mountains would be a separate entity. While the west breeds evergreen trees, liberal cities, perennial rain and gourmet coffee, the east is the opposite: a land of sunbaked hills and big blue skies stuffed with private vineyards, rodeo towns and huge Native American reservations.

The east's geographic identity is intrinsically linked to the mighty Columbia River, which has transformed both the landscape and the economy. This once-parched region now features gargantuan dams and ambitious irrigation projects that have converted barren valleys and scrubby steppe into a veritable Garden of Eden. Humanmade lakes have provided a nexus of outdoor recreation, while the rich, irrigated soil has propelled the region into an enological rival to California, producing some of the nation's youngest, fruitiest and most promising new wines.

When to Go

Spokane

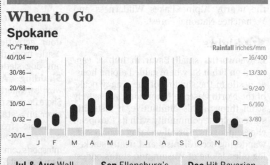

Jul & Aug Wall-to-wall sunshine for wine-tasting trips in the Columbia River Valley.

Sep Ellensburg's Labor Day Rodeo is Central Washington's biggest show.

Dec Hit Bavarian Leavenworth for the picturesque Christmas Lights Festival.

CENTRAL WASHINGTON

Caught in the foothills of the grandiose Cascade Mountains, central Washington is a geographic crossroads where dramatic alpine peaks fold with eerie suddenness into a barren steppelike desert broken only by the winding presence of the Columbia River and its irrigating dams.

Wenatchee and Leavenworth are the most interesting urban centers here and both are popular stopping-off points on the scenic **Cascade Loop drive**. (The drive starts and ends in Everett, about 25 miles north of Seattle, and takes in the North Cascades, the Methow Valley, the Wenatchee Valley, the Columbia River and some of the San Juan Islands over its 440 miles.) Aside from Leavenworth's Bavarian bonhomie, outdoor adventures are the main draw.

Leavenworth

POP 1993

Blink hard and rub your eyes. Yes, all your *Sound of Music* fantasies may have just come true. This is Leavenworth, a former lumber town that underwent a Bavarian makeover back in the 1960s after the rerouting of the cross-continental railway threatened to put it permanently out of business. Swapping wood for tourists, tiny Leavenworth has successfully reinvented itself as a traditional *Romantische Strasse* village, right down to the beer, sausages and lederhosen-loving locals (25% of whom are German). The crisp and clean mountain-scenery setting helps, as does the fact that Leavenworth serves as the main activity center for sorties into the nearby Alpine Lakes Wilderness and Wenatchee National Forest.

◉ Sights

Leavenworth's small Bavarian hub is centered on Front St, where gabled alpine houses nestle in the shadow of the craggy peaks of the North Cascade Mountains. A leisurely stroll through this diminutive, if distinctly surreal, alpine community, with its European cheesemongers, dirndl-wearing waitresses, wandering accordionists and neatly stacked log piles, is one of Washington state's oddest but most endearing experiences. Even the Bank of America and Starbucks signs are on homemade-looking wood panels in fancy Germanic fonts.

Leavenworth National Fish Hatchery   HATCHERY
(12790 Fish Hatchery Rd; admission by donation; ☉8am-4pm) 🌢 Of three thriving fish hatcheries on the Columbia River, this is the largest and, quite possibly, the most interesting. Created to provide a spawning ground for salmon that had been blocked from migrating upriver by the construction of the Grand Coulee Dam in the 1930s, the ongoing fish-rearing project produces some 1.6 million Chinook salmon a year. The young smolt are released into Icicle Creek each spring, from where they migrate to the Pacific.

From the hatchery, you can hike the mile-long **Icicle Creek Interpretive Trail** and learn about the local ecology and history.

Waterfront Park   PARK
Tucked out of view but surprisingly close, this green area provides Leavenworth with access to the Wenatchee River. Wander down 9th St and follow the leafy domain over a footbridge and onto Blackbird Island, where you can catch a glimpse of Sleeping Lady Mountain ringed by foliage. Interpretive signs furnish the route and help explain the local plant and animal life.

Nutcracker Museum   MUSEUM
(www.nutcrackermuseum.com; 735 Front St; admission $2.50; ☉2-5pm; 🐾) As much a gift shop as a place to peruse, the Nutcracker Museum specializes, as you'd guess, in an exceptional variety (around 5000 at last count) of nutcracker dolls. Ebony, metal, boxwood, ivory and porcelain – who knew cracking nuts could be so much fun?

🏃 Activities

It's no wonder Leavenworth is one of Washington's adventure capitals: there are outdoor activities galore during all seasons. Aside from the following you can also try out dog sledding with **Leavenworth Dog Sledding Adventures** (☑509-630-0456; www.leavenworthdogsledding.com; 15263 North Shore Dr; tours per person from $60) or tackle the river on a stand-up paddle board with gear available from **Leavenworth Mountain Sports** (☑509-548-7864; www.leavenworth-mtnsports.com; 220 US 2; ☉10am-6pm Mon-Fri, 9am-6pm Sat & Sun).

Hiking

Leavenworth offers ample opportunities for hiking. The most diverse selection of trails can be found in the nearby Alpine Lakes

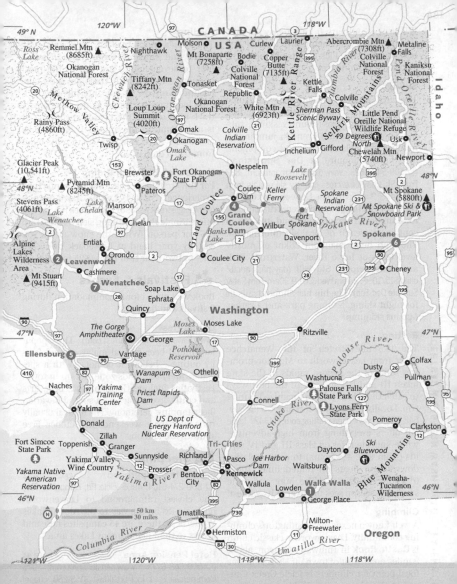

Central & Eastern Washington Highlights

❶ Pairing homegrown food with excellent **Walla Walla** (p199) vintages at the town's wineries or world-class restaurants.

❷ Warming up with bratwurst, beer and accordion music after frolicking (biking, skiing etc) in the wilderness around Bavarian-inspired **Leavenworth** (p186).

❸ Watching the sunset over the Cascades from the dining car of Amtrak's **Empire Builder** (p210).

❹ Admiring the state-of-the-art after-dark laser show at the awe-inspiring **Grand Coulee Dam** (p210).

❺ Mingling with students and supping good coffee at the **Ellensburg Rodeo** (p194).

❻ Reclining regally in the grandiose lobby of Spokane's **Davenport Hotel** (p207).

❼ Perusing the orchard-lined back roads around **Wenatchee** (p191), stopping at fruit stands and antique malls.

Wilderness and vary from an easy 3.5-mile river loop to a challenging two- to three-day backcountry slog. Pick up a trail map at the chamber of commerce.

Skiing

The area around Leavenworth has some diverse skiing opportunities, including downhill skiing, cross-country skiing, tubing, snowshoeing and even ski jumping. A number of hotels rent skis and equipment, or you can inquire at **Der Sportsman** (☑509-548-5623; www.dersportsmann.com; 837 Front St; 1-day bike/cross-country ski rentals from $25/14; ☺9am-6pm). The **Leavenworth Winter Sports Club** (www.skileavenworth.com) is a local umbrella organization, and its website contains a wealth of local ski information. The club helps maintain 26km of mostly level trails at Icicle River, Waterfront Park and **Leavenworth Ski Hill** (day pass adult/child $15/10; ☺3-7pm Wed & Fri, 9.30am-7pm Sat & Sun late Dec-Feb). The hill has 5km of trails lit for night skiing, a tubing park and a rather famous ski jump.

Rafting

The 18.5-mile stretch of the Wenatchee River from Leavenworth to Monitor promises some of the biggest rapids in the state (class III and IV) and one of the best ways to catch them is to join an organized rafting trip. Locally run **Osprey Rafting Co** (☑509-548-6800; www.ospreyrafting.com; 4342 Icicle Rd) offers everything from high-adventure white-knuckle rides on class III and IV rapids (from $78, 4½ hours) to contemplative downstream floats on rented inner tubes (day-long floats $46). The May and June snowmelt season sees the river at its wildest.

Climbing

A well-known nexus for Washington's climbing community, Leavenworth's classic climb is **Castle Rock** in Tumwater Canyon, about 3 miles northwest of town off US 2. A newer focal point for climbers is Icicle Creek Canyon in the Alpine Lakes Wilderness, where the challenging rock climbing requires a United States Forest Service (USFS) permit. **Snow Creek Wall** is an old stalwart in this area, but there are several hundred other climbs here, most of which have been developed in the last 15 years. Leavenworth Mountain Sports (p186) rents rock shoes, harnesses and other climbing gear.

Cycling

The **Devil's Gulch trail** (25 miles, four to six hours) and **Mission Ridge trail** (26 miles, four to seven hours) are two of the most popular off-road bike trails in the state. **Freund Canyon** is an intermediate 8.3-mile loop and is classed as the best single-track bike trail in the Leavenworth area. It is also home to the annual Bavarian Bike and Brews Race. Der Sportsman rents bikes from $25 a day.

Horseback & Sleigh Riding

For the archetypal Leavenworth wintertime experience, contact **Eagle Creek Ranch** (www.eaglecreek.ws; 7951 Eagle Creek Rd), which offers 'Jingle Bells'–evoking sleigh rides from $15 per person. When the snow clears you can try your hand at horseback riding on one- to two-hour trail rides ($25 to $78).

⭐ Festivals & Events

Book well ahead for accommodation during festivals and holidays.

Oktoberfest   BEER
(www.leavenworthoktoberfest.com) This popular annual beer festival makes a good family outing – believe it or not – with a special *kinderplatz* (kids zone) set up in town. Festivities include German food, beer, arts and crafts. live music and a special Bavarian 'beer-tapping' ceremony. The festival usually runs over three weekends in October. Free shuttles are laid on.

🛏 Sleeping

Eightmile Campground   CAMPGROUND $
(☑800-274-6104; 4905 Icicle Rd; campsites $16) The closest campground to Leavenworth on Icicle Rd on the way to the Alpine Lakes Wilderness; there are 45 campsites here and access to the Enchantment Lakes area.

Hotel Pension Anna   HOTEL $$
(☑509-548-6273; www.pensionanna.com; 926 Commercial St; r incl breakfast $155-250, chapel ste $240-360) The most authentic Bavarian hotel in town is also spotless and incredibly friendly. Each room is decorated in imported Austrian decor and the European-inspired breakfasts may induce joyful yodels. Our favorite room is the double with handpainted furniture, but the spacious suite in the adjacent St Joseph's chapel (that the owners rescued and moved here in 1992) is perfect for families.

CHRISTMAS LIGHTS

Leavenworth's alpine houses look like a Christmas card at the best of times, and no more so than in the first three weeks of December, when the locals relight the town three times on the first three Saturdays of the month. There's live music, carol singing and, of course, an appearance by Father Christmas.

Enzian Inn
HOTEL **$$**

(☑ 509-548-5269; www.enzianinn.com; 590 Hwy 2; d $110-205, ste $215-375; 🕾 🏊) A Leavenworth classic, with long-term owner Bob Johnson starting the day with a blast on his famous alpenhorn before breakfast. If this doesn't send you running for your lederhosen, cast an eye over the free putting green (with resident grass-trimming goats), the indoor and outdoor swimming pools, the panoramic upstairs restaurant, or the nightly pianist pounding out requests in the Bavarian lobby.

Bavarian Lodge
HOTEL **$$**

(☑ 509-548-7878; www.bavarianlodge.com; 810 Hwy 2; d/ste incl breakfast $155/319; 🎛 🕾 🏊) This lodge takes the Bavarian theme to luxury levels in a plush, clutter-free establishment with modern – but definably German – rooms complete with gas fires, king-size beds, funky furnishings and a serve-yourself buffet breakfast. Outside there's a heated pool and hot tub, while the suite rooms upstairs have huge Jacuzzi baths wedged into a cozy Bavarian turret.

Bavarian Ritz
HOTEL **$$**

(☑ 509-548-5455; 633 Front St; d/ste $89/240; 🎛 🕾 🏊) Wedged into Bavarian-style Front St, the Ritz is a vintage 1903 inn that was reincarnated in Leavenworth's 1960s German makeover. Promoting a wide selection of room types and a couple of decent downstairs restaurants, the facilities fall short of luxury status, though the vista-studded sundeck and the extravagant four-poster beds in the Royal King suites should keep visiting Europhiles happy.

Leavenworth Village Inn
HOTEL **$$**

(☑ 509-548-6620; www.leavenworthvillageinn. com; 1016 Commercial St; d/ste from $79/159; 🕾) Huge rooms at economical prices. Recent remodeling has ensured that this place is both modern and bereft of the frilly German touches ubiquitous elsewhere in town.

Run of the River Inn
B&B **$$$**

(☑ 509-548-7171; www.runoftheriver.com; 9308 E Leavenworth Rd; ste from $230; 🕾) A romantic dream: welcome to a stress-free, kid-free, smoke-free B&B where all the rooms are suites and breakfast is the tastiest and largest meal of the week. The suites are pure luxury, with Jacuzzis, fluffy bathrobes, fireplaces, hiking gear, binoculars (the inn is next to a bird refuge) and an old-fashioned typewriter just in case guests get poetically inspired. Very special.

✖ Eating

★München Haus
GERMAN **$**

(www.munchenhaus.com; 709 Front St; snacks from $6; ⊙ 11am-11pm May-Oct, closed Mon-Fri Nov-Apr; 🍴) The Haus is 100% alfresco, meaning that the hot German sausages and pretzels served up here are essential stomach-warmers in the winter, while the Bavarian brews do a good job of cooling you down in the summer. The casual beer-garden atmosphere is complemented by vibrant flower baskets, laid-back staff and a stash of top-quality relishes including cider kraut and mustard to spice up your bratwurst. There are even vegan varieties.

South
MEXICAN **$$**

(www.southleavenworth.com; 913 Front St; mains $15-21; ⊙ lunch & dinner) Sick of sausages and sauerkraut? (Most people crumble after three days. Divert here. The Mexican menu with Cuban and Peruvian inflections is cool and creative but always true to its Hispanic roots. Highlights of a made-from-scratch roll call are the self-proclaimed 'to-die-for' Oaxaca mole, the melt-in-your-mouth nachos and 30-odd types of tequila. It also offers (sigh) good old German sausage.

Café Christa
GERMAN **$$**

(www.cafechrista.com; upstairs 801 Front St; mains $13-20) Christa's features quaint European decor, discreet yet polite service and a menu that rustles up a plethora of old-world classics such as bratwurst, Wiener schnitzel and Jäger schnitzel served with sauce, red cabbage and spätzle. Even better, you can wash it all down with an accompanying stein of Hofbräuhaus Munich lager.

Pavs Cafe Bistro　　　　　　　FRENCH $$
(833 Front St; crepes $10-20; ⊗11:30am-9pm Mon-Fri, 9am-9pm Sat & Sun) Ah, *oui!* If another lick of accordion music will make you run screaming for the mountains, tuck instead into this wee French cafe serving delicious crepes, seafood and French-ified steaks and pastas. It's also one of the best choices in town for breakfast.

Andreas Keller　　　　　　　GERMAN $$
(www.andreaskellerrestaurant.com; 829 Front St; mains from $15; ⊗lunch & dinner) The definitive Leavenworth experience lurks in this cavernous basement or *rathskeller,* with a genuine Oktoberfest atmosphere inspired by lederhosen-clad accordionists crooning Bavarian drinking songs. To add to the authenticity, the head chef is German and prepares wonderful Wiener schnitzels, potato salad, sauerkraut, red cabbage and rye bread.

Visconti's　　　　　　　ITALIAN $$
(www.viscontis.com; 636 Front St; ⊗lunch & dinner) Another escape from Bavaria lets you head south (figuratively speaking) to Visconti's, where you may think you've reached Italy, so good is the ravioli – and the wines.

Icicle Brewery　　　　　　　PUB
(935 Front St; pub meals $6-10; ⊗noon-10pm) This pub is in the brewery itself, with big vats shining behind the bar. The modern, industrial-hip building brings you back to the Pacific Northwest with light meals like soups and Ploughman's plates that (like the five delicious beers on tap) all use local ingredients.

Gustav's Grill & Sports Pub　　　　　　PUB
(www.gustavsleavenworth.com; 617 US 2; sausages & sandwiches $6-7) In an onion-domed building on Hwy 2, Gustav's boasts a rooftop beer garden and lots of good Northwest brews on tap to complement its less remarkable sausages and deli sandwiches.

☆ Entertainment

Leavenworth Summer Theater　　　　THEATER
(☑box office 509-548-2000; Hwy 2 & Icicle Rd; tickets $14-30; ⊗shows Jul, Aug & Dec) Leavenworth's flirtation with kitsch doesn't end in the Bavarian village. If a Julie Andrews sound-alike singing 'Do-Re-Mi' doesn't send you rushing back to Seattle for a distorted grunge fix, proceed to the Ski Hill Amphitheater during the summer months for a full-length production of Rodgers and Hammerstein's *The Sound of Music,* performed against an authentic alpine backdrop.

ⓘ Information

Leavenworth Chamber of Commerce & Visitor Center (www.leavenworth.org; 940 US 2; ⊗8am-5pm Mon-Thu, 8am-6pm Fri & Sat, 10am-4pm Sun) If you're not immediately sold on the town's rather unusual German makeover, come here and they'll attempt to convince you otherwise.

Leavenworth Ranger Station (600 Sherbourne St; ⊗7:30am-4:30pm daily mid-Jun–mid-Oct, from 7:45am Mon-Fri mid-Oct–mid-Jun) Off US 2 at the east end of town; provides information on recreational opportunities and issues various types of permits.

ⓘ Getting There & Around

BUS

Northwestern Trailways (☑800-366-3830; www.northwesterntrailways.com) buses stop in Leavenworth twice daily on their way between Seattle ($34, three hours) and Wenatchee ($16, 40 minutes). The bus stop is on Hwy 2 by the post office.

Link Transit (www.linktransit.com) bus 22 passes up US 2 between Leavenworth and Wenatchee ($1.25, 50 minutes), via Peshastin and Cashmere, 20 times daily Monday to Friday (no weekend service).

TRAIN

The **Amtrak** (www.amtrak.com) *Empire Builder* stops twice daily at the town's Icicle Station on its route between Seattle and Chicago. Connections to Portland, OR, and Vancouver, British Columbia, run through Seattle.

Around Leavenworth

Alpine Lakes Wilderness

The Alpine Lakes Wilderness is a 614-sq-mile protected area of rough, crenellated mountains, glacier-gouged valleys, and – as the name implies – gorgeous sapphire lakes (more than 700 of them, in fact). Crisscrossed by trails and popularly accessed from the Icicle Canyon Rd west of Leavenworth, the wilderness offers a handful of easy day hikes along with plenty of more substantial backcountry jaunts that require good fitness, shrewd forward planning and a decent pair of walking boots.

The area's close proximity to Seattle makes this former logging and mining region popular with hikers; the Enchantment Lakes area requires a $5 permit in the summer (inquire at Leavenworth Ranger Station). Good entry points are from the Icicle

Rd (USFS Rd 7600) off Hwy 2 and on a dirt road just north of Tumwater campground on US 2.

The Icicle Gorge Trail is the most accessible hike here, an easy 3.6-mile river loop that gives you an enticing taste of what this pristine wilderness is all about. Other trailheads dot Icicle Rd and lead off into a network of popular trails. Pick up a leaflet at Leavenworth Chamber of Commerce & Visitor Center.

Lake Wenatchee

Swimming, boating and fishing entertain summertime visitors to Lake Wenatchee, 23 miles north of the city of Wenatchee (and actually much closer to Leavenworth). You can hike the 4.5-mile trail up Dirtyface Peak, cycle around the lake, or sign on with one of the rafting companies on Hwy 207 for a float trip.

Once there's snow on the ground, Lake Wenatchee becomes a great cross-country ski area, with 20 miles of marked and groomed trails, though skiers may have to dodge weekend snowmobilers. More trails crisscross the Lower Chiwawa River area off the Chumstick Hwy, including a 5-mile scenic loop trail (closed to snowmobiles) that follows the Wenatchee River. Alternatively, you can head further west into the Henry M Jackson Wilderness on USFS Rd 6500 (off Hwy 207) at Little Wenatchee Ford campground, where a number of trails hook up with the Pacific Crest Trail.

To reach the lake, head north on Chumstick Hwy, or take US 2 west of town, then turn north onto Hwy 207. Link Transit runs a bus up here six times daily (35 minutes). For further area details contact the Lake Wenatchee Ranger Station (22976 Hwy 207; ⊗8am-4:30pm Mon-Fri, plus Sat Mar-Sep).

Wenatchee

POP 32,373

In the age of video blogging and lightning-fast messaging, the definition of Wenatchee can be condensed into six familiar letters: 'apples'. pink lady, gala, braeburn, golden delicious; the varieties are endless in a city that not inaccurately describes itself as the 'Apple Capital of the World' (the region produces more than half of the total US crop). On the banks of the Columbia River, Wenatchee's position is eye-catching even if its mall, fast food and cheap-motel–infested suburbs aren't. The town itself isn't exactly teeming with pulsating distractions, but there are plenty of outdoor adventures nearby and, with its handy transport connections, Wenatchee is an OK place to crack open your suitcase for the night and sample a slice of apple pie.

◎ Sights

Ohme Gardens GARDENS
(www.ohmegardens.com; 3327 Ohme Rd; adult/child $7/3.50; ⊗9am-6pm Apr-Oct) Three miles north of town on Alt US 97, the Ohme showcases the mighty Columbia River at its best, with 9 acres of terraced alpine gardens emerging like an oasis from the barren rock.

Wenatchee Valley Museum & Cultural Center MUSEUM
(www.wenatcheevalleymuseum.com; 127 S Mission St; adult/child $5/2; ⊗10am-4pm Tue-Sat) Welcome to another good municipal museum, which places its main focus on – surprise, surprise – apples. Exhibits include a recreation of a 1920s apple-packing shed and a farm shop from the 1890s. Look out for memorabilia on local hero Clyde Pangborn, the first man to fly nonstop across the Pacific in 1931.

Washington Apple Commission Visitors Center VISITOR CENTER
(www.bestapples.com; 2900 Euclid Ave; ⊗8am-5pm Mon-Fri, 9am-5pm Sat, 10am-4pm Sun May-Dec) FREE Washington's, America's and – quite possibly – the world's self-styled apple capital is also home to this little-visited yet surprisingly interesting exposé on gala, fuji, golden delicious et al. Find out how apples are grown, harvested, transported and sold via a number of interpretive displays and an enlightening 20-minute video.

♣ Activities

Mission Ridge SKIING
(www.missionridge.com; full-day lift tickets adult/child $50/32; ⊗9am-4pm Thu-Mon late Nov-early Apr) Downhill skiers covet the dry powder covering the slopes of Mission Ridge, located 12 miles southwest of Wenatchee. The resort features a vertical drop of 2200ft and 35 runs with four lifts and two rope-tows.

Apple Capital Recreation Loop Trail WALKING, CYCLING
Wenatchee's interurban trail is a 10-mile walk- and bikeway that starts and finishes in Riverfront Park and stretches along

CENTRAL & EASTERN WASHINGTON WENATCHEE

WORTH A TRIP

CASHMERE

Stopping in this cute, midcentury-meets–Wild West brick town between Leavenworth and Wenatchee is a must if your family traditions involved Aplets & Cotlets (an American take on Turkish delight: a jellied fruit candy with nuts and dusted with powdered sugar). **Liberty Orchards** (117 Mission Ave; ⊙8:30am-5:30pm Mon-Fri, 10am-4pm Sat & Sun) FREE which have been producing these addictive sweets since the 1930s are based here and offer free tastings and tours through summer.

To work off your sugar high, visit **Apple Annie's Antique Gallery** (100 Apple Annie Ave; ⊙9am-6pm) and **Antique Mall at Cashmere** (603 Cotlets Way; ⊙9am-6pm), two of the largest antique shopping venues in the Pacific Northwest.

both sides of the Columbia River via some orchards, adjacent to downtown. Access to the park can be gained at the end of 5th St or by crossing a railway footbridge at the end of 1st St.

Riverfront Park Ice Arena   ICE SKATING
(25th St; admission $4; ⊙Oct-Mar) An indoor rink with public skating and ice hockey.

Arlberg Sports   BICYCLE RENTAL
(25 N Wenatchee Ave; per day $35; ⊙10am-6pm Mon-Sat, noon-5pm Sun) Next to the Convention Center.

🛏 Sleeping

If you don't go in for chain hotels, it will be a struggle to find an independent lodging in franchise-filled Wenatchee, where the arterial N Wenatchee Ave is studded with all number of Travelodges, Super 8s and Econo Lodges.

Wenatchee Confluence State Park   CAMPGROUND $
(☑509-664-6373; 333 Olds Station Rd; tent/RV sites $21/28) The campground, with 51 hookups and eight tent spaces, is on the north bank of the Wenatchee River. It's an ideal spot for active travelers: besides a swimming beach, there are athletic fields, tennis and basketball courts and 4.5 miles of trails.

Warm Springs Inn   B&B $$
(☑509-662-8365; www.warmspringsinn.com; 1611 Love Lane; r $115-140; ❋🛰) Situated on 10 acres by the Wenatchee River, this 1917 mansion turned B&B has six individually crafted rooms, river views, and a manicured English garden with a shaded gazebo. It's close enough to town to be convenient but far enough away to feel like you're in the country.

WestCoast Wenatchee Center Hotel   HOTEL $$
(☑509-662-1234; www.coasthotels.com; 201 N Wenatchee Ave; r from $110; ❋🛰🏊) Best of the bunch of chain hotels is this large central franchise that is handily connected to the convention center by a sky bridge and draws a regular business crowd. Rooms are well furnished, if a little characterless, and there's an above-average rooftop restaurant (the Wenatchee Roaster and Ale House) and a fitness center.

🍴 Eating

Tastebuds Coffee & Wine   CAFE, WINE BAR $
(www.tastebudscoffeewine.com; 212 5th St; appetizers from $7; ⊙8am-9pm Mon-Sat; 🛰) The idea goes something like this: take an aromatic European-style coffee bar, chuck in a few cool Northwest furnishings (fireplace, accented browns, and plenty of bottles on shelves) and, as the day wears on, let it metamorphose into a wine bar. There's food too, of course; more like appetizers than main meals (try the cheeses and rich tortes).

Cellar Café   CAFÉ $
(www.cellarcafe.org; 249 N Mission St; sandwiches around $9; ⊙9am-3pm Mon-Fri; 🍴) Putting up a brave rearguard action in Wenatchee's strip-mall zone, the Cellar is encased in a traditional craftsman house complete with outdoor seating and a koi pond. Made-from-scratch lunches include excellent wraps, quiches and a formidable apple crisp (this is 'apple town,' after all).

Owl Soda Fountain   SODA FOUNTAIN $
(25 N Wenatchee Ave; ⊙till 5pm) A classic old-fashioned soda fountain of 1950s vintage, with lurid color schemes, peanut-butter-and-jelly sandwiches, and humongous milkshakes plunked down on the bar in front of you. All that's missing is an Elvis impersonator with stick-on sideburns.

Inna's UKRAINIAN $$
(www.innascuisine.com; 26 N Wenatchee Ave; mains $15-20; ☺ lunch & dinner Tue-Sat) If you're craving borscht, piroshki or good old-fashioned Ukrainian dumplings, the search ends here. Run by a Ukrainian couple from Odessa, Inna's has added an Eastern European flavor to Wenatchee's clutch of above-average eateries.

ℹ Information

Wenatchee National Forest Headquarters (215 Melody Lane) North of town at the junction of Hwy 285 and US 2.
Wenatchee Valley Convention & Visitors Bureau (www.wenatcheevalley.org; Ste 100, 5 S Wenatchee Ave) For information and walking-tour maps.

ℹ Getting There & Away

AIR

Horizon Air services the **Pangborn Memorial Airport** (www.pangbornairport.com) in East Wenatchee, with four or five flights daily to and from Seattle (from $70 one way).

BUS

All bus and rail transit services are centralized at **Columbia Station** (300 S Columbia Ave), at the foot of Kittitas St. **Northwestern Trailways** (www.northwesterntrailways.com) runs daily buses to Seattle (direct), Spokane via Moses Lake, and Pasco via Yakima.

Apple Line (www.appleline.us) runs handy once-a-day services to destinations like Chelan Falls ($16) and south Ellensburg ($20).

You can get to the nearby towns of Leavenworth via Cashmere (bus 22, $2.50, 50 minutes) and Chelan via Entiat (bus 21, $2.50, one hour) on frequent **Link Transit buses** (www.linktransit.com). Buses are equipped with bike racks.

TRAIN

The **Amtrak** (www.amtrak.com) *Empire Builder* stops daily in Wenatchee on its way between Seattle and Chicago.

Yakima Valley

With its scorched hills interspersed with geometrically laid-out vine plantations and apple orchards, the Yakima River Valley glimmers like a verdant oasis in an otherwise dry and barren desert. Arising from the snowy slopes of Snoqualmie Pass and flowing deceptively southeast (and away from the Pacific) until it joins courses with the mighty Columbia, the fast-flowing Yakima River supports a lucrative agricultural industry that churns out copious amounts of cherries, vegetables and peaches, along with three-quarters of the US hop output, luscious wine grapes and the world's largest yield of apples.

Markedly drier and hotter than Washington's wet west coast, much of the valley survives on as little as 8in of rain a year (Seattle gets 37in) and temperatures can rise to over 100°F (38°C) in the summer.

A huge demand for agricultural labor to work in the fields and orchards during the fruit-picking season has brought a large Mexican population to the valley and, with 40% of Yakima county's population now registered as Hispanic, you'll hear *'buenos dias'* as often as 'good morning.' The vast Yakama Native American Reservation to the southwest adds a strong Native American element to the population mix.

Ellensburg

POP 18,468

Take an archetypal American small town; give it a stately college, a smattering of historic buildings, and more coffee bars per head than anywhere else in the US (allegedly); then throw in the largest and most lauded rodeo in the Pacific Northwest. Welcome to Ellensburg, a town where erudite college undergraduates rub shoulders with weekend cowboys in a collegiate town where two-thirds of the 16,000-strong population

CENTRAL & EASTERN WASHINGTON YAKIMA VALLEY

ROADSIDE FRUIT STANDS

Let Washington's mouthwatering fruit stands reignite your diet with something crisp, colorful and healthy. Apples are the most ubiquitous crop, but you can also find apricots, pears and countless others when the season's in full swing. One of the best tracts of road to 'shop' is the stretch of Hwy 2/97 going north between Wenatchee and Chelan on the east side of the Columbia River. Look out in particular for **Lone Pine Fruit & Espresso** (23041 Hwy 97), housed in a century-old apple-packing shed near Orondo, and B&B Fruit Stand, which has been in operation since the early 1960s, 2.5 miles north of the Odabashion Bridge.

are registered students. Like most Washington towns, Ellensburg has its fair share of peripheral motel and mall infestations, but body-swerve the familiar big boxes and you'll uncover a compact but select cluster of venerable red-brick buildings born out of the 'City Beautiful' movement in the early 1890s.

Ellensburg's location on the cusp of the Eastern Cascades and the flat, fertile Columbia River basin throws up two radically different types of adventure opportunities (rugged to the east, refined to the west). Seattleites regularly cross Snoqualmie Pass to sup local wine and enjoy seemingly endless summer sunshine. Easterners stop by on their way to the snowier mountains.

Once touted as the 'Pittsburg of the West' for its plentiful coal and iron-ore deposits, Ellensburg suffered the fate of many western towns in 1889 when a fire tore the heart out of nine blocks of its central business district. The present-day historical core, though small in size, is the result of an industrious postfire rebuilding process.

⊙ Sights

Downtown Historic District   HISTORIC SITE
Beautified by a compact yet charismatic grid of Victorian buildings, central Ellensburg deserves an unhurried morning or afternoon's exploration. Kick off at the friendly chamber of commerce, where you can get informative maps of the downtown historic district, roughly contained between Main St and 6th and 3rd Aves. Sprinkled with antique shops, galleries and cafes, the quarter is dominated by the **Davidson Building**, Ellensburg's signature postcard sight, built in 1889 by local attorney John B Davidson. Also worth checking out is the **Kittitas County Historical Museum** (www.kchm.org; donations accepted; ⊙10am-4pm Mon-Sat Jun-Sep, from noon Tue-Sat Oct-May), housed in the 1889 Cadwell Building, known mostly for its petrified-wood and gemstone collections but also boasting a cleverly laid-out history section documenting the backgrounds of Croatian, Arabic and Welsh immigrants. Equally intriguing are the paintings of native son John Clymer at the **Clymer Museum** (www.clymermuseum.com; 416 N Pearl St; ⊙10am-5pm Mon-Fri, 10am-4pm Sat, noon-4pm Sun) FREE, whose all-American subjects graced *Saturday Evening Post* covers in the 1950s and '60s.

For kids try the **Children's Activity Museum** (www.childrensactivitymuseum.org; 118 E 4th Ave; admission $4.25; ⊙10am-5pm Wed-Sat; 🖈), which has a miniature cowboy ranch, a science lab and other engaging hands-on exhibits.

**Chimpanzee & Human
Communication Institute**   WORKSHOPS
(☎509-963-2244; www.cwu.edu/~cwuchci; cnr Nicholson Blvd & D St; adult/student $11/8.50; ⊙9:15am & 10.45am Sat, 12:30pm & 2pm Sun Mar-Nov) As well as having a rather picturesque campus, Central Washington University has gained some renown for its studies of communication between humans and chimpanzees. Several of its chimps have learned to communicate using American Sign Language. On weekends the institute presents an informative, hour-long 'Chimposium' workshop that includes an audience with the chimps. Reservations are required.

**Olmstead Place State Park
Heritage Area**   HISTORIC PARK
(921 N Ferguson Rd; ⊙8am-5pm) FREE Four-and-a-half miles southeast of Ellensburg off I-90, the historical theme continues with log cabins, pioneer barns and other farm buildings dating from 1875 to 1890. They depict early homestead life in the Kittitas Valley.

Thorp Grist Mill   HISTORIC SITE
(www.thorp.org; ⊙11am-3pm Thu-Sat, noon-4pm Sun Jun-Sep) FREE Another view of frontier agriculture is on display in the small town of Thorp, 8 miles northwest of Ellensburg at what was once a de facto meeting place for local farmers. The mill, now a rural museum, dates from 1873.

🏃 Activities

South of Ellensburg, Hwy 821 through the Yakima Canyon offers a scenic alternative to busy I-82. Rafting on the Yakima River is a popular activity here, with **Rill Adventures** (www.rillsonline.com; Thorp Hwy) offering raft and kayak hire. Catch-and-release fishing is another drawcard.

🎊 Festivals & Events

★**Ellensburg Rodeo**   RODEO
(www.ellensburgrodeo.com) Ellensburg's ultimate festival takes place on Labor Day weekend in tandem with the Kittitas County Fair. It's ranked among the top 10 rodeos in the nation and is one of central Washington's biggest events. Come prepared to see some hard riding and roping – participants take this rodeo very seriously, as there is big money at stake.

THE GORGE AMPHITHEATER

Gorge-ous and 100% natural, 'The Gorge' is a stunning alfresco music venue perched on the banks of the Columbia River, 40 miles east of Ellensburg. Regularly touted as the most spectacular rock venue in North America, the steeply banked natural amphitheater with space for 25,000 on an expansive terraced lawn leaves most concert-goers at a loss for words. Numerous international stars have stepped up to the microphone here, including the Who, the Police, David Bowie and Van Morrison, and many of the sets have entered rock legend. Pearl Jam made its 2005–06 album *Live at the Gorge* into a box set, while the Dave Matthews Band has serenaded the impossibly crimson Columbia River sunsets more than 30 times.

For more information on summer concerts and tickets see www.gorgeconcerts.com.

🛏 Sleeping

Like many towns in Washington, the areas near the freeways are loaded with cheap and bland motels and chain hotels, but there are a few more interesting choices in the historic downtown.

Guesthouse Ellensburg B&B $$
(☎509-962-3706; www.guesthouseellensburg. com; 606 Main St; r $145) This unique guesthouse, handily located opposite the chamber of commerce on Main St, doubles as a wine shop and tasting room, and the proprietors certainly know their enology. Two restored Victorian rooms are furnished with English antiques, four-poster beds and flat-screen TVs, while downstairs in the tasting room you can discuss viticulture until the grapes ripen with free tasting sessions and generous discounts for guests.

Wrens Nest B&B B&B $$
(☎509-925-9061; www.wrensnest.com; 300 E Manitoba Ave; r from $90) This is a typical small-town B&B encased in a 1912 Craftsman-style home. Experienced B&Bers will appreciate the familiar touches: welcome tea and cookies, beyond-the-call-of-duty service, individually furnished rooms, relaxed guest-to-guest interaction and substantial (and creative) breakfasts.

🍴 Eating & Drinking

★ **Yellow Church Café** FUSION $$
(www.yellowchurchcafe.com; 111 S Pearl St; brunch $8-10, dinner $13-23; ⊙11am-8pm Mon-Fri, 8am-8pm Sat & Sun) This homey bright-yellow former church built by the German Lutherans in 1923 is now an unconventional restaurant that serves urban hipster-worthy food. The breakfast – including the aptly named St Benedict's eggs – has won widespread recommendations, while the elegant dinner options have been well matched with local wines from the expert owners, who also run the nearby Guesthouse Ellensburg.

Valley Café FUSION $$
(www.valleycafeellensburg.com; 105 W 3rd Ave; dinner mains $16-25) This diminutive art-deco construction, in business since 1938, has a restaurant and cafe, along with an excellent selection of Washington wines, nicely paired with the accompanying food. Check out the cioppino, the rack of lamb or the ahi tuna. The interior is furnished with unpretentious booths and there's also a takeout section.

D&M Coffee CAFE
(www.dmcoffee.com; 301 N Pine St; ⊙7am-5pm) 🖋 With allegedly more coffee bars per head than anywhere else in the US, you're certainly spoiled for choice when it comes to satisfying your morning caffeine habit in Ellensburg. D&M is the local roasting company, and the best of its quintet of local outlets is situated here, opposite the Kittitas County Museum. Funky stools and an academic atmosphere make it an ideal place to linger.

Iron Horse Micropub BREWPUB
(414 N Main St; beers on tap from $4; ⊙4-9pm Mon-Sat) The downtown outpost for one of the region's best microbreweries is a bright and hip, albeit small pub serving eight beers on tap and snacks. You can also check out the larger main brewery at 1000 Prospect St, about a mile from the town center.

ℹ Information

Ellensburg Chamber of Commerce (www. ellensburg-chamber.com; 609 N Main St; ⊙8am-5pm Mon-Fri, 10am-2pm Sat) For maps and information; the building is shared by the US Forest Service and Ellensburg Rodeo offices.

ⓘ Getting There & Away

Greyhound (www.greyhound.com) buses stop at the Pilot gas station at I-90 exit 106, 2 miles from the town center. The ticket window is in the Subway sandwich shop. Buses here leave for Seattle ($26, two hours, five daily), Spokane via Moses Lake ($40, four hours, three daily) and Yakima ($17, 45 minutes, three daily). Some Yakima buses continue on to the Tri-Cities and beyond.

Apple Line (www.appleline.us) runs one bus daily to Wenatchee, Chelan Falls, Pateros and Omak.

Bellair Shuttle (www.airporter.com) runs five daily buses to Sea-Tac Airport and Seattle to the east and Yakima to the west; fares are $7. It stops next to Starbucks on the Central Washington University campus.

Yakima

POP 95,512

Not long after the Northwest's weighty clouds have dumped most of their precipitation on Seattle and the Cascade Mountains they arrive in the parched east, lighter, whiter, or – if you're lucky – vanquished altogether. All the more reason to pull into balmy Yakima, the so-called 'Palm Springs of Washington' – not the state's prettiest or most interesting city, but certainly one of its sunniest. If you can see past the limitations of Yakima's rather dull downtown, the settlement's rural periphery beckons like an enologist's wet dream, a kind of Washingtonian Dordogne without the historic villages but with enough reputed vineyards to keep any French wine snob happy for days.

Founded on its present site in 1884, Yakima takes its name from the Yakama Native American people, who inhabited this valley for centuries before an 1855 treaty created the Yakama Native American Reservation.

One third of the city of Yakima's population is Hispanic.

◎ Sights & Activities

★ **Yakima Valley Museum**　MUSEUM
(www.yakimavalleymuseum.org; 2105 Tieton Dr; adult/senior $5/3; ◎10am-5pm Mon-Sat, closed Mon Nov-Mar, Children's Underground 1-5pm Tue-Fri, 10am-5pm Sat; ④) This highly educational and entertaining museum is one of the state's best. It tells the story of the region from a geographic and historical viewpoint, with a strong emphasis on agriculture and the Yakama Native American heritage. Prize exhibits include a number of horse-drawn conveyances and some early motor vehicles, plus a full working mockup of a Depression-era soda fountain. The **Children's Underground** does a good job of incorporating Yakima's human and natural history into a number of hands-on exhibits.

Adjacent to the museum is **Franklin Park**, a broad lawn planted with evergreens that features a playground, picnic tables, and – an important feature in sun-baked Yakima – a swimming pool.

Yakima Greenway　PARK
(www.yakimagreenway.org) 🚲 A pleasant oasis in an otherwise unremarkable city, the Greenway is best accessed via Sarg Hubbard Park at I-82 exit 33. It's a 10-mile path for walkers and cyclists that tracks the fast-flowing Yakima River through a string of parks and recreation areas. One good stop-off point is the **Yakima Area Arboretum** (www.ahtrees.org), just east of exit 34, where a collection of more than 2000 species of trees and shrubs spreads out over 46 acres of landscaped gardens. You can procure a free walking-tour brochure at the **Jewett Interpretive Center** (1401 Arboretum Dr; ◎9am-4pm Tue-Sat) ｜FREE｜.

Treveri Cellars　WINE TASTING
(71 Gangl Rd, Wapato; ◎noon-5pm Mon-Thu, 11am-7pm Fri & Sat, noon-4pm Sun) The only sparkling wines in the valley are made by Treveri, and they're so good they've been served at the White House. You'll have to drive to Wapato, about 15 miles south of Yakima, to go to the tasting room and if you do you'll probably end up buying a few bottles – they start at $14.

🛏 Sleeping

Birchfield Manor　B&B $$
(☏509-452-1960; www.birchfieldmanor.com; 2018 Birchfield Rd; manor r $119-159, cottage r $139-219; 🛜) Renowned for its flavorful food and well-stocked Washington wine cellar, the Birchfield offers unusual antique-filled rooms in a pleasant parklike setting 2 miles east of Yakima off Hwy 24. Five manor rooms are complemented by six guest cottages, some with double Jacuzzi. The manor, which makes a great alternative to the standard Yakima hotel chains, also has as a first-class restaurant.

Ledgestone Hotel　HOTEL $$
(☏509-453-3151; www.ledgestonehotel.com; 107 North Fair Ave; ste from $119; 🅿@🛜) The Ledgestone looks like just another roadside chain

CENTRAL & EASTERN WASHINGTON YAKIMA VALLEY

hotel, but it's not. All its rooms are one-bedroom suites with minikitchens, lounge areas, bathrooms and separate bedrooms (with their own flat-screen TVs). There's even a little office nook. Happily, the suites are sold at standard room prices and there's a fitness room, a laundry service and a few air miles thrown in for free.

✕ Eating

For a wine region, Yakima is disappointing in the food stakes, though a strong Hispanic community provides a good excuse to go Mexican.

Tacos Los Primos #2   MEXICAN $
(404 N 4th St; tacos $1.25; ⊘ lunch) It looks dirty and is parked humbly in front of Delaney's Lost Sock Laundromat, but this little taco shack churns out some of very Latino Yakima's best tacos, tortas, sopas and burritos for next to nothing. We highly recommend the spicy pork, but go for the *tripa* (intestines) if you're feeling adventurous.

Essencia Artisan Bakery   BAKERY $
(4 N 3rd St; sandwiches from $5; ⊘ 6am-4pm Mon-Fri, 7am-2pm Sat) Head to this homey bakery that's always full of locals for creative sandwiches (think ginger roast beef or brie and chicken), soups, salads, panini, homemade chai and of course the decent selection of breads and baked goods.

★Birchfield Manor Restaurant   FUSION $$$
(☑ 509-452-1960; www.birchfieldmanor.com; 2018 Birchfield Rd; mains from $20; ⊘ dinner) The revered Birchfield is a sublime dining experience offered in an intimate 1910 B&B. While the accommodation here is considered top end, the food is even better. Reservations must be made in advance and seating is at set times, but everything from the bread to the after-dinner chocolates to the knowledgeable service is impeccable. The highlights are the mains: salmon in puff pastry with chardonnay sauce, steak Diane in a brandy cream sauce, all expertly paired with local wines (the place has its own cellar). Exquisite!

☕ Drinking

Gilbert Cellars   CAFE
(www.gilbertcellars.com; 5 N Front St; ⊘ noon-9pm Mon-Thu, to 11pm Fri & Sat, to 5pm Sun) This refined downtown tasting room ($5 for five tastings) has the air of a classy wine bar. Service is knowledgeable but unpretentious and there are some excellent cheese-based snacks.

Northtown Coffee   CAFE
(www.northtowncoffee.com; 28 N 1st St; ⊘ 6am-midnight Mon-Fri, 7am-midnight Sat & Sun) A bit of Portland repositioned to central Washington (which is no bad thing), Northtown sells PDX's famous Stumptown coffee in cozy nooks. Get comfortable – it's open till midnight daily.

ℹ Information

Yakima Valley Visitors & Convention Bureau (www.visityakima.com; 10 N 8th St; ⊘ 9am-5pm Mon-Sat, 10am-4pm Sun)

Toppenish

POP 9095
If you make one stop off the wine trail in the Yakima Valley, make it off-the-wall Toppenish, a living art festival that has become locally famous for its 60 or more historic **murals** painted Banksy-style on most of the downtown buildings. Chronicling the events from Yakama and Northwestern history, the first mural was painted back in 1989. Later additions include evocative tableaux of the valley's more recent Mexican immigrants employed in the agricultural sector. Further information and mural guides can be procured from the **Toppenish Chamber of Commerce** (www.toppenish.net; 504 S Elm St; ⊘ 11am-4pm Mon-Sat).

Another Toppenish institution is the **American Hop Museum** (www.americanhopmuseum.org; 22 S B St; admission $3; ⊘ 10am-4pm May-Sep), a temptation for all beer lovers, that chronicles the history of the American hop-growing industry from its humble beginnings in New England in the early 1600s.

The history of the Yakama Native Americans is well documented at the **Yakama Indian Nation Cultural Center** (www.yakamamuseum.com; 280 Buster Rd; adult/child $6/4; ⊘ 8am-5pm Mon-Fri, 9am-5pm Sat & Sun), which exhibits costumes, baskets, beads and audiovisual displays, and includes a gift shop, library, restaurant and heritage theater (with occasional tribal dances).

An interesting historical curiosity is contained in an old fort complex preserved in the 200-acre **Fort Simcoe State Park** (5150 Fort Simcoe Rd; ⊘ interpretive center 9am-4:30pm Wed-Sun Apr-Oct), an oasis of green in the midst of scorched desert hills. It was built in 1855 but served as a fort for only three years until the creation of the Yakama Reservation in 1859. Listed on the National Register of Historical Places, the park now acts as an interpretive center with a handful of original buildings still intact.

CENTRAL & EASTERN WASHINGTON YAKIMA VALLEY

SOUTHEASTERN WASHINGTON

Parched, remote, and barely served by public transportation, southeastern Washington is the state's loneliest corner and is characterized by the dry volcanic plateaus and denuded lava flows of the inhospitable 'Scablands' region, exposed by the Missoula floods at the end of the last ice age. Tourism – and its attendant attractions – was on a backburner here until the early 1990s, when wine growers in and around Walla Walla began to realize the town's potential as a new Sonoma, and wine connoisseurs started arriving from around the globe. For many, the region's fortunes turned full circle.

Established as one of Washington's first permanent settlements in 1836 when Marcus Whitman rolled off the Oregon Trail and founded a mission in the foothills of the Blue Mountains, the southeast was once a hive of commercial activity that sat on the cusp of Washington's burgeoning frontier. But as the settlers pushed west in the late 19th century, the Columbia River Basin slipped into a self-imposed coma, made all the more terminal when the US government opened up the Hanford nuclear complex near Richland in 1942. Not surprisingly, the stigma of secret bomb-making factories and contaminated waste sites has been hard to dislodge, but delicious wines are overshadowing everything nowadays.

DON'T MISS

YAKIMA VALLEY WINE TOUR

The Yakima Valley American Viticultural Area (AVA) encompasses four sub-AVAs (Red Mountain, Rattlesnake Hills, Horse Heaven Hills and Snipes Mountain) and more than 80 wineries, most of them small, family-run affairs. These dry yet deceptively fertile fields produce some of the most delicious wines in the country; around 40% of Washington's wine grapes are grown here. **Wine Yakima Valley** (www.wineyakimavalley.org) has an up-to-date list of local wineries and **Yakima Valley Wine** (www.yakimavalleywine) is an excellent source of information for the entire valley.

The following tour takes in our favorite spots:

Start in the **Rattlesnake Hills AVA** that lazes next to the tiny town of **Zillah**. **Bonair Winery** (www.bonairwine.com; 500 S Bonair Rd, Zillah; ⊙10am-5pm), one of the valley's oldest, is a quintessential stop where you can picnic on the front lawn and chat with the friendly owners over their affordable red blends. For contrast head up the hill to **Silver Lake Winery** (www.silverlakewinery.com; 1500 Vintage Rd, Zillah; ⊙10am-5pm Apr-Nov, 11am-4pm Thu-Mon Dec-Mar), a favorite venue for fancy weddings thanks to its views over the whole valley.

Your next stop is **Prosser**, a midcentury movie-set-worthy town that's your best stop for lunch – for a kitsch surprise, beer and burgers try **Bern's Tavern** (618 6th St, Prosser; ⊙9am-10pm Sun-Thu, to 2am Fri & Sat). Get back to wines at picture-book-pretty **Chinook Wines** (www.chinookwines.com; Wine Country Rd, Prosser; ⊙tastings noon-5pm Sat & Sun May-Oct), known for its chardonnay and sauvignon blanc. **Vinter's Village** across the highway is in bland housing-community-like surrounds but holds some great wineries; try **Maison Bleue** (☑509-378-6527; www.mbwines.com; 357 Port Ave, Studio D, Prosser; ⊙by appointment) for Rhone-style syrah or **Airfield Estates** (www.airfieldwines.com; 560 Merlot Dr, Prosser; ⊙11am-5pm) for an easy-to-love unoaked chardonnay.

Your final stops are just up the hill from **Benton City** at the **Red Mountain AVA**, the smallest viticultural area in the US and one of the best. Meander up N Sunset Rd, stopping first at humble **Cooper Wine Company** (wwwcooperwinecompany.com; 35306 N Sunset Rd, Benton City; ⊙noon-5pm Fri-Mon) to ooh and aah over its L'Inizio bordeaux blend. Up the road and on a dirt path to the left is **Taptiel Estate** (www.taptiel.com; 20206 E 583 PR NE, Benton City; ⊙11am-5pm Fri-Sun Apr-Nov), great for syrah and cabernet sauvignons to sip over views of the valley. Last, take a detour to the grandest estate on the tour, **Terra Blanca** (www.terrablanca.com; 34715 N DeMoss Rd, Benton City; ⊙11am-6pm), where you can sample red and dessert wines in the castlelike tasting room or on the terrace overlooking manicured gardens, a pond, golden grasslands and mountains.

Tri-Cities

POP 188,981

Three cities (Pasco, Kennewick and Richland) situated at the confluence of three rivers (the Snake, Columbia and Yakima) sounds like a promising proposition, but while the Tri-Cities can offer plenty in the way of wine quaffing and water sports they rarely feature in the front line of Washington's tourist push. Part of the reason is that, historically, the Tri-Cities have been closely associated with the notorious Hanford site, the top-secret plutonium-processing plant that manufactured 'fat boy,' the atomic bomb dropped on Nagasaki in 1945, and subsequently stayed in operation throughout the Cold War. Although it has been largely decommissioned since the early 1990s, recent studies have revealed that Hanford's operations have leaked a significant amount of radioactive waste into the Columbia River.

Eschewing their nuclear image, the Tri-Cities have grown and prospered in recent years through wine production, agriculture and – ironically – a massive (and still ongoing) Hanford clean-up campaign (which still employs thousands).

◉ Sights & Activities

Columbia River Exhibition of History, Science & Technology   MUSEUM

(CREHST; www.crehst.com; 95 Lee Blvd, Richland; adult/student $5/4; ⊙10am-5pm Mon-Sat, noon-5pm Sun) CREHST documents Columbia River history, the journey of Lewis and Clark and, inevitably, the Hanford project.

East Benton County Historical Museum   MUSEUM

(www.ebchs.com; 205 Keewayden Dr, Kennewick; adult/child $4/1; ⊙noon-4pm Tue-Sat) This museum tracks local history and has some exhibits on 'Kennewick Man,' the 9300-year-old skeleton of a Caucasian male found on the banks of the Columbia in 1996 that blew the anthropological history of North America wide open.

Riverside Greenway   HIKING, CYCLING

To see the Tri-Cities in their best light, stay close to the broad Columbia River, which reveals its only stretch of free-flowing water at the **Hanford Reach National Monument**.

Kennewick's **Columbia Park** is a vast greenway complete with golf course, playing fields, campground and boat moorage, while the 23-mile paved **Sacagawea Heritage Trail** acts as a connecting hiking and biking artery between the three cities using the river as its marker.

🛏 Sleeping & Eating

Clover Island Inn   HOTEL $

(☏509-586-0541; www.hotelkennewick.com; 435 Clover Island Dr, Kennewick; r from $74; ❀ 🕸 🞱 ✿ 🞲) You won't have trouble finding an economical motel in the Tri-Cities but, if you want something a little plusher, hit the locally owned Clover Island Inn, which is situated on its own island in the Columbia River. This unique establishment boasts 152 rooms, its own boat dock and panoramic views from the top-floor Crow's Nest Restaurant. You can borrow bikes to use on the abundant paths for free.

Atomic Ale Brewpub & Eatery   PUB $$

(www.atomicalebrewpub.com; 1015 Lee Blvd, Richland; sandwiches $8, pizzas $9-14; ⊙closed Sun) A perceptible Hanford-inspired 'gallows humor' pervades this cheery microbrewery and eatery, well known for its wood-fired specialty pizzas and top-notch soups (try the red potato). But first blast off with a locally crafted Half-Life Hefeweizen, Plutonium Porter or Atomic Amber. Real intellectuals grab an Oppenheimer Oatmeal Stout.

❶ Getting There & Away

Greyhound (www.greyhound.com) and **Amtrak** (www.amtrak.com) share a terminal at 535 N 1st Ave in Pasco. Greyhound buses go to Spokane ($44, 2½ hours), Portland ($57, four hours) and Seattle ($57, 4½ hours) via Yakima and Ellensburg. Amtrak's *Empire Builder* stops here en route to Portland at 5:35am ($41, 4½ hours); eastbound, it passes through at 8:57pm on the way to Spokane ($23, 3½ hours) and Chicago.

Walla Walla

POP 32,148

'Walla Walla, so good they named it twice' – or so the understandably biased locals would have you believe. The quip probably seemed like a bad joke a couple of decades ago, when Walla Walla's most well-known landmark was the state's largest penitentiary. These days the naysayers are laughing on the other side of their faces. The reason: wine. Walla Walla and its surrounding vineyards now concoct some of the best vintages in the US, challenging California in the same way the 'Sunshine State' once took on the French. Furthermore, Walla Walla, more than any

Washington town, has fermented the ingredients to support a burgeoning wine culture, including a historic Main St, a handsome college, a warm summer climate and a growing clutch of fine restaurants where pairing wine and food is as common as pairing couples on a blind date.

Located in a rich agricultural area, Walla Walla supplements its much-sought-after vineyards with pea and asparagus production, apple orchards and its famous sweet onions. Equally distinctive in the undulating countryside are 454 wind turbines belonging to the massive Stateline Wind Energy Center, a groundbreaking environmental project that is a vital source of Washington's renewable energy.

◉ Sights

With its laid-back, small-town feel, excellent reds and plethora of unpretentious local wineries, Walla Walla is the best place in the state to indulge in a bit of wine touring. Expect tasting fees of $5 to $10. Meander the town's rural outskirts to taste wines in the fresh air, or stop by at an ever-expanding number of tasting rooms in town.

Historic Downtown   HISTORIC SITE
You don't need to be sloshed on wine to appreciate Walla Walla's historical and cultural heritage. Its Main Street has won countless historical awards, and to bring the settlement to life the local chamber of commerce has concocted some interesting walking tours, with a leaflet including maps and numbered icons.

The 1.5-mile 'Downtown Walk' starts at the 1928 Marcus Whitman Hotel and proceeds in a loop around the historic buildings of Main and Colville Sts. A couple of other walks showcase the historic homes that dot the suburbs with Queen Anne, neoclassical and Gothic Carpenter–style architecture. Also be sure not to miss the gorgeous Whitman College campus and the lush confines of Pioneer Park nearby.

Fort Walla Walla Park   HISTORIC SITE
This fine historic site showcases the original buildings from a US Army installation that existed here from its inception in 1858 until 1910 – everything from the officer's quarters to the quartermaster's stable. The grounds now house the Department of Veterans Affairs Medical Center. Slightly west of here is the Fort Walla Walla Museum (755 Myra Rd; adult/child $7/3; ◷ 10am-5pm; ⊞), a pioneer

village of 17 historic buildings, including a blacksmith shop, an 1867 schoolhouse, log cabins and a railway depot, arranged around a central meadow. On a hill above the village, the fort's old cavalry stables house the museum proper, with collections of farm implements, ranching tools and what could be the world's largest plastic replica of a mule team.

Whitman Mission   HISTORIC SITE
(www.nps.gov/whmi; Swegle Rd; ◷ 9am-4pm) ⚑ FREE An erstwhile stop on the Oregon Trail and infamous site of the 1847 Whitman 'massacre,' when white missionary Marcus Whitman and a dozen others were murdered by Cayuse Indians, this potent historic site 7 miles west of Walla Walla contains a museum and marked sites and monuments indicating where the mission once stood.

🏃 Activities

Halcyon bike rides between wineries are just the tip of the outdoor-activity iceberg in Walla Walla.

Amavi Cellars   WINE TASTING
(3796 Peppers Bridge Rd; ◷ 10am-4pm) South of Walla Walla, amid a scenic spread of grape and apple orchards, you can sample some of the most talked about wines in the valley (try the syrah and cabernet sauvignon). The classy yet comfortable outdoor patio has views of the Blue Mountains.

Waterbrook Wine   WINE TASTING
(www.waterbrook.com; 10518 W US 12; ◷ 11am-6pm Mon-Thu, to 8pm Fri & Sat) About 10 miles west of town, the pondside patio of this large winery is a great place to imbibe a long selection of wines on a sunny day. Outrageously good tacos (two for $6) are served on Friday and Saturday.

Dusted Valley Wines   WINE TASTING
(1248 Old Milton Hwy; ◷ noon-5pm Thu-Mon Apr-Nov) At this great example of one of the valley's better small wineries, the tasting room is attached to the owner's home. Imbibe in the garden and grab lunch at one of the food trucks that often park nearby.

Otis Kenyon   WINE TASTING
(23 E Main St; ◷ 11am-5pm Thu-Mon) One of the better tasting rooms in the downtown area: the decor isn't special, but the quirky story behind the label and the earthy syrah certainly are.

L'Ecole No 41
WINE TASTING

(41 Lowden School Rd; ⊙10am-5pm) Eleven miles west of Walla Walla just off W US 12, take a wine lesson at the bar of this hip, early-1900s schoolhouse (if only school was always this fun). The syrah and bordeaux earn easy As.

Canoe Ridge
WINE TASTING

(www.canoeridgevineyard.com; 1102 W Cherry St; ⊙11am-5pm) One of town's most interesting tasting rooms is situated in a newly restored 1905 streetcar engine house. Try the merlot and the cabernet sauvignon.

Umatilla National Forest
HIKING

(www.fs.fed.us/r6/uma) Three-quarters of this Blue Mountains protected area lies across the state border in Oregon. The Washington section contains plenty of hiking trails. Consult the Ranger Station (1415 W Rose St) in Walla Walla.

Ski Bluewood
SKIING

(www.bluewood.com; day pass adult/child $42/33; ⊕) Situated 52 miles northeast of Walla Walla near the town of Dayton, Bluewood is something of a revelation to most visitors, who (wrongly) assume that southeast Washington is flat and not particularly snowy. The ski area is small, with 20 runs, but has a high base elevation of 4545ft.

⭐ Festivals & Events

Walla Walla Sweet Onion Blues Fest
FOOD, MUSIC

(☑509-525-1031; www.sweetonions.org; ⊙mid-Jul) The Walla Walla Sweet Onion Blues Fest, held at Fort Walla Walla, celebrates the valley's renowned crop (now upstaged by the region's wine). There are food booths and recipe contests, as well as live music provided by touring blues acts.

Balloon Stampede
HOT-AIR BALLOONS

(⊙mid-May) The Balloon Stampede sees competitors launch dozens of hot air–filled craft at 6am.

🛏 Sleeping

Colonial Motel
MOTEL $

(☑509-529-1220; www.colonial-motel.com; 2279 Isaacs Ave; r from $70; ❋☎) A simple family-run motel halfway to the airport, the Colonial is welcoming and bike friendly with safe bike storage and plenty of local maps.

Marcus Whitman Hotel
HOTEL $$

(☑509-525-2200; www.marcuswhitmanhotel.com; 6 W Rose St; r $119-325; ❋☎❖) Walla Walla's best-known landmark is also the town's only tall building, impossible to miss with its distinctive rooftop turret. In keeping with the settlement's well-preserved image, the red-brick 1928 beauty has been elegantly renovated, with ample rooms in rusts and browns, embellished with Italian-crafted furniture, huge beds and killer views over the nearby Blue Mountains.

The on-site Marc restaurant is one of the town's fanciest eating joints.

Green Gables Inn
B&B $$

(☑509 525 5501; www.greengablesinn.com; 922 Bonsella St; r $165-225; ❋☎) While it's a long way from Prince Edward Island (the setting for *Anne of Green Gables)* this inn in a 1909 Craftsman-style home plays heavily on the classic book and features five rooms named after instances in LM Montgomery's famous novel. Enjoy candlelit breakfasts, a shady wraparound porch, and rooms replete with bathrobes and fresh flowers.

Inn at Abeja
INN $$$

(☑509-522-1234; www.abeja.net; 2014 Mill Creek Rd; r $245-295, ste $495; ☎) If you've got your own transportation and approximately $250 in spare change you can spend a night at this historic homestead and working winery set in the foothills of the Blue Mountains 4 miles east of Walla Walla. Luxury accommodation is in unique self-contained houses that each played a historical role at the farm (hayloft, mechanic's shed etc).

🍴 Eating

Walla Walla is defined by its wine and food, and its restaurants are befitting of a far larger city. There are so many great places to eat that we can't possibly list them all here. Find most places scattered around the small downtown core.

Graze
CAFE $

(5 S Colville St; sandwiches from $8; ⊙10am-7:30pm Mon-Sat, to 3:30pm Sun; ☑) Amazing sandwiches are packed for your picnic, or (if you can get a table) eaten at the simple cafe. Try the butternut-squash panini with mozzarella, roasted garlic, sage and provolone or the flank-steak *torta* with pickled jalapenos, avocado, tomato, cilantro and chipotle dressing. Plenty of vegetarian and nonvegetarian options.

WAITSBURG

Isolated and bucolic Waitsburg (21 miles north of Walla Walla on US 12) has become the unlikely location of a burgeoning restaurant and bar scene. If you want to get way out into the sticks but still get a New York City–style cocktail and really good coffee, this town is for you. Within the historic brick buildings of the few wide streets you'll find a handful of worth-the-drive restaurants, bars and cafes; there's Southern fare at **Whoopemup Hollow Cafe** (120 Main St; ⊘ 5-10pm Wed-Thu, 11:30am-2pm Sat & Sun) and superb tapas and cocktails at **Jimgermanbar** (119 Main St; ⊘ 5pm-late Thu-Mon).

Olive Marketplace & Café   CAFE $
(21 E Main St; breakfast & sandwiches $7-12; ⊘ 7am-9pm) In the historic 1885 Barrett Building, this breezy cafe-market serving breakfast and lunch is a good place to line your stomach for an impending wine tasting.

Colville Street Patisserie   BAKERY $
(40 S Colville St; ⊘ 9am-8pm Mon-Thu, to 10pm Fri & Sat, to 6pm Sun) Gorgeous pastries, outrageously delicious gelato and good coffee in a spacious, well-lit and modern space.

★**Saffron Mediterranean Kitchen**   MEDITERRANEAN $$$
(☑ 509-525-2112; www.saffronmediterraneankitchen.com; 125 W Alder St; mains $15-27; ⊘ 2-10pm, to 9pm winter) This place isn't about cooking; it's about alchemy: Saffron takes seasonal, local ingredients and turns them into pure gold. The Med-inspired menu lists dishes such as pheasant, ricotta gnocchi, amazing flatbreads and weird yogurt-cucumber combo soups that could stand up against anything in Seattle. Then there are the intelligently paired wines – and beers. It's insanely popular, so be sure to reserve.

Brasserie 4   FRENCH $$$
(☑ 509-529-2011; 4 E Main St; mains $15-25; ⊘ closed Mon, lunch Tue & dinner Sun) Sharing a latitude with Bordeaux and a French passion for growing grapes, it was only a matter of time before Walla Walla came over all *français*. Cool, minimalist Brasserie 4 is one of its best manifestations, where the wait staff knows its wines and the Gallic-inspired food is more than just a few pretentious names on the menu. Try the *moules frites* (mussels and fries), cheese plate or excellent steaks.

T-Maccarones   MEDITERRANEAN $$$
(☑ 509-522-4776; www.tmaccarones.com; 4 N Colville St; dinner mains $23-37; ⊘ dinner, breakfast Sun) Another good reason to come to Walla Walla is T-Maccarones, a contemporary restaurant with Italian inflections that's guaranteed to reignite your tired palate after a tough day in the wine-tasting rooms. Big hitters include pear salad, beef tenderloin, prawn polenta and a house fontina mac 'n' cheese. It's food as art, so book ahead.

Whitehouse-Crawford Restaurant   FUSION $$$
(☑ 509-525-2222; www.whitehousecrawford.com; 55 W Cherry St; mains from $20; ⊘ 5-10pm Wed-Mon) If you're feeling flush, bypass the town's ample cafes and make a beeline for this fine-dining establishment housed in an impressively renovated 1905 woodworking mill. Great local seafood and produce highlight the seasonally (and daily) varying menu.

Marc   FRENCH $$$
(☑ 509-525-2200; www.marcuswhitmanhotel.com; 6 W Rose St; mains from $20) Widely lauded fine dining in the Marcus Whitman hotel; try to bag the private chef's table in the kitchen, where you'll get a special meal prepared for you as you watch.

Drinking

Laht Neppur   BREWPUB
(53 S Spokane St) This place is totally devoid of any wine-town pretension but full of stuff every small-town brewpub should have: friendly locals, laughter, sports on TV and peanut shells on the floor. The decent beer is brewed in nearby Waitsburg, but skip the food.

Coffee Perk   CAFE
(4 1st St; 🛜) A student hangout notable for its giant old-fashioned bookcase stocked with everything from Dickens to Mark Twain's *Innocents Abroad*. If the literature doesn't perk you up, the coffee will.

☆ Entertainment

Walla Walla Symphony CLASSICAL MUSIC
(www.wwsymphony.com) Yes, the supposed rural backwater of Walla Walla has had a symphony orchestra since 1907 and the group is currently led by musical director Yaacov Bergman. Tackling everything from Holst to Gershwin, it runs an annual six-concert series in the Cordiner Hall at Whitman College.

Harper Joy Theatre THEATER
(N Park St & Boyer Ave; adult/senior $12/8) Walla Walla's culture vultures wander over to Whitman College's theater department for renditions of Shakespeare, Rodgers and Hammerstein, and plenty of local fare.

❶ Information

Chamber of Commerce (www.wallawalla.org; 29 E Sumach St; ☺ 8:30am-5pm Mon-Fri, 9am-4pm Sat & Sun May-Sep) For information on wine tasting and maps of four fascinating urban walking tours call in here.

❶ Getting There & Around

AIR

Alaska Airlines has two daily flights to Seattle-Tacoma International Airport (from $210 return) from the **Walla Walla Regional Airport** (www.wallawallaairport.com), northeast of town off US 12.

The local bus service is operated 6:30am to 5:30pm weekdays by **Valley Transit** (www.valleytransit.com).

BUS

Greyhound (www.greyhound.com) buses run once daily to Seattle ($67, seven hours) via Pasco, Yakima and Ellensburg; change buses in Pasco for Spokane. Comfortable **Grape Line** (www.grapeline.us) buses run thrice daily to Pasco ($15)

Pullman

POP 29,913

Another of Washington's liberal university towns, Pullman lies in the midst of the golden Palouse region, a fertile pastiche of rolling hills and well-tilled agricultural fields replete with wheat, lentils, barley and peas that is excellent for cycling.

◉ Sights & Activities

Washington State University UNIVERSITY
(WSU; www.wsu.edu) Situated 7 miles west of the Idaho state line, most of Pullman's sights are related directly to expansive WSU, which accommodates more than 22,000 students and one of Washington's leading agricultural schools. In this small 'city within a city' is the WSU's **Museum of Art** (Fine Arts Center, cnr Stadium Way & Wilson Rd; ☺ 10am-4pm Mon-Wed & Fri, 1-5pm Sat & Sun, 10am-10pm Tue) **FREE**, which mounts some lively, well-curated shows featuring Northwestern artists.

Other WSU museums include the **Jacklin Collection** (room 124, Webster Physical Sciences Bldg; ☺ 8am-5pm Mon-Fri) **FREE**, showcasing more than 2000 specimens of petrified wood and the **Museum of Anthropology** (110 College Hall; ☺ 9am-4pm Mon-Fri) **FREE**, which documents fossils relating to human evolution.

🛏 Sleeping & Eating

Hilltop Inn & Restaurant INN $$
(☎ 509-332-0928; 928 NW Olsen St; r from $125; ❇ 🛜 ☒), If you're staying over, try this place about a mile outside of town.

Ferdinand's CAFE $
(☎ 509-335-2141; 101 Food Quality Bldg, WSU Creamery; milkshakes $3.50; ☺ 9:30am-4:30pm Mon-Fri) Don't miss Ferdinand's, which sells the locally concocted Cougar Gold cheese (white sharp cheddar, sold by the can) along with milkshakes, ice cream and a decent espresso.

❶ Information

Pullman Chamber of Commerce (www.pullman-wa.com; 415 N Grand Ave) For a full lowdown on the area and its facilities.

❶ Getting There & Away

Northwestern Trailways (www.northwesterntrailways.com) links Pullman to other cities such as Spokane ($24, 1½ hours) from the **bus station** (NW 1002 Nye St) behind the Dissmore supermarket.

NORTHEASTERN WASHINGTON

Bordered by Canada to the north and Idaho to the east, northeastern Washington is dominated by the understated yet populous city of Spokane, and is internationally famous for producing one of the 20th century's greatest engineering marvels: the gargantuan Grand Coulee Dam. However, the region is little visited and only a few small towns scatter the protected hills and boreal pine forests of the Okanogan and Colville National Forests. Climatically, the northeast is a transition zone, with a dry belt running immediately east of the Cascade Mountains, while wetter, more humid air seeps into the verdant Kettle River and Selkirk Mountain ranges closer to Idaho. This precipitous region marks Washington's only real incursion into the Rocky Mountains.

Spokane

POP 210,103

Washington's second-biggest population center (edging out Tacoma by about 10,000 people) is a welcome break after the treeless monotony of the eastern Scablands. Situated at the nexus of the Pacific Northwest's so-called 'Inland Empire,' this understated yet confident city sits clustered on the banks of the Spokane River. Though rarely touted in national tourist blurbs, Spokane hosts the world's largest mass-participation running event (May's annual Bloomsday), a stunning gilded-age hotel (the Davenport) and a spectacular waterfall throwing up angry white spray in the middle of its downtown. It was also the childhood home of that famous old crooner Bing Crosby, and remains the smallest city to have ever hosted an Expo (the 1974 World's Fair). Prepare yourself for some interesting revelations: there's more to this modest metropolis than meets the eye.

◉ Sights

Riverfront Park PARK

(www.spokaneriverfrontpark.com; ⛱) The former site of Spokane's 1974 World's Fair and Exposition, this park provides a welcome slice of urban greenery in the middle of downtown. It has been redeveloped in recent years with a 17-point sculpture walk, along with plenty of bridges and trails to satisfy the city's abundance of amateur runners.

The park's centerpiece is Spokane Falls, a gushing combination of scenic waterfalls and foaming rapids that can get pretty tempestuous after heavy rain. There are various viewing points over the river, including a short gondola ride (adult/child $7.75/4; ⊙11am-6pm Sun-Thu, to 10pm Fri & Sat Apr-Sep), which takes you directly above the falls, or the cheaper and equally spectacular Monroe Street Bridge, built in 1911 and still the largest concrete arch in the USA.

Originally part of a railway depot built in 1902, the 151ft clocktower in the center of the park has become the city's signature sight. The kitschy Pavilion is a small amusement park in the summer and an ice rink in the winter. The adjacent Imax Theater (☑ tel, info 509 625 6686; adult/child US$8/6; ⊙shows hourly noon-7pm daily Mar-Oct, Fri-Sun & holidays Oct-Mar) seats 385 people and boasts a 53ft-high screen.

Like some relic from an old-fashioned fairground, the 1909 hand-carved carousel (admission $2; ⊙noon-5pm weekends & holidays) is a kids classic and, along with the larger-than-life Radio Flyer Wagon sculpture, should keep families occupied for a couple of hours. A miniature tour train ($5) can cart you from A to B in the park, or you can join the walkers and joggers on the Spokane River Centennial Trail (www.spokanecentennialtrail.org), which extends for 37 miles to the Idaho border and beyond.

Riverside State Park PARK

(www.riversidestatepark.org) ⭐ Track the Centennial Trail 3 miles to the west and you'll end up here in 10,000 acres of protected forest and trails where you can run, walk or cycle to your heart's content. Among the park's natural highlights is the Bowl & Pitcher, a deep gorge with huge boulders at a bend in the river 2 miles north of the southern entrance. A swinging suspension bridge, built in the 1930s by the Civilian Conservation Corps, crosses the river here.

History also has its place in the park. Fur trader David Thompson of the North West Company built a trading post in 1810 just north of Nine Mile Falls, beyond the Centennial Trail's northern endpoint. The site is commemorated by the Spokane House Interpretive Center (⊙10am-6pm Thu-Mon Jun-Aug) FREE, where several modest exhibits tell the story with photos and dioramas.

Nearby, you can explore one of Thompson's trapping routes, looking much as it may have looked in his time, at the Little Spokane River Natural Area. A 3.6-mile hiking and cross-country skiing trail through the protected wetland begins about half a mile beyond Spokane House along Hwy 291. Great blue herons nest in the cottonwoods and Native American pictographs can be found at Indian Painted Rocks. The area is perhaps best appreciated in a kayak.

Gonzaga University UNIVERSITY

(www.gonzaga.edu) Founded in 1887 by the Jesuit Order, Gonzaga University is famous for its college basketball team and one particularly celebrated former student: the incomparable Harry Lillis 'Bing' Crosby, who came here to study in 1920.

Bing Crosby Memorabilia Room MUSEUM
(502 E Boone Ave; ☉8am-midnight daily during school year, hours vary Jun-Sep) The immortal Bing Crosby donated a comprehensive collection of his recordings and paraphernalia to alma mater Gonzaga University, and these are displayed in this room at the Crosby Student Center. A bronze statue of the crooner – who, though born in Tacoma, moved to Spokane at the age of three in 1906 – stands out front, with his prized golf clubs in tow.

Jundt Art Museum MUSEUM
(202 E Cataldo Ave; ☉10am-4pm Mon-Thu, 10am-9pm Fri, noon-4pm Sat, hours vary Jun-Sep) In the university art center at the end of Pearl St is this museum housing a good collection of classical sculpture and painting, as well as an 18ft chandelier by glass artist Dale Chihuly.

Northwest Museum of Arts & Culture MUSEUM
(www.northwestmuseum.org; 2316 W 1st Ave; adult/child $7/5; ☉10am-5pm Wed-Sun) Encased in a striking state-of-the-art building in the historic Browne's Addition neighborhood, this museum has – arguably – one of the finest collections of indigenous artifacts in the Northwest. Leading off a plush glass foyer overlooking the Spokane River are four galleries showcasing Spokane's history, as well as a number of roving exhibitions that change every three to four months. Your ticket also earns you the right to visit the adjacent English Tudor–revival **Campbell House**.

🏃 Activities

While Walla Walla and the Yakima Valley are the most obvious stops on the Washington wine-tasting circuit, Spokane has also developed a decent clutch of wineries and tasting rooms with knowledgeable staff on hand to help decipher the flavors.

Running aside, Spokane's outdoor activities center around golf and skiing. In addition to Mt Spokane Ski & Snowboard Park, there are several trails for cross-country skiing in, and just past, nearby Mt Spokane State Park.

Arbor Crest Wine Cellars WINE TASTING
(4705 N Fruithill Rd; ☉noon-5pm) The hilltop location with views over Spokane; the landmark estate; blooming grounds; and live music performances on Wednesdays and the weekends throughout summer all make this winery and vineyard a destination in itself. The wines add to the romance (it's no wonder this is a popular spot for weddings). Try any of the great-value reds.

Caterina Winery WINE TASTING
(www.caterinawinery.com; 905 N Washington; ☉noon-6pm Wed-Sun) For wholesome reds, including some widely lauded cabernet sauvignons, try this kid-friendly winery on the northern outskirts of Riverfront Park.

GHOST TOWNS

Northeast Washington may lack the coffee flavors of Seattle and the alternative music of Olympia, but it does harbor some classic American ghost towns.

The eeriest of the stash is **Molson**, 4 miles south of the Canadian border near Oroville. It's a former mining town that suffered the misfortune of going bust not once but twice in the early years of the 20th century. Molson mark 1 was founded in 1900 by John W Molson of beer-brewing fame, and within a year it had morphed into a viable settlement of 300 fuelled by mining speculation. But the speculators had overpredicted. The still nascent town's fortunes nosedived the following year as the mines dried up, and the population fell to almost single figures. The rebirth came in 1905 with the arrival of the Great Northern Railroad, which led to the development of a new town sited half a mile to the north. New Molson thrived until the late 1920s, when the Great Depression put a brake on its delicate economy. The final curtain fell in 1935 with the cessation of railroad operations.

Today, ghostly remnants of Old Molson make up a rather spooky indoor and outdoor museum complete with bank, law office, store and various outbuildings. It's run by the Molson Historical Society; entrance to these dusty relics is by donation.

After exhuming the ghosts of Molson, you can head to two more skeletal settlements: **Nighthawk**, a railroad and mining nexus founded in 1903, and **Bodie**, founded in 1896 by overoptimistic gold prospectors.

Spokane

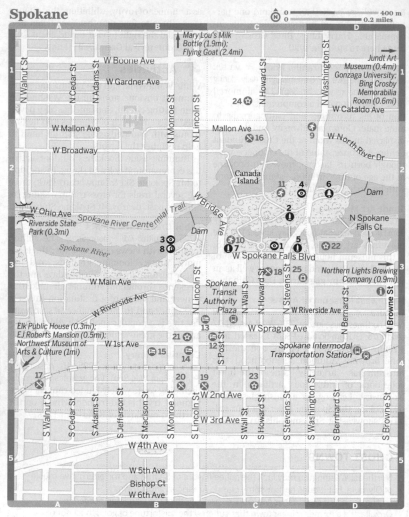

0 ____ 400 m
0 ____ 0.2 miles

Mary Lou's Milk Bottle (1.9mi); Flying Goat (2.4mi)

W Boone Ave

W Gardner Ave

N Walnut St
N Cedar St
N Adams St

W Mallon Ave

W Broadway

N Monroe St
N Lincoln St
N Howard St
N Washington St

Jundt Art Museum (0.4mi) Gonzaga University; Bing Crosby Memorabilia Room (0.6mi)

W Cataldo Ave

Mallon Ave ⊗ 16

24 ⊗

Canada Island

⊗ 9

W North River Dr

11 ⊕   4 ◎   6 ⊕   Dam

2 ⊕

N Spokane Falls Ct

W Ohio Ave
Riverside State Park (0.3mi)

Spokane River Centennial Trail

W Bridge Ave

Dam

Spokane River

3 ◎   10 ⊕
8 ⊙   7 ⊕
W Spokane Falls Blvd   ⊕ 1   5 ⊕   ⊗ 22

18 ⊗ 25
Northern Lights Brewing Company (0.9mi) ⊕

W Main Ave

W Riverside Ave

N Lincoln St
N Wall St
N Howard St
N Stevens St
N Bernard St
N Browne St

Spokane Transit Authority Plaza

W Riverside Ave

Elk Public House (0.3mi);
EJ Roberts Mansion (0.5mi);
Northwest Museum of Arts & Culture (1mi)

13 ⊙

W 1st Ave   21 ⊛   ⊗ 12   S Post St

W Sprague Ave

Spokane Intermodal Transportation Station ⊕

⊙ 15   14 ⊙

17 ⊙

20 ⊗   19 ⊗   23 ⊛

W 2nd Ave

W 3rd Ave

S Walnut St
S Cedar St
S Adams St
S Jefferson St
S Madison St
S Monroe St
S Lincoln St
S Wall St
S Howard St
S Stevens St
S Washington St
S Bernard St
S Browne St

W 4th Ave

W 5th Ave

Bishop Ct

W 6th Ave

Latah Creek Wine Cellars   WINE TASTING
(www.latahcreek.com; 13030 E Indiana Ave; ☺9am-5pm) If white's more your tipple, try the sweet riesling and chardonnays at Latah Creek Wine Cellars, east of the city off I-90 exit 289.

Mt Spokane Ski & Snowboard Park   SKIING
(www.mtspokane.com; day pass adult/child $49/39; ⊛) This refreshingly unhyped ski resort features a 2100ft vertical drop. The resort can be found 31 miles northeast of Spokane at the end of Hwy 206.

⛷ Festivals & Events

Bloomsday Run   RUNNING
(www.bloomsdayrun.org) The race attracts up to 60,000 runners, walkers and wheelchair racers every year on the first Sunday in May. The course bisects downtown and garners plenty of local enthusiasm. Also see p208.

Hoopfest   BASKETBALL
(www.spokanehoopfest.net) An enormous outdoor basketball tournament held at Riverfront Park and in the downtown streets in late June.

Spokane

🛏 Sleeping

Goodbye, boring franchise accommodation; hello, classy independent hotels. Spokane has some of the best. Read on...

Hotel Ruby   BOUTIQUE MOTEL $
(☑ 509-747-1041; www.hotelrubyspokane.com; 901 W 1st Ave; r $68-110; ✳🢁🢄) This is basically just a run-of the mill motel with a hip red-and-black color scheme. Clean and efficient, it has an unbeatable downtown location.

Riverside State Park   CAMPGROUND $
(☑ 888-226-7688; 4427 N Aubrey L White Parkway; tent/RV sites $23/32) Located at the Bowl and Pitcher area on a bend in the Spokane River, this pleasant campground 5 miles northwest of downtown has 32 sites, showers, restrooms and a store.

★ **Davenport Hotel**   HISTORIC HOTEL $$
(☑ 509-455-8888;   www.thedavenporthotel.com; 10 S Post St; Davenport Tower/Davenport Hotel r from $120/130; ✳🢁🢄) As much historic monument as luxury sleepover, the Davenport is one of the most memorable hotels in the Pacific Northwest. The ostentatious lobby extracts a sharp intake of breath from most visitors; everything from the huge fireside vases to the garbage buckets in the restrooms exhibit incredible attention to detail. The truly lavish guest rooms feature beautifully hand-carved custom-made beds.

Even if you're not staying here, be sure to check out the ornate Marie Antoinette Ballroom. The newer, funkier Davenport Tower wing showcases an improbable safari theme

(think stuffed animals and zebra-striped chairs) yet still manages to look sophisticated.

The winner of copious awards, this AAA four-diamond beauty was constructed in 1914 to the design of talented local architect Kirtland Cutter.

Montvale Hotel   BOUTIQUE HOTEL $$
(☑ 509-747-1919; www.montvalehotel.com; 1005 W 1st Ave; r $90-200; ✳🢁) Built in 1899 to house miners and laborers who wearily landed here, Spokane's oldest hotel targets a more discerning clientele nowadays. Upstairs, a refined inner quadrangle with atrium ceilings and a roaring fireplace has a distinctly European feel. Rooms continue the Continental theme, mixing plush old-world furnishings with plenty of up-to-date gadgets. In the basement you'll find Catacombs, a medieval-themed pub.

Hotel Lusso   BOUTIQUE HOTEL $$
(☑ 509-747-9750; www.hotellusso.com; 808 W Sprague Ave; r from $100; ✳🢁) Offering a heritage-style plushness that's on par with its illustrious neighbor the Davenport (the hotels are also under the same management), excellent-value Hotel Lusso is a labyrinth of twisting and turning hallways leading to rooms with glittering marble bathrooms and solid wooden furnishings. Service is equally spiffy. Ask for a room facing the street rather than the alley.

EJ Roberts Mansion B&B   B&B $$$
(☑ 509-456-8839; www.ejrobertsmansion.com; 1923 W 1st Ave; ste $140-200; 🢁) You haven't really absorbed Spokane until you've sniffed around

the upper-crust Browne's Addition and its stately homes. After nearly 25 years of renovation, this historic 1889 Queen Anne mansion that once belonged to a local railroad tycoon is in business as a plush five-suite B&B. Retaining its Victorian essence without being too frilly, expect exquisite breakfasts and service.

✕ Eating

Spokane's surprises continue with an impressive variety of excellent restaurants, from retro diners to classy local-ingredient enthusiasts and gluten-free menus.

Flying Goat   PIZZERIA $
(3318 W Northwest Blvd; pizzas $10-15; ⊘11am-late) Perennially packed with happy dinners noshing on the city's best pizzas and knocking back craft beers. Thin-crust artisanal pies come in creative combos like green-curry chicken (recommended) or pulled pork and caramelized onion, and there are 15 beers on tap, including local brews from Northern Lights. The ambience is laid-back, modern-pub style and distinctly Pacific Northwest.

Elk Public House   PUB $
(1931 W Pacific Ave; lunch $8-10) Situated on a leafy street corner in the salubrious and fun Browne's Addition, the Elk is a favorite neighborhood pub that turns out a kicking soup-and-sandwich lunch menu best enjoyed alfresco on the street. Also featured is a menu of Northwest beers plus live music at weekends.

Frank's Diner   BREAKFAST $
(www.franksdiners.com; 516 W 2nd Ave; breakfast $5-10) A little west of downtown is this enchantingly restored vintage railway car that knocks out a classic breakfast, including good eggs and no-frills biscuits and gravy. Frank's operated as a Seattle diner from 1931 until it was moved to Spokane in 1991. Arrive early to beat the queues.

Mary Lou's Milk Bottle   DINER $
(802 W Garland Ave; burgers $5-8; ⊘11am-8pm) Only in America! A tiny diner shaped like a milk bottle (honest!) that does made-from-scratch cheeseburgers, and milkshakes that come in the jug they were mixed in.

★ Mizuna   FUSION $$
(☑509-747-2004; 214 N Howard St; mains lunch/dinner $10/28; ⊘11am-10pm Mon-Sat, 4-10pm Sun; ☑) Take a well-lit and spacious antique brick building, add some stained glass and simple wooden furniture and top the tables with fresh flowers. Now serve incredibly fresh and flavorful dishes like lemongrass green curry with scallops and clams or a Berkshire pork tenderloin with caramelized pear and bacon relish. Add an equally good vegetarian menu and wash it all down with exquisite wines. Heaven.

Steam Plant Grill   FUSION $$
(www.steamplantgrill.com; 159 S Lincoln St; mains $15-23; ⊘lunch & dinner) Set in the neo-industrial confines of Kirtland Cutter's once-legendary old steam plant, this unfussy, eye-catching restaurant serves everything from a Thai chicken wrap to pub-style fish

---

BLOOMSDAY

It is said that Spokane breeds two sorts of citizens: those who run Bloomsday and those who watch. Born out of the 1970s running craze, the 12km Bloomsday Run professes to be the largest timed road race in the world. There's merit in the claim. Outstripping the longer and more arduous New York Marathon, Spokane's annual May dash regularly garners a minimum 50,000 participants and reached a peak of 61,298 runners in 1996.

Bloomsday was the brainchild of local runner and schoolteacher Don Kardong, a US representative in the 1976 Olympic marathon (where he finished a respectable fourth in two hours 11 minutes), who suggested putting to good use Spokane's fine riverside trails in the wake of the 1974 World's Fair. An impressive 1000 runners turned out for the first race in 1977, which was won by the gazellelike Frank Shorter. The event mushroomed the following year when the presence of US marathon legend Bill Rodgers cemented its lofty reputation. Good organization, an attractive course and high-class opposition have since made Bloomsday one of the highlights of the US running calendar, with its manageable 7.5-mile (12km) course attracting many runners for whom a marathon is a step too far.

For entry details check the official race website at www.bloomsdayrun.org.

and chips. Beers are brewed on site courtesy of Coeur d'Alene Brewing Company.

Clinkerdagger
FUSION $$

(☑509-328-5965; www.clinkerdagger.com; 621 W Mallon Ave; mains around $20; ☺ lunch & dinner) If you want good food and a classic Spokane Falls view, this is the place for you. Wedged into the old-fashioned Flour Mill, the Clinkerdagger has wraparound windows and a dining deck jutting out over the river. The food is as elegant as the setting and includes grilled king salmon and rock-salt-roasted prime ribs.

Wild Sage American Bistro
NORTHWESTERN $$$

(www.wildsagebistro.com; 916 W 2nd Ave; mains $15-34; ☺4-9pm Sun-Thu, to 10pm Fri & Sat) The intimate yet simple decor and fresh local ingredients, creatively and elegantly prepared, get Wild Sage consistently rated as one of Spokane's top dining spots. The cioppino, goat's-cheese-stuffed chicken and coconut-cream layer cake come highly recommended, and there's a gluten-free menu, an excellent selection of wines and a popular happy hour (4pm to 5pm Monday to Thursday).

🍷 Drinking & Entertainment

From opera to billiards, Spokane has the best nighttime-entertainment scene east of the Cascades.

Northern Lights Brewing Company
BREWPUB

(www.northernlightsbrewing.com; 1003 E Trent Ave) FREE A student hangout situated near Gonzaga University, Spokane's best microbrewery serves all kinds of weird and wonderful flavors, including an enticing blueberry cream ale and an eye-watering chocolate *dunkel* (dark German beer), all of which are brewed right on the premises. Foodwise, check out the cod and chips cooked in batter made with the brewery's own pale ale.

Opera House
LIVE MUSIC

(www.spokanecenter.com; 334 W Spokane Falls Blvd) Part of the Spokane Convention Center at Riverfront Park, the Opera House hosts touring companies and the Spokane Symphony.

Bing Crosby Theater
THEATRE

(www.mettheater.com; 901 W Sprague Ave) The former Met, now named after local hero Bing, presents concerts, plays, film festivals and the Spokane Opera in a fairly intimate setting.

Spokane Interplayers Ensemble
THEATER

(www.interplayers.com; 174 S Howard St) Spokane's local theater offers Broadway-style entertainment from September to June.

Spokane Veterans Memorial Arena
MUSIC, SPECTATOR SPORT

(www.spokanearena.com; 720 W Mallon Ave) Catch major touring acts at this 12,500-seat hall opposite the Flour Mill.

🛍 Shopping

Auntie's Bookstore
BOOKS

(www.auntiesbooks.com; 402 W Main Ave) Auntie's Bookstore is a fantastic bookshop with an excellent travel section, plenty of erudite book readings and the fine on-site Liberty Café with salads, sandwiches and coffee.

ℹ Information

Spokane Area Visitor Information Center

(www.visitspokane.com; 201 W Main Ave, at Browne St; ☺8:30am-5pm Mon-Fri, 9am-6pm Sat & Sun) The visitor information center provides a raft of information.

ℹ Getting There & Away

AIR

From **Spokane International Airport** (www.spokaneairports.net), 8 miles southwest of downtown off US 2, Alaska, Delta, US Airways and United airlines all offer daily services to destinations including Seattle, Portland, San Francisco, Denver, Minneapolis, Salt Lake City and Phoenix.

BUS

All buses arrive at and depart from the **Spokane Intermodal Transportation Center** (221 W 1st Ave), a combination bus-and-train station. **Greyhound** (www.greyhound.com) buses head off daily to Seattle ($36, six hours, three daily) and Pasco ($44, 2½ hours), the former via Moses Lake and Wenatchee.

TRAIN

The **Amtrak** (www.amtrak.com) Chicago–Seattle *Empire Builder* divides in Spokane, with trains heading to both Portland via Pasco and Seattle via Wenatchee once a day in either direction. Fares are Chicago $163, Portland $53 and Seattle $46.

ℹ Getting Around

Spokane Transit (www.spokanetransit.com) buses depart from streets bordering the Plaza, a huge indoor transit station at Sprague Ave and Wall St. Bus fares are $1.50. Bus 64 runs hourly on weekdays between the Plaza and Spokane International Airport, from 6:20am to 5:50pm.

Grand Coulee Dam Area

While the more famous Hoover Dam (conveniently located between Las Vegas and the Grand Canyon) gets around 1.6 million visitors per year, the much larger (four times) and arguably more significant Grand Coulee Dam (inconveniently located far from everything) gets only a trickle of tourism. If you're lucky enough to find yourself out this way don't miss a stop here: it's one of the country's most spectacular displays of engineering and you'll get to enjoy it crowd free.

Utilizing the raw power of the mighty Columbia River was always going to be logistically difficult. The problem was solved in the 1930s by the building of the gargantuan dam, still the largest concrete structure in the US and also the country's largest producer of electricity. Aside from providing enough hydroelectric power to fuel multiple cities, the dam irrigates more than half a million acres of central Washington and provides year-round recreation (and tourist dollars) for millions of people. All told, its economic importance dwarfs its significant physical presence.

The towns servicing the dam – Grand Coulee, Electric City and Elmer City – are sleepy and bland, but the surrounding gorge scenery is spectacular. Grand Coulee has a small heritage area and walking-tour maps are available at most hotels and at the Grand Coulee Visitor Arrival Center.

Grand Coulee Dam

The **Grand Coulee Visitor Arrival Center** (☏509-633-9265; ☉9am-5pm) details the history of the dam and surrounding area with movies, photos and interactive exhibits, while free guided **tours** of the facility run on

the hour from 10am until 5pm (May to September) and involve taking a glass-walled elevator 465ft down an incline to the Third Power Plant, where you can view the tops of the generators from an observation deck.

Similarly spectacular is the newly updated (with a $1.6-million injection in 2012) nightly **laser show** (☉after dark May-Sep) – purportedly the world's largest – which illustrates the history of the Columbia River and its various dams against a gloriously vivid backdrop.

Folks from all around Washington and beyond descend on Grand Coulee each year for one of the state's best firework displays from the top of the dam on July 4. Crowds usually number over 50,000 and for many the show is a family tradition that goes back generations.

Accommodations in Grand Coulee itself can be found in a number of places (book well in advance in summer months), none better than the **Columbia River Inn** (☏509-633-2100; www.columbiariverinn.com; 10 Lincoln St, Coulee Dam; r/ste $105/205; ☒) opposite the visitor arrival center. It offers a swimming pool, a gym-sauna and modern, cozy rooms. The area's cuisine is mostly of the diner-style fried variety, save at **Fusion Cafe & Espresso** (Hwy 155, bwtn Grand Coulee & Electric City; sandwiches from $7; ☉lunch & dinner), a simple place serving fresh soups, sandwiches, burgers and a daily special always 'made from scratch.'

Lake Roosevelt National Recreation Area

A 150-mile-long reservoir held back by the Grand Coulee Dam, Lake Roosevelt is a major recreation area that is popular with anglers, boaters, canoeists and waterskiers.

Dry, sunny weather prevails here, drawing people to camp and play on the lake's

---

THE EMPIRE BUILDER ACROSS THE CASCADES

With its two-level superliner carriages and grand imperial name, Amtrak's Seattle-to-Chicago *Empire Builder* runs along the former Great Northern Railroad on a route that is a proverbial A to Z of the American West. Yet, unlike other more tourist-oriented trains, it's not prohibitively expensive: a standard 'coachliner' seat can cost as little as $150, while roomettes with private bathrooms go from $420. Throw in forests, prairies, ghost mining towns and snowcapped mountains and you're onto one of the biggest bargains in the US, a magnificent journey significant not just for its amazing scenery but also for the fascinating insights into American life that you see on board. A mostly windows viewing car makes the view that much better.

For reservations and further details, see www.amtrak.com.

southern white-sand beaches. As the lake inches its way north to Canada, the desert cliffs and high coulee walls give way to rolling hills and orchards, becoming dense forests of ponderosa pine around Kettle Falls.

As recreation areas go, Lake Roosevelt remains refreshingly undeveloped, and few roads penetrate its isolated shoreline. To explore the area at any great length you'll need a boat. The lake offers a plethora of boat launches, with fees starting at $6 for seven days and $40 for a year. One of the best places to organize other water-based activities – such as fishing, canoeing and waterskiing – is at the **Keller Ferry Campground** (☑509-633-9188; campsites May-Sep $10, Oct-Apr $5), located 14 miles north of the town of Wilbur. The free **Keller Ferry** (◷6am-11pm) crosses Lake Roosevelt near the campground, linking to Hwy 21 and providing access to the Sanpoil River and the town of Republic to the north.

To uncover the history of the area visit **Fort Spokane Museum & Visitor Center** (◷10am-5pm May 26-Oct 10) `FREE` off Hwy 25, 23 miles north of Davenport, where original fort buildings from 1880 tell the story of how white settlers attempted to quell the region's Native American tribes.

Your best bet for general information about the area is the **Lake Roosevelt National Recreation Area Headquarters** (www.nps.gov/laro; 1008 Crest Dr; ◷8am-4pm), in Coulee Dam. Park admission is free.

Okanogan River Valley

A geographical extension of British Columbia's Okanagan region, the Okanogan (note the subtle change of spelling) forms Washington's biggest yet most sparsely populated county and remains one of the lesser-known parts of the state. With much of the land given over to the Colville Indian Reservation, there are not a lot of obvious attractions here, though if you wander under the radar you'll uncover eerie ghost towns and lonely mountain ranges.

Okanogan – which derives from the native Salish word for 'rendezvous' – is also the name of the diminutive county capital (population 2568) that lies 29 miles to the east of Twisp at the nexus of US 20 and US 97. In recent decades Okanogan has effectively merged with the nearby town of Omak (population 4881), though neither settlement is a budding tourist center.

Omak is famous for its August **Omak Stampede**, a well-known local spectacle that includes the notorious 'Suicide Race,' a 210ft plunge down a 60-degree slope on horseback followed by the fording of the 50yd-wide Okanogan River. Not surprisingly, the event has raised the ire of numerous animal-rights groups.

If you pass through here, it's worth stopping at **Fort Okanogan State Park** (junction of US 97 & Hwy 17; ◷9am-5pm Wed-Sun May-Sep) `FREE`, 4 miles northeast of the town of Brewster. It tells the story of the valley's original Native American inhabitants and relates how three different fur-trading companies successively occupied the site of the old fort in the early 19th century.

The varied landscape around Okanogan and Omak offers plenty of outdoor possibilities, including a small ski center at the **Loup Loup Ski Bowl** (www.skitheloup.com; day pass adult/child $38/24; ◷Dec-Mar; ⚐), just off US 20, 18 miles west of Okanogan. Hiking and biking are also popular here in the summer.

Colville National Forest

Wedged into Washington's northeastern corner abutting the borders of Idaho and Canada lies the 1.1-million-acre Colville National Forest, a vast and relatively remote corner of the state that spans the Kettle River and Selkirk Mountains ranges and is bisected in the west by the Columbia River and Lake Roosevelt. Lying in the foothills of the Rocky Mountains, this wild region is home to grizzly bears, cougars and the last herd of caribou in the lower 48 states. Some of the loveliest scenery can be found in the isolated Salmo-Priest Wilderness Area, which is crisscrossed by hiking trails. Colville makes a good base for exploring the Selkirks and the Pend Oreille River area.

Colville

The area's main settlement is a small town embellished with parks and some gracious older buildings. It acts as a good base camp for exploring Lake Roosevelt and the surrounding national forest.

SCENIC DRIVE – SHERMAN PASS

The 35 miles of Hwy 20 between Kettle Falls and the town of Republic has been designated the **Sherman Pass Scenic Byway**, and interpretive sites along the route have been beefed up in recent years. Eleven miles west of Kettle Falls on Hwy 20 (at Canyon Creek, mile 335) you'll find the **Log Flume Heritage Site** in the middle of a ponderosa pine forest. The site provides a snapshot of logging history, with several interpretive displays along a mile-long, winding, wheelchair-accessible trail. Further on is the **Growden Heritage Site**, which relates stories of the Civilian Conservation Corps in the 1930s and '40s; while closer to Republic, near the crest of the 5575ft pass, is the **White Mountain Interpretive Center**, with stunning views toward British Columbia, Canada.

A new mock train depot in Kettle Falls acts as an excellent information portal for the drive. It's situated on the corner of US 395 and Juniper St and is open daily year-round.

◉ Sights & Activities

Fort Colville Museum HISTORIC SITE
(www.stevenscountyhistoricalsociety.org; 700 N Wynne St; adult/child $5/2; ◷10am-4pm Mon-Sat, 1-4pm Sun May-Sep) Colville town's most notable attraction has as its centerpiece Keller House, a large bungalow with attractive Craftsman details, built in 1910. Dispersed around the house are reconstructed versions of a pioneer blacksmith's shop, schoolhouse, trapper's cabin, sawmill and a fire lookout tower. The 7-acre park grounds are great for a picnic.

Little Pend Oreille National Wildlife Refuge WILDLIFE RESERVE
(www.fsw.gov/littlependoreille) Bird-watchers should swing down to this 41,573-acre refuge where McDowell Lake attracts waterfowl. To reach the **refuge headquarters** (1310 Bear Creek Rd; ◷7:30am-4pm), take US 20 for about 8 miles east of Colville, then turn south on Narcisse Creek Rd. The Mill Butte Trail starts from the refuge headquarters, gaining 600ft in 3 miles. Free camping is available on six designated sites within the refuge from April to December. There's no drinking water available.

49 Degrees North SKIING
(www.ski49n.com; 3311 Flowery Trail Rd, Chewelah; day pass adult/child $57/48; ◷closed Wed & Thu except holidays; ⊛) Despite having little star appeal, 49 Degrees is actually the state's second-largest ski area, after Crystal Mountain. Hidden in the Selkirk Mountains 42 miles due north of Spokane on US 395, there are an incredible 75 runs here, served by five chairlifts, along with a good 25ft dumping of winter snow.

The beginner's runs are particularly good, and the area is often sold as a family resort. Expect ski clubs and childcare but no overnight facilities. A Nordic center with 16km of trail was added in 2006. If you're approaching from Colville, 49 Degrees is located 30 miles to the southeast near the town of Chewelah, about 25 miles south of the true 49th parallel (the US–Canada border).

🛏 Sleeping & Eating

Cheap accommodations around Colville is plentiful in motels and campgrounds.

Douglas Falls Grange Park Campground CAMPGROUND
(☏509-684-7474; Douglas Falls Rd; ◷May-Sep) Free camping alongside Mill Creek 7 miles north of town.

Selkirk Motel MOTEL $
(☏509-684-2565; 369 S Main St; r $50-110; ⊛🖥) Fulfills the three Cs: comfortable, convenient and clean. Several rooms also have kitchenettes.

Stephani's Oak Street Grill INTERNATIONAL $$
(157 N Oak St; mains $14-21; ◷11am-9pm Tue-Sat) For catfish, Cajun chicken, steak or an Asian stir-fry, head here.

ⓘ Information

Colville Chamber of Commerce (www.colville. com; 121 E Astor St; ◷9am-noon & 1-4pm) For local information.
Colville National Forest Ranger Station (765 S Main St; ◷7:30am-4:30pm Mon-Fri) Has the lowdown on hiking and camping.

Portland

Includes →

Best Places to Eat

- → Higgins (p232)
- → Paley's Place (p232)
- → Laurelhurst Market (p234)
- → Bamboo Sushi (p233)
- → Pok Pok (p233)

Best Places to Stay

- → Ace Hotel (p229)
- → Nines (p229)
- → Hawthorne Portland Hostel (p230)
- → Kennedy School (p230)
- → Jupiter Hotel (p230)

Why Go?

Dynamic yet mellow, Oregon's largest metropolis boasts a vibrant downtown across the Willamette River from charming neighborhoods full of friendly – and often zany – people. It hums with a youthful vitality and is home to a landslide of liberal idealists, but it's located in a state where back roads brim with Republican red. Here Gore-Tex rain jackets in fine restaurants are as common as sideburns on a hipster. A haven for eco-activists, cyclists, grungesters, outdoor nuts, vegans, gardeners and dog-lovers, all supporting countless brewpubs, coffeehouses, knitting circles, lesbian potlucks and book clubs, Portland is a livable metropolis with pretty neighborhoods and a friendly, small-town atmosphere. It's an up-and-coming destination that has finally found itself but keeps redefining its ethos with every controversy (fluoride, anyone?). Racially progressive, culturally diverse and politically charged, the city is also – as many folks from out of state have discovered – an awesome spot to plant roots, settle in and chill out for while.

When to Go
Portland

Apr–May Long-awaited springtime flowers start blooming.

Jun–Sep Festivals galore, including the Oregon Brewer's Festival and the Bite of Oregon.

Nov–Mar Rainy season: visit museums, galleries, coffee shops, brewpubs...

Kettle Falls

The question that tickles most people to Kettle Falls is: where are the falls? The answer is: they've disappeared. The original Kettle Falls, a series of cascades and rapids that was once a favored fishing spot for Native Americans, was inundated in the late 1930s by water that backed up behind the new Grand Coulee Dam (ultimately forming present-day Lake Roosevelt). The spectacular natural sight wasn't the only casualty. A town that had been founded 3 miles south of the falls in the 1880s had to be uprooted piece by piece and moved a few

miles east to be rebuilt alongside the existing settlement of Meyers Falls (bisected by a much smaller waterfall). The two towns amalgamated in the 1940s to form 'new' Kettle Falls. These days it is largely a blue-collar lumber settlement set in an attractive valley that – somewhat ironically – acts as a base for water activities on the lake that once drowned it.

To get a glimpse of the town before its relocation, drop by the **Kettle Falls Interpretive Center** (⊙11am-5pm Wed-Sat May-Sep), just north of US 395, to see a giant photo mural showing the predam Columbia as it crashed through Kettle Falls.

Portland Planning

A visit to Portland doesn't require too much detailed planning. There are plenty of hotels of all kinds and budgets in and around the city, and only the most popular ones book up (usually in summer). You can walk into most restaurants, even the fanciest ones, in a hiking jacket and jeans. Dinner reservations are taken at some of the most popular restaurants (others don't take reservations for groups under six). Portland is a laid-back kinda town.

OFF THE BEATEN PATH: SAUVIE ISLAND

About a 20-minute drive from downtown is **Sauvie Island** (www.sauvieisland.org), an agricultural oasis providing an excellent break from Portland's bustle. Its flat, 12-mile country-road loop also makes it a popular place for weekend cyclists.

The 12,000-acre **Sauvie Island Wildlife Area** includes a wetland sanctuary for thousands of migratory ducks, geese, tundra swans, bald eagles and Sandhill cranes. Permanent residents include peregrine falcons, great blue herons, foxes and beavers.

During summer, don't miss the opportunity to pick strawberries, peaches, corn and flowers – try **Kruger's** or **Sauvie Island Farms**, both on NW Sauvie Island Rd.

Beach-heads should visit **Walton Beach**, a decent stretch of sand on the island's eastern side. Leashed dogs are allowed, but fires and camping are not. Nudies can head toward **Collins Beach** at the northern end, past the pavement.

The refuge and beaches require a $7 parking permit; get one from the Fish & Wildlife Office or an island store.

Transportation

➔ **Public transportation** Transit buses, the streetcar and the MAX light-rail system all link up and can get you nearly everywhere (www.trimet.org). Taxi companies are abundant, and another (more green) option is bike pedicab services.

➔ **Bicycle** Portland's often named 'the most bike-friendly city in the US.' Bicycle lanes are plentiful and several shops rent bikes. For bike maps see www.portlandoregon.gov/transportation/34809.

➔ **Car** Parking on the east side of the city is generally easy to find; downtown, SmartPark garages offer affordable parking (www.portlandoregon.gov/transportation/35272). Northwest neighborhoods and the Pearl District often have metered parking; finding a spot here can be harder. Car-share programs like Zipcar are popular.

For more details on transportation options in the city, see p242.

PORTLANDERS

Simpsons creator Matt Groening, notorious figure skater Tonya Harding and Nobel Prize–winning chemist Linus Pauling all hail from Portland.

For Kids

➔ Oregon Zoo (p219)

➔ Children's Museum (p219)

➔ Oregon Museum of Science & Industry (p223)

➔ Oaks Amusement Park (p223)

➔ PlayDate PDX (☑503-227-7529; www.playdatepdx.com; 1434 NW 17th Ave)

Oregon Fast Facts

➔ **Nickname** Beaver State

➔ **Population** 3.9 million

➔ **Capital** Salem

➔ **Home of** Crater Lake, Nike, spotted owls

Resources

➔ **Travel Portland** (www.travelportland.com) What to do, where to go, how to save...

➔ **Portland Food and Drink** (www.portlandfoodanddrink.com) Unbiased reviews of Portland's restaurants.

➔ **Portland Monthly Mag** (www.portlandmonthlymag.com) Interesting local content.

➔ **Oregon Live** (www.oregonlive.com) News, sport and entertainment.

History

The Portland area was first settled in 1844 when two New Englanders bought a claim for 640 acres on the Willamette's west bank. They built a store, plotted streets and decided to name the new settlement after one of their hometowns: a coin toss resulted in Portland winning over Boston, and the new town was up and running.

Portland's location near the confluence of the Columbia and Willamette Rivers helped drive the young city's growth. San Francisco and the Californian gold rush clamored for Oregon lumber, while the growing population of settlers in the Willamette Valley demanded supplies. Both relied upon Portland for services.

The city's status got a boost when the Northern Pacific Railroad arrived in 1883, linking the Pacific Northwest to the rest of the country. In the late 1880s the first bridges were built across the Willamette River, and the city spread eastward. Portland kept growing steadily, also benefiting from the WWII shipbuilding boom.

Today over half a million people live in the Greater Portland area. Shipping operations have since moved north of downtown, the Old Town has been revitalized and the once-industrial Pearl District now brims with expensive lofts and sophisticated boutiques. Big sports and outdoor-clothing manufacturers like Nike, Adidas and Columbia Sportswear help drive the economy, along with high-tech companies like Intel and Tektronix.

◉ Sights

◉ Downtown

Downtown Portland is an urban success story. An activist city government began work in the 1970s to ensure that Portland's business and nightlife did not flee the city center, and downtown Portland remains a vibrant destination both day and night.

But with success comes certain problems – like parking. You may get lucky and find a metered street space, but there also are six **SmartPark** parking buildings that charge $1.60 per hour (similar to the price of metered parking). Check www.portlandoregon.gov/transportation/35272 for their locations and hours.

★**Pioneer Courthouse Square**　LANDMARK
(Map p220) The heart of downtown Portland, this brick plaza is nicknamed 'Portland's living room' and is the most visited public space in the city. When it isn't full of Hacky Sack players, sunbathers or office workers lunching, the square hosts concerts, festivals, rallies, farmers markets – and even summer Friday-night movies (aka 'Flicks on the Bricks'; details at www.thesquarepdx.org).

One of Portland's grandest Victorian hotels once stood here, but it fell into disrepair and was torn down in 1951. Later the city decided to build Pioneer Courthouse Sq, and grassroots support resulted in a program that encouraged citizens to buy and personalize the bricks that eventually built the square. Names include Sherlock Holmes, William Shakespeare and Elvis Presley.

Across 6th Ave is the **Pioneer Courthouse**. Built in 1875, this was the legal center of 19th-century Portland.

South Park Blocks　PARK
Two important museums flank the South Park Blocks, the 12-block-long greenway that runs through much of downtown. The blocks themselves are a fine, leafy refuge from downtown's bustle, and host a farmers market and occasional art shows.

The **Oregon Historical Society** (Map p220; ☑503-222-1741; www.ohs.org; 1200 SW Park Ave; adult/child 6-18yr $11/5; ☺10am-5pm Mon-Sat, noon-5pm Sun) is the state's largest historical museum, and dedicates most of its space to the story of Oregon and the pioneers who made it. There are interesting sections on Native American tribes and the travails of the Oregon Trail. Temporary exhibits furnish the downstairs space.

Across the park, the excellent **Portland Art Museum** (Map p220; ☑503-226-2811; www.portlandartmuseum.org; 1219 SW Park Ave; adult/child $15/free; ☺10am-5pm Tue, Wed & Sat, to 8pm Thu & Fri, noon-5pm Sun) has exhibits that include Native American carvings, Asian and American art and English silver. The museum also houses the Whitsell Auditorium, a first-rate theater that frequently screens rare or international films. Blockbuster exhibits are mounted regularly.

At the southern end of the South Park Blocks is **Portland State University**, the city's largest university.

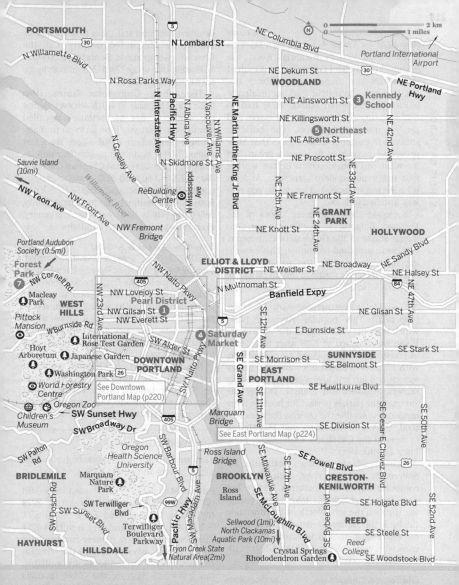

Portland Highlights

1 Exploring the many restaurants and galleries in the chic **Pearl District** (p221).

2 Sampling a wide variety of microbrews in one of the 50-plus **breweries** (more than any other city in the world; p235).

3 Watching a movie, drinking a beer or spending the night at the eclectic **Kennedy School** (p238).

4 Wandering through craft stalls at the **Saturday Market** (p218), grabbing a bite and taking in street performers' antics.

5 Partying with the 'Last Thursday' crowds on NE Alberta in the **Northeast** (p222), where

artists, musicians and buskers compete for attention.

6 Catching a flick at one of the many **movie houses** (p238) offering second-run screenings for around $5.

7 Taking a walk in **Forest Park** (p223), the country's largest urban park, with more than 70 miles of woodsy trails.

Portland Building LANDMARK

(Map p220; cnr SW 5th Ave & SW Main St) This controversial 15-story building (1982) was designed by Michael Graves and catapulted the postmodern architect to celebrity status. However, the people working inside the blocky, pastel-colored edifice have had to deal with tiny windows, cramped spaces and general user-unfriendliness. The building suffered from major design flaws that later proved very costly to fix – not a great start for what was considered to be the world's first major postmodern structure. At least it's been made somewhat green: an eco roof was installed in 2006.

Towering above the main doors of the Portland Building is Portlandia, an immense statue of the Goddess of Commerce, Portland's supposed patroness. This crouching figure is, at 36ft, the second largest hammered-copper statue in the US (after the Statue of Liberty).

★ Tom McCall Waterfront Park PARK

(Map p220) This popular riverside park, which lines the west bank of the Willamette River, was finished in 1978 after four years of construction. It replaced an old freeway with 1.5 miles of paved sidewalks and grassy spaces, and attracts heaps of joggers, in-line skaters, strollers and cyclists. During the summer, the park is perfect for hosting large outdoor events like the Oregon Brewers Festival. Walk over the Steel and Hawthorne bridges to the Eastbank Esplanade, making a 2.6-mile loop.

Salmon Street Springs Fountain, on Salmon St near the river, cycles through computer-generated patterns. On hot days kids (and adults) take turns plunging through the jets. North of the Burnside Bridge is the Japanese-American Historical Plaza, a memorial to Japanese Americans who were interned by the US government during WWII.

Old Town & Chinatown NEIGHBORHOOD

The core of rambunctious 1890s Portland, the once-seedy Old Town used to be the lurking ground of unsavory characters, but today disco queens outnumber drug dealers. It's one of the city's livelier places after dark, when nightclubs and bars open their doors and the hipsters start showing up.

Running beneath Old Town's streets are the shanghai tunnels, a series of underground corridors through which unscrupulous people would kidnap or 'shanghai' drunken men and sell them to sea captains looking for indentured workers. Call the Cascade Geographic Society (☑503-622-4798; adult/child under 12yr $13/8; ☉tours by appointment) for tours.

The ornate Chinatown Gates (Map p220; cnr W Burnside St & NW 4th Ave) define the southern edge of Portland's so-called Chinatown – but you'll be lucky to find any Chinese people here at all. There are a few token Chinese restaurants, but the main attraction is the Classical Chinese Gardens (Map p220; ☑503-228-8131; www.lansugarden.org; 239 NW Everett St; adult/child $8/7; ☉10am-6pm). It's a one-block haven of tranquility, reflecting ponds and manicured greenery. Free tours available with admission.

Saturday Market & Around MARKET

(☑503-222-6072; www.portlandsaturdaymarket.com; SW Ankeny St & Naito Pkwy; ☉10am-5pm Sat & 11am-4:30pm Sun Mar-Dec) The weekend Saturday Market is a fun and popular outdoor crafts fair with booths selling paper, wood, glass and metal crafts of all kinds, along with jewelry, ceramics and body products. There are street entertainers, concerts and food booths too.

Nearby is the lovely Victorian-era Skidmore Fountain, along with the New Market Theater, built in 1871 as Portland's first theater for stage productions. It's now home to shops and restaurants.

◉ West Hills

This area is known for its exclusive homes, windy streets and Forest Park.

Pittock Mansion HISTORIC BUILDING

(☑503-823-3623; www.pittockmansion.org; 3229 NW Pittock Dr; adult/child 6-18yr $8.50/5.50; ☉11am-4pm) This grand and beautiful 1914 mansion was built by pioneer-entrepreneur Henry Pittock, who revitalized the *Oregonian* newspaper. Guided tours are available, but it's worth visiting the (free) grounds simply to have a picnic while taking in the spectacular views.

★ International Rose Test Garden GARDENS

(☑503-823-3636; www.rosegardenstore.org/rosegardens.cfm; 400 SW Kingston Ave; ☉7:30am-9pm) FREE These gardens practically gave Portland its 'Rose City' nickname. They sprawl across 4.5 acres of manicured lawns, fountains and flowerbeds, and on a clear day you can catch peeks of downtown and Mt Hood. Over 500 rose varieties grow in the permanent gardens, including many old and rare ones. From April through September the scent and colors are intoxicating. Call ☑503-823-3664 for tours.

Japanese Garden　　　　　　GARDENS
(☑503-223-1321; www.japanesegarden.com; 611 SW Kingston Ave; adult/child 6-17yr $9.50/6.75; ☉noon-7pm Mon, 9am-7pm Tue-Fri & Sun, 9am-9pm Sat) This tranquil, formal garden is made up of 5.5 acres of tumbling water, koi ponds, ornamental cherry trees, a ceremonial teahouse (no drinks served!) and a sand garden. Tours are available, and hours are limited in winter.

★ Oregon Zoo　　　　　　　　ZOO
(☑503-226-1561; www.oregonzoo.org; 4001 SW Canyon Rd; adult/child 3-11yr $11.50/8.50; ☉9am-6pm; 👪) In summer ride the Zoo Train from the rose gardens to this excellent and beautiful zoo. There's a primate house, a 'penguinarium' and a large African animals area, among many other impressive exhibits. Enclosures are spacious and seminatural, and big-name concerts take place on the zoo's lawns in summer. But despite its excellence, the zoo is reinventing itself – in future years, a California condor exhibit and an extensive elephant exhibit are set to open (along with others). Hours vary seasonally.

Children's Museum　　　　　MUSEUM
(☑503-233-6500; www.portlandcm.org; 4015 SW Canyon Rd; admission $10; ☉9am-5pm; 👪) Parents can seek solace at this museum, a great place to keep kids busy with interesting learning activities and exhibits. There's a clay studio, a construction zone, a 'grocery store,' a pet hospital and a baby room for kids under three, plus more.

World Forestry Center　　FORESTRY INTERPRETATION CENTER
(☑503-228-1367; www.worldforestry.org; 4033 SW Canyon Rd; adult/child 3-18yr $9/6; ☉10am-5pm; 👪) The center highlights the importance of the world's forests, with a focus on Pacific Northwest forests and their role in providing water, recreation, habitat and resources.

Hoyt Arboretum　　　　　　GARDEN
(☑503-865-8733; www.hoytarboretum.org; 4000 Fairview Blvd; ☉trails 6am-10pm, visitor center 9am-4pm Mon-Fri, 11am-3pm Sat & Sun) **FREE** Twelve miles of trails wind through this 187-acre ridgetop garden above the city zoo. It's home to over 6000 species of both native and exotic plants and trees, and offers easy walks any time of year.

Portland Audubon Society　　SANCTUARY
(☑503-292-6855; www.audubonportland.org; 5151 NW Cornell Rd; ☉9am-5pm, nature store 10am-6pm Mon-Sat, to 5pm Sun) Nestled in a gulch beside Forest Park, the Wildlife Care Center here treats injured native wildlife. You can also visit the nature store, then walk along 4.5 miles of forested trails in the nature sanctuary.

PORTLAND: A BRIEF ORIENTATION

Portland lies just a few miles south of the Washington border; it's about 15 minutes from the border metropolis of Vancouver, WA (note: this is a very different city from Vancouver, BC, in Canada). It's also way inland, about a 1½-hour drive from the Pacific Coast.

The Willamette River flows through the center of town, dividing the city into east and west. Burnside St divides north from south, organizing the city into four quadrants: Northwest, Southwest, Northeast and Southeast. Make sure you understand this, as the same address could exist on both NE Davis St and NW Davis St, which are on opposite sides of the river! (There's also North Portland, which oddly enough is more to the west of NE Portland, but many tourists don't make it this far.)

Northwest and Southwest Portland include downtown, historic Old Town, the chic postindustrial Pearl District and exclusive West Hills. Close to downtown but across the river is the Lloyd District, an extension of downtown that's anchored by a glass-towered convention center and a big shopping mall.

Northeast and Southeast Portland are mostly tree-lined, late-19th-century residential neighborhoods, each with its own trendy cluster of shops and restaurants. Popular commercial streets include N Mississippi Ave, NE Alberta St, SE Hawthorne Blvd and SE Division St. Sellwood is furthest south and is a pretty neighborhood with antique stores and yuppies.

Downtown Portland

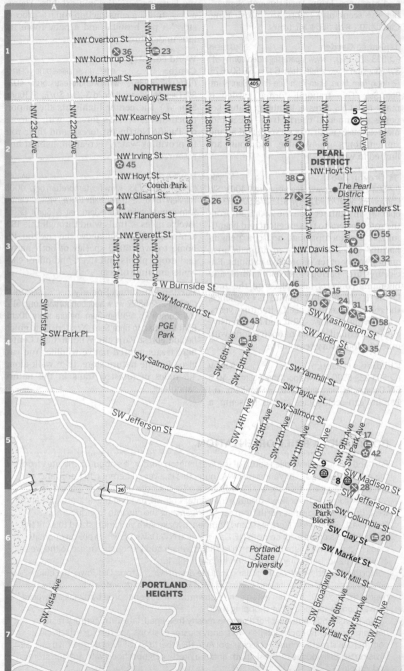

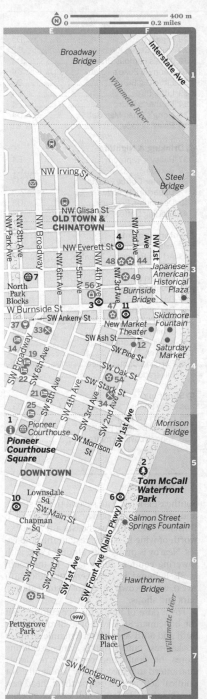

PORTLAND SIGHTS

Northwest

When Portlanders talk about 'Northwest,' they are usually referring to the attractive neighborhood surrounding NW 21st and 23rd Aves, north of W Burnside St. The residential heart of late-19th-century Portland, this area hums with street life.

Fashionable NW 23rd Ave brims with clothing boutiques, home-decor shops and cafes. Restaurants – including some of Portland's finest – lie mostly along NW 21st Ave. This is a great neighborhood for strolling, window-shopping and people-watching. Parking is tough but not impossible.

Just east of Northwest, the **Pearl District** is an old industrial precinct that has transformed itself into Portland's swankiest neighborhood. Warehouses have been converted to fancy lofts commanding some of the highest real-estate prices in Oregon. It's a great place to walk around, checking out upscale boutiques, trendy restaurants and Portland's highest concentration of art galleries. Every first Thursday of each month, many galleries extend their evening hours and show off new exhibits (www.firstthursdayportland.com).

Be sure to visit the **Museum of Contemporary Craft** (Map p220; ☎503-223-2654; www.museumofcontemporarycraft.org; 724 NW Davis St; admission $4; ⏰11am-6pm Tue-Sat, to 8pm 1st Thu of every month) with a fine, growing collection of excellent regionally made crafts, especially ceramics.

The Pearl is bordered by NW 9th Ave, NW 14th Ave, W Burnside St and NW Lovejoy St, though it's creeping northward toward the river.

Northeast

Most of Portland's east side is residential, but just across the Willamette River the modern Lloyd District is like an extension of downtown. Here lies the nation's first full-blown shopping mall, the **Lloyd Center** (www.lloydcenter.com; 2201 Lloyd Center), along with the twin-glass-tower **Oregon Convention Center** (Map p224; www.oregoncc.org; 777 NE Martin Luther King Jr Blvd) and the **Moda Center** (Rose Garden Arena; Map p224; ☎503-235-8771; www.rosequarter.com; 300 N Winning Way), home of the Trail Blazers.

Further up the Willamette, N Mississippi Ave has experienced an amazing revival in the past few years. Run-down buildings have been transformed into trendy shops, cafes and restaurants – with the main anchor being

Downtown Portland

the **ReBuilding Center** (☎ 503-331-1877; www.rebuildingcenter.org; 3625 N Mississippi Ave), a cool recycling warehouse full of donated housing materials where you can find nearly anything building-related. Amnesia Brewing (p236), which makes excellent beer, is also based here.

Northeast of Mississippi, creatively spunky NE Alberta St is another success story. The stretch between NE 15th and NE 33rd Aves has revamped itself from a ribbon of vacant buildings, dubious bars and drug dealing into one of Portland's hippest streets. Despite the gentrification, it's still ethnically diverse and home to small art galleries, boutiques, studios, bars and cafes. Don't miss **Last Thursday** (www.lastthursdayonalberta.com), an art walk with plenty of entertainment, taking place every last Thursday of the month.

◉ Southeast

Southeast is laced with several trendy streets and good walking parks. The corner of E Burnside and 28th Ave boasts a few blocks' worth of wine bars, fine restaurants and cafes. Nearby is pretty **Laurelhurst Park**, with towering conifers and a lake. To the south is SE Belmont St (between 32th and 35th Aves), with its own stretch of casual eateries, bars and shops.

For a dose of hippie-hipster culture, visit the bohemian SE Hawthorne Blvd (between 30th and 50th Aves). It's a dynamic string of bookstores, cutesy shops, vintage-clothing stores, brewpubs and cafes. You're almost guaranteed to be accosted by panhandlers or political activists; to escape them, head east to **Mt Tabor Park**, a small extinct volcano that has great walking trails and good city views. Nearby is SE Division St, another long stretch of popular restaurants and shops surrounded by residential neighborhoods.

Finally, way to the south lies Sellwood, an old working-class neighborhood known for its antique stores.

Oregon Museum of Science & Industry
MUSEUM

(OMSI; Map p224; www.omsi.edu; 1945 SE Water Ave; adult/child 3-13yr $13/9.50; ⏱9:30am-5:30pm Sun-Thu, to 9pm Fri & Sat; ♿) This excellent museum offers hands-on science exhibits for kids, along with other special, temporary exhibits like *Mummies of the World*. There's also an Omnimax theater, planetarium shows and a submarine tour (all carry a separate charge). Parking is extra; $2 admission first Sunday of each month.

Crystal Springs Rhododendron Garden
GARDENS

(☎503-771-8386; www.rhodies.org/xtal/csg_index.htm; 6015 SE 28th Ave; admission Thu-Mon $4,

Tue & Wed free, 12yr & under free; ⏱dawn-dusk) To the south is this 5-acre garden near Reed College. Its large, beautiful grounds are covered with more than 2000 full-grown rhododendrons, azaleas and other plants, plus a large lagoon; peak bloom is late April into May. Free admission from October through February.

🏃 Activities

Oaks Bottom Wildlife Refuge WILDLIFE REFUGE
Located in Sellwood, this large wetland of around 140 acres has a nearby bike path and good bird-watching.

Oaks Amusement Park AMUSEMENT PARK
(☎503-233-5777; www.oakspark.com; 7805 SE Oaks Park Way; individual rides $1.25, ride bracelets $12.25-25; ♿) Sellwood amusement park popular with families. Lots of fun rides, plus go-karts and a classic roller-skating rink. Check website for hours, as they vary with the seasons and for each attraction.

PINCH THOSE PENNIES – PORTLAND FOR FREE

Dead broke, or just don't feel like spending a fortune? Check out **Around the Sun** (www.aroundthesunblog.com).

Plenty of events are cheap or free; see www.travelportland.com/things-to-see-and-do/attractions/free-attractions and www.travelportland.com/things-to-see-and-do/attractions/annual-events. Here's our list of a few free (or cheap) Portland attractions:

➡ International Rose Test Garden (p218)

➡ Hoyt Arboretum (p219)

➡ Forest Park (p224)

➡ Crystal Springs Rhododendron Garden (p223) Free admission Tuesday and Wednesday; otherwise $3.

➡ Saturday Market (p218)

➡ Powell's City of Books (p241)

➡ Portland Audubon Society (p219)

➡ Portland Art Museum (p216) Free admission from 5pm to 8pm on the last Friday of each month.

➡ Portland Children's Museum (p219) Free admission from 4pm to 8pm on the first Friday of each month.

➡ Museum of Contemporary Craft (p221) Free admission on the first Thursday of each month.

➡ Oregon Zoo (p219) Admission only $4 on the second Tuesday of each month.

➡ Oregon Museum of Science & Industry (p223) (OMSI) Admission only $2 on the first Sunday of each month.

➡ World Forestry Center (p219) Admission only $3 on the first Wednesday of each month.

East Portland

Hiking

Forest Park　　　　　　HIKING
(www.forestparkconservancy.org) With over 5000
acres under its belt, this is the USA's largest park within city limits. There are more
than 80 miles of trails for hikers, runners
and dog-walkers, and some excellent fire
roads for cyclists. The **Wildwood Trail** starts
at the Hoyt Arboretum and winds through
30 miles of forest, with many spur trails al-
lowing for loop hikes. Some other trailheads

forest offers a nature center, streamside wildlife and 8 miles of trails, including a 3-mile paved bike path. Late March brings wondrous displays of trillium, a wild marsh lily. Located south of Sellwood, in Southwest Portland.

Cycling

Portland has been voted the USA's top bike-friendly city (most recently by *Bicycling Magazine*) and also boasts the highest percentage of bicycle commuters. For you, this means that great trails for both road and mountain bikes exist, including pleasant paths along the Willamette River downtown, and the fine 21-mile **Springwater Corridor** (www.40mileloop.org/trail_springwater-corridor.htm), which heads out to the suburb of Boring.

Mountain bikers can head to **Leif Erikson Doctor**, an easy dirt logging road leading 11 miles into Forest Park and offering occasional peeks over the city. Most hiking trails here are off-limits to bikes, so please don't ride them. For single-track and technical trails, the Hood River and the Mt Hood area (both about an hour's drive away) have great options.

For scenic farm country, head to **Sauvie Island**, 10 miles northwest of downtown Portland. This island, the largest in the Columbia River, is prime cycling land – it's flat, it has relatively little traffic and much of it is a wildlife refuge.

Try to snag a free *Portland by Bicycle* (www.portlandoregon.gov/transportation/39402) or *Bike There!* map ($9) from a visitor center or a bike shop; both detail bike-friendly streets and trails.

If you're a visiting cyclist and want to meet like-minded folk, check out Friendly Bike Guesthouse (p230). And for local bike news, see www.bikeportland.org.

A few cycling events worth taking part in:

Bridge Pedal CYCLING EVENT
(www.bridgepedal.com) Thousands of Portlanders bike over bridges closed or partially closed to vehicular traffic; held in August.

Pedalpalooza CYCLING FESTIVAL
(www.pedalpalooza.org) Three-week celebration in June of the city's uniquely creative bike culture, including the world's largest naked bike ride.

Sunday Parkways CYCLING EVENT
(www.portlandsundayparkways.org) A few Sundays a year, Portland closes off certain

into Forest Park begin at the western ends of NW Thurman and NW Upshur Sts.

Tryon Creek State Natural Area STATE PARK
(503-636-9886; www.oregonstateparks.org; 11321 SW Terwilliger Blvd) This verdant 670-acre

East Portland

streets to motor vehicles so cyclists (especially families) can ride without worrying about cars. Food, entertainment and bike-themed booths too.

On the Water

Summer in Portland means finding cool things to do in the heat, and fortunately there are a few.

On hot days, visit the Salmon Street Springs Fountain or the **Jamison Square Fountain** (Map p220; 810 NW 11th Ave), both of which attract splashing kids as the mercury rises.

Matt Dishman Community Center SWIMMING
(☑503-823-3673; www.portlandoregon.gov/parks/60933; 77 NE Knott St) Swimmers should grab their suits and beeline to the indoor pool here; it's just north of the Lloyd District. Check hours beforehand.

US Grant Park SWIMMING
(☑503-823-3674; cnr NE 33rd Ave & NE US Grant Pl) For an outdoor experience, try the pool here. Call for hours.

North Clackamas Aquatic Park AQUATIC PARK
(☑503-557-7873; www.ncprd.com/aquatic-park; 7300 SE Harmony Rd, Milwaukie; admission $8, under 3yr free) About 10 miles south of downtown Portland are these water slides and indoor wave pool. There's also a climbing wall (extra cost), along with adults-only hot tub. Hours vary widely, so call ahead.

eNRG Kayaking KAYAKING
(☑503-772-1122; www.enrgkayaking.com; 1701 Clackamette Dr, Oregon City) Located in Oregon City, about a half-hour drive from downtown Portland, is this outfitter that offers kayak rentals, instruction and tours, plus stand-up paddleboarding (SUP) on the Willamette.

Portland Kayak Company KAYAKING
(☑503-459-4050; www.portlandkayak.com; 6600 SW Macadam Ave) Kayaking rentals, instruction and tours including a three-hour circumnavigation of Ross Island on the Willamette River.

Spa Services & Massage

The following spas all offer massage services.

Dragontree Spa SPA

(☑ 503-221-4123; www.thedragontree.com; 2768 NW Thurman St) Hedonism on earth, with a full range of spa services in gorgeous surroundings.

Loyly SPA

(Map p224; ☑ 503-236-6850; www.loyly.net; 2713 SE 21st Ave) Scandinavian-style steam and sauna facilities, plus Swedish massage.

Common Ground SPA

(☑ 503-238-1065; www.soakandsauna.org; 5010 NE 33rd) Best for its large, outdoor soaking pool in a Zen-like patio.

🍴 Courses

Portland's Culinary Workshop COOKING

(☑ 503-512-0447; www.portlandsculinaryworkshop.com; 807 N Russell St) From beginner to professional cooking courses, including seafood, barbecuing, Mexican, Thai, gluten-free, pastries and cakes...

Elements Glass GLASSBLOWING

(☑ 503-228-0575; www.elementsglass.com; 1979 NW Vaughn St) Glass-artist wannabes can take a beginners course at Portland's largest glassblowing shop, just north of the Pearl District.

Mazamas ADVENTURE SPORTS

(☑ 503-227-2345; www.mazamas.org; 527 SE 43rd Ave) Plug into the outdoor-adventure community with courses on mountaineering, rock climbing and Nordic skiing, among others, run by this educational organization.

FH Steinbart Co BREWING

(Map p224; ☑ 503-232-8793; www.fhsteinbart.com; 234 SE 12th Ave) A store offering beer-making classes, along with a great selection of home-brewing equipment.

820 Lounge BAR

(☑ 503-284-5518; www.mintand820.com; 816 N Russell St) Learn to make avocado daiquiris with Lucy Brennan, one of the nation's top mixologists. Classes take place monthly on Saturdays.

Collage CRAFT

(☑ 503-249-2190; www.collagepdx.blogspot.com; 1639 Alberta St) Craft classes galore – make glass pendants, acrylic paintings, sun prints, Japanese-bound books, do print-making, soldering and more. Cheap $5 classes on Friday too.

If you're in the area for while and want to take a specific class, consider **Portland Community College** (www.pcc.edu), which offers courses on nearly anything you can think of.

PORTLAND COURSES

OFFBEAT PORTLAND

Portland is certainly eccentric – 'Keep Portland Weird' is the city's unofficial motto. For more oddball attractions, check www.hiddenportland.com.

Voodoo Doughnut (Map p220; ☑ 503-241-4704; www.voodoodoughnut.com; 22 SW 3rd Ave; ⊙ 24hr) There's nothing quite like this standing-room-only, downtown hole-in-the-wall (pun intended). It bakes up creative, sickly-sweet treats – go for the surprisingly good bacon-maple bar or the 'cock-n-balls' (shaped like a...well, yes). Also at 1501 NE Davis.

Mill Ends Park (Map p220) Having the largest park (Forest Park) within city limits perhaps isn't an oddity, but having the smallest one might be. Mill Ends Park – located on the median strip at SW Naito Parkway and Taylor St – is a circle of green 24in in diameter (it's the reputed home of leprechauns).

Stark's Vacuum Museum (Map p224; ☑ 503-232-4101; www.starks.com/about_us/vacuum; 107 NE Grand Ave; ⊙ 8am-7pm Mon-Fri, 9am-4pm Sat) Located in a vacuum-cleaner store (no surprise there). It'll really suck you in.

Vaux Swifts (www.audubonportland.org/local-birding/swiftwatch) Every September, tens of thousands of these little birdies roost in Chapman Elementary School's old brick chimney. Seeing them spiral down in their multitudes, right at sunset, is an unforgettable sight.

Pdx Adult Soapbox Derby (www.soapboxracer.com; ⊙ 3rd Sat in Aug) Great spectator fun, when homemade, nonmotorized vehicles (from Mr Potato Head models to aerodynamic speedsters) swoosh down Mt Tabor's sinewy road, driven by costumed contestants.

☞ Tours

Portland Walking Tours WALKING TOUR
(☑503-774-4522; www.portlandwalkingtours.com)
Food, chocolate, underground and even
ghost-oriented tours.

Pedal Bike Tours BICYCLE TOUR
(Map p220; ☑503-243-2453; www.pedalbiketours.
com; 133 SW 2nd Ave) Bike tours with all sorts
of themes – history, food carts, beer – or
head to the coast or gorge.

Portland Spirit CRUISE
(☑503-224-3900; www.portlandspirit.com) Tour
Portland from the water; cruises offer sightseeing, historical narratives and/or meal
combinations.

EverGreen Escapes ECOTOUR
(☑866-203-7603, 503-252-1931; www.evergreen-
escapes.com) Half- and full-day tours of Portland and its surrounding regions. Also overnight and multiday 'escapes'.

Forktown FOOD TOUR
(☑503-234-3663; www.forktown.com) Experience Stumptown's neighborhood eateries
from your taste buds' point of view.

Pubs of Portland Tours BEER TOUR
(☑512-917-2464; www.pubsofportlandtours.com)
Visit several breweries and brewpubs with
guides who will educate you on the beer-
brewing process, various styles of beer and
essentially how to taste the stuff.

✯✯ Festivals & Events

There's some sort of festival in Portland
nearly every summer weekend; even each
neighborhood seems to have its own. For
monthly listings, check www.travelport-
land.com/things-to-see-and-do/attractions/
annual-events.

Portland International Film Festival FILM
(www.nwfilm.org; ⊙mid-late Feb) Oregon's biggest film event highlights almost 100 films
from over 30 countries, screened in several
movie houses downtown.

Portland Rose Festival ROSE FESTIVAL
(www.rosefestival.org; ⊙late May–mid-Jun)
Rose-covered floats, dragon-boat races,
a riverfront carnival, fireworks, roaming
packs of sailors and the crowning of a Rose
Queen all make this Portland's biggest
celebration.

Queer Pride Celebration GAY & LESBIAN
(www.pridenw.org; ⊙mid-Jun) Keep Portland
queer: enjoy a kick-off party, take a cruise or
join the parade along with Dykes on Bikes.

Oregon Brewers Festival BEER
(www.oregonbrewfest.com; ⊙Jul) In the last full
weekend in July you can quaff microbrews
from near and far in Waterfront Park – everyone's happy and even nondrinkers have
fun. Plenty of food stalls.

Waterfront Blues Festival BLUES FESTIVAL
(www.waterfrontbluesfest.com; ⊙early Jul) Enjoy
top blues acts, music and partying at Waterfront Park; proceeds go to the Oregon Food
Bank.

Bite of Oregon FOOD
(www.biteoforegon.com; ⊙early Aug) All the food
(and beer) you could think of consuming,
much of it from great local restaurants – and
some of it from Portland's now-famous food
carts. Good microbrews too. The festival
benefits Special Olympics Oregon.

Art in the Pearl ART
(www.artinthepearl.com; ⊙1st Mon in Sep & weekend prior) On Labor Day weekend, over 100
carefully selected artists come together to
show and sell their fine works. Plenty of food
and live music.

Holiday Ale Festival BEER
(www.holidayale.com; ⊙early Dec) This five-day
celebration takes place under covered tents
in Pioneer Sq, and you have to be at least 21.
Seasonal beers are a highlight, and there's
mead too.

🛏 Sleeping

Tariffs listed are for the summer season,
when reservations are a good idea. Prices at
top-end hotels are highly variable depending on occupancy and day of the week. Ask
about discounts; AAA membership can often get you 10% off. Portland has all of the
chain hotels and budget motels, though
their locations won't all be downtown. Parking costs listed are per day.

🛏 Downtown & Northwest

Northwest Portland Hostel HOSTEL $
(Map p220; ☑503-241-2783; www.nwportlandhos-
tel.com; 425 NW 18th Ave; dm $20-29, d with shared
bath $65; ❋@🖨) Perfectly located between
the Pearl District and NW 21st and 23rd
Aves, this friendly and clean hostel takes

up four old buildings and features plenty of common areas (including a small deck) and bike rentals. Dorms are spacious and private rooms can be as nice as in hotels, though all share outside bathrooms. Non-HI members pay $3 extra.

★ **Ace Hotel** BOUTIQUE HOTEL **$$**
(Map p220; ☎ 503-228-2277; www.acehotel.com; 1022 SW Stark St; d with shared/private bath from $135/185; ✳ @ ☸) Portland's trendiest place to sleep is this unique hotel fusing classic, industrial, minimalist and retro styles. From the photo booth and sofa lounge in its lobby to the recycled fabrics and furniture in its rooms, the Ace makes the warehouse feel work. A Stumptown coffee shop on the premises adds even more comfort. Parking costs $25.

Inn at Northrup Station BOUTIQUE HOTEL **$$**
(Map p220; ☎ 503-224-0543; www.northrupstation.com; 2025 NW Northrup St; d from $174; ✳ @) Almost over the top with its bright color scheme and funky decor, this supertrendy hotel boasts huge artsy suites, many with patio or balcony, and all with kitchenettes or full kitchens. There's a cool rooftop patio with plants, and complimentary streetcar tickets are included (the streetcar runs just outside).

Crystal Hotel HOTEL **$$**
(Map p220; ☎ 503-972-2670; www.mcmenamins.com/CrystalHotel; 303 SW 12th Ave; r $85-165; ✳ ☎) Room furnishings that blend Grateful Dead–inspired psychedelia with the interior of a Victorian boudoir can only mean one thing. Welcome to the latest McMenamins hotel, an action-packed accommodations option, bar, cafe and restaurant that shares a name and ownership with the famous ballroom across the road. Parking costs $25.

Mark Spencer Hotel HOTEL **$$**
(Map p220; ☎ 503-928-4853; www.markspencer.com; 409 SW 11th Ave; d from $169; ✳ ☎ ☸) A no-nonsense downtown option is this simple yet slightly refined choice, hosting spacious, good rooms, all with kitchens. There's complimentary tea with cookies in the afternoon, and evening wine receptions. Don't be afraid of the alleyway-like entrance – they're friendly inside. Parking costs $18 (hybrids pay half).

Nines BOUTIQUE HOTEL **$$$**
(Map p220; ☎ 877-229-9995; www.thenines.com; 525 SW Morrison St; r from $209; ✳ @ ☎ ☸) The ultimate in uberfancy celebrity-like luxury. Take the elevator to reception on the 8th floor, where the huge lobby rises six stories and is flooded in light from the glass roof. And don't miss the Departure Lounge on the 15th floor, a restaurant-bar with an outstanding patio and views. Reserve well ahead for availability and best prices. Parking costs $39 (hybrids pay half).

Hotel Vintage Plaza HOTEL **$$$**
(Map p220; ☎ 800-263-2305; www.vintageplaza.com; 422 SW Broadway; r from $199; ✳ @ ☎) For muted luxury there's this historic and tasteful hotel with a wine theme. Rooms are large, stylish and lovely; the king suites are huge at 700 sq ft, and some have large soaking tubs. Good restaurant, daily wine reception and pet friendly. It's a Kimpton, which means it does its part for the environment by recycling, using ecofriendly products and conserving resources. Parking costs $37 (hybrids pay half).

Hotel Lucia BOUTIQUE HOTEL **$$$**
(Map p220; ☎ 866-986-8086; www.hotellucia.com; 400 SW Broadway; d from $229; ✳ ☎ ☸) Those seeking luxurious tranquility in busy downtown Portland should head to this minimalist hotel with a rich, earthy color scheme and cutting-edge artwork in the lobby. There are pillow-top mattresses, iPod docking stations and flat-screen TVs, and plush robes come standard. Parking costs $35.

Hotel Monaco BOUTIQUE HOTEL **$$$**
(Map p220; ☎ 888-207-2201; www.monaco-portland.com; 506 SW Washington St; r from $199; ✳ @ ☎ ⊞ ☸) The lavishly loud lobby is decorated with colorful furniture, patterned carpeting and brightly painted walls. The spacious rooms are a bit less whimsical though still somewhat extravagant in their decoration. There's a wine reception in the afternoon and the hotel's supremely pet friendly – a lab roams the premises and goldfish are available for company. Parking costs $38.

Hotel Modera BOUTIQUE HOTEL **$$$**
(Map p220; ☎ 877-484-1084; www.hotelmodera.com; 515 SW Clay St; r from $199; ✳ @ ☎) New, slick and almost futuristic-looking hotel with attractive front courtyard boasting a living wall of native plants. Hip rooms with huge glass walls. Parking costs $27.

Governor Hotel HOTEL **$$$**
(Map p220; ☎ 503-224-3400; www.governorhotel.com; 614 SW 11th Ave; r from $199; ✳ @ ☎) Those

not looking for newfangled frills will likely appreciate the Governor, an old-fashioned hotel with a grand lobby and spacious, classy executive-style rooms. For even more hedonistic comfort, go for the penthouse suites, with glamorous terraces overlooking the city. Parking costs $36.

Heathman Hotel   LUXURY HOTEL $$$
(Map p220; ☑ 503-241-4100; www.heathmanhotel. com; 1001 SW Broadway; d from $249; ✳ @ ☎ ✿) A Portland institution, the Heathman has top-notch services and one of the best restaurants in the city. Rooms are elegant, stylish and luxurious, and the location is very central. Parking costs $32.

Hotel deLuxe   HOTEL $$$
(Map p220; ☑ 503-219-2094; www.hoteldeluxeportland.com; 729 SW 15th Ave; r from $199; ✳ ☎ ✿) Historic hotel with old-Hollywood movie theme and tasteful, modernized rooms. Get a suite for more space and ask for an upper-floor exterior room if you want views. Parking costs $28.

Benson Hotel   HOTEL $$$
(Map p220; ☑ 503-228-2000; www.bensonhotel. com; 309 SW Broadway; d from $199; ✳ ☎ ✿) The lobby is at this decadent and historic hotel is lined with walnut and filled with huge chandeliers, marble floors and an elegant bar-restaurant. Great location, though some rooms can be small. Parking costs $31.

🛏 Northeast & Southeast

Friendly Bike Guesthouse   GUESTHOUSE $
(☑ 503-799-2615; www.friendlybikeguesthouse. com; 4039 N Williams Ave; dm $36, tw per person $45, r $76; ☎) Smack on N Williams, one of Portland's main cycling thoroughfares, is this unique bike-oriented guesthouse. Rooms all share bathrooms in this pretty house, and there's a kitchen, laundry facilities, secure lockups for your ride and even a basement workshop for tune-ups. It's all so very Portland. Located 2 miles north of the Lloyd District.

White Eagle   HOTEL $
(☑ 503-282-6810; www.mcmenamins.com; 836 N Russell St; dm $45-50, d $50-65; ☎) In a small but hip industrial part of town is this old renovated hotel, another in the McMenamins empire. Nightly live rock-and-roll music creeps up from the downstairs saloon – where you check in – so it's easy to rock into the night. Then just stumble up-

stairs into one of the 11 spartan but lovely rooms (all with sinks in-room and shared bathrooms down the hall) and relish in your great-value deal.

Hawthorne Portland Hostel   HOSTEL $
(Map p224; ☑ 503-236-3380; www.portlandhostel. org; 3031 SE Hawthorne Blvd; dm $28, d with shared bath $60; @ ☎) ✏ This ecofriendly hostel has good vibes and a great Hawthorne location. The private rooms are good and dorms spacious; all share outside bathrooms. There are summertime open-mic nights in the grassy backyard, and bike rentals available. Very environmentally conscious; composts and recycles, uses rainwater to flush toilets, and has a nice eco-roof. Discounts to those bike touring.

★ Kennedy School   HOTEL $$
(☑ 503-249-3983; www.mcmenamins.com; 5736 NE 33rd Ave; d $115-155; ☎) Portland's most unusual institution, this former elementary school is now home to a hotel (sleep in old classrooms!), a restaurant with a great garden courtyard, several bars, a microbrewery and a movie theater. Guests can use the soaking pool for free, and the whole school is decorated in McMenamins' funky art style – mosaics, fantasy paintings and historical photographs. It's a unique stay and very Portland.

Jupiter Hotel   BOUTIQUE MOTEL $$
(Map p224; ☑ 503-230-9200; www.jupiterhotel. com; 800 E Burnside St; d from $159; ✳ ☎ ✿) The hippest hotel in town, this slick, remodeled motel is within walking distance of downtown and right next to Doug Fir, a top-notch live-music venue. Standard rooms are tiny – go for the Metropolitan instead – and ask for a pad away from the bamboo patio if you're more into sleeping than staying up late. Kitchenettes and bike rentals are available; walk-ins after midnight get a discount.

Clinton Street Guesthouse   GUESTHOUSE $$
(☑ 503-234-8752; www.clintonstreetguesthouse. com; 4220 SE Clinton St; d incl breakfast $100-145; ✳ ☎) Four simple but beautiful rooms (two with shared bathroom) are on offer in this lovely Craftsman house in a residential neighborhood. Furnishings are elegant, the linens luxurious, and your hosts gracious. There are many restaurants within walking distance.

Bluebird Guesthouse   GUESTHOUSE $$
(Map p224; ☑ 503-238-4333; www.bluebirdguesthouse.com; 3517 SE Division St; r inc breakfast $120;

✳🕏) Nicely located on a lively section of SE Division, this pleasant guesthouse is in a beautiful old arts-and-crafts house with country kitchen. Seven tasteful rooms are available, two with private bathroom, and plenty of good restaurants and shops are within walking distance. Continental breakfast included. Prices vary depending on month.

Caravan   BOUTIQUE HOTEL **$$**
(☑ 503-288-5225; www.tinyhousehotel.com; 5009 NE 11th St; r $125) Only in Portland: stay in a tiny house (100 to 200 sq ft – smaller than some hotel rooms!), complete with kitchen and bathroom, in the artsy Alberta neighborhood. Just three of these efficiently designed mobile dwellings are available. Follows the latest trend to 'live large in small spaces' – even temporarily.

Lion & the Rose   B&B **$$$**
(☑ 800-955-1647; www.lionrose.com; 1810 NE 15th Ave; d $200-250; ✳🕏) Located at the edge of upscale Irvington, this turreted Queen Anne mansion is almost over the top with its fine antiques and flowery decoration. All seven rooms come with private bathroom (one has its private bathroom down the hall), and the large basement apartment has a kitchenette. This gay-friendly place is close to shops, bars, cafes and the MAX. Discounts outside summer.

🍴 Eating

Portland has become nationally recognized for its food scene, with dozens of young, top-notch chefs pushing the boundaries of ethnic and regional cuisines. Casual clothes are acceptable even at higher-end places, where reservations are a good idea.

Fast-food lovers should consider looking up the various branches of Burgerville (local, seasonal ingredients; www.burgerville.com) and Laughing Planet (vegetarian-friendly burritos; www.laughingplanetcafe.com), but the city's best fast food is dished up at the more than 600 food carts.

🍴 Downtown & Northwest

Office workers and students flock to pods of food carts in the area: SW 5th Ave and SW Stark; SW Alder and 9th; SW 3rd between Washington and Stark; and SW 4th between Hall and College.

St Honoré Boulangerie   BAKERY, CAFE **$**
(☑ 503-445-4342; www.sainthonorebakery.com; 2335 NW Thurman St; light meals $5-10; ☉ 7am-8pm) Popular for its luscious breads and pastries, this modern-rustic bakery in the Northwest district also serves savory dishes like panini sandwiches, gourmet salads and puff pastries stuffed with vegetables. Try your luck at snagging a precious sidewalk table on a warm sunny day.

TOP PORTLAND FOOD CARTS

Stumptown is famous – *really* famous – for its food carts. For a good guide, see www.foodcartsportland.com; for some of the best, just read on.

Nong's Khao Man Gai (Map p220; ☑ 971-255-3480; www.khaomangai.com; SW 10th Ave & SW Alder St; mains $7; ☉ 10am-4pm Mon-Fri) Tender poached chicken with rice. That's it – and enough. Also at 411 SW College St and 609 SE Ankeny St.

Viking Soul Food (www.vikingsoulfood.com; 4262 SE Belmont Ave; mains $5-6; ☉ noon-8pm Tue-Thu, 11:30am-9:30pm Fri & Sat, 11:30am-8:30pm Sun) Delicious sweet and savory wraps.

Rip City Grill (www.ripcitygrill.com; cnr SW Moody Ave & Abernethy St; sandwiches $5-7; ☉ 10am-2pm Mon-Fri) The tri-tip steak sandwich is not to be missed.

Pepper Box (www.pepperboxpdx.com; 2737 NE Martin Luther King Jr Blvd; tacos & quesadillas $3.50-4; ☉ 9am-2pm Tue-Fri, to 1pm Sat) Awesome breakfast tacos and fancy quesadillas.

Thrive Pacific NW (www.thrivepacificnw.com; mains $5-8) Organic, free-range and gluten-free exotic food bowls. See website for changing location and hours.

Sip (☑ 503-680-5639; www.sipjuicecart.com; 2210 NE Alberta St; ☉ 9am-3pm) Fresh, organic and vegan juices, smoothies and even milkshakes. Also at 3029 SE 21st Ave.

Potato Champion (Map p224; ☑ 503-683-3797; www.potatochampion.tumblr.com; 1207 SE Hawthorne Blvd; ☉ noon-3am Tue-Sun; 🍴) Twice-fried fries and exotic dipping sauces. Open very late!

Little Big Burger   BURGERS $

(Map p220; ☑ 503-274-9008; www.littlebigburger. com; 122 NW 10th Ave; burgers $4; ☺11am-10pm) A simple six-item menu takes fast food to the next level with mini burgers made from prime ingredients. Try a beef burger topped with cheddar, Swiss, chevre or blue cheese, with a side of truffled fries – then wash it down with a gourmet root-beer float. Several locations; check website.

Kenny & Zuke's   DELI $$

(Map p220; ☑ 503-222-3354; www.kennyandzukes. com; 1038 SW Stark St; sandwiches $10-15; ☺7am-8pm Mon-Thu, to 10pm Fri, 8am-10pm Sat, to 8pm Sun) The only place in the city for real Jewish deli food: bagels, pickled herring, homemade pickles and latkes. But the real draw is the house pastrami, cut to order and gently sandwiched in one of the best Reubens you'll ever eat. Bustles for breakfast, too. Also in North Portland.

★Higgins   FRENCH $$$

(Map p220; ☑ 503-222-9070; www.higginsportland.com; 1239 SW Broadway; lunch mains $10-19, dinner mains $21-37; ☺11:30am-midnight Mon-Fri, 4pm-midnight Sat & Sun) 🥢 In 1994 chef-owner Greg Higgins opened the doors to one of Portland's groundbreaking restaurants. These days, Higgins feels more classically elegant than cutting edge, but it still features French-inspired dishes using seasonal Northwest ingredients. The beer list is the best in town; ask for pairing suggestions for any course.

Paley's Place   FRENCH, FUSION $$$

(Map p220; ☑ 503-243-2403; www.paleysplace. net; 1204 NW 21st Ave; mains $23-36; ☺5:30-10pm Mon-Thu, to 11pm Fri & Sat, 5-10pm Sun) 🥢 Established by Vitaly and Kimberly Paley, this is one of Portland's premier restaurants, offering a creative blend of French and Pacific Northwest cuisines. Whether it's seared Alaskan halibut or crispy sweetbreads with fava-bean puree, you can count on fresh ingredients, excellent service and a memorable experience.

Andina   PERUVIAN $$$

(Map p220; ☑ 503-228-9535; www.andinarestaurant.com; 1314 NW Glisan St; lunch mains $14-17, dinner mains $22-30; ☺11:30am-2:30pm & 5-9:30pm Sun-Thu, to 10:30pm Fri & Sat) A modern take on traditional Peruvian food produces delicious entrees like quinoa-crusted scallops on a bed of wilted spinach, or

slow-cooked lamb shank in cilantro-black-beer sauce. For lighter fare, hit the bar for tapas, great cocktails and Latin-inspired live music.

Little Bird   FRENCH $$$

(Map p220; ☑ 503-688-5952; www.littlebirdbistro. com; 219 SW 6th Ave; lunch mains $14-27, dinner mains $20-27; ☺11am-midnight Mon-Fri, 5pm-midnight Sat & Sun) Sister restaurant to lower E Burnside's renowned Le Pigeon is this quaint French bistro. Folks swoon over the duck-leg cassoulet and chicken-fried trout; don't miss the pricey but sublime desserts ($9). Also serves one of Portland's best burgers ($12).

Irving Street Kitchen   NORTHWESTERN $$$

(Map p220; ☑ 503-343-9440; www.irvingstreetkitchen.com; 701 NW 13th Ave; mains $17-26; ☺5:30-10pm Mon-Thu, to 11pm Fri, 10am-2:30pm & 5:30-11pm Sat, 5-9pm Sun) Pacific Northwest cuisine with a Southern touch, this upscale restaurant serves exceptional dishes like bourbon-soaked Chinook salmon, wild mushroom and mascarpone ravioli, and seared duck breast with grits. The wine list is notable, and save room for the butterscotch pudding served in Mason jars. Also does brunch.

Clyde Common   EUROPEAN $$$

(Map p220; ☑ 503-228-3333; www.clydecommon. com; 1014 SW Stark St; lunch mains $9-14, dinner mains $19-24; ☺11:30am-11:45pm Mon-Thu, to 12:45am Fri, 9am-12:45am Sat, 9am-3pm Sun) Attached to the hip Ace Hotel, this spot is Euro bistro meets cool Scandinavian chic. Be ready for communal tables, where you'll dig into ricotta and chard ravioli, seared trout over bulgur or lamb with tarragon pesto. Great wines by the glass and unique cocktails, which are churned out from the bar by expert hands.

Jake's Famous Crawfish   SEAFOOD $$$

(Map p220; ☑ 503-226-1419; 401 SW 12th Ave; lunch mains $10-16, dinner mains $19-39; ☺11.30am-10pm Mon-Thu, to midnight Fri & Sat, 3-10pm Sun) Saunter into this classic joint, reservation in hand. You'll need it – some of Portland's best seafood can be found here within an elegant old-time atmosphere. The oysters are divine, the crab cakes a revelation and the macadamia-crusted wild halibut your ticket into heaven. Come at happy hour for more affordable treats.

Northeast & Southeast

¿Por Qué No? Taquería
MEXICAN $
(☑503-467-4149; www.porquenotacos.com; 3524 N Mississippi Ave; tacos $3-4, mains $6.50-11; ⊙11am-10pm Mon-Sat, to 9:30pm Sun) ✐ Pricey for a taqueria, but the ingredients are good, and so is the vibe. Great tacos, or try the Bryan's Bowl – essentially a tortilla-less burrito in a bowl – and down it with a pomegranate margarita. It's a tiny place, and the line often goes out the door. Another branch at 4635 SE Hawthorne has a funky back patio.

Pine State Biscuits
SOUTHERN $
(Map p224; ☑503-477-6605; www.pinestatebiscuits.com; 2204 NE Alberta St; biscuit sandwiches $4-8; ⊙7am-3pm Mon-Wed, to 11pm Thu & Sun, to 1am Fri & Sat) Immensely popular for its heart-stopping fried chicken, bacon and cheese biscuit sandwiches, with possible egg and gravy additions. Plenty of sides, with interesting drinks like local apple cider or gourmet chocolate milk. Also at corner SE Division St and SE 11th Ave.

Little T American Baker
BAKERY $
(Map p224; ☑503-238-3458; www.littletbaker.com; 2600 SE Division St; mains $7-10; ⊙7am-5pm Mon-Sat, 8am-2pm Sun) Best baguette in town, as well as quiches and salads for lunch. Don't forget dessert – order a delicious pastry like the poached-pear danish, pistachio bear claw, almond currant roll, sweet-potato cinnamon doughnut, chocolate-praline croissant...

Bamboo Sushi
SUSHI $$
(Map p224; ☑503-232-5255; www.bamboosushi.com; 310 SE 28th Ave; nigiri $4-7, mains $10-14; ⊙4:30-10pm) ✐ Bamboo claims to be the first 'certified sustainable' sushi restaurant in the world, and – this being Portland – we believe it. Eco-food twist aside, it's hard to find fish that tastes this good. And don't forget the cooked dishes either, like the Alaskan black cod with orange and ginger. Eating green never felt so good. Also at 836 NW 23rd Ave.

Pok Pok
THAI $$
(Map p224; ☑503-232-1387; www.pokpokpdx.com; 3226 SE Division St; mains $11-16; ⊙11:30am-10pm) Spicy Thai street food with a twist draws crowds to this famous eatery; don't miss the renowned chicken wings. To endure the inevitable long wait, try a tastier-than-it-sounds drinking vinegar nearby at the restaurant's bar, Whiskey Soda Lounge. There's a second location at 1469 NE Prescott St.

Toro Bravo
SPANISH $$
(☑503-281-4464; www.torobravopdx.com; 120 NE Russell St; tapas $7-12, mains $11-19; ⊙5-10pm Sun-Thu, to 11pm Fri & Sat) Sure, you could order the house bacon and manchego burger here and be happy, but it's the endless list of tapas that should guide your taste buds – try the grilled corn with cilantro pesto or basque piperade with duck egg. Be prepared for a wait – this place has an enduring reputation for deliciousness.

Smallwares
FUSION $$
(☑503-229-0995; www.smallwarespdx.com; 4605 NE Fremont St; small plates $8-15; ⊙5-10pm) Self-proclaimed as serving 'inauthentic Asian cuisine,' this open-kitchen-industrial eatery is all about ubercreative small plates that are meant to be shared. Try the chicken 'lollipops' with *sriracha* mayo, crab noodle soup, oxtail curry or pear kimchi. And don't miss the fried kale with candied bacon. Inauthentic indeed!

Navarre
EUROPEAN $$
(Map p224; ☑503-232-3555; www.navarreportland.blogspot.com; 10 NE 28th Ave; small plates $4-8, large plates $10-18; ⊙4:30-10:30pm Mon-Thu, to 11:30pm Fri, 9:30am-11:30pm Sat, to 10:30pm Sun) A paper-list menu at this industrial-elegant restaurant lists various small plates (don't call them tapas), which rotate daily – though a few popular dishes are fixed commodities. Expect a simple and truly delicious approach to crab cakes, lamb and roasted veggies. Weekend brunch is just as good.

Old Salt Marketplace
AMERICAN $$
(☑971-255-0167; www.oldsaltpdx.com; 5027 NE 42nd Ave; mains $15-20; ⊙5pm-midnight) ✐ Combining restaurant, bar, bakery, 'American' butcher shop, deli and even a cooking school under one roof is this supper house highlighting well-sourced ingredients. The aesthetic is salvaged wood and the kitchen focuses on the open hearth where most dishes are cooked. Excellent roast beef, duck and pork, and great biscuits.

Pambiche
CUBAN $$
(Map p224; ☑503-233-0511; www.pambiche.com; 2811 NE Glisan St; mains $12-17; ⊙11am-10pm Mon-Thu, to midnight Fri, 9am-midnight Sat, to 10pm Sun) Portland's best Cuban food, with a trendy and riotously colorful atmosphere. All your regular favorites like *ropa vieja* are available, but leave room for dessert. Lunch is a good deal, but happy hour is even better (2pm to 6pm

Monday to Friday, 10pm to midnight Friday and Saturday). Be prepared to wait for dinner.

Farm Café   AMERICAN, NORTHWEST $$

(Map p224; ☑ 503-736-3276; www.thefarmcafe. com; 10 SE 7th Ave; mains $10-15; ⊙ 5-10:30pm Sun-Thu, to 11:30pm Fri & Sat; ☑) ◢ From outside it's just an old white house, and you'll wonder what all the fuss is about. This is it: well-priced, vegetarian-friendly dishes (plus a few good lamb and fish options) that are lovingly prepared and made using only local and organic ingredients. Add some good cocktails and a relaxing backyard patio, and you've got a memorable dining experience.

Country Cat   SOUTHERN $$

(☑ 503-408-1414; www.thecountrycat.net; 7937 SE Stark St; mains $13-18; ⊙ 9am-2pm & 5pm-close) Located in the Montavilla neighborhood (about 4.5 miles east of downtown), which is starting to establish itself as a foodie destination with a few key eateries. Choose Southern specialties like skillet-fried chicken, paprika-marinated shrimp and barbequed duck leg with braised green beans. Early birds will find buttermilk pancakes, brisket sandwiches and shrimp 'n' grits.

Ken's Artisan Pizza   PIZZA $$

(Map p224; ☑ 503-517-9951; www.kensartisan.com; 304 SE 28th Ave; small pizzas $11-14; ⊙ 5-10pm Mon-Sat, 4-9pm Sun) Glorious wood-fired, thin-crust pizzas that serve one or two, with toppings like prosciutto, house-made pancetta and green garlic. Supertrendy atmosphere, with huge sliding windows that open to the street on warm nights. Expect a long wait – no reservations taken.

★ Laurelhurst Market   AMERICAN $$$

(Map p224; ☑ 503-206-3097; www.laurelhurst-market.com; 3155 E Burnside St; mains $21-29; ⊙ 5-10pm) Hugely popular and vegetarian-unfriendly is this hip and meaty spot, where grass-fed steaks, pork chops and mussels *frites* (french fries) dominate the menu. Just be prepared to wait, unless you have a reservation. There's also a small butcher counter selling quality meats and great lunchtime sandwiches.

DOC   ITALIAN $$$

(☑ 503-946-8592; www.docpdx.com; 5519 NE 30th Ave; mains $18-27; ⊙ 6-10pm Tue-Sat) ◢ Enter this tiny Northeast establishment and find yourself in the middle of the kitchen, a purposeful way to introduce you to an intimate dining experience that marries Northwest

---

BRUNCH, ANYONE?

Portlanders love brunch, and on weekends you'll see long lines at all the popular spots. Weekend hours are usually from 9am to 2pm; some places are only open Saturday and Sunday. Note that some of the regular restaurants we list, especially Simpatica and Woodsman Tavern, also offer excellent brunches.

Tasty n Sons (☑ 503-621-1400; www.tastyntasty.com; 3808 N Williams Ave) Superb small plates in a high-ceilinged warehouse. Wait guaranteed.

Screen Door (Map p224; ☑ 503-542-0880; www.screendoorrestaurant.com; 2337 E Burnside St) Heavenly fried chicken and exceptional French toast. Wait guaranteed.

Tin Shed (☑ 503-288-6966; www.tinshedgardencafe.com; 1438 NE Alberta St) Hot NE Alberta spot with awesome outside patio.

Mother's Bistro (Map p220; ☑ 503-464-1122; www.mothersbistro.com; 212 SW Stark St) Upscale downtown brunch spot; try the salmon hash. Guaranteed wait on weekends.

Broder (Map p224; ☑ 503-736-3333; www.broderpdx.com; 2508 SE Clinton St) Danish pancakes, Swedish hash, Norwegian potato crepes...

Hazel Room (Map p224; ☑ 503-756-7125; www.thehazelroom.com; 3279 SE Hawthorne Blvd) Stunning biscuit sandwiches and breakfast plates, served all day.

Olympic Provisions (☑ 503-894-8136; www.olympicprovisions.com; 1632 NW Thurman St) Just a few items like biscuits with sausage gravy, keilbasa hash and three kinds of Benedict. Also at 107 SE Washington St.

Beast (☑ 503-841-6968; www.beastpdx.com; 5425 NE 30th Ave) Four-course prix-fixe brunch on Sunday (10am and noon seatings only). Reserve ahead.

ingredients with simple Italian cooking. Expect tender pastas, perfectly cooked meats and a memorable cheese course. Splurge for wine pairings and you won't be disappointed.

Ox STEAKHOUSE **$$$**
(☑ 503-284-3366; www.oxpdx.com; 2225 Martin Luther King Jr Blvd; mains $19-38; ☺ 5-10pm Tue-Sun) Currently Portland's most popular restaurant is this upscale, Argentine-inspired steakhouse. Start with the bone marrow clam chowder, then go for the gusto: the grass-fed beef rib eye ($38). Or if there's two of you, the asado ($60) is a good choice for trying several different cuts. Reserve, and bring a fat wallet.

Castagna EUROPEAN **$$$**
(Map p224; ☑ 503-231-7373; www.castagnarestaurant.com; 1752 SE Hawthorne Blvd; prix fixe $55/95, wine pairings $35; ☺ 5:30-10pm Wed-Sat) At this elegantly upscale prix-fixe restaurant, chef Justin Woodward transforms seasonal ingredients into works of art with truly amazing textures and flavors (think hot-smoked halibut belly with lovage). Don't miss dessert, which can include a blackberry-mezcal sorbet with corn mousseline. More familiar á la carte dishes grace the menu at the attached cafe.

Nostrana ITALIAN **$$$**
(Map p224; ☑ 503-234-2427; www.nostrana.com; 1401 SE Morrison St; mains $17-28; ☺ 11:30am-2pm & 5-10pm Sun-Thu, to 11pm Fri & Sat) Award-winning chef Kathy Whims makes meals special at this gem of an Italian restaurant. Choose from wood-fired pizzas (served uncut for authenticity), pappardelle with rabbit sugo and flat-iron steak with arugula, which round out the classic Italian dishes. Happy hour runs after 9pm and offers good deals.

Simpatica Dining Hall AMERICAN **$$$**
(Map p224; ☑ 503-235-1600; www.simpaticapdx.com; 838 SE Ash St; prix fixe $38-55; ☺ prix-fixe dinners 7:30pm Fri & 7pm Sat, brunch 9am-2pm Sun) One of Portland's most popular Sunday brunch spots (hello, fried chicken and waffles!) also serves great prix-fixe dinners. Make new friends at long communal tables, which hold lovely soups, rustic pastries and well-prepared meat dishes – all made with seasonally appropriate ingredients and served family-style.

Ned Ludd AMERICAN **$$$**
(☑ 503-288-6900; 3925 NE Martin Luther King Jr Blvd; small plates $8-21; ☺ 5pm-close Wed-Sat, 9am-2pm & 5pm-close Sun) 🌱 Too quintessentially Portland, this offbeat, upscale joint exudes thick artisan vibes, from its rustic-peasant decor to the prominent brick wood-fired oven where all dishes are cooked. The beautifully presented small plates are rotated daily. Not a place to simply fill your tummy, but rather to sample eclectic 'American craft' delicacies. Also does a good brunch.

Woodsman Tavern AMERICAN **$$$**
(☑ 971-373-8264; www.woodsmantavern.com; 4537 SE Division St; mains $24-30; ☺ 5-10pm Mon-Fri, 9am-2pm & 5-10pm Sat & Sun) Hip, upscale restaurant decked out in wood and some industrial furniture. Beautifully presented food; start with some seafood or country ham plates, and end with the whole roasted trout. Great brunch too, with choices like salmon croquettes and smoked barley porridge with poached egg.

Bar Avignon EUROPEAN **$$$**
(Map p224; ☑ 503-517-0808; www.baravignon.com; 2138 SE Division St; mains $18-23; ☺ 5pm-close) A romantic setting for snacky plates to share (try the Netarts Bay oysters), or real entrees like seared pork chop with cherry glaze and red-pepper fettucine with smoked mushrooms and chevre. You'll want to linger over a special bottle of wine at the bar, or at a sidewalk table. Happy hour offers some good deals.

🍸 Drinking & Nightlife

Portland is famous for its coffee, and also offers a wide range of excellent bars, from dives to hipster joints to pubs and ultramodern lounges.

For funky atmospheres with OK beer, there's no beating **McMenamins** (www.mcmenamins.com). The empire includes brewpubs all over the Pacific Northwest, each offering their own ales along with brews from other producers. Thirsty parents should head to especially family-friendly **Laurelwood Brewing Co** (☑ 503-282-0622; 5115 NE Sandy Blvd), though many brewpubs welcome kids until 9pm or so.

Check out www.barflymag.com for opinionated, spot-on reviews. Oregon bars and pubs are legally required to be nonsmoking.

★**Barista**   CAFE
(Map p220; ☑ 503-274-1211; www.baristapdx.com; 539 NW 13th Ave; ☺ 6am-6pm Mon-Fri, 7am-6pm Sat & Sun) One of Portland's best coffee shops, owned by award-winning barista Billy Wilson and known for its lattes. They source their beans from specialty roasters. Also at 529 SW 3rd Ave and 1725 NE Alberta St.

★**Hair of the Dog Brewing**   BREWPUB
(Map p224; ☑ 503-232-6585; www.hairofthedog. com; 61 SE Yamhill St; ☺ 11:30am-8pm Tue-Sun, to 10pm Fri & Sat) HOTD brews unusual beer styles, some of which are 'bottle-conditioned' – the brewing cycle is finished inside the bottle. This results in complex flavors and high alcohol content, and the beer ages like a fine wine. Interested? Try the beer flight. Snacky foods too.

Amnesia Brewing   BREWPUB
(☑ 503-281-7708; www.amnesiabrews.com; 832 N Beech St; ☺ 3pm-midnight Mon, noon-midnight Tue-Sun) This hip Mississippi St brewery has a very casual feel and picnic tables out front. For excellent (and, despite the name, memorable) beer, try the Desolation IPA, Amnesia Brown or Wonka Porter. An outdoor grill offers burgers and sausages, and there's live music on weekends.

Horse Brass Pub   PUB
(☑ 503-232-2202; www.horsebrass.com; 4534 SE Belmont St; ☺ 11am-2:30am) Portland's most authentic English pub, cherished for its dark-wood atmosphere, excellent fish 'n' chips (or try the artery-clogging scotch egg) and nearly 60 beers on tap. Also serves 'proper 20oz Imperial pints.' Play some darts, watch soccer on TV and just take it all in.

Coava Coffee   CAFE
(Map p224; ☑ 503-894-8134; www.coavacoffee. com; 1300 SE Grand Ave; ☺ 6am-6pm Mon-Fri, 7am-6pm Sat, 8am-6pm Sun) The decor takes the concept of 'neo-industrial' to extremes, but most people love that – and Coava delivers where it matters. The pour-over makes for a fantastic cup of java, and the espressos are exceptional too.

Bailey's Taproom   BREWPUB
(Map p220; ☑ 503-295-1004; www.baileystaproom. com; 213 SW Broadway; ☺ 2pm-midnight) Unique and popular brewpub offering a rotating selection of 20 eclectic beers from Oregon and beyond. Cool digital menu board lets you know about the beers, and how much

of each is left. No food served, but you can bring stuff in from outside.

Belmont Station   BREWPUB
(☑ 503-232-8538; www.belmont-station.com; 4500 SE Stark St; ☺ noon-11pm) More than 20 excellent rotating taps in a simple 'biercafé' with sidewalk seating. Attached to one of the city's best bottle shops, which sells over 1200 beers (!) and offers a small cash discount.

Departure Lounge   BAR
(Map p220; ☑ 503-802-5370; www.departureportland.com; 525 SW Morrison St; ☺ 4pm-midnight Sun-Thu, to 1am Fri & Sat) This rooftop restaurant-bar, atop the 15th floor of the Nines Hotel, fills a deep downtown void: a cool bar with unforgettable views of Pioneer Courthouse Sq and the Willamette River. The vibe is distinctly spaceship LA, with mod couches and sleek lighting. Hit happy hour from 4pm to 6pm (or late night) for select $6 drinks and less pricey appetizers.

Ristretto Roasters   CAFE
(☑ 503-288-8667; www.ristrettoroasters.com; 3808 N Williams Ave; ☺ 6:30am-6pm Mon-Sat, 7am-6pm Sun) Medium-roast, small-batch and single-origin coffee beans that result in a mellow, more subtle cup of java. Free cuppings (tasting sessions) Fridays at 1pm. Also at 555 NE Couch St and 2181 NW Nicolai St (in a cool Schoolhouse Electric building).

Breakside Brewery   BREWPUB
(☑ 503-719-6475; www.breakside.com; 820 NE Dekum St; ☺ 3-10pm Mon-Thu, noon-11pm Fri & Sat, noon-10pm Sun) Over 20 taps of some of the most experimental, tasty beer you'll ever drink, laced through with fruits, vegetables and spices. Past beers have included a Meyer lemon *kolsch*, mango IPA and beet beer with ginger. For dessert, pray it has the salted-caramel milk stout. Good food and nice outdoor seating too.

Stumptown Coffee Roasters   CAFE
(☑ 503-230-7702; www.stumptowncoffee.com; 4525 SE Division St; ☺ 6am-7pm Mon-Fri, 7am-7pm Sat & Sun) The first microroaster to put Portland on the coffee map, and still its most famous coffee shop. Proud to deal directly with coffee farmers to ensure quality beans. See the website for other Portland (and US) locations.

Green Dragon   BREWPUB
(Map p224; ☑ 503-517-0660; www.pdxgreendragon.com; 928 SE 9th Ave; ☺ 11am-11pm Sun-Wed, to 1am Thu-Sat) Owned by Rogue Breweries but

serves a whopping 62 guest taps – and an eclectic mix to boot. Decent pub-fare food too. Located in an echoey eastside warehouse space; sit in the patio on warm days.

Rontoms
BAR

(Map p224; 503-236-4536; 600 E Burnside St; ⊗4:30pm-2:30am) First the downside – the food's just OK, the service is mediocre and if you're not a hipster you'll feel out of place. But if it's a nice day, the large patio in back is the place to be. It's at the corner of E Burnside and 6th (too cool for a sign).

Hopworks Urban Brewery
BREWPUB

(503-232-4677; www.hopworksbeer.com; 2944 SE Powell Blvd; ⊗11am-11pm Sun-Thu, to midnight Fri & Sat;) All organic beers made with local ingredients, served in an eco-styled building with bicycle frames above the bar. Good selection of food in a family-friendly atmosphere, and the back deck can't be beat on a warm day. Also at 3947 N Williams Ave.

Sterling Coffee Roasters
CAFE

(Map p220; www.sterlingcoffeeroasters.com; 417 NW 21st Ave; ⊗7am-4pm Mon-Fri, 8am-4pm Sat & Sun) Very small but elegant coffee shop roasting complex, flavorful beans. Simple menu, with great cappucinos and espressos; knowledgeable baristas. Also at 1951 W Burnside (where it's called Coffeehouse Northwest).

Saraveza
PUB

(503-206-4252; www.saraveza.com; 1004 N Killingsworth St; ⊗11am-midnight) Bottle shop–pub best for its American craft beer, served by award-winning 'beertenders.' Choose from over 250 bottles of the stuff, including nine on draft. Also good for its savory and sweet pasties (hand pies).

Kir Wine Bar
WINE BAR

(Map p224; 503-232-3063; www.kirwinebar.com; 22 NE 7th Ave; ⊗from 5pm Tue-Sat) Small, intimate wine bar offering around 50 quality, unique wines by the glass, including 10 rosés in summer. Also has a good variety of gourmet small plates. Come during happy hour (5pm to 6pm) for half-off wines.

Hale Pele
TIKI BAR

(503-662-8454; www.halepele.com; 2733 NE Broadway; ⊗5pm-midnight Tue-Sat, 10am-2pm Sun) *The* kitschy tiki bar (aren't they all?) to come to for 'historical' tropical cocktails, all made from fresh juices, hand-crafted syrups and premium spirits. Try the popular

Suffering Bastard, made with ginger beer, bourbon, gin and lime. Also does exotically tinged Sunday brunch.

Victory Bar
BAR

(Map p224; 503-236-8755; www.thevictorybar.com; 3652 Division St; ⊗5pm-12:30am Sun-Wed, to 1am Thu & Sat, to 1:30am Fri) Great cocktails, great beer selection, great venison burger (and spaetzle) and great happy hour. That's all we're going to say and all you need to know.

Cascade Brewing
BREWPUB

(Map p224; 503-265-8603; www.cascadebrewing.com; 939 SE Belmont St; ⊗noon-10pm Sun & Mon, to 11pm Tue-Thu, to midnight Fri & Sat) Excellent brewery specializing in sour beers, many made from fruit – they'll bring more tang into your life. If you can't decide, try the samplers (or the honey-ginger-lime...mmm). It all goes well with the gourmet food on the nice, big patio.

Deschutes Brewery
BREWPUB

(Map p220; 503-296-4906; www.deschutesbrewery.com; 210 NW 11th Ave; ⊗11am-11pm Sun-Thu, to midnight Fri & Sat) This is the Portland branch of this Bend brewery, but the stuff is brewed here, too – which keeps pints fresh and tasty. The Mirror Pond Ale and Obsidian Stout have won 'best of show' at the International Brewing Awards (the Oscars of beer brewing).

Upright Brewing
BREWPUB

(503-735-5337; www.uprightbrewing.com; 240 N Broadway, Suite 2; ⊗4:30-9pm Fri, 1-6pm Sat & Sun) Basement brewery with intimate tasting room for sampling French and Belgian farmhouse-inspired ales. Only open Friday to Sunday (unless there's a home Trail Blazers game, when hours are extended); cash or checks only.

Heart
CAFE

(Map p224; 503-206-6602; www.heartroasters.com; 2211 E Burnside St; ⊗7am-7pm) Artsy-industrial atmosphere on busy E Burnside; check out its large visible roaster. A bit too hipster-y for some, and service can be spotty, but most of the beans are well (and lightly) roasted.

Courier Coffee Roasters
CAFE

(Map p220; 503-545-6444; www.couriercoffeeroasters.com; 923 SW Oak St; ⊗7am-5pm Mon-Fri, 9am-4pm Sat & Sun) Small-batch roaster with friendly baristas and a great macchiato. Exceptional pastries too. Go for an iced drink on a hot day. It's a small space, so don't expect to hang out too long. It delivers its roasted beans by cargo bike, among other sustainable practices.

☆ Entertainment

The best guide to local entertainment is the free *Willamette Week* (www.wweek.com), which comes out on Wednesday and lists theater, music, clubs, cinema and events in the metro area. Also try the *Portland Mercury* (www.portlandmercury.com).

Live Music

For summer outdoor concerts, check what's happening at the Oregon Zoo (p219).

Doug Fir Lounge   LIVE MUSIC
(Map p224; ✆503-231-9663; www.dougfirlounge. com; 830 E Burnside St) Paul Bunyan meets the Jetsons at this ultratrendy venue that has transformed the LoBu (lower Burnside) neighborhood from seedy to slick. Doug Fir books edgy, hard-to-get talent, drawing crowds from tattooed youth to suburban yuppies. Its decent restaurant has long hours; located next to the rock-star-quality Jupiter Hotel.

Mississippi Studios   LIVE MUSIC
(✆503-288-3895; www.mississippistudios.com; 3939 N Mississippi Ave) Recently expanded but still intimate; good for checking out budding acoustic talent, along with more established musical groups. Excellent sound system and good restaurant-bar with patio next door. Located right on trendy N Mississippi Ave.

Crystal Ballroom   LIVE MUSIC
(Map p220; ✆503-225-0047; www.mcmenamins. com; 1332 W Burnside St) Major acts have played at this large and historic ballroom, including the Grateful Dead, James Brown and Jimi Hendrix. The 'floating' dance floor makes dancing a balancing act. If you like '80s music, head to Lola's Room downstairs on Friday night.

Jimmy Mak's   IA77
(Map p220; ✆503-295-6542; www.jimmymaks. com; 221 NW 10th Ave; ☺music from 8pm) Stumptown's premier jazz venue, serving excellent Mediterranean food in its fancy dining room. There's a casual bar with pool tables and darts in the basement.

LaurelThirst Public House   LIVE MUSIC
(Map p224; ✆503-232-1504; www.laurelthirst.com; 2958 NE Glisan St) Great acoustic bands spill the crowds onto the sidewalk at this dark, funky neighborhood joint. The music – which plays every night – is usually free (or the cover might only be $5). Check out the Freak Mountain Ramblers on Sunday night.

Goodfoot   LIVE MUSIC
(Map p224; ✆503-239-9292; www.thegoodfoot. com; 2845 SE Stark St) Very neighborly spot with affordable music acts in the basement, plus good dancing (especially Friday nights) and a great sound system. Upstairs is a bar with booths, cheap pool tables, stiff drinks and creative art on the walls. Check out the open-mic night on Monday.

Dante's   LIVE MUSIC
(Map p220; ✆503-345-7892; www.danteslive. com; 350 W Burnside St) This steamy red bar books vaudeville shows along with national acts like the Dandy Warhols and Concrete Blonde. Drop in on Sunday night for the eclectic Sinferno Cabaret, and on Monday night for Karaoke from Hell.

Cinemas

Portland has plenty of multiplex cinemas, but it's the great selection of old personality-filled theaters – often selling beer and pizza, along with cheap tickets – that makes going to the movies a joy here.

Laurelhurst Theater   CINEMA
(Map p224; ✆503-232-5511; www.laurelhursttheater.com; 2735 E Burnside St) Great gourmet-pizza-and-microbrew theater with nearby nightlife.

Bagdad Theater   CINEMA
(Map p224; ✆503-249-7474; www.mcmenamins. com; 3702 SE Hawthorne Blvd) Another awesome McMenamins venue with bargain flicks; on Tuesday they're only $2.

Kennedy School   CINEMA
(✆503-249-3983; www.mcmenamins.com; 5736 NE 33rd Ave) McMenamins' premiere Portland venue. Watch $3 movies in the old school gym. Check the website for current showings.

Cinema 21   CINEMA
(Map p220; www.cinema21.com; 616 NW 21st Ave) Portland's premiere art-house and foreign-film theater, though the seats aren't the most comfortable.

Hollywood Theatre   CINEMA
(✆503-281-4215; www.hollywoodtheatre.org; 4122 NE Sandy Blvd) Historic art-deco spot playing

classic, foreign and quirky independent movies. Microbrews, wine and pizza too.

Clinton Street Theater
CINEMA

(Map p224; ☑ 503-238-5588; www.clintonsttheater.com; 2522 SE Clinton St) Old neighborhood theater screening independent and revival films. *The Rocky Horror Picture Show* plays every Saturday night at midnight, and has done so for over 35 years.

Mission Theater
CINEMA

(Map p220; ☑ 503-223-4527; www.mcmenamins.com; 1624 NW Glisan St) Come early for a front-row balcony seat at this beautiful McMenamins theater.

Theater & Performing Arts

Arlene Schnitzer Concert Hall
CLASSICAL MUSIC

(Map p220; ☑ 503-228-1353; www.pcpa.com/schnitzer; 1037 SW Broadway) The Oregon Symphony performs in this beautiful, if not acoustically brilliant, downtown venue.

Artists Repertory Theatre
THEATER

(Map p220; ☑ 503-241-1278; www.artistsrep.org; 1515 SW Morrison St) Some of Portland's best plays, including regional premieres, are performed in two intimate theaters.

Keller Auditorium
THEATER

(Map p220; ☑ 503-248-4335; www.pcpa.com/keller; 222 SW Clay St) The Portland Opera and Oregon Ballet Theatre stage performances here, along with some Broadway productions.

Portland Center Stage
THEATER

(Map p220; ☑ 503-445-3700; www.pcs.org; 128 NW 11th Ave) The city's main theater company now performs in the Portland Armory – a newly renovated Pearl District landmark with state-of-the-art features.

Gay & Lesbian Venues

For current listings see *Just Out* (www.justout.com), Portland's free gay biweekly. Or check out *Gay and Lesbian Community Yellow Pages* (www.pdxgayyellowpages.com) for other services. For more information, see www.travelportland.com/lgbt.

Stark St, around SW 10th St, has several edgy gay bars. For an upscale, mixed-crowd bar, lesbians should head east to **Crush** (Map p224; www.crushbar.com; 1400 SE Morrison St).

CC Slaughters
CLUB

(Map p220; ☑ 503-248-9135; www.ccslaughterspdx.com; 219 NW Davis St) Popular and long-running nightclub with big, loud dance floor, laser light show and good DJs. When you tire of shaking bootie, head over to the Rainbow Room, the relaxed lounge where you can actually have a conversation. Cheap drinks from 10pm to 11pm on Friday and Saturday, plus a Sunday-night drag show and fun themed nights.

Silverado
CLUB

(Map p220; ☑ 503-224-4493; www.silveradopdx.com; 318 SW 3rd Ave) Almost nightly stripper shows (Monday is karaoke) catering to men. Mixed crowd, cheap drinks, potential groping and muscled dancers, so bring plenty of dollar bills and expect a wild time.

Hobo's
RESTAURANT, PIANO BAR

(Map p220; ☑ 503-224-3285; www.hobospdx.com; 120 NW 3rd Ave) Past the old historic storefront here is a classy restaurant–piano lounge popular with older gay men. It's a quiet, relaxed place and good for a romantic dinner or drink; for some activity, head to the pool tables in back. Live music starts at 8pm from Wednesday to Sunday.

Darcelle XV
CABARET

(Map p220; ☑ 503-222-5338; www.darcellexv.com; 208 NW 3rd Ave; ☺ shows Wed-Sat) Portland's Vegas-style cabaret show, featuring glitzy drag queens in big wigs, fake jewelry and overstuffed bras. Musical performances are spiced with corny comedy while hapless audience members are picked out and teased. Male strippers perform at midnight on Friday and Saturday.

Sport

Trail Blazers
SPECTATOR SPORT

(www.nba.com/blazers) Rip City's major league basketball team; they play at the Moda Center (formerly the Rose Garden Arena).

Winter Hawks
SPECTATOR SPORT

(www.winterhawks.com) Beervana's major junior hockey team.

Timbers
SPECTATOR SPORT

(www.portlandtimbers.com) PDX's major-league soccer franchise.

Portland Thorns
SPECTATOR SPORT

(www.portlandtimbers.com/thornsfc) The City of Roses' professional women's soccer team, which plays in the National Women's Soccer League (NWSL). The team won the league's inaugural championship in 2013!

Rose City Rollers
SPECTATOR SPORT

(www.rosecityrollers.com) Roller derby in Stumptown? You bet.

🛍 Shopping

Portland's downtown shopping district extends in a two-block radius from Pioneer Courthouse Sq. **Pioneer Place** – an upscale mall – is between SW Morrison and SW Yamhill Sts, east of the square. Large shopping mall the Lloyd Center is on the eastside.

The Pearl District is full of high-end galleries, boutiques and home-decor shops – and don't miss Powell's City of Books. On the first Thursday of each month galleries stay open longer and people fill some of the Pearl's streets amid a party atmosphere. And on weekends there's the fun Saturday Market.

Northwest's fanciest shopping street is NW 23rd Ave, nicknamed 'trendy-third.' This is where Portland's branches of Gap, Pottery Barn and Restoration Hardware live, among many other fancy stores and people.

Eastside has many trendy shopping streets that also host restaurants, cafes and bars. SE Hawthorne Blvd is the biggest of these, N Mississippi Ave is the most recent and NE Alberta is the most artsy and funky.

If you're feeling up for the drive, find outlet malls at Woodburn Company Stores (in Woodburn, about 30 miles south of Portland) or Columbia Gorge Premium Outlets (in Troutdale, just east of Portland). And for some fun, off-the-beaten-path shops, visit www.portlandpicks.com.

★ Powell's City of Books
BOOKS

(Map p220; ☑503-228-4651; www.powells.com; 1005 W Burnside St; ☺9am-11pm) One of the USA's largest independent bookstores, with a whole city block of new and used titles. Has other branches around town, including at 3723 and 3747 SE Hawthorne.

Music Millennium
MUSIC

(Map p224; ☑503-231-8926; www.musicmillennium.com; 3158 E Burnside St; ☺10am-10pm Mon-Sat, 11am-9pm Sun) In an age of dying record shops, this place is a revelation. Extensive collections of everything from classic rock to straight-up classical. Check the listings of live in-store performances and grab a 'Keep Portland Weird!' sticker while you're here.

Union Rose
CLOTHING

(☑503-287-4242; www.unionrosepdx.com; 7909 SE Stark Ave; ☺10am-6pm Mon-Sat, 11am-5pm Sun) Located to the east in the increasingly hip neighborhood of Montaville is this women's clothing boutique showcasing unique, locally designed and handcrafted goods. Feminine without the fluff. Also some men's and kids' things.

Next Adventure
OUTDOOR EQUIPMENT, CLOTHING

(Map p224; ☑503-233-0706; www.nextadventure.net; 426 SE Grand Ave; ☺10am-7pm Mon-Fri, to 6pm Sat, 11am-5pm Sun) Awesome outdoor store with plenty of sport clothing (including discounted items) and gear for hiking, camping, skiing and whatever else you had in mind. Also a downstairs 'bargain basement' of used clothing and gear.

Flutter
GIFTS

(☑503-288-1649; www.flutterclutter.com; 3948 N Mississippi Ave; ☺11am-6pm Mon-Sat, to 5pm Sun) Cool N Mississippi Ave shop with reclaimed and refurbished items for the home, vintage jewelry, birdcages, Gothic wedding gowns, ornate pillows and feathery hats.

Frock Boutique
CLOTHING

(☑503-595-0379; www.frockboutique.com; 1439 NE Alberta St; ☺10am-6pm Tue-Sat, to 4pm Sun & Mon) One of Alberta St's most whimsical and eclectic clothing stores. Screen-printed T-shirts, sundresses, woolen hats, jewelry, onesies for babies and more (even for the guys).

Land
GIFTS

(☑503-451-0689; www.landpdx.com; 3925 N Mississippi Ave; ☺10am-6pm) Unique, fun and crafty gifts of all kinds, plus an art gallery upstairs. Famous as the setting for the *Portlandia* 'Put a bird on it' episode.

Mag-Big
GIFTS

(Map p224; ☑503-236-6120; www.magbig.com; 3279 SE Hawthorne Ave; ☺11am-7pm Tue-Sun) Consignment store offering the work of around 500 local artists, designers and craftspersons. Score a dress made from vintage bedsheets, a pair of acorn earrings or some vegan soap. Art viewings and sewing classes too.

Queen Bee Creations
BAGS

(☑503-232-1755; www.queenbee-creations.com; 3961 N Williams Ave; ☺10am-7pm Mon-Sat, 11am-5pm Sun) One-of-a-kind faux-leather and supercute bags, wallets and bike panniers sewn on-site.

Halo Shoes
SHOES

(Map p220; ☑503-331-0366; www.haloshoes.com; 938 NW Everett St; ☺11am-6pm Mon-Sat, noon-5pm Sun) Gorgeous, high-end designer shoes for both women and men, with knowledge-

A ROSE, BY ANY OTHER NAME...

Portland seems to have endless nicknames; here are a few:

➡ **City of Roses** Roses do well here.

➡ **PDX** Portland's airport code.

➡ **Stumptown** Many stumps were created to make this town.

➡ **Bridge City** There are 10 bridges over the Willamette!

➡ **River City** Referring to the Willamette, not the nearby Columbia.

➡ **Beervana** Local microbrews are tops.

➡ **Rip City** Coined by a sportscaster during a Trail Blazer game.

➡ **Little Beirut** Courtesy of George HW Bush, during his visit here.

➡ **P-Town** It's shorter than Portland.

➡ **Portlandia** Due to the hit cable show.

able service personnel to go along. You'll need a very fat wallet, but you won't get better-quality shoes. Nice handbags too.

Tender Loving Empire GIFTS
(Map p220; ☑ 503-243-5859; www.tenderlovingempire.com; 412 SW 10th Ave; ☺ 11am-6pm) Small gift shop selling unique and fun handmade goods. Also multitasks as an independent record label, screen-printing shop and art gallery. Can you guess it's really into promoting local art and creativity?

Hand Eye Supply CLOTHING, TOOLS, STATIONERY
(Map p220; ☑ 503-575-9769; www.handeyesupply.com; 23 NW 4th Ave; ☺ 11am-6pm) For the hip industrial artist or craftsperson who needs to look good while creating. There's tough workwear, fancy pencils and markers, good-looking shop tools, upscale leather tool bags and slick toolboxes.

Broadway Books BOOKS
(☑ 503-284-1726; www.broadwaybooks.net; 1714 NE Broadway; ☺ 10am-7pm Mon-Sat, noon-5pm Sun) Good general, independent bookstore with especially strong literary fiction, biography and Judaica sections.

In Other Words BOOKS
(☑ 503-232-6003; www.inotherwords.org; 14 NE Killingsworth St; ☺ noon-7pm Tue-Sat) Nonprofit feminist bookstore parodied in *Portlandia* episodes. Plenty of community events take place here, and it's a valuable resource center as well.

❶ Information

EMERGENCY & MEDICAL SERVICES

Call ☑ 911 for medical, fire or crime emergencies.

Legacy Good Samaritan Medical Center
(☑ 503-413-7711; www.legacyhealth.org; 1015 NW 22nd Ave) Convenient to downtown.

Portland Police (☑ 503-823-0000; www.portlandoregon.gov/police; 1111 SW 2nd Ave)

INTERNET ACCESS

Practically all coffee shops have wi-fi. All libraries in Multnomah County (Portland's county) have free internet access and wi-fi.

Backspace (☑ 503-248-2900; www.backspace.bz; 115 NW 5th Ave; ☺ 7am-midnight Mon-Fri, 10am-midnight Sat & Sun) This youth-oriented hangout has arcade games, Stumptown coffee, vegetarian snacks, live music, long hours and – of course – internet access.

Central Library (☑ 503-988-5123; www.multcolib.org; 801 SW 10th Ave) Downtown; for other branches check the website.

MEDIA

KBOO 90.7 FM (www.kboo.fm) Progressive local radio station run by volunteers; alternative news and views.

Portland Independent Media Center (www.portland.indymedia.org) Open publishing source of community news and lefty activism.

Portland Mercury (www.portlandmercury.com) The free local sibling of Seattle's the *Stranger*.

Willamette Week (www.wweek.com) Free weekly covering local news and culture.

MONEY

Portland is full of banks with exchange services and ATMs. **Travelex** (☑ 503-281-3045; ☺ 5:30am-4:30pm) is at the Portland airport, in the main ticket lobby.

POST

Post Office (Map p220; ☑ 503-525-5398; www.usps.com; 715 NW Hoyt St; ☺ 8am-

6:30pm Mon-Fri, 8:30am-5pm Sat) Many branches around town.

TOURIST INFORMATION

Nature of the Northwest Visitor Center (☏971-673-2331; www.naturenw.org; 800 NE Oregon St, Suite 965; ☺9am-12:30pm & 1-4pm Mon-Fri) Offers geologic information on Oregon; has books, brochures and all kinds of maps.

Portland Oregon Visitors Association (Map p220; www.travelportland.com; 701 SW 6th Ave; ☺8:30am-5:30pm Mon-Fri, 10am-4pm Sat, to 2pm Sun) Superfriendly volunteers staff this office in Pioneer Courthouse Sq. There's a small theater with a 12-minute film about the city, and Tri-Met bus and light-rail offices inside.

❶ Getting There & Away

AIR

Award-winning **Portland International Airport** (PDX; ☏503-460-4234; www.flypdx.com; 7000 NE Airport Way) provides service all over the country, as well as to several international destinations. Amenities include restaurants, money changers, bookstores (including three Powell's branches) and other services like free wi-fi. It's also well connected to downtown and other parts of Portland via light rail.

BUS

Greyhound buses leave from its **depot** (Map p220; ☏503-243-2361; www.greyhound.com; 550 NW 6th Ave) and connect Portland with cities along I-5 and I-84. Destinations include Chicago, Boise, Denver, San Francisco, Seattle and Vancouver, BC.

If you're traveling between Portland, Seattle and Vancouver, BC, try **Bolt bus** (☏877-265-8287; www.boltbus.com), which provides service in large buses with wi-fi and power outlets.

TRAIN

Amtrak (☏503-273-4865; www.amtrak.com; 800 NW 6th Ave), at Union Station, offers services up and down the West Coast. The *Empire Builder* travels to Chicago, the *Cascades* goes to Vancouver, BC, and the *Coast Starlight* runs between Seattle and LA.

❶ Getting Around

TO/FROM THE AIRPORT

PDX is about 10 miles northeast of downtown, next to the Columbia River. Tri-Met's light-rail MAX line takes about 40 minutes to get from downtown to the airport. If you prefer a bus, **Blue Star** (☏503-249-1837; www.bluestarbus.

com) offers shuttle services between PDX and several downtown stops.

Taxis charge around $34 (not including tip) from the airport to downtown.

BICYCLE

It's easy riding a bicycle around Portland, often voted 'the most bike-friendly city in America.'

Clever Cycles (☏503-334-1560; www.clever-cycles.com/rentals; 900 SE Hawthorne Blvd)

Everybody's Bike Rentals (☏503-358-0152; www.pdxbikerentals.com; cnr NE 19th Ave & Going St)

Waterfront Bicycle Rentals (☏503-227-1719; www.waterfrontbikes.com; 10 SW Ash St; per day $40)

BUS, LIGHT RAIL & STREETCAR

Portland has a good public-transportation system, which consists of local buses, streetcars and the MAX light rail. All are run by Tri-Met, which has an **information center** (☏503-238-7433; www.trimet.org; 701 SW 6th Ave; ☺8:30am-5:30pm Mon-Fri) at Pioneer Courthouse Sq.

Tickets for the transportation systems are completely transferable within two hours of the time of purchase. Buy tickets for local buses from fare machines as you enter; for streetcars, you can buy tickets either at streetcar stations or on the streetcar itself. Tickets for the MAX must be bought from ticket machines at MAX stations (*before* you board); there is no conductor or ticket-seller on board (but there *are* enforcers).

If you're a night owl, be aware that there are fewer services at night, and only a few run past 1am; check the website for details on a specific line.

CAR

Most major car-rental agencies have outlets both downtown and at Portland's airport (PDX). Many of these agencies have added hybrid vehicles to their fleets. **Zipcar** (www.zipcar.com) is a popular car-sharing option, but there are many.

CHARTER SERVICE

For custom bus or van charters and tours, try **EcoShuttle** (☏503-548-4480; www.ecoshuttle.net). Its vehicles run on 100% biodiesel.

PEDICAB

For an ecofriendly option, contact one of the several pedicab operators in town, including **PDX Pedicab.** (☏503-828-9888; www.pdxpedicab.com). It utilizes bicycle pedicabs with 'drivers' that pedal you around downtown.

The Willamette Valley & Wine Country

Includes ➡

Best Places to Eat

➡ Painted Lady (p247)

➡ Red Hills Market (p247)

➡ Bistro Maison (p250)

➡ Crescent Cafe (p249)

➡ Beppe & Gianni's Trattoria (p258)

Best Places to Stay

➡ Allison Inn & Spa (p247)

➡ Abbey Road Farm B&B (p247)

➡ C'est La Vie Inn (p257)

➡ McMenamins Hotel Oregon (p249)

Why Go?

The Willamette Valley is world famous for its fabulous and plentiful wineries, which could easily take several days to explore. However, they're not the region's only highlight. Visit humble Salem, Oregon's capital city, for its museums and stately buildings. Nearby is an amazing waterfall-filled state park, along with a lovely abbey that's home to a 2.5lb hairball (no joke). Pause in dynamic and liberal Eugene, full of energetic college students, pretty riverside parks and fine restaurants. And don't forget historic Oregon City, the lovely McKenzie River area and the region's wealth of festivals.

The Willamette Valley is well located: head east to the Columbia River Gorge, north to Washington and west to the coast. Everything is so close by you'll want to linger for longer than you planned, so stretch that schedule and put on your explorer's hat – you'll need it.

When to Go
Eugene

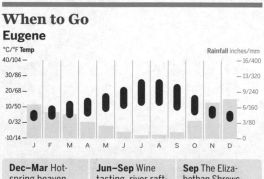

Dec–Mar Hot-spring heaven at Bagby, Beiten-bush or the Belknap Hot Springs Lodge.

Jun–Sep Wine tasting, river rafting, and walking behind waterfalls at Silver Falls State Park.

Sep The Eliza-bethan Shrews-bury Renaissance Faire and the artsy Fall Festival.

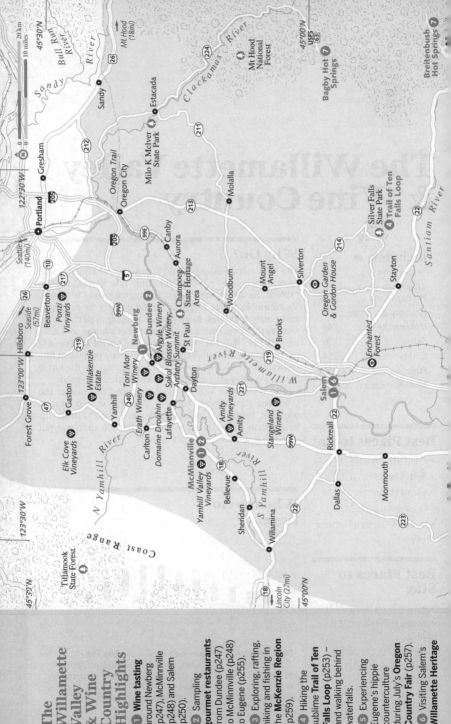

The Willamette Valley & Wine Country Highlights

1 **Wine tasting** around Newberg (p247), McMinnville (p248) and Salem (p250).

2 Sampling **gourmet restaurants** from Dundee (p247) to McMinnville (p248) to Eugene (p255).

3 Exploring, rafting, hiking and fishing in the **McKenzie Region** (p259).

4 Hiking the sublime **Trail of Ten Falls Loop** (p253) – and walking behind waterfalls.

5 Experiencing Eugene's hippie counterculture during July's **Oregon Country Fair** (p257).

6 Visiting Salem's **Willamette Heritage**

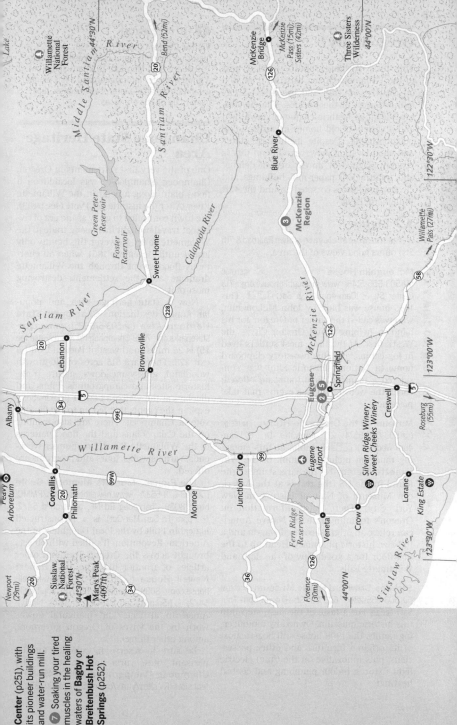

Center (p251), with its pioneer buildings and water-run mill.

⑦ Soaking your tired muscles in the healing waters of **Bagby** or **Breitenbush Hot Springs** (p252).

Oregon City

POP 32,000

This little Portland suburb, nestled next to the Willamette River, was the final stop on the Oregon Trail and the first US city founded west of the Rockies. The city features a bit of historic character downtown and a variety of old homes in surrounding neighborhoods. Despite its historic status and good location, however, Oregon City is visually plagued by an expanse of defunct and unattractive paper-mill buildings and electric generators corseted around the 42ft Willamette Falls.

◉ Sights

A free **municipal elevator** (btwn Railroad & 7th Sts) offers good views of the area.

McLoughlin House   HISTORIC
(☑503-656-5146; www.mcloughlinhouse.org; 713 Center St; ☺10am-4pm Fri & Sat) **FREE** This 1845 house was built by John McLoughlin, who was called the 'father of Oregon' for his hand in helping found Oregon City – the West's first. At the time, most settlers lived in log cabins, and this two-story clapboard home (a National Historic Site) was considered a mansion. Free tours are offered; check the website for free events that take place here.

Museum of the Oregon Territory   MUSEUM
(☑503-655-5574; 211 Tumwater Dr; ☺11am-4pm Wed-Sat) **FREE** Exhibits at this engaging museum include a chunk of the **Willamette Meteorite**, the largest meteorite found in the US (the rest is at the American Museum of Natural History in New York City). There's also information on Oregon's founding fathers, Native American relics, an original covered wagon and a full-size historic pharmacy. Head up to the 3rd floor for a good view of the dam and Willamette Falls.

Stevens-Crawford House Museum MUSEUM
(☑503-655-2866; 603 6th St; ☺noon-4pm Thu-Sat) **FREE** For a taste of the past, step into this historic museum. Owned by a pioneering family, the 1908 house still boasts most of its original furniture and other possessions, plus innovative (at the time) electric light fixtures, indoor plumbing and central heating!

❶ Information

Visitor Center (☑503-657-9336; www.historicoregoncity.com; 1726 Washington St; ☺9:30am-5pm Mon-Sat, 10:30am-5pm Sun) A good place for information and a few pioneer exhibits from an old interpretive center that used to be on the premises.

Champoeg State Heritage Area

One of the very first settlements in Oregon, Champoeg (shampoo-e) was located on a flood plain along a bend in the Willamette River. After the historic 1843 vote (see p433), the town continued to grow as the era of riverboat travel brought increasing trade to the Willamette Valley. However, this bounty only lasted until December 1861, when an enormous flood swept through the Willamette drainage and the settlement, destroying most of it.

Now a state heritage area and popular family destination, **Champoeg State Heritage Area** (☑503-678-1251; www.oregonstateparks.org; 7679 Champoeg Rd NE; day-use fee $5) is 25 miles southwest of Portland, off I-5 exit 278. There are 615 acres of old-growth woodland, grassy meadows, nature trails, historic sites and campgrounds. Films and displays at the **visitors center** (☺9am-5pm) explain the events that led up to the famous vote at Champoeg. There are also exhibits on the Calapooians and the flood patterns of the Willamette River. On summer weekends, various walks, tours and programs are offered.

The **Pioneer Mothers Memorial Cabin** (☑503-678-5537; www.newellhouse.com/PMMC.html; 8089 Champoeg Rd NE; adult/child $4/2; ☺1-5pm Fri-Sun Mar-Oct) is a reconstructed log cabin built by the local Daughters of the American Revolution. It's filled with objects brought across the Oregon Trail and other articles of frontier life. The 1852 **Robert Newell House** (☑503-678-5537; www.newellhouse.com; 8089 Champoeg Rd NE; adult/child $4/2; ☺1-5pm Fri-Sun Mar-Oct) houses Native American artifacts and inaugural gowns worn by the wives of Oregon governors, among other things.

Be sure to reserve in summer for the pleasant sites, yurts and cabins at the **Champoeg Campground** (☑800-452-5687; tent sites/RV sites/yurts/cabins $19/24/36/39).

Newberg & Dundee

The gateways to wine country, these small cities were originally founded as Quaker settlements. Now little of those original quiet ways remain, and strip malls and modern services are much of what you'll see. There are excellent restaurants here, however, along with upscale places to sleep. Dundee is 2 miles west of Newberg, on Hwy 99W. For transportation information see McMinnville (p250).

◉ Sights

Hoover-Minthorn House   MUSEUM
(☑503-538-6629; 115 S River St, Newberg; adult/child 10yr & under $3/50¢; ⊙1-4pm Wed-Sun Mar-Nov, 1-4pm Sat & Sun Dec & Feb, closed Jan) This house is where Herbert Hoover (the 31st president of the USA) grew up. Built in 1881, the restored home is now a museum of period furnishings and early Oregon history.

🛏 Sleeping & Eating

The closest camping is at Champoeg State Heritage Area, about 7 miles southeast of Newberg. Inexpensive chain hotels and motels exist in Newberg.

Expect mostly local and seasonal ingredients at the region's top-drawer restaurants, along with changing menus and exceptional wine lists.

★**Allison Inn & Spa**   RESORT $$$
(☑877-294-2525, 503-554-2525; www.theallison.com; 2525 Allison Lane, Newberg; d from $330; ❋🛜❋🛝) 🍴 If luxury is what you seek, then you seek the Allison. From its spacious, plush rooms to its relaxing soaking tubs to its excellent restaurant and great services (including a spa), your needs will be met. Great stone landscaping, with its own vineyard nearby, and it's ecofriendly to boot – solar panels grace most roofs, while hybrid/electric cars have their own parking spots.

★**Abbey Road Farm B&B**   B&B $$$
(☑503-852-6278; www.abbeyroadfarm.com; 10501 NE Abbey Rd, Carlton; d $225; ❋🛜) For the ultimate country experience, head 8 miles west of Newberg to this working farm with lush vegetable garden and farm animals. Your hosts John and Judi have created a serene spot with modern comforts – you'll sleep in unique silos converted into five contemporary rooms with simple luxuries like Jacuzzis and memory-foam beds. You can milk goats and sample the cheese Judi makes. A three-bedroom house is also available.

★**Red Hills Market**   AMERICAN $
(☑971-832-8414; www.redhillsmarket.com; 155 SW 7th St, Dundee; mains $9-13; ⊙7am-8pm) This deli-market offers great atmosphere, with its wines and gourmet food products surrounding diners in the main room. Head to the back patio to enjoy your toasted, open-faced 'craft' sandwich, made from fancy charcuterie. A few salads and wood-fired pizzas are also available.

Dundee Bistro   NORTHWESTERN $$
(☑503-554-1650; www.dundeebistro.com; 100 SW 7th St, Dundee; mains $14-29; ⊙11:30am-9pm) Modern, popular restaurant, owned by Ponzi Vineyards and with wine-tasting room next door. Dishes like dry aged New York steak and pappardelle pasta with lamb *sugo* (a rich sauce) grace the menu, while the gourmet pizza offers a more casual option. On warm days go for the great back patio.

★**Painted Lady**   NORTHWESTERN $$$
(☑503-538-3850; www.thepaintedladyrestaurant.com; 201 S College St, Newberg; prix fixe $65-85; ⊙5-10pm Wed-Sun) 🍴 Accomplished chefs Allen Routt and Jessica Bagley use their wide travel and culinary experiences at this renowned restaurant in a renovated 1890s Victorian house. The multicourse menus include an appetizer, main dish and dessert (vegetarian choices available), with the option for a wine pairing.

Tina's   NORTHWESTERN $$$
(☑503-538-8880; www.tinasdundee.com; 760 Hwy 99W, Dundee; mains $28-34; ⊙11:30am-2pm & 5-9pm Tue-Fri, 5-9pm Sat & Sun) 🍴 This small, renowned and French-influenced restaurant does meat dishes like wild salmon, pork, rabbit and duck to perfection. Lunch is a more casual and affordable alternative, with mains in the $12 to $14 range. Expect local, organic and seasonal ingredients.

Red Hills Provincial Dining NORTHWESTERN $$$
(☑503-538-8224; www.redhills-dining.com; 276 Hwy 99W, Dundee; mains $28-30; ⊙5-9pm Tue-Sun) 🍴 Just off Hwy 99 is this excellent, award-winning restaurant in an old arts-and-crafts house. The European-influenced dishes range from grilled halibut with tarragon aioli to *favette* pasta with prosciutto to pork osso buco. Don't miss the desserts.

OREGON'S WINE BOUNTY

Oregon's first wineries started up in the 1850s, but it wasn't until the late 1960s and early 1970s that the region's modern winemaking potential started to bear fruit. The northern Willamette Valley's mild climate and long summers foster the delicate pinot noir grape, and pinot gris, chardonnay and riesling as well.

Most vineyards are family owned and welcome visitors to their tasting rooms, which range from grand edifices to homey affairs tucked into the corner of fermentation rooms. Before heading out, you may want to check wineries' tasting-room hours and tasting fees (usually $5 to $10). Get a winery map at McMinnville's Chamber of Commerce (p250; or see www.willamettewines.com), which will help you get a feel for the region's more than 400 wineries. And remember to pack a lunch; wineries usually can't offer food, but sometimes have picnic grounds.

You don't have to visit wineries to sip the region's wines, however. Some of the bigger wineries' tasting rooms have been popping up in many of the area's downtowns. And there are always the region's fine restaurants, with their excellent wine lists.

A Few Wineries

Argyle Winery (☑888-427-4953; www.argylewinery.com; 691 Hwy 99W, Dundee) Impressive sparkling wines.

Chehalem (☑503-538-4700; www.chehalemwines.com; 106 S Center St, Newberg) Private tastings at the winery; public tastings at its Newberg tasting room.

Domaine Drouhin (☑503-864-2700; www.domainedrouhin.com; 6750 Breymen Orchards Rd, Dayton) For grand atmosphere and panoramic views.

ℹ Information

Chamber of Commerce (☑503-538-2014; www.chelamvalley.org; 115 N College St, Newberg; ⊙9am-5pm Mon-Fri, 11am-5pm Sat & Sun) Local information, along with a wine-educational video and tasting room (usually open summer weekends).

McMinnville

POP 33,000

At the heart of the region's wine industry lies busy and modern McMinnville, mostly charmless except for its historic, red-brick downtown district. Here you'll find art galleries, boutiques, wine-tasting rooms and fine restaurants. There are some fine old buildings; see the tourist office for a pamphlet. The main regional attractions are the area's fine wineries, of course.

◉ Sights & Activities

★**Evergreen Aviation & Space Museum**   MUSEUM
(☑503-434-4180; www.evergreenmuseum.org; 500 NE Captain Michael King Smith Way; adult/child 5-16yr incl 3-D movie $25/23; ⊙9am-5pm) A mile east of McMinnville, this museum showcases Howard Hughes' *Spruce Goose*, the world's largest wood-framed airplane. In

1947, with Hughes at the wheel, the airplane flew for just under a mile – and never took off again. Plenty of other aircraft are on display, including propeller planes, small jets, fighters, biplanes and helicopters. A different building offers extensive and excellent space-exploration exhibits. There's also has a 3-D digital theater, along with two cafes and gift shops. Tours available.

★**Evergreen Wings & Waves Waterpark**   WATER PARK
(☑503-434-4185; www.evergreenmuseum.org; 500 NE Captain Michael King Smith Way; visitors under/over 42in $27/32, dry passes $12; ⊙10am-8pm, varies with season) A must on a hot summer day, this impressive indoor water park is next to the Evergreen Aviation & Space Museum and quite unmissable – a retired Boeing 747 lies atop the building. Inside are 10 water slides (including four that come out of the 747), a wave pool, splashing play structure, leisure pool and bubbly toddler area. Plenty of lifeguards keep everyone safe.

✸ Festivals & Events

Turkey Rama   FOOD
(⊙Jul) Anchored by 'the world's largest' turkey barbecue.

Eyrie Vineyards (☎503-472-6315; www.eyrievineyards.com; 935 NE 10th Ave, McMinnville) The first pinot noir and chardonnay plantings in the Willamette Valley, and the first pinot gris plantings in the USA. Tasting room in McMinnville.

Sokol Blosser Winery (☎800-582-6668; www.sokolblosser.com; 5000 Sokol Blosser Lane, Dundee) A view of Mt Hood goes nicely with the pinot noir here.

Willakenzie Estate (☎503-662-3280; www.willakenzie.com; 19143 NE Laughlin Rd, Yamhill) Tucked in the beautiful rolling Chehalem Hills near Yamhill.

Yamhill Valley Vineyards (☎503-843-3100; www.yamhill.com; 16250 NW Oldsville Rd, McMinnville) Try the pinot gris; west of McMinnville.

Wine Tours

If you'd rather just sit back, drink and be driven, wine tours are offered. A few are listed below.

EcoTours of Oregon (☎503-245-1428; www.ecotours-of-oregon.com) Wine country tours, among many others.

Equestrian Wine Tours (☎503-864-2336; www.equestrianwinetours.com) Tour on horseback.

Grape Escape (☎503-283-3380; www.grapeescapetours.com) Long-running outfit offering a variety of wine tours.

Oregon Wine Tours (☎503-681-9463; www.orwinetours.com) Custom wine tours.

UFO Festival UFOS
(www.ufofest.com; ⊙May) Join with other believers to celebrate the aliens among us. Or just come for the food and costume parade.

🛏 Sleeping

There are many chain hotels and motels in McMinnville, along with 28 B&Bs in the county.

⭐**McMenamins Hotel Oregon** HOTEL $
(☎503-472-8427; www.mcmenamins.com; 310 NE Evans St; d $75-145; ✳🛜🐾) Expect the typical McMenamins eccentricities at this funky hotel, like eclectic artwork; there's also an unbeatable rooftop restaurant-pub, mandatory for drinks on warm summer nights. Most of the classic old rooms share bathrooms, which are kept in good order.

Joseph Mattey House B&B B&B $$
(☎503-434-5058; www.josephmatteyhouse.com; 10221 NE Mattey Lane; d $165-190; ✳🛜) About 3 miles northeast of town is this 1892 Queen Anne Victorian farmhouse featuring country-style atmosphere, charming old details and four comfortable rooms with quilts, lace and private bathrooms. There's a great wraparound porch, plus a vineyard right past the lawn, and it's run by English owners.

Steiger Haus B&B B&B $$
(☎503-472-0821; www.steigerhaus.com; 360 Wilson St; d $95-150; ✳🛜) This friendly, casual home offers a little paradise right in downtown McMinnville. It's on a half-acre and features a hilly, woodsy backyard with good bird-watching. Five comfortable bedrooms are available, each with its own bathroom and some with a deck just outside.

Youngberg Hill Vineyard & Inn INN $$$
(☎888-657-8668; www.youngberghill.com; 10660 SW Youngberg Hill Rd; d incl breakfast $220-350; ✳@🛜) You'll get panoramic views from this luxury inn atop a 700ft hill. The eight rooms and suites are very nice, but reserve ahead of time – especially for summer weekends, which are popular for weddings. Afternoon wine reception also included; it's about 8 miles west of town.

🍴 Eating

There's good eating in McMinnville. For average pub fare with above-average views, head to the Hotel Oregon's rooftop resto-pub.

⭐**Crescent Cafe** AMERICAN $$
(☎503-435-2655; 526 NE 3rd St; mains $8-11; ⊙7am-1pm Wed-Fri, 8am-1pm Sat & Sun) Truly excellent breakfast spot with gourmet treats

CELEBRATING WINE

Held in late July, the **International Pinot Noir Celebration** (www.ipnc.org; McMinnville) is an important testing ground for pinot noir wines from all over the world. The three-day festival is immensely popular despite costing $975 per person (including some meals); there's a public tasting ($125) on Sunday.

A more egalitarian event, the **McMinnville Wine & Food Classic** (www.sipclassic.org) is held at the aviation museum in March.

like creamed chicken and biscuits with eggs, or grilled ham and cheddar sandwich with caramelized onions (the menu changes seasonally). If available, try the blood orange mimosa and cinnamon roll. Gourmet sandwiches for lunch. Expect a long wait on weekends.

La Rambla   SPANISH **$$**
(☑503-435-2126;   www.laramblaonthird.com; 238 NE 3rd St; tapas $6-16; ☺11:30am-2:30pm & 4-9pm Sun-Thu, 11:30am-10pm Sat & Sun) Try as many dishes as possible by ordering several tapas at this upscale, atmospheric restaurant. Pasta and paella mains are also available if you don't want to share.

Golden Valley Brewery   AMERICAN **$$**
(☑503-472-2739;   www.goldenvalleybrewery.com; 980 NE 4th St; mains $9-31; ☺11am-10pm Mon-Sat, to 9pm Sun) This top-notch brewery-restaurant offers great salads, sandwiches and pastas, along with gourmet burgers and steaks – made from meat from its own ranch!

★**Bistro Maison**   FRENCH **$$$**
(☑503-474-1888; www.bistromaison.com; 729 NE 3rd St; mains $24-28; ☺11:30am-2pm & 5-8pm Wed-Thu, 11:30am-2pm & 5-9pm Fri, 5-9pm Sat, noon-8pm Sun) This European eatery is one of McMinnville's best restaurants, serving up exceptional French dishes like duck *confit cassoulet* and *cote de boeuf*. Try the ground-to-order, dry-aged sirloin hamburger for lunch (mains $12 to $15). The lovely garden patio is mandatory on warm summer nights.

Joel Palmer House   NORTHWESTERN **$$$**
(☑503-864-2995; www.joelpalmerhouse.com; 600 Ferry St; prix fixe $49-80; ☺4:30-9:30pm

Tue-Sat) ✐ Renowned for its dishes laced with wild mushrooms (often hand-picked by the chef, Christopher Czarnecki), this highly lauded restaurant is just a few miles northwest of McMinnville. It's one of Oregon's finest eateries, turning local ingredients into unforgettable fine cuisine.

Thistle   NORTHWESTERN **$$$**
(☑503-472-9623; www.thistlerestaurant.com; 228 NE Evans St; mains $24-27; ☺5:30-9pm Tue-Sat) ✐ Small but top-drawer restaurant run by Eric Bechard, an award-winning chef who fiercely believes in using local, organic ingredients whenever possible. The menu changes daily and is posted on a chalkboard, and while portions are small they are well created and truly delicious.

❶ Information

Chamber of Commerce (☑503-472-6196; www.mcminnville.org; 417 NW Adams St; ☺9am-5pm Mon-Fri)

❶ Getting There & Around

Renting a car is the best way to see this region, especially if you want to visit wineries. For wine-tour information see the Oregon's Wine Bounty boxed text on p248.

Caravan Airport Transportation (www.caravanairporttransportation.com) and **Royal Shuttle** (☑503-554-0005) provide shuttle services from Portland's airport.

Valley Retriever (www.kokkola-bus.com) has buses to Corvallis, Salem, Portland and the coast. **Yamhill County Transit Area** (www.yctransitarea.org) provides bus service around Yamhill County, with connections to the Portland MAX system and Salem.

Salem

POP 157,000

The state capital is a peaceful and homely university city that exudes a slightly conservative air and is a popular destination for conferences. Salem makes a good day trip from Portland as it's just an hour's drive south. Highlights include the state capitol itself and a few museums, along with a pleasant riverfront park complete with carousel. Outside the city limits are more interesting destinations like a spectacular state park, an interesting hilltop abbey and a beautiful themed garden.

◎ Sights

Willamette Heritage Center MUSEUM
(☑503-585-7012; www.willametteheritage.org; 1313 Mill St SE; adult/child 6-17yr $6/3; ☉10am-5pm Mon-Sat) This interesting 5-acre complex houses grassy gardens, two gift shops, a clutch of pioneer buildings and two museums.

The **Mission Mill Museum**, the **Jason Lee House** (1841), the **John Boon House** (1847), the **Methodist Parsonage** (1841) and an **old Presbyterian church** (1858) all look pretty much as they did in the 1840s and 1850s. The **Thomas Kay Woolen Mill** was built in 1889 and was powered by a mill race (waterway), a section of which still runs through the grounds. Free access to museum grounds.

Oregon State Capitol LANDMARK
(900 Court St NE) FREE The state's first capitol building burned down in 1855, and a domed classic-Roman edifice was built to replace it. Unfortunately, that building also burned down (in 1935), and the current capitol building was completed in 1938. Bauhaus and art-deco influences are apparent, especially in the strident bas-relief in the front statuary and the hatbox-like cupola. The building is faced with white Danby Vermont marble, and the interior is lined with rose travertine from Montana.

The most notable features of the capitol are four Works Progress Administration–era **murals** lining the interior of the rotunda. There's also a galleria with changing exhibits, plus a cafe. Surmounting the capitol building's top is the gleaming **Oregon Pioneer**, a 23ft-high gilded statue depicting a stylized, early male settler.

Free tours are offered daily; call ahead to check schedules. In spring and summer you can also take a 'Tower Tour,' which goes up 121 spiral steps to the rooftop (weather permitting).

Willamette University UNIVERSITY
(☑503-370-6267; www.willamette.edu; 900 State St) Just south of the capitol, Willamette University was the first university in the western USA and is well respected for its liberal-arts undergraduate program and law school. The Visitor Information Center has a walking-tour leaflet of the university.

The oldest remaining building on the campus is **Waller Hall**, built between 1864 and 1867. The **Hallie Ford Museum of Art** (900 State St; adult/under 12yr $3/free; ☉10am-5pm Tue-Sat, from 1pm Sun) houses works from Europe, the Middle East, Africa and Asia, along with the Pacific Northwest.

Bush's Pasture Park PARK
One of Oregon's leading citizens of the late 19th century was Asahel Bush, a newspaperman and a highly successful banker who began building his rambling Italianate residence in 1877. Designed to be a self-sufficient farm, the grounds are now preserved as Bush's Pasture Park and include a large rose garden, a playground, picnic areas and walking trails.

The **Bush House Museum** (☑503-363-4714; www.salemart.org; 600 Mission St SE; adult/child 6-15yr $6/3; ☉1-4pm Wed-Sun, closed Jan & Feb) is open as a showplace of Victorian design. Note the marble fireplaces, 10 in all. Most of the wallpaper is from the original 1878 construction and was made in France. The house is open for guided tours only, given on the hour.

The reconstructed stable is now the **Bush Barn Art Center** (☑503-581-2228; www.salemart.org; ☉10am-5pm Tue-Fri, noon-5pm Sat & Sun), which features several galleries. The main floor holds the fine work of regional artists and craftspeople, which is for sale.

Deepwood Estate HISTORIC HOUSE
(☑503-363-1825; www.historicdeepwoodestate.org; 1116 Mission St SE; adult/child 6-12yr $4/2; ☉tours on the hour 9am-noon Wed-Mon, hours vary outside summer) Not far from the Bush House, this 1894 Queen Anne mansion is topped by turrets and bejeweled with decorative moldings and beautiful stained-glass windows. There's free access to the grounds, which contain a nature trail and a formal English tea garden. The mansion is only open for guided tours.

AC Gilbert's Discovery Village MUSEUM
(☑503-371-3631; www.acgilbert.org; 116 Marion St NE; child under 2yr $3.50, 3-59yr $7, senior over 60yr $5.50; ☉10am-5pm Mon-Sat, noon-5pm Sun) Built to honor Salem native AC Gilbert, who invented the Erector Set, this hands-on children's museum – located in two colorful arts-and-crafts houses – combines educational exhibits with plenty of play areas. The highlight has to be the outdoor tower maze, with wood bridges and climbing structures; it's great for energetic little bodies. Adults and toddlers have their own sections too.

IN HOT WATER

A couple hours' drive east of Salem is one of Oregon's best soaks – **Bagby Hot Springs** (www.bagbyhotsprings.org). You'll need to hike 1.5 miles through lush forest to reach these clothing-optional springs, but then you'll be rewarded with rustic private bathhouses and hollowed-log tubs. Be prepared to wait your turn on weekends. A $5 per-person fee is collected by an attendant near the trailhead.

To get to Bagby from Estacada, head 26 miles south on Hwy 224. This road turns into Forest Rd 46; keep going straight for 3.5 more miles, then turn right onto Forest Rd 63 and go 3.6 miles to USFS Rd 70. Turn right again and go about 6 miles to the parking area.

There's another good soak at **Terwilliger Hot Springs** (aka Cougar Hot Springs;, about 40 miles east of Eugene), a beautiful cluster of terraced outdoor pools framed by large rocks. They're rustic but well maintained, with the hottest on top. Clothing is optional, no alcohol is allowed and it's day-use only. From the parking lot, you'll have to walk a quarter-mile to the springs. There's a fee of $6 per person. To get here, turn south onto Aufderheide Scenic Byway from Hwy 126 and drive 7.5 miles.

For a more developed soaking experience there's **Breitenbush Hot Springs** (☑ 503-854-7174; www.breitenbush.com), located east of Salem off Hwy 46, just past the town of Detroit. This peaceful retreat offers beautiful hot springs, along with massages, yoga, vegetarian food and simple lodgings. Day-use fees range from $15 to $28 per adult and require reservations. Call or check the website for directions.

Elsinore Theatre HISTORIC BUILDING
(☑ 503-375-3574; www.elsinoretheatre.com; 170 High St SE) This dazzling Tudor-Gothic landmark, opened in 1926 and once a silent-movie theater, is now primarily a venue for theater and concerts. Classic movies are shown weekly from October to May, with live accompaniment (for silent movies) on a 1778-pipe Wurlitzer organ – one of the finest in the country. Tours by appointment.

★ Festivals & Events

Oregon State Fair CARNIVAL
(www.oregonstatefair.org; ☺ Aug) Salem's biggest party of the year; held at the fairgrounds and Expo Center for the 10 days prior to Labor Day.

Salem Art Fair & Festival ART
(www.salemart.org/?page_id=130; ☺ 3rd weekend Jul) Over 200 artists from around the country bring their work to the state's largest juried art show, held at Bush Pasture Park.

🛏 Sleeping & Eating

Salem offers all the usual chain motels and hotels.

Bookmark B&B B&B $
(☑ 503-399-2013; evhopkinsbb@comcast.net; 975 D St NE; d with shared bath $90) Located next door to Betty's B&B and hosted by friendly Evelyn Hopkins, this is a more casual and homey stay. Choose from two lovely rooms within the main house. Above the garage in back is a beautiful and cozy two-bedroom apartment, good value and more private (four people here pay only $120).

Salem Campground & RVs CAMPGROUND $
(☑ 800-826-9605; www.salemrv.com; 3700 Hagers Grove Rd SE; tent sites $21, RV sites $31-34; 🖥🐾) Located behind Home Depot, Salem's closest campground features nearly 200 jam-packed campsites not far from a noisy highway. There are showers, a market and playground, but for a bit more nature head to Silver Falls State Park (p254).

Betty's B&B B&B $$
(☑ 503-399-7848; www.salemoregonbedandbreakfast.com; 965 D St; d $110; 🌀🌐🐾) Just two rooms – each with their own bathroom and decorated with antiques – are available at this small B&B run by your hospitable and knowledgeable host, Betty DeHamer. Breakfast is a gourmet affair, often made with produce from the garden, and the house is a restored arts-and-crafts bungalow.

Grand Hotel HOTEL $$
(☑ 877-540-7800; www.grandhotelsalem.com; 201 Liberty St SE; d incl breakfast from $129; 🌀@🌐🐾) This upscale hotel is next to the city's conference center. Most standard rooms have sitting areas, and all are stylish and modern. It's geared toward business travelers, with amenities like indoor pool, spa, gym, restaurant and lounge; breakfast is a buffet.

Word of Mouth Bistro
AMERICAN $

(☑503-930-4285; www.wordofsalem.com; 140 17th St NE; mains $9-13; ☺7am-3pm) If crème brûlée French toast sounds good, then beeline to this friendly and excellent bistro. Other tasty (and unusual) treats include the blueberry pancakes, asparagus and brie omelette and prime rib Benedict. Gourmet sandwiches, salads and burgers rule the lunch menu.

Wild Pear
AMERICAN $

(☑503-378-7515; www.wildpearcatering.com; 372 State St; mains $8-13; ☺10:30am-6pm Mon-Sat) Popular modern deli serving up tasty soups, sandwiches and salads, along with fancier options like a lobster melt. There's also a Greek wrap, artichoke fritters, pizzas, home-made pastries and even a surprisingly good pho (Vietnamese noodle soup) – all combined with good, efficient service.

Best Little Roadhouse
AMERICAN $$

(☑503-365-7225; www.bestlittleroadhouse.com; 1145 Commercial St SE; mains $9-22; ☺11am-11pm Sun-Thu, to midnight Fri & Sat; 🖼) This family-friendly dining spot has a comfortable modern atmosphere with separate bar area and sports on TV. Out back is a mini-golf course sporting waterfalls and fake-rock features, as well as a great shady patio for warm weather. The menu is lined with typical meat-and-salad items, and there are local microbrews on tap.

❶ Information

Visitors Information Center (www.travel-salem.com; 181 High St NE; ☺8:30am-5pm Mon-Fri, 10am-4pm Sat)

❶ Getting There & Around

The Salem Airport is about 4 miles west of downtown, though there are no commercial flights. The **Hut Airport Shuttle** (☑503-364-4444; www.portlandairportshuttle.com) provides frequent service between Salem and Portland International Airport.

For long-distance bus services there's **Greyhound** (☑503-362-2428), at the Amtrak Station. Trains stop at the **Amtrak Station** (☑503-588-1551; www.amtrak.com; 500 13th St SE). **Cherriots** (☑503-588-2877; www.cherriots.org; 285 Church St NE) buses serve the city; there's no weekend or holiday service.

Around Salem

There are plenty of interesting attractions around Salem to keep you busy.

⊙ Sights

Enchanted Forest
AMUSEMENT PARK

(☑503-371-4242; www.enchantedforest.com; 8462 Enchanted Way SE, Turner; adult/child 3-12yr $10.50/9.50) Located 7 miles south of Salem, this children's theme park is a fun fantasyland offering rides (extra charge), a European village, Western town and storybook themes, among other things. There are water light shows and a comedy theater in summer. Picnic grounds, gift shops and food services are also available. Opening hours vary widely so check the website for details.

Oregon Garden
GARDENS

(☑503-874-8100; www.oregongarden.org; 879 W Main St; adult/student 12-17yr $11/8; ☺9am-6pm) Plant-lovers shouldn't miss this garden, located 15 miles east of Salem outside Silverton. Over 20 specialty gardens are showcased on 80 acres, including a Northwest plant collection, miniature conifer section, children's garden and even a pet-friendly garden. There are 5 miles of walking trails, with a tram for those with mobility issues. Plenty of events take place, including classes, lectures and outdoor summer concerts. Opening hours and admission prices vary year-round. A large hotel resort is also on the premises, with wedding and conference facilities.

Gordon House
HISTORIC BUILDING

(☑503-874-6066; www.thegordonhouse.org; 869 W Main St; tours $10) Next to the Oregon Garden is Gordon House, the only building in Oregon designed by Frank Lloyd Wright. It was built in 1964 and moved to its present location in 2002. Call ahead for tours as opening hours/days vary.

Mount Angel
TOWN

The little town of Mount Angel, with its Bavarian-style storefronts and lovely abbey, is like an old-world holdover in the Oregon countryside. Visit in mid- to late September, during **Oktoberfest** (www.oktoberfest.org), for maximum effect; thousands show up for the music, beer and dances. Gothic-like **St Mary Parish Church** (1910) is worth a visit for its mural-covered walls.

Open to everyone, the **Mount Angel Abbey** (☑503-845-3030; www.mountangelabbey.org; 1 Abbey Dr) is a delightful Benedictine monastery on grassy grounds set atop a hill that overlooks town. There's a modernist library designed by Finnish architect Alvar Aalto, plus a quirky museum featuring a 2.5lb pig hairball and deformed calves (among other

WINERIES AROUND SALEM

One of Oregon's most-respected wine growers is **Willamette Valley Vineyards** (☑ 800-344-9463; www.wvv.com; 8800 Enchanted Way, Turner), on an imposing hilltop south of town.

Stangeland Winery (☑ 503-581-0355; www.stangelandwinery.com; 8500 Hopewell Rd NW), north of Salem in the Eola Hills, is a smaller winery with good Pinot Noir.

amazing taxidermy). Lodging is available to those seeking a spiritual retreat.

Mount Angel is 18 miles northeast of Salem on Hwy 214.

★**Silver Falls State Park**　　　PARK
(☑ 503-873-8681; day-use fee $5, tent sites/RV sites/cabins $19/24/39) Oregon's largest state park, Silver Falls, 26 miles east of Salem on Hwy 214, is an easy day trip from Portland, Salem and Eugene. It offers camping, swimming, picnicking, and bicycle and horseback riding. Best of all are the hikes, the most famous being the **Trail of Ten Falls Loop**, a relatively easy 8-mile loop that winds up a basalt canyon through thick forests filled with ferns, moss and wildflowers. Featured on this hike are 10 waterfalls, several of which you can walk behind. A few roadside trailheads access this hike, but the most services are at the South Falls day-use area, the park's main entrance.

Corvallis

POP 56,000

Proud to be the home of Oregon State University (OSU), Corvallis is a bustling, youthful city on the edge of the Willamette River, and is surrounded by miles of farms, orchards and vineyards. Downtown storefronts are filled with bakeries, bookstores and cafes, while the upscale riverfront area offers pleasant walking along with stylish restaurants and pubs. The university campus, where nearly half of the city's population studies or works, dominates just a few blocks to the west.

Corvallis is an easy place to spend a day just hanging out, and it's also a good base from which to explore the surrounding region.

◉ Sights

Peavy Arboretum & McDonald State Forest　　　FOREST
Both of these areas are administered by OSU and are popular with dog walkers. Peavy Arboretum has several interpretive trails that wind through 40 acres of forest. You can continue into McDonald State Forest, a research forest with several miles of hiking and mountain-bike trails. From Corvallis, take Hwy 99W north for about 5 miles, then turn left at Arboretum Rd and go almost a mile.

Marys Peak　　　MOUNTAIN
At 4097ft, Marys Peak, in the **Siuslaw National Forest**, is the highest peak in the Coast Range. Several hikes are strewn around the summit, and on a clear day there are views across the valley from the Pacific Ocean to the glacier-strewn Central Oregon Cascades.

To reach the summit, drive on Hwy 20 – past the nearby town of Philomath – and then take Hwy 34 for 8.5 miles. Turn right on Marys Peak Rd and go 9.5 miles to the Summit Trailhead; from the summit it's a half-mile walk. A Northwest Forest Pass (available at Peak Sports) or $5 day-use fee (payable on the spot) is required; there's also a campground nearby. Marys Peak Rd is closed above Mile 5.5 from about December to April.

✯ Festivals & Events

da Vinci Days　　　CULTURE
(www.davincidays.org; ⊘ 3rd weekend Jul) Kinetic sculpture and home-built electric-car races are highlights of this funky arts-and-science celebration.

Shrewsbury Renaissance Faire　　　CULTURE
(www.shrewfaire.com; ⊘ 2nd weekend Sep) Costumed players roam an Elizabethan marketplace, engaging visitors in late-16th-century small talk; held in nearby Kings Valley.

Fall Festival　　　MUSIC
(www.corvallisfallfestival.org; ⊘ last weekend Sep) At Corvallis' premier festival live music fills the streets and top Northwest artists showcase their work.

⌂ Sleeping

Expect prices to skyrocket during key football games, graduation and other key university or citywide festivals and events.

Super 8 Motel MOTEL **$**
(☑541-758-8088; www.super8.com; 407 NW 2nd St; d $74-94; ✹@☎☒☒) Decent budget motel with basic rooms and a pleasant location right next to the river. Larger rooms with two beds face the river. Weekdays are cheaper.

Corvallis/Albany KOA CAMPGOUND **$**
(☑800-562-8526; http://koa.com/campgrounds/albany; 33775 Oakville Rd; tent sites/cabins $29/60, RV sites $34-40; ☎☒☒) Pleasant RV-oriented campground with small pool, arcade, mini-golf course and playground. Six cabins have shared outside bathrooms. Located 5 miles east of Corvallis and 4.5 miles west of Hwy 5, just off Hwy 34.

Hanson Country Inn B&B **$$**
(☑541-752-2919; www.hcinn.com; 795 SW Hanson St; d $135-250; ✹☎☒) This wonderful Dutch-colonial farmhouse – set on 6 acres in the countryside, just minutes from downtown – once hosted travel writer Bill Bryson. The four rooms are comfortable and spacious, and two boast private decks. Two-bedroom cottage available; cats and a dog on the premises.

Harrison House B&B B&B **$$**
(☑800-233-6248, 541-752-6248; www.corvallis-lodging.com; 2310 NW Harrison Blvd; d $139-159, ✹@☎) Dutch colonial B&B near the campus offering five tasteful and comfortable rooms, each with private bathroom (one is a cottage suite). The friendly hosts have plenty of information on the area, there are cozy common areas in which to socialize, and complimentary drinks – including wine – are offered.

✗ Eating

McMenamins on Monroe AMERICAN **$**
(☑541-758-0080; www.mcmenamins.com; 2001 NW Monroe Ave; mains $8-12; ☉11am-11pm Mon, to midnight Tue-Wed, to 2am Thu-Sat, noon-11pm Sun) You can't go wrong with any McMenamins venue, where basic comfort foods like cheeseburgers and pepperoni pizzas (along with its own microbrews) are served up in creative interiors – check out the amazing copper trellis with painted ceramic sinks here. There is another branch at 420 NW 3rd St.

Baguette VIETNAMESE **$**
(☑541-752-9960; 121 SW 3rd St; sandwiches $5.50; ☉11am-8pm Mon-Sat) For a good, cheap lunch you can't do much better than this place.

Vietnamese sandwiches come with fresh ingredients in French-style baguette rolls. You have nine choices here, from Asian BBQ pork to marinated chicken to sautéed tofu with curry and lemongrass. Shrimp and veggie rolls too.

Beanery CAFE **$**
(☑541-753-7442; 500 SW 2nd St; drinks $3.50-4.50, snacks $4-7; ☉6am-10pm Sun-Thu, to 11pm Fri & Sat; ☑) Popular corner coffee shop grinding up local beans and offering snacks like soups, salads, sandwiches and wraps. Milkshakes and smoothies too. Live music on weekends; two other locations in town.

Luc NORTHWESTERN **$$**
(☑541-753-4171; www.i-love-luc.com; 134 SW 4th St; mains $16-21; ☉4:30-9pm Wed-Sun) Small, elegant restaurant with fantastic food. It's a short menu but what's there counts: think butter-poached salmon in a white bean ragout and rabbit medallions with applewood bacon. There are only 13 tables, so reserve ahead.

❶ Information

Visit Corvallis Information Center (☑800-334-8118; www.visitcorvallis.com; 420 NW 2nd St; ☉9am-5pm Mon-Fri) Located in the Chamber of Commerce, across from the Super 8 Motel.

❶ Getting There & Around

The nearest airport is in Eugene; **Hut** (☑541-753-7831; www.hutshuttle.com) has shuttle services. **Greyhound** (☑541-757-1797; www.greyhound.com; 153 NW 4th St) and **Valley Retriever** (☑541-265-2253; www.kokkola-bus.com) provide the city's long-distance bus services.

Local (free) bus service is provided by **Corvallis Transit** (CTS; ☑541-766-6998; www.corvallistransit.com). For an eco-transportation choice around town, contact **Corvallis Pedicab** (☑541-609-8949; www.corvallispedicab.com) or rent a bike at **Peak Sports** (☑541-754-6444; www.peaksportscorvallis.com; 121 NW 2nd St).

Eugene
POP 158,000

Full of youthful energy, liberal politics, alternative lifestylers and with a fun-loving atmosphere, eclectic Eugene is a vibrant stop along your I-5 travels. Also known as 'Tracktown,' the city is famous for its track-and-field champions – Nike was born here, after all. And while Eugene maintains a working-class base in timber and manufacturing, some of the state's most unconventional citizens live here as well – ex-hippie activists, eco-green anarchists, upscale entrepreneurs and high-tech heads.

Eugene offers a great art scene, exceptionally fine restaurants, boisterous festivals, miles of riverside paths and several lovely parks. Its location at the confluence of the Willamette and McKenzie Rivers, just west of the Cascades, means plenty of outdoor recreation in the area – especially around the McKenzie River region, Three Sisters Wilderness and Willamette Pass.

Sixty miles to the west is the Oregon coast, easily accessible via pretty Hwy 126. The city is also at the south end of the Willamette Valley, which boasts several world-class wineries. Eugene is an awesome place, for both energetic visitors and those lucky enough to settle here.

◎ Sights

5th Street Public Market
MARKET

(☑541-484-0383; www.5stmarket.com; cnr 5th Ave & High St) An old mill now anchors several dozen restaurants, cafes and boutique stores around a pretty central courtyard. Musicians and other performers occasionally entertain here. For great fun and a quintessential introduction to Eugene's peculiar vitality, don't miss the **Saturday Market** (☑541-686-8885; www.eugenesaturdaymarket.org), held each Saturday from April through mid-November at E 8th Ave and Oak St. Between Thanksgiving and Christmas it's renamed the **Holiday Market** (☑541-686-8885; www.holidaymarket.org) and moves indoors to the Lane Events Center at 13th Ave and Jefferson St.

WINERIES AROUND EUGENE

Nestled in the hills at the southern end of the Willamette Valley are some exceptional wineries. These include lovely **Silvan Ridge** (☑541-345-1945; www.silvanridge.com; 27012 Briggs Hill Rd; ⊙noon-5pm), 11 miles southwest of Eugene. Nearby is **Sweet Cheeks** (☑877-309-9463; www.sweetcheekswinery.com; 27007 Briggs Hill Rd), with its beautiful tasting room. And **King Estate** (☑541-942-9874; www.kingestate.com; 80854 Territorial Rd; ⊙11am-9pm) is a huge producer with a very fine restaurant.

University of Oregon
UNIVERSITY

(☑541-346-1000; www.uoregon.edu) Established in 1872, the University of Oregon is the state's foremost institution of higher learning, with a focus on the arts, sciences and law. The campus is filled with historic ivy-covered buildings and includes a **Pioneer Cemetery**, with tombstones that give vivid insight into life and death in the early settlement. Campus tours are held in the summer.

Museum of Natural & Cultural History
MUSEUM

(☑541-346-3024; http://natural-history.uoregon.edu; 1680 E 15th Ave; adult/3-18yr $3/2, Wed free; ⊙11am-5pm Wed-Sun) Housed in a replica of a Native American longhouse, this museum features a variety of displays on Northwest Native American culture and artifacts, including basketry and the world's oldest shoes. A new natural-history exhibit showcasea Oregon fossils. Fun, hands-on 'laboratory' activities introduce kids and families to the fundamentals of science.

Jordan Schnitzer Museum of Art
MUSEUM

(☑541-346-3027; http://jsma.uoregon.edu; 1430 Johnson Lane; adult/child $5/free; ⊙11am-5pm Tue-Sun, to 8pm Wed) This renowned museum offers a 13,000-piece rotating permanent collection of world-class art, with an Asian art specialty. Highlights can include a 10-panel Korean folding screen and a standing Thai Buddha in gold leaf. Free admission on the first Friday of each month. Excellent cafe on the premises.

Lane County Historical Museum
MUSEUM

(☑541-682-4242; 740 W 13th Ave; adult/child 15-17yr $5/1; ⊙10am-4pm Tue-Sat) Most prominent at this good museum is a transportation collection that includes Oregon's oldest, best-preserved running gear (undercarriage) for a covered wagon. A Victorian parlor, historic kitchen exhibit and old logging tools are other historic artifacts worth a gander.

Skinner Butte
VIEWPOINT

A hike up wooded Skinner Butte, directly north of downtown, provides a good orientation and a little exercise (drive up if you're feeling lazy). Eugene Skinner established the city's first business on the narrow strip of land along the Willamette River below, which is now **Skinner Butte Park**; there's a great playground for kids. If you're a rock climber, don't miss the columnar basalt formations along the butte's lower western side.

Follow the path around the north side of Skinner Butte to the **Owens Memorial Rose Garden**, a lovely park with picnic benches and rose bushes (best June to August), along with the country's oldest black tartarian cherry tree, planted around 1847.

Alton Baker Park PARK
(100 Day Island Rd) Heaven for cyclists and joggers is this popular, 400-acre riverside park, which provides access to the **Ruth Bascom Riverbank Trail System**, a 12-mile bikeway that flanks both sides of the Willamette. There's good downtown access via the De-Fazio Bike Bridge.

Hendricks Park Rhododendron Garden GARDENS
Thousands of rhododendrons and azaleas erupt into bloom here in the spring, along with dogwoods and daffodils, peaking in May. The garden is part of a larger park that features native trees and shrubs, and during the rest of the year it's a quiet retreat with occasional lovely views worthy of a picnic. To get there head south on Agate St, turn left on 21st and left again on Fairmont, then right on Summit.

Science Factory MUSEUM
(☑541-682-7888; www.sciencefactory.org; 2300 Leo Harris Pkwy; admission $4, 2yr & under free; ☺10am-4pm Wed-Sun, daily Jul & Aug; ◈) Parents and kids will love this children's museum, located in Alton Baker Park. Hands-on exhibits and live lizards and frogs are among the highlights; weekend planetarium shows cost extra. Expansive lawns outside for picnics and expending youthful energy.

Activities

Pacific Tree Climbing Institute TREE CLIMBING
(☑866-653-8733; www.pacifictreeclimbing.com) Release your inner child and learn how to climb trees with this Eugene-based organization. Both day trips and overnight expeditions (that include spending the night up in a tree!) are available, and you won't need any climbing experience to partake – though being in good shape helps.

Festivals & Events

Oregon Bach Festival MUSIC
(☑800-457-1486; www.oregonbachfestival.com; ☺late-mid-Jul) The great composer takes center stage, but other classical heavyweights like Beethoven, Brahms and Dvorak get a look-in as well.

Oregon Country Fair CARNIVAL
(☑541-343-4298; www.oregoncountryfair.org; ☺late Jun–mid-Jul) This is a riotous celebration of Eugene's folksy, hippie past and present.

Oregon Festival of American Music MUSIC
(OFAM; ☑541-687-6526; www.ofam.org; ☺early Aug) American music is celebrated with a week-long concert series of jazz and contemporary show tunes.

Eugene Celebration CARNIVAL
(☑541-681-4108; www.eugenecelebration.com; ☺late Aug) Takes over downtown with parades, art shows and a lively street fair.

Sleeping

Prices can rise sharply during key football games and graduation.

Campus Inn MOTEL $
(☑541-343-3376; www.campus-inn.com; 390 E Broadway; d $70-80; ❄@❷❂) Very pleasant motel near the university with spacious business-style rooms in simple, stylish decor. Go for the $10 upgrade; it's worth it for a bigger bed and more space. Small gym, communal Jacuzzi and upstairs outside patio available.

Eugene Whiteaker Hostel HOSTEL $
(☑541-343-3335; www.eugenehostels.com; 970 W 3rd Ave; tent sites per person $15, dm $25, r $40-70, all incl breakfast; @❷) This casual hostel is in an old rambling house. There's a kitchen for cooking, an artsy and musical vibe (guitars available for all), nice front and back patios to hang out in, and a free simple breakfast. There's an annex down the street.

Armitage Park Campground CAMPGROUND $
(☑541-682-2000; 90064 Coburg Rd; tent & RV sites $30; ❄) Pleasant large, grassy park on the outskirts of Eugene. Go for a site at the back for more privacy. No showers; reserve for summer weekends.

★**C'est La Vie Inn** B&B $$
(☑541-302-3014; www.cestlavieinn.com; 1006 Taylor St; d $150-170; ❄@❷) This gorgeous Victorian house, run by a friendly French woman and her American husband, is a neighborhood show-stopper. Beautiful antique furniture fills the living and dining areas, while the three tastefully appointed rooms offer comfort and luxury. Also available is an amazing suite with kitchenette ($260).

Excelsior Inn   INN $$

(☑541-342-6963,   800-321-6963;   www.excelsiorinn.com; 754 E 13th Ave; d incl breakfast $135-300; ❋❀❈❈) A stately, elegant and very comfortable inn with 14 rooms, each named after a famous composer. Reproduction antiques and wood floors blend with modern amenities for a luxurious experience, and one of Eugene's finest restaurants is on the premises.

Oval Door B&B   B&B $$

(☑541-683-3160; www.ovaldoor.com; 988 Lawrence St; d $89-185; ❋@❀) This friendly B&B has six homey rooms, all with private bath and individual, tasteful decor. It has a great location near the center, yet is in a residential neighborhood. Gourmet breakfast is served and the interior is 'shoes off' during rains.

Campbell House   INN $$

(☑800-264-2519, 541-343-1119; www.campbellhouse.com; 252 Pearl St; r incl breakfast $139-389; ❋@❀❈) A large inn with 18 rooms and lovely common spaces, Campbell House's lush garden is popular for weddings. Choose from small, cozy rooms, spacious suites with Jacuzzi and fireplace, or a two-bedroom suite ($389). Well located on a hill in an upscale neighborhood.

Secret Garden Inn   BOUTIQUE HOTEL $$

(☑541-484-6755, 888-484-6755; www.secretgardenbbinn.com; 1910 University St; d incl breakfast $125-350; ❋@❀) This beautiful three-story house has 12 spacious rooms (each with private bathroom), antique furniture and plenty of common areas. There's a nice back deck, lush gardens all around and it's near the university. Hot breakfast.

✗ Eating

Two exceptional natural-food grocery stores are **Kiva** (☑541-342-8666; www.kivagrocery.com; 125 W 11th Ave; ⊘9am-8pm) and **Sundance** (☑541-343-9142; www.sundancenaturalfoods.com; 748 E 24th Ave; ⊘7am-11pm); the latter has hot food and salad bars.

Papa's Soul Food Kitchen   SOUTHERN $

(☑541-342-7500; 400 Blair Blvd; mains $7-11; ⊘noon-2pm & 5-10pm Tue-Fri, 2-10pm Sat) This popular Southern-food spot grills up awesome jerk chicken, pulled-pork sandwiches, crawfish jambalaya and fried okra. The best part is the live blues music, which keeps the joint open late on Friday and Saturday nights. Nice back patio.

Original Pancake House   BREAKFAST $

(☑541-343-7523; www.originalpancakehouse.com; 782 E Broadway; mains $7-11; ⊘6am-2pm Mon-Fri, to 3pm Sat & Sun) Excellent place for breakfast. Go for bacon waffles, mandarin orange crepes, green chili and cheese omelette or one of the dozen kinds of pancakes (blueberry, peach, coconut, chocolate chip...). The Dutch Baby is its signature dish.

Belly Taquería   MEXICAN $

(☑541-687-8226; www.eatbelly.com; 291 E 5th Ave; tacos $3-4, tostadas $5-6; ⊘5-9pm Mon-Thu, to 10pm Fri & Sat) Corn tortilla tacos are on tap here – order the *carnitas* (slow-cooked pork), *camarones* (shrimp), scallops (beer-battered and fried) or *lengua* (tongue – don't knock it till you try it). Good tostadas and quesadillas, plus excellent key lime pie.

Newman's Fish 'n Chips   AMERICAN $

(☑541-344-2371; 1545 Willamette St; mains $6.50-12; ⊘11am-7pm Mon-Fri, to 6:30pm Sat) Fish market offering Eugene's best fish and chips (cod, halibut or salmon). Also shrimp and scallops plates. Order at the takeout window and eat outside under the covered patio.

Sweet Life Patisserie   BAKERY $

(☑541-683-5676; www.sweetlifedesserts.com; 755 Monroe St; pastries $2-5; ⊘7am-11pm Mon-Fri, from 8am Sat & Sun) 🍴 Eugene's best dessert shop; think pecan sticky buns, savory croissants and *pain au chocolat*. Even the day-old pastries are delicious (and half-off). Organic coffee too.

★ Beppe & Gianni's Trattoria   ITALIAN $$

(☑541-683-6661; www.beppeandgiannis.net; 1646 E 19th Ave; mains $15-25; ⊘5-9pm Sun-Thu, to 10pm Fri & Sat) One of Eugene's most beloved restaurants and certainly its favorite Italian food. Homemade pastas are the real deal here, and the desserts are excellent. Reservations only for groups of eight or more; otherwise, expect a wait.

McMenamins North Bank   AMERICAN $$

(☑541-343-5622; www.mcmenamins.com; 22 Club Rd; mains $9-20; ⊘11am-11pm Sun-Thu, to midnight Fri & Sat) Gloriously located on the banks of the mighty Willamette, this relatively modest (for a McMenamins) pub-restaurant boasts some of the best views in Eugene. Grab a riverside patio table on a warm, sunny day and order a cheeseburger with the Hammerhead ale – you can't get more stylin'.

Marché
NORTHWESTERN $$$

(📞 541-342-3612; www.marcherestaurant.com; 296 E 5th Ave; lunch mains $13-18, dinner mains $23-29; ⏰ 7am-11pm Sun-Wed, to midnight Thu-Sat) 🅿️ Renowned Eugene restaurant that bases its menu on fresh, seasonal and local produce and meats. There are gourmet sandwiches and wood-oven-fired pizzas for lunch, with dinner dishes like poached black cod, spring lamb navarin and goat cheese and green garlic soufflé. Also open for breakfast.

🍸 Drinking & Entertainment

Ninkasi Brewing Company
BREWPUB

(📞 541-344-2739; www.ninkasibrewing.com; 272 Van Buren St; ⏰ 10am-6pm Tue-Fri, 9am-4:30pm Sat) Head to this tasting room to sample some of Oregon's best microbrews. Sweet outdoor patio and snacks available, and there's usually a food cart or two nearby. Brewery tours given.

Steelhead Brewing Co
BREWPUB

(📞 541-686-2739; www.steelheadbrewery.com; 199 E 5th St; ⏰ 11:30am-11:30pm Sun-Thu, to 1am Fri & Sat) Popular, award-winning brewpub with typical pub food on the menu, plus around 10 homemade brews including seasonal and dark beers. Try the beer sampler; you get six 4oz tastes. Great atmosphere, with comfy wingback chairs and sports on TV.

Full City Coffee Roasters
CAFE

(📞 541-465-9270; www.full-city.com; 295 E 13th Ave; drinks $3-5; ⏰ 6am-6pm Mon-Fri, 7am-6pm Sat, 7am-5pm Sun) Good coffee shop that roasts its beans daily. Also at 842 Pearl St.

Sam Bond's
LIVE MUSIC

(📞 541-431-6603; www.sambonds.com/calendar; 407 Blair Blvd) Eugene's favorite live-music venue, located in an old garage. Nightly entertainment from 9pm on, with good organic pizza, happy-hour pints for $3.50, free bluegrass jams on Tuesday and nice outdoor patio for those sweltering summer nights.

ℹ️ Information

Springfield Visitor Center (📞 541-743-8767; 3312 Gateway St; ⏰ 9am-6pm)
Visitor Center (📞 541-484-5307; www.eugene-cascadescoast.org; 754 Olive St; ⏰ 8am-5pm Mon-Fri)

ℹ️ Getting There & Around

The **Eugene Airport** (📞 541-682-5544; www.flyeug.com; 28801 Douglas Dr) is about 7 miles northwest of the center. **Greyhound** (📞 541-344-6265; www.greyhound.com; 987 Pearl St) provides long-distance services to Salem, Corvallis, Portland, Medford, Grants Pass, Hood River, Newport and Bend. **Porter Stage Lines** (www.porterstageline.com) goes to the coast.

Trains leave from the **Amtrak station** (📞 541-687-1383; www.amtrak.com; cnr E 4th Ave & Willamette St) for Portland, Seattle and Vancouver, BC (among other places). Local bus service is provided by **Lane Transit District** (📞 541-682-6100; www.ltd.org; 3500 E 17th Ave). For bike rentals, head to **Bicycle Way of Life** (📞 541-344-4150; www.bicycleway.com; 556 Charnelton St; ⏰ 10am-7pm Mon-Fri, to 5pm Sat & Sun).

McKenzie Region

The single name 'McKenzie' identifies a beautiful and mysterious river, a mountain pass, a spectacular historic highway and one of Oregon's most extraordinary and wondrous natural areas. Premiere recreational opportunities abound, from fantastic fishing to exceptional hiking to racy rafting trips.

The little community of McKenzie Bridge, 50 miles east of Eugene on Hwy 126, offers several serene accommodations, a couple of restaurants and a market. Four miles east from here the highway splits and continues east as Hwy 242 (the Old McKenzie Hwy) over the Cascades toward McKenzie Pass on its way to Sisters, 34 miles distant (the pass is closed approximately November to June). Hwy 126 continues north along the McKenzie River to US 20, which crosses the Cascades at Santiam Pass (4817ft; open year-round).

🏃 Activities

Hiking

One of Oregon's showcase 'Wild & Scenic Rivers,' the McKenzie is graced with the 26-mile **McKenzie River National Recreation Trail**, which follows the here-again, gone-again cascading river from its inception near the town of McKenzie Bridge. There are entry trailheads at several places along Hwy 126.

A good day hike is the 5-mile **Clear Lake Loop**, accessible via either Clear Lake Resort or Coldwater Cove Campground. It circles Clear Lake while passing a large spring, several groves of old-growth forest and an extensive lava flow.

Another series of easy hikes begins at the **Sahalie Falls**, where a footbridge crosses the upper falls viewpoint to join the McKenzie

River Trail for a 2-mile stroll to Carmen Reservoir past **Koosah Falls**. On the highway side of the river is the more developed and shorter **Waterfall Trail**, which links Sahalie with Koosah Falls. Parts of this trail are wheelchair accessible.

Day hikes also reach the calm, emerald-colored **Tamolitch Pool** (aka Blue Pool) from the south. To reach the trailhead, turn off Hwy 126 at Trail Bridge Reservoir, following the gravel road to the right. The 2-mile trail passes through a mossy lava flow before coming upon the mighty McKenzie River surging up in a cliff-lined bowl of rock.

Fishing

The McKenzie River is one of the best fishing streams in Oregon, and the slower water and deep pools west of Blue River also offer good fishing. Check regulations with the **Fish & Wildlife Office** ([phone]541-726-3515; www.dfw.state.or.us; 3150 E Main St) in Springfield. For fishing guides and equipment rental, check www.mckenzieguides.com.

Rafting

White-water rafting trips are popular on the McKenzie River's class I to III rapids from April to October. **High Country Expeditions** ([phone]888-461-7238; www.hcexpeditions.com; 59296 N Belknap Springs Rd, McKenzie Bridge) and **Oregon Whitewater Adventures** ([phone]800-820-7238; www.oregonwhitewater.com; 39620 Deerhorn Rd, Springfield) operate on the McKenzie.

🛏 Sleeping

There are many lovely summer **campgrounds** ([phone]877-444-6777; www.recreation.gov; campsites $10-20) in the area, which include **Paradise** (old-growth grove near white water), **McKenzie Bridge** (Douglas fir and cedar trees), **Delta** (scenic and enchanting) and **Ice Cap Creek** (a cliff-top location near a reservoir and waterfalls). Limited reservations are possible. Contact the McKenzie Ranger Station (p261) for more information.

Reserve rooms in summer. The following are located from east to west.

Clear Lake Resort CABIN $
([phone]541-967-3917; www.campingfriend.com/clearlakeresort; 13000 Hwy 20; tent sites $18, cabins $64-117; 🅿) Eighteen miles east of McKenzie Bridge and 4 miles south of Hwy 20 are these rustic lakeside cabins, which are great if you like roughing it (just a little).

More modern cabins with inside bathroom are available; older ones share outside bathrooms. Rowboat rentals available. Bring all bedding, towels, food and cooking gear.

Harbick's Country Inn MOTEL $
([phone]541-822-3805; www.harbicks-country-inn.com; 54791 McKenzie Hwy, Rainbow; d $70-110; ✴🛜) Attractive motel with both older rooms and gorgeous remodeled ones (some with flat-screen TVs, kitchenette and jetted tubs). Nice grassy view out back. There's also a large apartment available that sleeps five. Harbick's also manages the riverfront cottages and houses for **Holiday Farm Resort** (cottages $175-550).

Belknap Hot Springs Lodge RESORT $$
([phone]541-822-3512; www.belknaphotsprings.com; 59296 Belknap Springs Rd; tent/RV sites $25/35, d $100-155, cabins $130-425, houses $225-325; ✴🐾🛜) Located 5 miles east of McKenzie Bridge, this large mountain resort has something for everyone – camping, RV sites, rustic cabins, modern lodge rooms and even mountain homes (off-site). The reason to visit or stay, however, is the spring-fed pools (nonguest fee $7 to $12).

Caddisfly Resort CABIN $$
([phone]541-822-3556; www.caddisflyresort.com; 56404 McKenzie Hwy; cabins $110; ✴🛜🐾) Friendly place in McKenzie Bridge with just three rustic 'cottages' (two share a wall). All have a fully stocked kitchen, fireplace and deck near the river; two have separate bedroom plus sleeping loft, while the last is a one-bedroom cabin. They sleep four to seven people and are a great deal, so reserve well ahead.

Eagle Rock Lodge B&B $$
([phone]541-822-3630; www.eaglerocklodge.com; 49198 McKenzie Hwy, Vida; d $130-225; ✴🛜) Gorgeous B&B with eight rooms (some with fireplace and Jacuzzi) and over 4 acres of lovely lawns, gardens and patios. Located right next to the river, with a great deck nearby. Gourmet three-course breakfast.

McKenzie River Inn B&B $$
([phone]541-822-6260; www.mckenzieriverinn.com; 49164 McKenzie Hwy, Vida; d $98-185; ✴🛜🐾) Homey B&B for those who need a comfortable but not luxurious room. All rooms have river view and the 'cabins' have kitchens and can sleep up to six. Breakfast available for rooms only.

✗ Eating

Takoda's AMERICAN $

(☑541-822-1153; 91806 Mill Creek Rd, Rainbow; mains $7-14; ☺8am-9pm) Located near the Shell station about 10 miles west of McKenzie Bridge is this popular restaurant serving up a variety of interesting sandwiches, burgers and pizza. For something special, try the marionberry chicken.

Rustic Skillet AMERICAN $

(☑541-822-3400; www.rusticskillet.com; 54771 McKenzie Hwy, Rainbow; mains $6-16; ☺6:30am-2pm) Go back in time at this very casual diner, which offers up pancakes and three-egg omelets for breakfast and a variety of sandwiches and burgers for lunch. Homemade pies and a nice patio are highlights. Hours may extend in summer.

❶ Information

McKenzie Ranger Station (☑541-822-3381; www.fs.fed.us/r6/willamette; 57600 McKenzie Hwy; ☺8am-4:30pm Mon-Sat) Can help with trails and campgrounds, and sells permits.

❶ Getting There & Away

Lane Transit District (☑541-687-5555; www.ltd.org) Bus 91 from Eugene provides services along Hwy 126 to the McKenzie Ranger Station.

Columbia River Gorge

Best Places to Eat

➡ Celilo Restaurant
& Bar (p270)

➡ Nora's Table (p270)

➡ Double Mountain
Brewery (p270)

Best Places to Stay

➡ McMenamins Edgefield
(p263)

➡ Skamania Lodge (p267)

➡ Celilo Inn (p273)

Why Go?

Cleanly dividing Oregon and Washington is the spectacular Columbia River Gorge, carved some 15,000 years ago by cataclysmic glaciers and floods. Driving east on I-84 (or on the scenic Historic Columbia River Hwy) has you passing high waterfalls and nearly vertical mountain walls, all the while paralleling the mighty Columbia.

Hikers have plenty to keep them busy in the gorge, which features many steep, lovely trails that lead through canyons lined with ferns and rivers, and across wildflower fields to grand vistas. Summer wind sports are legendary – the gorge channels westerlies inland against the current, creating world-class windsurfing and kiteboarding conditions. There are also mountain-biking and rafting possibilities, especially around Hood River. Not into strenuous activity? The gorge offers highlights such as lovely waterfalls, agricultural bounties (don't miss the cherries in July!) and fine wine tasting. This is a special place, so take time to enjoy it.

When to Go
Hood River

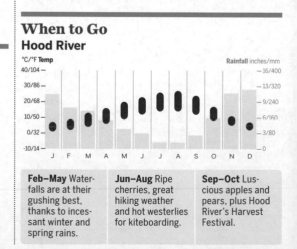

Feb–May Waterfalls are at their gushing best, thanks to incessant winter and spring rains.

Jun–Aug Ripe cherries, great hiking weather and hot westerlies for kiteboarding.

Sep–Oct Luscious apples and pears, plus Hood River's Harvest Festival.

The Western Gorge & Columbia River Highway

Finished in 1915, the Historic Columbia River Hwy winds its scenic way between Troutdale and The Dalles. Also known as US 30, this thoroughfare was the first paved road in the Northwest and America's first scenic highway; it was also the last leg of Lewis and Clark's Corps of Discovery expedition and the hellish finale for Oregon Trail pioneers.

The Columbia River Hwy offers access to gushing waterfalls in spring, wildflower displays in summer and awe-inspiring views all year round. Hikers have plenty of trailheads to choose from, and cyclists can cruise two stretches of the old highway renovated for nonvehicular use. It's slow going on busy weekends, however, and windy enough that trailers are not recommended.

For great views, head to **Portland Women's Forum Park** – it's just a parking lot but one of the best viewpoints into the gorge. Another great must-see panoramic spot is nearby **Crown Point**, which marks the western edge of the gorge. Here, the 1916 **Vista House** (☉10am-4pm) FREE, an art nouveau–style rotunda, houses an **information center** (☑503-695-2230; www.vistahouse.com; ☉9am-6pm), gift shop and snack stand. And everyone stops at **Multnomah Falls**, Oregon's tallest waterfall at 620ft, with a 1-mile hike to the top. There's a **US Forest Service visitors center** (☑503-695-2372; ☉9am-5pm) and refreshment stand at the base of the falls. Finally, hikers will love the very popular **Eagle Creek Trail** (see p266), the gorge's premier walk; just be prepared for high trails with steep drop-offs.

There's camping at **Ainsworth State Park** (☑800-551-6949; www.oregonstateparks.org; tent/RV sites $17/20; ☉Mar 15-Oct 31) though it caters more to RVs with crowded campsites and highway noise. For a special atmosphere, stay at the unforgettable **McMenamins Edgefield** (☑503-669-8610; www.mcmenamins.com/54-edgefield-home; 2126 SW Halsey St, Troutdale; dm $30, d with shared bath $70-115, with private bath $120-155; 🅿🛜) in Troutdale, worth a visit for its bars and restaurants alone. The **Multnomah Falls Lodge** (☑503-695-2376; www.multnomahfallslodge.com; ☉8am-9pm) offers a fine Northwest-style dining option right at Multnomah Falls.

To reach the historic highway, take exit 17 or 35 off I-84.

Cascade Locks

An early transportation center, Cascade Locks (at exit 44 off I-84) gets its name from the navigational locks, completed in 1896, that cut through the treacherous rapids here (now submerged). The town flourished throughout the 1930s, when the area was home to thousands of Bonneville Dam construction workers. At the locks, note the wooden Native American fishing platforms.

◉ Sights & Activities

Cascade Locks Historical Museum MUSEUM (☑541-374-8535; Port Marina Park; ☉noon-5pm May-Sep, sometimes closed Mon) FREE Housed in an old lockmaster's three-story residence (1905) across from the locks, this museum features Native American artifacts, a fish wheel and a basement taxidermy collection – including a very surprised bobcat.

Columbia Gorge Sternwheeler CRUISE (☑800-224-3901; www.portlandspirit.com; adult/child 4-12yr $28/18; ☉May-Oct) Sightsee the Columbia River on a sternwheeler. Embark from the eastern end of Marine Park, where there are picnic tables, a cafe and gift shop. There are also jet-boat rides and other types of cruises.

🛏 Sleeping & Eating

A couple of campgrounds, a few motels and some diners offer the basics. Most travelers stay in Hood River, 14 miles to the east, or across the river at elegant Skamania Lodge (p267).

For a fast-food treat, get a giant soft-serve cone at **East Wind Drive-in** (☑541-374-8380; 395 NW Wanapa St; burgers $4-7; ☉7am-8pm).

Bonneville Dam

This **dam** (☑541-374-8820; ☉9am-5pm) FREE was one of the largest New Deal projects of the Depression era. Completed in 1937, it was the first major dam on the Columbia River. Dam construction brought thousands of jobs, and the cheap electricity produced by the dam promised future industrial employment. Bonneville's two hydroelectric powerhouses back up the Columbia River

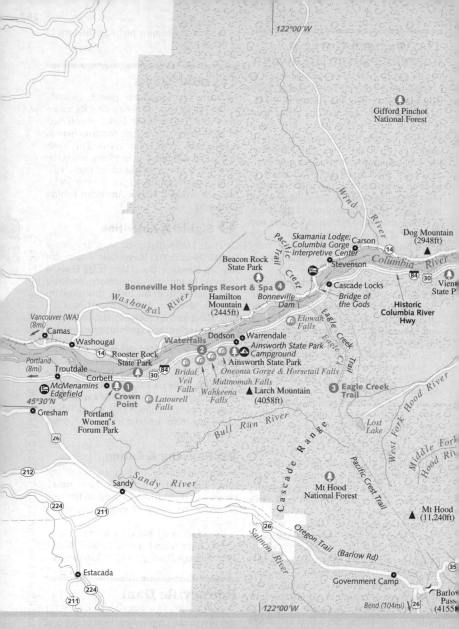

Columbia River Gorge Highlights

❶ Enjoying incredible panoramic views from Crown Point's **Vista House** (p263).

❷ Counting dozens of gushing **waterfalls** (p272) up and down the gorge.

❸ Hiking up the premier **Eagle Creek Trail** (p266) to heart-skipping heights.

❹ Soaking away your aches at **Bonneville Hot Springs Resort & Spa** (p267).

❺ Catching the wind while windsurfing or kiteboarding around **Hood River** (p267).

❻ Exploring the impressive **Maryhill Museum of Art**

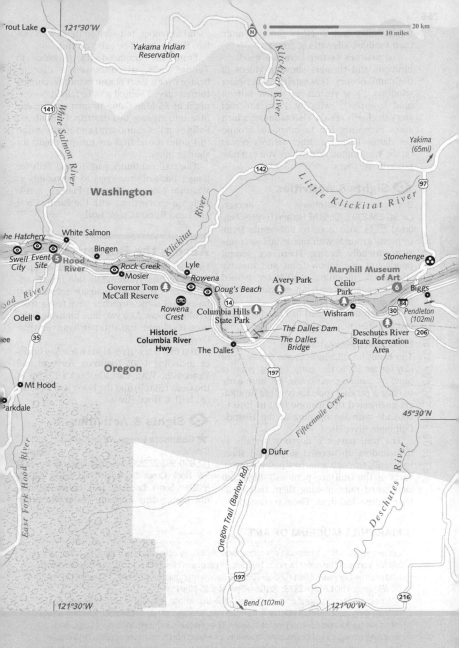

121°30'W

Trout Lake

Yakama Indian
Reservation

Klickitat River

20 km
10 miles

Yakima
(65mi)

142

97

Little Klickitat River

Washington

White Salmon River

Klickitat River

The Hatchery
White Salmon

Swell City
Event Site
Hood River
Bingen
Rock Creek
Mosier
Lyle
Rowena

Stonehenge

Maryhill Museum
of Art

Avery Park
Celilo
Park

Biggs

84

Governor Tom
McCall Reserve

Rowena
Crest

Doug's Beach

14

Wishram

30
Pendleton
(102mi)

206

Hood River

Odell

35

Columbia Hills
State Park

The Dalles Dam
The Dalles
Bridge

Deschutes River
State Recreation
Area

Historic
Columbia River
Hwy

The Dalles

197

45°30'N

Oregon

Mt Hood

Parkdale

East Fork Hood River

Fifteenmile Creek

Deschutes River

Dufur

Oregon Trail (Barlow Rd)

197

Bend (102mi)

121°30'W

216

121°00'W

(p266), on the Washington
side.

7 Tasting the gorge's spring
and summer **fruit bounties**
or indulging in **wine tasting**
(p267).

for 15 miles and together produce more than 1 million kilowatts of power.

The **visitors center** here has good exhibitions and theaters showing videos of the dam's history. Downstairs, underwater windows allow visitors to watch salmon (and lampreys!) swim by. From the roof you can clearly see the **fish ladders**, which allow migrating fish to negotiate around the dams. There's another visitors center on the Washington side, where you can take powerhouse tours.

◉ Sights & Activities

Bonneville Fish Hatchery   HATCHERY
(☑ 541-374-8393; 70543 NE Herman Loop; ⊙ 7am-dusk) **FREE** Next door to Bonneville Dam, in pretty grounds with picnic tables, is this visitor-friendly facility. There are several ponds full of rainbow trout and massive sturgeon – including a 10-footer named Herman – along with an educational exhibit, gift shop and small cafe.

To reach the dam and fish hatchery, take exit 40 off I-84.

Eagle Creek Recreation Area   PARK
The beautiful, 13.2-mile **Eagle Creek Trail** (day-use fee $5) is the gorge's most popular hike; on summer weekends, get here early to snag a parking spot. Early gorge promoters engineered this historic trail in 1910 to coincide with the opening of the Historic Columbia River Hwy.

The trail passes a dozen waterfalls as it meanders up wooded slopes and sheer rock walls through a narrow basalt canyon. Parts of the trail are perilously high and lack guard rails, making them dangerous for children and dogs. These sections have metal aid ropes, but even so those with vertigo issues should be extra careful.

From the trailhead it's 6 miles to **Tunnel Falls**, which crosses a dizzying bridge over a 150ft chasm before reaching a tunnel carved behind a waterfall. Stay overnight at 7.5 Mile Camp to turn a tiring day hike into an easy two-day trip. **Punchbowl Falls** (4 miles round-trip) and **High Bridge** (6.4 miles round-trip) are turning points for shorter hikes.

The trail continues past Tunnel Falls for longer backcountry loops to viewpoints at Wahtum Lake and Benson Plateau, accessible via connections with the Pacific Crest Trail and Ruckel Creek Trail.

Across the Border

Driving Hwy 14 on the Columbia River Gorge on the Washington side has its advantages – there are roadside recreational lakes, and some stretches have fewer trees to block views. As a two-lane highway, however, it's slower and also much curvier than Oregon's I-84.

You can reach Hwy 14 via a few key bridges including I-205 (between Portland and Vancouver, WA), Cascade Lock's Bridge of the Gods ($1 toll) and the Hood River Bridge ($1 toll) at Hood River.

◉ Sights & Activities

★**Columbia Gorge Interpretive Center**   MUSEUM
(☑ 800-991-2338; www.columbiagorge.org; 900 SW Rock Creek Dr; adult/child 6-12yr $10/6; ⊙ 10am-5pm) Located just below Skamania Lodge, this museum weaves together

---

MARYHILL MUSEUM OF ART

Eccentric Sam Hill, a railroad executive and visionary (among other things), is responsible for some of the most famous building projects in the gorge, including this impressive and worthwhile **museum** (☑ 509-773-3733; www.maryhillmuseum.org; 35 Maryhill Museum Dr, WA; adult/child 7-18yr $9/3; ⊙ 10am-5pm Mar 15-Nov 15).

Spectacularly located on a bluff above the Columbia, this old mansion boasts an outstanding collection of Native American baskets and other artifacts, including a seal-intestine parka and carved walrus tusks. Other notable exhibits include a large and amazing collection of chess sets, a variety of French fashion mannequins, and sculptures by Auguste Rodin. Outside are garden sculptures and picnic tables with fine views. There's also a cafe on premises.

In 2012 the Maryhill opened a new wing, adding more collection rooms, educational and research spaces and outdoor areas with expansive views of the gorge.

The museum is in Washington, just across the Columbia; cross The Dalles bridge and head west for 3 miles.

the many threads that form the area's history – Native Americans, early explorers, pioneer settlers, logging, fishing, shipping, power generation and recreation. It also claims to have the 'world's largest rosary collection.'

Beacon Rock State Park PARK
(☑509-427-8265; www.parks.wa.gov; Hwy 14, mile 35; day-use fee $10) Washington's Beacon Rock, the core of an ancient volcano, is a prominent state park about 7 miles west of the Bridge of the Gods. It offers hiking, mountain-biking and horseback-riding trails, picnicking, camping and river access.

The ascent up 848ft **Beacon Rock** is a 0.9-mile trail with 52 switchbacks; views are grand. For a longer hike, climb 2445ft **Hamilton Mountain** (nearly 8 miles round-trip; about 4½ hours); going just 1.25 miles leads to Hardy and Rodney Falls.

Beacon Rock is one of the few **rock-climbing** sites in the gorge. The majority of climbs are trad and multipitch, and for experienced climbers only. To protect raptor nests, climbing is not allowed from February to mid-July.

Dog Mountain HIKING
(day-use fee $5) It's a steep 3.8 miles up the popular **Dog Mountain Trail**, but this is the best place in the gorge for late-spring wildflowers. Once on top of Dog Mountain, the views of the Columbia River and nearby Cascade volcanoes are spectacular. Allow approximately five hours round-trip and take a jacket – it's windy up there.

🛏 Sleeping

★**Skamania Lodge** HOTEL $$
(☑800-221-7117; www.skamania.com; 1131 SW Skamania Lodge Way; d $140-250; ❈ �es 🐾 🐶) Up the hill from the bridge is the gorge's biggest and cushiest resort. Facilities include hiking trails, tennis courts, a spa, an indoor swimming pool, an 18-hole golf course with shop and even a zip-line course. There are 254 beautiful lodge rooms and suites with either forest or river views, plus two restaurants.

Rates vary depending on occupancy; reserve ahead in summer.

Bonneville Hot Springs Resort & Spa HOTEL $$$
(☑866-459-1678; www.bonnevilleresort.com; 1252 E Cascade Dr; d from $229, pool day use Mon-

THE FRUIT LOOP

Covering 35 miles along scenic fertile lands, the Hood River County Fruit Loop takes you by family fruit stands, U-pick orchards, lavender fields, alpaca farms and winery tasting rooms. There are blossoms in spring, berries in summer, and apples and pears in fall – with plenty of festivals and celebrations throughout the seasons (except for winter). It's a good way to sample the area's agricultural bounties while appreciating the local scenery too. For more information and a list of events, check www.hoodriverfruitloop.com.

Thu $15, Fri-Sun $25; ❈ @ 🛜 🐾) With a grand five-star lobby and 78 stylish rooms (nearly half with private balcony hot tubs), this resort offers fine dining and full spa services. There's an elegant 25m indoor pool filled with mineral water, plus indoor and outdoor Jacuzzis.

The resort is about 4 miles west of the Bridge of the Gods; look for the entrance road ('Hot Springs Way') across from the Bonneville Dam visitor center road. Sunday through Thursday rates are $50 less.

❶ Information

US Forest Service Information Center
(☑509-427-2528; ⊙10am-5pm) In Skamania Lodge.

Hood River

One of the best windsurfing and kiteboarding destinations in the world is the dynamic town of Hood River. Strong river currents, prevailing westerly winds and a vast body of water provide the perfect conditions for these wind sports, attracting sometimes hundreds of photogenic enthusiasts who zip back and forth across the wide Columbia River.

But Hood River offers more than awesome winds. South of town, the Hood River drains a wide fertile valley planted with orchards. During spring, the area fills with the scent and color of pink and white blossoms, and roadside fruit stands peddle apples, pears, cherries, berries and vegetables.

Premier wineries have also taken hold in the region, providing good wine-tasting opportunities. Hwy 35, which traverses the valley, continues south 40 miles to Mt Hood, Oregon's best-known mountain and a mecca for more great outdoor activities.

⊙ Sights

Hood River County Historical Museum
MUSEUM

(☑541-386-6772; 300 E Port Marina Dr; admission $5, 10yr & under free; ⊙10am-5pm Mon-Sat, 1-5pm Sun; ⛴) Newly renovated, this worthwhile museum depicts the history of Hood River County and the mid-Columbia River region, with displays on Native American artifacts and quirky things like fishing lures. Watch a video on Japanese American history, and have your kids play in the fun children's 'exploration space.'

Mt Hood Railroad
RAILROAD

(☑800-872-4661; www.mthoodrr.com; 110 Railroad Ave) Built in 1906, the railroad once transported fruit and lumber from the upper Hood River Valley to the main railhead in Hood River. The vintage trains now transport tourists beneath Mt Hood's snowy peak and past fragrant orchards, on various excursions. See the website for the various schedules and fares. Reserve in advance.

Lost Lake
LAKE

(day-use fee per vehicle $7) Take your own postcard photo of Mt Hood from Lost Lake, which frames the white peak rising from a deep-blue lake amid thick green forest. This inland side trip offers relief when the gorge gets too hot. To reach Lost Lake, which is 25 miles south of Hood River, take Hwy 281 from Hood River to Dee and follow the signs. Canoe and paddle boat rentals are available at the **resort** (www.lostlakeresort.com) here.

Saturday Market
MARKET

(⊙May-Sep) If you happen to be around town from May to September, check out the Saturday market at 5th and Columbia Sts for crafts, live music and fresh fruits.

🏃Activities

Windsurfing and kiteboarding are huge in the Columbia River Gorge area. For details, see the boxed text below.

Lovers of the grape can visit over a dozen wineries in the region for wine-tasting adventures; try nearby **Cathedral Ridge Winery** (☑800-516-8710; www.cathedralridgewinery.com; 4200 Post Canyon Dr). Stop by the Chamber of Commerce for a 'Columbia Gorge Wine Map,' which outlines all of them; you can also check www.columbiagorgewine.com.

SLICING UP THE COLUMBIA

On hot summer days, the inland desert climate of Eastern Oregon attracts cool air from the Pacific Coast, creating fierce winds that shoot westward 80 miles through the narrow walls of the Columbia River Gorge. These westerlies, which directly oppose the river's flow, create some of the world's most optimal conditions for windsurfing, which has been popular around Hood River since the 1980s. Kiteboarding, that more edgy cousin of windsurfing, also offers exciting speeds and airy acrobatics. On a good day you can witness hundreds of colorful sails cutting through the water at breathtaking speeds, in daring displays of athleticism and beauty.

Good put-in spots in Washington include **Swell City**, the **Hatchery** and **Doug's Beach** (all for the experienced). In Oregon, Hood River's **Event Site** is a major put-in location for intermediates and gets crowded; other good spots include **Rock Creek** and **Rowena**. Beginners should head to the **Hook**. Wind conditions change frequently, making some locations better than others on any given day; for current conditions check www.iwindsurf.com.

For beginners, taking a windsurfing or kiteboarding lesson is mandatory. **Big Winds** (☑888-509-4210; www.bigwinds.com; 207 Front St) is the biggest operator in the area and in downtown Hood River. **Brian's Windsurfing** (☑541-377-9463; www.brianswindsurfing.com; 400 Portway Ave, Hood River) and **Hood River Water Play** (☑541-386-9463; www.hoodriverwaterplay.com; Port of Hood River Marina) are other good options. All rent stand-up paddling (SUP) equipment too.

Cyclists, walkers, runners and skaters share the pavement on the refurbished stretch of the **Historic Columbia River Highway** between Hood River and Mosier. No cars are permitted on the 4.5-mile road, which passes through two old highway tunnels and is popular with families. To reach the trailhead, head east out of downtown, cross Hwy 35, and continue up the hill to the parking area ($5 parking fee).

Mountain Biking

Head south of town for great mountain biking. Most of the area's trails are off Hwy 35 and Forest Rd 44 (which branches off Hwy 35 about 20 miles south of Hood River). Good local rides include Post Canyon, Surveyor's Ridge and Nestor Peak.

Discover Bicycles   CYCLING
(☑ 541-386-4820; www.discoverbicycles.com; 210 State St; ⏰ 10am-6pm Mon-Sat, to 5pm Sun) Rents road, hybrid and mountain bikes ($30 to $50 per day) and can give advice.

Rafting

For white-water rafting, head to the White Salmon, Hood or Klickitat Rivers. Stand up paddling (SUP) is becoming popular on the Columbia.

Wet Planet   RAFTING
(☑ 877-390-9445; www.wetplanetwhitewater.com; 860 Hwy 141) White-water rafting trips and kayaking classes; located nearby in White Salmon, WA.

✯ Festivals & Events

Blossom Festival   FLOWERS
(⏰ 3rd weekend Apr) The Hood River Valley springs to life in April with the Blossom Festival. Local orchard tours are the highlight, along with food, music and crafts in town.

Harvest Festival   FOOD
(⏰ Oct) The fall version of the Blossom Festival.

🛏 Sleeping

There are around a dozen B&Bs in town. Listed here are summer weekend rates; during the off season and on weekdays prices can drop. Reservations should be made in summer.

Gorge View B&B   B&B $
(☑ 541-386-5770; www.gorgeview.com; 1009 Columbia St; dm $50, d $110-115; ✳ @ 🛜) Catering to outdoor sports enthusiasts is this tasteful yet casual B&B. There's a four-bunk room for single travelers, along with peeks at the river views from the living room. Three rooms share a common bathroom; one has private bath. There's also a two-bedroom apartment available. Open May to September only.

Vagabond Lodge   MOTEL $
(☑ 541-386-2992; www.vagabondlodge.com; 4070 Westcliff Dr; d $80-125; ✳ 🛜 ✳) Some rooms at this basic but friendly motel have river views, and suites come with amenities like fireplace, kitchenette and Jacuzzi. It's next to the highway but near woodsy areas and next door to the Columbia Gorge Hotel (and its pleasant gardens).

Viento State Park   CAMPGROUND $
(☑ 541-374-8811; www.oregonstateparks.org; I-84, exit 56; tent/RV sites $17/20) Located 8 miles west of Hood River is this campground with showers between the highway and river; note it's next to the train tracks too (noisy trains). River access.

Columbia River Gorge Hostel   HOSTEL $
(☑ 509-493-3363; www.bingenschool.com; cnr Cedar & Humboldt Sts; dm/r from $19/49) Located in Bingen, WA, this quirky and spartan hostel is in an old, historic school two blocks up from the main highway. Lodgings are in the old basic classrooms (dorms have many beds) and facilities include a kitchen and old gym. Call beforehand as office/check-in hours are limited.

Hood River B&B   B&B $
(☑ 541-387-2997; www.hoodriverbnb.com; 918 Oak St; d $85-145; ✳ @ 🛜) Friendly owners Jane and Jim Nichols have made their casual B&B into a homey and comfortable place to stay. Choose from one of four rooms, two with private bathrooms. There are partial river views from the breakfast room, and it's very close to downtown.

Inn of the White Salmon   INN $$
(☑ 509-493-2335; www.innofthewhitesalmon.com; 172 West Jewett Blvd; d $129-189; ✳ 🛜) Over in White Salmon, WA, is this very pleasant and contemporary 18-room inn with comfortable rooms and a lovely patio-garden out back. There's also a very nice

eight-bed dorm room available (single bunk $29, queen bunk for two $40), along with a common-use kitchenette area.

Lakecliff B&B
B&B $$

(☑541-386-7000; www.lakecliffbnb.com; 3820 Westcliff Dr; d $175-195; ✸🔊) Sitting on a cliff overlooking the Columbia River, this B&B offers four spacious rooms with private baths – most have gas fireplaces and amazing views. The 3 acres of lawns are popular for weddings in summer, and you can enjoy breakfast on the back deck while watching the windsurfers. Two-night minimum.

Hood River Hotel
HISTORIC HOTEL $$

(☑541-386-1900; www.hoodriverhotel.com; 102 Oak St; d $99-179; ✸🔊✸) Located right in the heart of downtown, this fine 1913 hotel offers comfortable old-fashioned rooms with four-post or sleigh beds, some with tiny baths. The suites have the best amenities and views. Kitchenettes are also available, and there's a restaurant and sauna on the premises.

Columbia Gorge Hotel
HOTEL $$$

(☑800-345-1921; www.columbiagorgehotel.com; 4000 Westcliff Dr; d $169-369; ✸@🔊✸) Hood River's most famous place to stay is this historic Spanish-style hotel, set high on a cliff above the Columbia. The atmosphere is classy and the grounds lovely, and there's a fine restaurant on the premises. River-view rooms cost more, but are worth it.

✗ Eating & Drinking

Hood River is blessed with many great places to eat, not limited to the followong listings.

★ Nora's Table
NORTHWESTERN $$

(☑541-387-4000; www.norastable.com; 110 5th St; breakfast mains $8-10, dinner mains $12-27; ⊘8am-noon & 5-9pm May-Oct, 8am-noon & 5-9pm Fri-Sun, 5-9pm Mon-Thu Nov-Apr) 🍴 One of the region's best restaurants, serving exotic breakfast treats like curried potatoes with kale hash and fried oysters, and ricotta, lemon and almond-filled challah French toast. Dinner mains are limited, but local, sustainable meats and vegetables are used, and even the wines are only from the Columbia Gorge.

★ Celilo Restaurant & Bar
NORTHWESTERN $$$

(☑541-386-5710; www.celilorestaurant.com; 16 Oak St; mains $18-27; ⊘11:30am-3pm & 5-9pm) 🍴

For upscale dining there's Celilo, a modern and beautiful restaurant with walls that open to the sidewalk on warm afternoons. Main dishes can include the house-made pappardelle pasta with lamb meat balls, or braised pork shoulder in miso-mushroom broth (check the website for the current menu). Lunch is more affordable and casual.

Doppio Coffee
CAFE $

(☑541-386-3000; www.doppiohoodriver.com; 310 Oak St; mains $8-9; ⊘7am-7pm Sun-Thu, to 8pm Fri & Sat) Very popular and trendy coffeehouse serving up egg sandwiches for breakfast and panini and salads for lunch.

Especially pleasant on warm days, when the window-walls go up and the place opens to the outside. Dog-friendly patio.

Double Mountain Brewery
BREWPUB $$

(☑541-387-0042; www.doublemountainbrewery. com; 8 4th St; sandwiches $7.50-10, pizzas $16-22; ⊘11:30am-11pm Sun-Thu, to midnight Fri & Sat) For a casual bite, step into this hugely popular brewpub-restaurant for a tasty sandwich or excellent brick-oven pizza. The menu is limited, but the food is great and the beer even better. Live music on weekends.

Full Sail Brewpub
BREWPUB $$

(☑541-386-2247; www.fullsailbrewing.com; 506 Columbia St; mains $10-15; ⊘11am-9pm) Hood River's main brewpub offers salads, sandwiches and burgers, along with great river views and decent beer.

An outdoor patio is a plus on sunny days, and there are free 30-minute tours in the afternoon.

ℹ Information

Chamber of Commerce (☑541-386-2000; www.hoodriver.org; 720 E Port Marina Dr; ⊘9am-5pm Mon-Fri year-round, 10am-5pm Sat & Sun Apr-Oct)

US Forest Service Office (☑541-308-1700; 902 Wasco St; ⊘8am-4:30pm Mon-Fri) For hiking and camping information.

ℹ Getting There & Away

Greyhound (☑541-386-1212; www.greyhound. com; 110 Railroad Ave) buses stop at Mt Hood Railroad. Amtrak's *Empire Builder* stops daily at Bingen, on the Washington side of the gorge, along its Portland–Spokane leg.

THE FALL OF CELILO

On March 10, 1957, the newly constructed gates of the Dalles Dam closed for the first time, nearly halting the mighty Columbia. Eight miles upstream, it took only a few hours for Celilo Falls – an important Native American fishing ground – to be forever buried under the rising floodwaters. It was the end of a Native American identity, tradition and livelihood that dated back over 10,000 years.

Over millennia, thousands of Native American peoples from as far away as the Great Plains and Alaska would gather at Celilo Falls – also known as Wyam ('the echo of falling water') – to fish for salmon, trade goods and socialize. Lewis and Clark stopped by in 1805 and were amazed by the variety and numbers of people they encountered here.

Celilo Falls' tallest drop only stood at 22ft, but in volume the falls were the sixth largest in the world. Native Americans would risk their lives on rickety wooden platforms over the rushing currents while using dip nets to catch their 60lb quarry. It was a dangerous occupation – if they fell, survival was unlikely – but a good day could yield tons of fish.

Native American tribes were financially compensated for the submergence of the falls, but their cultural loss is priceless. Today, over 55 years later, Celilo Falls is still mourned by those who remember its glory and significance. In fall 2015 a memorial by Maya Lin (who designed the Vietnam Veterans Memorial in Washington, DC) is set to be dedicated in Celilo Park; see www.confluenceproject.org.

The Dalles & Around

Located about 85 miles east of Portland, The Dalles features a decidedly different climate – much drier and sunnier. Though steadfastly unglamorous and down to earth (except for a few historic buildings), the city offers good outdoor recreation; there's decent camping and hiking, and fierce winds that are excellent for windsurfing and kiteboarding. The region hosts several good wineries and is also the nation's largest producer of sweet cherries. The Dalles has also gone high-tech – Google has built a large server facility here to utilize the area's cheap hydroelectric power.

◉ Sights

★ Columbia Gorge Discovery Center
MUSEUM

(☑541-296-8600; www.gorgediscovery.org; 5000 Discovery Dr; adult/child 6-16yr $9/5; ⊘9am-5pm) This excellent museum covers the history of the gorge, from its creation by cataclysmic floods to the hardships pioneers had traversing it, to early settlements and transport in the area to the construction – and consequences – of its dams.

The Lewis and Clark wing has an exhibit on animals the corps had to kill (including 190 dogs and a ferret); there's also a bird of prey educational program every day at 11am and 2pm, where live raptors are featured.

Other amenities include a large theater, outside picnic tables and a cafe with an outside deck. The discovery center is 2 miles west of the city.

Fort Dalles Museum
MUSEUM

(☑541-296-4547; www.fortdallesmuseum.org; 500 W 15th St; adult/child 7-17yr $5/1; ⊘10am-5pm, hours vary seasonally, closed Oct-Feb) This museum was once part of an 1856 fort and is Oregon's oldest history museum. It's a fascinating place full of historical items; highlights include an albatross-feather muff, human hair wreaths, a child's casket with window face hole and a bonnet worn at Ford Theatre the night Abraham Lincoln was assassinated. There are several antique cars, stagecoaches and even a horse-drawn hearse. Across the street is a rare example of the area's Swedish architecture.

The Dalles Dam & Lock
DAM

(☑541-296-1181) The Dalles Dam, built in 1957, produces enough electricity to power 800,000 homes. Access to this power came at a price, however. The dam's reservoir, Lake Celilo, flooded the culturally rich area around Celilo Falls, which was for thousands of years a Native American meeting place and fishery.

In Seufert Park, east on the frontage road from I-84 exit 87, is **Dalles Dam Visitors Center** (☑541-296-9778; Clodfelter Way; ⏲9am-5pm May-Sep). Here you'll find the usual homage to hydroelectricity, along with exhibits on local history and a live fish cam to view migratory salmon. **Tours** are given on Saturdays and Sundays at 10:30am, 12:30pm and 2:30pm.

Columbia Hills State Park   PARK
(☑509-767-1159; Hwy 14, mile 85; day-use fee for stays longer than 15min $10) Some of the most famous remaining **pictographs** (painted figures) along the Columbia River are at this Washington state park. The pictograph area can be visited only on a free guided **tour** at 10am on Friday and Saturday from April to October; reservations are required. The park's **petroglyphs** (carved figures) can be seen any time from April to October without a tour.

Rock climbers practice their moves on the basalt walls of **Horsethief Butte**, just east of the park entrance, and this section of the Columbia River is a good place for beginning windsurfers to catch some wind without strong river currents. The park also offers fishing and swimming in Horsethief Lake, as well as camping and hiking.

Rowena Crest   VIEWPOINT
On top of Rowena Crest are spectacular views and vast meadows now preserved as a wildflower sanctuary. **Governor Tom McCall Reserve**, on Rowena Plateau, is one of the best places to see native plants. Springtime wildflowers include balsamroot, wild parsley, penstemon and wild lilies. A 2-mile hike climbs 1000ft and ends at **McCall Point**, which offers even better views.

To reach this section of the Historic Columbia River Hwy from The Dalles, follow W 6th St westward out of town until it becomes US 30. From the west, take I-84 exit 69 at Mosier, and travel east on US 30.

🏃 Activities

Hood River may be the gorge's windsurfing capital, but the wind blows hard at The Dalles too. Right in town, **Riverfront Park** (exit 85) is a good spot for beginners. **Avery Park**, 8 miles from town, offers access to the river from the Washington side. A favorite entry point with strong west winds is **Celilo Park**, about 10 miles east of town.

Sunshine Mill   WINE TASTING
(☑541-298-8900; 901 East 2nd St; ⏲noon-6pm Sat-Thu, to 10pm Fri) Atmospherically located in an old flour mill, this wine bar is an

---

TOP SEVEN WATERFALLS

Waterfalls are at their gushiest in spring. The following are all off US 30 and listed from west to east.

➡ **Latourell Falls** (249ft) The first major waterfall as you come east on US 30. Hike 10 minutes to reach it, or go a mile to the top.

➡ **Bridal Veil Falls** (140ft) Two-tiered falls reached via an easy half-mile walk. A separate wheelchair-accessible trail leads to great views.

➡ **Wahkeena Falls** (242ft) Hike up the Wahkeena Trail, join Trail No 441 and head down to Multnomah Falls. Return via the road for the 4.8-mile loop.

➡ **Multnomah Falls** (620ft) The gorge's top attraction. A 1-mile trail leads to the top. Continue up forested Multnomah Creek and the top of Larch Mountain (another 7 miles).

➡ **Oneonta Falls** (65ft) Located within the lovely, half-mile Oneonta Gorge. Carefully scamper over log jams and wade in water up to waist-high. Fun and worth it!

➡ **Horsetail Falls** (176ft) Just east of Oneonta Gorge. A 2.6-mile loop begins here, passing through Ponytail Falls (and with an optional side trail to Triple Falls). Walk a half-mile east on US 30 (passing the Oneonta Gorge) to return.

➡ **Elowah Falls** (230ft) More isolated but pretty falls about 1 mile off the highway. Hike to the top, then take a 0.7-mile side trail to McCord Creek Falls (2.5 miles round-trip).

awesome place to take a break, nibble on snacks and taste some wine from two boutique wineries. Cool industrial-art touches; check out the 'man-lift' elevator and Thomas Edison–designed motor in a nearby room. Live music on Fridays from 7pm to 10pm.

There are plans to add a hotel and restaurant on the premises sometime in the next few years.

✖ Festivals & Events

Fort Dalles Days   MUSIC
(⊘Jul) One of The Dalles' biggest summer events is Fort Dalles Days, when there's music, dances, a parade and a popular rodeo.

🛏 Sleeping

Big event weekends means skyrocketing hotel prices; check ahead. There are plenty of chain motels and hotels in town.

Windrider Inn   GUESTHOUSE $
(☑541-296-2607; www.windriderinn.com; 200 West 4th St; d $45-59; ✳🖥🐾) For a *very* casual stay, there's this small guesthouse with a hostel-like feel. Mostly long-term guests stay here, especially in the summer, when it's usually booked; call a few days ahead to see if anything's open. All rooms have private bath, but only two are en suite. Kitchen use and small pool available. No breakfast.

★ Celilo Inn   BOUTIQUE MOTEL $$
(☑541-769-0001; www.celiloinn.com; 3550 E 2nd St; d from $139; ✳🖥🐾) The beautifully remodeled Celilo Inn was once an old motel, but is now a slick and trendy stay with gorgeous contemporary rooms, many offering views of The Dalles' bridge and dam (worth it at only $10 to $20 more). Luxurious touches include flat-screen TVs and a cool pool for those guaranteed hot summer days. Discount on weekdays.

Cousins' Country Inn   MOTEL $$
(☑800-848-9378; www.cousinscountryinn.com; 2114 West 6th St; d $85-159; ✳🖥🐾) This upscale motel offers 97 beautiful modern rooms, the fanciest (in 'The Barn') with gas fireplace, outdoor deck or patio and huge shower stalls with triple heads. Even regular rooms have flat-screen TVs, and some come with kitchenette. The swimming pool is a plus, and the restaurant with 'saloon' is just across the parking lot.

✖ Eating

Petite Provence   CAFE $
(☑541-506-0037; 408 East 2nd St; mains $9-12; ⊘7am-3pm) It's a little taste of Paris in The Dalles. One of a few branches in the region, this attractive cafe-bistro serves up luscious pastries, along with tasty breakfast treats and gourmet sandwiches, salads and soups for lunch. Fancy dinners are offered the first Friday and Saturday of the month (mains $13 to $19).

Anzac Tea Parlour   CAFE $
(☑541-296-5877; www.anzactea.com; 218 W 4th St; drinks & snacks $2-9; ⊘11am-4pm Wed-Sat) Australian-style high tea is served in this romantic old house. Choose from more than 60 exotic teas, and nibble on savory meat pies, quiches, crumpets and – of course – Vegemite sandwiches. It's small and hours are limited, so reserve ahead to guarantee a table.

Cousins' Restaurant & Saloon   AMERICAN $$
(☑541-298-2771; www.cousinsrestaurants.com; 2116 West 6th St; mains $10-26; ⊘6am-10pm Sun-Thu, to 11pm Fri & Sat; 🖥) 'Hello cousin!' might be the first thing you hear after coming through the mooing and baaing sounds the front doors make. Specializing in homestyle comfort food such as meatloaf, chicken pot pie and turkey with dressing, this old-fashioned place offers plenty of other good food, with large portions and friendly service. Great for breakfast.

Baldwin Saloon   AMERICAN $$
(www.baldwinsaloon.com; 205 Court St; mains $11-20; ⊘11am-10pm Mon-Sat) It doesn't look like much from the outside, but this 1876 building holds a colorful past – it's been a bar, a brothel and a coffin storage warehouse. Today it's a casual restaurant with an interesting brick interior full of large oil paintings. Food choices include a dozen salads, sandwiches, natural beef burgers and pasta dishes. There's a historic bar, plus live piano music on Friday and Saturday from 7pm to 9pm.

ℹ Information

Chamber of Commerce (☑800-255-3385, 541-296-2231; www.thedalleschamber.com; 404 W 2nd St; ⊘8am-5pm Mon-Fri year-round, 10am-4pm Sat & Sun Memorial Day–Labor Day) Pick up brochures of the city's historic buildings and murals.

COLUMBIA RIVER GORGE THE DALLES & AROUND

ℹ Getting There & Around

Link (www.gorgetranslink.com/transit-wasco. html; ⌚8am-5pm Mon-Fri) Weekday, door-to-door service (fare $1.50) within The Dalles and around (and connects with Greyhound); reserve 24 hours ahead.

Greyhound (☑541-296-7595; 201 Federal St) Provides long-distance transportation. Amtrak stops at Wishram, on the Washington side of the Columbia River.

Eastern Gorge

East of The Dalles the sights get fewer, but there are a few worthy places to check out.

⊙ Sights

Stonehenge   MONUMENT
Not one for small gestures, Sam Hill (see boxed text, p266) built a full-scale replica of Salisbury Plain's Stonehenge on the cliffs above the Columbia River, about a mile east of The Dalles bridge in Washington. Dedicated as a peace memorial to Klickitat County's soldiers killed in WWI, his Stonehenge was built of poured concrete and represents an intact site (unlike its tumbled-down English cousin).

Hill planned that his Stonehenge would line up for celestial events such as equinoxes. It's a popular place for odd rites and ceremonies, and offers great views of the gorge.

Deschutes River State Recreation Area   PARK
(☑541-739-2322, 800-551-6949; www.oregon stateparks.org; tent/RV sites $9/20) The Deschutes River, Oregon's second largest, cuts through Central Oregon and meets the Columbia at this fine state park, 15 miles east of The Dalles. There are expansive green lawns and beautiful riverside camp-sites here; reserve in summer.

From the south end of the park, riverside **hiking trails** pass old homesteads, springs and groves of willow and locust trees. Keep an eye out for raptors and migrating song-birds.

There is also a **mountain-biking trail** (originally a rail bed) that runs about 17 miles upriver from here.

🏃 Activities

Maryhill Winery   WINE TASTING
(☑877-627-9445; www.maryhillwinery.com; 9774 Hwy 14, Goldendale, WA; ⊙10am-6pm) Boasting expansive gorge views from a high bluff is this beautiful winery. Grab your glass of grape-derived ambrosia and peer over the stone terrace down to the scenic vineyards and Columbia River. The 4000-seat amphitheater below offers big-name music concerts in the summer. The winery is 1 mile west of the Maryhill Museum of Art.

Central Oregon & the Oregon Cascades

Best Places to Eat

➡ Zydeco (p288)
➡ Jen's Garden (p284)
➡ The Porch (p284)
➡ Kokanee Cafe (p282)
➡ Rendezvous Grill & Tap Room (p279)

Best Places to Stay

➡ Timberline Lodge (p279)
➡ McMenamins Old St Francis School (p287)
➡ Oxford Hotel (p287)
➡ Five Pine Lodge (p283)

Why Go?

Love mountain tops? Well, that's what Central Oregon and its Cascades are all about. You can practically skip your way from peak to snowy peak here, from Mt Hood, to Jefferson, to Bachelor, to Three Fingered Jack and the lovely Sisters volcanoes. As you can imagine, there's plenty of awesome skiing and mountaineering, along with stellar hiking and camping. And it's not just mountain-lovers who come here – world-class mountain biking, golfing, rafting, kayaking, fishing and rock climbing are also on offer. Did we mention there's nearly 300 days of sunshine every year?

As much as the outdoors may beckon, the lively city of Bend provides plenty of good food and accommodations. Or head nearby to the sweet little town of Sisters for a more quaint and personal atmosphere. Add a must-stop visit to Mt Hood's historic Timberline Lodge, or a getaway break in the region's many peaceful lakeside resorts, and you'll find that Central Oregon's many attractions are hard to beat.

When to Go
Bend

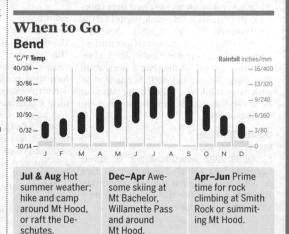

Jul & Aug Hot summer weather; hike and camp around Mt Hood, or raft the Deschutes.

Dec–Apr Awesome skiing at Mt Bachelor, Willamette Pass and around Mt Hood.

Apr–Jun Prime time for rock climbing at Smith Rock or summiting Mt Hood.

Mt Hood

The state's highest peak, Mt Hood (11,240ft), pops into view over much of northern Oregon whenever there's a sunny day, exerting an almost magnetic tug on skiers, hikers and sightseers. In summer, wildflowers bloom on the mountainsides and hidden ponds shimmer in blue, making for some unforgettable hikes; in winter, downhill and cross-country skiing dominates people's minds and bodies. Timberline Lodge, a handsome wood gem from the 1930s, offers glorious shelter and refreshments to both guests and nonguests all year round – and shouldn't be missed.

Mt Hood rises above the Western Cascades, a ridge of older volcanoes stretching between Mt Rainier and Mt Shasta. These volcanoes erupted between 20 and 40 million years ago, and their peaks have long since eroded. Mt Hood began to burp toward the end of the last ice age, and geologists believe that the mountain's last major eruption was about 1000 years ago.

Mt Hood is accessible year-round on US 26 from Portland (56 miles), and from Hood River (44 miles) on Hwy 35. Together with the Columbia River Hwy, these routes comprise the Mt Hood Loop, a popular scenic drive. Government Camp, at the pass over Mt Hood, is the center of business on the mountain.

🏃 Activities

If you park at certain designated winter recreational areas from November 1 to April 30 (ie for cross-country skiing or snowshoeing), you'll need a Sno-Park permit (daily $3, three-day $7, annual $20). These are available at gas stations, some Government Camp businesses and at Timberline Lodge.

During the rest of the year, a Recreation Pass (daily $5, annual $30) is required to park at most hiking trailheads; buy them at ranger stations and from some Government Camp businesses.

Downhill Skiing

Mt Hood Meadows   SKIING
(☑503-337-2222; www.skihood.com; lift tickets adult/child 7-14yr $74/39) The largest ski area on Mt Hood; often has the best conditions. Facilities include two day lodges with nine snack bars and restaurants.

Timberline   SKIING
(☑503-272-3158; www.timberlinelodge.com; lift tickets adult/child 15-17yr/child 7-14yr $68/56/42) Boasts the longest ski season in North America; its legendary lodge is a must-visit for bar drinks, fireplace sit-downs and upscale dinners.

Mt Hood SkiBowl   SKIING
(☑503-272-3206; www.skibowl.com; lift tickets adult/child 7-12yr $49/30) The region's largest night-ski area and the closest skiing to Portland, making it popular with Portlanders who buzz out for an evening of skiing. Overall, it's smaller than Meadows or Timberline.

Cooper Spur Ski Area   SKIING
(☑541-352-6692; www.cooperspur.com) On the northeast slopes of Mt Hood; caters to beginners and families, with mostly beginner/intermediate runs and a tubing area. See the website for ticket prices.

Cross-Country Skiing

Trillium Lake, near the campground of the same name, is a very popular cross-country ski loop. **White River Canyon** is another good trail, and starts at a Sno-Park on Hwy 35 (about 4 miles north of Hwy 26).

Mt Hood Meadows Nordic Center (☑503-337-2222; www.skihood.com) offers around 10 miles of groomed wooded trails. Several other free (ungroomed) trails start from the same parking area, including an easy 1.3-mile trail to Sahalie Falls and another, more challenging one, to Elk Meadows.

Teacup Lake (www.teacupnordic.org) has 12 miles of groomed trails and a variety of terrain.

Hiking

An outstanding guide that includes Mt Hood hikes is William L Sullivan's *100 Hikes in Northwest Oregon*. It's also worth visiting a ranger station for maps and information on the many hikes in the area. A Northwest Forest Pass ($5) is required at most trailheads.

A popular trail loops for 7 miles via lovely **Ramona Falls**, which tumbles 120ft down a face of mossy columnar basalt. To reach the trailhead from Zigzag, turn north onto Lolo Pass Rd for 4 miles, then turn right on USFS Rd 1825 for 3 miles.

Hike a mile up from US 26 to **Mirror Lake**, which reflects Mt Hood beautifully. You can hike a half-mile around the lake,

Central Oregon & the Oregon Cascades Highlights

① Hiking and camping in the wonderfully forested foothills around **Mt Hood** (p276).

② Carving powder in winter (and summer!) above **Timberline Lodge** (p279).

③ Photographing summer wildflowers in the **Three Sisters Wilderness** (p284).

④ Sampling the finest cuisine in **Bend** (p287), after golfing, rafting, skiing or mountain biking nearby.

⑤ Setting up a multipitch climb at spectacular **Smith Rock** (p286).

⑥ Peeking through a lava tube at **Newberry National Volcanic Monument** (p289).

⑦ White-water rafting or fly-fishing on the famous **Deschutes River** (p280).

CLIMBING MT HOOD

Mt Hood (11,240ft) is the second-most-climbed peak over 10,000ft in the world, after Japan's Mt Fuji. This isn't to say Mt Hood does not require both climbing skills and stamina; nearly every year, a few people die making the ascent. Climbing is best between May and mid-July, and a typical climb from Timberline Lodge (where registration is mandatory) takes eight to 10 hours round-trip for a fit person. If you're not an experienced climber, be safe and go with a guide service, such as **Northwest School of Survival** (☑ 503-668-8264; www.nwsos.com) or **Timberline Mountain Guides** (☑ 541-312-9242; www.timberlinemtguides.com).

Portland's Mazamas (p227) is a mountaineering and hiking club (not a guide service) that sponsors climbs of many Northwest peaks, including Mt Hood. Membership isn't necessary, though mountaineering experience might be. And for climbing Mt Hood, experience certainly won't hurt.

then 2 miles beyond the lake to a ridge top. The trail begins between Miles 51 and 52 on US 26, about 1.5 miles west of Government Camp.

Walk 2 miles (one way) on the gentle Old Salmon River Trail, through old-growth forest along the Salmon River. To reach the trailhead, turn south from Zigzag on Salmon River Rd and drive 2.6 miles. The trail follows the road, but the walk is still outstanding.

The mother of all trails is the (approximately) 40-mile Timberline Trail, which circumnavigates Mt Hood along a scenic wilderness of waterfalls, quiet reflecting lakes, wildflower meadows and mountain vistas. At research time, however, part of the trail was washed out, with no timetable for when it would be repaired. The trail can be access from several points – noteworthy sections include the hike to McNeil Point and the short climb to Bald Mountain, both offering breathtaking scenery. From Timberline Lodge, Zigzag Canyon Overlook is a 4.5-mile round-trip through meadows of wildflowers to a canyon vista. Some trails can be snowbound until late July and fording rivers can be a challenge, so stop in at a ranger station for details before you decide on which part of the trail to take on.

Mountain Biking

When the snow is gone, Mt Hood SkiBowl is transformed into a mountain-bike downhill arena; bike rentals are available. If you're more the cross-country type, cross US 26 to the free Government Camp recreation trail network. The Crosstown Trail is a fairly easy 3-mile single track between Glacier View and the Summit Ski Area. More challenging trails sprout from it.

Most of the cross-country ski trails in the area are good for summertime mountain biking.

🛏 Sleeping

Most area **campsites** cost $13 to $20 per night and have drinking water and vault toilets. Reserve ahead on busy weekends (☑ 877-444-6777; www.reserveusa.com), though some walk-in sites are usually set aside. For more information contact a nearby ranger station.

Tollgate and Camp Creek Campgrounds are further down US 26 with some nice streamside sites. Still Creek Campground is near Government Camp. Large and popular Trillium Lake Campground has great views of Mt Hood. Frog Lake Campground lies on the shores of tiny Frog Lake. Off the beaten track is Cloud Cap Campground, with easy access to the Timberline Trail. Nottingham and Sherwood Campgrounds are toward the east, on Hwy 35.

Huckleberry Inn   INN $
(☑ 503-272-3325; www.huckleberry-inn.com; 88611 E Government Camp Loop; r $85-180; 🕾) Simple and comfortably rustic rooms are available here, and there are bunk rooms that sleep up to 14. It's in a great central location in Government Camp, and has a casual restaurant (which doubles as the hotel's reception). Holiday rates go up 20%.

**Lost Lake
Resort & Campground**   LODGE, CAMPGROUND $
(☑ 541-386-6366; www.lostlakeresort.org; USFS Rd 1340; tent/RV sites $25/30, d $125-175, cabins $80-180; 🐾) Six lodge rooms with kitchenettes, 127 campsites and seven rustic cabins (pit toilets and showers outside) are nestled on

Mt Hood's northern flank. There's a small store and motorless boat rentals; fishing is possible. Monday to Thursday nights are cheaper.

Mt Hood Village RV Resort CAMPGROUND $
(☎ 800-255-3069; www.mthoodvillage.com; 65000 E US 26; tent sites $25, RV sites $42-52, yurts $42-60, cabins $60-95; ☞☒☒) The area's largest RV park; also has tent sites, yurts and cabins. Amenities include showers, indoor swimming pool, fitness center, store and a variety of sporting options (volleyball and basketball courts, horseshoes).

★Timberline Lodge LODGE $$
(☎ 800-547-1406; www.timberlinelodge.com; d $115-290; ☞☒) More a community treasure than a hotel, this gorgeous historic lodge offers a variety of rooms, from bunk rooms that sleep up to 10 to deluxe fireplace rooms. Huge wooden beams tower over multiple fireplaces, there's a year-round heated outdoor pool, and the ski lifts are close by. Enjoy amazing views of Mt Hood, nearby hiking trails, two bars and a good dining room.

Best Western Mt Hood Inn HOTEL $$
(☎ 503-272-3205; www.bestwestern.com/mthoodinn; 87450 E Government Camp Loop; d $109-189; ☒☞☒) Pleasant rooms (some with kitchenette and Jacuzzi) are on tap at this lodge-like hotel. Located at the entrance to Government Camp, close to Mt Hood SkiBowl and within stumbling distance of the Ice Axe Grill and its microbrewery.

Doublegate Inn B&B $$
(☎ 503-622-0629; www.doublegateinn.com; 26711 E Welches Rd; d $139-169; ☞) Lovely B&B in Welches boasting three very comfortable and beautiful rooms of different sizes, each with private bath. There's a second-story deck with peeks at the nearby Salmon River. Reservations necessary.

Summit Meadow Cabins CABIN $$
(☎ 503-272-3494; www.summitmeadow.com; cabins $190-265) These five rustically comfortable cabins, each with different amenities (but all with kitchen), lie just south of Government Camp in the Trillium Lake basin. They make great bases for nature getaways. Trails surround the cabins; during winter, it's a 1.5-mile cross-country ski in. Two-night minimum stay on weekends, when rates are higher. Reservations required.

✖ Eating & Drinking

The Huckleberry Inn serves a decent family dinner.

★Rendezvous Grill & Tap Room AMERICAN $$
(☎ 503-622-6837; www.rendezvousgrill.net; 67149 E US 26, Welches; lunch mains $9-16, dinner mains $13-22; ☉ 11:30am-9pm) In a league of its own is this excellent restaurant with outstanding dishes, such as citrus-curry wild salmon and chargrilled pork chop with apple-fennel chutney. Lunch means gourmet sandwiches, burgers and salads on the outdoor patio.

Ram's Head Bar AMERICAN $$
(www.timberlinelodge.com; Timberline Lodge; mains $8-20; ☉ 11am-11pm, hours vary outside summer) Located on the open 2nd floor of Timberline Lodge is this casual bar-eatery with great views of Mt Hood. It's a great place to hang out and nibble on cheese plates or upscale soups, salads and sandwiches. In winter, snag a window seat and order a hot buttered brandy, spiced cider or microbrew – and you'll be in heaven.

Barlow Trail Roadhouse AMERICAN $$
(☎ 503-622-1662; 69580 E US 26; mains $8-14; ☉ 8am-9pm Mon-Thu, 7am-9pm Fri & Sat, 7am-8pm Sun) Old-fashioned catery serving sandwiches, salads, steaks and a dozen kinds of burgers. Good stick-to-your-ribs breakfasts.

Cascade Dining Room NORTHWESTERN $$$
(☎ 503-272-3104; www.timberlinelodge.com; dinner mains $28-40; ☉ 7:30-10am, 11:30am-2pm & 6-8pm) Chef Jason Stoller Smith prepares fine cuisine with a Northwestern emphasis at Timberline Lodge's elegant restaurant. The wine cellar is award-winning (boasting more than 300 Oregon pinots) and the staff is knowledgeable; this is the place for that special meal with great views and atmosphere. Reserve for dinner; breakfast and lunch are more casual.

Ice Axe Grill BREWPUB
(☎ 503-272-3172; www.iceaxegrill.com; 87304 E Government Camp Loop; mains $12-18; ☉ 11am-10pm) Government Camp's only brewery-restaurant, the Ice Axe offers a friendly, family-style atmosphere and pub fare including good pizzas, shepherd's pie and upscale burgers. Veggie chili and lentil burgers too.

TIMBERLINE LODGE

The building of Timberline Lodge (p279) in 1936 and 1937 was a huge project for the Works Progress Administration (WPA), which employed up to 500 workers to hand-construct the 43,700-sq-ft log-and-stone lodge.

To emphasize the natural beauty of the area, architects quarried local stone and cut local timber, also designing the six-sided central tower to echo the faceted peak of Mt Hood. The steeply slanted wings leading away from the common rooms are meant to shed the heavy snowfalls and resemble mountain ridges.

The interior of the lodge is where the workmanship is most evident. The central fireplace rises 92ft through three floors of open lobby. All the furniture was made by hand in WPA carpentry halls, and murals and paintings of stocky, stylized workers – in the style of Socialist Realist art – adorn the walls.

Timberline Lodge is a hotel, ski resort, restaurant and National Historic Landmark. Anyone can stop by for a refreshment and look around – this building belongs to the wider community more than anything. And yes, some exterior shots of *The Shining* really were filmed here.

ⓘ Information

For maps, permits and information contact regional ranger stations, which include:

Hood River Ranger Station (📞541-352-6002; 6780 Hwy 35, Parkdale; ⊙8am-4:30pm Mon-Fri)

Mt Hood Information Center (📞503-272-3301; 88900 E US 26; ⊙9am-5pm) Located in Government Camp, in the Mt Hood Cultural Center and Museum building.

Zigzag Ranger Station (📞503-622-3191; 70220 E Hwy 26; ⊙7:45am-4:30pm Mon-Sat)

ⓘ Getting There & Away

BUS

There are several public transportatin options from Portland to the Mt Hood area. The **Park & Ride bus** (www.skihood.com/Plan-Your-Trip/Transportation-Options/Park-and-Ride) transports skiers from three Tri-Met stops in Portland to Mt Hood Meadows on winter weekends and holidays.

Central Oregon Breeze (📞800-847-0157; www.cobreeze.com) provides transportation from Bend to Portland, with possible stops in Government Camp (reserve 24 hours ahead). **Sea to Summit** (📞503-286-9333; www.seatosummit.net) provides winter transportation from Portland to various ski resorts. It also has airport shuttles and private charter services.

CAR

Check road conditions with the Oregon Department of Transportation (ODOT) **TripCheck Traveler Information System** (📞800-977-6368, 503-588-2941; www.tripcheck.com). State law requires traction devices to be carried in vehicles during winter (in certain areas), and trailers are sometimes banned.

Maupin & the Lower Deschutes River

The Lower Deschutes River boasts some of the Northwest's most renowned whitewater rafting. For a dramatic peek at white water without getting wet, head to **Sherars Falls**, about 9 miles north of Maupin. You might see Native Americans dip-net fishing on wooden platforms right above the water. Maupin provides most of the area's services.

🏃 Activities

Rafting

The Lower Deschutes River is ideal for rafting, with about 100 miles of mostly class III rapids flowing thtough stark canyon landscapes and basalt cliffs before mingling with the Columbia to the north. Most expeditions are one-day adventures that leave from Harpham Flat, about 5 miles upstream from Maupin (the nearest town), and end about 15 miles down the river at Sandy Beach. Longer two- and three-day excursions are also available.

A boater pass is required for all floaters (per person per day $2 weekdays, $6 to $8 weekends). It's available online at www.boaterpass.com, which also has details on this local system.

Maupin's outfitters include the following:

All Star Rafting RAFTING
(☑800-909-7238; www.asrk.com; 405 Deschutes Ave)

Deschutes River Adventures RAFTING
(☑800-723-8464; www.800 rafting.com; 602 Deschutes Ave)

Imperial River Company RAFTING
(☑800-395-3903; www.deschutesriver.com; 304 Bakeoven Rd)

Fly-Fishing

Fly-fishing on the Deschutes River is challenging and world renowned – the remoteness of desert canyons makes it an unforgettable experience. In May and June, the stonefly hatch drives Redside trout (and anglers) into a frenzy, while fall means steelhead trout are in the crosshairs.

The **Deschutes Canyon Fly Shop** (☑541-395-2565; www.flyfishingdeschutes.com; 599 S US 197) and **Deschutes Angler** (☑541-395-0995; www.deschutesangler.com; 504 Deschutes Ave), both in Maupin, are great places to buy gear and get advice. Call the **Fish & Wildlife Bureau** (☑541-296-4628; www.dfw.state.or.us/fish/The_Dalles; 3701 W 13th St), in the Dalles, for current regulations.

🛏 Sleeping & Eating

Near Maupin are Bureau of Land Management (BLM) inexpensive campgrounds with minimal facilities (bring water or a filter). Contact the **BLM Visitor Center** (☑541-395-2778; 7 N Hwy 197; ⊙10am-5pm Thu-Sun May-Sep), just west of the Deschutes River Bridge, for details. Both the Oasis and Imperial River Company have restaurants, and there are others in town.

Oasis CABIN, CAMPGROUND $
(☑541-395-2611; www.deschutesriveroasis.com; 609 US 97 S; RV & tent sites $20, cabins $45-85; ❀❀) These 11 tiny cabins are simple but well equipped, and most have kitchenettes. There's a small restaurant on the premises, and raft shuttle services are offered. RV and campsites are nearby, closer to the river.

Maupin City Park CAMPGROUND $
(☑541-395-2252; 206 Bakeoven Rd; tent/RV sites $24/32; ❀) Near the Imperial River Company, this pleasant campground has running water, showers and RV hookups – along with a boat ramp (day use $4 to $5). Kayaks and floats available to rent.

Imperial River Company MOTEL $$
(☑800-395-3903; www.deschutesriver.com; 304 Bakeoven Rd; d from $99; ❀❀❀) Maupin's best stay is this modern riverside lodge, featuring a good variety of rooms that range from small and subdued to huge and magnificent. Rooms with river views cost significantly more, while prices are lower from Sunday to Thursday. The restaurant boasts an awesome patio with log furniture over the river.

❶ Information

Visitor Center (☑541-395-2599; Hwy 197; ⊙11am-4pm Thu-Sun) Located just north of Maupin, 1.5 miles up from the river.

Warm Springs Indian Reservation

Home to three Native America groups – the Wasco, the Warm Springs and the Paiute – Warm Springs Indian Reservation stretches from the peaks of the Cascades in the west to the banks of the Deschutes River to the east. The Wasco and Warm Springs tribes were confined here after a treaty with the US government in 1855; the Paiute were moved here after the Bannock War of 1878.

The **Pi Ume Sha Treaty Days Celebration** is held on the third weekend of June at Warm Springs, with competitive dancing, horse races and a rodeo. For details contact the **Confederated Tribes of Warm Springs** (☑541-553-1161; www.warmsprings.com; 1233 Veterans St, Warm Springs).

Don't miss the excellent **Warm Springs Museum** (☑541-553-3331; www.museumatwarmsprings.org; 2189 US 26, Warm Springs; adult/child 5-12yr $7/3.50; ⊙9am-5pm), a wonderful evocation of traditional Native American life and culture, with artifacts, audiovisual presentations and re-created villages.

The tribe-owned **Kah-Nee-Ta Resort** (☑800-554-4786; www.kahneeta.com; 6823 Hwy 8; RV sites $49, tipis $69, d Sun-Thu from $140, Fri & Sat from $169) is popular with families, especially sun-starved Portlanders. Facilities include a hotel, a spa, a golf course, tennis courts, horseback riding, kayaking, fishing and a double-Olympic-size spring-fed pool; there's a $5 day-use parking fee.

Mt Jefferson & the Metolius River

The Metolius River bursts in all its glory from a ferny hillside, flowing north through a beautiful pine-filled valley as it passes beneath rugged Mt Jefferson, Oregon's second-highest peak (10,495ft). This gorgeous, peaceful region offers fine recreational opportunities that include great hiking and mountain biking, world-class trout fishing, riverside campgrounds and comfortable lodges. Summer is fabulous and popular, but consider coming in fall when the crowds disperse and temperatures remain mild. In winter there's good cross-country skiing.

To find the head of the Metolius, turn north from US 20 onto Camp Sherman Rd (USFS Rd 14), then turn right at the marked sign and continue 1.4 miles. A short path leads through a forest of ponderosa pines to remarkable **Metolius Springs**, where the river flows out of a hillside.

🏃 Activities

Hiking

Trails lead from the Metolius Valley up into the **Mt Jefferson Wilderness Area**. For a serious but fabulous day hike, head up to Canyon Creek Meadows, where summer produces a vibrant wildflower display and great views onto the rugged 7841ft **Three Fingered Jack** (4.5 miles round-trip; $5 day-use pass required). To reach the trailhead from Sisters, drive 13 miles northwest on US 20. Just south of Suttle Lake, turn north on Jack Lake Rd (USFS Rd 12). It's about 8 miles to the trailhead, at Jack Lake Campground.

From the same access road there is a shorter hike that leads to three mountain lakes. One mile from the turnoff of US 20, take a west-turning fork (USFS Rd 1210) toward **Round Lake**. From here an easy 2-mile trail leads past tiny Long Lake to **Square Lake**, the highest of the trio. Note that this area is still recovering from a large 2003 fire.

For less strenuous yet still excellent walking, follow the trails on either side of the Metolius River, accessed from Camp Sherman or any campground.

🛏 Sleeping & Eating

The tiny community of Camp Sherman (around 15 miles north of Sisters) provides a few resorts, two seasonal restaurants, a store and not much else.

Area campsites include **Camp Sherman** (Forest Rd 1419; tent & RV sites $16) and **Riverside** (Forest Rd 14; walk-in tent sites $12), north and south of Camp Sherman respectively. Both have water and vault toilets, and are by the river. For more information about area campgrounds, visit the **Sisters Ranger Station** (☑541-549-7700; www.fs.fed.us/r6; 2002 Forest Service Loop; ☺8am-4:30pm Mon-Fri).

Metolius River Lodges   CABIN $$
(☑800-595-6290; www.metoliusriverlodges.com; 12390 SW Forest Service Rd 1419; cabins $126-315; ☎) Just across the bridge from Metolius River Resort is this casual place with 13 cozy and comfy cabins – both attached and stand-alone – right next to the river. Many have kitchens and fireplaces, and some boast decks over the water (the Salmonfly cabin has the best view).

Metolius River Resort   CABIN $$$
(☑800-818-7688; www.metoliusriverresort.com; 25551 SW Forest Service Rd 1419; cabins $245; ☎) More like small houses, the 11 lovely cabins at this pleasant spot all have two bedrooms and well-equipped kitchens. They sleep two to six people and each is decorated differently (as they're owned by different people). The river is nearby.

★**Kokanee Cafe**   NORTHWESTERN $$$
(☑541-595-6420; www.kokaneecafe.com; mains $22-27; ☺5-9pm mid-May–mid-Oct) Located at the Metolius River Resort, this log-cabin restaurant offers fine Northwestern cuisine that includes the use of game, organic meats and wild fish. Dishes include things like seafood fettuccine, lamb shank and roasted salmon. Eclectic wine list. Reserve ahead.

Hoodoo Mountain Resort

Oregon's oldest downhill **ski area** (☑541-822-3799; www.hoodoo.com; Hwy 20; regular lift tickets adult/child 6-12yr $45/31) is 25 miles northwest of Sisters at the crest of the Cascades. Though it's small, Hoodoo has variety in its terrain, with good snow and some surprisingly challenging skiing. For conditions call ☑541-822-3337.

There's night skiing Friday and Saturday. Hoodoo also has groomed cross-country ski trails (Nordic pass $14), though many free, ungroomed trails start at the Sno-Parks near Santiam Pass.

Sisters

POP 2100

Straddling the Cascades and high desert, where mountain pine forests mingle with desert sage and juniper, lies the darling town of Sisters. Once a stagecoach stop and trade town for loggers and ranchers, Sisters is today a bustling tourist destination whose main street is lined with boutiques, art galleries and eateries housed in Western-facade buildings. Visitors come for the mountain scenery, spectacular hiking, fine cultural events and fantastic climate – there's plenty of sun and little precipitation here. And while the town's atmosphere is a bit upscale, people are still friendly and the back streets still undeveloped enough that deer are often seen nibbling in neighbors' garden plots.

Festivals & Events

Sisters Rodeo   CARNIVAL

(☑800-827-7522; www.sistersrodeo.com; ☉2nd weekend Jun) The town shows its cowboy spirit at the Sisters Rodeo, complete with parade, toe-tappin' music and rodeo queens.

Outdoor Quilt Show   CULTURE

(☑541-549-0989; www.sistersoutdoorquiltshow. org; ☉mid-Jul) A month after the rodeo is the wildly popular Outdoor Quilt Show. Over a thousand quilts are on display throughout the packed-out town, including many hung up outside buildings.

Sleeping

Unless you camp, sleeping in Sisters is expensive; head to Bend (19 miles southeast) for budget motels. Nonreservable campsites (without showers) are available at the pleasant **City Park Camping** (tent sites $15, RV sites $15-40), at the southern end of Sisters. Reserve accommodations in summer – but especially during weekends and festivals, when prices can skyrocket.

**Band/Sisters Garden
RV Resort**   CAMPGROUND $

(☑888-503-3588; www.bendsistersgardenrv.com; 67667 US 20 W; tent & RV sites $48-53, cabins $58-73, cottages $175; ☞⛱) Comfortable sites about 3.5 miles southeast of Sisters and 15 miles northwest of Bend. Fun activities include mini-golf, a fishing pond and a swimming pool with hot tub; there's also a store.

★**Five Pine Lodge**   HOTEL $$

(☑866-974-5900; www.fivepinelodge.com; 1021 Desperado Trail; d $170-257, cabins $179-317; ✱@☞⛱) Five Pine is a superb Craftsman-style lodge with gorgeous, luxurious rooms, most of which have two floors, fireplace and balcony or patio, plus bathtubs that open to the sitting area and fill from a ceiling spigot (really). Cabins are also available, and use of the gym next door is included. Complimentary wine reception in evening and bike rental included.

Blue Spruce B&B   B&B $$

(☑888-328-9644; www.bluesprucebnb.com; 444 S Spruce St; d $169-189; ✱☞) This fine B&B offers four spacious, themed rooms, all with fireplace, king bed, TV and private bath sporting jetted tub. There's a large grassy backyard and a great deck, and the breakfast is gourmet.

Sisters Motor Lodge   MOTEL $$

(☑541-549-2551; www.sistersmotorlodge.com; 511 W Cascade St; r $119-225; ✱☞⛱) Eleven cozy, clean and spacious rooms, each one unique, at this older but excellent lodge. Expect homey decor and quilts on the beds, and modern comforts such as a DVD player. Kitchenettes and two-bedroom suites are available, and there's a peaceful little patio in the back.

Sisters Inn & Suites   MOTEL $$

(☑541-549-7829; www.sistersinnandsuites.com; 605 N Arrowleaf Trail; d $99-129; ✱@☞⛱) At the edge of town is this motel with wonderful, spacious rooms, all boasting slick contemporary decor, refrigerator, microwave and either patio or balcony. Kitchenettes available.

Eating & Drinking

Seasons Café & Wine Shop   SANDWICHES $

(☑541-549-8911; 411 E Hood St; sandwiches $7-8; ☉11am-3pm Mon-Sat) Line up with the locals at this popular sandwich shop and order the turkey with cranberry sauce or Black Forest ham with Gruyère cheese (21 kinds of sandwiches total!). There is also salads, quiche and lots of wine.

Sisters Coffee Company   CAFE $

(☑541-549-8976; www.sisterscoffee.com; 273 W Hood Ave; drinks $2.50-4; ☉6am-6pm) Local, upscale bean roaster with high ceilings, stone fireplace, wonderfully comfortable furniture and lots of antlers on the walls. The coffee and pastries are good; head upstairs for seating with a view.

★ **The Porch** AMERICAN **$$**
(☑541-549-3287; www.theporch-sisters.com; 243 N Elm St; small plates $6-12, mains $15-17; ⊗5-9pm Tue-Sat) Located in a cute blue house is this highly regarded eating establishment. It's mostly small plates like Parmesan truffle fries, creamy butternut squash risotto or duck confit lasagna, with only two or three 'all mine' mains like rosemary pork loin and red wine braised lamb shank. Whatever you order, it'll likely be superb.

★ **Jen's Garden** FRENCH **$$$**
(☑541-549-2699; www.intimatecottagecuisine.com; 403 E Hood Ave; mains $26; ⊗5-9pm Wed-Sun) One of Central Oregon's finest restaurants, this intimate spot has a limited but quality menu; expect dishes such as grilled duck breast with ginger glaze or slow poached trout roulade. A five-course menu runs $55, or choose the three-course menu for $42. Reserve ahead.

Three Creeks Brewing BREWPUB
(☑541-549-1963; www.threecreeksbrewing.com; 721 Desperado Ct; ⊗11:30am-10pm Sun-Thu, till 11pm Fri & Sat) The place to go for handcrafted beer in Sisters. Order a beer flight to wash down that Three Alarm burger (with jalapeños) or Thai chicken rice bowl. Plenty of other sandwiches, salads, pizza and meat dishes available.

❶ Information

Chamber of Commerce (☑541-549-0251; www.sisterscountry.com; 291 Main St; ⊗10am-4pm Mon-Sat)

Sisters Ranger Station (☑541-549-7700; www.fs.fed.us/r6/centraloregon; 2002 Forest Service Loop; ⊗8am-4:30pm Mon-Fri) For camping and hiking information.

❶ Getting There & Away

Valley Retriever (www.kokkola-bus.com) Connects Sisters with Bend, Newport, Corvallis, Salem, McMinnville and Portland; the buses stop at the corner of Cascade and Spruce Sts.

McKenzie Pass Area

From the lava fields of 5325ft McKenzie Pass (open approximately June to October) you'll find stunning views of the Cascade Range and one of the youngest and largest lava flows in the continental USA. Intriguing hikes are scattered through the area.

Perched on a swell of frozen rock at McKenzie Pass, **Dee Wright Observatory** is a small fortress that was built out of lava in 1935 by the Civilian Conservation Corps. It surveys a desolate volcanic landscape, but on a clear day you can witness a dozen volcanic cones and mountain peaks from its arched windows. Nearby, a half-mile interpretive trail winds through the lava.

Two free primitive campgrounds (no water) in the area are **Scott Lake Campground** and **Lava Camp Lake Campground**, both with lakeside campsites. The campsites can't be reserved.

A $5 day-use pass (available at ranger stations) is required for the following activities. The **Upper & Lower Proxy Falls** tumble over glacier-carved walls to disappear into lava flows. A 1.2-mile loop trail begins directly east of Mile 64, about 12 miles east of McKenzie Bridge.

The **Pacific Crest Trail** crosses McKenzie Pass a half-mile west of the Dee Wright Observatory. It's 2.5 miles across barren lava flows to a spectacular viewpoint atop **Little Belknap Crater**. Bring water and sun protection.

The **Obsidian Trail** is a very popular access point into the Three Sisters Wilderness, but requires a $6 limited-entry permit (available through www.recreation.gov). The full loop to Obsidian Cliffs and back is 13 miles, but for a shorter hike go just 2.5 forested miles to a 50ft-high lava flow with exhilarating views of the Three Sisters.

Three Sisters Wilderness

This beautiful 283,400-acre region spans the Cascade Range and is highlighted by the glaciered Three Sisters, three recent volcanic peaks each topping 10,000ft. The west slope of the wilderness is known for dense old-growth forest laced with strong rivers and streams. The glorious **Pacific Crest Trail** traverses the area, easily accessed from Hwy 242 at McKenzie Pass.

USFS Rd 19, also known as the **Aufderheide Scenic Byway**, edges the westernmost wilderness boundary as it makes the 76-mile connection between Rainbow on Hwy 126 and Westfir (near Oakridge on Hwy 58). From **French Pete Campground**, one popular trail along this route leads up **French Pete Creek** through old-growth forest for about 3 miles.

Another good hike is to **Green Lake Basin**, on a high plateau between 9173ft Broken Top and 10,358ft South Sister. These celadon-green lakes are the centerpiece of a tremendous wildflower display in July and August, when the area throngs with crowds – especially on weekends. Park at the Green Lakes Trailhead along Hwy 46, above Sparks Lake, and hike north. The 4.4-mile trail is fairly steep but passes some great waterfalls.

Strong, experienced and prepared hikers should consider climbing **South Sister**. It's Oregon's third-highest peak, but during summer the southern approach doesn't demand any technical equipment. The steep 6-mile trail (4900ft elevation gain) begins near Devils Lake (just off the Cascade Lakes Hwy) and is passable only in late summer.

For more information on this region contact either the **McKenzie River Ranger District** (57600 McKenzie Hwy, McKenzie Bridge; ⊗ 8am-4:30pm, reduced hours winter) or the Bend-Fort Rock Ranger District (p288). Note that a Northwest Forest Pass is required to park at the Green Lake Basin and South Sister trailheads.

Bend

POP 78,000

Bend is where all outdoor-lovers should live – it's an absolute paradise. You can ski fine powder in the morning, paddle a kayak in the afternoon and take in a game of golf into the evening. Or would you rather go mountain biking, hiking, mountaineering, stand-up paddleboarding, fly-fishing or rock climbing? It's all close by, and top-drawer. Plus, you'll probably be enjoying it all in great weather, as the area gets nearly 300 days of sunshine each year.

With the lovely Deschutes River carving its way through the heart of the city, Bend also offers a vibrant and attractive downtown area full of shops, galleries and upscale dining. South of downtown, the Old Mill District has been renovated into a large shopping area full of brand-name stores, fancy eateries and modern movie theaters. Bend has also become a beer-lover's frothy wet dream; it has more breweries per capita than any other city in Oregon (more than a dozen).

Not all of Bend is pretty, though – US 97 (3rd St) is a long commercial strip of cheap motels, fast-food restaurants and run-of-the-mill services. But something has had to support Bend's fast-growing population, which skyrocketed nearly 50% in the last decade. While the economic slowdown has definitely affected the city's booming growth in recent years, Bend is likely to remain a mecca for those who seek to integrate the outdoors into their active lifestyles.

◉ Sights & Activities

Beautiful **Drake Park**, right downtown, is a good place to start exploring Bend's many miles of riverfront walking trails.

★**High Desert Museum**   MUSEUM
(☑ 541-382-4754; www.highdesertmuseum.org; 59800 S US 97; adult/child 5-12yr May-Oct $15/9, Nov-Apr $12/7; ⊗ 9am-5pm) Don't miss this excellent museum about 3 miles south of Bend on US 97. It charts the exploration and settlement of the West, using reenactments of a Native American camp, a hard rock mine and an old Western town. The region's natural history is also explored; kids love the live snake, tortoise and trout exhibits, and watching the birds of prey and otters is always fun.

Deschutes Historical Museum   MUSEUM
(☑ 541-389-1813; www.deschuteshistory.org; 129 NW Idaho Ave; adult/child 13-17yr $5/2; ⊗ 10am-4:30pm Tue-Sat) Located in an old grade school, this museum houses Native American and pioneer artifacts. There's also historical information on the area's logging, railroad and fur-trapping industries.

Mountain Biking

Bend is a mountain-biking paradise, with hundreds of miles of awesome trails to explore. For a good bike trails map, get the *Bend, Central Oregon Mountain Biking and XC Skiing* map ($12; www.adventuremaps.net), available at the Visit Bend tourist office (p288) and elsewhere.

The king of Bend's mountain-biking trails is the **Phil's Trail** (www.ormtb.com) network, which offers a variety of excellent fast single-track forest trails just minutes from town. If you want to catch air, don't miss the Whoops Trail.

The 8.5-mile (one way) **Upper Deschutes River Trail** runs from Meadow Day-Use Area (6 miles west of Bend, off Hwy 46; $5 day-use fee from May to September), past Lava Island Falls and Dillon Falls to Benham

SMITH ROCK, COVE PALISADES & MILL CREEK

Best known for its glorious rock climbing, **Smith Rock State Park** (⟦☎⟧800-551-6949; www.oregonstateparks.org; 9241 NE Crooked River Dr; day use $5) boasts rust-colored 800ft cliffs that tower over the pretty Crooked River. Nonclimbers have several miles of fine hiking trails, some of which involve a little simple rock scrambling. Nearby Terrebonne has a climbing store, along with some restaurants and grocery stores. There's **camping** (⟦☎⟧800-551-6949; www.oregonstateparks.org; 9241 NE Crooked River Dr; sites per person $5) right next to the park, or at Skull Hollow (no water; campsites $5), 8 miles east. The nearest motels are a few miles south in Redmond.

Just a couple miles north of Smith Rock, **Peter Skene Ogden State Scenic Viewpoint** highlights a stunning 300ft-deep gorge. You can walk over the old highway bridge and look down at the Crooked River waaay below.

Rent **boats** (⟦☎⟧541-546-3521) at the marina in spectacular Lake Billy Chinook, in **Cove Palisades State Park** (⟦☎⟧541-546-3412; www.oregonstateparks.org; day-use fee $5). Or hike the 7-mile **Tam-a-láu Trail** for spring wildflowers and great views. There's **camping** (⟦☎⟧800-551-6949; www.oregonstateparks.org; tent/RV sites $20/26, cabins $80) near the lake, or motels 15 miles northeast in Madras.

The gently sloping Ochoco Mountains undulate across much of Central Oregon, offering good hikes near Prineville in the **Mill Creek Wilderness**. For a good hike, follow US 26 east from town for 9 miles, and head north on USFS Rd 33 for about 10 miles to Wildcat Campground. From here a trail winds along the East Fork of Mill Creek through a lovely pine forest, eventually reaching **Twin Pillars**, a couple of spirelike volcanic crags (16.5 miles round-trip). The **Prineville Ranger Station** (⟦☎⟧541-416-6500; www.fs.usda.gov/centraloregon; 3160 NE 3rd St; ⟦⊙⟧7:45am-4:30pm Mon-Fri) has a list of nearby USFS campgrounds. There are plenty of accommodations in Prineville.

Falls. It's a lovely riverside route that's good for beginners and experts alike.

Rent mountain bikes at **Pine Mountain Sports** (⟦☎⟧541-385-8080; www.pinemountainsports.com; 255 SW Century Dr) or **Hutch's Bicycles** (⟦☎⟧541-382-9253; www.hutchsbicycles.com; 725 NW Columbia St). Both offer free or inexpensive community rides. For mountainbike tours and shuttles, **Cog Wild** (www.cogwild.com; 255 SW Century Dr) can't be beat.

Water Sports

One of Bend's many charms is the pretty Deschutes River, which runs right through town and offers many opportunities for watery fun.

Rent kayaks, canoes, floats and stand-up paddleboards (SUPs) from **Tumalo Creek Kayak & Canoe** (⟦☎⟧541-317-9407; www.tumalocreek.com; 805 Industrial Way); classes, tours and shuttles are also available. **Sun Country Tours** (⟦☎⟧800-408-8251; www.suncountrytours.com; 531 SW 13th St) is another popular company that does SUP, floating and rafting. Or experience white water with **Ouzel Outfitters** (⟦☎⟧800-788-7238; www.oregonrafting.com); it also rents rafts and inflatable kayaks.

✦ Festivals & Events

Pole Pedal Paddle OUTDOORS
(www.pppbend.com; ⟦⊙⟧mid-May) Pole Pedal Paddle is a huge event that showcases Bend's extraordinary outdoor resources – it includes skiing, mountain biking, running and canoeing/kayaking.

Bend Summer Festival PERFORMING ARTS
(www.c3events.com/events/Bend-Summer-Festival; ⟦⊙⟧2nd weekend Jul) If you happen to be in Bend in July, check out the Bend Summer Festival, which features artists, street performers, live music, plenty of food and lots of fun.

⌂ Sleeping

There's a countless supply of cheap motels, hotels and services on 3rd St (US 97). The Mill Inn has one dorm room for penny-pinchers. During special festivals and events, Bend's lodging rates head north.

Mill Inn INN $
(⟦☎⟧877-748-1200, 541-389-9198; www.millinn.com; 642 NW Colorado Ave; dm $35, d incl breakfast $90-130; ⟦☎⟧) A 10-room boutique hotel with small, classy rooms decked out in velvet

drapes and comforters; four share outside baths. Full breakfast and hot tub use is included, and there's a nice back patio and basement recreation room. Budget travelers should go for the one (tight) dorm room.

Motel West MOTEL **$**
(☑541-389-5577; 228 NE Irving St; d $79; 🖥🕸) The rooms at this slightly atypical motel are a notch up from the usual, with stylish comforters and drapes. It's just off the main commercial drag.

Tumalo State Park CAMPGROUND **$**
(☑800-551-6949, 541-388-6055; www.oregon stateparks.org; 64120 OB Riley Rd; tent/RV sites $26/21, yurts $39; 🕸) Riverside spots are best at this piney campground 5 miles northwest of Bend off US 20. Showers and flush toilets available.

Bend Riverside Motel MOTEL **$**
(☑541-389-2363, 800-284-2363; www.bend riversidemotel.com; 1565 NW Wall St; d $78-159; 🕸🖥🕸) Unmemorable rooms at this motel-condo compound, but a wide range of them. Worth it if you get a good river-view room (check beforehand if you care); some have kitchen and fireplace. Indoor heated pool, with gated parking and a pleasant nearby park.

★McMenamins Old St Francis School HOTEL **$$**
(☑541-382-5174; www.mcmenamins.com; 700 NW Bond St; d $135-175, cottages $185-395; 🕸🖥) One of McMenamins' best venues, this old schoolhouse has been remodeled into a classy 19-room hotel – two rooms have side-by-side clawfoot tubs! The fabulous tiled saltwater Turkish bath is worth the stay alone, though nonguests can soak for $5. A restaurant-pub, three other bars, a movie theater and creative artwork complete the picture.

Hillside Inn B&B **$$**
(☑541-389-9660; www.bendhillsideinn.com; 1744 NW 12th St; ste $180-195; 🖥🕸) Just two large suites are on tap at this stylish B&B, located in a peaceful residential street close to downtown. Both are beautiful with outdoor sitting areas, and one has kitchen facilities. There's a common living room for hanging out, and breakfast is made to order. Hot tub available.

Pine Ridge Inn INN **$$**
(☑541-389-6137, 800-600-4095; www.pin eridgeinn.com; 1200 SW Century Dr; d $169-249;

🕸🖥) For modern luxury lodging there's this splendid place just outside downtown. Many of the spacious suites have jetted tubs, romantic fireplaces and great views of the Deschutes River and Old Mill District, and all come with balcony or patio. It's just five minutes from the riverside trail. A full, hot breakfast included.

★Oxford Hotel BOUTIQUE HOTEL **$$$**
(☑877-440-8436; www.oxfordhotelbend.com; 10 NW Minnesota Ave; d $289-549; 🕸🖥🕸) 🌱
Bend's premier boutique hotel, and very popular. The smallest rooms are huge (470 sq ft) and decked out in eco-features including soy-foam mattresses, cork flooring, 35% bamboo towels and dual-flush toilets. High-tech aficionados will love the iPod docks and smart-panel work desk (connecting your computer to the flat-screen TV). Suites with kitchen and steam shower are available, and the basement restaurant is slick.

✕ Eating

McMenamins Old St Francis School has a bar-restaurant with typical pub fare and long hours; it also has three other bars. The brewpubs listed under Drinking & Nightlife also serve good food.

★Chow AMERICAN **$$**
(☑541-728-0256; www.chowbend.com; 1110 NW Newport Ave; mains $8-14; ⊘7am-2pm) 🌱 The signature poached egg dishes here are spectacular and beautifully presented, coming with sides like crab cakes, house-cured ham and cornmeal crusted tomatoes (don't miss their house-made hot sauces). Or try the caramelized banana French toast, or bacon biscuits with thyme. Gourmet sandwiches and salads are for lunch, with many vegetables grown in the garden. Good cocktails too.

Jackson's Corner AMERICAN **$$**
(☑541-647-2198; www.jacksonscornerbendor.com; 845 NW Delaware Ave; mains $10-26; ⊘7am-9pm; 🍴) Very popular with families is this homey corner restaurant with a marketlike feel. Homemade pizzas and pastas are always good, as are the organic salads (add on chicken, steak or prawns). There's a kids menu and outside seating for sunny days; just remember to order at the counter first.

10 Below Restaurant & Lounge NORTHWESTERN **$$**
(☑541-382-1010; www.oxfordhotelbend.com; 10 NW Minnesota Ave; mains $10-25; ⊘6am-2pm & 5-10pm) 🌱 Nestled in the basement of the

Oxford Hotel is this upscale restaurant serving breakfast, lunch and dinner. Expect classy, well-prepared and delicious food. The $10 lunch special is quick and good value, while dinner means fancy dishes made with locally produced meats. The pork-belly tacos are delicious happy-hour specials.

★ Zydeco
AMERICAN $$$

(☑ 541-312-2899; www.zydecokitchen.com; 919 NW Bond St; mains $16-27; ⏰ 11:30am-2:30pm & 5-9pm Mon-Thu, 5-10pm Fri & Sat, 5-9pm Sun) One of Bend's best restaurants, and with good reason. Start with the duck fries (french fries cooked in duck fat) or tricolored beet salad with goat's cheese, then move onto your main course: roasted wild mushroom pork tenderloin, sesame-encrusted ahi tuna or New Zealand rack of lamb with dijon mustard. Reserve ahead.

Ariana
EUROPEAN $$$

(☑ 541-330-5539; www.arianarestaurantbend. com; 1304 NW Galveston Ave; mains $20-27; ⏰ 5-9pm Tue-Sat) ✔ Cozy and intimate, Ariana is housed in an old bungalow and serves excellent European-inspired cuisine. Start with the beef carpaccio before leading into wild seared scallops or rack of lamb with salsa verde. Reserve ahead – there are only 12 tables, with outdoor seating in summer.

Blacksmith
AMERICAN $$$

(☑ 541-318-0588; www.bendblacksmith.com; 211 NW Greenwood Ave; mains $14-31; ⏰ 4-11pm Mon-Thu, till midnight Fri & Sat, 4-9pm Sun) Under new ownership, this upscale restaurant offers cowboy comfort food with a twist, such as cider-brined pork chop with brussels sprouts, Cajun beef medallions and grilled shrimp with house-made grits. Happy hour promises $9 natural-beef burgers and a mac 'n' cheese 'flight' (three tastes of their smoked, bacon and truffle mac 'n' cheeses).

🍷 Drinking & Nightlife

For something unique (and if you're into cycling), check out www.cyclepub.com. For a beer tour, try www.bendbrewbus.com or www.getitshuttle.com. Several distilleries in town are also popular.

Crux
BREWPUB

(☑ 541-385-3333; www.cruxfermentation.com; 50 SW Division St; ⏰ 11:30am-10pm Tue-Sun) Bend's latest brewpub darling, located in an industrial neighborhood (don't let the 'no trespassing' and 'private road' signs put you off). It has an awesome casual atmosphere, with fermentation tanks behind glass windows housing the unique experimental beers that this place puts out. Try the beer flight, which comes with six 5oz pours. Outdoor seating, family friendly and a good range of foods made with beer.

Deschutes Brewery & Public House
BREWPUB

(☑ 541-382-9242; www.deschutesbrewery.com; 1044 NW Bond St; ⏰ 11am-11pm Mon-Thu, till midnight Fri & Sat, till 10pm Sun) Bend's first microbrewery serves up plenty of food at its beautiful and huge two-story restaurant with balcony seating. Handcrafted beers including Mirror Pond Pale Ale, Black Butte Porter and Obsidian Stout; its Red Chair NWPA was voted 'world's best beer' in 2012 by the World Beer Awards. Free daily tours are given every hour from 1pm to 4pm at its plant at 901 SW Simpson Ave.

Bend Brewing Co
BREWPUB

(☑ 541-383-1599; www.bendbrewingco.com; 1019 NW Brooks St; ⏰ 11:30am-9pm Sun-Thu, till 10pm Fri & Sat) This casual pub-restaurant has a good location near the river, with a great patio for warm days. Order one of the award-winning brews, such as the hoppy Elk Lake India Pale Ale, or the robust Pinnacle Porter. On Mondays, you get $5 off certain growlers. Typical pub food (burgers and salads) is also available.

Thump Coffee
CAFE

(☑ 541-388-0226; www.thumpcoffee.com; 25 NW Minnesota Ave, No 2; ⏰ 6am-5:30pm Mon-Fri, 7am-5:30pm Sat, 7am-4:30pm Sun) Some of Bend's best coffee can be found at this elegant little coffee shop downtown, which roasts its own beans.

ℹ Information

Bend-Fort Rock Ranger District (☑ 541-383-4000; www.fs.usda.gov/main/centraloregon/home; 63095 Deschutes Market Rd; ⏰ 7:45am-4:30pm Mon-Fri) For camping and hiking information, plus trail conditions. A better-located visitor center on Hwy 46, toward Mt Bachelor, is being planned.

Visit Bend (☑ 800-949-6086; www.visitbend.com; 750 NW Lava Rd; ⏰ 9am-5pm Mon-Fri, 10am-4pm Sat) Great information, plus maps and recreation passes.

ℹ Getting There & Around

The Redmond Municipal airport is located 18 miles north of Bend; several bus companies provide shuttle service.

Central Oregon Breeze (☎800-847-0157; www.cobreeze.com) offers transportation to Portland two or more times daily. You can connect to Sisters, Willamette Valley destinations and the coast with **Valley Retriever** (www.kokkola-bus.com) and **Porter Stage Lines** (www.kokkola-bus.com). **Grant County People Mover** (www.grantcountypeoplemover.com) goes to the John Day area three times weekly.

High Desert Point (www.highdesert-point.com) buses link Bend with Chemult, where the nearest train station is located (65 miles south). It also has bus services to Eugene, Ontario and Burns.

Cascades East Transit (www.cascadeseast-transit.com) is the regional bus company in Bend, covering La Pine, Mt Bachelor, Sisters, Prineville and Madras. It also provides bus transportation within Bend.

The greenest way of getting around town is by renting a bicycle (see p286). For a pedicab tour, contact **Get It Shuttle** (www.getitshuttle.com).

Mt Bachelor

Just 22 miles southwest of Bend is Oregon's best skiing – glorious Mt Bachelor (9065ft). Here, Central Oregon's cold, continental air meets up with the warm, wet Pacific air. The result is tons of fairly dry snow and plenty of sunshine – excellent conditions for skiing. With 370in of snow a year, the season begins in November and can last until May.

At **Mt Bachelor Ski Resort** (☎800-829-2442; www.mtbachelor.com; lift tickets adult/child 6-12yr/child 13-18yr $59/36/49), rentals are available at the base of the lifts. In Bend, you can stop for gear at **Powder House** (☎541-389-6234; www.powderhousebend.com; 311 SW Century Dr). **Shuttle buses** (www.mtbachelor.com) run several times a day to Mt Bachelor from Bend.

Mt Bachelor grooms about 35 miles of cross-country trails, though the day pass (weekends and holidays $17, weekdays $14) may prompt skiers to check out the free trails at Dutchman Flat Sno-Park, just past the turnoff for Mt Bachelor on Hwy 46. This is as far as the snowplows maintain the highway during winter.

If there's adequate snow at lower elevations you can also cross-country ski from the Virginia Meissner or Swampy Lakes Sno-Parks, between Bend and Mt Bachelor on Hwy 46. To use all these Sno-Parks you'll need a Sno-Park permit, which is available

from area businesses ($3 for one day, $7 for three days, $20 for an annual pass).

In summertime you can go hiking and mountain biking on the mountain, and take the chairlift to a meal at Pine Marten Lodge, which has restaurants offering incredible mountain views.

Newberry National Volcanic Monument

This relatively recent volcanic region (day use $5), highlighted by the Newberry Caldera, showcases 400,000 years of volcanic activity.

◉ Sights & Activities

Newberry Crater   VOLCANO
Newberry Crater was formed by the eruption of what was one of the largest and most active volcanoes in Oregon. Successive flows cover 500 sq miles. As with Crater Lake, the summit of the volcano collapsed after a large eruption, creating a caldera.

Initially a single body of water, **Paulina Lake** and **East Lake** are now separated by a lava flow and a pumice cone. Due to the lakes' great depths and the constant flow of fresh mineral spring water, stocked trout thrive here. Looming above is 7985ft **Paulina Peak**.

A short trail halfway between the two lakes leads to the **Big Obsidian Flow**, an enormous deposit on the south flank of Newberry Crater. The **Newberry Crater Rim Loop Trail** circles Paulina Lake and is a good place for hiking and mountain biking.

To get there from US 97, take Paulina East Lake Rd to Newberry Caldera.

Lava Formations

For spectacular views, drive to the summit of **Lava Butte**, a perfect cone rising 500ft above the surrounding lava flows; get a permit from the welcome station first.

Four miles west of the visitor center is **Benham Falls**, a good picnic spot on the Deschutes River. About 1 mile south of the visitors center, **Lava River Cave** (☉9am-4pm, hours vary outside summer) is the only lava tube that's developed for visitor (bring a flashlight or rent a lantern for $5).

About 6000 years ago, a wall of molten lava 20ft deep flowed down from Newberry Crater and engulfed a forest of mature trees, resulting in the **Lava Cast Forest**.

The mile-long interpretive trail here is 9 miles east of US 97 on Lava Cast Forest Rd.

🛏 Sleeping

The monument's various campgrounds usually stay open from late May to October. Contact the Bend-Fort Rock Ranger District in Bend (p288) for more information.

There are a few cheap motels and restaurants in La Pine, about 30 miles south of Bend.

East Lake Resort MOTEL, CABIN $
(☑ 541-536-2230; www.eastlakeresort.com; 22430 E Lake Rd; d $75, cabins $139-169; 🛜 🐾) This resort offers 12 rustic but comfortable cabins with kitchenettes; some boast lake views. There are also four motel-type rooms with outside coin-operated showers, a grocery store, a tackle shop, a cafe and boat rentals. Tent/RV sites are also available ($20/25). Located 18 miles east of Hwy 97.

LaPine State Park CAMPGROUND $
(☑ 541-536-2071, 800-452-5687; www.oregonstateparks.org; 15800 State Recreation Rd; tent & RV sites $22, rustic/deluxe cabins $42/81; 🐾) Just north of La Pine and 4 miles west of US 97, this piney campground has sites near the Deschutes River, along with hot showers and flush toilets.

Paulina Lake Lodge CABIN $$
(☑ 541-536-2240; www.paulinalakelodge.com; cabins $100-265; 🐾) Thirteen miles east of Hwy 97 is this rustically pleasant resort with a handful of log cabins (sleeping up to 10). Each has its own kitchen and bath; some are more 'upscale' than others. There's also a restaurant, bar, small store and tackle shop; you can rent kayaks, canoes, paddle boats and stand-up paddleboards.

ℹ Information

Start your visit at the **Lava Lands Visitor Center** (☑ 541-593-2421; 58201 S Hwy 97; ⊙ 9am-5pm mid-Jun–Labor Day weekend, limited hours low season), about 13 miles south of Bend. The center is closed some days outside the peak season; check the website before you visit to make sure it will be open.

Cascade Lakes

Long ago, lava from the nearby volcanoes choked this broad basin beneath the rim of the Cascade Range. Lava flows dammed streams, forming lakes. In other areas, streams flowed underground through the porous lava fields to well up as lake-sized springs. Still other lakes formed in the mouths of small, extinct craters.

Hwy 46, also called the Cascade Lakes Hwy, loops roughly 100 miles between high mountain peaks, linking together this series of lovely alpine lakes (though many of them aren't visible from the road). Cyclists pedal the road in summer, while skiers and snowmobilers take over during winter. There are several trailheads in the area. Beyond Mt Bachelor, the road is closed from November to May.

Tiny **Todd Lake** offers views of Broken Top and relative seclusion, as getting there requires a quarter-mile hike. **Sparks Lake**, in a grassy meadow popular with birds, is in the process of transforming itself into a reedy marsh. **Hosmer Lake** is stocked with catch-and-release Atlantic salmon, making it popular with anglers (and osprey and beavers). **Little Lava Lake** is the source of the mighty Deschutes River. The Deschutes is dammed at **Crane Prairie Reservoir**, where ospreys fish in the shallow lake water and use dead trees for nesting.

🛏 Sleeping

There are public campgrounds at each of the lakes along the route. Some have resort cabins on their shores, ranging from rustic to upscale. Not all are open year-round; check ahead of time. Reserve well ahead in summer. Restaurants, groceries and boat rentals are usually available.

Cultus Lake Resort CABIN $
(☑ 541-408-1560; www.cultuslakeresort.com; cabins $85-140; 🐾) Offers 23 homey cabins with a two-night minimum; week-only from July 4 to Labor Day. There's also a restaurant and marina.

Elk Lake Resort CABIN $
(☑ 541-480-7378; www.elklakereservations.net; cabins $29-135, homes $150-199; 🐾) This resort has cabins ranging from very rustic (no electricity, outside bath, bring your own linens) to comfortably cozy. Upscale homes, along with camping and RV sites, are also available.

Twin Lakes Resort CABIN $$
(☑ 541-382-6432; www.twinlakesresort.net; cabins from $120) The cabins here are simple yet comfortable, and can sleep up to 16. All have lake views. One cabin for two is available for $70.

Willamette Pass

Southeast from Eugene, the Willamette River leaves its wide valley and is immediately impounded into reservoirs. By Oakridge, the Willamette is restored to a rushing mountain river, and Hwy 58 climbs steadily up the Cascade Range's densely forested western slope.

At the Cascade crest, near Willamette Pass, are some beautiful lakes and wilderness areas, and Oregon's second-highest waterfall, 286ft **Salt Creek Falls**. There's good hiking here, and in winter the area is popular for downhill and cross-country skiing. Along the way, you can soak in warm waters at undeveloped **McCredie Hot Springs**; It's close to the road and clothing-optional. The unpaved turnout is just past Blue Pool Campground, about 50 miles east of Eugene.

◉ Sights

Waldo Lake   LAKE
At an elevation of 5414ft on the very crest of the Cascades, Waldo Lake has no stream inlets – the only water that enters is snowmelt and rainfall. It is one of the purest bodies of water in the world and is the source of the Willamette River. The lake is amazingly transparent – objects 100ft below the surface are visible. Not only is It Oregon's second-deepest lake (420ft), it's also the state's second-largest lake (10 sq miles). No motorized gas boats are allowed, but afternoon winds make the lake popular for sailing. Three lovely USFS campgrounds flank the eastern half of the lake.

The west and north sides of the lake are contained in the **Waldo Lake Wilderness Area**, a 148-sq-mile expanse that abuts the Three Sisters Wilderness and is filled with tiny glacial lakes, meadows and hiking trails.

Odell & Crescent Lakes   LAKES
Immediately on the eastern slope of Willamette Pass is gorgeous Odell Lake, resting in a steep glacial basin. Hiking trails lead into relatively unexplored wilderness from lakeside campgrounds. In winter, the lake becomes a popular cross-country skiing destination.

A rustic lodge and popular campground ring Crescent Lake, which is popular for water-skiing, fishing and swimming. It's about 9 miles south of Willamette Pass just off Hwy 58 (about 3 miles down National Forest Rd 60).

🏃 Activities

Hiking
A day-use pass ($5) is required for the following hikes. Trails are snow-free from July to October.

The 22-mile **Waldo Lake Trail** encircles Waldo Lake and is bikable. A less ambitious hike leads 3.4 miles from North Waldo Campground to rocky beaches at the outlet of the Willamette River; make it an 8-mile loop by returning via **Rigdon Lakes**, which lie at the base of a volcanic butte. Note that this hike is popular with mountain bikers, and goes through a 2006 fire area.

From the west end of Odell Lake, energetic hikers should consider the 5.3-mile one-way hike to **Yoran Lake** for a great view of 8744ft Diamond Peak. A popular hike from Odell Lake Resort leads 3.8 miles to **Fawn Lake**, below two rugged peaks.

Skiing
The **Willamette Pass Resort** (☎ 541-345-7669; www.willamettepass.com; Hwy 58; lift tickets adult/child 6-10yr $49/30), 70 miles southeast of Eugene and 70 miles southwest of Bend, has steep slopes and great views. Most of the 29 runs are rated intermediate to advanced, with a vertical drop of 1563ft. Six-person gondolas run all year for both skiers and hikers/mountain bikers. The Pacific Crest Trail is less than a mile away (no bikes).

The resort also has 12 miles of groomed cross-country ski trails. **Odell Lake** is another popular spot for cross-country skiing.

🛌 Sleeping

There are many campgrounds in the area.

Westfir Lodge   LODGE $
(☎ 541-782-3103; www.westfirlodge.com; 47365 1st St, Westfir; d $75-90; ▣ 🐾) A stone's throw from Oregon's longest covered bridge is this spacious lodge with eight homey guest rooms, one of them an eight-bed dorm ($30 per bed). Some rooms share baths down the hall. Check out the central vault, left over from when this building used to be a lumber company office. Breakfast costs extra.

Odell Lake Resort   LODGE, CAMPGROUND $
(☎ 541-433-2540; www.odelllakeresort.com; 21501 East Odell Rd; campsites $14-18, d $65-85, cabins $100-320; 🐾🐾🐾) This casual family resort has small lodge rooms with a pleasant common living room. Also available are about a dozen cabins, each with kitchen and

fireplace, that sleep up to 16. There's a restaurant, along with bike and boat rentals. Located 6 miles east of Willamette Pass and just off Hwy 58, right on Odell Lake.

North Waldo
Lake Campground   CAMPGROUND $
(off USFS Rd 5897; campsites $20; ⊘Jun-Oct) Campgrounds don't get much better than this lovely and rustic spot on Waldo Lake, but bring repellant. Located 11 miles off Hwy 58 near the end of USFS Rd 5898.

Willamette Pass Inn   MOTEL $$
(✉541-433-2211;   www.willamettepassinn.com; 19821 Hwy 58; d Sun-Thu $96-120, Fri, Sat & holidays $112-135, cabins $155; 含❀) This is the closest motel to the ski area, with very spacious and beautiful rooms, most boasting fireplaces and kitchenettes. Privately owned cabins are also available. It's 7 miles east of Willamette Pass.

Crescent Lake Resort   LODGE $$
(✉541-433-2505;   www.crescentlakeresort.com; National Forest Rd 60; cabins $95-215; 含❀) A variety of cabins (sleeping up to five) are on tap here, most with kitchen and some with fireplace; there's a three-night minimum from June to August and during holidays. Aquacycles, kayaks and mountain bikes are available for rent (snowmobiles in winter), and there's a restaurant with a nice patio too.

ℹ Information

Willamette pass divides two national forests. For details on the Deschutes National Forest, contact the **Crescent Ranger District** (✉541-433-3200; 136471 Hwy 97 Nth, Crescent; ⊘8am-4:30pm Mon-Fri). For information on the Willamette National Forest, including Waldo Lake, contact the **Middle Fork Ranger Station** (✉541-782-2283; www.fs.fed.us/r6/willamette; 46375 Hwy 58, Westfir; ⊘8am-4:30pm Mon-Fri).

Oregon Coast

Best Places to Eat

➡ Rising Star Cafe (p304)

➡ Blackfish Cafe (p307)

➡ Local Ocean Seafoods (p310)

➡ Waterfront Depot (p314)

Best Places to Stay

➡ Wildspring Guest Habitat (p321)

➡ Tu Tu' Tun Lodge (p322)

➡ Newport Belle (p309)

➡ Heceta Head Lighthouse B&B (p312)

Why Go?

A drive along Oregon's coast is a must-do any time of year. Rocky headlands loom high above the ocean, providing astounding vistas, while craggy rocks lie scattered along the shoreline like oceanic sentinels. The Coast Range is deeply etched by great rivers and patched with forests, offering outdoor enthusiasts excellent boating, fishing and hiking. The Oregon Dunes – among the largest coastal dunes in the world – stretch for more than 50 miles, and just offshore, gray whales migrate from Alaska to Mexico and back.

Thanks to a far-sighted government in the 1910s, Oregon's 363-mile Pacific Coast was set aside as public land and strung with more than 70 state parks and protected areas. The northern Oregon coast has developed more quickly than the southern end, offering travelers a choice between bustling beach resorts and blissfully laid-back retreats. Everyone from campers to gourmet-lovers will find a plethora of ways to enjoy this exceptional region.

When to Go
Newport

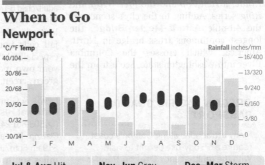

| Jul & Aug Hit the beach or go camping – but be prepared for crowds and high prices. | Nov–Jun Gray whales migrate north (March to June) or south (November to February). | Dec–Mar Storm-watchers' heaven: the crowds are gone and there's plenty of bargain lodging. |

NORTHERN OREGON COAST

Oregon's northern coast stretches from the mouth of the Columbia River south to Florence. Here lie the state's biggest and most touristy beach towns – Seaside, Cannon Beach and Lincoln City – while Depoe Bay is great for whale-watching and Newport is famous for its excellent aquarium.

Because of its popularity, the northern coast tends to get clogged with weekend visitors from Portland and the Willamette Valley. Since US 101 is mostly a two-lane highway, traffic can slow to 20mph in sections – especially with the many RVs on the road. Expect to join the masses during summer months, when the beaches fill with crowds and lodging prices skyrocket.

Astoria

POP 10,000

Named after America's first millionaire, John Jacob Astor, Astoria sits at the 5-mile-wide mouth of the Columbia River and was the first US settlement west of the Mississippi. The city has a long seafaring history and has seen its old harbor, once home to poor artists and writers, attract fancy hotels and restaurants in recent years. Inland are many historical houses, including lovingly restored Victorians – a few converted into romantic B&Bs.

◉ Sights & Activities

Astoria has been the setting and shooting location for movies such as *The Goonies, Kindergarten Cop* and the *Free Willy* and *Ring* series. Adding to the city's scenery is the 4.1-mile **Astoria-Megler Bridge**, the longest continuous truss bridge in North America, which crosses the Columbia River into Washington state. See it from the

Astoria Riverwalk, which follows the trolley route. Pier 39 is an interesting covered wharf with an informal cannery museum and a couple of places to eat.

★**Columbia River Maritime Museum**   MUSEUM
(☎503-325-2323; www.crmm.org; 1792 Marine Dr; adult/child 6-17yr $12/5; ☺9:30am-5pm) Astoria's seafaring heritage is well interpreted at this wave-shaped museum. It's hard to miss the Coast Guard boat, frozen in action, through a huge outside window. Other exhibits highlight the salmon-packing industry, local lighthouses and the river's commercial history; also check out the Columbia River Bar exhibit and 3-D theater.

Astoria Column   LANDMARK
(☎503-325-2963; www.astoriacolumn.org; Coxcomb Hill; parking $1) Rising high on Coxcomb Hill, the Astoria Column (built in 1926) is a 125ft tower painted with scenes from the westward sweep of US exploration and settlement. The top of the column (you'll need to go up 164 steps) offers excellent views over the area.

Flavel House   HISTORIC BUILDING
(www.cumtux.org; 441 8th St; adult/child 6-17yr $5/4; ☺10am-5pm) The extravagant Flavel House was built by Capt George Flavel, one of Astoria's leading citizens during the 1880s. This Queen Anne house has been repainted in its original colors and the grounds have been returned to Victorian-era landscaping; it has great views of the Columbia River too.

Oregon Film Museum   MUSEUM
(☎503-325-2203; www.cumtux.com; 636 Duane St; adult/child 6-17yr $4/2; ☺10am-5pm) Just below Flavel House is this small but fun museum, located in the old county jail. Two rooms and jail cells honor movies filmed in Oregon, especially Astoria's own *The Goonies*. Make your own movie clips and see yourself on a green screen.

Lewis & Clark National Historical Park   HISTORIC SITE
(☎503-861-2471; www.nps.gov/lewi; 92343 Fort Clatsop Rd; adult/child 15yr & under $3/free; ☺9am-6pm Jun-Aug, till 5pm Sep-May) Five miles south of Astoria, this historical park holds Fort Clatsop, a reconstructed fort similar to the one the Corps of Discovery occupied during their miserable winter of 1805–06. There's expedition history and artifacts at the visitor center, and costumed

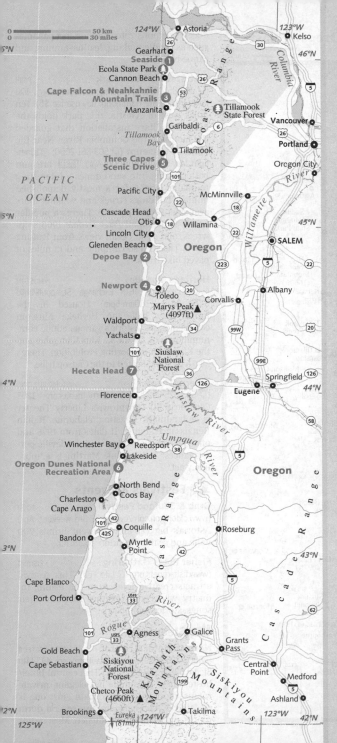

Oregon Coast Highlights

1 Nibbling fish 'n chips, crab cakes or chowder in towns such as **Seaside** (p300).

2 Spotting gray whales during their migrations at **Depoe Bay** (p307).

3 Hiking the **Cape Falcon** and **Neahkahnie Mountain Trails** (p303) for awesome views.

4 Checking out the jellyfish, sea otters and sharks at Newport's **Oregon Coast Aquarium** (p308).

5 Cruising and taking in the views along the stunning **Three Capes Scenic Drive** (p305).

6 Camping and hiking among the towering sands of the **Oregon Dunes National Recreation Area** (p315).

7 Counting lighthouses – like the super-photogenic one at **Heceta Head** (p312) – along the coast.

Northern Oregon Coast

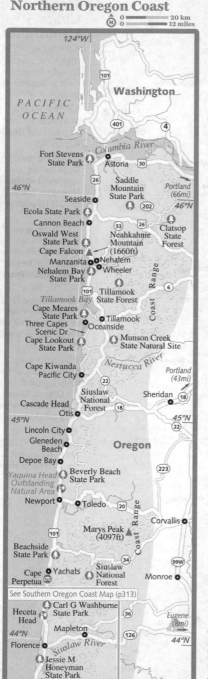

PACIFIC OCEAN

Washington

Oregon

See Southern Oregon Coast Map (p313)

docents demonstrate common fort pastimes such as candle-making, leather-tanning and canoe-building.

Fort Stevens State Park PARK
(📞503-861-1671; www.oregonstateparks.org; 100 Peter Iredale Rd, Hammond; day-use fee $5) Ten miles west of Astoria, this park holds the historic military installation that guarded the mouth of the Columbia River. Near the **Military Museum** (📞503-861-2000; ⊘10am-6pm May-Sep, to 4pm Oct-Apr) **FREE** are gun batteries dug into sand dunes – interesting remnants of the fort's mostly demolished military buildings (truck and walking tours available; $4 per person). There's a popular beach at the small *Peter Iredale* 1906 shipwreck, and good ocean views from Parking Lot C. There's also camping and 12 miles of paved bike trails.

Heritage Museum MUSEUM
(www.cumtux.org; 1618 Exchange St; adult/child 6-17yr $4/3; ⊘10am-5pm) Housed in the former city hall, the Heritage Museum commemorates Astoria's various ethnic communities. Look for the Ku Klux Klan robes and the Klan letter supporting Prohibition. There's also a room dedicated to the Clatsop tribe.

Liberty Theater HISTORIC BUILDING
(📞503-325-5922; www.liberty-theater.org; 1203 Commercial St) Downtown's Liberty Theater is a landmark boasting elaborate Italian Renaissance styling. It dates from 1925 and once hosted silent films and vaudeville performances; today, Pink Martini is a more likely act.

🎉 Festivals & Events

Crab & Seafood Festival FOOD
(www.oldoregon.com/events; ⊘3rd weekend Apr) Astoria's biggest annual event brings 200 wine and seafood vendors together.

Fisher Poets Gathering FISHING
(www.fisherpoets.org; ⊘late Feb) This festival attracts creative folks from the fishing industry who come together to share their songs, stories and poetry.

🛏 Sleeping

Norblad Hotel & Hostel HOTEL, HOSTEL $
(📞503-325-6989; www.norbladhotel.com; 443 14th St; dm $30, d $59-89; 🐾🖧) This central hotel/hostel offers six simple but elegant, private rooms, most with shared bath (just one is en suite; $74). There are also several dorm rooms and a communal kitchen. Most rooms

share outside baths but some have flat-screen TVs and peeks of the river.

Grandview B&B
B&B $$

(☑800-488-3250; www.grandviewbedandbreak-fast.com; 1574 Grand Ave; d $69-160; ☎) This sprawling, slightly outdated B&B features nine rooms, each with private bath and some with great views (a few are crowded with beds). Common spaces are limited and Charleen, the owner, does not allow alcohol on the premises.

Fort Stevens State Park
CAMPGROUND $

(☑503-861-1671; www.oregonstateparks.org; 100 Peter Iredale Rd, Hammond; tent sites/RV sites/yurts/cabins $21/27/41/85) About 560 sites (most RVs) are available at this popular campground 10 miles west of Astoria. Great for families; reserve in summer.

★Commodore Hotel
BOUTIQUE HOTEL $$

(☑503-325-4747; www.commodoreastoria.com; 258 14th St; d with shared/private bath from $89/149; ☎) Hip travelers should beeline to this slick and trendy hotel, which offers small, chic, minimalist rooms. Choose either private bathrooms or go Euro-style (sinks in rooms but baths down the hall; 'deluxe' rooms have better views). Great 'living room'–style lobby with attached cafe. Room 309 has the best river view.

Hotel Elliott
HISTORIC HOTEL $$

(☑503-325-2222; www.hotelelliott.com; 357 12th St; d incl breakfast $129-209; ✳☎) Standard rooms have charming period elegance at this historic hotel. For more space, get a suite (the 'presidential' boasts two bedrooms, two baths, a grand piano and rooftop deck). There's also a rooftop terrace with great views, and a wine bar open Wednesday to Sunday.

Franklin Street Station B&B
B&B $$

(☑503-325-4314; www.astoriaoregonbb.com; 1140 Franklin St; d $80-135; ☎) Well-located B&B offering six classic rooms, each with private bath and some with balconies and river views. Most rooms have TV, refrigerator and microwave; go for the Starlight attic room for a cozy romantic feel.

Rose River Inn B&B
B&B $$

(☑503-325-7175; www.roseriverinn.com; 1510 Franklin Ave; d $95-150; ☎) This friendly, casual country-style B&B offers five handsome rooms (all with private bathroom), including a two-bedroom suite. The breakfast room offers river views; a chihuahua roams the premises. Kids over 16 only.

Cannery Pier Hotel
HOTEL $$$

(☑503-325-4996, 888-325-4996; www.cannerypier hotel.com; 10 Basin St; d Sun-Thu $269, Fri & Sat $319; ☎) Located on a pier at the west end of town, this luxurious hotel offers fine rooms right over the water, with balconies, bridge views, contemporary furnishings and bathtubs that open to the room. Perks include afternoon wine socials, continental breakfast and a free ride in a vintage car. Spa on the premises.

✖ Eating & Drinking

Astoria is flush with good restaurants. Beer drinkers note: Rogue Brewery has a branch at 100 39th St (Pier 39).

Astoria Coffeehouse & Bistro
AMERICAN $

(☑503-325-1787; www.astoriacoffeehouse.com; 243 11th St; mains $10-22; ⊗7am-8pm Sun-Thu, till 9pm Fri & Sat, till 5pm Sun) Small, hip cafe with attached bistro offering an eclectic menu like Peruvian root vegetable stew, wasabi wonton prawns, chili-relleno burger, fish tacos, pad Thai and mac 'n' cheese. Great sidewalk seating.

Blue Scorcher Bakery Café
CAFE $

(☑503-338-7473; www.bluescorcher.com; 1493 Duane St; mains $7-13; ⊗8am-5pm; ☑⛟) ✔ Artsy, organic co-op coffeehouse and bakery. Tasty salads, sandwiches, pizza and egg dishes for breakfast. Vegetarian/vegan-friendly; doughnut-free.

Drina Daisy
BOSNIAN $$

(☑503-338-2912; www.drinadaisy.com; 915 Commercial St; lunch mains $9-16, dinner mains $15-25; ⊗11am-9pm Wed-Thu & Sun, till 10pm Fri & Sat) Excellent Bosnian food that includes rotisserie lamb, stuffed cabbage leaves and spinach pitas. There's Turkish coffee to sip and baklava for dessert.

Fort George Brewery
BREWPUB $$

(☑503-325-7468; www.fortgeorgebrewery.com; 1483 Duane St; mains $9-14; ⊗11am-11pm Mon-Thu, till midnight Fri & Sat, noon-11pm Sun) Atmospheric brewery-restaurant in a historic building – this was the original settlement site of Astoria. Today you can get gourmet burgers, house-made sausages, organic salads and a few eclectic dishes. Afternoon brewery tours on weekends.

T Paul's Urban Café   INTERNATIONAL $$

(☑503-338-5113; www.tpaulsurbancafe.org; 1119 Commercial St; mains $11-19; ☺11am-9pm Mon-Thu, to 10pm Fri & Sat) With a slick yet funky atmosphere, this popular cafe serves up a large variety of gourmet quesadillas, sandwiches, salads and pastas. Another branch is at 360 12th St.

Bridgewater Bistro   NORTHWESTERN $$$

(☑503-325-6777; www.bridgewaterbistro.com; 20 Basin St; lunch mains $9-14, dinner mains $22-30; ☺11:30am-9pm) Fine dining with great water views in a beautiful lofty space. There are fancy sandwiches, salads and burgers for lunch, and gourmet seafood and steak dishes for dinner. Sunday brunch too.

Wet Dog Café   BREWPUB

(☑503-325-6975; www.wetdogcafe.com; 144 11th St; mains $10-20; ☺11am-9pm Mon-Thu, till 9:30pm Fri, 8am-9:30pm Sat, 8am-9pm Sun) 🍴 For casual dining there's this large, quirky brewery-restaurant, with beers like Poop Deck Porter and Bitter Bitch IPA. The grub is typically publike, and there are good water views. Live music on weekends.

ⓘ Information

Visitor Center (☑503-325-6311; www.old oregon.com; 111 W Marine Dr; ☺9am-5pm) Sells permits such as the Oregon Pacific Coast Passport (p294) and State Park Recreation Pass.

ⓘ Getting There & Around

Bikes & Beyond (☑503-325-2961; www.bikesandbeyond.com; 1089 Marine Dr; ☺10am-6pm Mon-Sat, 11am-4pm Sun) Rents one-speed beach cruisers for $5 per hour or $20 per day.

Northwest Point (☑503-484-4100; www.northwest-point.com) Twice-daily buses head to Seaside, Cannon Beach and Portland.

Pacific Transit (☑360-642-9418; www.pacifictransit.org) Buses go over the border to Washington.

Riverfront Trolley ($1) Astoria's trolley goes from the Port of Astoria to Pier 39. It runs from noon to 6pm in summer and is shut down from January to March.

Sunset Empire Transit (☑503-861-7433; www.ridethebus.org; 900 Marine Dr) Local transportation; buses also head to Warrenton, Cannon Beach and Seaside.

Seaside

POP 6500

Oregon's largest resort town is popular, gaudy and unpretentious Seaside, which attracts families and young folks looking for a fun and affordable beach getaway. On summer weekends and during holidays or festivals the town's central precinct – dominated by ice-cream shops, video-game arcades and gift stores – is thronged with tourists and takes on a carnival-like atmosphere. Bicycles and surreys have the run of Seaside's 2-mile boardwalk, called 'the Prom,' but at least most of the miles of sandy beach are relatively peaceful. During spring break, expect a wilder party atmosphere.

◎ Sights

Seaside Aquarium   AQUARIUM

(☑503-738-6211; www.seasideaquarium.com; 200 N Promenade; adult/child 6-13yr $8/4; ☺9am-7pm; ⊕) Families with kids will enjoy this aquarium on the promenade. Don't expect anything like Newport's cutting-edge version, but rather a few fish tanks, a touch pool and a small indoor seal tank where you can feed the splashy critters. A recent addition is the 'Tsunami Fish' – an Asian fish that stowed away in a wooden boat set adrift by the 2011 Japanese tsunami.

Seaside Museum & Historical Society   MUSEUM

(☑503-738-7065; 570 Necanicum Dr; adult/senior $3/2; ☺10am-4pm Mon-Sat) Curious about Seaside's past? This museum displays old

---

THE LONG WALK – THE OREGON COAST TRAIL

The **Oregon Coast Trail** (OCT; www.oregon.gov/oprd/parks/Pages/oct_main.aspx) is an adventurous 400-mile route that runs through sandy beaches, verdant forests and rocky headlands, as well as coastal towns and cities. It preserves public access lands and provides wonderful wildlife-viewing opportunities.

The OCT isn't necessarily a hard route, but it'll take about a month to hike the whole thing. This is best done north to south due to prevailing winds and available literature. Hike it all or just a few sections of it, and enjoy the spectacular views – there's one around every corner or two.

photos and relics; ask about Lewis and Clark's saltworks' history and summer re-enactments here.

🏃 Activities

Join the pedaling hordes on the promenade by renting bikes and four-wheel surreys at **Prom Bike & Hobby Shop** (☑503-738-8251; 622 12th Ave). It also offers tandems, skates and strollers (and more). For advice on where to hit the waves, there's **Cleanline Surf Company** (☑503-738-7888; www.cleanlinesurf.com; 60 N Roosevelt Dr); it rents surfboards, kayaks and stand-up paddleboards.

**Saddle Mountain
State Natural Area** HIKING
(☑503-368-5943; www.oregonstateparks.org) About 13 miles east of Seaside on US 26, this park features a popular 2.5-mile hiking trail that starts at 1650ft elevation and heads through alpine wildflower meadows to the top of Saddle Mountain (3283ft). Views of the Columbia River and the Pacific coastline are absolutely spectacular, but the trail is steep and grueling. Bring layers and be prepared for changeable weather.

🎉 Festivals & Events

**Seaside Beach Volleyball
Tournament** SPORTS
(www.seasidebeachvolleyball.com; ⊙2nd weekend Aug) If you're here in mid-August, check out the largest amateur beach-volleyball tournament in the world.

Hood to Coast Relay RACE
(www.hoodtocoast.com; ⊙4th weekend Aug) In August, the Hood to Coast Relay jams the main road between Portland and Seaside and packs out the town.

🛏 Sleeping

Reserve in July and August, when two-night minimums might be required on weekends.

Seaside International Hostel HOSTEL $
(☑503-738-7911; www.seasidehostel.net; 930 N Holladay Dr; dm/d $29/69; @�📶♿🐾) For budget lodgings you can't beat this family-friendly hostel, offering good dorms and private rooms with bath – most opening to the parking area. There's a kitchen and TV room, but the highlight is the grassy backyard overlooking a river. Canoe and kayak rentals available. Cyclists and those who get here by bus get a $2 discount off dorm rates.

**Bud's RV Park
& Campground** CAMPGROUND $
(☑503-738-6855; 4412 Hwy 101 N; tent/RV sites $26/39; 🐾) This campground has RV and tent sites near the highway, plus full grocery store with crab pots and razor clam digging gear for rent. Located about 4 miles north of Seaside. For more tent camping try Astoria (15 miles north; see p296) or Cannon Beach (7 miles south; see p301).

Inn of the Four Winds INN $$
(☑800-818-9524; www.innofthefourwinds.com; 820 N Promenade; d $159-299; 🐾) One of Seaside's most luxurious stays is this intimate inn with only 14 rooms. All are beautiful and most come with gas fireplace and an outside seating area boasting ocean views. Tempur-Pedic mattresses and flat-screen TVs are de rigueur, but best of all might be the complimentary cookies that greet you upon arrival.

Gearhart Hotel HOTEL $$
(☑503-717-8159; www.mcmenamins.com; 1157 N Marion Ave, Gearhart; d weekdays $150-190, weekends $195-225; 🐾🍴) The McMenamin brothers extend their empire to the beach with this, their latest hotel venue, located in Gearhart (3 miles north of Seaside). All 18 comfortable, wood-paneled rooms have private bathroom, and are decorated with the quirky art that has made the McMenamin brand famous. Below is a restaurant-bar with awesome outdoor patio that looks over golf links.

Sandy Cove Inn BOUTIQUE MOTEL $$
(☑503-738-7473; www.sandycoveinn.biz; 241 Ave U; d $99-199; 🐾🍴) This friendly, family-run motel has 18 boutique rooms; all are different and tastefully decorated with fun themes and antiques. Jacuzzi suites, two houses and a condo are also available (sleeping up to 12). It's at the north end of town, three blocks from the beach.

Beachside Inn MOTEL $$
(☑800-845-1284; www.beachsideinnseaside.com; 300 5th Ave; d $105-175; 🐾) Just a couple of blocks from the beach and close to downtown Seaside is this handful of cute rooms and multi-bedroom units, all tastefully furnished with soft pastels and pleasant decor. Most have a small kitchen, while others have just a microwave, coffeemaker and fridge – but all are comfortable and clean.

Hillcrest Inn
HOTEL $$

(☑503-738-6273; www.seasidehillcrest.com; 118 N Columbia; d $120; ❋ ⊛) This Cape Cod–style inn offers a wide variety of simple but comfortable rooms and suites, some with kitchenette, jetted tubs and partial ocean views (rooms 123 and 129 are especially good). They sleep up to six. There's a nice grassy common area, and the beach is a block away. It's great value; reserve way ahead for the really budget rooms ($40 and $72).

Gilbert Inn
INN $$

(☑503-738-9770; www.gilbertinn.com; 341 Beach Dr; d $119-159; ⊛) This 1892 Queen Anne house is located in a neighborhood of apartments, but it's just a block from the beach. The nine guest rooms, all carpeted and decorated in traditional style, have private bathrooms; the attic room is huge. Children over 18 only; minimal breakfast.

✖ Eating

Seaside Coffee House
CAFE $

(5 N Holladay Dr; ⊘6am-4pm Mon & Tue, till 5pm Wed-Fri, 7am-5pm Sat, 7am-4pm Sun) For good coffee in a casual atmosphere try this comfortable and friendly coffee shop. There's oatmeal for breakfast and grilled sandwiches for lunch. Or get a banana fudge latte and lose yourself in a sofa.

Pacific Way Bakery & Cafe
NORTHWESTERN $$

(☑503-738-0245; www.pacificwaybakery-cafe. com; 601 Pacific Way; mains $14-29; ⊘11am-3:30pm & 5-9pm Thu-Mon) Located in Gearhart, about 3 miles north of Seaside, this jewel of a restaurant is worth the trip. It serves excellent sandwiches and salads for lunch, while dinner means treats such as tequila-lime chicken or pan-roasted ling cod – though gourmet pizza is also available. The bakery next door (open 7am to 1pm Thursday to Monday) has folks lining up outside.

Norma's
SEAFOOD $$

(☑503-738-4331; www.normasseaside.com; 20 N Columbia; mains $13-25; ⊘11am-10pm) Look for the lighthouse shape atop this family-friendly restaurant, which serves up a medley of seafood dishes, from halibut steaks to Alaska king crab to four kinds of fish 'n chips. Steaks, pasta, salads and plenty of sandwiches also available.

McKeown's
AMERICAN $$

(☑503-738-5232; www.mckeownsrestaurant. com; 1 N Holladay Dr; mains $10-21; ⊘11am-9pm

Mon-Fri, 8am-9pm Sat & Sun; ⊞) Family-friendly and popular, this restaurant serves good breakfast, lunch and dinner, offering something for everyone. Come during happy hour for cheap appetizers, and if you're super hungry on Sunday morning then the famous buffet is a must.

❶ Information

Visitors Bureau (☑503-738-3097; www. seasideor.com; 7 N Roosevelt Dr; ⊘8am-5pm Mon-Sat, 11am-4pm Sun)

❶ Getting There & Away

Northwest Point buses to Portland, Astoria and Cannon Beach stop daily at **Del's Service Station** (☑503-738-3651; www.northwest-point.com; 1215 S Holladay Dr). **Sunset Empire Transportation District** (☑503-861-7433; www.ridethebus. org) has similar services.

Cannon Beach
POP 1700

Charming Cannon Beach is one of the most popular beach resorts on the Oregon Coast. Several premier hotels here cater to a fancier clientele, as do the town's many boutiques and art galleries. In summer the streets are ablaze with flowers. Unlike Seaside's Coney Island–like atmosphere, Cannon Beach is toned down and much more refined. Lodging is expensive, and the streets are jammed: on a warm sunny Saturday, you'll spend a good chunk of time just finding a parking spot.

Just offshore is another reason for the town's popularity. Glorious Haystack Rock is a magnet for beachgoers – providing great photo opportunities and tide-pooling possibilities – and the wide sandy beach stretches for miles.

◉ Sights & Activities

If you want to check out the local surfing, visit **Cannon Beach Surf** (☑503-436-0475; www.cannonbeachsurf.com; 1088 S Hemlock St)for board rentals and lessons. Landlubbers who like to pedal can rent three-wheeled sand bicycles at **Family Fun Cycle** (☑503-436-2247; 1160 S Hemlock St). The chamber of commerce has a list of area hikes. Horseback riding is available at Sea Ranch RV Park.

Ecola State Park
PARK

(☑503-436-2844; day-use fee $5) Located just north of town, Ecola State Park offers seclusion and great picnicking. Short paths at

OREGON COAST FOR FAMILIES

The Oregon Coast is a great destination for families. Cities like Seaside and Newport have affordable accommodations, good beaches and family atmosphere. Here are some particularly fun places to take the kids:

Seaside Aquarium (p298) Slightly cheesy, but you can feed the seals!

Oregon Coast Aquarium (p308) Cutting edge, with plenty for kids to see and do.

Hatfield Marine Science Center (p308) Educational, surprisingly good and free (but donations are welcome).

Umpqua Discovery Center (p316) Learn interactively about the area's cultural history.

Prehistoric Gardens (p321) Large-scale dinosaur replicas; need we say more?

Ecola Point lead over the headland to dramatic views of Cannon Beach's sandy shore, sharply punctuated by stone monoliths and all hunkered beneath the Coast Range.

Leading north from here is an 8-mile stretch of the **Oregon Coast Trail** (see p298), which follows the same route traversed by the Corps of Discovery in 1806. Highlights on this trail include a sandy cove at **Indian Beach** (which is popular with surfers and stood in for La Push beach in the original *Twilight* movie) and **Tillamook Head** (which offers awesome views).

Haystack Rock   LANDMARK
Haystack Rock is Cannon Beach's iconic symbol, a beautiful hulking monolith that rises 235ft and has had cameos in several movies. It's part of the Oregon Islands National Wildlife Refuge and home to a variety of seabirds, including the charmingly cute tufted puffin.

During low tide you can walk out to the rock and investigate tide pools and sea caves. In summer, volunteers are on hand to help protect the area and provide infomation (www.cannon-beach.net/hrap). Please do not remove anything from the tide pools.

The closest access to Haystack Rock is at the end of Gower St, a mile south. Note that there's another monolith also confusingly called Haystack Rock, off Cape Kiwanda to the south.

⭐ Festivals & Events

Sandcastle Day   CULTURE
(⊙ Jun) Cannon Beach's largest festival (held in June, dates depend on tides) has teams competing for originality and execution in sand sculpture.

🛏 Sleeping

Cannon Beach is pretty exclusive; for budget choices head 7 miles north to Seaside (p298). For vacation rentals, check out www.visitcb.com.

Sea Ranch RV Park   CAMPGROUND $
(☎ 503-436-2815; www.searanchrv.com; 415 Fir St; tent sites $33, RV sites $38-43, cabins $85-95; 🐾) Pleasant Sea Ranch, on quiet Ecola Creek, is across from the turnoff to Ecola State Park and a seven-minute walk to the center. On the premises are an espresso bar, a 'wellness center' and a horseback riding operation. Feral bunnies and racoons abound so watch your food.

Wright's for Camping   CAMPGROUND $
(☎ 503-436-2347; www.wrightsforcamping.com; 334 Reservoir Rd; tent sites $32; 🐾) Family-run campground with clean bathhouse and 20 pleasant, spacious sites in a woodsy forest. Plenty of tall trees – bring your hammock. Open May to September (check for exact dates).

Waves Motel   MOTEL $$
(☎ 800-822-2468; www.thewavesmotel.com; 188 W 2nd St; d $139-459; 🐾) Disregard the word 'motel' here – this place is more like an upscale inn. Furnishings are elegant and the rooms comfortable and bright, and some come with kitchens, two bedrooms and decks overlooking the beach. Also on offer are suites, a two-bedroom townhouse and three-bedroom beach house next door at the Argonauta Inn, which is run by the same management and shares the same website and prices.

Cannon Beach Hotel   HISTORIC HOTEL $$
(☎ 503-436-1392; www.cannonbeachhotellodgings.com; 1116 S Hemlock St; d incl breakfast $139-269; 🐾) If you don't need much space, check out this classy, centrally located hotel with just 10 rooms. Standard rooms are lovely but very small; even the regular suites are tight. A good breakfast at the cafe on the premises is included.

Blue Gull Inn Motel MOTEL **$$**

(☎800-507-2714; www.haystacklodgings.com; 487 S Hemlock St; d $119-219; 🐾📶🖥) These are some of the more affordable rooms in town, with comfortable atmosphere and toned-down decor, except for the colorful Mexican head-boards and serapes on the beds. Kitchenette and Jacuzzi units available. Run by Haystack Lodgings, which also manages six other properties in town and does vacation rentals.

★**Ocean Lodge** HOTEL **$$$**

(☎503-436-2241, 888-777-4047; www.theocean lodge.com; 2864 S Pacific St; d $269-399; 🖥📶🖥) This gorgeous place has some of Cannon Beach's most luxurious rooms, many with ocean view and all with fireplace and kitchenette. A complimentary continental breakfast, an 800-DVD library and pleasant sitting areas are available to guests. Located on the beach at the south end of town.

✖ Eating & Drinking

Sleepy Monk Coffee CAFE **$**

(☎503-436-2796; www.sleepymonkcoffee.com; 1235 S Hemlock St; ⏱8am-2pm Mon & Tue, till 4pm Fri-Sun) 🍴 For organic, certified fair-trade coffee, try this little coffee shop on the main street. Sit on an Adirondack chair in the tiny front yard and enjoy the rich brews, all tasty and roasted on the premises. Good home-made pastries too.

Lumberyard AMERICAN **$$**

(☎503-436-0285; www.thelumberyardgrill.com; 264 3rd St; mains $8-28; ⏱noon-9pm Mon, Thu & Sun, till 10pm Fri & Sat) This casual eatery has something for everyone, including rotisserie specialties, pasta, pizzas, salads, steaks and six kinds of burgers (get one with four patties and finish it within 30 minutes for a free T-shirt!). There are booths for cozy dining, a front patio for warm days and a bar area for easy drinking.

> ### SO HIP IT YURTS
>
> Many Oregon state parks along the coast offer modern yurts for 'luxury' camping. These sport canvas walls, windows, electricity and heat (bath-rooms are usually outside). Furniture such as bunk beds and tables are included, but bring bedding. Yurts are immensely popular in summer, so reserve way ahead.

★**Newman's at 988** FRENCH, ITALIAN **$$$**

(☎503-436-1151; www.newmansat988.com; 988 S Hemlock St; mains $22-36; ⏱5:30-9pm daily Jul–mid-Oct, Tue-Sun mid-Oct–Jun) Expect a fine-dining experience at this small, quality restaurant on the main drag. Award-winning chef John Newman comes up with a fusion of French and Italian dishes such as marinated rack of lamb and char-grilled portabella mushrooms with spinach and Gorgonzola. Desserts are sublime.

Irish Table IRISH **$$$**

(☎503-436-0708; www.theirishtablerestaurant. com; 1235 S Hemlock St; mains $20-29; ⏱5:30-9pm Fri-Tue) 🍴 Excellent restaurant serving a fusion of Irish–Pacific Northwest cuisine, using local and seasonal ingredients. The menu is small and simple, but the choices are tasty, eg vegetarian shepherd's pie, lamb loin chops and seared Piedmontese flat iron steak. Don't miss the homemade desserts.

ℹ Information

Chamber of Commerce (☎503-436-2623; www.cannonbeach.org; 207 N Spruce St; ⏱10am-5pm) Has good local information, including tide tables.

ℹ Getting There & Around

Northwest Point (www.northwest-point.com) Buses head from Astoria to Portland (and vice versa) every morning, stopping at Cannon Beach; buy tickets at the Beach Store, next to Cannon Beach Surf. The **Cannon Beach Shuttle** (The Bus; ☎503-861-7433; www.ridethebus. org) runs the length of Hemlock St to the end of Tolovana Beach; the schedule varies depending on the day and season. Both buses go to Seaside or Astoria too.

Tillamook County Transportation (The Wave; ☎503-815-8283; www.tillamookbus. com) buses go south toward Manzanita and Lincoln City several times daily.

Manzanita
POP 600

One of the more laid-back beach resorts on Oregon's coast is the hamlet of Manzanita, boasting lovely white-sand beaches and a slightly upscale clientele. It's much smaller and far less hyped than Cannon Beach, and still retains a peaceful atmosphere. You can relax on the beach, take part in a few activities and hike on nearby Neahkahnie Mountain, where high cliffs rise dramatically above the Pacific's pounding waves.

🏃 Activities

Hiking

Five miles north is **Oswald West State Park** (☑503-368-3575), a beautiful preserve with dense coastal rainforest and two headlands. For a good hike, take the 2.4-mile trail to **Cape Falcon**, which offers expansive views and good birdwatching. For more exercise, climb 2.5 miles to the top of 1660ft **Neahkahnie Mountain**, which towers above Nehalem Bay and offers amazing views – on a clear day, you can see 50 miles out to sea.

Cycling, Surfing & Kayaking

Surfers and body boarders can head a quarter-mile from the highway parking lot to **Short Sand Beach**, which offers good waves. Rent bicycles (or kites) from **Manzanita Bikes & Boards** (☑503-368-3337; www.manzanitabikesandboards.com; 170 Laneda Ave; bicycle rental per hour $9). There are kayaking opportunities just 4 miles south in Wheeler.

🛏 Sleeping & Eating

For vacation rentals, see www.manzanita rentals.com.

Inn at Manzanita   INN $$
(☑503-368-6754; www.innatmanzanita.com; 67 Laneda Ave; d $179-199; 🐾🍴) This very pleasant inn is right on the main street. There are 14 cozy rooms, all with fireplace, balcony and jetted tub. The larger suites are best for families and come with kitchenette; there's also a large three-bedroom penthouse apartment ($385). Two-night minimum in summer.

Sunset Surf Motel   MOTEL $$
(☑503-368-5224; www.sunsetsurfocean.com; 248 Ocean Rd; d $84-174; 🐾🍴🐾) Beachside motel with wide range of rooms (including one-bedroom units) in three buildings. Many rooms are large, with kitchenettes and ocean views. Room 27 has one of the best views.

⭐ **Coast Cabins**   APARTMENT $$$
(☑503-368-7113; www.coastcabins.com; 635 Laneda Ave; d $215-425; 🐾) Just six luxurious suites are available at this lovely retreat near the entrance to town. All come with contemporary furnishings and kitchenette, half are two-story affairs and four have private outdoor Jacuzzi. The simple, lovely gardens provide plenty of privacy.

⭐ **Bread & Ocean**   AMERICAN $
(☑503-368-5823; www.breadandocean.com; 154 Laneda Ave; panini $8.50; ⊘7:30am-2pm Wed-Sat, 8am-2pm Sun) 🍴 You'll have to line up for exceptional panini, pasta salads and baked goods at this small but excellent bakery-deli, a beloved local institution. Most meats are baked on the premises. The cute garden patio is a must on warm days.

Manzanita News & Espresso   CAFE $
(☑503-368-7450; 500 Laneda Ave; ⊘7:30am-5pm) This friendly, slightly funky and cozy cafe has good coffee and pastries, along with an interesting selection of magazines for sale. Nice outdoor seating for those warm summer days.

ℹ Getting There & Away

Tillamook County Transportation (The Wave; ☑503-815-8283; www.tillamookbus.com) Buses stop on 5th St near Laneda Ave and connect to Tillamook, Cannon Beach and Portland a few times daily.

Nehalem & Wheeler

Nearly 4 miles south of Manzanita, the Nehalem River creates a wide estuarial valley and bay that are protected from the ocean by a 3-mile sand spit. Straddling the river, the historic fishing villages of Nehalem and Wheeler have become centers for antiques and river recreation – and are home to a couple of truly fine restaurants.

🏃 Activities

Nehalem Bay State Park (☑503-368-5154; www.oregonstateparks.org; 9500 Sandpiper Lane; day-use fee $5) has a good 2-mile walk, or sandy bike ride, on the Spit Trail, which finishes up at the end of a peaceful peninsula. Meanwhile, the quiet, bird-rich waters of Nehalem Bay are good for contemplative kayaking and birdwatching; rent kayaks and canoes at **Wheeler Marina** (☑503-368-5780; www.wheelermarina.net; 580 Marine Dr; per hour single/double kayaks $22/28, canoes $28).

🛏 Sleeping & Eating

Bunk House   MOTEL $
(☑503-368-2865; www.thebunkhousemotel. biz; 36315 N US 101; d $46-126; 🐾) Located in Nehalem, this is a homely spot with seven good rooms (the cheapest share a bathroom) and two cabins. All rooms are clean and cozy, with quilts on the beds, and some

have full kitchen and dining areas. Casual restaurant on premises.

Nehalem Bay State Park
CAMPGROUND $

(☑503-368-5154, 800-452-5687; www.oregonstateparks.org; 9500 Sandpiper Lane; campsites/yurts $24/36; 🐾) On the dunes of Nehalem Spit, 3 miles south of Manzanita off US 101, this big campground has showers, equestrian facilities, a boat ramp and even an airstrip.

Old Wheeler Hotel
HOTEL $$

(☑877-653-4683; www.oldwheelerhotel.com; 495 Hwy 101; d $99-160; @🛜) This lovely historic hotel, with views of Nehalem Bay, is located 4 miles south of Manzanita in Wheeler. The eight rooms are classically styled and decorated with antiques, and some have a Jacuzzi. There's a two-room suite, a couple of pleasant common areas and continental breakfast is included.

★ Rising Star Cafe
CAFE $$

(☑503-368-3990; www.risingstarcafe.com; 92 Rorvik St; mains $14-24; ⊙noon-3pm & 5-8pm Wed, Thu & Sat, 5-8pm Fri, 10am-3pm Sun) Just a handful of tables sit in this fine restaurant, which looks more like a greasy-spoon shack. The exquisitely prepared dishes will soon set you straight, however, making it hard to choose between the North Coast cioppino (fish stew) with roasted vegetables, halibut and shrimp Française in a citrus beurre blanc and slow-roasted pumpkin risotto. If you're here on Sunday, don't miss the brunch.

Nehalem River Inn
NORTHWESTERN $$$

(☑503-368-7708; www.nehalemriverinn.com; 34910 Hwy 53; mains $16-32; ⊙5:30-9pm Thu-Sat, 9am-2pm Sun) 🍴 Located between Nehalem and Wheeler, 1.3 miles up Hwy 53 from Hwy 101, lies this highly regarded farm-to-table restaurant. Mostly organic and very local ingredients are used to create homey yet complex dishes like roasted bone marrow, Gruyère mac 'n' cheese and cinder-brined pork porterhouse. Leave room for dessert – chocolate *pot de crème* is often on the menu.

Tillamook

POP 5000

Best known for its huge cheese industry, Tillamook is a nondescript town that's worth a brief stop to down some dairy. Cheese production began in Tillamook in the 1890s, when an English cheesemaker brought his cheddar-making techniques to the fledgling dairies along Tillamook Bay.

Nearly a million people stop here annually to visit the famed Tillamook Cheese Factory, which produces 167,000 pounds of cheese every day.

South of Tillamook, US 101 loses the beaches and headlands and follows the Nestucca River through pastureland and logged-off mountains. The slower but prettier Three Capes Scenic Drive begins in Tillamook and follows the coast.

◉ Sights & Activities

Pioneer Museum
MUSEUM

(☑503-842-4553; www.tcpm.org; 2106 2nd St; adult/child 10-17yr $4/1; ⊙10am-4pm Tue-Sun) This worthwhile museum has a great taxidermy room and some very interesting pioneer artifacts. There are also curiously carved Neahkahnie stones (actually beeswax) meant to point to a legendary buried treasure, plus an Abraham Lincoln room with a sexy Norman Rockwell print of the president.

Tillamook Naval Air Museum
MUSEUM

(☑503-842-1130; www.tillamookair.com; 6030 Hangar Rd; adult/child 6-17yr $9/5; ⊙9am-5pm) Aircraft-lovers shouldn't miss the large collection of fighter planes and the 7-acre blimp hangar. It's 2 miles south of town; there are plans to move the planes to Madras in 2016.

Munson Creek Falls
WATERFALL

At Munson Creek State Natural Site, 7 miles south off US 101, an easy quarter-mile hike through old-growth spruce reaches Munson Creek Falls, the highest waterfall in the Coast Range at 319ft (though some figures incorrectly claim it's 266ft).

Tillamook Forest Center
MUSEUM

(☑866-930-4646; www.tillamookforestcenter.org; 45500 Wilson River Hwy; ⊙10am-5pm, limited hours outside summer, closed late Nov-Feb) FREE Located 22 miles east of Tillamook on Hwy 6, this excellent forest center educates the public on forest fires and the area's first white settlers. Cross a 250ft-long suspension bridge, watch salmon migrating, climb a (reproduction) fire lookout tower and tour the surrounding forest.

Tillamook Cheese Factory
CHEESE TASTING

(☑800-542-7290; www.tillamookcheese.com; 4175 N US 101; ⊙8am-8pm mid-Jun–Labor Day, till 6pm rest of year) Two miles north of town is this tourist wonderland. Line up for free cheese samples, lick down an ice-cream cone or peek

THREE CAPES SCENIC DRIVE

Cape Meares, Cape Lookout and Cape Kiwanda are some of the coast's most stunning headlands, strung together on a slow, winding and sometimes bumpy 40-mile alternative to US 101. It's a very worthwhile drive, though in March 2013 a section of road north of Cape Meares began sinking and was closed. Repairs are ongoing, so you might have to drive to Cape Meares via Netarts and Oceanside, then backtrack.

The forested headland at **Cape Meares** offers good views from its lighthouse, which is 38ft tall (Oregon's shortest). Short trails lead to Oregon's largest Sitka spruce and the 'Octopus Tree', another Sitka shaped like a candelabra.

A panoramic vista atop sheer cliffs that rise 800ft above the Pacific makes **Cape Lookout State Park** a highlight. In winter, the end of the cape, which juts out nearly a mile, is thronged with whale-watchers. There are wide sandy beaches, hiking trails and a popular campground near the water.

Finally there's **Cape Kiwanda**, a sandstone bluff that rises just north of the little town of Pacific City. You can hike up tall dunes, or drive your truck onto the beach. It's the most developed of the three capes, with plenty of services nearby – don't miss **Pelican Pub & Brewery** (mains $12-32; ⊗ 8am-10pm Sun-Thu, till 11pm Fri & Sat) if you like beer. Watch the dory fleet launch their craft or, after a day's fishing, land as far up the beach as possible.

into the factory floor assembly line; there's a cafe, gift shop and fudge counter too.

Blue Heron French Cheese Company CHEESE TASTING
(☑ 800-275-0639; www.bluehe111oregon.com; 2001 Blue Heron Dr; ⊗ 8am-8pm Jun-Aug, till 6pm Sep-May) The Blue Heron French Cheese Company, just north of town, offers much less hype than the Tillamook Cheese Factory. There are cheese, wine and jam tastings, along with a gourmet food gift shop. Its farm-animal petting pen and picnic grounds make it more of a country experience.

Pacific Seafood OYSTER SHUCKING
(☑ 503-377-2323; 5150 Oyster Dr; ⊗ 10am-8pm Jun-Sep, till 7pm Oct-May) To witness some of the fastest oyster shucking you'll ever see, head to Pacific Seafood in Bay City. The casual restaurant offers simple seafood dishes ($8 to $18) and a fish counter, but in the back is the assembly-line processing of oysters. Go early – the shuckers are sometimes done by noon.

🛏 Sleeping

Western Royal Inn MOTEL $
(☑ 503-842-8844; www.westernroyalinn.com; 1125 US 101; d $90; 🐾) Right next to Blue Heron French Cheese Company is this decent motel with spacious rooms. To avoid highway noise get a suite with bedroom in the back.

ℹ Information

Chamber of Commerce (☑ 503-842-7525; 3705 N US 101; ⊗ 9am-5pm Mon-Fri, 10am-2pm Sat & Sun) In the parking lot of the Tillamook Cheese Visitors Center.

ℹ Getting There & Away

Tillamook County Transportation (The Wave; ☑ 503-815-8283; www.tillamookbus.com) buses provide service within Tillamook city. They also depart from 2nd and Laurel Sts to Oceanside and Netarts on the capes, as well as to Manzanita, Lincoln City and Portland.

Lincoln City

POP 8000

More a sprawling modern beach resort than a serene seaside retreat, Lincoln City is a long series of commercial strips, motels, eateries and gift shops that front a fairly wide and lackluster stretch of sandy beach. As a local once put it, 'Lincoln City is five towns brought together in 1965 by the fact they needed a sewer system.' But the resort does serve as the region's principal commercial center, while boasting the Oregon Coast's most affordable beachfront accommodations, and the surrounding area features some good hikes.

From mid-October to Memorial Day, over 2000 brightly colored glass floats – hand-blown by local artisans – are hidden weekly along beaches as part of an ongoing (off-season) promotion.

◉ Sights

**North Lincoln
Historical Museum** MUSEUM
(☑541-996-6614; www.northlincolncounty
historicalmuseum.org; 4907 SW US 101; ☉noon-
5pm Wed-Sun) **FREE** This good museum
highlights Lincoln City's history with Native
American basketry, pioneer artifacts, glass
floats and exhibits on its past industries.

**Jennifer Sears
Glass Art Studio** GLASSBLOWING
(☑541-996-2569; www.jennifersearsglassart.com;
4821 SW Hwy 101) Like glassblowing? Then
don't miss the Jennifer Sears Glass Art Studio where you can learn to blow your own
float – or just watch someone else do it.

🏃 Activities

Hiking

At **Cascade Head**, two Nature Conservancy
trails access a 1200ft-high ocean vista. The
first is Cascade Head (north entrance), a
mile-long upper trail that leaves from Cascade Head Rd (USFS Rd 1861), 4 miles north
of the Hwy 18 junction. The second is Trail
1310, a 3-mile lower trail that scales the
headland from the end of Three Rocks Rd.

At the end of USFS Rd 1861 is the steep
2.6-mile trail down to **Harts Cove**, a remote
meadow along a cliff-lined bay frequented
by sea lions.

Some trails are closed January to July;
call the **Hebo Ranger Station** (☑503-392-
3161) for current information.

Other Activities

Canoeing and kayaking are possible on Devil's
Lake, east of town, and on Siletz Bay. Several
operators offer horseback riding on the beach,
including **Green Acres Beach & Trail Rides**
(☑541-603-1768; www.beach-rides.com).

Blue Heron Landing WATER SPORTS
(☑541-994-4708; 4006 W Devil's Lake Rd; ☉9am-
7pm mid-Mar–Sep) Rent kayaks, paddle boats
and bicycles.

Oregon Surf Shop SURFING
(☑541-996-3957; www.oregonsurfshop.com; 3001
SW US 101; ☉10am-6pm Mon-Sat, 1-6pm Sun)
Surfing advice and rentals.

🎉 Festivals & Events

Kite Festivals KITE FLYING
(☉Jun & Oct) The self-proclaimed 'Kite Capital
of the World,' Lincoln City hosts two kite festivals each year. Enormous kites – some over

LINCOLN CITY MUST-DOS

Shirley Brey (of Brey House B&B) has
some tips on what not to miss in Lincoln
City:

➡ Cascade Head – Great for hiking.

➡ The Beach – You can walk for miles in
either direction, and also go horseback
riding.

➡ Marionberry Cobbler – Every other
restaurant seems to offer it, and it's
good everywhere!

100ft in length – take off to twist and dive in
the ocean breezes.

**Siletz Bay
Sandcastle Contest** SANDCASTLES
(☉early Aug) Have a fun time checking out
amazing sand sculptures at this competition – or even participate yourself!

🛏 Sleeping

There are many hotels and motels on or
near Lincoln City's main drag, and endless
vacation rentals available online.

Historic Anchor Inn INN $
(☑541-996-3810; www.historicanchorinn.com; 4417
SW US 101; d $79-89; 🐾🖥) This is like no place
you've ever stayed. It's super quirky and
funky – in a good way – from the float collection and full-size boat in the front to the
museum-like kitschy decor in the hallways.
The breakfast room is worth the price of
admission alone. Kitchen, game room, sun-
deck, backyard and free popcorn are pluses.

Devil's Lake State Park CAMPGROUND $
(☑541-994-2002, 800-551-6949; www.oregon-
stateparks.org; 1452 NE 6th Dr; tent sites/RV sites/
yurts $21/27/40; 🖥) Located not far from the
beach, Devil's Lake includes showers, flush
toilets and fishing and boating on a freshwater lake.

Looking Glass Inn HOTEL $$
(☑541-996-3996, 800-843-4940; www.looking
glass-inn.com; 861 SW 51st St; d $114-149; @🐾🖥)
Simple but clean and comfortable rooms in
various sizes are featured at this modern
and friendly hotel. Some have kitchenette,
fireplace and jetted tubs; two-bedroom
suites are available. It's only a half-block
from the beach, and very dog-friendly.

Brey House B&B B&B **$$**
(☑ 877-994-7123, 541-994-7123; www.breyhouse.
com; 3725 NW Keel Ave; d $109-159; 🐾) For a personal experience, stay at this homey, Cape Cod–style B&B just a block from the beach (great ocean views from the common areas). There are four comfortable rooms, each with private bath and fireplace, and a suite with kitchen is available. For the best view snag the captain's suite.

Ester Lee Motel MOTEL **$$**
(☑ 888-996-3606, 541-996-3606; www.esterlee.
com; 3803 SW Hwy 101; d $97-167; @🐾🐾) A good range of plain yet comfortable rooms and cottages, some with kitchenette, fireplace and/or Jacuzzi, but all with ocean views. Located on a high, tsunami-resistant bluff; walk down to the beach.

Salishan Spa & Golf Resort HOTEL **$$$**
(☑ 800-452-2300; www.salishan.com; 7760 N US 101, Gleneden Beach; r from $199; @🐾🐾🐾) This four-star luxury resort boasts a top-notch 18-hole golf course, tennis courts and a gorgeous spa. Rooms are tastefully done, very spacious and have gas fireplaces; some boast water views. Also on-site are fancy shops, a video game room, an indoor pool and a fine dining room.

✗ Eating

The Salishan Spa & Golf Resort offers premier Northwestern cuisine and a legendary wine cellar.

★ **Blackfish Cafe** NORTHWESTERN **$$**
(☑ 541-996-1007; www.blackfishcafe.com; 2733 NW US 101; mains $16-28; ⊙ 11:30am-3pm & 5-9pm Wed-Mon) 🍴 Blackfish Cafe specializes in cutting-edge cuisine highlighting fresh seafood and local, seasonal vegetables. Chef Rob Pounding is an accomplished master at creating simple but delicious dishes; try his signature Northwest cioppino. Reserve in summer.

Kyllo's Seafood Grill AMERICAN **$$**
(☑ 541-994-3179; www.kyllosrestaurant.com; 1110 NW 1st Ct; mains $10-24; ⊙ 11:30am-8:30pm Sun-Thu, till 9am Fri & Sat) One of Lincoln City's few restaurants with an ocean view, popular Kyllo's offers good clam chowder, seafood, salads, pastas, burgers and steaks. A local called it 'the best seafood on the coast.' Outdoor tables are a must on hot days.

Wildflower Grill AMERICAN **$$**
(☑ 541-994-9663; 4250 NE US 101; mains $10-16; ⊙ 7am-4pm Sun & Mon, 7am-4pm & 5-9pm Tue-Sat) Located at the north end of town, this diner serves up tasty sandwiches, burgers and salads. Try the oyster po'boy, wilted spinach salad or crab benedict. Great for breakfast; get a table overlooking the big pond in back.

Bay House NORTHWESTERN **$$$**
(☑ 541-996-3222; www.thebayhouse.org; 5911 SW US 101; mains $27-39; ⊙ 5-9pm) Chef Kevin Ryan presides over the kitchen at this elegant establishment, creating a fine and changing seafood and meat menu (posted daily on the website). Only the freshest top-quality ingredients are used, and the view is stunning. Try the five-course tasting menu ($57).

ℹ Information

Visitor Center (☑ 541-994-3302; www.oregon-coast.org; 540 NE US 101; ⊙ 10am-5pm) In the cultural center building.

ℹ Getting There & Around

The local **LINC bus** (☑ 541-265-4900; www.co.lincoln.or.us/transit/pdfs/LincolnCityLoop.pdf) provides services within Lincoln City, while **Lincoln County Transit** (☑ 541-265-4900; www.lincoln.or.us/transit) buses connect to Newport and Yachats.

Depoe Bay

POP 1400

Located 10 miles south of Lincoln City, little Depoe Bay is edged by modern timeshare condominiums but still retains some original coastal charm. It lays claim to having the 'world's smallest navigable harbor' and being the 'world's whale-watching capital' – pretty big talk for such a pint-sized town. Whale-watching and charter fishing are the main attractions in the area, though 5 miles south of town there is also the Devil's Punchbowl, an impressive collapsed sea cave that churns with waves and offers good tide pools nearby (get there via Otter Crest Loop, a scenic road).

The **chamber of commerce** (☑ 541-765-2889; www.depoebaychamber.org; 223 SW US 101, Suite B; ⊙ 11am-3pm Sun-Wed, 9am-3pm Thu-Sat) is next to the Mazatlan restaurant. An impressive **Whale Watching Center** (☑ 541-765-3304; www.whalespoken.org; 119 SW US 101; ⊙ 9am-5pm) has good exhibits and provides

OREGON COAST DEPOE BAY

binoculars and views out to sea. There's also a **Whale, Sealife & Shark Museum** (☑541-765-2219; 234 SW US 101; adult/child 4-12yr $5/3; ☺9am-5pm), wonderful if you like dioramas. For whale-watching, contact **Dockside Charters** (☑800-733-8915; www. docksidedepoebay.com).

🛏 Sleeping & Eating

Trollers Lodge   MOTEL $
(☑800-472-9335; www.trollerslodge.com; 355 SW US 101; d $67-97; ☎❄) Come here for a dozen cute rooms and one- and two-bedroom suites (some with kitchenette), all decked out in casual country style. There's a grassy yard with gas grill and picnic tables.

Inn at Arch Rock   INN $$
(☑800-767-1835; www.innatarchrock.com; 70 NW Sunset St; d $89-179; ☎❄) This friendly, upscale inn has very comfortable rooms and suites, most with sea view. They range widely in size and amenities; some have fireplace, kitchenette and sitting areas. There's a grassy backyard and private beach cove access.

Tidal Raves   SEAFOOD $$
(☑541-765-2995; www.tidalraves.com; 279 US 101; mains $13-25; ☺11am-9pm) Both the food and the view are awesome at this popular restaurant overlooking the ocean. Seafood is a specialty, from grilled wild salmon to razor clam steaks to the shrimp in green curry. Good salads, soups and sandwiches also.

Newport

POP 10,000

Home to Oregon's largest commercial fishing fleet, Newport is a lively tourist city with several fine beaches and a world-class aquarium. In 2011 it became the host of NOAA (National Oceanic and Atmospheric Administration). Good restaurants – along with some tacky attractions, gift shops and barking sea lions – abound in the historic bayfront area, while bohemian Nye Beach offers art galleries and a friendly village atmosphere. The area was first explored in the 1860s by fishing crews who found oyster beds at the upper end of Yaquina Bay.

⊙ Sights

★**Oregon Coast Aquarium**   AQUARIUM
(☑541-867-3474; www.aquarium.org; 2820 SE Ferry Slip Rd; adult/child 3-12yr/child 13-17yr $18.95/11.95/16.95; ☺9am-6pm; 🖑) The region's top attraction, this cutting-edge aquarium is especially fun if you have kids along. Marine celebrities include seals, sea otters and a giant octopus (or two), and there's an impressive deep-sea exhibit where you walk under Plexiglas tunnels and get an eyeful of sharks and rays swimming by. The jellyfish exhibit is a surreal experience, while the touch tank appeals to everyone. There's also a good cafe.

★**Yaquina Head**
Outstanding Natural Area   PARK
(☑541-574-3100; 750 NW Lighthouse Dr; admission $7; ☺sunrise-sunset, interpretive center 10am-6pm) Stretching a mile out to sea is the popular Yaquina Head, a grassy headland just north of Newport. Short trails lead to viewing areas for shorebirds, harbor seals and whales, and the tide pools are the best-managed on the coast. Visit the excellent **interpretive center** to explore different marine environments and the history of the coast's lighthouses. The coast's tallest (93ft), still-functioning **lighthouse** is at the tip of the headland and offers tours by docents in period costumes.

Hatfield Marine
Science Center   SCIENCE CENTER
(☑541-867-0100; www.hmsc.oregonstate.edu; 2030 SE Marine Science Dr; ☺10am-5pm) FREE
This excellent science center has great exhibits, especially on wave energy and the local fishing industry. There's a touch tank and you can see the octopus being fed. Outside, a section of the Misawa dock from Japan is exhibited; the dock floated all the way across the Pacific after the 2011 tsunami. Admission is free, but donate a few dollars to help run programs.

Yaquina Bay State Park   PARK
(☑museum 541-265-5679; ☺lighthouse 11am-5pm, museum 11am-5pm) Situated on a bushy

---

CANYON WAY BOOKSTORE

Still hanging on after the internet age, the **Canyon Way Bookstore** (☑541-265-8319; www.canyonway.com; 1216 SW Canyon Way; ☺10am-5pm Mon-Thu, till 8pm Fri, 11am-4pm Sat) is a Newport institution offering a fine choice of books, with especially good history, mystery and children's sections. An on-site restaurant provides good homemade meals, a peaceful patio and occasional live music.

bluff above the north entrance of the bay, this park is popular for beach access and views over Yaquina Bay. Visit the **Yaquina Bay Lighthouse** – not to be confused with the Yaquina Head Lighthouse, 3 miles north – built in 1871. The living quarters are preserved as an informal **museum**.

Burrows House Museum MUSEUM
(☑541-265-7509; www.oregoncoast.history. museum; 545 SW 9th St; ⏲11am-4pm Thu-Sun) **FREE** This museum displays an impressive collection of Siletz artifacts, a rectangular grand piano and a hand-carved 'Dining Room' sign for the first resort hotel on the Oregon Coast, among other things.

Pacific Maritime & Heritage Center MUSEUM
(☑541-265-4261; www.oregoncoast.history.museum; 333 SE Bay Blvd; ⏲11am-4pm Thu-Sun) This new museum, on the bayfront, educates the public on the central Oregon coast's maritime history and fishing industry, displaying such artifacts as a hand-hewn Siletz canoe and a couple of ship steering wheels.

☞ Tours

Marine Discovery Tours WHALE-WATCHING
(☑800-903-2628; www.marinediscovery.com; 345 SW Bay Blvd; adult/child $36/18) This tour operator sets out on two-hour cruises to view whales and other marine life.

✴ Festivals & Events

Newport Seafood & Wine Festival FOOD & WINE
(www.seafoodandwine.com; ⏲last weekend Feb) The Newport Seafood & Wine Festival is one of the coast's premier events.

🛏 Sleeping

There are plenty of economy hotels to be found on US 101.

South Beach State Park CAMPGROUND $
(☑541-867-4715; www.oregonstateparks.org; tent sites/RV sites/yurts $21/27/40; 🐾) Two miles south on US 101, this 227-site campground is especially good for large groups and has showers, flush toilets, 27 yurts and various walking trails.

★ Newport Belle B&B $$
(☑541-867-6290; www.newportbelle.com; 2126 SE Marine Science Dr, South Beach Marina, H Dock; d $150-165; ⏲Feb-Oct; 🛜) For a unique stay there's no beating this stern-wheeler B&B.

The five small but lovely and shipshape rooms all have private baths and water views, while the common spaces are wonderful for relaxing. Best for couples; reservations required.

Sylvia Beach Hotel HOTEL $$
(☑541-265-5428; www.sylviabeachhotel.com; 267 NW Cliff St; d incl breakfast $115-220) This book-themed hotel offers simple and classy rooms, each named after a famous author and decorated accordingly. The best are higher up, and the 3rd-floor common room has a wonderful ocean view and is great for talking to fellow guests. Full breakfast is included; reservations required. Note there are no TVs, phones or wi-fi. Cat on premises.

Grand Victorian B&B B&B $$
(☑800-784-9936; www.grandvictorianor.com; 105 NW Coast St; d $100-180; 🛜) Three rooms (two share one bathroom) are nestled in this green, three-story, shoes-off Victorian home. They're all beautiful and decorated with antiques; the suite is huge, with ocean view. A two-bedroom cottage next door is also available ($180). Note they do afternoon high tea on the premises, open to the public.

Elizabeth Street Inn HOTEL $$
(☑877-265-9400; www.elizabethstreetinn.com; 232 SW Elizabeth St; d incl breakfast $160-190; 🅿🛜🅰🐾) This lovely hotel has 68 elegantly furnished rooms, all with fireplace and balcony overlooking the ocean. There's a common-use pool and Jacuzzi, and complimentary afternoon clam chowder!

Rogue Ales Public House APARTMENT $$
(☑541-961-0142; www.rogue.com/locations/bb.php; 740 SW Bay Blvd; apt $110-130; 🛜🐾) Just three one- or two-bedroom apartments huddle above this pub-restaurant – the original Rogue Ales brewery site – all with comfortable modern furnishings (including washer/dryer) and kitchenette. Rather than breakfast, 22oz beers come with the package, making it a true 'Bed and Beer.'

Agate Beach Motel MOTEL $$
(☑800-755-5674; www.agatebeachmotel.com; 175 NW Gilbert Way; ste $139-159; 🛜🐾) Located 1.5 miles north of Newport down a short gravel road, this is a good place to be isolated from the busy city. Ten spacious one-bedroom suites, all with kitchens and front decks, are available. Past the grassy grounds are faraway ocean views.

✗ Eating

Tables of Content in the Sylvia Beach Hotel is open to nonguests, but reservations are necessary (prix fixe dinners $23.50).

Panini Bakery   BAKERY **$**
(☑541-265-5033; 232 NW Coast St; mains $6-8, pizzas $17-21; ☺7am-7pm) Lines form out the door at this tiny bakery-cafe. Exceptional pizza, bread and pastries.

★Local Ocean Seafoods   SEAFOOD **$$**
(☑541-574-7959; www.localocean.net; 213 SE Bay Blvd; mains $11-23; ☺11am-8:30pm Sun-Thu, till 9pm Fri & Sat) ✔ Popular and with good reason – the food is freshly prepared and very tasty here. Try the crab po'boy, smoked king salmon salad or pan-fried oysters. The wharf views are pretty, especially on warm days when the walls open up.

Nana's Irish Table   IRISH-AMERICAN **$$**
(☑541-574-8787; www.nanasirishpub.com; 613 NW 3rd St; mains $10-14; ☺11am-11pm Sun-Thu, till midnight Fri & Sat) Great hangout pub in Nye Beach, with good atmosphere and reasonable prices. The 'Bunratty Reuben' sandwich comes locally recommended, or try the sheperd's pie or Irish sausage rolls. Nice front patio for warm days.

Brewer's on the Bay   AMERICAN **$$**
(☑541-867-3664; 2320 SW OSU Dr; mains $6-16; ☺11am-9pm Sun-Thu, till 10pm Fri & Sat) This casual eatery serves up clam chowder, BLTs, pulled pork sliders, Kobe beef burgers and salads. The view of Yaquina Bay is a plus, and the bar's a great hangout. Walk through Rogues' giant fermentation tanks to get there (tours available).

La Maison   BAKERY **$$**
(☑541-265-8812; 315 SW 9th St; mains $11-15; ☺9am-3pm) Sweet little bakery-cafe serving up French crepes and omelettes for breakfast, and gourmet sandwiches and salads for lunch. Try the duck-egg quiche lorraine. Awesome bread, pastries and cakes too.

Saffron Salmon   NORTHWESTERN **$$$**
(☑541-265-8921; www.saffronsalmon.com; 859 SW Bay Blvd; mains $14-27; ☺11:30am-2:15pm & 5-9pm Thu-Tue) ✔ Once you get past the stellar wall-to-wall view, dig into the sautéed prawns, spicy seafood stew or grilled lamb burger stuffed with goat's cheese. Reserve for dinner.

LOCAL KNOWLEDGE

TRIP TO TOLEDO

A Newport local offers the following tip: 'Go up Bay Blvd 12 miles to Toledo, a pretty town with lumber baron houses that would be overrun except for the paper mill. It's a beautiful windy drive along the Yaquina River.'

❶ Information

Visitor Center (www.newportchamber.org; 555 SW Coast Hwy; ☺8am-5pm Mon-Fri, 10am-3pm Sat)

❶ Getting There & Around

The free daily shuttle **Newport City Loop** (☑541-265-4900; www.thecityofnewport. net) stops at key locations around town ($1 for nonhotel guests) and runs from around 7:30am to 5pm daily.
Bike Newport (☑541-265-9917; 150 NW 6th St) For bike rentals.
Lincoln County Transit (☑541-265-4900; www.co.lincoln.or.us/transit) Connects Newport with Lincoln City and Yachats.
Valley Retriever Buslines (☑541-265-2253; www.kokkola-bus.com; 956 SW 10th St) Heads to Portland, Corvallis and other inland locations.

Yachats

POP 690

One of the Oregon Coast's best-kept secrets is the neat and friendly little town of Yachats (ya-*hots*). Lying at the base of massive Cape Perpetua, Yachats offers the memorable scenery of a rugged and windswept land. People come here and to small, remote inns and B&Bs just south of town to get away from it all, which isn't hard to do along this relatively undeveloped coast.

For a bit of Yachats' history, visit the **Little Log Church & Museum** (☑541-547-3976; 328 W 3rd St; admission by donation, ☺noon-3pm Fri-Wed). Lining the town is the 804 coast trail, providing a lovely walk and access to tide pools and fabulous ocean vistas. It hooks up with the Amanda trail to the south, eventually arriving at Cape Perpetua Scenic Area.

🛏 Sleeping

Rock Park Cottages   COTTAGES **$**
(☑541-547-3214; www.rockparkcottages.com; 431 W 2nd St; d $75-85; 🐾🐕) Five cute and comfy

cottages with kitchenette are available here, some with peeks at the ocean. Most are studios, but cottage one has a separate bedroom and there's also a large A-frame that sleeps up to six and is great for families ($130).

Ya'Tel Motel
MOTEL $

(☎ 541-547-3225; www.yatelmotel.com; cnr US 101 & 6th St; d $64-84; @ 🛜 🐾) This nine-room motel has personality, along with spacious, clean rooms, some with kitchenette. A large room that sleeps six is available ($109). Look for the sign that could say something like 'Always clean, usually friendly.'

Deane's Oceanfront Lodge
MOTEL $$

(☎ 541-547-3321; www.deaneslodge.com; 7365 US 101; d $89-119; 🛜 🐾) Located a couple miles north of town, this cute place has 16 tidy and differently themed rooms, most with ocean view. Special amenities include glass-block showers, vintage kitchenettes (in just two rooms), grassy yard over the beach and covered back patio. There's also a duplex that sleeps six.

Overleaf Lodge
HOTEL $$$

(☎ 800-338-0507; www.overleaflodge.com; 280 Overleaf Lodge Lane; d from $195; @ 🛜) Just north of the center is this fancy resort-spa offering elegantly simple and spacious rooms, all with ocean views and some with balconies, fireplaces and Jacuzzis. Cottages are available, and continental breakfast is included.

✗ Eating

The **Adobe Resort** (☎ 541-547-3141; www.adobe resort.com; 1555 US 101; mains $16-22) has a dining room with great ocean views.

★ Green Salmon Coffee House
CAFE $

(☎ 541-547-4409; www.thegreensalmon.com; 220 US 101; mains $7-11; ⊙ 7:30am-2pm; 🖉) 'Organic' and 'fair trade' are big words at this eclectic cafe, where locals meet for tasty breakfast items (pastries, lox bagel, homemade oatmeal). Lunch means gourmet sandwiches, fancy salads and wraps, and there's a wide range of teas. Vegan menu available, plus used book exchange.

Ona
NORTHWESTERN $$

(☎ 541-547-6627; www.onarestaurant.com; 131 US 101; mains $16-30; ⊙ 11am-9pm) Yachats' most elegant restaurant, Ona has an upscale yet still casual atmosphere. Pasta, seafood and meats rule the mains, though there are also a few soups, salads and burgers. Happy hour

runs 4pm to 6pm daily and offers great food deals, and patio seating is available.

Drift Inn
AMERICAN $$

(☎ 541-547-4477; www.the-drift-inn.com; 124 N US 101; mains $9-23; ⊙ 8am-9pm) Wood booths mean cozy dining at this very popular restaurant. A decent range of dishes meets everyone's needs: seven kinds of salads, plenty of seafood (such as crab ravioli), pasta, burgers, steaks, sandwiches and rice bowls. Early birds can peck at the raspberry crepes and spinach frittata. Live music nightly at 6:30pm.

❶ Information

Visitor Center (☎ 800-929-0477; www.yachats.org; cnr US 101 & 3rd St; ⊙ 10am-4pm) Next to C&K Market.

❶ Getting There & Away

Lincoln County Transit (☎ 541-265-4900; www.co.lincoln.or.us/transit) Connects Yachats with Newport and Lincoln City.

South of Yachats

Beginning at Cape Perpetua and continuing south about 20 miles is some spectacular shoreline. This entire area was once a series of volcanic intrusions which resisted the pummeling of the Pacific long enough to rise as oceanside peaks and promontories. Acres of tide pools are home to starfish, sea anemones and sea lions. Picturesque Heceta Head Lighthouse rises above the surf, while tiny beaches line the cliffs.

⊙ Sights & Activities

★ Cape Perpetua Scenic Area
PARK

Located 3 miles south of Yachats, this volcanic remnant – one of the highest points on the Oregon Coast – was sighted and named by England's Capt James Cook in 1778. Famous for its dramatic rock formations and crashing surf, the area contains numerous trails that explore ancient shell middens, tide pools and old-growth forests. Views from the cape are incredible, taking in coastal promontories from Cape Foulweather to Cape Arago. There's a day-use fee of $5.

The **visitor center** (☎ 541-547-3289; www. fs.usda.gov/siuslaw; ⊙ 10am-4pm daily Mar-May, Sep & Oct, till 5pm daily Jun-Aug, closed Tue Nov-Feb) details human and natural histories, and has displays on the Alsi tribe. For spectacular ocean views, head up Overlook Rd to the Cape Perpetua day-use area.

Deep fractures in the old volcano allow waves to erode narrow channels into the headland, creating effects such as **Devil's Churn**, about a half-mile north of the visitor center. Waves race up this chasm, shooting up the 30ft inlet to explode against the narrowing sides of the channel.

For an easy hike, take the paved **Captain Cook Trail** (1.2 miles round-trip) down to tide pools near Cooks Chasm, where at high tide the geyser-like spouting horn blasts water out of a sea cave.

The **Giant Spruce Trail** (2 miles round-trip) leads up Cape Creek to a 500-year-old Sitka spruce with a 15ft diameter. The **Cook's Ridge-Gwynn Creek Loop Trail** (6.5 miles round-trip) heads into deep old-growth forests along Gwynn Creek; follow the Oregon Coast Trail south and turn up the Gwynn Creek Trail, which returns via Cook's Ridge.

Heceta Head Lighthouse　　　LIGHTHOUSE
(☑ 541-547-3416; www. hecetalighthouse.com; day-use fee $5; ⊙ 11am-3pm Mar-Apr & Oct, to 5pm Jun-Sep, varies rest of year) Built in 1894 and towering precipitously above the churning ocean, this lighthouse, 13 miles south of Yachats on US 101, is supremely photogenic and still functions. Tours are available.

Sea Lion Caves　　　CAVES
(☑ 541-547-3111; www.sealioncaves.com; 91560 US 101; adult/child 6-12yr $14/8; ⊙ 9am-6pm) Fifteen miles south of Yachats is an enormous sea grotto that's home to hundreds of groaning sea lions. An elevator descends 208ft to a dark interpretive area, and an observation window lets you watch Steller's sea lions jockeying for the best seat on the rocks.

There are also outside observation areas, as from late September to November there are no sea lions in the cave.

🛏 Sleeping

The following are ordered north to south.

Beachside State Park　　　CAMPGROUND $
(☑ 800-551-6949; www.oregonstateparks.org; tent sites/RV sites/yurts $21/26/40; ☻) Five miles north of town on US 101, nearly 80 sites and two yurts are available (along with showers and flush toilets) at this beachside campground.

Ocean Haven　　　INN $$
(☑ 541-547-3583; www.oceanhaven.com; 94770 US 101 S; d $105-165; ☎) This casual five-room inn 8 miles south of Yachats is run by an eccentric couple who have banned Hummers from their parking lot. All rooms come with kitchenettes and awesome ocean views, and the rustic cabin has hosted author Robert Bly. Whimsical details add personality to an already quirky place.

SeaQuest Inn B&B　　　B&B $$$
(☑ 800-341-4878; www.seaquestinn.com; 95354 US 101 S; d $180-210; @ ☎) This gorgeous B&B, 7 miles south of Yachats, is located in a large wood-shingle, driftwood-decorated house that has stunning ocean views and artsy touches. Seven luxurious rooms (four with their own Jacuzzi) boast private decks and ocean views; the huge suite ($325) is heaven for romantic couples.

★**Heceta Head Lighthouse B&B**　　　B&B $$$
(☑ 866-547-3696; www.hecetalighthouse.com; 92072 Hwy 101 S; d $209-315; ☎) This 1894 Queen Anne B&B can't help but attract passersby. Located near the lighthouse trail, it's 13 miles south of town on US 101. Inside there are six pretty rooms, all simply furnished with period antiques, along with a classy, museum-like atmosphere. Breakfast is a seven-course gourmet sensation and reservations are definitely recommended.

SOUTHERN OREGON COAST

The flip side of its northern coastal counterpart, Oregon's southern coast is further from the major inland metropolises and consequently gets less attention, less traffic, less bustle and more solitude. Much of the coastline here is nearly pristine, with a wild and dramatic feel. Beautiful clean rivers gush from inland mountainsides down to the sea, offering exceptional salmon and steelhead fishing along with boating recreation. Life is laid-back and relatively subdued; if you find a sandy beach at the end of a hiking trail, chances are you'll have it to yourself.

Despite its remoteness, the southern coast is slowly attracting development and a finer class of tourism, and you won't have a hard time finding the occasional upscale resort, world-class golf course or amazing gourmet restaurant – if that's what you're looking for. Harboring a milder climate (and less precipitation) than the north has its advantages as well, and the scenic drives – especially from Port Orford to Brookings – boast some of the most memorable coastal views you'll ever set eyes on.

Florence

POP 8500

Much of Florence consists of a long, mind-numbing commercial strip that serves the needs of tourists and passing dune-buggy enthusiasts buzzing a path to the Oregon Dunes National Recreation Area just further south. Find your way to the Old Town neighborhood, however, and you'll see another, more charming side of the town: a quaint waterfront district nestled along the scenic Siuslaw River next to the Oregon Coast's prettiest harbor.

◉ Sights & Activities

Old Town   NEIGHBORHOOD

Boardwalks, fun shops, good restaurants and great views of the Siuslaw Bridge make Old Town a top place to explore. The **Siuslaw Pioneer Museum** (☑ 541-997-7884; cnr Maple & 2nd Sts; admission $3; ⊗ noon-4pm) is located in a 1905 schoolhouse and displays exceptional farming, fishing and logging artifacts, along with pioneer items and Native American relics.

Darlingtonia Wayside   PARK

Three miles north of downtown Florence on US 101 is Darlingtonia Wayside, where a short boardwalk overlooks a surreal bog of insect-eating pitcher plants (*Darlingtonia californica,* also known as cobra lilies).

Sand Master Park   SANDBOARDING

(☑ 541-997-6006; www.sandmasterpark.com; 5351 US 101; ⊗ 9am-6:30pm) Yes, sandboarding. Like snowboarding, but on sand. Try it on the dunes at the northern edge of Florence. Sandboard rentals and lessons are on offer, and on Saturdays (in summer) free sand sculpture classes are given for those not keen on sand rashes.

Sandland Adventures   DUNE BUGGYING

(☑ 541-997-8087; www.sandland.com; 85366 US 101 S; ⊗ 9am-6pm; ⛟) This place offers fun for the entire family, from dune-buggy tours to mini-golf to go-karts to bumper boats. There's even a 12-minute train ride and water-balloon fights. In summer, reserve ahead for the dune buggy tours.

Southern Oregon Coast

0 — 30 km
0 — 20 miles

Carl G Washburne State Park

Heceta Head

Devil's Elbow State Park

Florence

Jessie M Honeyman State Park

Siuslaw National Forest

Siuslaw River

Eugene (36mi)

Tahkenitch Lake

See Northern Oregon Coast Map (p296)

Reedsport

Winchester Bay

Umpqua River

PACIFIC OCEAN

Oregon Dunes National Recreation Area

North Bend

Coos Bay

Charleston

Cape Arago

Sunset Bay State Park

Oregon

Bullards Beach State Park

Coquille

Bandon

Myrtle Point

Middle Fork River

Langlois

Floras Lake

Powers

Cape Blanco State Park

Port Orford

Humbug Mountain State Park

Wild Rogue Wilderness Area

Rogue River

Illahe

Gold Beach

Agness

Galice

Cape Sebastian

Cape Sebastian State Park

Kalmiopsis Wilderness

Grants Pass (17mi)

Samuel H Boardman State Park

Alfred A Loeb State Park

Chetco Peak (4660ft)

Harris Beach State Park

Brookings

Takilma

California

Crescent City

Eureka (81mi)

C&M Stables HORSEBACK RIDING

(☑541-997-7540; www.oregonhorsebackriding.com; 90241 N US 101; rides per person from $50) There's horseback riding on beaches and trails 8 miles north of Florence at these stables.

⚜ Festivals & Events

Rhododendron Festival PARADE

(☺3rd weekend May) A beauty pageant, parade and flower show are highlights of the three-day Rhododendron Festival, which has been celebrated for more than 100 years to honor the ubiquitous shrubbery.

🛏 Sleeping

For camping south of Florence, check out the Oregon Dunes National Recreation Area. About 4 miles north of town is pleasant Alder Dune Campground (☑541-547-3679; 89630 US 101; sites $22).

Port of Siuslaw Campground CAMPGROUND $

(☑541-997-3040; www.portofsiuslaw.com; cnr 1st & Harbor Sts; tent sites $22-26, RV sites $26-32; 🛜🅿) RV-oriented, but tents accepted. Pleasant and very centrally located close to the old town, at the Marina (some sites have water views).

Blue Heron Inn B&B B&B $$

(☑800-997-7780; www.blueheroninnflorence.com; 6563 Hwy 126; d $125-150; 🛜) Four beautiful rooms are available at this pleasant B&B, 2.5 miles east of Florence right on Hwy 126. The owners are friendly and knowledgeable; there's a basement movie room and a great river view from the living room. Breakfast is gourmet. Best for ages 14 and up.

Edwin K B&B B&B $$

(☑800-833-9465; www.edwink.com; 1155 Bay St; d $160-185; 🛜) Sitting across the street from the Siuslaw River is the flowery Edwin K, which comes with six comfortable rooms. All are spacious, and three have Jacuzzi tubs. A gourmet breakfast is served, and a huge apartment with kitchen that sleeps four is also available.

Landmark Inn MOTEL $$

(☑800-822-7811; www.landmarkmotel.com; 1551 4th St; d $80-145; 🛜) This pretty hilltop inn is a fine deal, offering a dozen tasteful and spacious rooms and suites, some with kitchen and three with Jacuzzi (one on a tiny private outdoor deck). A good choice for families; get suite 10 for a great view of the Siuslaw River. There's a sauna too.

🍴 Eating

Lovejoy's Restaurant & Tearoom FUSION $

(☑541-902-0502; www.lovejoysrestaurant.com; 195 Nopal St; mains $7-9; ☺11am-2:30pm Tue-Sat) Darling little place serving up seafood treats (clam chowder, crab cakes), sandwiches and wraps, quiches and salads, and various luscious desserts (lemon curd cheesecake, brownie sundae). High tea – good for lunch – starts at 11am.

★ Waterfront Depot NORTHWESTERN $$

(☑541-902-9100; www.thewaterfrontdepot.com; 1252 Bay St; mains $12-16; ☺4-10pm) This cozy, atmospheric joint is one of Florence's best restaurants. Come early to snag one of the few waterfront tables, then enjoy your Jambalaya pasta or crab-encrusted halibut. There are excellent small plates, a great wine list and desserts are spectacular. Reserve ahead – it's well priced and very popular.

Spice ASIAN $$

(☑541-997-1646; www.spiceinflorence.com; 1269 Bay St; mains $8-18; ☺3-9pm Tue-Sun) For a variety of different Asian (and more) cuisines, and all surprisingly well prepared, head to Spice. There is a *pho* noodle bowl from Vietnam, Bulgogi barbecue from Korea, lamb *koftas* from Armenia and tandoori chicken from India. On Friday, the seafood buffet ($18) is a great deal. Small plates too.

ℹ Information

Visitor Center (☑541-997-3128; www.florencechamber.com; 290 US 101; ☺9am-5pm Mon-Fri, 10am-2pm Sat, plus 11am-3pm Sun May-Oct)

LOCAL KNOWLEDGE

SWEET HIKING

What's the best-kept secret in the area? One local recommends hiking to Sweet Creek Falls, an easy 2.2-mile round-trip journey that starts 15 miles east of Florence on Hwy 126, toward Eugene.

Not only is the hike itself beautiful, but you'll pass several pretty waterfalls to end at the multi-tiered Sweet Creek Falls (day-use fee $5). It's a secret, so that's all we'll say.

❶ Getting There & Around

Porter Stage Lines (☑ 541-269-7183; www.porterstageline.com) has daily buses to Coos Bay and Eugene. Within town, hop on the **Rhody Express** (☑ 541-902-5067; www.ltd.org/rhody), which runs hourly 10am to 6pm Monday to Friday.

Oregon Dunes National Recreation Area

Stretching for nearly 50 miles between Florence and Coos Bay, the Oregon Dunes form the largest expanse of oceanfront sand dunes in the USA. The dunes tower up to 500ft and undulate inland as far as 3 miles to meet coastal forests, harboring curious ecosystems that sustain an abundance of wildlife, especially birds. The area inspired Frank Herbert to pen his epic sci-fi *Dune* novels.

The very northern and southern sections of the dunes are dominated by dune buggies and dirt bikes (off-highway vehicles, or OHVs); avoid hiking in these areas. It's possible to rent vehicles south of Florence and around Winchester Bay. The central section of the dunes is closed to OHVs, and instead preserved for wildlife and more peaceful human activities such as hiking and canoeing.

🏃 Activities

A day-use fee of $5 is required at the trailheads listed below. Or buy a $30 Northwest Forest Pass at the Oregon Dunes NRA Visitors Center in Reedsport.

From the **Stagecoach Trailhead** (look for the 'Siltcoos Recreation Area' sign 7 miles south of Florence), three short trails along a river and wetlands afford good wildlife viewing. One of these, the **Waxmyrtle Trail**, winds to the beach for 1.5 miles along the Siltcoos River, where herons, deer and waterfowl can be seen. Other trails lead to a freshwater lagoon or up to a forested vista point.

At Carter Lake Campground, 12 miles north of Reedsport, the **Taylor Dunes Trail** leads a half-mile to a viewing area. You can hike beyond here through dunes to meet the **Carter Dunes Trail** and head to the beach (3 miles round-trip). The **Oregon Dunes Day Use Area**, about 2-miles south, has good viewing platforms and also serves as a trailhead for a 2-mile round-trip hike to the beach.

The challenging 6-mile loop **Tahkenitch Dunes Trail** starts from Tahkenitch Campground, 8 miles north of Reedsport.

You'll reach the beach in about 2 miles, then walk south about a mile to signs for the **Threemile Lake Trail**, which returns to the campground via a freshwater lake and deep forests.

For the area's biggest dunes (including the tallest at 500ft), take the **John Dellenbeck Trail**, 10.5 miles south of Reedsport, which leads out across a wilderness of massive sand peaks before reaching the beach. The round-trip hike is 6 miles and involves some tough dune climbing, though there's a 1-mile interpretive loop on packed gravel if you just want to take a look.

🛏 Sleeping

There are cheap motels around Florence and Reedsport. Campgrounds from north to south include (but are not limited to) the following:

Jessie M Honeyman Memorial State Park   CAMPGROUND $
(☑ 800-452-5687, 541-997-3641; www.oregonstateparks.org; 84505 US 101 S; tent sites/RV sites/yurts $21/26/39; 🐾) Located 3 miles south of Florence on Cleawox Lake; popular for its easy access to the dunes. The lake is great for swimming. Rent canoes and kayaks at the park concession.

Tahkenitch Campground   CAMPGROUND $
(☑ 877-444-6777; campsites $20; 🐾) A good woodsy place to ditch those OHVs; also has trailheads. Located on US 101, 8 miles north of Reedsport.

Umpqua Lighthouse State Park   CAMPGROUND $
(☑ 800-452-5687, 541-271-4118; www.oregonstateparks.org; 460 Lighthouse Rd; tent sites/RV sites/yurts/cabins/deluxe yurts $19/24/36/39/76; 🐾) Pleasant, wooded campsites adjacent to tiny Lake Marie, which warms up nicely in summer. Four miles south of Reedsport.

William M Tugman State Park   CAMPGROUND $
(☑ 541-759-3604, 800-452-5687; 72549 US 101; tent sites/yurts $20/39; 🐾) On US 101, 8 miles south of Reedsport, this is a large campground with grassy open areas and easy access to Eel Lake, popular for fishing and kayaking.

❶ Information

Get information at the **Oregon Dunes NRA Visitors Center** (☑ 541-271-6000; www.stateparks.com/oregon_dunes.html; 855 Highway Ave;

HALL LAKE

Want to know where the locals go? Then just take Wildwood Dr, directly across from William M Tugman State Park, go half a mile and you'll see the sign for Hall Lake Day Use Area on your left. You can walk around the lake in about a half-hour, climbing sand dunes along the way for an ocean view; in the future, the trail might extend to encircle nearby Schuttpelz Lake.

⊙ 8am-4:30pm May-Sep, closed Sat & Sun rest of year) in Reedsport; it's in the same building as the chamber of commerce.

Reedsport

POP 4150

Five miles from where the mighty Umpqua River joins the Pacific Ocean is Reedsport, the historic port that ushered out the immense bounty of logs cut in the wide Umpqua River drainage. Today Reedsport is a small town getting smaller, but it still boasts a few area attractions. Its location in the middle of the Oregon Dunes makes it an ideal base for exploring the region.

Take the kids to **Umpqua Discovery Center** (☑ 541-271-4816; www.umpquadiscovery-center.com; 409 Riverfront Way; adult/child 5-16yr $8/4; ⊙ 9am-5pm; ⊕) to explore the area's cultural and natural history through colorful murals and a few interactive displays. A free platform offers good views of the Umpqua River, and there are casual eateries nearby.

About 4 miles south of town you can tour of the 1894 **Umpqua River Lighthouse** (☑ 541-271-4631; 1020 Lighthouse Rd; admission $5; ⊙ 10am-4:30pm May-Oct, hours vary rest of year); the lighthouse's museum (200yd away) is free. Opposite is a **whale-watching platform**, and a nearby **nature trail** rings freshwater Lake Marie, which is popular for swimming. There's camping in the area.

A herd of about 120 Roosevelt elk loiter at **Dean Creek Elk Viewing Area**, a roadside wildlife refuge 3 miles east on Hwy 38. These elk are Oregon's largest land mammal.

There are several inexpensive motels on Hwy 101, the main drag through town; for

something a bit more special, head to Winchester Bay (just 3 miles south) and check into the **Salmon Harbor Landing Motel** (☑ 541-271-3742; www.salmonharborlanding.com; 265 8th St; d $59-69). Not far from here is the Salmon Harbor Marina, with seafood shacks.

Need more? Contact the **chamber of commerce** (☑ 541-271-3495; www.reedsportcc.org; 855 Highway Ave; ⊙ 8am-4:30pm).

Coos Bay & North Bend

The no-nonsense city of Coos Bay (population 16,000) and its modest neighbor North Bend (population 10,000) make up the largest urban area on the Oregon Coast. Coos Bay boasts the largest natural harbor between San Francisco and Seattle, and has long been a major shipping and manufacturing center for most of southern Oregon. It was also once the largest timber port in the world. Today the logs are gone, but the tourists have taken their place.

⊙ Sights & Activities

Coos Bay NEIGHBORHOOD

The **Coos Art Museum** (☑ 541-267-3901; www.coosart.org; 235 Anderson Ave; admission $5; ⊙ 10am-4pm Tue-Fri, 1-4pm Sat), in a historic art-deco building, provides a hub for the region's art culture. Rotating exhibits from the museum's permanent collection are displayed, along with occasional shows of local artists' works. The old-style movie house **Egyptian Theatre** (☑ 541-269-8650; www.egyptian-theatre.com; 229 S Broadway) has fun Egyptian motifs and an original Wurlitzer organ.

Heaven for those with a sweet tooth, **Cranberry Sweets** (☑ 541-888-9824; www.cranberrysweets.com; 1005 Newmark Ave; ⊙ 9:30am-5:30pm Mon-Sat, 11am-5pm Sun) has its factory here; watch candy being made, and sample it – try the popular cheddar fudge.

Coos Historical & Maritime Museum MUSEUM

(☑ 541-756-6320; www.cooshistory.org; 1220 Sherman Ave; adult/senior $4/2) In North Bend, just south of the McCullough Bridge, this museum displays exhibits from Native American culture to maritime shipwrecks. Stay tuned: It's due to move into new quarters on Coos Bay's waterfront in mid-2014.

✳️ Festivals & Events

Oregon Coast Music Festival   MUSIC
(www.oregoncoastmusic.com; ☺Jul) Coos Bay's Oregon Coast Music Festival takes place over two weeks in July.

🛏 Sleeping

Both towns have cheap motels along their main drags. There are campgrounds to the south, near Charleston, or north in the Oregon Dunes National Recreation Area (p315).

Bay Bridge Motel   MOTEL $
(✆800-557-3156; 66304 US 101, North Bend; d $60-85; 🕿) This typical motel is located just north of the McCullough Bridge and has typical amenities, but most of the 11 rooms boast very atypical bay views. A few have kitchenette.

Edgewater Inn   MOTEL $$
(✆541-267-0423, 800-233-0423; www.theedgewaterinn.com; 275 E Johnson Ave, Coos Bay; d from $100; @🕿🏊💪) Tucked in behind Safeway and Fred Meyer's, this pleasant motel features clean, good-sized rooms (some with kitchenette and Jacuzzi). Get an upper room for views over the river; they're only $5 more. A business center, gym and indoor pool are fun diversions.

This Olde House B&B   B&B $$
(✆541-267-5224; www.thisoldehousebb.com; 202 Alder Ave, Coos Bay; d $105-185; 🕿💪) Not every B&B can claim to have hosted Robert Plant, even if they had no idea who he was at the time. There are five homey rooms at this casual B&B, all with private bath; the Redwood Room boasts the best amenities and view. Reservations are mandatory (even if you're a rock star).

🍴 Eating

Pancake Mill   AMERICAN $
(✆541-756-2751; www.pancakemill.com; 2390 Tremont, US 101; mains $6-11; ☺6am-3pm) This no-nonsense diner is popular for its tasty breakfasts and lunches. It's typical stuff – scrambles, omelettes, waffles and (of course) pancakes for breakfast, with sandwiches and burgers for lunch. Specialties like chicken pasta salad and chili nacho plates make things interesting. Plenty of pies and cakes too.

Fishermen's Seafood Market   SEAFOOD $$
(✆541-290-1007; 200 S Bayshore Dr; mains $9-16; ☺10:30am-7pm Mon-Wed, Fri & Sat, till 6pm

Thu) Best for takeout, this seafood shack on the bayfront has only two tables and a fish counter. Order fish-and-chips or a clam basket and head outside; there are plenty of benches on the nearby boardwalk.

ℹ️ Information

Coos Bay Visitor Center (✆541-269-0215; www.oregonsbayareachamber.com; 50 Central Ave; ☺9am-5pm Mon-Fri, 11am-3pm Sat, 10am-2pm Sun)

North Bend Visitor Center (✆541-756-4613; www.northbendcity.org; 1380 Sherman Ave; ☺10am-5pm Mon-Fri, till 4pm Sat, till 3pm Sun)

ℹ️ Getting There & Around

Porter Stage Lines (✆541-269-7183; 126 Market Ave), next to the old Tioga Hotel in Coos Bay, goes to Florence and Eugene.

Curry Public Transit's **Coastal Express** (✆800-921-2871; www.currypublictransit.org) shuttles connect Coos Bay/North Bend with Bandon, Port Orford, Gold Beach and Brookings.

Loop Bus (✆541-267-7111; www.coostransit.org) provides weekday services around Coos Bay, North Bend and Charleston.

Charleston & Around

Charleston is a tiny bump of civilization on the Cape Arago Hwy, a commercial fishing port that sits just 8 miles southwest of bustling Coos Bay but feels worlds away. It makes a good jumping-off point to a trio of splendid state parks on the Cape Arago headlands.

👁 Sights & Activities

Sunset Bay State Park   PARK
(✆541-888-4902; www.oregonstateparks.org; 89814 Cape Arago Hwy) Three miles southwest of town on Cape Arago Hwy, this state park is nestled in a small, protected bay that once served as a safe harbor for fishing boats, and possibly pirates as well. Today it's popular with swimmers, hikers and tide-pool explorers. A 6-mile, cliff-edge stretch of the Oregon Coast Trail continues south from here to link all three state parks. Cape Arago Lighthouse sits just offshore on a rocky crag.

Shore Acres State Park   PARK
(✆541-888-3732; www.shoreacres.net; Cape Arago Hwy; day use $5) Beautiful rehabilitated gardens are the highlight of this unusual state park, 4 miles southwest of town on Cape

Arago Hwy. Louis Simpson, an important shipping and lumber magnate, was exploring for new stands of lumber in 1905 when he discovered this wildly eroded headland. After buying up the 320 acres for $4000 he built a three-story mansion here, complete with formal gardens. It burned down in 1921. A trail leads to a glass-protected observation building on the cliffs where the mansion once stood, and then continues on to the beach.

Cape Arago State Park
PARK

(☑ 800-551-6949; www.oregonstateparks.org; Cape Arago Hwy) A mile beyond Shore Acres State Park is **Simpson Reef Viewpoint**, where you can spot shorebirds, migrating whales and several species of pinnipeds. Head another 0.5 miles to Cape Arago State Park and the terminus of Cape Arago Hwy, where grassy picnic grounds make for great perches over a pounding sea. Trails lead down to the beach and fine tide pools, while the **Oregon Coast Trail** heads back north to Shore Acres and Sunset Bay.

South Slough National Estuarine Research Reserve
MUSEUM

(☑ 541-888-5558; www.southsloughestuary.org; 61907 Seven Devils Rd; ☺10am-4:30pm Tue-Sat) Charleston sits at the mouth of South Slough, a tidal river basin that turns into a vast, muddy estuary full of wildlife. Four miles south of Charleston on Seven Devils Rd is this excellent interpretive center, which has exhibits on estuarine ecology, also showcased in a 12-minute video. It runs events and programs all year long.

Several **walking trails**, ranging from 0.25 to 3 miles, offer glimpses of the local ecology. Canoeing is also possible in the area, but you'll need your own canoe.

🛏 Sleeping & Eating

Captain John's Motel
MOTEL $

(☑ 541-888-4041; www.captjohnsmotel.com; 63360 Kingfisher Dr; d $69-79; @🛜🐾) Popular with anglers, Captain John's keeps room smells down by providing an outside crab-cooking facility for guests. Some rooms have a kitchenette ($15 extra). It's a bit run-down, but tolerable for a night. It's right near the boat docks.

Sunset Bay State Park
CAMPGROUND $

(☑ 541-888-4902, 800-551-6949; www.oregonstateparks.org; 89814 Cape Arago Hwy; tent sites/RV sites/yurts $19/24/36; 🐾) Three miles southwest of town, this is a busy, sheltered beachside campground with 130 sites, eight yurts, showers and flush toilets.

Bastendorff Beach County Park
CAMPGROUND $

(☑ 541-888-5353, 541-396-7755; 63379 Bastendorff Beach Rd; tent sites/RV sites/cabins $20/20/35; 🐾) Two miles southwest of town, just off Cape Arago Hwy, this park has more than 90 pleasant wooded campsites in a developed campground near the beach.

Portside Restaurant
AMERICAN $$

(☑ 541-888-5544; www.portsidebythebay.com; 63383 Kingfisher Dr; mains $11-29; ☺11:30am-11pm) Seafood dominates the menu at this good long-running restaurant, though there are a few terrestrial choices including chicken, beef and pasta. The best part might be the great bay view. There's live music in the lounge on weekends.

ℹ Information

The **visitor center** (☑ 541-888-2311; 91143 Cape Arago Hwy; ☺9am-5pm Mon-Sat, noon-5pm Sun) sits at the west end of the bridge.

Bandon
POP 3100

The cute little town of Bandon happily sits at the bay of the Coquille River. Its Old Town district has been gentrified into a picturesque harborside location that offers pleasant strolling, window-shopping and sweets-tasting. The area's most noteworthy industry is cranberry farming, with neighboring bogs yielding a considerable percentage of the cranberry harvest in the US. Nearby is a world-class golf resort.

◉ Sights & Activities

Bandon Historical Society Museum
MUSEUM

(☑ 541-347-2164; 270 Fillmore Ave; admission $2; ☺10am-4pm Mon-Sat) This museum has exhibits on the area's historical industries and the Coquille Native Americans, along with memorable photos of Bandon's two devastating fires (1914 and 1936) and various shipwrecks.

Game Park Safari
ZOO

(☑ 541-347-3106; www.gameparksafari.com; adult/child 7-12yr/child 2-6yr $17.50/10/7; ☺9am-6pm Mar-Nov, 10am-5pm Sat & Sun Jan & Feb) For something different, visit Game Park Safari,

7 miles south on US 101, where you can see lions and tigers and bears (oh my), among other exotic animals. There's baby-animal petting too.

Table Rock & Face Rock   LANDMARKS
South of town, and not obvious from the highway, are miles of sandy beaches broken by outcroppings of towering rocks; these are home to myriad sea birds, sea lions and tide pools. Look for whales in spring.

At Coquille Point, at the end of SW 11th St, steps lead down to a beach interspersed with rocky crags and monoliths. Table Rock lies just offshore and is protected as the Oregon Islands National Wildlife Refuge.

A few blocks to the south is Face Rock, a huge monolith with a human profile. Native American legends tell of a maiden and her pet kittens turned to stone by an evil sea god; they all now rise as sea stacks. A path winds along the headland and to the beach.

**Bandon Beach
Riding Stables**   HORSEBACK RIDING
(☑ 541-347-3423; 54629 Beach Loop Dr) Three miles south of downtown; offers horseback riding on the beach.

✯ Festivals & Events

Cranberry Festival   CULTURE
(☉ 2nd weekend Sep) The Cranberry Festival, Bandon's largest civic event, features a parade, craft fair and the glorious crowning of the Cranberry Queen.

🛏 Sleeping

There are several cheap motels on the road into and out of town.

Sea Star Guesthouse   GUESTHOUSE $
(☑ 541-347-9632; www.seastarbandon.com; 370 1st St; d $75-115; 🐾) This pretty harborside guesthouse offers six pleasant rooms, all comfortable and tastefully decorated, and each with its own amenities. The biggest suite has a loft and water views, and sleeps up to six.

Sunset Oceanfront Lodging   MOTEL $$
(☑ 800-842-2407; www.sunsetmotel.com; 1865 Beach Loop Rd; d $75-175; 🐾🍽🐾) Just south of town, this large motel complex offers a wide range of comfortable lodgings, from 'economy rooms' with no view to studios, suites, apartments and beach cottages, some with great views. Pool available.

Windermere   MOTEL $$
(☑ 541-347-3710; www.windermereonthebeach.com; 3250 Beach Loop Rd; d $135-198; 🐾🐾) Very pleasant and spacious rooms here range from simple affairs to more upscale suites with kitchenette, fireplace and private balcony or deck. All have stunning ocean views. Located about 2 miles southwest of the center.

Bullards Beach State Park   CAMPGROUND $
(☑ 800-551-6949, 541-347-2209; www.oregonstateparks.org; US 101; RV & tent sites/yurts $24/36; 🐾) On US 101, 2 miles north of town, are 185 RV and tent sites, plus 13 yurts, hot showers, flush toilets and easy beach access. Historic lighthouse nearby, too. It's 2 miles north of Bandon.

✗ Eating

Bandon Dunes Golf Resort, north of town, has good restaurants and an English pub. Got a sweet tooth? Sample candy at **Cranberry Sweets** (☑ 541-347-9475; www.cranberrysweets.com; 280 1st St SE; ☉ 9:30am-5:30pm).

Bandon Coffee Café   CAFE $
(☑ 541-347-1144; www.bandoncoffee.com; 365 2nd St; snacks under $8; ☉ 6am-4pm Mon-Sat, till 3pm Sun) This casual and popular coffee shop offers light meals such as sandwiches, burgers, pitas and bagels, along with pastries, gourmet coffee and a warm atmosphere.

Alloro Wine Bar & Restaurant   ITALIAN $$
(☑ 541-347-1850; www.allorowinebar.com; 375 2nd St; mains $15-29; ☉ 4-9pm Sun-Thu, till 10pm Fri & Sat) This small and fancy restaurant boasts an Italian-influenced menu and a wide-ranging wine list. Order the lamb osso buco, roasted duck with cranberry-cherry salsa or the *cacciucco*, a Tuscan-style fish stew.

Lord Bennett's   AMERICAN $$
(☑ 541-347-3663; www.lordbennett.com; 1695 Beach Loop Rd; lunch mains $10-13, dinner mains $17-29; ☉ 11am-2pm Fri & Sat, 10am-2pm Sun, 5-9pm daily) A Bandon institution, this upscale restaurant has fine panoramic sea views and dishes such as wild prawns, Kobe beef burgers, calamari steaks and fettuccine with crab legs – all served with the appropriate sides. There's Sunday brunch too.

Tony's Crab Shack   SEAFOOD $$
(☑ 541-347-2875; www.tonyscrabshack.com; 155 1st St; mains $8-15; ☉ 10:30am-7pm Mon-Fri, till 8pm Sat & Sun) What could be better than eating fresh fish at a seafood shack on a waterside dock? At Tony's you'll choose from

CATCHING A BREEZE ON FLORAS LAKE

Unassuming Langlois, 14 miles south of Bandon, is the closest town to Floras Lake, a covert **windsurfing**, **kitesurfing** and **kayaking** destination. Only a thin sand spit separates this shallow springwater lake from the ocean. Summer is the peak season, though winter storms also attract adventurers. To reach the lake, head 1 mile south of Langlois on US 101, turn west onto Floras Lake Rd and follow the signs for 2.7 miles.

There are **campsites** (tent/RV sites $12/16) at the lake with showers available but no RV hookups. For more comfort, check into the lovely four-room **Floras Lake House B&B** (541-348-2573; www.floraslake.com; 92870 Boice Cope Rd; d $160-180; closed Nov-Feb;) nearby. There's a small market (famous for its hot dogs) and a cafe in Langlois.

Equipment rental and lessons are available at the lake from **Floras Lake Windsurfing** (541-348-9912; www.floraslake.com/flw2.html; Boice Cope Rd; 10am-6pm Memorial Day–Labor Day); take the short, unmarked path next to RV site 22, or ask at Floras Lake House for information.

pasta specials like smoked salmon alfredo, sandwiches like hot crab and shrimp, and house specials like fish tacos or Pacific halibut. Casual atmosphere, with outside tables for warm days.

ℹ Information

For information, try the **Chamber of Commerce** (541-347-9616; www.bandon.com; 300 2nd St; 10am-5pm).

ℹ Getting There & Around

Beachside Bike Rentals (541-347-1995; www.southcoastbicycles.com; 805 2nd St) The place to go for bikes.

Coastal Express (Curry Public Transport; 800-921-2871; www.currypublictransit.org) Shuttles connect Bandon with Coos Bay/North Bend, Port Orford, Gold Beach and Brookings.

Port Orford

POP 1200

Perched on a grassy headland and wedged between two magnificent state parks, the hamlet of Port Orford is one of Oregon's true natural ocean harbors (most others are situated along river mouths). It's on one of the most scenic stretches of coastal highway and there are stellar views even from the center of town. While Port Orford is still a small place, the outside world has discovered its charms: an upscale retreat is nestled a half-mile from the center, and in 2010 renowned glass artist Chris Hawthorne opened a fancy gallery, along with the area's finest restaurant.

◎ Sights & Activities

Port Orford Heads State Park PARK
(541-332-0521; www.oregonstateparks.org; Coast Guard Rd; 10am-3:30pm Wed-Mon) A short drive along Coast Guard Rd leads to this state park, which has the best location in town. A couple of 20-minute loop trails offer fine panoramic views and a closer look at coastal flora. Deer and bunnies live on the grassy picnic grounds surrounding the **Lifeboat Station Museum** (541-332-0521; 10am-3:30pm Wed-Mon), which was formerly a Coast Guard station. Check out the 36ft 'unsinkable' motor lifeboat on display.

Cape Blanco State Park PARK
(541-332-6774; www.oregonstateparks.org; US 101) Nine miles north of Port Orford, off US 101, this rugged promontory is the second most westerly point of the continental USA and host to a fine state park with hiking trails spreading out over the headland. Sighted in 1603 by Spanish explorer Martin d'Anguilar, Cape Blanco juts far out into the Pacific, withstanding lashing winds that can pass 100mph. Visitors can tour the **Cape Blanco Lighthouse** (541-332-2207; www.oregonstateparks.org; US 101; admission $2; 10am-3:30pm Wed-Mon), built in 1870, the oldest and highest operational lighthouse in Oregon.

A mile east is **Hughes House** (541-332-0248; www.oregonstateparks.org; 10am-3:30pm Wed-Mon) FREE, a restored Victorian home built in 1898 by Patrick Hughes, an Irish dairy rancher and gold miner.

**Humbug Mountain
State Park** PARK

(✆541-332-6774) Six miles south of Port Orford, mountains edge down to the ocean, and heavily wooded Humbug Mountain rises 1750ft from the surf. When European settlers first came to the area in 1851, the Tututni Native Americans lived in a large village along the beach just north of here. Hike a 3-mile trail that leads through the coast's largest remaining groves of Port Orford cedar to the top of the mountain for dramatic views of Cape Sebastian and the Pacific Ocean.

Prehistoric Gardens PARK

(✆541-332-4463; 36848 US 101; adult/child 3-12yr $10/8; ⊙9am-6pm; 🚼) Twelve miles south of Port Orford, your kids will scream at the sight of a Tyrannosaurus rex in front of this dinosaur park. Life-size replicas of the extinct beasties are set in a lush, first-growth temperate rainforest; the huge ferns and trees set the right mood for going back in time. Family-run for nearly 60 years.

🛏 Sleeping

Red Fish restaurant has a luxurious upstairs suite with ocean view ($350).

**Humbug Mountain
State Park** CAMPGROUND $

(✆541-332-6774, 800-551-6949; www.oregonstateparks.org; US 101; tent/RV sites $17/20; 🐾) Nearly 100 comfortable, sheltered sites with access to showers and flush toilets available at this park, 6 miles south of Port Orford on US 101.

Cape Blanco State Park CAMPGROUND $

(✆541-332-6774, 800-551-6949; www.oregonstateparks.org; US 101; tent & RV sites/cabins $20/39; 🐾) Located on US 101, 9 miles northeast of town on a high, sheltered rocky headland with beach access and great views of the lighthouse. Showers, flush toilets and boat ramp available.

Compass Rose B&B B&B $$

(✆541-322-7076; www.compassroseportorford.com; 42497 Gull Rd; d $155-180; 🌐) This huge and gorgeous B&B is set on 12 acres of woodland with glimpses of a nearby lake. It has four beautiful and contemporary rooms, all with private bathroom, and there are spacious common areas. A full breakfast is included, as are visits to the bunny hutch. It's just north of town, 1 mile down Paradise Point Rd.

Castaway-by-the-Sea Motel MOTEL $$

(✆541-332-4502; www.castawaybythesea.com; 545 W 5th St; d $85-145; @🌐🐾) Thirteen modern, pleasant and spacious ocean-view rooms are available here, some with kitchenette and loft, but all with great ocean views. Trivia: the Castaway claims to be the most westerly motel in the continental US.

★**Wildspring Guest Habitat** CABIN $$$

(✆866-333-9453; www.wildspring.com; 92978 Cemetery Loop; d incl breakast $278-308; @🌐) A few acres of wooded serenity greet you at this quiet retreat, set in a sheltered grove a half-mile from town. Five luxury cabin suites, all filled with elegant furniture and modern amenities such as radiant-floor heating and slate showers, make for a very comfortable and romantic getaway. It has an outdoor Jacuzzi with spectacular views.

🍴 Eating

For seafood-at-the-dock atmosphere there's **Griffs** (✆541-332-8985; Port Orford Dock; mains $10-15; ⊙10:30am-8pm), a greasy-spoon shack at the port.

Crazy Norwegian AMERICAN $

(✆541-322-8601; 259 6th St; mains $7-15; ⊙11:30am-8pm Wed-Sun) A casual family spot famous for its excellent fish and chips and seafood combos. Soup, salad and sandwich fans won't be disappointed either, and there are homemade cakes and pies aplenty. Just be prepared to wait at peak times.

★**Red Fish** NORTHWESTERN $$$

(✆541-336-2200; www.redfishportorford.com; 517 Jefferson St; mains $21-29; ⊙11am-9pm Mon-Fri, 9am-9pm Sat & Sun) 🍴 At first glance this slick, sea-view restaurant would seem better located in Portland's Pearl District – especially since ex-Salishan chef now presides over the kitchen. Red Fish boasts the freshest seafood in town, so take advantage: try the grilled jerk wild salmon or pan-seared halibut. Weekend brunch too.

Paula's Bistro FRENCH $$$

(✆541-322-9378; www.paulasbistro.com; 236 6th St; mains $24-30; ⊙5-9pm Wed-Sat) 🍴 The limited but quality menu at this excellent French restaurant includes dishes like lamb chops with duck savory, chicken gorgonzola pasta and cassoulet royal (a baked bean casserole). Don't miss the crème brûlée if it's on the menu.

ℹ Information

The **visitor center** (☑ 541-332-4106; www.
portorford.org/visitorcenter.html; 520 Jefferson
St; ⊙ 9am-4pm) is at Battle Rock Park (in the
center of town).

ℹ Getting There & Around

Curry Public Transit's **Coastal Express** (☑ 800-
921-2871; www.currypublictransit.org) shuttles
connect Port Orford with Coos Bay/North Bend,
Bandon, Gold Beach and Brookings.

Gold Beach

POP 2300

At the mouth of the Rogue River, Gold
Beach got its start when the precious ore
was discovered here in 1853. The mines
didn't strike it rich compared to other
places, but the town remained. Then in
the early 20th century, salmon-rich waters
caught the fancy of gentleman anglers such
as Jack London and Zane Grey. Still a place
for fishing vacations, Gold Beach's other
big attraction is jet-boat excursions up the
Rogue River, one of Oregon's wildest and
most remote. Wildlife-viewing is good, with
deer, elk, otters, beavers, eagles and osprey.

◉ Sights & Activities

Cape Sebastian State Park   PARK
The coast around Gold Beach is spectacular.
Take a break at Cape Sebastian State Park, a
rocky headland 7 miles south, for a panorama
stretching from California to Cape Blanco.
Flex your legs on a 1.5-mile walking trail to
the cape; from December to April, keep your
eyes peeled for whales.

Curry Historical Society Museum   MUSEUM
(☑ 541-247-9396; 28419 Ellensburg Ave; adult/
child 16yr & under $2/50¢; ⊙ 10am-4pm
Tue-Sat, closed Jan) The Curry Historical
Society Museum has displays on the area's
mining, logging and Native American
histories.

Jerry's Rogue Jets   JET-BOATING
(☑ 800-451-3645; www.roguejets.org; river trips
adult/child 4-11yr from $50/25) Ready for a jet-
boat trip? Hold onto your hat and see Jerry's
Rogue Jets, at the port. They also run a large
gift shop with small museum on the history
of the Rogue River, near the main office.

Shrader Old Growth Trail   HIKING
Drive about 8 miles up USFS Rd 33 and turn
right on USFS Rd 090; after 2 miles you'll

reach the Shrader Old Growth Trail, which
wanders for 1.5 miles through towering
Douglas fir and Port Orford cedar. There are
other hiking options in the area, including
on the 40-mile Rogue River National Recreation Trail.

🛏 Sleeping

There's great riverside camping up USFS
Rd 33.

Motel 6   MOTEL $
(☑ 541-247-4533; www.motel6-gold-beach.com;
94433 Jerry's Flat Rd; d $86; ☎🐾) This is not
your mother's Motel 6. The ubiquitous
economy motel chain is going upscale, with
hip styling, bright colors and fancy-looking
flooring. Think of it as an affordable boutique motel; the upstairs rooms have river
views. There are private Jacuzzi rooms, with
one communal Jacuzzi.

Secret Camp RV Park   CAMPGROUND $
(☑ 541-247-2665; www.secretcamprvpark.com;
95614 Jerry's Flat Rd; tent/RV sites $18/40; ☎🐾)
Three miles east of town, this nature-sur-
rounded haven, complete with small creek, offers pretty sites for campers and full hookups
for RV enthusiasts. Fire pits, horseshoes and
volleyball are available. Free showers.

Ireland's Rustic Lodges   LODGE $$
(☑ 541-247-7718; www.irelandsrusticlodges.com;
29346 Ellensburg Ave; d $119-149; ☎🐾) A wide
variety of accommodations awaits you at
this woodsy place. There are regular suites
with kitchenette, rustic one- and two-
bedroom cabins, beach houses or even RV
sites. A glorious garden sits in front while
beach views are out back. Three communal
Jacuzzis with faraway ocean views, too.

★ Tu Tu' Tun Lodge   LODGE $$$
(☑ 800-864-6357; www.tututun.com; 96550 N Bank
Rogue Rd; d from $290; @🐾) One of Oregon's
most exclusive hideaways is 7 miles up the
Rogue River. The luxurious rooms and suites
all come with river views, while a few boast
fireplaces and private outdoor Jacuzzi. It's a
romantic spot with a small golf course and
an excellent dining room. Three houses also
available.

🍴 Eating

Indian Creek Café (☑ 541-247-0680; 94682
Jerry's Flat Rd; mains $7-12; ⊙ 5:30am-2pm) is
great for breakfast.

Patti's Rollin 'n Dough Bistro   AMERICAN $
(☑541-247-4438; 94257 N Bank Rogue Rd; mains
$8-13; ⊙9am-3pm Tue-Sat, till 2pm Sun) ✐ This
tiny bistro has a limited menu and hours,
and the food is usually exceptional. Gourmet burgers, sandwiches and salads are the
norm, created with organic and local ingredients where possible.

Anna's by the Sea   NORTHWESTERN $$
(☑541-247-2100; www.annasbythesea.com; 29672
Stewart St; mains $18-21; ⊙5-8:30pm Wed-Sat)
One of Gold Beach's best restaurants, this
homey spot serves up just a few key mains
like black rock cod with sweet onions, oven-
seared breast of duck and chicken thighs in
chantrelle gravy. Great wine list, but don't
expect upscale: it's self-proclaimed as 'Re-
jecting trendy from the start.'

Porthole Café   AMERICAN $$
(☑541-247-7411; 29975 Harbor Way; mains $7-17;
⊙11am-10pm) Casual harborside restaurant
with a varied menu: lots of sandwiches
(reuben, tuna melt), burgers (chili, porta-
bella, mushroom and Swiss), salads (sesame
chicken, fajita), seafood (chipotle fish and
chips) and meats (prime rib, top sirloin).
Has good water views.

Bridge   NORTHWESTERN $$$
(☑541-247-6465; 94321 Wedderburn Loop; mains
$15-24; ⊙11am-4pm & 5-9pm Tue-Sat, 4-9pm
Sun) The Bridge offers gourmet dishes like
spicy shell pasta with shrimp, braised pork
shank, classic gumbo and cioppino. Casual
restaurant-bar atmosphere with peeks at
the river from some tables.

BROOKINGS AS WWII BOMB SITE

Brookings was the site of one of the two
mainland air attacks the US suffered
during WWII. A seaplane launched from
a Japanese submarine in September
1942 succeeded in bombing Mt Emily,
behind the city (there were no casual-
ties). The main goal of the attack was
to burn the forests, but they failed
to ignite. The Japanese pilot of that
same seaplane returned to Brookings
20 years later and presented the city
with his samurai sword, which was in
his plane during the bombing; it's now
displayed in Brookings' library.

---

❶ Information

Ranger Station (☑541-247-3600; 29279
Ellensburg Ave; ⊙8:30am-12:30pm & 1:30-
4:30pm Mon-Fri)
Visitor Center (☑800-525-2334; www.gold
beach.org; 94080 Shirley Lane; ⊙9:30am-
4:30pm Mon-Fri, 10am-5pm Sat & Sun)

❶ Getting There & Around

Curry Public Transit's **Coastal Express** (☑800-
921-2871; www.currypublictransit.org) shuttles
connect Gold Beach with Bandon, Coos Bay/
North Bend, Port Orford and Brookings.

Brookings
POP 6500

Just 6 miles from the California border,
Brookings is a balmy commercial town on
the bay of the Chetco River. Tourists are
drawn here for the world-class salmon and
steelhead fishing upriver, while the coastline
to the north is some of Oregon's most gor-
geous. Winter temperatures hover around
60°F (15°C), making Brookings the state's
'banana belt' and a mecca for retirees. The
city is also a leader in Easter lily-bulb pro-
duction; in July, fields south of town are
filled with bright colors and a heavy scent.

Roads lead inland from Brookings up
the Chetco River to the western edge of the
Kalmiopsis Wilderness. Oregon's only red-
wood forests are also found in this area.

◉ Sights & Activities

**Chetco Valley
Historical Society Museum**   MUSEUM
(☑541-469-5650; 15461 Museum Rd; admission by
donation; ⊙noon-4pm Sat & Sun) Once a stage-
coach stop, the 1857 Blake House is now
home to this museum. Stop in to see a quilt
from 1844, an old Native American cedar
canoe and an iron face supposedly cast re-
sembling Queen Elizabeth I. Outside is the
'world's largest Monterey cypress.' Off-hours
private tours are possible; call Julie Paine on
☑541-469-3144.

Azalea Park   PARK
(Azalea Park Rd) This is a glorious, hilly park
showcasing hundreds of azaleas, along with
other pretty flora. Blooms are best from April
to June. On Memorial Day weekend, the park
becomes the focus of the annual **Azalea
Festival**, with a floral parade and craft fair.
There are Sunday concerts in July and Au-
gust and a holiday light show in December.

Samuel H Boardman State Park PARK

Four miles north of Brookings, US 101 winds over 11 miles of headlands through Boardman State Park, which contains some of Oregon's most beautiful coastline. Along the highway are a number of roadside turnouts and picnic areas with short trails leading to secluded beaches and dramatic viewpoints. Marching far out to sea are tiny island chains, home to shorebirds and braying sea lions.

Pretty **Lone Ranch Beach**, the southernmost turnoff, has picnic opportunities and tide pools in a sandy cove studded with triangular sea stacks. Half a mile north is the turnoff to **Cape Ferrelo**, with great ocean vistas. A further mile north is **House Rock Viewpoint**, a high windy promontory with more stunning views.

North of the Thomas Creek Bridge (Oregon's highest at 345ft) is the turnoff for **Natural Bridge Viewpoint**, where you can see rock arches – the remnants of collapsed sea caves – just off the coast. And at **Arch Rock Point**, about a mile north, are interesting, eroded volcanic headlands.

Harris Beach State Park PARK

(✆541-469-2021; www.oregonstateparks.org; 1655 US 101 N) This pleasant state park is about a mile north of town. There are views of Goat Island, Oregon's largest offshore island and a bird sanctuary, from the picnic area.

Alfred A Loeb State Park PARK

(✆541-469-2021; www.oregonstateparks.org; North Bank Chetco River Rd) Nature trails at lush Alfred A Loeb State Park, about 9 miles east of town on North Bank Chetco Rd, showcase two of Oregon's rarest and most cherished trees – redwood and myrtle. Hike the gorgeous 1.2-mile Redwood Nature Trail loop; the trailhead is on Chetco River Rd, 0.25 miles past the park's entrance.

🛏 Sleeping

Westward Inn MOTEL $

(✆541-469-7471; www.westwardinn.com; 1026 Chetco Ave; d $75-99; 🖥🐾) Very nice hotel rooms on tap here, some with ocean view. Clean, comfortable and good value.

Harris Beach State Park CAMPGROUND $

(✆541-469-2021; www.oregonstateparks.org; 1655 US 101 N; tent sites/RV sites/yurts $20/26/39; 🐾) Camp above the beach at one of 150 sites here. Six yurts, showers, flush toilets and coin laundry are among the amenities. Located about a mile north of town.

South Coast Inn B&B B&B $$

(✆800-525-9273; www.southcoastinn.com; 516 Redwood St; d $119-159; @🖥) Bernard Maybeck designed this lovely arts-and-crafts-style house in 1917. It offers four rooms, one cottage and an apartment. It's filled with antiques, and a gorgeous stone fireplace dominates the living room. The gardens are lovely.

🍴 Eating

The port has seafood and the excellent **Zola's Pizzeria** (✆541-412-7100; 16362 Lower Harbor Rd; pizzas $15-30; ⊘11am-9pm Mon-Sat, till 8pm Sun).

Mattie's Pancake & Omelette AMERICAN $

(✆541-469-7211; www.mattiespancakehouse.com; 15975 US 101 S; mains $7-13; ⊘6am-1:45pm Mon-Sat) This casual breakfast and lunch spot offers 18 kinds of omelettes (such as crab and Swiss cheese) along with pancakes (yes! chocolate chip!) and waffles. Sandwiches and salads for lunch.

Art Alley Grille AMERICAN $$

(✆541-469-0800; www.artalleygrille.com; 515 Chetco Ave; mains $16-23; ⊘11am-2pm Tue, 11am-2pm & 5-9pm Wed-Sat) Brookings' best restaurant. Lunch (upstairs at 'The Snug') means $8 to $9 homemade salads and sandwiches; sit on a verandah in good weather. Dinner is downstairs and choices include great pasta, seafood and meat dishes.

ℹ Information

Brookings Welcome Center (✆541-469-4117; brookingswc@traveloregon.com; 14433 Hwy 101 S; ⊘9:30am-4:30pm Mon-Sat, 11am-4:30pm Sun) Lots of brochures and good information.

Chamber of Commerce (✆541-469-3181; www.brookingsharborchamber.com; 16330 Lower Harbor Rd; ⊘9am-5pm Mon-Fri year-round, plus 11am-3pm Sat May-Sep)

ℹ Getting There & Around

Curry Public Transit's **Coastal Express** (✆800-921-2871; www.currypublictransit.org) shuttles connect Brookings with Bandon, Coos Bay/North Bend, Port Orford and Gold Beach.

Daily **Southwest Point** (✆541-813-1223; www.southwest-point.com; 624 Railroad St) shuttles connect Brookings with Grants Pass, Medford, Ashland and Klamath Falls.

Ashland & Southern Oregon

Best Places to Eat

➡ New Sammy's Cowboy Bistro (p329)

➡ Crater Lake Lodge Dining Room (p341)

➡ Steamboat Inn (p338)

➡ Morning Glory (p328)

Best Places to Stay

➡ Crater Lake Lodge (p341)

➡ Wolf Creek Inn (p333)

➡ Country Willows (p328)

➡ Out 'n' About Treesort (p335)

Why Go?

With a warm, sunny and dry climate that belongs in nearby California, Southern Oregon, the state's 'banana belt,' is an exciting place to visit. Rugged and remote landscapes are entwined with a number of designated 'wild and scenic' rivers, which are famous for their challenging white-water rafting, world-class fly-fishing and excellent hiking. There's good birding in the area – especially for bald eagles – and exceptional lakes to visit, including spectacular Crater Lake.

Gold and timber originally brought pioneers to Southern Oregon cities, and today the migration continues with families and retirees seeking affordable housing. Downtowns have been revitalized, and there's plenty of culture: Ashland is home to the renowned Oregon Shakespeare Festival, while nearby Jacksonville hosts the music-lovers' Britt Festival. Located between Seattle and San Francisco, Southern Oregon is certainly worth more than a gas break if you're cruising the I-5.

When to Go
Ashland

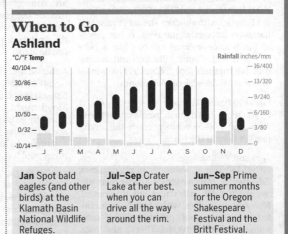

Jan Spot bald eagles (and other birds) at the Klamath Basin National Wildlife Refuges.

Jul–Sep Crater Lake at her best, when you can drive all the way around the rim.

Jun–Sep Prime summer months for the Oregon Shakespeare Festival and the Britt Festival.

Ashland

POP 21,000

This pretty city is the cultural center of Southern Oregon thanks to its internationally renowned Oregon Shakespeare Festival (OSF), which runs for nine months of the year and attracts hundreds of thousands of theatergoers from all over the world. The festival is so popular that it's Ashland's main attraction, packing it out in summer and bringing in steady cash flows for the many fancy hotels, upscale B&Bs and fine restaurants in town. Even without the OSF, however, Ashland is still a pleasant place where trendy downtown streets buzz with well-heeled shoppers and youthful bohemians. In late fall and early winter – those few months when the festival doesn't run – folks come to ski at nearby Mt Ashland. And wine-lovers take note – the area has several good wineries worth seeking out, exploring and tasting, of course.

◎ Sights & Activities

Schneider Museum of Art MUSEUM
(☑541-552-6245; www.sou.edu/sma; 1250 Siskiyou Blvd; suggested donation $5; ⊙10am-4pm Mon-Sat) Ashland's culture extends beyond the OSF; if you like contemporary art, check out this Southern Oregon University museum. The university also puts on theater performances of its own, along with classical concerts and opera performances.

Scienceworks MUSEUM
(☑541-482-6767; www.scienceworksmuseum.org; 1500 E Main St; adult/child 2-12yr $9/7; ⊙10am-6pm; ⋅) Families with children shouldn't miss this hands-on interactive museum. It has plenty of fun science-oriented exhibits like a bubble room, hall of optical illusions and shadow wall that captures your silhouette. Free admission first Wednesday of each month.

Lithia Artisans Market MARKET
If you're in town on a weekend between April and mid-November, catch this crafty market behind the plaza.

Jackson Wellsprings SPA
(☑541-482-3776; www.jacksonwellsprings.com; 2253 Hwy 99; ⊙8am-midnight, shorter hours winter) For a good soak check out this casual, New Age–style place, which boasts a mineral-fed swimming pool, private soaking tubs, saunas and steam rooms. There's also yoga, massages and spa services, plus camping. It's 1 mile north of town.

Kokopelli RAFTING
(☑866-723-8874; www.kokopelliriverguides.com; 2475 Siskiyou Blvd) Rafting trips on the Rogue River.

Mt Ashland Ski Resort SKIING
(☑541-482-2897; www.mtashland.com; lift passes adult/child 7-12yr $43/33) Powdery snow is abundant at this resort 16 miles southwest of town on 7533ft Mt Ashland.

Siskiyou Cyclery CYCLING
(☑541-482-1997; www.siskiyoucyclery.com; 1729 Siskiyou Blvd; ⊙10am-6pm Mon-Sat, 11am-4pm Sun) Rent a bike and explore the countryside on Bear Creek Greenway.

Lithia Park ICE-SKATING
You can ice-skate at lovely, 93-acre Lithia Park, which winds along Ashland Creek above the center of town (in summer it offers live concerts, duck ponds and picnic tables).

⌂ Sleeping

From May to October, try to arrive with reservations. Rooms are cheaper in Medford (p330), 12 miles north of Ashland. There's camping, RV sites and tipis at Jackson Wellsprings (p326).

Ashland Hostel HOSTEL $
(☑541-482-9217; www.theashlandhostel.com; 150 N Main St; dm $28, d $45-94; ⊛⊚) Central and somewhat upscale hostel (shoes off inside!). Most private rooms share bathrooms; some are connected to dorms. Hangout spaces include the cozy basement living room and shady front porch. No alcohol or smoking on the premises; call ahead as reception times are limited.

Ashland Motel MOTEL $
(☑541-482-2561; www.ashlandmotel.com; 1145 Siskiyou Blvd; d $95-110; ⊛⊚⊛) The Ashland Motel might look like the same old thing from the outside, but remodeled rooms here are surprisingly hip and contemporary with a simple, industrial look. There's a swimming pool too.

Manor Motel MOTEL $
(☑541-482-2246; www.manormotel.net; 476 N Main St; d $87-129; ⊛⊚⊛) Cute motel with 12 pleasant rooms and one- and two-bedroom units near downtown; kitchenettes available. The Garden Suite has its own private garden.

Ashland & Southern Oregon Highlights

1 Strutting with the Bard at Ashland's **Oregon Shakespeare Festival** (p329).

2 Counting bald eagles in **Klamath Basin National Wildlife Refuges** (p345).

3 Rafting down the mighty **Rogue River** (p341), Oregon's premier white water.

4 Spelunking the main grotto at **Oregon Caves National Monument** (p335).

5 Exploring the historic downtown streets of **Jacksonville** (p331).

6 Fly-fishing the world-class waters of the **North Umpqua River** (p337).

7 Taking the scenic Rim Drive around gorgeous **Crater Lake** (p338).

Cedarwood Inn   MOTEL $

(☎800-547-4141; www.ashlandcedarwoodinn.com; 1801 Siskiyou Blvd; d from $72; ✳🛜🐾🏊) Pleasant spacious motel on a relatively quiet avenue with an outdoor pool. There's also a large indoor Jacuzzi and steam room. Kitchenettes available. Reserve ahead as it's a good deal and fills up fast; price varies according to vacancy rates.

Ashland Commons   HOSTEL, APARTMENT $

(☎541-482-6753; www.ashlandcommons.com; 437 Williamson Way; dm $26, s $45-65, d $60-80; ✳🛜) Interesting dorm or private room accommodations provided within three large apartments. All vary in atmosphere, and are either two- or four-bedroom, with kitchen and living areas. Great for large groups, as entire apartments can be rented.

Glenyan Campground   CAMPGROUND $

(☎877-453-6926; www.glenyanrvpark.com; 5310 Hwy 66; tent/RV sites from $24/33; 🛜🐾🏊) This shady and pleasant 12-acre campground about 5 miles southeast of Ashland. Reserve a creekside spot, as they're the best. Playground, games room and store available.

★**Country Willows**   B&B $$

(☎541-488-1590; www.countrywillowsinn.com; 1313 Clay St; d $165-290; ✳@🛜🏊) Only minutes from downtown is this luxurious B&B on 5 acres in the 'countryside'. The nine rooms, suites and a cottage sport a mix of antiques and contemporary furniture; some suites are as big as small apartments and have a kitchenette or private deck. The gorgeous breakfast room is next to the swimming pool.

Palm   BOUTIQUE HOTEL $$

(☎541-482-2636; www.palmcottages.com; 1065 Siskiyou Blvd; d $98-239; ✳🛜🐾🏊) Fabulous small motel remodeled into 16 charming garden cottage rooms and suites (some with kitchens). It's an oasis of green on a busy avenue, complete with grassy lawns and a saltwater pool. A house harbors three large suites ($299).

Columbia Hotel   HOTEL $$

(☎541-482-3726; www.columbiahotel.com; 262 1/2 E Main St; d $89-179; ✳🛜) Awesomely located 'European-style' hotel – which means most rooms share outside bathrooms. It's the best deal in downtown Ashland, with 24 quaint vintage rooms (no TVs), a nice lobby and a historic feel. The rooms are on the 2nd floor and there's no elevator.

Chanticleer Inn   B&B $$

(☎541-482-1919, 800-898-1950; www.ashland-bnb.com; 120 Gresham St; d $170-205; ✳🛜) This lovely arts-and-crafts-style B&B comes with six elegant rooms and friendly host Ellen Campbell. The common areas are comfortable and tasteful, and the gardens are filled with lush plants. It's in a peaceful residential neighborhood very close to the center.

Ashland Springs Hotel   HISTORIC HOTEL $$

(☎541-488-1700; www.ashlandspringshotel.com; 212 E Main St; d from $179; ✳🛜) This is a beautiful, renovated, historic landmark hotel with small but pleasant rooms and a noteworthy restaurant, Larks. Snag an upper corner room for great light and views. Great downtown location.

Iris Inn   B&B $$

(☎541-488-2286; www.irisinnbb.com; 59 Manzanita St; d $190; ✳🛜) Well-located and long-running B&B in a 1905 Victorian, with five lovely rooms and a garden deck, patio and gazebo. There are afternoon drinks and gourmet breakfast, and it's easy walking distance to downtown.

Ashland Creek Inn   HOTEL $$$

(☎541-482-3315; www.ashlandcreekinn.com; 70 Water St; d $265-425; ✳🐾🏊) This gorgeous creekside inn offers 10 impeccable and eclectic suites, each with a nice living area. Most have a kitchenette and private deck over the water. There's a small but pretty garden and deck areas in which to relax, and a multi-course breakfast is included.

Arden Forest Inn   B&B $$$

(☎541-488-1496; www.afinn.com; 261 W Hersey St; d $195-230; ✳🛜🏊) This lovely and comfortable B&B has five tastefully decorated rooms (including a two-bedroom suite), a wonderful large garden and theater-loving hosts. There's a casual and liberal atmosphere, the gourmet breakfast is bountiful, and it's very gay-friendly.

✖ Eating

There are plenty of great eating choices in Ashland, which levies a 5% restaurant tax. Dinner reservations in summer are a good idea at the fancier spots.

★**Morning Glory**   CAFE $

(☎541-488-8636; www.morninggloryrestaurant.com; 1149 Siskiyou Blvd; mains $11-13; ⏱8am-1:30pm) This colorful, casual cafe is one of

Ashland's best breakfast joints. Creative dishes include the Alaskan crab omelette, vegetarian hash with roasted chilis and shrimp cakes with poached eggs. For lunch there's gourmet salad and sandwiches. Go early or late to avoid a long wait.

Ashland Food Cooperative   SELF-CATERING **$**
(☑541-482-2237; www.ashlandfood.coop; 237 N 1st St; ☺7am-9pm) Head to this awesome food co-op if you've scored a kitchenette in your hotel room. All the typical healthy foods are available, along with a small cafe-deli and to-go food bar.

Agave   MEXICAN **$**
(☑541-488-1770; www.agavetaco.net; 92 N Main St; tacos $2.75-4.50; ☺11am-9pm Sun-Thu, till 10pm Fri & Sat) Tasty and creative tacos are cooked up at this small, trendy joint. There's the regular stuff like carnitas and grilled chicken, but for something more exotic go for the shredded duck or sautéed main lobster ($8.25). A few salads and tamales too.

★Smithfields   STEAKHOUSE **$$**
(☑541-488-9948; www.smithfieldsashland.com; 36 S 2nd St; mains $17-27; ☺11:30am-2:30pm & 5-9pm Tue-Fri, 10am-2:30pm & 5-9pm Sat & Sun) Excellent, meat-centric (and boasts it) restaurant. Start with the roasted bone marrow and head straight into the char-grilled hanger steak, duck leg confit or cider-braised pork belly. Lunch means fancy sandwiches, and don't miss weekend brunch for gourmet meaty treats.

Dragonfly   INTERNATIONAL **$$**
(☑541-488-4855; www.dragonflyashland.com, 241 Hargadine St; mains $13-25; ☺8am-3pm & 5-9pm) 🍃 Great international creativity served here; there's coconut French toast for breakfast, free-range chicken tamales for lunch and wok-fried rice bowls for dinner (among many other options). Pretty garden patio in back.

Standing Stone Brewery   AMERICAN **$$**
(☑541-482-2448; www.standingstonebrewing.com; 101 Oak St; mains $10-17; ☺11am-midnight) Popular and hip brewery-restaurant with burgers, salads, sandwiches and wood-fired pizzas, along with a few seafood dishes. Wash it all down with some microbrews or a cocktail. Great back patio.

★New Sammy's Cowboy Bistro   FRENCH, AMERICAN **$$$**
(☑541-535-2779; 2210 S Pacific Hwy, Talent; mains $25-28, prix fixe $45; ☺noon-1:30pm & 5-9pm Wed Sun) 🍃 Some consider this funky spot, run by an eclectic couple, Oregon's best restaurant. There are only a handful of tables and the wine selections are spectacular. Mains

---

OREGON SHAKESPEARE FESTIVAL

The Pacific Northwest is a hot spot for both traditional and innovative theater, and one top highlight is definitely Ashland's wildly popular Oregon Shakespeare Festival (OSF). Despite being deeply rooted in Shakespearean and Elizabethan drama, the festival also features plenty of revivals and contemporary theater from around the world.

As a young town, Ashland was included in the Methodist Church's cultural education program, called the Chautauqua Series. By the 1930s, one of the venues, Chautauqua Hall, had deteriorated to a dilapidated wooden shell. Angus Bowmer, a drama professor at the local college, noted the resemblance of the roofless structure to drawings of Shakespeare's Globe Theatre. He convinced the town to sponsor two performances of Shakespeare's plays and a boxing match (the Bard would have approved) as part of its 1935 Fourth of July celebration. The plays proved a great success, and the OSF was off and running.

Eleven productions run from February to October in three theaters near Main and Pioneer Sts: the outdoor **Elizabethan Theatre** (open June to October), the **Angus Bowmer Theatre** and the intimate **Thomas Theatre**. Children under six are not allowed. There are no Monday performances.

Performances sell out quickly; obtain tickets in advance at www.osfashland.org. You can also try the **box office** (☑541-482-4331; 15 S Pioneer St; tickets $25-95) for last-minute tickets. Popular backstage **tours** (adult/child 6-17yr $15/11) also need to be booked well in advance.

Check the OSF Welcome Center (p330) for other events, which may include scholarly lectures, play readings, concerts and pre-show talks.

are few but the flavor combinations can be incredible; many vegetables come from the garden outside. Located in Talent, about 2 miles north of Ashland. Reserve a week in advance for dinner; limited winter hours.

Amuse FRENCH $$$
(☑541-488-9000; www.amuserestaurant.com; 15 N 1st St; mains $22-28; ⊙5:30-9pm Tue-Sun) Fine French bistro serving dishes like Parisian gnocchi, grilled Painted Hills rib eye and truffle-roasted game hen. Dessert means bittersweet chocolate truffle cake and warm beignets with crème anglaise. Reserve ahead.

🍷 Drinking

Caldera Tap House BREWPUB
(☑541-482-4677; www.calderabrewing.com; 31 Water St; ⊙2pm-close) Popular, casual brewpub with outdoor decks under a street overpass. Typical pub grub, with award-winning ales and lagers to accompany it; there is live music two to three times per week. Also has a much fancier restaurant at 590 Clover St (dinner mains $10 to $21).

Rogue Valley Roasting Co CAFE
(☑541-488-5902; www.ashlandcoffee.com; 917 E Main St; ⊙6:45am-6pm) This quality coffeehouse serves up dark roasts and organic beans, along with gourmet teas and a few light snacks. The atmosphere is laid-back and there's some outdoor seating.

Noble Coffee CAFE
(☑541-488-3288; www.noblecoffeeroasting.com; 281 4th St; ⊙7am-4pm) Some of Ashland's best organic coffee, freshly roasted and pressed, siphoned or dripped to your specifications. Nice atmosphere too.

🛍 Shopping

Dagoba CHOCOLATE
(☑541-482-2001; www.dagobachocolate.com; 1105 Benson Way; ⊙10am-4pm Mon-Fri) Chocolate-lovers shouldn't miss a visit to the factory store and tasting room.

ℹ Information

Ashland Chamber of Commerce (☑541-482-3486; www.ashlandchamber.com; 110 E Main St; ⊙9am-5pm Mon-Fri) An information booth at the Plaza is open summer weekends only.
OSF Welcome Center (76 N Main St; ⊙10am-6pm Tue-Sun) Helps with OSF-related questions.

ℹ Getting There & Around

The nearest airport is 15 miles north in Medford. **Cascade Airport Shuttle** (☑541-488-1998; www.cascadeshuttle.com) provides services from the airport to Ashland; reserve ahead. Local bus transportation is provided by **Rogue Valley Transportation District** (RVTD; ☑541-779-2877; www.rvtd.org).

Medford

POP 76,000

Southern Oregon's largest metropolis, Medford is well known for its fruit industry, especially pears and wine grapes. In the past decade the city has grown tremendously, drawing thousands of California retirees with its sunny warm weather. It's also well located, with plenty of affordable accommodations, and Ashland, Jacksonville, Crater Lake, Oregon Caves National Monument and the Rogue River valley are all a day trip away.

⊙ Sights & Activities

Harry & David's Country Village GOURMET FOOD STORE
(☑541-864-2278; www.harryanddavid.com; 1314 Center Dr; ⊙9am-8pm Mon-Sat, 9am-7pm Sun) Medford's most famous tourist attraction is this outlet store of the giant mail-order fruit company. It offers nearby **plant tours** (☑877-322-8000; tours $5) with advance reservations.

Tou Velle State Park PARK
About 6 miles north of Medford on the Rogue River, this state park is popular for swimming and picnicking. About a mile beyond is **Table Rocks**, impressive 800ft mesas that speak of the area's volcanic past and are home to unique plant and animal species. Flowery spring is the best time for hiking to the flat tops, which were revered Native American sites.

From downtown, follow Riverside Ave north and turn right on Table Rock Rd. After Tou Velle State Park, fork either left to reach the trailhead to Lower Table Rock (3.5-mile round-trip hike) or right for Upper Table Rock (2.5-mile round-trip hike). The **Bureau of Land Management** (BLM; ☑541-618-2200; www.or.blm.gov; 3040 Biddle Rd) has information and offers guided springtime hikes.

📖 Sleeping & Eating

Medford's Riverside Ave has plenty of budget and midrange motels, but the cheapest can be a bit grungy and most are within earshot of the I-5.

Medford Inn   MOTEL $
(☑ 541-773-8266; www.medfordinnsuites.com; 1015 S Riverside Ave; d $65-80; ❄ 🐶 🛜 ✈ 🏊) Despite being on a busy avenue, this is a pleasant, large motel with spacious, clean rooms and atmosphere. All rooms come with refrigerator and microwave, and there's a pool and small garden patio area.

Cedar Lodge   MOTEL $
(☑ 541-773-7361; www.cedarlodgemotorinn.com; 518 N Riverside Ave; d $55; ❄ 🛜 ✈ 🏊) There are good standard rooms at Cedar Lodge, some with microwave and refrigerator. One of the better places on this drag, it boasts a small outdoor swimming pool.

White House   B&B $$
(☑ 541-301-2086; www.thewhitehouse-bedand-breakfast.com; 212 Valley View Dr; r $135) Just one large lovely room with sitting room is generally available at this friendly B&B. If you're in a group or family and are willing to share the bathroom, you can take another room ($50). It's in a residential neighborhood and a gourmet breakfast will be cooked to order for you.

Buttercloud Bakery & Cafe   AMERICAN $
(☑ 541-973-2336; www.buttercloudbakery.com; 310 Genessee St; biscuit sandwiches $6.25-6.75; ⊙ 7am-3pm Tue-Sat, 8am-2pm Sun) For a breakfast treat, head on over to this small but bright bakery-cafe. Biscuit sandwiches are the highlight here; order them with toppings like eggs, bacon, brisket, spinach, roasted peppers and goat's cheese. A few soups, salads and sides are also available, along with luscious pastries.

Porters   AMERICAN $$
(☑ 541-857-1910; www.porterstrainstation.com; 147 N Front St; mains $10-31; ⊙ 5-9pm Sun-Thu, till 9:30pm Fri & Sat) This gorgeous arts-and-crafts-style restaurant is decked out in dark-wood booths and boasts an awesome patio next to the train tracks. Steak, seafood and pasta dishes dominate the menu, though the food won't blow you away. The attached bar stays open later.

Downtown Market Co   AMERICAN $$
(☑ 541-973-2233; www.downtownmarketco.com; 231 E Main St; mains $9-12; ⊙ 11am-4pm Mon-Fri, noon-4pm Sat) Gourmet market that also offers cooking classes in its open back kitchen. Come here for good sandwiches (changed daily), soups and salads. There are also incredible-looking desserts.

ℹ Information

Visitor Center (☑ 541-776-4021; www.travel medford.org; 1314 Center Dr; ⊙ 9am-6pm) Right next to Harry & David's.

ℹ Getting There & Around

The Rogue Valley International Medford Airport is 2.5 miles north of town, off Biddle Rd.

Greyhound (☑ 541-779-2103; www.greyhound. com; 220 S Front St) Buses (via South West-point shuttles; www.southwest-point.com) run to Ashland, Klamath Falls and Brookings.

Rogue Valley Transit District (RVTD; ☑ 541-779-5821; www.rvtd.org; 200 S Front St) Provides local bus transportation.

Jacksonville

This former gold-prospecting town is the oldest settlement in Southern Oregon and a National Historic Landmark. Small but endearing, the town's main drag – California St – is like a step back in time, lined with well-preserved brick-and-wood buildings dating from the 1880s. Today, folks come to stroll around downtown and enjoy the old-time atmosphere while exploring the many boutiques and galleries. Although summertime is great, Jacksonville has a certain magic touch in winter, when the crowds are lighter and the old-fashioned 'Victorian Christmas' holiday celebrations take hold.

Don't miss the Britt Festival, a world-class musical experience that runs all summer long. And in the surrounding Applegate Valley there are several wineries to visit, offering more varietals than just pinot noir; see www.applegatewinetrail.com for more.

⊙ Sights

Jacksonville Cemetery   CEMETERY
(www.friendsjvillecemetery.org) A well-maintained, 32-acre cemetery, it is worth a wander to explore historic pioneer gravesites chronicling wars, epidemics and other untimely deaths. For two days in October, the 'Meet the

BRITT FESTIVAL

In 1963, Portland conductor John Trudeau came to Jacksonville with a few friends, and they found themselves on the former hillside estate of Peter Britt (1819–1905), a Swiss photographer who made a name for himself after immigrating to Oregon. These musicians noticed the exceptional acoustics of the hillsides surrounding Britt's old home, and that same year built a plywood stage for a local orchestral performance. Thus was born the Pacific Northwest's first outdoor music festival.

In 1978 a pavilion was constructed and the festival continued to grow and attract top-notch artists. The nonprofit Britt Festival (www.brittfest.org; ☉ Jun-Sep) is now a premier music festival attracting tens of thousands of revelers; it also sponsors educational programs through the Britt Institute. For more information, head to the festival's website. And for more on Peter Britt and his many talents, go to www.peterbritt.org.

Pioneers' program has volunteers in period costumes leading tours. The chamber of commerce has helpful literature with maps.

☞ Tours

Trolley Tours   SIGHTSEEING TOUR
(adult/child 6-12yr $5/3) These narrated tours provide a good historical overview of the town; they run daily May through October.

🛏 Sleeping

Jacksonville has limited and mostly upscale accommodations (reserve ahead). There's more choice and less expensive accommodations 6 miles east in Medford (p330).

Cantrall-Buckley
Campground   CAMPGROUND $
(www.co.jackson.or.us/page.asp?navid=3271;   154
Cantrall Rd; campsites $16; ☉ May-Sep) Located in Ruch, 10 miles west of Jacksonville on Hwy 238, this first-come, first-served campground (showers available) is shaded by oak, fir and madrone trees. The pleasant Applegate River flows nearby.

Touvelle House   B&B $$
(☎ 541-899-8938, 800-846-8422; www.touvelle house.com; 455 N Oregon St; d $159-199; ✳@⊛⊛) This gorgeous arts-and-crafts-style house offers six elegant rooms, all different sizes and with different decoration but each with feather bed, down comforter and private bathroom. It's on spacious grounds with a pool (the only one in town!), just two blocks from downtown.

Jacksonville Inn   HOTEL $$
(☎ 541-899-1900; www.jacksonvilleinn.com; 175 E California St; d incl breakfast $159-199; ✳⊛⊛) This historic 1863 hotel is right downtown and has beautiful, classic rooms with flowery (but tasteful) decoration. There are also four lovely cottages a couple of blocks away, plus an excellent upscale restaurant and bistro.

Apothecary Inn   B&B $$
(☎ 541-899-3998; www.apothecaryinn.com; 830 Upper Applegate Rd; d $135 & $165; ✳⊛) There are just two rooms at this countryside B&B, cheerfully run by a young couple. On the grounds are miniature donkeys, llamas, chickens and Nigerian dwarf goats; there are also vegetable and herb gardens and a small orchard. It's about 9 miles south of Jacksonville.

Magnolia Inn   B&B $$
(☎ 866-899-0255; www.magnolia-inn.com; 245 N 5th St; d $144-174; ✳⊛⊛) The Magnolia is a pleasant nine-room B&B boasting a guest kitchen (food warm-up only; no cooking) with a great covered verandah nearby. All rooms have private bathroom and are differently decorated with antiques; breakfast is included.

Wine Country Inn   HOTEL $$
(☎ 541-899-3953, 800-253-8254; www.country-houseinnsjacksonville.com; 830 N 5th St; d $118-129; ✳⊛⊛) This modern hotel offers 27 spacious, simple and elegant contemporary rooms, some with Jacuzzi. It's just outside the heart of town.

✕ Eating

The Jacksonville Inn has a fine restaurant with some of the town's best food; head to its more casual bistro for less pricey selections and no reservations needed.

Mustard Seed Cafe
AMERICAN $

(☑541-899-2977; 130 N 5th St; mains $7-10; ☺7am-2pm Wed-Sat, till 1pm Sun) Awesome breakfast spot with great-value menu. Come early for breakfast, which means French toast, biscuits and gravy, scrambles and 'nearly famous' cinnamon rolls. For lunch there are eight kinds of burger, along with gourmet salads and grilled sandwiches.

GoodBean Coffee
CAFE $

(☑541-899-8740; www.goodbean.com; 165 S Oregon St; drinks & snacks under $5; ☺6am-7pm) This is a casual, trendy coffee shop with brick walls and sidewalk tables. Gourmet beans and bagel and panini sandwiches are available.

C Street Bistro
AMERICAN $$

(☑541-261-7638; www.cstbistro.com; 230 East C St; mains $12-19; ☺10:30am-2:30pm Tue-Sat, 5:30-8:30pm Thu-Sat) Casual bistro serving tasty signature sandwiches and grilled cheese panini for brunch and lunch. For dinner expect dishes like crispy duck leg confit, pappardelle shrimp pesto and gourmet burgers.

❶ Information

Chamber of Commerce (☑541-899-8118; www.jacksonvilleoregon.org; 185 N Oregon St; ☺10am-5pm Mon-Fri, till 3pm Sat & Sun)

❶ Getting There & Away

RVTD bus 30 runs from Medford. For bike rentals, check with **Cycle Analysis** (☑541-899-9190; 535 N 5th St).

Grants Pass

POP 35,000

As a modern and not particularly scenic city Grants Pass isn't a huge tourist destination, but its location on the banks of the Rogue River makes it a portal to adventure. White-water rafting, fine fishing and jet-boat excursions are the biggest attractions, and there's also good camping and hiking in the area.

If you're here on a Saturday between mid-March and Thanksgiving be sure to check out the **Outdoors Growers' Market**, a farmers and craft market that draws the city together. Grants Pass is also the gateway to Oregon Caves National Monument.

◉ Sights

Wildlife Images
WILDLIFE CENTER

(☑541-476-0222; www.wildlifeimages.org; 11845 Lower River Rd; adult/child 4-13yr $15/9; ☺tours 9:30am, 11:30am, 1:30pm & 3:30pm daily mid-Mar–Oct) Animal-lovers shouldn't miss this nonprofit rehabilitation center for native creatures in trouble. It's about 13 miles from Grants Pass, near Merlin; visits are by tour only (reserve a day ahead).

🛏 Sleeping

There are plenty of economy motels lining 6th and 7th Sts.

Buona Sera Inn
MOTEL $

(☑541-476-4260; www.buonaserainn.com; 1001 NE 6th St; d $85-100; ☎☀) Lovingly renovated motel with 14 comfortable, and even slightly luxurious, country-style rooms. All have quality linens and boast a refrigerator and microwave; some come with kitchenette.

Schroeder Park
CAMPGROUND $

(☑800-452-5687; 605 Schroeder Lane; tent sites/RV sites/yurts $19/22/30) This pleasant riverside campground is about 4 miles west of town, on the south side of the river. There are around 50 sites with showers, two yurts, flush toilets, a dog park, a playground and a boat ramp.

Valley of the Rogue State Park
CAMPGROUND $

(☑541-582-1118; www.oregonstateparks.org; 3792 N River Rd; tent sites/RV sites/yurts $19/24/36) Around 12 miles east of town, this riverside campground has 168 sites and six yurts. There are showers, flush toilets and a boat ramp.

★ Wolf Creek Inn
HOTEL $$

(☑541-866-2474; www.historicwolfcreekinn.com; 100 Front St; d incl breakfast $105-135; ☀☎☀) Located 20 miles north of Grants Pass, this historic hotel and stagecoach stop once hosted celebrities like Jack London, Clark Gable and Mary Pickford. There are only nine period rooms available (room 9 is the biggest). Restaurant available.

Motel del Rogue
MOTEL $$

(☑541-479-2111; www.moteldelrogue.com; 2600 Rogue River Hwy; r $90-145; ☀☎☀) Friendly motel about 2.5 miles east of town, on the Rogue River. Fourteen sweet and homey rooms are available, most with kitchenette, back deck and river views. It's a well-cared-for and charming place with personality.

THE UNIQUE KALMIOPSIS WILDERNESS

One of Oregon's largest wilderness areas, the remote Kalmiopsis Wilderness is famous for its rare plant life and the state's oldest peaks, the Klamath Mountains. About 150 million years ago, offshore sedimentary beds buckled up into mountains separated from North America by a wide gulf. Vegetation evolved on its own, so by the time the mountains fused to the continent the plant life was very different from that of the mainland. The area also has the country's largest exposed serpentine rock formations.

Unusual and unique plant species are showcased on the steep 0.8-mile hike to **Babyfoot Lake**. The pink-flowered *Kalmiopsis leachiana* and rare Port Orford cedar are found almost nowhere else on earth. Watch meadows for the carnivorous *Darlingtonia* (also called the pitcher plant or cobra lily) that traps insects for nourishment. To get to the trailhead, turn onto Eight Dollar Mountain Rd and follow the signs for 17 winding miles (this road is impassable in winter). There are many other hikes in the area.

Another section of the Kalmiopsis is accessible from the coastal town of Brookings. For more information and hiking trails, enquire at the ranger stations in Cave Junction (p336) and Gold Beach (p342).

Weasku Inn Resort INN $$$
(☑ 800-493-2758; www.countryhouseinns.com; 5560 Rogue River Hwy; d from $199, cabins from $225; ❉ ☏) Situated about 5 miles east of town, this grand old 1923 lodge once hosted Clark Gable (room 4) and Walt Disney (room 2). Five luxuriously rustic rooms and 12 cabins are available; some cabins have private Jacuzzi but all overlook the Rogue River. Continental breakfast is included.

✖ Eating

Rogue Coffee Roasters CAFE $
(☑ 541-476-6134; www.roguecoffeeroasting.com; 237 SW G St; coffee & snacks under $5; ☺ 7am-5pm Mon-Wed, to 7pm Thu & Fri, 8am-5pm Sat, to 2pm Sun) Organic, shade-grown and fair-trade coffees, along with gourmet teas and a few pastries.

Twisted Cork AMERICAN $$
(☑ 541-295-3094; www.thetwistedcorkgrantspass.com; 210 SW 6th St; mains $11-17; ☺ 11am-8pm Tue-Thu, till 9pm Fri & Sat, till 3pm Mon) Small, upscale restaurant in a central downtown location. It's open to a gift shop next door, lending it an odd commercial atmosphere, but the food is good. There are gourmet pastas, specialty flatbread dishes and fancy seafood courses – plus plenty of wines, of course.

Taprock AMERICAN $$
(☑ 541-476-2501; www.taprock.com; 940 SE 7th St; mains $11-22; ☺ 8am-10pm Sun-Thu, till 11pm Fri & Sat) Gorgeous, multimillion-dollar restaurant perched above the Rogue River. The menu has something for everyone – steaks, burgers, seafood, sandwiches and salads. Also does breakfast. Awesome deck seating with water views.

Middle Rogue Farm Cafe AMERICAN $$
(☑ 541-476-6882; 2315 Upper River Rd Loop; mains $7-10) ✿ Casual farm-to-table cafe out in the country offering quality sandwiches and salads – many of the ingredients are grown on the premises. A great spot for lunch; sit outside on sunny days. To get here, take G St southwest 1.4 miles, then turn left on Upper River Rd Loop. Call to check hours.

❶ Information

Tourism Office (☑ 541-450-6180; www.visitgrantspass.org; 1995 NW Vine St; ☺ 8am-5pm Mon-Fri) Right off I-5, exit 58.

❶ Getting There & Away

Greyhound (☑ 541-476-4513; www.greyhound.com; 460 NE Agness Ave) Off I-5 near exit 55, about 2 miles from downtown.

Oregon Caves National Monument

This popular tourist destination lies 19 miles (and a winding 40-minute drive) east of Cave Junction on Hwy 46. The Oregon Caves began as seafloor limestone deposits that were eventually hoisted into the Siskiyou Mountains. Molten rock forced its way into rock faults to form marble, and acidified groundwater seeped through cracks to carve underground channels. Surface erosion eventually created an opening for air to enter, causing water to mineralize and create myriad formations, such as cave popcorn, pearls, moonmilk, classic pipe organs, columns and stalactites.

⊙ Sights & Activities

Oregon Caves CAVE
(☑ 541-592-2100; www.nps.gov/orca; 19000 Caves Hwy; tours adult/child $8.50/6; ☉ tours 9am-6pm Jun-Sep, varies rest of year) The cave – there's only one – contains about 3 miles of passages, explored via 90-minute walking tours that expose visitors to dripping chambers and 520 rocky steps. The trail, which requires ducking at times, follows an underground waterway called the River Styx. Guided tours (the only way to access the cave) run at least hourly; they run half-hourly in July and August. Dress warmly, wear good shoes and be prepared to get dripped on. Due to safety, children less than 42in tall are not allowed on tours.

A handful of short nature trails surround the area, such as the 0.75-mile **Cliff Nature Trail** (offering good views) and the 3.3-mile **Big Tree Trail** (which loops through old-growth forest to a huge Douglas fir). Some fine **wineries** are also found in the area.

Kerbyville Museum MUSEUM
(☑ 541-592-5252; 24195 Redwood Hwy; adult/child 6-16yr $5/2; ☉ 10am-3pm Mon-Sat, noon-3pm Sun May-Sep, limited hours Apr & Oct, closed Nov-Mar) Surprisingly good museum for the tiny town of Kerby, 2 miles north of Cave Junction, with fascinating old relics from Native American baskets to taxidermy and an old View-Master stereoscope (the idea which started at the Oregon Caves Chateau's dining room). Also a scary surgical kit, linotype machine and military collection. Tour the nearby historic house too.

Great Cats World Park ZOO
(☑ 541-592-2957; www.greatcatsworldpark.com; 27919 Redwood Hwy; adult/child 4-12yr $14/10; ☉ 10am-6pm Jun-Aug, varies rest of year) For something completely different, check out this park 1.5 miles south of Cave Junction. This zoo/interactive big cat preserve proves cats *are* trainable – even if they're big enough to eat your head.

🛏 Sleeping & Eating

The Oregon Caves Chateau has a dining room and cafe.

Holiday Motel MOTEL $
(☑ 541-592-3003; 24810 Redwood Hwy; d $68-78; ❄🕾) Pleasant and friendly little motel with a handful of simple and clean rooms. Two kitchenettes and a cabin that sleeps up to six is available ($88). Located in Kerby, 2 miles north of Cave Junction.

Country Hills Resort CAMPGROUND, CABIN $
(☑ 541-592-3406; www.countryhillsresort.com; 7901 Caves Hwy; tent/RV sites $17/25, d $69, cabins $80-99) This rustic resort has five comfortable country-style rooms and six cabins with kitchenettes. It also offers creekside camping and full-hookup RV sites. It's 8 miles from Cave Junction, on the way to Oregon Caves; reserve in summer.

Cave Creek Campground CAMPGROUND $
(☑ 541-592-4000; campsites $10) About 15 miles up Hwy 46, this campground is nearly 4 miles from the caves and has a 1.8-mile trail leading there. There are vault toilets, picnic tables and drinking water; no showers or hookups.

★ Out 'n' About Treesort TREE HOUSE $$
(☑ 541-592-2208; www.treehouses.com; 300 Page Creek Rd, Takilma; tree houses incl breakfast $120-300; 🐾) A must for families with inquisitive kids, this rustic but fun place offers 15 different tree houses, from small, round rooms 47ft up, to more terrestrial suites with kitchens. Some share outside bathrooms. Zip lines and horseback riding are available, and minimum-night stays apply in summer. It's in Takilma, 12 miles south of Cave Junction. Reservations are crucial.

Oregon Caves Chateau HOTEL $$
(☑ 541-592-3400; www.oregoncaveschateau.com; 20000 Caves Hwy; r $109-199; ☉ mid-May–late Sep) Situated near the cave's entrance, this impressive, historic lodge has huge windows facing the forest, 23 simple, vintage rooms and a fine dining room (mains $21 to $30) overlooking a plunging ravine; the dining room is open mid-May through September from 5.30pm to 8pm nightly. Snacks and great milkshakes are served at the old-fashioned soda fountain. The cafe is open 7am to 5pm daily the same months as the dining room; mains are $8 to $12.

Taylor's Country Store DELI $
(☑ 541-592-5358; www.taylorsausage.com/store; 202 S Redwood Hwy; mains $3-8; ☉ 6am-7pm Mon-Thu, till 8:30pm Fri, 7am-7pm Sat, 8am-7pm Sun) Wonderfully local joint with tables surrounded by large meat counter and refrigerated cases. Good for breakfast, while lunch means hot or cold deli sandwiches and burgers. Fancier dinners on weekends, with live music Friday evenings.

Wild River Brewing & Pizza Co   PIZZERIA **$$**
(🖉541-592-3556; www.wildriverbrewing.com; 249 Redwood Hwy; pizzas $12-25; ⊙11am-9pm) Another link in this small but good restaurant chain. There are large family tables inside, but if it's sunny, the back deck (overlooking a creek) is the place to be. Also lots of sandwiches.

❶ Information

Cave Junction, 28 miles south of Grants Pass on US 199 (Redwood Hwy), provides the region's services.

Illinois Valley Visitor Center (🖉541-592-4076; 201 Caves Hwy; ⊙9am-4pm Mon-Fri, 10am-4:30pm Sat & Sun) Information on the area.

Wild Rivers Ranger District (🖉541-592-4000; www.fs.fed.us/r6/rogue-siskiyou; 26568 Redwood Hwy; ⊙8am-4:30pm Mon-Fri)

Roseburg

POP 21,500

Sprawling Roseburg lies in a valley near the confluence of the South and North Umpqua Rivers. The city is mostly a cheap, modern sleepover for travelers headed elsewhere (such as Crater Lake), but it does contain a cute historic downtown area and is surrounded by award-winning wineries. Two exceptional area sights include a regional museum and drive-through safari park.

◉ Sights & Activities

Douglas County Museum   MUSEUM
(🖉541-957-7007; www.co.douglas.or.us/museum; 123 Museum Dr, I-5 exit 123; adult/child $5/free; ⊙10am-5pm Tue-Sat; 🐾) Don't miss this excellent museum, which displays the Umpqua River Valley's cultural and natural histories. Especially interesting are the railroad derailment photos, logging exhibit and local wine history. Kids have interactive areas and live snakes to look at.

Wildlife Safari   ZOO
(🖉541-679-6761; www.wildlifesafari.net; 1790 Safari Rd, I-5 exit 119; adult/child 4-12yr $18/12; ⊙9am-5pm; 🐾) Ten miles southwest near Winston is where you drive your car (convertibles, motorcycles and pets not allowed!) around a 600-acre park dotted with inquisitive ostriches, camels, giraffes, lions, tigers and bears – among other exotic animals. Includes a small zoo where 'encounters' are available.

🛏 Sleeping & Eating

Roseburg is host to plenty of budget and mid-range hotel chains, most just off I-5 on NW Garden Valley Blvd, or on NE Stephens St.

Rose City Motel   MOTEL **$**
(🖉541-673-8209; 1142 NE Stephens St; d $60-66; 🅿❄🛜) A cheap motel on a busy avenue, but it's a great deal and pride in the place shows – there are plants here and there, and whimsical touches abound. Kitchenettes are available, and there's a nice little garden in back.

Hokanson's Guest House   B&B **$$**
(🖉541-672-2632; www.hokansonsguesthouse.com; 848 SE Jackson St; d $115-135; 🛜🐾) Just three charming rooms are available at this downtown B&B, each with a private bathroom. The 1882 Victorian is filled with antiques, and a Siamese cat roams the premises (but not in guest areas unless he's 'invited').

McMenamins Roseburg Station Pub   AMERICAN **$**
(www.mcmenamins.com; 700 SE Sheridan St; mains $7-11; ⊙11am-11pm Mon-Thu, till midnight Fri & Sat, noon-10pm Sun) This is a beautiful, cozy pub-restaurant in classic McMenamins style – old-fashioned and tasteful. Typical burgers, sandwiches and salads dominate the menu. It's in an old train depot; sit and order a microbrew on the sunny patio in summer.

Brix 527   CAFE **$**
(🖉541-440-4901; 527 SE Jackson St; mains $8-13; ⊙7am-8pm Mon-Sat, till 3pm Sun) A modern, hip cafe, Brix serves omelettes, pancakes and French toast for breakfast, and burgers, gourmet sandwiches and salads for lunch. Its 'Chill Lounge' is next door, with a fancier atmosphere and full dinner menu.

❶ Information

Fish & Wildlife Office (🖉541-440-3353; 4192 N Umpqua Hwy; ⊙8am-5pm Mon-Fri)

Roseburg Visitor Center (🖉800-444-9584, 541-672-9731; www.visitroseburg.com; 410 SE Spruce St; ⊙9am-5pm Mon-Fri, 9am-4pm Sat, 10am-4pm Sun)

❶ Getting There & Away

Greyhound (🖉541-673-3348; www.greyhound.com; 835 SE Stephens St). Provides long-distance bus services.

North Umpqua River

From Roseburg, Hwy 138 winds east toward Crater Lake along the lovely North Umpqua, a designated 'wild and scenic' river, and one of the best-loved fly-fishing streams in Oregon. Deep forests crowd the river's boulder-strewn edge while volcanic crags rise above the trees. This corridor contains one of Oregon's greatest concentrations of waterfalls, and there are short hikes to most of them.

Between Idleyld Park and Diamond Lake are dozens of mostly USFS campgrounds, many right on the river. In summer, plan on pitching a tent unless you've reserved accommodations at one of the resorts.

ℹ Information

Colliding Rivers Information Center (☏541-496-0157; 18782 N Umpqua Hwy, Glide; ⊙9am-5pm May-Sep)

Diamond Lake Ranger District (☏541-498-2531; 2020 Toketee-Rigdon Rd, Idleyld Park, Idleyld; ⊙8am-4:30pm Mon-Fri)

Diamond Lake Visitors Center (☏541-793-3379; USFS Rd 4795; ⊙10am-4pm Thu-Sun)

North Umpqua Ranger District (☏541-496-3532; 18782 N Umpqua Hwy, Glide; ⊙8am-4:30pm Mon-Fri) Adjacent to the Colliding Rivers Information Center.

Steamboat & Around

Steamboat is excellent for fishing and rafting, and especially for the many hikes in the surrounding area.

🏃 Activities

Fish & Wildlife Office   FISHING
(☏541-440-3353) Fly-fishing is heaven here, offering steelhead, cutthroat trout, and chinook and coho salmon. Consult the Fish & Wildlife Office for limits and restrictions.

North Umpqua Outfitters   RAFTING
(☏888-454-9696; www.nuorafting.com) Frothy rapids above Steamboat make this part of the river good for rafting and kayaking. North Umpqua Outfitters offers guided raft trips.

North Umpqua Trail   HIKING
The 79-mile North Umpqua Trail begins near Idleyld Park and passes through Steamboat en route to the Pacific Crest Trail near Lemolo Lake.

Mott Bridge   HIKING
A worthwhile day hike to Mott Bridge travels 5.5 gentle miles upstream through old-growth forest; it starts from the **Wright Creek Trailhead**, a few miles west of Steamboat on USFS Rd 4711.

Indian Mounds Trail   HIKING
From the Susan Creek day-use area (just west of Susan Creek campground), the 1.2-mile Indian Mounds Trail passes **Susan Creek Falls** before climbing up to a vision-quest site.

Fall Creek Falls   HIKING
About 4 miles east of Susan Creek day-use area is the 1-mile hike to the double-tier Fall Creek Falls; **Job's Garden Trail** is a 0.4-mile offshoot halfway up that leads to columnar basalt formations.

Steamboat Falls   HIKING
Turn up USFS Rd 38 at Steamboat to reach Steamboat Falls, where sea-run salmon and steelhead struggle to the top of the fast-moving falls from May to October. The best views are from the Steamboat Falls Campground, across the bridge.

Toketee Falls   HIKING
Twenty-one miles east of Steamboat is the stunning, two-tiered Toketee Falls, flowing over columnar basalt. To reach it turn off on USFS Rd 34; the hike there is just 0.4 miles. For a special treat, visit clothing-optional **Umpqua Hot Springs** (Northwest Forest Pass required, or pay $5 on-site); keep heading 2 miles up USFS Rd 34 past Toketee Falls, then turn right on Thorn Prairie Rd (USFS Rd 3401; possibly unsigned). After another 2 miles you'll reach the short trailhead.

Watson Falls   HIKING
Two miles past Toketee Junction on Hwy 138 is Watson Falls, which at 272ft is one of the highest waterfalls in Oregon. The 0.4-mile path begins at the picnic area on USFS Rd 37, but you can also see it from the parking lot.

🛏 Sleeping

There are several campgrounds on Hwy 138.

Dogwood Motel   MOTEL $
(☏541-496-3403; www.dogwoodmotel.com; 28866 N Umpqua Hwy; d $70-75; ❊ 🛜 🐾) At the well-maintained Dogwood, log cabins house six dark, rustic and tidy rooms, some with

kitchenettes. There's also a two-bedroom house that can sleep six. A pretty garden out back offers a wood gazebo and koi pond, along with a picnic area. Located 11 miles east of Glide.

Susan Creek CAMPGROUND $
(campsites $14) A lovely place with showers, 13 miles east of Glide.

Boulder Flat CAMPGROUND $
(campsites $10) A primitive spot with no water, 36 miles east of Glide with views of a spectacular lava formation down the river. Bring drinking water.

Umpqua's Last Resort CAMPGROUND, CABIN $$
(☑541-498-2500; www.golastresort.com; 115 Elk Ridge Lane, Idleyld Park; tent & RV sites $23-36, cabins $59-79) It's hardly fancy – the small cabins on a sunny, grassy hill just hold a bed (bring your own sleeping bag/linens) – but they're decent enough. The larger ones are much more comfortable, with sofa, refrigerator and TV. All cabins share outside bathrooms. Located about 8.5 miles east of Steamboat.

★ **Steamboat Inn** INN $$$
(☑800-840-8825; www.thesteamboatinn.com; 42705 N Umpqua Hwy; d $185-300; ❋☎❀❀) The Steamboat offers lovely wood-paneled suites and cabins next to the river, along with larger modern cottages and houses nearby. All have comfortable amenities, and some come with a fireplace, kitchenette and soaking tubs. Its renowned restaurant is open to nonguests (prix-fixe dinner $50 to $90; reserve ahead). Located 38 miles east of Roseburg.

Diamond Lake

This beautiful, deep-blue lake attracts motor-boat and RV enthusiasts in summer, with activity centered on a bustling full-service resort. There are fishing, boating and swimming possibilities, along with a 12-mile paved bike path around the lake. Winter brings cross-country skiers.

Rising to the east of Diamond Lake is pointy **Mt Thielsen**, a 9182ft basalt spire. A 5-mile trail (10 miles round-trip; Northwest Forest Pass required or pay $5 on-site) begins 1 mile north of the junction of Hwys 138 and 230 and stops 80ft short of the summit, which is attainable only with technical climbing skills.

Diamond Lake Campground (☑541-793-3310; www.diamondlake.net/summer.html; USFS Rd 4795; campsites $16-22) has 238 sites and offers plenty of camping amenities at the north end of the lake. It's such a popular place that you should reserve in summer.

Diamond Lake Resort (☑800-733-7593, 541-793-3333; www.diamondlake.net; 350 Resort Dr; d from $99) offers motel-type rooms, studios, Jacuzzi suites and two-bedroom cabins with kitchens. Dining options include a cafe, a pizzeria and sports grill with outdoor patio. There's a small store, and boats, canoes, kayaks, bicycles, fishing gear and ski equipment are all available for rent.

Lemolo Lake

Ten miles north of Diamond Lake is Lemolo Lake, a much quieter, family-oriented resort with views across the reservoir to faraway Mt Thielsen.

The 1.7-mile hike to **Lemolo Falls** is worth the off-road drive. Turn off Hwy 138 onto USFS Rd 2610 (Lemolo Lake Rd) for 4.2 miles, then left onto USFS Rd 3401 (Thorn Prairie Rd) for half a mile. Then turn right onto USFS Rd 800 for 1.8 miles, and another right at USFS Rd 840 for 0.3 miles.

Poole Creek Campground (☑541-498-2531; USFS Rd 2610; tent sites $15) is a popular, woodsy, USFS-maintained ground – the best sites are right near the lake. There's also a boat ramp; bring mosquito repellant.

Lemolo Lake Resort (☑541-643-0750; www.lemololakeresort.com; 2610 Birds Point Rd; hookups $30, r $89-149, cabins $149-250) is a casual and funky place with a nondescript RV campsite, A-frame cabins, a boat ramp, a small store and a cafe-restaurant. Boat rentals are available, but you'll have to bring your own alcohol and TV. It's 5 miles off Hwy 138, up Lemolo/Birds Point Rd.

Crater Lake National Park

The gloriously blue waters of Crater Lake reflect surrounding mountain peaks like a giant dark-blue mirror, making for spectacular photographs and breathtaking panoramas. **Crater Lake** (☑541-594-2211; www.nps.gov/crla; admission for up to 7 days per vehicle $10) is Oregon's only national park and also the USA's deepest lake at 1943ft deep.

The park's popular south entrance is open year-round and provides access to Rim Village and Mazama Village, as well as the park

Crater Lake National Park

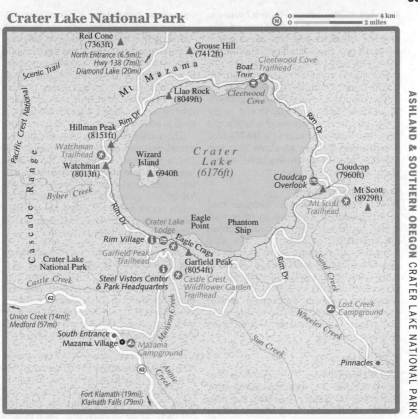

headquarters at the Steel Visitors Center. In winter you can only go up to the lake's rim and back down the same way; no other roads are plowed. The north entrance is only open from early June to late October, depending on snowfall.

It's best to top up your gas tank before arriving at Crater Lake. There's reasonably priced gas at Mazama Village (summertime only); the closest pumps otherwise are in Prospect, Diamond Lake and Fort Klamath.

Summer is often cold and windy, so dress warmly.

🏃 Activities

For more activities around Crater Lake, check out the good website www.thingstodonearcraterlake.com.

Rim Drive   SCENIC DRIVE
(☉ Jun–mid-Oct) You can hike and cross-country ski in the area, but most visitors just

cruise the 33-mile loop Rim Drive, which offers over 30 viewpoints as it winds around the edge of Crater Lake. A paved side road on the east side leads to amazing views from **Cloudcap Overlook**, almost 2000ft above the lake. Another nearby side road leads about 7 miles southeast to the **Pinnacles**, a valley of pumice and ash formations carved by erosion into 100ft spires called hoodoos. Without any stops, it takes an hour to do this drive (but you'll want to stop!).

Hiking

Crater Lake has over 90 miles of hiking trails, though some higher ones aren't completely clear of snow until late July. From the east edge of the Rim Village parking lot, a 1.7-mile trail leads up 8054ft **Garfield Peak** to an expansive view of the lake; in July the slopes are covered with wildflowers. A strenuous 5-mile round-trip hike takes you to an even better lake vista atop 8929ft **Mt Scott**, the highest point in the park. For a steep but shorter hike, trek up 0.7 miles to the **Watchman**, an old lookout tower on the opposite side of the lake that boasts one of the park's best views. For flower enthusiasts, there is an easy 1-mile nature trail near the Steel Visitors Center that winds through the **Castle Crest Wildflower Garden Trail**.

The popular and steep mile-long **Cleetwood Cove Trail**, at the north end of the crater, provides the only water access at the cove. Two-hour **boat tours** (☑888-774-2728; www.craterlakelodges.com; adult/child 3-11yr from $35/21; ☺ Jul–mid-Sep) are available; reserve ahead as these are popular.

Cross-Country Skiing

In winter, only the southern entrance road to Rim Village is kept plowed to provide access to several Nordic trails. Rentals are unavailable, so bring your own skis. Snowshoes are provided for free ranger-led **snowshoe walks**, which are held on weekends from Thanksgiving through March. Only experienced skiers should attempt the dangerous, avalanche-prone loop around Crater Lake, which takes two to three days and requires a backcountry permit from park headquarters.

☞ Tours

Crater Lake Trolley   SIGHTSEEING TOUR
(☑541-882-1896; www.craterlaketrolley.com; adult/child 5-13yr $25/15; ☺ Jul-Sep) Two-hour ranger-guided trolley tours that go all the way around the lake on Rim Dr, with occasional stops. They leave from Rim Village; call ahead to reserve.

🛏 Sleeping & Eating

Other than Crater Lake Lodge (the only lodging at the lake itself) and Mazama Village (7 miles from the rim), the nearest noncamping accommodations are 20 to 40 miles away. Park lodging is closed from mid-October to late May, depending on snowfall. Fort Klamath has several good lodgings. Union Creek and Prospect and the Diamond Lake area all have nice, sometimes woodsy places. The drive-through towns of Chemult and Chiloquin have budget motels that are much less scenic. Finally, if you don't mind driving all day, there's lots of accommodations in Medford, Roseburg or Klamath Falls.

The park's eating facilities are limited, though you can always bring a picnic and find a fabulously scenic spot. Rim Village has a small cafe and there's an upscale dining room nearby at the lodge. Mazama Village has a small store, gift shop and decently priced restaurant called **Annie Creek** (Mazama Village; mains lunch $9-11, dinner $13-18; ☺ breakfast, lunch & dinner Jun-Sep).

Mazama Campground   CAMPGROUND $
(☑888-774-2728; www.craterlakelodges.com; tent/RV sites from $21/29; 🛜🐾) Located 7 miles from the lake and open approximately mid-June through September (depending on weather), this is the park's main campground. There are over 200 wooded sites, showers and a laundry; some sites are first-come, first-served.

Lost Creek Campground   CAMPGROUND $
(☑541-594-3100; campsites $10) Open mid-July to mid-September, this nonreservable campground is 3 miles southeast of the lake and offers just 16 tent sites. Water is available, but there are no showers. Was closed in 2013 due to budget cuts, but this may change in the future.

Cabins at Mazama Village   CABIN $$
(☑541-830-8700; www.craterlakelodges.com; d $140) These 40 pleasant rooms (no TV or telephones) are open late May to mid-October, and located in attractive four-plex buildings. They're 7 miles from Crater Lake,

---

MT MAZAMA

The ancient mountain whose remains now form Crater Lake was Mt Mazama, a roughly 12,000ft volcanic peak that was heavily glaciered and inactive for many thousands of years until it came back to life 7700 years ago. A catastrophic explosion scattered ash for hundreds of miles as flows of superheated pumice solidified into massive banks. These eruptions emptied the magma chambers at the heart of the volcano, and the summit cone collapsed to form the caldera.

Only snowfall and rain contribute to the lake water. This purity and the lake's great depth give it that famous blue color. Sparse forests can be seen growing in pumice and ash in the Pumice Desert, just north of Crater Lake along N Entrance Rd.

with a small grocery store and gas pump nearby. Reserve as early as possible.

★**Crater Lake Lodge**   LODGE **$$$**
(☑888-774-2728; www.craterlakelodges.com; d $165-292; 🐾) Open from late May to mid-October, this grand old lodge has 71 simple but comfortable rooms (no TV or telephones), but it's the common areas that are most impressive. Large stone fireplaces, rustic leather sofas and a spectacular view of Crater Lake from the outside patio make this place special. There's a fine dining room too.

★**Crater Lake Lodge Dining Room**   NORTHWESTERN **$$$**
(☑541-594-2255; www.craterlakelodges.com; mains $24-39; ⏱7-10:30am, 11:30am-2:30pm & 5-10pm) Crater Lake's finest dining is at the lodge, where you can feast on Northwestern cuisine from a changing menu. Try for a table with a lake view (there are only a few). Longer hours mid-June through September; dinner reservations recommended.

🛏 Fort Klamath & Around

Fort Klamath is about 24 miles from Crater Lake.

Crater Lake Resort   CABIN **$**
(☑541-381-2349; www.craterlakeresort.com; 50711 Hwy 62; d $75-115; 🐾🛜🐾) This friendly, good-value place is just south of Fort Klamath and boasts 11 excellent, well-maintained cabins with kitchens and decks (some overlooking a creek). There are expansive lawns, and tent and RV sites are available ($20 to $30). Open May to October.

Sun Pass Ranch   B&B **$$**
(☑541-381-2882; www.sunpassranch.com; 52125 Hwy 62; r $125; 🐾🛜🐾) This friendly B&B is on 110 acres (it's a working cattle ranch) and offers five very comfortable, wood-paneled rooms, three with private bathroom. The home is beautiful and – unsurprisingly – has a bit of a Western motif. Nearby activities include fly-fishing, kayaking, biking and hiking.

Jo's Motel   MOTEL **$$**
(☑541-381-2234; www.josmotel.com; 52851 Hwy 62; tent/RV sites $20/30, d $95-150; 🐾🐾) Five well-kept and wood-paneled two-room suites with kitchens are available at this friendly motel. Bigger groups can go for the

stand-alone cabins with a loft that sleep six. There are sites for campers and RV fans too, along with a tiny organic grocery store and deli. Open February to October.

Crystalwood Lodge   B&B **$$**
(☑866-381-2322; www.crystalwoodlodge.com; 38625 Westside Rd; d $95-165; 🛜🐾) Possibly the most dog-friendly B&B in Oregon is run by a woman who's done the Iditarod, and her sled dogs live on premises. Seven no-nonsense rooms and a full kitchen available. The lodge is set on 130 acres, with dog-washing facilities, a fishing pond, hiking trails, birding and canoeing all possible. It's 15 miles south of Fort Klamath, and about 32 miles from Crater Lake.

ℹ️ Information

Rim Visitor Center (☑541-594-3090; ⏱9:30am-5pm May-Sep) At Rim Village itself.
Steel Visitors Center (☑541-594-3100; ⏱9am-5pm May-Oct, 10am-4pm Nov-Apr) Three miles south of Rim Village; provides good information.

Rogue River

The Rogue is a legendary white-water river that flows from its headwaters at Crater Lake to its terminus at Gold Beach, on the Pacific Ocean – 215 miles total. A good stretch of the river has been designated 'wild and scenic' (thus protected), and celebrities such as Zane Grey and Ginger Rogers have lived along its banks. The Rogue is prized for awesome steelhead and trout fishing, along with exceptional hiking, but it's also famous for world-class rafting.

For the serious adventurer, the Rogue offers everything from pulse-thumping class IV rapids near the Wild Rogue Wilderness to more gentle waters upriver. A convenient base is the busy city of Grants Pass (see p333). For those more into an afternoon float amid natural surroundings, there's the Shady Cove area.

Some of the many outfitters that run the Rogue include the following:

High Country Expeditions   RAFTING
(☑888-461-7238; www.hcexpeditions.com)

Orange Torpedo Trips   RAFTING
(☑541-476-5061; www.orangetorpedo.com)

Rogue Wilderness Adventures　　RAFTING
(☑800-336-1647; www.wildrogue.com; 325 Galice Rd, Merlin)

Sundance Kayak　　KAYAKING
(☑541-386-1725; www.sundancekayak.com)

Wild Rogue Wilderness

Famous for its turbulent class IV rapids, the Rogue River departs civilization at Grave Creek and winds for 40 untamed miles through a remote canyon preserved within rugged Bureau of Land Management (BLM) land and the Wild Rogue Wilderness. This stretch is not for amateurs – a typical rafting trip here takes three to four days, and hiring an outfitter is mandatory for all but the most experienced.

Contact the BLM's **Smullin Visitor Center** (☑541-479-3735; www.blm.gov/or/resources/recreation/rogue; 14335 Galice Rd, Galice; ◷7am-3pm) for information. The center also issues rafting permits, which are required to float the Rogue without an outfitter (for details go to www.blm.gov/or/resources/recreation/rogue/about-permits.php).

The **Rogue River Trail** is a highlight of the region, and is at the west end of the Rogue River. This 40-mile track, best hiked in spring or fall, follows the rapids from Grave Creek to Illahe. Once used to transport mail and supplies from Gold Beach, the route follows a relatively easy grade through scrub oak and laurel past historic homesteads and cabins.

The full hike takes four to five days, but rustic lodges along the way (see boxed text) can make your itinerary flexible.

A 7-mile round-trip hike to **Whiskey Creek Cabin** from Grave Creek makes a good day trip.

Shady Cove

Although the real action is far downriver most people find more peaceful adventures in the gentle waters north of scrappy Shady Cove, which has plenty of services. For general information visit the **McGregor Park Visitors Center** (☑541-878-3800; 100 Cole M Rivers Dr; ◷10am-5pm Memorial Day-Labor Day); it's near the Cole M Rivers Fish Hatchery.

For raft rental options, check out **Raft the Rogue** (☑800-797-7238; www.rafttherogue.com; 21171 Hwy 62).

About 12 miles north of Shady Cove is **McGregor Park**, a popular raft put-in and picnic spot. Up by the dam is the large **Cole M Rivers Fish Hatchery**, where you can feed the fish for $0.25.

Area campgrounds include the expansive, well-serviced **Joseph Stewart State Park** (☑800-452-5687, 541-560-3334; www.oregonstateparks.org; tent/RV sites $17/20) and the more rustic **Rogue Elk Campground** (☑541-774-8183; 27766 Hwy 62; campsites $20-24). For more comfort there's the decent **Royal Coachman Motel** (☑541-878-2481; www.royalcoachmanmotel.com; 21906 Hwy 62; d $59-79; ❄) and the much fancier **Edgewater Inn** (☑888-811-3171; www.edgewaterinns.com; 7800 Rogue River Dr; d from $110; ❄ ⚌ ⚌).

Prospect & Union Creek

Past Shady Cove, about 17 miles north, the valley walls close in, and the silvery river quickens and channels a gorge through thick lava flows. Dense forests robe the steep mountainsides, surrounding sparsely populated Prospect and Union Creek with uncrowded hiking trails, quiet camping and rustic lodging convenient to Crater Lake.

A mile south of Prospect on Mill Creek Dr is the 0.3-mile trail to **Mill Creek Falls** (173ft). A side shoot leads to the **Avenue of Giant Boulders**, where the Rogue River crashes through rocky boulders (scrambling required).

A good 4.6-mile hike (one way) starts from either the Woodruff Bridge picnic area or the River Bridge campground; you'll get views of the pretty **Takelma Gorge**. You can also hike 3.5 miles (one way) between **Natural Bridge**, where the Rogue River borrows a lava tube and goes underground for 200ft, and the magical **Rogue River Gorge**, where a narrow, turbulent section of river cuts a sheer-walled cleft into a lava flow.

Mill Creek, **River Bridge** and **Natural Bridge** campgrounds are primitive with no water (campsites $8 to $10; Natural Bridge is close to a lava tube). **Union Creek** (campsites $14) and **Farewell Bend** (campsites $18) campgrounds do have water; make reservations for these two through www.roguerec.com.

For detailed camping and much more hiking information, contact the **High Cascades Ranger Station** (☑541-560-3400; 47201 Hwy 62, Prospect; ◷8am-4:30pm Mon-Fri).

The grand old **Prospect Hotel** (☑800-944-6490; www.prospecthotel.com; 391 Mill Creek Dr; d $140-205; ❄ ⚌) has small, charming B&B rooms (along with modern motel rooms), a wraparound porch and a worthy dining

ⓘ ROGUE RIVER TRAIL LODGING

Lodging along the Rogue River Trail includes the accommodations listed below. Rates run from $110 to $160 per person and typically include breakfast, dinner and a packed lunch; reserve ahead. Riverside camping is also a possibility; contact the Smullin Visitor Center.

Black Bar (☑541-479-6507; www.black-barlodge.com; Merlin)

Clay Hill (☑503-859-3772; www.clayhill-lodge.com)

Half Moon Bar (☑888-291-8268; www.halfmoonbarlodge.com)

Marial Lodge (☑541-474-2057)

Paradise (☑888-667-6483; www.paradise-lodge.com)

room (open 5pm to 9pm summer only). The **Union Creek Resort** (☑866-560-3565; www.unioncreekoregon.com; 56484 Hwy 62; d $63-68, cabins from $105; ⊛) is an old 1930s lodge with nine wood-paneled rooms (shared bathrooms outside) and a couple dozen rustic cabins that sleep two to 13 people; there's a restaurant nearby.

There are also a few restaurants and other services in the town of Prospect.

Klamath Falls

POP 21,000

Sleepy is a good way to describe Klamath Falls. It has a lot of growth potential, boasting over 300 days of sunshine, affordable real estate, spectacular countryside and great recreational opportunities. But for now, it's still a small town with friendly people and an attractive downtown.

K-Falls (as locals call it) is set on the shores of Lake Ewana, though the water is not visible from most of town. There are some key things to see, including the nearby Klamath Basin National Wildlife Refuges (p345), which boasts a huge population of wintering bald eagles – along with over 350 other species of birds. Check out the surrounding high desert mountain terrain – amazing Crater Lake National Park (p338) is only 60 miles north, and there are lots of area lakes and fishing streams to explore.

And for those into outdoor sports, you can boat, raft, fish and bike – plenty to keep you active and busy.

⊙ Sights & Activities

Downtown has quite a few old but noteworthy buildings – take a walk and discover them (the visitor center has a pamphlet). In winter there's **snowshoeing** and **cross-country skiing** west on Hwy 140 at Lake of the Woods and north at Crater Lake.

Klamath County Museum   MUSEUM
(☑541-883-4208; www.co.klamath.or.us/museum; 1451 Main St; adult/child 13-17yr $5/4; ⊙9am-5pm Tue-Sat) Learn about the area's history at this slightly quirky museum in the old armory. Along with natural-history dioramas and fine Native American basketry, look for the pelican figurine collection. The museum also maintains historic artifacts housed in the 1905 **Baldwin Hotel** (☑541-883-4207; 31 Main St; admission with tour $5; ⊙10am-4pm Tue-Sat Jun-Aug).

Favell Museum of Western Art & Indian Artifacts   MUSEUM
(☑541-882-9996; www.favellmuseum.org; 125 W Main St; adult/child 6-16yr $10/5; ⊙10am-5pm Tue-Sat) Good upscale museum (for K-Falls) with Native American tools, basketry and bead work – check out the over 60,000 arrowheads on display, including one made of opal. Miniature guns and local artwork gallery as well.

Hutch's   CYCLING
(☑541-850-2453; www.hutchsbicycles.com; 808 Klamath Ave; ⊙9am-6pm Mon-Sat, 11am-5pm Sun) Rents bikes and offers free bike rides in summer. Ask about the **OC&E Woods Line State Trail**, which follows a historical rail bed for 100 miles.

Adventure Center   RAFTING
(☑541-488-2819; www.raftingtours.com) Ashland-based; offers rafting trips on the Upper Klamath River.

⊨ Sleeping & Eating

Quality Inn   HOTEL $
(☑541-882-4666; www.choicehotels.com/hotel/or413; 100 Main St; d $70-90; ⊛⊛⊛⊛) There are fine, modern and spacious rooms at the Quality Inn that are a couple of steps up from basic budget motels. Amenities include a fitness center, Jacuzzi and small outdoor pool. Hot breakfast included and nice, central location at the southern entrance into town.

BALD EAGLE WATCHING

Every November, hundreds of bald eagles travel from Canada and Alaska to winter in the Klamath Basin, feeding on the area's rich waterfowl populations. December through February are prime viewing months, when you can spot dozens of these national symbols along the Lower Klamath Refuge and Tule Lake. To catch them flying out from their night roosts at first light, head to Bear Valley Refuge, an old-growth hillside off Hwy 97 (turn west onto the Keno–Worden road just south of Worden, and after the railroad crossing go left onto a dirt road for half a mile; park on the shoulder).

In spring and summer you can also watch nesting bald eagles along the west side of Upper Klamath Lake and at Klamath Marsh National Wildlife Refuge. For more on bird life in the area, see www.klamathbirdingtrails.com.

Maverick Motel MOTEL $
(☎ 541-882-6688; www.maverickmotel.com; 1220 Main St; d weekday $45-55, weekends $55-65; ✻ @ ☎ ☜ ☒) Your typical budget motel. Get a room with two beds on the 2nd floor, overlooking the back street – these tend to be bigger, brighter and quieter than the ones in the front, and have peeks at faraway mountains. Located right next to the Creamery.

Klamath Falls KOA CAMPGROUND $
(☎ 541-884-4644; www.koa.com/where/or/37107; 3435 Shasta Way; tent sites $25, RV sites $34-37, cabins $54; ☎ ☒) This decent KOA is 3 miles southeast of the center. It has a small outdoor pool and playground. Prices are cheaper during the week.

Running Y Ranch RESORT $$
(☎ 877-656-7784; www.runningy.com; 5500 Running Y Rd; d from $129; ✻ ☎ ☒ ☒) This upscale resort is about 6 miles from downtown K-Falls. It's mostly dotted with private vacation homes, but the lodge offers 88 lovely and contemporary rooms ($10 extra for views). There are tennis courts, a swimming pool and gym with sauna and Jacuzzi. The restaurant has a great patio overlooking the golf course.

Lake of the Woods Resort RESORT $$
(☎ 866-201-4194; www.lakeofthewoodsresort.com; 950 Harriman Rte; RV sites $35-45, cabins $159-325; ☒ ☒) Located 32 miles west of Klamath Falls is this pleasant, rustic, family resort with around 30 cabins. The marina rents boats; you can also rent mountain bikes in summer and snowshoes in winter. There's a restaurant, lounge and small store on the premises. Two-night minimum; discount on weekdays.

Leap of Taste CAFE $
(☎ 541-850-9141; www.aleapoftaste.com; 907 Main St; mains $7-8; ⊙ 7:30am-6:30pm Mon-Fri, 9am-4pm Sat) ✔ Popular and trendy eatery serving up cold or hot gourmet sandwiches (half or whole), along with a few soups, salads and pizza by the slice. Nice atmosphere, with sofas and wood tables. Organic coffee as well.

Tobiko JAPANESE $$
(☎ 541-884-7874; 618 Main St; sushi $4-12, small plates $8-12; ⊙ noon-2pm & 5-9pm Mon-Thu, till 10pm Fri, 5-10pm Sat, 5-9pm Sun) With a look that belongs more in a big city than small K-Falls, upscale and stylish Tobiko serves up creative sushi rolls – along with tempura vegetables, seared ahi tuna and sake-steamed clams. Asian-influenced cocktails available.

Creamery AMERICAN $$
(☎ 541-273-5222; www.kbbrewing.com/brewpub; 1320 Main St; mains $11-12; ⊙ 11am-9:30pm) One of the hippest places in town, the Creamery is a large brewpub-restaurant with all the usual favorites like burgers, pastas, salads and sandwiches. Microbrews include its decent Butt Crack Brown. There's a great patio for sunny days.

❶ Information

Discover Klamath Visitor Center (☎ 541-882-1501; www.discoverklamath.com; 205 Riverside Dr; ⊙ 9am-6pm Mon-Fri, 10am-2pm Sat) Area information.

Klamath Falls Ranger District (☎ 541-883-6714; www.fs.fed.us/r6/frewin; 2819 Dahlia St; ⊙ 8am-4:30pm Mon-Fri)

❶ Getting There & Away

Klamath Falls airport (☎541-883-5372; www.
flykfalls.com; 6775 Arnold Ave) 5 miles southeast of town.

BTS (☎541-883-2877; www.basintransit.com;
1130 Adams St) Provides regional bus services
to surrounding cities from Monday to Saturday.

Amtrak (☎541-884-2822; www.amtrak.com;
1600 Oak Ave) is at Spring St and Oak Ave.

Klamath Basin National Wildlife Refuges

The Klamath Basin is a broad, marshy
floodplain extending from the southern
base of Crater Lake into the northernmost
part of California. The surrounding region
offers some of the finest bird-watching in
the West: six wildlife refuges, totaling more
than 300 sq miles, support concentrations of
more than a million birds.

In the **Upper Klamath National Wildlife
Refuge**, tule rushes fill the northwestern
shore of shallow, marshy Upper Klamath
Lake. Here there's shelter for colonies of
cormorants, egrets, herons, cranes, pelicans and many varieties of ducks and geese.

A 9.5-mile canoe trail starts at Rocky Point
Resort, 24 miles northwest of Klamath Falls
off Hwy 140.

West of Worden, down near the state border, **Bear Valley Refuge** is known mostly
as a wintering area for bald eagles; 500 to
1000 birds gather here between December
and March.

The **Lower Klamath National Wildlife
Refuge** lies mostly in California. This mix
of open water, shallow marsh, cropland and
grassy upland offers the best year-round
viewing and great access for motorists: a
10-mile auto tour begins off Hwy 161 (State
Line Rd). Get information beforehand
in Klamath Falls or at the **Refuge Headquarters** (☎530-667-2231; www.fws.gov/
klamathbasinrefuges; 4009 Hill Rd) in Tulelake,
California.

If you're in the area on President's Day
weekend in mid-February, check out the four-
day **Winter Wings Festival** (www.winterwings-
fest.org), which draws together bird-lovers of
all kinds for lectures, workshops, field trips
and wildlife art at the Oregon Institute of
Technology in Klamath Falls.

Eastern Oregon

Includes ➡

Best Places to Eat

➡ Coco's Grill (p355)

➡ Vali's Alpine Restaurant (p356)

➡ Terminal Gravity Brewing (p353)

➡ Snaffle Bit (p362)

Best Places to Stay

➡ Enterprise House B&B (p353)

➡ Bronze Antler B&B (p354)

➡ Pine Valley Lodge (p358)

➡ Hotel Prairie (p361)

Why Go?

Eastern Oregon is sure to amaze. Among its extensive farmlands and desert plateaus are stunning attractions: the gorgeous snowy peaks of the Wallowa Mountains; Hells Canyon, which dips deeper than the Grand Canyon; the John Day Fossil Beds, with their eerily colorful hills and rock formations; and the incredible glacier-carved valleys of the Steens Mountain range.

This slice of Oregon was the last arduous passage the pioneers traversed on their journey west; in some places you can see where their wagon ruts carved out the Oregon Trail. Gold was discovered in the region in the 1860s – making and breaking dozens of towns and cities – and there's also rich Native American history in towns like Joseph.

With a rodeo in every town and the Old West still palpable in spots, visiting eastern Oregon is like a trip back in time – but forget the covered wagons and bring the digital camera instead.

When to Go
Pendleton

Jul–Oct Drive the stunning Steens Mountain Loop or hike in high Wallowas.

Spring or Fall Avoid the high-summer heat, and yell 'giddyup' at Pendleton's Round-Up.

Nov–Mar Colder weather makes hot springs more decadent, and there are ski resorts too.

Pendleton

POP 17,000

Eastern Oregon's largest city, 'wild and woolly' Pendleton is a handsome old town famous for its wool shirts and big-name rodeo. It has managed to retain a glint of its old-time atmosphere and cow-poking past, and nestles between steep hills along the Umatilla River.

All around are farms and ranchlands, though in the last few years a microbrewery has popped up as a sign of the times, along with a million-dollar steakhouse complex. With its art galleries, antique shops, fancy Western-wares stores and budding music scene, Pendleton has become one of eastern Oregon's most popular destinations.

◉ Sights

The paved River Walk, atop a levee, follows the Umatilla for 2.8 miles and is a great place for a stroll; keep an eye out for herons and other water birds.

**Umatilla County
Historical Museum**   MUSEUM

(☎541-276-0012; www.heritagestationmuseum.org; 108 SW Frazer Ave; adult/family $5/10; ☺10am-4pm Tue-Sat) The worthwhile Umatilla County Historical Museum is in Pendleton's old railroad station. There are pioneer exhibits and Native American artifacts; check out the caboose and one-room schoolhouse.

Tamástslikt Cultural Institute   MUSEUM

(☎541-996-9748; www.tamastslikt.org; 47106 Wild Horse Blvd; adult/child $8/6; ☺9am-5pm, closed Sun Oct-Mar) Witness Oregon's past from a Native American perspective at the spacious Tamástslikt Cultural Institute, east of Pendleton off I-84 exit 216. State-of-the-art ex-

hibits weave voices, memories and artifacts through an evolving history of the region. There's a cafe on the premises.

Round-Up Hall of Fame   MUSEUM

(☎541-278-0815; 1114 SW Court Ave; adult/child 10yr & under $5/2; ☺10am-4pm Mon-Sat) If you miss the Pendleton Round-Up, visit the Round-Up Hall of Fame. Here you can see the excitement of past round-ups via photographs, saddles won in competitions and other memorabilia.

☞ Tours

**Pendleton
Underground Tours**   SIGHTSEEING TOUR

(☎800-226-6398, 541-276-0730; www.pendletonundergroundtours.org; 37 SW Emigrant Ave; tours per person $15; ☺closed Tue & Sun) At the end of the 19th century, a shady network of businesses boomed beneath Pendleton's storefronts, driven underground by Prohibition and social tensions. Saloons, Chinese laundries, opium dens, card rooms and other questionable businesses found cozy tunnels in which to operate. Pendleton Underground Tours lets you explore the town's infamous underground past, as well as an above-ground early-1900s brothel. Tours last 1½ hours; reservations required. Children under six are not allowed.

Pendleton Woolen Mills   MILL TOUR

(☎541-276-6911; www.pendleton-usa.com; 1307 SE Court Pl; ☺8am-6pm Mon-Sat, 9am-5pm Sun) World-famous Pendleton Woolen Mills has been weaving blankets for more than one hundred years, and is especially known for Native American designs. Free, short factory tours are given at 9am, 11am, 1:30pm and 3pm Monday to Friday year-round.

🛏 Sleeping

There are several chain motels and hotels off I-84 and on Dorion Ave.

Rugged Country Lodge   MOTEL $

(☎541-966-6800, 877-778-4433; www.ruggedcountrylodge.com; 1807 SE Court Ave; d $60-65; ❊🖀❊) On the eastern edge of town is this out-of-the-ordinary, great-deal motel featuring stylish rooms with personal touches such as down pillows, quality linens and Pendleton blankets. Most rooms line inside hallways, making them quiet and giving them a homelike quality. A good breakfast and homemade cookies are included.

ROUND UP FOR THE RODEO

The rowdy **Pendleton Round-Up** (☎800-457-6336; www.pendletonroundup.com; 1205 SW Court Ave), called 'the USA's best rodeo,' is an all-out Dionysian celebration featuring cowboy breakfasts, dances, bull riding and an Indian Pageant. There's also a big-name music concert. Reserve tickets and lodging way in advance. It's held the second full week in September.

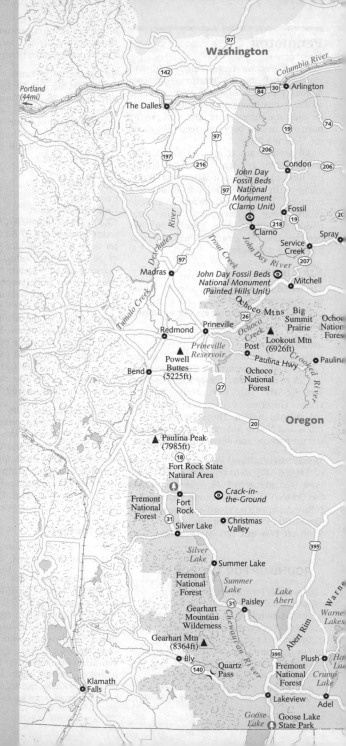

Eastern Oregon Highlights

1 Whooping it up at the **Pendleton Round-Up** (p347), an awesome rodeo.

2 Finding scenic heaven at **Hells Canyon** (p357), North America's deepest river gorge.

3 Trekking in the **Eagle Cap Wilderness** (p356), with or without a llama to help.

4 Oohing and aahing at the fantastic colors and rock formations of **John Day Fossil Beds** (p362).

5 Being amazed by the glacier-scoured valleys in the majestic **Steens Mountain** (p367) region.

6 Cruising the amazing rock formations at **Succor Creek** and **Leslie Gulch** (p365).

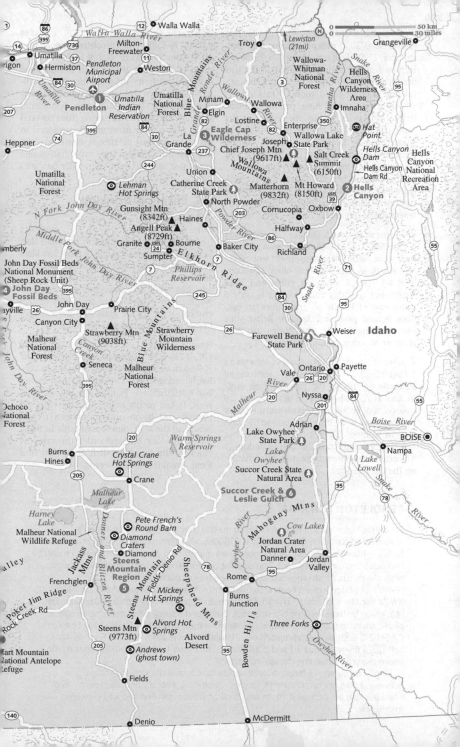

Working Girls Old Hotel
HOTEL $

(☎541-276-0730; www.pendletonunderground-tours.org; 17 SW Emigrant Ave; d $75-95; ❉🖵) Run by Pendleton Underground Tours, this one-time bordello offers five large, beautiful and antique-filled rooms. Only one is en suite; two rooms have private hallway baths (only three rooms are rented at the same time, unless everyone's willing to share baths). There's a kitchen, dining room and parlor for all guests to share, and the downtown location is convenient.

This place is best for those who are self-sufficient and don't need much service (there's no reception). Children over 16 only; reservations required.

Wild Horse Resort & Casino
CAMPGROUND $

(☎541-278-2274, 800-654-9453; www.wildhorseresort.com; 46510 Wildhorse Blvd; tent sites/tipis $15/19, RV sites $29-34; ⏲office 7am-10pm; 🖵❉🖵) There's plenty of grass and little shade, but this tidy campground is only 5 miles east of Pendleton and offers an outdoor heated pool and Jacuzzi. Bring your own bedding for the tipis. Rates are 30% cheaper Monday through Thursday.

Emigrant Springs State Park
CAMPGROUND $

(☎541-983-2277, 800-551-6949; www.oregonstateparks.org; 65068 Old Emigrant Trail; tent/RV sites $17/20, cabins $24-39; ❉) Located 26 miles east of Pendleton, this pleasant woodsy campground is at an elevation, so it stays cool in summer. There's freeway noise, but quieter cabins are available (bring bedding). The park has some interpretive information on the Oregon Trail.

Pendleton House B&B
B&B $$

(☎541-276-8581; www.pendletonhousebnb.com; 311 N Main St; d $135; ❉🖵🖵) Near downtown is this pink 1917 Italian Renaissance mansion with its original furniture, wallpaper and even drapes. The home's details are amazing (especially the communal shower), and there's a relaxing front covered patio with wicker furniture. Be prepared to get to know your neighbors, however – the five beautiful rooms (two with half-baths) share just one full bath. A friendly dog lives here.

✕ Eating & Drinking

Great Pacific Wine & Coffee Co
AMERICAN $

(☎541-276-1350; www.greatpacific.biz; 403 S Main St; drinks $1.50-4, mains $6-9; ⏲10am-9pm Mon-Sat) This trendy-for-Pendleton coffee shop serves up hot and cold sandwiches, salads, baked stuffed croissants and gourmet Naples-style pizzas. There are plenty of java choices, wine by the glass and even microbrews on tap. Occasional live music.

Rainbow Cafe
AMERICAN $$

(☎541-276-4120; www.rainbowcafependleton.com; 209 South Main St; mains $9-12; ⏲6am-2am Mon-Sat, till midnight Sun) This historic and casual bar-restaurant is Pendleton's oldest business. It has plenty of personality, with old photos and bison and pronghorn trophy heads on the wall, plus a pool table in back. Sit at the long bar and order the rainbow chicken, the signature dish, then chat to a local. Breakfast is also served.

PENDLETON FOR KIDS

Pendleton has a few fun spots for kids to release their energy. The **Children's Museum of Eastern Oregon** (☎541-276-1066; www.cmeo.org; 400 S Main St; admission $3.50; ⏲10am-5pm Mon-Sat; 🖵) is more like a mini-theme park, with tiny replica market, firehouse and pizza restaurant. The science, art and 'shadow' offer educational angles, while the musical instruments and costumes are just plain fun.

If it's a hot day, make a beeline to the **Family Aquatic Center** (☎541-276-0104; 1901 NW Carden Ave; adult/child 3-1/yr $6/4; ⏲noon-8pm approximately Memorial Day-Labor Day; 🖵), which features an Olympic-size pool, diving and wading pools, curly water slides, picnic areas and concession stands. Meanwhile the **Pendleton Center for the Arts** (☎541-278-9201; www.pendletonarts.org; 214 North Main; ⏲10am-4pm Tue-Fri, noon-4pm Sat) FREE offers various art and craft classes, and their teen program includes music, film-making and costume-design workshops.

Finally, if you need a family-friendly place to eat, take the kids to Prodigal Son Brewery. There are two children's spaces – including a library and play room – and while the kids are occupied, mom and dad can have a relaxing and well-deserved microbrew.

Hamley's Steakhouse AMERICAN $$

(☑541-278-1100; www.thehamleysteakhouse.com; 8 SE Court Ave; mains $10-33; ⊙5-9pm Sun-Thu, till 10pm Fri & Sat) This 150-seat steakhouse has been gorgeously done up with wood floors, stone accents and tin ceilings. There's a bar with sports on TV and the restrooms have 'interesting' art work. Food is decent, with large portions. Hamley's empire also includes a first-rate Western store, saddle-making workshop, cafe and wine cellar.

Prodigal Son Brewery PUB

(☑541-276-6090; www.prodigalsonbrewery.com; 230 SE Court Ave; mains $8-14; ⊙11am-10pm Tue-Thu, till 11pm Fri & Sat, noon-9pm Sun; ⊕) Pendleton's award-winning brewery is a popular place, even with families (there are two kids' rooms). It has a great atmosphere and serves up eight beers on tap, plus a typical pub menu that includes eight burgers, various salads and some surprises like Scotch egg and onion tarts.

ⓘ Information

Pendleton Chamber of Commerce (☑800-547-8911, 541-276-7411; www.pendleton-chamber.com; 501 S Main St; ⊙8:30am-5pm Mon-Fri)

ⓘ Getting There & Away

Pendleton Municipal Airport is 5 miles west of town on US 30. Greyhound runs east- and westbound buses (both twice daily) from the **Double J Drive Thru** (☑541-276-1551; 801 SE Court Ave; ⊙office 11am-noon & 4-5pm Mon-Sat).

La Grande

POP 13,000

Early French traders, upon seeing this broad, seemingly circular valley, declared it to be La Grande Ronde (Big Circle). Indeed, from the historical marker on US 30 above town, it does seem as if the mountain peaks form a giant ring around the valley.

The Oregon Trail crossed this valley, and the pioneers rested here in preparation for traversing the challenging Blue Mountains. Some saw the valley's agricultural potential and its pretty Grande Ronde River, and decided to settle down instead. Today La Grande is home to Eastern Oregon University and provides services to the region; it also offers a surprising wealth of outdoor recreation, though the city itself isn't all that memorable.

◉ Sights

Oregon Trail Interpretive Park PARK

(☑541-963-7186; I-84, exit 248; day-use fee $5; ⊙9am-7pm Tue-Sun Memorial Day-Labor Day) This park gives a visceral feeling of what travel was like for Oregon Trail pioneers crossing the Blue Mountains. A half-mile paved interpretive path winds through the forest to ruts left by pioneer wagons – still visible after 150 years. The center is 13 miles west of La Grande and 3 miles on well-marked roads from the freeway exit.

Union County Museum MUSEUM

(☑541-562-6003; 333 South Main St; admission $5; ⊙10am-4pm Mon-Sat) Located in Union, about 15 miles southeast of La Grande, is this interesting museum. The histories of Union, Wallowa and other counties are chronicled here; interesting relics include an old bank vault, a vintage Barbie doll collection, and antique kitchen and bath re-creations (check out the huge copper bathtub). There's also a 'Cowboy' room. Out back is a pioneer cabin and blacksmith shop.

⁂ Activities

Catherine Creek State Park HIKING

(☑800-551-6949; Hwy 203) There's good hiking and camping at this park, about 23 miles southeast of La Grande. You can access the Eagle Cap Wilderness from a trail here, and there are mountaintop views from another hike nearby.

Spout Springs Ski Resort SKIING

(☑541-566-0320; www.spoutspringsskiresort.com; 79327 Hwy 204; lift tickets adult/child 12-17yr $35/30) A small, low-key ski resort about 20 miles east of La Grande with night skiing, plus several miles of groomed cross-country ski trails. Good for beginners and families. For another nearby ski area, see Anthony Lakes (p359).

Fishing FISHING

There are several scenic rivers, lakes and reservoirs in the area for hooking rainbow trout, steelhead and bass. The Grande Ronde River, Morgan Lake, Catherine Creek and Thief Valley Reservoir are a few places to try your luck. Contact the **Fish & Wildlife Office** (☑541-963-2138; 107 20th St; ⊙8am-5pm Mon-Fri) in La Grande for current regulations and information.

🛏 Sleeping

La Grande has a lack of interesting lodging in town, but there are a couple of places within a dozen miles that are atmospheric.

Union Hotel
HOTEL $

(☑541-562-1200; www.thehistoricunionhotel.com; 326 N Main St; d $65-119, tent sites $11-16, RV sites $26-37, tipis $16-22; ❋🌐🐾) Fifteen miles southeast of La Grande, in the town of Union, is this very atmospheric old hotel. All 16 rooms are decorated individually, and none has a TV or telephone, though three come with kitchenette (there are common rooms with a TV and library). Friendly sheep dog on premises.

Royal Motor Inn
MOTEL $

(☑541-963-4154; www.royalmotorinn.net; 1510 Adams Ave; d $59; ❋🌐🐾) Decent, central motel with good budget rooms, some with newer pillowtop mattresses.

Catherine Creek State Park
CAMPGROUND $

(☑800-551-6949; Hwy 203; campsites $9; 🐾) Some 23 miles southeast of La Grande, past Union, this beautiful state-park campground has a clear fishing creek, though campsites are primitive.

Hilgard Junction State Park
CAMPGROUND $

(☑800-551-6949; I-84 exit 252; campsites $9; 🐾) Only 8 miles west of La Grande, this lovely riverside park is convenient but gets highway noise. Campsites are primitive; boat launch available.

Hot Lake Springs
HOTEL $$

(☑541-963-4685; www.hotlakesprings.com; 66172 Hwy 203; d from $144; ❋🌐) Eight miles southeast of La Grande is this grand, restored hotel in a historic building that was once a hospital. There's also a spa, restaurant, museum, art gallery, bronze foundry (tours available) and several hot-spring pools. Each of the 22 big, beautiful suites has its own theme, and breakfast is included – along with a movie in the hotel's theater. The hotel is closed from mid-December to February.

🍴 Eating

Nells-N-Out
AMERICAN $

(☑541-963-5733; 1704 Adams Ave; mains $3-8; ◷11am-10pm) Long-running drive-thru burger joint likely offering eastern Oregon's best fast food. Choose from 16 burgers, plus hot dogs, sandwiches, wraps, salads and sides like battered green beans and jalapeño poppers. The milkshakes are legendary. A few shady picnic tables available.

Ten Depot Street
AMERICAN $$

(☑541-963-8766; www.tendepotstreet.com; 10 Depot St; mains $11-25; ◷5-10pm Mon-Sat) This longtime local favorite offers some classics – such as prime rib and seafood fettuccine – along with a few surprises like the Thai salad and lentil-pecan vegan burger. Classy atmosphere, with a good selection of microbrews available.

Mt Emily Ale House
PUB $$

(☑541-962-7711; www.mtemilyalehouse.com; 1202 Adams Ave; mains $8-15; ◷4:30-10pm Mon-Thu, 11:30am-10pm Fri & Sat) Attractive brewery-restaurant serving a decent variety of burgers, salads, gourmet pizzas, rice bowls and – of course – craft ales. Beer samplers (six 3oz tastes) are available if you can't decide.

ℹ Information

Chamber of Commerce (☑800-848-9969, 541-963-8588; www.visitlagrande.com; 207 Depot St; ◷9am-5pm Mon-Fri)

ℹ Getting There & Around

Greyhound (☑541-963-5165; 2204 East Penn Ave; ◷office 8:30-11am & 4-6:30pm Mon-Fri) Buses leave twice daily in both east- and westbound directions.

NEO Transit (☑541-426-3840; www.sites.google.com/a/neotransit.org/index) Daily bus services to Baker City, from Monday to Friday; leaves from several stops around town. Links with Enterprise and Joseph twice a week. Also provides in-town bus services.

Enterprise

POP 2000

Enterprise is a small, friendly place that's less expensive and upscale than its nearby sister town of Joseph, just 6 miles away. However, it shares with Joseph an attraction for artists, as well as an exceptional location surrounded by grassy meadows, pine forests and the stunning Wallowa Mountains. Some of Enterprise's original buildings are still intact and there's a good selection of traveler's services, making it an ideal base for exploring northeastern Oregon – such as Hells Canyon and, of course, the Wallowas.

🎊 Festivals & Events

Hells Canyon Mule Days   FIESTA
(www.hellscanyonmuledays.com; ⊘Sep) On the weekend after Labor Day, Enterprise is host to Hells Canyon Mule Days, a three-day event featuring a parade, quilt show, cowboy poetry and barrel racing.

🛏 Sleeping

Note that during certain events (especially Chief Joseph Days, held the last full weekend in July in Joseph) accommodations become scarce and prices skyrocket.

Ponderosa Motel   MOTEL $
(☑541-426-3186; 102 E Greenwood St; d $70-80; ✱🐾🖥) Right in downtown is this well-run motel with attractive wood-and-stone facade. The excellent rooms are clean and comfortable, with lodgelike furniture.

Wilderness Inn   MOTEL $
(☑541-426-4535; www.wildernessinn.hotels.office live.com; 301 W North St; d $70-80; ✱🐾🖥) A good budget choice, this basic motel has spacious rooms with flat-screen TVs. Rooms in back have two beds and offer more peace as well as mountain views (from higher floors). Sauna available.

ALL ABOARD!

Railroad buffs and scenery-lovers shouldn't miss the **Eagle Cap Excursion Train** (☑800-323-7330; www. eaglecaptrainrides.com), a slow-moving, nostalgic train ride that follows the Grande Rhone and Wallowa Rivers through rugged canyons and pleasant scenery. If you're lucky, you'll spot a Rocky Mountain elk or black bear, but you're much more likely to see bald eagles. And cows, of course – sometimes traipsing right on the tracks!

Connecting Elgin with Joseph, the train runs for 38 miles (round-trip), mostly on Saturday from June to October. The 3½-hour trip costs $75 for adults, less for seniors and kids. And every once in a while, the train gets 'robbed' – with play money handed over – or a historian or wildlife biologist makes a special appearance. But even if you just experience the train ride by itself, it's sure to be memorable.

★ Enterprise House B&B   B&B $$
(☑541-426-4238; www.enterprisehousebnb. com; 508 S 1st St; d $121-189; ✱🐾) Enterprise's most majestic place to stay is this 1910 colonial revival mansion with wraparound porch and fancy wine cellar. The five antique-filled rooms are all lovely, and the common areas elegant. At research time this place was for sale, but likely will remain a B&B.

Barking Mad Farm   B&B $$
(☑541-215-2758; www.barkingmadfarm.com; 65156 Powers Rd; d $135-195; ✱🐾🖥) This countryside B&B – on 42 acres – has just three large, comfortable rooms, two with great mountain views and one with private deck. There's a wonderful front porch, plus relaxing backyard with great Wallowa views. Dog and cat on premises. Located a mile down Fish Hatchery Rd (from which Powers Rd spurs straight off), just before entering Enterprise from the west.

🍴 Eating

El Bajio   MEXICAN $
(☑541-426-3322; 100 W North St; mains $7-13; ⊘11am-10pm) Some say El Bajio serves the tastiest and best-value Mexican food in town. Don't be put off by the building's facade; it's nicer inside, and friendly.

Red Rooster Cafe   AMERICAN $
(☑541-426-2233; 309 W Main St; mains $8-11; ⊘7am-2pm Wed-Sat, 8am-2pm Sun) There's a definite chicken theme at this casual diner, where breakfast means cage-free egg Benedicts and scrambles, plus pancakes and French toast. Sandwiches, soups and salads for lunch, and homemade pie for dessert.

★ Terminal Gravity Brewing   PUB $$
(☑541-426-3000; www.terminalgravitybrewing. com; 803 SE School St; mains $9-12; ⊘11am-9pm Sun-Tue, till 10pm Wed-Sat) One of Oregon's best breweries. There's limited inside seating, but on a warm day you'll want to be at a picnic table outside with a tasty IPA and buffalo burger anyway. Sandwiches and salads dominate the menu, with a few specials like beer mac 'n' cheese.

ℹ Information

Chamber of Commerce (☑800-585-4121, 541-426-4622; www.wallowacountychamber. com; 309 South River St; ⊘8am-5pm Mon-Sat)

ⓘ Getting There & Away

NEO Transit (☎541-426-3840; www.sites.
google.com/a/neotransit.org/index) Monday to Saturday services from Enterprise
to Joseph and Wallowa Lake (June to September). Year-round buses twice weekly link
Joseph, Enterprise and La Grande.

Joseph

POP 1100

If ever there was a trendy eastern Oregon
town, it's Joseph. You can see its wealth right
on the brick sidewalks, where well-groomed
planter boxes and huge bronze statues sit
proudly on downtown street corners. Many
of the old storefronts are now glitzy boutiques, peddling everything from inexpensive souvenirs to huge, expensive bronzes.
There seem to be more galleries than anything else, and Valley Bronze – one of the nation's largest foundries – anchors the artistic
heart of this old frontier town.

Even while Joseph feels more like Santa
Fe than your typical backcountry Western
town, it has just enough boots-and-jeans
street life to keep it from seeming completely fake. And simply heading a few blocks out
of downtown brings you back into beautiful
countryside – just a mile south is Wallowa
Lake, a glacial basin flanked by gorgeous
towering peaks. Joseph is also a good base
for exploring the region's many other recreational highlights; there's even a tiny ski
resort, Ferguson Ridge, about 8 miles away.

Public transportation services are the
same as those for Enterprise.

◉ Sights & Activities

The Wallowa-Whitman National Forest and
the Hells Canyon National Recreation Area
are laced with mountain-biking trails, including the pretty, 10-mile Wagon Loop Rd;
the Redmont Trail Network has great singletrack. When snow falls, the area is good for
cross-country skiing.

Valley Bronze   FOUNDRY
(☎541-432-7445; www.valleybronze.com; 18 S Main
St) Joseph is most noted for its cast-bronze
sculpture, thanks in part to Valley Bronze.
Foundry tours are $15 per person and by
reservation only.

Wallowa County Museum   MUSEUM
(☎541-432-6095; 110 S Main St; adult/child 7-18yr
$4/2; ◉10am-4pm Memorial Day-late Sep) The
Wallowa County Museum, housed in an 1888

bank building, is notable for its displays on
local pioneer and Nez Percé histories; check
out the 'ladies jail' out the back.

✪ Festivals & Events

Chief Joseph Days   CULTURE
(☎541-432-1015; www.chiefjosephdays.com; ◉late
Jul) Chief Joseph Days, held over four days in
late July, features a rodeo, Native American
dancing and cowboy breakfasts.

Bronze Blues & Brews Festival   MUSIC
(www.bronzebluesbrews.com; ◉mid-Aug) The
Bronze Blues & Brews Festival sees good
jazz, microbrews and bronze sculptures on
display.

⊨ Sleeping

Accommodations in Joseph are expensive;
Enterprise (6 miles to the north) has budget
choices. Reserve ahead in summer, especially during festivals.

Mountain View Motel & RV Park   MOTEL $
(☎541-432-2982, 866-262-9891; www.rvmotel.
com; 83450 Joseph Hwy; tent/RV sites $20/30,
r $75-105; ❋⬚❂) Located a mile from
Joseph, on the way to Enterprise, is this
fine, friendly spot with nine great rooms
(that sleep up to five), a few with kitchens
and all with back decks boasting Wallowa
views. Nice campsites and RV hookups too.

Indian Lodge Motel   MOTEL $
(☎541-432-2651; www.indianlodgemotel.com; 201
S Main St; d $100-110; ❋⬚) This is Joseph's
only motel, with 16 neat plain rooms and a
great downtown location. Off-site cottages
($119 to $195) also available. Reserve well in
advance.

Hurricane Creek Campground CAMPGROUND $
(Mile 7, Hurricane Creek Rd; campsites $6) Campers who don't need many amenities should
try this primitive but beautiful campground
about 7 miles south of Enterprise. Bring
water or a filter.

★ Bronze Antler B&B   B&B $$
(☎866-520-9769, 541-432-0230; www.bronze
antler.com; 309 S Main St; d $129-250; ❋⬚) This
restored arts-and-crafts home offers three
elegant rooms, each with private bath, plus
one luxurious suite with steam shower and
jets in the tub. There's also a bocce court in
the yard, and your friendly hosts know the
area well. A cat roams the premises.

JOSEPH TO HALFWAY – OR BUST

From Joseph, paved USFS Rd 39 skirts the eastern Wallowas and heads south to Hwy 86, just east of Halfway. Part of the Hells Canyon Scenic Byway, this drive links the northern and southern halves of the Wallowas. It also provides access to Hells Canyon Overlook, 3 miles off USFS Rd 39 on USFS Rd 3965, the only canyon viewpoint you can drive to over a paved surface.

It's 73 miles between Joseph and Halfway along this route. USFS Rd 39 is usually closed November through May (dependent on the weather; it's groomed for snow-mobiles and cross-country skiing). There are trailheads and campsites along the way, but no gas stations or other services.

Chandler's Inn   B&B **$$**
(☑541-432-9765; www.josephbedandbreakfast.com; 700 S Main St; d $85-160; ❋ 🐾 🛜 🐾) With more of a Western lodge feel than a typical B&B, this casual spot offers eight themed rooms, including a couple of two-bedroom suites and a cozy cabin. Great mountain views from the 2nd-story hot tub.

🍴 Eating & Drinking

If you like whiskey, vodka or rum, check out the beautiful tasting room of family-run **Stein Distillery** (☑541-432-2009; www.steindistillery.com; ⊙11am-5pm Mon-Sat, 10am-2pm Sun), two doors down from Mutiny Brewing.

★ Coco's Grill   AMERICAN **$$**
(☑541-432-2626; 507 N Main St; mains $9-16; ⊙4-8pm Mon & Tue, 11:30am-8pm Wed-Sat) Some of the best food in Wallowa County is made at this fine eatery. On a warm day, grab a seat on the front patio and order a gourmet burger or thin-crust pizza, both fired in a special wood-stone oven. Shrimp skewers, Thai chicken stir-fry or choice beef medallions are also on offer, plus a variety of exotic tapas.

Caldera's   AMERICAN **$$**
(☑541-432-0585; www.calderasofjoseph.com; 300 N Lake St; mains $9-15; ⊙1-9pm Thu-Mon) This tiny restaurant, really part of a gift shop, is gorgeously decorated in an art-nouveau style. Expect just a few special dishes like baked pesto polenta, butternut squash ravioli or pan-seared scallops. Don't miss the stunning glass-tiled restrooms.

Mutiny Brewing Company   BREWPUB
(☑541-432-5274; www.mutinybrewing.com; 600 N Main St; mains $8-12; ⊙11am-9pm Tue-Sun) Joseph's main brewery is a casual place with pleasant front garden tables – excellent on warm days. The menu has a few creative dishes such as a curry rice bowl and home-made chicken pot pie, and even the local, grass-fed burger is exceptional.

Red Horse Coffee Traders   CAFE
(☑541-432-3784; 306 N Main St; ⊙7am-5pm Mon-Sat, 8am-5pm Sun) Organic beans are roasted on-site at this small coffeehouse. There are also a few snacks, smoothies and exotic teas. Nice outside seating near a stream.

ℹ Information

Visitor Center (cnr Main St & Joseph Ave; ⊙9:30am-5pm) Small wood shack near the bronze statue of Chief Joseph.
Wallowa Mountains Forest Service Office (☑541-426-4978; 201 E Second St; ⊙7:45am-4:30pm Mon-Fri) Sells passes and has maps and information on Hells Canyon, the Eagle Cap Wilderness and the Wallowas. Located in the old elementary school.

Wallowa Mountains

Rising precipitously from the flatlands in Oregon's far northeastern corner, the Wallowas have 19 peaks over 9000ft. Ice Age glaciers carved sharp crags and deep canyons into the mountains, and the moraines of one such glacier now impound Wallowa Lake. Much of the high country, including the only remaining glacier (Alpine Glacier) and eastern Oregon's highest peak (the 9838ft Sacajawea), is part of the Eagle Cap Wilderness, a 715-sq-mile natural area studded with alpine meadows and lakes.

Trails, campgrounds and fishing holes are popular during the high season. In particular, the lovely state park at Wallowa Lake takes on a carnival atmosphere on summer weekends. Some secondary roads over the Wallowa Mountains are closed between November and May, so check ahead.

Wallowa Lake

Located 6 miles from Joseph, Wallowa Lake was formed when glaciers plowed down out of the Wallowas, pushing huge piles of displaced rock. These rock moraines eventually stopped the progress of the glacier, which melted, creating a lake basin. Today the lake is surrounded by dramatic peaks, including the 9617ft Chief Joseph Mountain. Speaking of Chief Joseph, his gravesite is near the north shore of Wallowa Lake, less than a mile south of Joseph and right on the highway.

◉ Sights & Activities

Wallowa Lake State Park   PARK
(☏541-432-4185; www.oregonstateparks.org; 72214 Marina Lane) Pretty Wallowa Lake State Park is the center of activities at the lake's south end. A swimming beach and a boat launch bustle madly in summer, and you can rent a variety of boats at the marina here, along with fishing gear. The best hiking is from the end of Wallowa Lake Rd.

Wallowa Lake Tramway   TRAM RIDE
(☏541-432-5331; www.wallowalaketramway.com; 59919 Wallowa Lake Hwy; adult/child 13-17yr/child 4-12yr $26/21/17; ☉10am-5pm late May-Sep) The Wallowa Lake Tramway leaves from Wallowa Lake and climbs 3700ft to the top of 8150ft Mt Howard. The 15-minute ride is thrilling enough, but the real rewards are the easy alpine hikes around Mt Howard's summit, with views onto Hells Canyon, the Wallowas and Idaho's Seven Devils. A restaurant serves food at the summit.

🛏 Sleeping & Eating

Reserve in summer.

Wallowa Lake State Park   CAMPGROUND $
(☏800-551-6949, 541-432-4185; www.oregon-stateparks.org; 72214 Marina Lane; tent/RV sites $20/25, yurts $38; 🐾) This popular lakeside state park offers more than 200 campsites, along with two yurts. Flush toilets, showers and firewood are available.

Flying Arrow Resort   CABIN $$
(☏541-432-2951; www.flyingarrowresort.com; 59782 Wallowa Lake Hwy; cabins $95-450; 🛜) This friendly resort is awesome, boasting 37 spacious cabins of all sizes, each with its own kitchen and many with a deck overlooking the Wallowa River. One six-bedroom lodge that sleeps 14 is available.

Wallowa Lake Lodge   LODGE $$
(☏541-432-9821; www.wallowalake.com; 60060 Wallowa Lake Hwy; d $99-185, cabins $160-275; 🛜) This 1923 lodge, on the shores of the lake, has both charming lodge rooms and rustic but comfortable lakeside cabins. Two-bedroom units are available. There's a great stone fireplace in the lobby, and a restaurant on the premises. No TVs or telephones.

Eagle Cap Chalets   LODGE $$
(☏541-432-4704; www.eaglecapchalets.com; 59879 Wallowa Lake Hwy; d $109-129, cabins $149-229; 🛜🏊♿🛜) Choose from simple and unpretentious motel rooms, cabins or condos. There's a mini-golf course for the kids, and a pool, hot tub and espresso bar for everyone else.

★ Vali's Alpine Restaurant   HUNGARIAN $$
(☏541-432-5691; 59811 Wallowa Lake Hwy; mains $12-18; ☉5pm & 7pm seatings Wed-Sun Memorial Day-Labor Day, Sat & Sun only rest of year) Hungarian specialties such as cabbage rolls, chicken paprika, beef kabobs and schnitzel are all excellent here, though dishes change daily. Do not miss dessert. Credit cards are not accepted, and reservations are required. Call ahead to check opening hours.

Glacier Grill   AMERICAN $$
(☏541-432-9292; 72784 Marina Dr; mains $7-17; ☉8am-8pm Mon-Thu, till 9pm Fri & Sat) Family dining room that offers sandwiches, burgers and salads for lunch, plus steaks (with plenty of sides) for dinner. Fried foods like fish-and-chips and chicken or clam strips too.

Eagle Cap Wilderness

Glacier-ripped valleys, high mountain lakes and marble peaks are some of the rewards that long-distance hikers find on overnight treks into the beautiful Eagle Cap Wilderness, nicknamed 'America's Little Switzerland.'

A major trailhead starts at the south end of Wallowa Lake Rd. One popular trail is the 6-mile jaunt to gorgeous Aneroid Lake, where you can camp; hike 2.5 miles further to reach Tenderfoot Pass. A longer trek is the Hurricane Creek Trail, which provides access to the Lakes Basin area (10 miles one way). Another popular destination is the Ice Lake Trail, an 8-mile hike with spectacular views of surrounding peaks. Day-use fees of $5 apply to some area hikes.

For easier, organized hiking, consider using horses or llamas to help out. **Eagle Cap Wilderness Pack Station** (☏541-432-4959; www.eaglecapwildernesspackstation.com; 59761 Wallowa Lake Hwy) offers a variety of horseback trips, from hour-long rides to extended pack tours. For llama excursions, contact **Wallowa Llamas** (☏541-742-2961; www.wallowallamas.com; 36678 Allstead Lane, Halfway). It runs multiday trips in the region.

Go skiing in the backcountry with **Wing Ridge Ski Tours** (☏541-398-1980; www.wing-ski.com; 500 N River St, Enterprise). It supplies guides and hut stays, though for the latter you'll need to bring your own food.

Hells Canyon

Over its 13-million-year life span, the Snake River, which neatly straddles the border between Oregon and Idaho, has carved out the deepest river gorge in North America – yes, at 8000ft from highest peak to river, it's deeper than the Grand Canyon (though not nearly as dramatic). The river originates in Yellowstone National Park and ends at the Columbia River near Pasco, Washington – running more than 1000 miles in total.

The prehistoric people who dwelt along Hells Canyon left pictographs, petroglyphs and pit dwellings. The Shoshone and Nez Percé tribes battled for dominance along this stretch of the Snake, with the Nez Percé winning out. Relics of the mining era, from the 1860s to the 1920s, are also found throughout the canyon, and tumbledown shacks remain from the unlikely settlement attempts of turn-of-the-century homesteaders.

Note that the Hells Canyon area, especially at low elevations, gets triple-digit temperatures from late spring through early fall; also, some trails can be under snow as late as July. Contact the Wallowa Mountains Forest Service Office (p355) in Joseph for details.

◉ Sights & Activities

Hat Point
VIEWPOINT

(USFS Rd 4240) High above the Snake River, the Hat Point fire lookout tower (elevation 6982ft) offers great views. On each side of the canyon, mountains soar toward 10,000ft, with the Seven Devils on the Idaho side and the towering Wallowas on the Oregon side.

From Hat Point, a **hiking trail** edges off the side of the canyon. It's a steep 2 miles to

another vista from the top of the river cliffs, then another 4 miles down to the river itself.

To reach Hat Point from Joseph, follow Hwy 350 about 30 miles to the little hamlet of Imnaha. From here, a good gravel road climbs up the Imnaha River canyon to Hat Point. Allow at least 1½ hours each way for the 23.5-mile drive from Imnaha to Hat Point (16% grade the first 6 miles); you'll be stopping for photos along the way. The road is generally open from June until October.

There are no services at Hat Point (other than picnic tables and restrooms), and Imnaha has very few supplies. Get what you need in Joseph and come with a full tank of gas.

Imnaha River Valley
VALLEY

Just west of Hells Canyon, the Imnaha River digs a parallel canyon that offers pastoral scenery in addition to astounding cliff faces.

The gravel Imnaha River Rd follows this narrow valley between Imnaha and the junction of USFS Rd 39 for about 40 miles. The northern end is very dramatic, as the river cuts more and more deeply through stair-stepped lava formations. The southern end is bucolic, with meadows and old farmhouses flanking the river.

North of Imnaha, a gravel-dirt road continues for 20 miles to Cow Creek Bridge, where the **Imnaha River Trail** begins (about 4 miles one way). Two miles beyond the bridge is the start of the **Nee-Me-Poo Trail** (which traces the path of Chief Joseph and the Nez Percé); it climbs 3.7 miles to a viewpoint over the Snake River.

Hells Canyon Dam
CANYON

Hells Canyon's most spectacular scenery is perhaps along the Snake River itself, following 25 miles of paved road (Idaho's Rte 454) toward Hells Canyon Dam; here dramatic canyon walls loom almost vertically. The road goes up the Idaho border but is accessed via the southern end of the Wallowa Mountain Loop, near Oxbow. Just past the dam the road ends at the **Hells Canyon Visitors Center** (☏541-785-3395; ⊙8am-4pm May-Sep) and boat launch. Miles beyond here, the Snake drops 1300ft in elevation through wild scenery and equally wild rapids, and the area can only be accessed via jet boat or raft.

There's also a gravel road that goes up the Snake River on the Oregon side, but it stops short of the dam. It accesses Bureau of Land Management (BLM) land, and some trailheads and rustic campgrounds. There's no bridge linking this gravel road to Rte 454 over the Snake.

Hells Canyon Adventures (☏800-422-3568; www.hellscanyonadventures.com) is the area's main tour outfitter, running a variety of jet-boat trips from May through September. Reservations are required.

There are several good **hiking trails** on the way to the dam; Allison Creek (on the Idaho side), about 4.5 miles round-trip, is an especially good one. Longer trails are possible; check with the Hells Canyon Visitors Center, from where there's also the mile-long Stud Creek hike downriver.

🛏 Sleeping

Enterprise, Joseph and Halfway are all day trips away from Hells Canyon, but you can also stay overnight in the area. There's a free primitive campsite near Hat Point. Imnaha has food and water (and some basic RV sites), but for gas you'll have to go to Joseph.

Ollokot (campsites $8) and **Blackhorse** (campsites $8) are two campgrounds at the southern end of the canyon, right on USFS Rd 39, midway between Halfway and Joseph. The **BLM campsites** `FREE` are rustic sites on the Oregon side of the Snake River.

Hells Canyon Park   CAMPGROUND $
(☏800-422-3143; tent/RV sites $10/16) Pretty campsite on the Idaho side of Snake River.

Copperfield Park   CAMPGROUND $
(☏800-422-3143; tent/RV sites $10/16; 🛜) Pleasant campsite at Oxbow.

Hells Canyon B&B   B&B $
(☏541-785-3373; www.hcbb.us; 49922 Homestead Rd; d $80; ❄🛜) Simple but great-value B&B in the Oxbow area.

Imnaha River Inn   INN $$
(☏866-601-9214; www.imnahariverinn.com; 73946 Rimrock Rd; s/d from $70/130) Beautiful inn 5 miles north of Imnaha.

Halfway

POP 280

An idyllic little town, Halfway lies on the southern edge of the Wallowa Mountains and is surrounded by beautiful meadows dotted with old barns and hay fields. It's a friendly spot with just enough tourist services to make it a decent base to explore the Hells Canyon Dam area. The **Pine Ranger Station** (☏541-742-7511; 38470 Pine Town Lane; ⊙7:30-11:45am & 12:30-4:30pm Mon-Fri mid-Apr–mid-Dec) is 1 mile south of Halfway and acts as the region's tourist information.

The **Pine Valley Museum** (admission by donation; ⊙10am-4pm Fri, Sat & Sun Memorial Day-Labor Day) is located right in the middle of town and has a few of the region's old photos and relics (check out the albino porcupine). If it's closed, ask around town for someone who might have the key.

🛏 Sleeping & Eating

Halfway has just two average dining options – Wild Bill's or Stockman's, both on the main drag. If you just need the basics, Stockman's has the cheapest rooms in town ($25 to $45; shared baths).

Halfway Motel   MOTEL $
(☏541-742-5722; www.halfwaymotel-rvpark.com; 170 S Main St; RV sites $25, d $65-75; ❄🛜🐾) Both old and new rooms are available at this reasonable motel. Go for the newer ones on the 2nd floor (facing the back) to enjoy peaceful meadow views. The themed older rooms are smaller and cheaper, but still comfortable. RV hookups are available.

★ **Pine Valley Lodge**   LODGE $$
(☏541-742-2027; www.pvlodge.com; 163 N Main St; d incl breakfast $85-140; ❄🛜🐾) Halfway's fanciest accommodations, with 14 lovely and very comfortable rooms in four buildings, all surrounded by flowery gardens. There's a great porch with wicker rocking chairs, and one cabin is also available (from $150). Some rooms have kitchenette.

Inn at Clear Creek Farm   B&B $$
(☏541-742-2238; www.clearcreekinn.com; 48212 Clear Creek Rd; d $95-150; ❄🛜) This gorgeous inn, 4 miles northwest of Halfway, is also a working cattle ranch. It offers six elegant rooms, including a family suite; meals (except for the included breakfast) are extra. No shoes are allowed inside, so bring your slippers!

Baker City

POP 9800

Back in the old days, Baker City was the largest metropolis between Salt Lake City and Portland, and was also the commercial and cultural capital of eastern Oregon.

The 1860s gold rush helped establish the town, enriching its coffers while making it party central for the region – a heady mix of miners, cowboys, shopkeepers and loggers kept the city's many saloons, brothels and gaming halls boisterously alive.

The good old times are long gone now, but the city's wide downtown streets and historical architecture recall its rich bygone days. Today, travelers come not only for a peek at the city's swaggering history, but to explore the area's outdoor attractions. There's good skiing in winter, while fishing, hiking and boating are great in summer – and the Eagle Cap Wilderness and Wallowa Mountains aren't too far away.

◎ Sights & Activities

Old Downtown Area   NEIGHBORHOOD
The old downtown retains much of its late-19th-century Victorian Italianate architecture. A brochure describing a **walking tour** of historic buildings in the city center is available from the visitors bureau. To ogle the 80.4oz Armstrong Nugget, found in the area in 1913, visit the US Bank (2000 Main St) during regular banking hours.

Housed in a 1921 natatorium (indoor swimming pool) is the very worthwhile **Baker Heritage Museum** (☑541-523-9308; 2480 Grove St; adult/child 13-17yr $6/5; ⊙9am-4pm late Mar-Oct). On display are machinery and antiques from Baker City's frontier days, along with a notable collection of semiprecious stones, fossils and petrified wood. Don't miss the fluorescent rock room and 950lb crystal.

Historic Adler House (☑541-523-9308; 2305 Main St; admission $6; ⊙10am-2pm Fri-Mon Memorial Day-Labor Day) is great if you like fully restored Victorian houses. If you're planning to visit this museum and the Baker Heritage Museum, buy a $10 ticket for both.

★**National Historic
Oregon Trail Interpretive Center**   MUSEUM
(☑541-523-1843; www.oregontrail.blm.gov; 22267 Hwy 86; admission adult/child $8/free; ⊙9am-6pm Apr-Oct, 9am-4pm Nov-Mar) This excellent interpretive center is the nation's foremost memorial to the pioneers who crossed the West along the Oregon Trail. Lying atop a hill 7 miles east of Baker City, it contains interactive displays, artifacts and films that stress the day-to-day realities of the pioneers. Outside you can stroll along the 4.2-mile interpretive path system and spot the actual Oregon Trail.

Anthony Lakes   HIKING, SKIING
About 30 miles northwest of Baker City, this area offers great scenery, along with camping and fishing. Several hiking trails lead to other small lakes, including a short but steep climb up Parker Creek to Hoffer Lakes (1 mile one way). Another short hike goes from Elkhorn Crest Trail up to Black Lake (1 mile one way).

In winter, ski-heads should beeline to nearby **Anthony Lakes Mountain Resort** (☑541-856-3277; www.anthonylakes.com; 47500 Anthony Lakes Hwy), which offers dry, fluffy powder and the highest base elevation in Oregon (7100ft). The resort grooms nearly 20 miles of cross-country trails.

EASTERN OREGON BAKER CITY

THE BLUE MOUNTAINS

Rising to the west from ranch land near Baker City, the Blue Mountains were responsible for the 1860s gold strikes that established towns such as Sumpter, Granite and Baker City. Ghost-town enthusiasts will find the Blue Mountains dotted with old mining camps, but there are also high mountain lakes, river canyons and hiking trails. And if you're crazy about trains, don't miss the narrow-gauge **Sumpter Valley Railroad** (☑800-523-1235; www.sumptervalleyrailroad.org). The railroad is open for train rides (two hours round-trip) weekends and major holidays, Memorial Day weekend to the last weekend in September. See the website for further details.

A good way to explore the Blue Mountains is via the **Elkhorn Drive Scenic Byway**, which circles Elkhorn Ridge. It takes all day to properly explore this 106-mile loop that includes Baker City, Phillips Reservoir, Sumpter, Granite and Haines; it also skirts the Anthony Lakes area, which offers camping, fishing and hiking. Part of the loop (between Granite and Anthony Lakes) is often closed from late October to mid-June, so call or visit the Baker Ranger District in Baker City for road conditions.

✹ Festivals & Events

Miners Jubilee CULTURE
(☉mid-late Jul) Area events include this Miners Jubilee, with art and quilt shows, and a rodeo.

Hells Canyon Rally MOTORCYCLE SHOW
(www.hellscanyonrally.com; ☉mid-Jul) The Hells Canyon Rally brings hundreds of motorcycle aficionados into town for a motorcycle show and rides into the scenic surrounding region.

🛏 Sleeping

Beaten Path B&B B&B $
(☑541-523-9230; www.abeatenpathbb.com; 2510 Court Ave; d $95; ✳☎) Located in a residential district, this friendly B&B is in an 1888 historical home. Two large, comfortable Victorian-style rooms are available, but only one is rented at a time since there's one bath (unless you're willing to share it). Gourmet breakfast.

Bridge St Inn MOTEL $
(☑541-523-6571, 800-932-9220; www.bridgestreet inn.net; 134 Bridge St; d $42-58; ✳☎✳) The motel rooms here are decent and though their layout is a bit eccentric, the Nitty Gritty Dirt Band once slept here and that's worth something. Get a room facing the back for peace. Hot breakfast offered.

Union Creek Campground CAMPGROUND $
(☑541-894-2393; Hwy 7 at Phillips Reservoir; tent sites $12, RV sites $20-32; ☉May-Sep) Located about 18 miles southwest of Baker City is this pleasant campground in a conifer forest around a reservoir popular with fishermen and boaters.

Anthony Lakes Campground CAMPGROUND $
(☑541-894-2393; 47500 Anthony Lakes Hwy; campsites $10-14; ☉Jul-Sep) Though it's 35 miles from town, this rustic but splendid campground is worth the drive (bring mosquito repellent!). It's high up and opens only after the snow melts, so call first.

Geiser Grand Hotel HOTEL $$
(☑541-523-1889, 888-434-7374; www.geisergrand. com; 1996 Main St; d $99-159; ✳☎✳) Baker City's downtown landmark and fanciest lodging is this meticulously restored Italian Renaissance Revival building. The elegant rooms are spacious and decorated with old-style furniture, while the restaurant offers fine food and has a stunning stained-glass ceiling. There's a great old saloon, too.

✗ Eating

The Geiser Grand Hotel has a fancy dining room.

Earth & Vine Wine Bar AMERICAN $
(☑541-523-1687; 2001 Washington Ave; mains $9-12; ☉11am-9pm Mon-Thu, till 10pm Fri, 8am-10pm Sat, 8am-8pm Sun) Upscale yet friendly and casual wine-bar eatery. There's wine-friendly choices like hummus and meat and cheese plates, plus fondue, wraps, salads and toasted sandwiches. Wines by the glass and even 'on tap,' with occasional special tastings.

Barley Brown's Brewpub PUB $$
(☑541-523-4266; www.barleybrowns.com; 2190 Main St; mains $9-18; ☉4-10pm Mon-Thu, till 11pm Fri & Sat) Baker City's only microbrew pub, with comfortable atmosphere boasting tin ceilings and plenty of wooden booths. The regular pub menu features more than just pub food – think Kobe beef burgers, eggplant parmesan, jalapeño chicken pasta. Wash it all down with one of the tasty brews on tap.

Corner Brick Bar & Grill AMERICAN $$
(☑541-523-6099; 1840 Main St; lunch $6-11, dinner $10-15; ☉11am-9pm Mon-Thu, till 10pm Fri & Sat) Very nice atmospheric restaurant serving up sandwiches (try the jalapeño pesto), salads and wraps. There's pasta with homemade sauces for dinner, along with a few tasty mains and a two-for-$25 steak special.

❶ Information

Visitors Bureau (☑541-523-5855; www. visitbaker.com; 490 Campbell St; ☉8am-5pm Mon-Sat, 9am-2pm Sun)
Whitman Ranger District (☑541-523-4476; 3285 11th St; ☉7:45am-4:30pm Mon-Fri) For area camping and hiking information.

❶ Getting There & Away

Baker Truck Corral (☑800-231-2222; 515 Campbell St; ☉9am-3pm Mon-Fri) Greyhound bus stop; twice-daily east- and west-bound services.

John Day

POP 1750

Smack near the middle of eastern Oregon, this unpretentious, one-stoplight town strings along a narrow passage of the John Day River Valley. It's a utilitarian but decent enough place to base yourself while exploring the scenic region, and hosts a few interesting museums as well.

◉ Sights

Kam Wah Chung State Heritage Site
HISTORIC SITE

(☑541-575-2800; 125 NW Canton St; ⊘9am-5pm May-Oct) **FREE** Don't miss this site, located in an 1865 building that served primarily as an apothecary for the noted Chinese herbalist and doctor Ing Hay. But it was also a community center, temple, general store and opium den for the Chinese population that reworked the area's mine tailings.

A nearby interpretive center offers a 19-minute video; free tours of the heritage site leave from here.

Grant County Ranch & Rodeo Museum
MUSEUM

(☑541-575-0278; 241 E Main St; adult/child/11yr & under $3/free; ⊘10am-4pm Thu-Sat May-Sep) Rodeo-lovers should visit this small museum, which showcases fine saddles and lots of rodeo photos. The friendly guys there really know the local rodeo and ranch scene. Call for off-hours visits.

Grant County Historical Museum
MUSEUM

(☑541-575-0362; 101 S Canyon City Blvd; adult/child 6-18yr $4/2; ⊘9am-4:30pm Mon-Sat May-Sep) Located just 2 miles south of downtown John Day, in the center of tiny Canyon City, this interesting museum houses gold-rush memorabilia, lots of polished agates and some stuffed two-headed calves. Outside is frontier poet Joaquin Miller's cabin.

⏏ Sleeping & Eating

See John Day Fossil Beds National Monument (p363) for other accommodations in the area. There are a few chain hotel/motels in town.

★ Hotel Prairie
HOTEL $

(☑541-820-4800; www.hotelprairie.com; 112 Front St; d incl breakfast $79-139; ⊛⊛) Actually located in Prairie City, 13 miles east of John Day, is this historic 1905 hotel with nine suites (one with kitchenette). There's a subdued, classy atmosphere and rooms are simple but comfortable; out back is a nice modern patio for hanging out. Cafe on premises.

Dreamers Lodge
MOTEL $

(☑800-654-2849; 144 N Canyon Blvd; d from $63; ⊛⊛⊛⊛) One of John Day's better-value places, this decent motel offers good-sized rooms (the ones with two beds are huge) and it's off the main drag.

Clyde Holliday State Park
CAMPGROUND $

(☑800-551-6949, 541-932-4453; www.oregon-stateparks.org; Hwy 26, Mile 155, Mt Vernon; tent & RV sites $22, tipis $39; ⊛) Six miles west of John Day, this pleasant, shady campground (with tipis) lies next to the John Day River, though it's also close to the road.

Outpost
AMERICAN $

(☑541-575-0250; www.gooutpost.com; 201 W Main St; mains $8-21; ⊘5:30am-9pm Mon-Sat, till 8pm Sun) There's something for everyone at this Western-style joint: soups, salads, sandwiches, pizzas, burgers and steaks, and

EASTERN OREGON JOHN DAY

RAFTING THE JOHN DAY

From Clarno Bridge (on Hwy 218) to Cottonwood Bridge (on Hwy 206), a distance of 70 miles, the John Day River cuts a deep canyon through basaltic lava flows on its way to the Columbia River. No public roads reach the canyon here; along the river are the remains of homesteads, Native American petroglyphs and pristine wildlife habitats.

Plan to float the John Day in spring or early summer, when the toughest rapids are class III or IV, depending on the water levels. Most trips take four days and some rafters float the John Day on their own (permit required). Shuttle service and raft rentals are available from **Service Creek Stage Stop** (☑541-468-3331; www.servicecreeklodge.com; 38686 Hwy 19).

For specific advice, contact the **Prineville BLM office** (☑541-416-6700; 3050 NE 3rd St; ⊘7:45am-4:30pm Mon-Fri) and see www.blm.gov/or/resources/recreation/johnday.

Among the companies that run trips are the following:

Oregon River Experiences (☑800-827-1358; www.oregonriver.com)

Oregon Whitewater Adventures (☑800-820-7238; www.oregonwhitewater.com)

Ouzel Outfitters (☑800-788-7238; www.oregonrafting.com)

pasta and fajitas; and homemade cinnamon rolls for breakfast. There's a good atmosphere with upscale rustic decor.

★ **Snaffle Bit**   AMERICAN $$
(☑541-575-2426; 830 S Canyon City Blvd; mains $9-29; ◎5-9pm Tue, 11am-2:30pm & 4:30-9pm Wed-Fri, 4:30-10pm Sat) Some of the county's best steaks are at this no-nonsense, friendly restaurant with a nice fountain patio. Also on the menu are salads, pasta, hamburgers and Mexican specialties. Large portions. Reservations are a good idea.

ⓘ Information

Chamber of Commerce (☑541-575-0547; www.gcoregonlive.com; 301 W Main St; ◎9am-4pm Mon-Fri)

Malheur National Forest Ranger Station (☑541-575-3000; www.fs.fed.us/r6/malheur; 431 Patterson Bridge Rd; ◎8am-4:30pm Mon-Fri)

ⓘ Getting There & Away

People Mover Bus (☑541-575-2370; www.grantcountypeoplemover.com; 229 NE Dayton) Curb-to-curb services to Bend on Monday, Wednesday and Friday.

Strawberry Mountain Wilderness

Named for the wild strawberries that thrive on its mountain slopes, the Strawberry Range is covered with ponderosa and lodgepole pines growing on glacier-chiseled volcanic peaks that are 15 million years old. The Strawberry Mountains contain deceptively high country: much of the wilderness is above 6000ft, and the highest peak – Strawberry Mountain – rises to 9038ft.

A popular and rewarding 2.8-mile round-trip hike winds up a steep valley to **Strawberry Lake**. About 1 mile past the lake is **Strawberry Falls**. To reach the trailhead, follow the signs 11 miles south from Prairie City.

Circle around to the south side of the wilderness area on Hwy 14 and paved USFS Rds 65 and 16, past old ponderosa pines and wide meadows, to find more trails. Hike into **High Lake Basin** (2.6 miles round-trip) from a trailhead high up the mountainside. From USFS Rd 16, turn on USFS Rd 1640 toward **Indian Springs Campground**. The trailhead is 11 miles up a steep gravel road.

There are several good campgrounds, including **Trout Farm** (☑541-820-3800; County Rd 62; campsites $8), a lovely stream-side spot 15 miles south of Prairie City. Water available.

For more information, contact the **Prairie City Ranger District** (☑541-820-3800; 327 Front St; ◎8am-4:30pm Mon-Fri) in Prairie City.

John Day Fossil Beds National Monument

Within the soft rocks and crumbly soils of John Day country lies one of the world's greatest fossil collections. Discovered in the 1860s by clergyman and geologist Thomas Condon, these fossil beds were laid down between six and 50 million years ago, when this area was a coastal plain with a tropical climate. Roaming the forests at the time were saber-toothed, felinelike nimravids, bear-dogs, pint-sized horses and other early mammals.

The fossils of more than 2200 different plant and animal species have been found here. The national monument includes 22 sq miles at three different units: Sheep Rock Unit, Painted Hills Unit and Clarno Unit. Each has hiking trails and interpretive displays. To visit all of the units in one day requires quite a bit of driving, as more than 100 slow miles of curving roads separate the fossil beds – it's best to take it easy and spend the night somewhere.

Note that this is a National Monument, and no fossil, rock or plant collecting is allowed. Also note it gets very hot in July and August.

◉ Sights & Activities

Sheep Rock Unit   GEOLOGICAL SITE
Featuring the most walks and hikes, this unit is also closest to the Thomas Condon Paleontology Center. Above loom majestic, layered mountains tilted and eroding into spectacular formations that date back 28 million years. Fossils are continually being exposed here.

From the Blue Basin Area, two hikes lead out to the fossil formations. The **Island in Time Trail** is a well-maintained, mile-long (round-trip) path that climbs up a narrow waterway to a badlands-basin of highly eroded, uncannily green sediments. The longer **Blue Basin Overlook Trail** is a 3-mile loop with amazing vistas of the John Day Valley.

Painted Hills Unit GEOLOGICAL SITE
Because no cap rock protects them from erosion, the Painted Hills have eroded into low-slung, colorfully banded hills that were originally formed about 30 million years ago. A series of eruptions drifted into beds hundreds of feet deep, layering the brick-red, yellow, black, beige and ocher-hued ash that you now see. It's a fabulous, uncommon sight.

Interpretive walks include the easy half-mile (round-trip) **Leaf Hill Trail**, which winds over the top of a banded hill, and the 1.5-mile (round-trip) **Carroll Rim Trail**, which goes to the top of a high bluff for great views.

Clarno Unit GEOLOGICAL SITE
The oldest, most remote fossil beds in the area are at the base of the John Day River's canyon. The 40-million-year-old Clarno Unit exposes mud flows that washed over an Eocene-era forest. The **Clarno Formation** eroded into white cliffs topped with spires and turrets of stone. There are three half-mile (round-trip) interpretive trails, including one that passes through large boulders containing fossils of an ancient forest, and another that leads to the base of **Palisades Cliff** and some petrified logs.

Thomas Condon Paleontology Center MUSEUM
(☏541-987-2333; www.nps.gov/joda; 32651 Hwy 19, Kimberly; ☺10am-5pm, occasional closed days) Visit the excellent Thomas Condon Paleontology Center 2 miles north of US 26 at the Sheep Rock Unit. Displays include a three-toed horse and petrified dung-beetle balls, along with many other fossils and geologic history exhibits. Note that staffing issues mean the center is closed occasionally.

Cant Ranch House HISTORIC HOUSE
(☺9am-4pm Mon-Thu & most Fri) The Cant Ranch House, near the paleontology center, offers a peek into settlers' early lives, and has picnic grounds and a riverside trail.

🛏 Sleeping & Eating

The town of John Day has a few accommodations. Public campgrounds in the area include **Lone Pine** (campsites $5) and **Big Bend** (campsites $5); both are nice riverside places on Hwy 402, north of the Sheep Rock Unit and 2 to 3 miles east of Kimberly (no water at either site). Over toward the Clarno Unit and 7 to 11 miles south of Fossil are **Bear Hollow** (campsites 1st night $10, later nights $5) and **Shelton Wayside** (campsites 1st night $10, later nights $5), both with woodsy campsites (no water at Bear Hollow).

Service Creek Lodge GUESTHOUSE $
(☏541-468-3331; www.servicecreek.com; 38686 Hwy 19; d incl breakfast from $85; ❈🛜) Twenty miles southeast of Fossil (which is near the Clarno Unit), this fine lodge has six awesome, comfortable rooms (some share baths) with a common living room. There's also a restaurant, a small store and rafting services. Reception is at the restaurant.

Fish House Inn INN $
(☏541-987-2124; www.fishhouseinn.com; 110 Franklin St, Dayville; tent/RV sites $15/25, d $50-70; ❈🛜🐕) Five nice rooms (two with shared bath) are available at this inn in Dayville, less than 10 miles southeast of the Sheep Rock Unit. There's also a pleasant area for tents and RVs. Three-bedroom house available ($125). Note that no breakfast is served.

OFF THE BEATEN TRACK

FOSSIL

Close to the Clarno Unit of the John Day Fossil Beds National Monument is this small, nondescript town. Not only does Fossil have an interesting name, it's located at the 45th parallel, which is generally regarded as being halfway between the equator and North Pole.

If you have a few hours to spare, **hunt for fossils** behind Wheeler High School ($5 per person, open May to October). It's self-serve, with buckets and tools provided; there's a caretaker on weekends. The **Fossil Museum** (☺1-4pm Mon & Wed-Sun; free) is another attraction, with interesting local relics. Finally there's the **Oregon Paleo Lands Institute**, a small educational facility which offers local information and a small geography display room (limited open days).

Need a bed for the night? Check into the **Fossil Motel & RV Park** (☏541-763-4075; 105 1st St; d $60-89, RV sites $30), which has a handful of homey and outdated but good-sized rooms.

Historic Oregon Hotel
HOTEL $

(☎541-462-3027; 104 E Main St; dm $20, d $45-69; 🛜) This pleasant old-style hotel is in the little town of Mitchell, about 10 miles southeast of the Painted Hills Unit. Plain homey rooms are featured, most with shared bath and no TVs. There's one dorm, plus a kitchenette room for $89. It's popular with cyclists.

Lands Inn B&B
B&B $

(☎541-934-2333; www.landsinn.net; 45457 Dick Creek Lane; campsites $25, cabins $45-95; ☉ Jun-Sep; 🛜🐾) 🐾 Possibly the world's only B&B with its own airstrip, this mountain hideaway is 6 miles north of Hwy 26 and 13 miles south of Kimberly (then 5 miles up a dirt road!). It has several different cabins, most with outside bath, plus campsites. Breakfast is extra ($12), however, and all electricity is solar (so can be spotty). Reservations required.

Wilson Ranches Retreat B&B
B&B $$

(☎866-763-2227; www.wilsonranchesretreat. com; 16555 Butte Creek Rd; d $99-139; ❄🛜) Six homey and comfortable guest rooms of different sizes (and all sharing baths) are available at this good B&B, which is also a working ranch. There are pleasant common spaces, and horseback riding is available. It's 2.5 miles northwest of Fossil. Call ahead.

Ontario

POP 11,300

Oregon's most easterly city, Ontario and its environs are often considered to be an extension of Idaho's fertile Snake River valley. The Malheur, Payette and Owyhee Rivers join the Snake's wide valley here, with irrigated farms producing a variety of crops – the region's economic backbone. The city itself is a bit homely and not worth more than a brief stop on your way somewhere more exciting.

Note that Ontario shares the same time zone, Mountain Standard Time, with Idaho – it's one hour ahead of Pacific Standard Time.

⊙ Sights

Four Rivers Cultural Center
MUSEUM

(☎541-889-8191; www.4rcc.com; 676 SW 5th Ave; adult/child 6-14yr $4/3; ☉9am-5pm Mon-Fri, 10am-5pm Sat) A far cry from your typical small-town museum, this center celebrates the region's diversity, focusing on Paiute Native Americans, Basque sheep-herders, and Japanese American and Mexican American farm workers. There's a Japanese garden out back.

🛏 Sleeping

Ontario Inn
MOTEL $

(☎541-823-2556; www.ontarioinnmotel.com; 1144 SW 4th Ave; d $55-66; ❄🛜❄) Pleasant, friendly, family-run motel with slightly outdated but clean rooms. One big plus: bagels and fruit for breakfast.

Lake Owyhee State Park
CAMPGROUND $

(☎541-339-2331; www.oregonstateparks.org; 1298 Lake Owyhee Dam Rd; tent/RV sites $17/20, tipis $36; ❄) Some 40 miles south of Ontario is this desertlike state park, on the shores of Lake Owyhee. It's at the end of a long, one-way road, but getting here is half the fun – and there are tipis to rent.

Farewell Bend State Recreation Area
CAMPGROUND $

(☎541-869-2365; www.oregonstateparks.org; I-84 exit 353; tent/RV sites $18/22, cabins $42; ❄) A good camping spot relatively close to Ontario is this large oasis at the Snake River's Brownlee Reservoir, 25 miles northwest of town.

Virtue House B&B
B&B $$

(☎541-889-1996; www.virtuehouse.com; 788 SW 2nd St; cottages $100; ❄@❄) For something a little different, rent out this darling one-bedroom cottage in a residential area. You'll get all the benefits of your own private little house, and the 'hosts' (who live nearby) will cook you a full breakfast in the morning. Call ahead.

🍴 Eating & Drinking

Romio's Pizza & Pasta
ITALIAN $$

(☎541-889-4888; www.romios-pizza.com; 375 S Oregon St; mains $10-13, pizzas $11-22; ☉11am-8pm Mon-Thu, till 9pm Fri-Sun) Consistently good pizzas, topped with treats such as fresh garlic, artichoke hearts, feta cheese and bacon. Plenty of sandwiches, salads and pasta too, along with a few calzones. Romantic atmosphere with some half-round booths.

Ogawa's Teriyaki Hut
ASIAN FUSION $$

(☎541-889-2725; www.ogawasrestaurant.com; 375 E Idaho Ave; mains $9-17; ☉11am-8pm Mon-Thu, till 9pm Fri & Sat) As exotic as Ontario can get. Try a 'wicked' rice bowl (chicken, beef, seafood etc) or a gourmet burger. There are also bento boxes, nigiri and sushi rolls. The *mafa* chicken (a unique fried chicken with vegetables; only available a couple times per week) is locally recommended.

Jolts & Juice CAFE
(cnr SW 3rd Ave & S Oregon Sts; snacks $4-8, drinks $1.50-3.50; ⊘6am-8pm Mon-Thu, till 9pm Fri, 7am-9pm Sat, 7am-4pm Sun) Ontario's best coffee shop, with artsy vibe and pleasant sidewalk seating. Order your favorite specialty coffee drink, fresh juice or smoothie; there are sandwiches and salads if you need nourishment.

ℹ Information

Chamber of Commerce (☑541-889-8012; www.ontariochamber.com; 876 SW 4th Ave; ⊘9am-5pm Mon-Fri) Near the Four Rivers Cultural Center in a strip mall.

ℹ Getting There & Around

Greyhound (☑541-889-7651; 842 SE 1st Ave) Located at the Malheur Council on Aging, with east- and west-bound services twice daily.

Jordan Valley

POP 180

The closest thing to civilization in the southeastern corner of Oregon is tiny Jordan Valley (Mountain Standard Time). Known for its Basque heritage, this pit stop has an interesting rebuilt *frontón,* a stone ball court used for playing the traditional Basque game of *pelota*. There is a motel and a surprisingly good restaurant-inn.

Basque Station Motel (☑541-586-2244; 801 Main St; d $54-64; ▣) is nothing fancy, with large rooms overlooking a serene meadow out back. Check-in is at the gas station.

Order *bacalao* (dried salt cod), Basque-style chorizos or just broiled lamb chops at **Old Basque Inn** (☑541-586-2800; 306 Wroten St; mains $7-19; ⊘7am-2:30pm & 5-10pm Mon-Sat, 7am-10pm Sun), an old Basque boarding house. There are five homey rooms upstairs with shared baths (doubles $65, including breakfast).

Burns

POP 2900

Named by a wistful early settler for Scottish poet Robert Burns, this isolated high-desert town was established in 1883 as the watering hole and social center for incoming settlers and roving cowhands. Today, Burns (don't mistake it for Burns *Junction* – essentially just a highway junction southwest of Jordan Valley) has a decent number of services and is a convenient jumping-off point for trips south into the Malheur National Wildlife Refuge and Steens Mountain area.

SUCCOR CREEK & LESLIE GULCH

It takes a little doing to get to the wildly eroded Owyhee River country, but sections of this 35-mile gravel drive (and its 14.5-mile side branch) are unforgettable. Running between Adrian and a junction with US 95, 18 miles north of Jordan Valley, this scenic route passes grand desert landscapes and spectacular rock peaks.

Take the gravel road 8 miles south of Adrian; the sign should say 'Succor Creek State Park.' You'll drive through sagebrush and rolling hills for about 10 miles, then start descending. A couple of miles later are amazing vertical walls of volcanic tuff hundreds of feet high. The **Succor Creek State Natural Area** sits at the other end of the canyon, with free basic campsites (no water), wildlife-watching opportunities and stunning vistas.

The scenery is even more spectacular at **Leslie Gulch**, 26 miles further south on a 14.5-mile dead-end side branch off the main gravel road. A narrow creek channel goes through vividly colored volcanic rock eroded into amazing pinnacles and turreted formations, at last reaching Lake Owyhee Reservoir. There's free primitive camping at **Slocum Creek campground** (covered picnic tables, fire pits, gravel sites), which is open March to November. Watch for rattlesnakes.

Driving on gravel roads is slow going, so leave yourself plenty of time and take food, lots of water and a full tank of gas. Also note that it gets *very* hot here in summer and you're unlikely to get cell service. For more information, contact the **Vale BLM** (☑541-473-3144; www.blm.gov/or/districts/vale).

◉ Sights & Activities

Harney County Historical Museum
MUSEUM

(☑541-573-5618; 18 West D St; admission $4; ⊙10am-4pm Tue-Sat Apr-Sep) Lots of historical relics – from photos to coins to guns to a document sentencing a hanging – are on exhibit at this museum; if you're a couple, the $5 admission covers you both.

Crystal Crane Hot Springs
SPRING

(☑541-493-2312; www.cranehotsprings.com; 59315 Hwy 78; ⊙9am-9pm) This rustic resort, 25 miles southeast of Burns and 3 miles northwest of Crane, is a little oasis and worth a stop. The springs flow into a large pond ($3.50 day use) and are also piped into tubs in small private bathhouses ($7.50 per person per hour; reserve on weekends).

⌑ Sleeping

Crystal Crane Hot Springs
CABIN $

(☑541-493-2312; www.cranehotsprings.com; 59315 Hwy 78; tent sites $15, RV sites $18-20, cabins $45-67; 🛜🐾) This very casual 'resort' is 25 miles from Burns, and an oasis in the desert. Accommodations are rustic, with simple cabins that share outside baths. Hot-spring and kitchen use is included, and there's a common room. There's also two houses available to rent and you can even stay in tipis ($20 to $55).

Silver Spur Motel
MOTEL $

(☑541-573-2077; www.silverspurmotel.com; 789 N Broadway Ave; d from $49; ✳🛜🐾) Your typical budget motel, with small and plain but clean rooms.

Burns RV Park
CAMPGROUND $

(☑800-573-7640; www.burnsrvpark.com; 1273 Seneca Dr; tent sites $18, RV sites $33-36; 🛜🐾) Just a quarter-mile east of Burns, on the main road, is this pleasant RV and camping park. Sites are decent, and some have shade.

Idlewild Campground
CAMPGROUND $

(☑541-573-4300; Hwy 395; campsites $10) North of town 17 miles, just off Hwy 395, this public campground is in the Malheur National Forest. It's peaceful, with pleasant sites among Jeffrey pines.

Sage Country Inn
B&B $$

(☑541-573-7243; www.sagecountryinn.com; 351½ W Monroe St; d $100-115; ✳🛜) Burns' most charming lodging by far, this beautiful old house has three well-furnished rooms, each with its own bath. Grassy gardens surround the place, and it's right near downtown.

✖ Eating & Drinking

Broadway Deli
CAFE $

(☑541-573-7020; 530 N Broadway Ave; sandwiches $6-11; ⊙8am-4pm Mon-Fri, 11am-3pm Sat) Fine sandwiches and salads are sold at this small, simple deli. Soups, smoothies and homemade pies and cakes are also available, and the service is old-fashioned.

Meat Hook
STEAKHOUSE $$

(☑541-573-7698; 673 W Monroe St; mains $8-18; ⊙4-9pm Mon & Thu-Sun) Ignore the name – some decent steaks can be had at this restaurant (though side dishes are average). Comfortable, carpeted dining room, and the chef might come out to see how you're doing.

★ Rhojo's
AMERICAN $$$

(☑541-573-7656; 83 W Washington; mains $21-25; ⊙11am-2pm Sun-Thu, 11am-2pm & 6-9pm Fri, 6-9pm Sat) Some of eastern Oregon's best food can be found at this nondescript little restaurant. Dishes change daily, but expect things like hand-made ravioli stuffed with mozzarella or grilled NY strip topped with Gorgonzola. Gourmet soups and sandwiches for lunch. Note that opening hours/days may vary.

Bella Java & Bistro
CAFE

(☑541-573-3077; 314a N Broadway; ⊙7:30am-3pm Mon-Fri, 9am-2pm Sat) Get your caffeine jolt at this pleasant coffee shop, decorated with tin ceilings and a couple of sofas. There's espresso or mocha, along with chai, Italian sodas and fruit smoothies.

❶ Information

BLM Office (☑541-573-4400; www.blm.gov/or/districts/burns; 28910 US 20W, Hines; ⊙7:45am-4:30pm Mon-Fri)

Chamber of Commerce (☑541-573-2636; www.harneycounty.com; 484 N Broadway; ⊙9am-5pm Mon-Fri)

Emigrant Creek Ranger District (☑541-573-4300; www.fs.usda.gov/malheur; 265 US 20S, Hines; ⊙8-11:30am & 12:30-4:30pm Mon-Fri)

❶ Getting There & Away

Eastern Point Shuttle (☑541-573-5500; 63 N Buena Vista Ave) Runs out of Figaro's Pizza, with one daily service to Ontario and Bend.

Malheur National Wildlife Refuge

South of Burns, covering 290 sq miles of lake, wetland and uplands, is this important breeding and resting refuge for birds traveling along the Pacific Flyway. Over 320 species can be observed here, including swans, loons, grebes, pelicans, herons, egrets, spoonbills, ibis, woodpeckers, flycatchers, warblers, finches and many raptors. It's a veritable birdwatchers' paradise. Waterfowl migration at Malheur peaks in March, shorebirds arrive in April and songbirds wing-in during May. During summer, waterfowl families skim across the ponds and lakes. In fall, birds come through on their way south. Mosquitoes are bad from June to August, so bring repellent.

There's limited gas at the Narrows RV Park and in Frenchglen, but it's best to fill up in Burns.

◉ Sights & Activities

The refuge's two big, shallow lakes attract waterfowl, but the best place for wildlife-viewing is often south along the Donner und Blitzen River, where wide, grassy marshes and ponds shelter many animals. The gravel Central Patrol Rd runs between the refuge headquarters and Frenchglen, paralleling the river and providing some 40 miles of good access into the backcountry. A few walks (most of them short) lead to ponds, a canal and a reservoir; many are along the Central Patrol Rd. Snag a brochure at the refuge headquarters for details.

Adjacent to the wildlife refuge, 55 miles south of Burns and east of Hwy 205, is Diamond Craters, a geographically interesting and concentrated area of volcanic craters, cinder cones and other lava formations that were formed as recently as 2500 years ago. Pick up a brochure for a self-guided tour from various tourist locations to sniff out the highlights.

Northeast of the Diamond Craters area and a mile off Lava Bed Rd is Pete French's Round Barn (1883), a historic 100ft-wide structure used to train draft horses. A nearby visitors center and gift shop (☑541-493-2070; www.roundbarn.net; 51955 Lava Bed Rd; ⊗9am-5pm, limited hours outside summer) is run by friendly Dick Jenkins, who has owned the Round Barn and conducted past tours; he's a wealth of local information.

🛏 Sleeping & Eating

Hotel Diamond   B&B $
(☑541-493-1898; www.historichoteldiamond.com; 49130 Main St; d $81-105; ⊗Mar-Oct; ❈ 🛜 ❈) This atmospheric hotel, in the hamlet of Diamond, is decorated with antiques and offers eight lovely rooms with quilt bedspreads. Both new and older rooms are available, and some share baths. Continental breakfast is included, with other meals available to guests and visitors alike (reservations required for dinner).

Narrows RV Park   CAMPGROUND $
(☑541-495-2006; www.thenarrowsrvpark.com; 33468 Sodhouse Lane; tent sites $12, RV sites $26-28; 🛜 ❈) At the junction of Hwy 205 and Sodhouse Lane, 28 miles south of Burns, this cheery RV park offers campers a desert refuge. There's a restaurant, 'saloon,' convenience store, espresso shop and gas. You can even stay in a yurt ($38; reserve in advance).

Malheur Field Station   HOSTEL, TRAILER PARK $
(☑541-493-2629; www.malheurfieldstation.org; 34848 Sodhouse Lane; RV sites $19, dm $22-30, trailer d $70-90; ⊗May-Sep; ❈ 🛜 ❈) About 4.5 miles west of the Refuge Headquarters, on a gravel side road, this collection of rustic buildings offers RV hookups, simple dormitories, kitchenette trailers and no-nonsense meals. Bring your own bedding, a towel, toiletries and a flashlight – lights out at 10pm for star-gazing! It's best for those who like to be out in nature, without many amenities. Reserve way ahead (especially for meals) as staffing is limited; educational courses and bird-guiding available.

❶ Information

Refuge Headquarters & Visitors Center
(☑541-493-2612; www.fws.gov/malheur; 36391 Sodhouse Lane; ⊗8am-4pm, limited hours outside summer) Six miles east of Hwy 205, this center on Sodhouse Lane has information, maps, a little museum and good bird-watching for songbirds.

Steens Mountain

The highest peak in southeastern Oregon, Steens Mountain (9773ft) is part of a massive, 30-mile-long fault-block range that was formed about 15 million years ago. On the western slope of the range, Ice Age glaciers bulldozed trenches that formed massive U-shaped gorges and hanging valleys. To the east, 'the Steens' – as the range is usually referred to – drop off to the Alvord Desert, 5000ft below.

Sights & Activities

Beginning in Frenchglen, the 56-mile, gravel **Steens Mountain Loop Road** is Oregon's highest road and offers the range's best sights, with awesome overlooks and access to camping and hiking trails. You'll see sagebrush, bands of juniper and aspen forests, and finally fragile rocky tundra at the top. **Kiger Gorge viewpoint** is especially stunning; it's 25 miles up from Frenchglen.

Road improvements have made the loop road open to most vehicles; ask at Frenchglen. It takes about two hours all the way around if you're just driving through, but you'll want to see the sights so give yourself much more time. You can also see the eastern side of the Steens via the Fields–Denio Rd, which goes through the Alvord Desert. Take a full gas tank and water, and be prepared for weather changes at any time of year.

Sleeping & Eating

Frenchglen (population 12) has one charming hotel with dining room, a small store with seasonal gas pump and not much else. There are camping options on the Steens Mountain Loop Rd, such as the BLM's pretty Page Springs. A few other campgrounds, further into the loop, are very pleasant but accessible in summer only; Page Springs is open year-round. Water is available at all of these campgrounds (sites $6 to $8). Free backcountry camping is also allowed in the Steens.

★ **Frenchglen Hotel**   HOTEL $
(541-493-2825; fghotel@yahoo.com; 39184 Hwy 205, Frenchglen; d $75-115; mid-Mar–Oct;) This historic hotel dates from the 1910s and features eight small but cute rooms, all sharing outside baths. A newer section of the hotel (called the Drovers' Inn) has five rooms, each with private bath. Dinners ($22 to $25; reservations required) are family style and served promptly at 6:30pm. Breakfast and lunch is also available, without reservations.

Steens Mountain Wilderness Resort   CAMPGROUND, CABIN $
(800-542-3765; www.steensmountainresort.com; 35678 Resort Lane, off Steens Mountain Loop Rd; tent sites $15, RV sites $25-30, cabins $65-190;) Three miles from Frenchglen, just before Page Springs campground, this 'resort' has nine decent single-wide trailers ('modular cabins') of various sizes spread out over a sparse hillside with low trees. All have kitchen areas; most require that you bring linens and bedding. Campsites and RV sites are available.

Alvord Desert

Once a large, 200ft-deep lake, the stunning Alvord Basin is now a series of playas – beige-white alkali beds that have resulted from centuries of evaporation. They alternate startlingly with sagebrush prairies and old ranches, while Steens Mountain looms dramatically to the west. The 66-mile, gravel Fields–Denio Rd (slowly being paved) between the hamlet of Fields and Hwy 78, is well maintained and open year-round.

MUSTANGS: WILD SYMBOLS OF THE WEST

One of the highlights of exploring the Steens could be spotting a herd of wild mustangs. Descended from domesticated horses that escaped from Native Americans, early Spanish explorers and pioneers, these free-roaming herds are managed by the Bureau of Landmanagement (BLM), which culls the animals (usually for adoption) to keep them healthy, maintain desired characteristics and prevent overpopulation.

Several different herds can be seen, each with their own distinctive markings. The most famous – and rarest – bunch are the Kiger mustangs, who were discovered in 1977 during a round-up and are considered to have descended directly from original Spanish stock. They number less than 100 and are generally dun in color, sometimes sporting a dark dorsal stripe and zebra-like markings on their legs. Their rugged handsomeness and vitality attracted the attention of DreamWorks, whose animated 2003 film *Spirit: Stallion of the Cimarron* was based on a Kiger mustang.

One of the best places to spot these animals is on the southern leg of the Steens Mountain Loop Rd. Keep your eyes peeled as you explore this area – if luck is on your side, you may get a glimpse of these wild symbols of the West.

About 23 miles north of Fields is rustic but worthy Alvord Hot Springs (fee $5); look for the small metal shelter 100yd off the road. Some 30 miles north of Fields, a side road goes a few miles to Mickey Hot Springs, a miniature Yellowstone with bubbling mud pots, steam vents and – beware – pools too hot for bathing (keep dogs leashed). Mann Lake, 42 miles north of Fields, offers fishing, birdwatching and primitive campsites (no water).

There's free backcountry camping around the edge of the Alvord Desert (windy). There's also camping down a dirt road directly across from Alvord Hot Springs. Bring food, water and sun protection; there are no services or cell service along the Fields–Denio Rd. For more details, contact the BLM office (p366) in Hines.

In the hamlet of Fields, Fields Station (☑ 541-495-2275; www.thefieldsstation.com; 22276 Fields Dr; ⊙ store 8am-6pm Mon-Sat, 9am-5pm Sun, cafe 8am-4:30pm Mon-Sat, 9am-4:30pm Sun) has a small store and a cafe. It's a near-mandatory stop for gas, snacks, good burgers and sublime milkshakes. Rooms are available to rent here ($65). There's also the tiny Alvord Inn (☑ 541-589-0575; www.alvordinn.com; d $70); minimum two-night stay.

Hart Mountain National Antelope Refuge

From the tiny town of Plush, Hart Mountain Rd crosses the Warner Lakes Basin, climbs into the spectacular, near-vertical Hart Mountain fault block (peak elevation over 8000ft) and emerges onto the prairie-like expanses of the Hart Mountain National Antelope Refuge. Roughly 3700 pronghorn antelope are protected within the refuge's 435 sq miles – a shadow of the millions of pronghorns that once roamed North America, but at least the population has remained steady.

Pronghorns are not true antelopes, and have horns rather than antlers, shedding only the outer hairy sheath and growing a new covering each year. Pronghorns are the world's second-fastest land animal (after the cheetah), having been clocked at more than 60mph.

The refuge also protects bighorn sheep, reintroduced to Hart Mountain in the 1950s and now living on the steep western side of the refuge. Cougar, bobcat, coyote, mule deer and a wide variety of birds (including sage grouse) inhabit the area.

Hart Mountain has an extensive network of 4WD trails and single-tracks through isolated areas, making for good hiking and mountain biking. At Petroglyph Lake, a short loop around the lake makes for great petroglyph-spotting, or hike along Skyline Drive (open in summer; 4WD vehicles only), where you have a decent chance at spotting antelope or sage grouse.

At the often unstaffed refuge headquarters (☑ 541-947-2731; ⊙ 7am-4:30pm Memorial Day-Labor Day, otherwise closed Sat & Sun) you can pick up brochures any time and use the area's only potable water and toilet facilities. Pitch a tent at the free Hot Springs Campground, about 4 miles south of HQ. There's a lovely wooded creek plus an open-air bathhouse that traps a hot spring – just the thing after a dusty day of exploring. There's an undeveloped hot-spring pool nearby.

If you're just passing through, allow two to three hours to travel the 75 miles between Plush and Frenchglen (about 50 miles is on a slow gravel surface); make sure you have plenty of gas. Call in winter or after heavy rains to check the refuge's roads are passable.

Vancouver, Whistler & Vancouver Island

Best Places to Eat

➡ Forage (p388)

➡ Hudson's on First (p412)

➡ Araxi Restaurant & Bar
(p398)

➡ Flying Pig (p388)

➡ Red Fish Blue Fish (p407)

Best Places to Stay

➡ Free Spirit Spheres (p415)

➡ Wickaninnish Inn (p420)

➡ Rosewood Hotel Georgia
(p383)

➡ Nita Lake Lodge (p397)

➡ Fairmont Pacific Rim
(p386)

Why Go?

Visitors to Canada's westernmost province are never short of superlatives when typing their travel blogs. It's hard not to be moved by looming mountains, wildlife-packed forests and uncountable kilometers of pristine coastline that slow your heartbeat like a spa treatment. But British Columbia (BC) is much more than just a nature-hugging diorama.

Cosmopolitan Vancouver is an animated fusion of cuisines and cultures from Asia and beyond, while historic Victoria and resort town Whistler have their own vibrant, alluring scenes. And for sheer character, it's hard to beat the province's kaleidoscope of quirky little communities, from the rustic Sunshine Coast to the laid-back Southern Gulf Islands.

Wherever you head, of course, the great outdoors will always be calling. Don't just point your camera at it. BC is unbeatable for the kind of life-enhancing skiing, kayaking, hiking and biking you'll want to brag about to everyone back home.

When to Go
Vancouver, BC

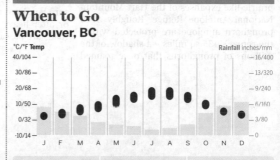

Dec–Mar Powder action stripes the slopes of Whistler and Blackcomb Mountains.

Jul & Aug Beaches, patios and a plethora of overlapping festivals enliven Vancouver.

Sep & Oct Great surfing and the start of storm-watching season lure many to Tofino.

Advance Planning

July and August make up the peak season for much of this region, so book hotels in advance during that time. The same applies in winter to popular ski-resort areas like Whistler, where the powder-loving peak is December and January. During the summer stretch, it's also a good idea to book for specific nights in top-end Vancouver restaurants and for seats at popular events like Bard on the Beach. BC Ferries services are often very busy on public-holiday weekends; if you're traveling on major routes with a car, consider booking ahead.

TRANSPORTATION

The sheer size of BC can be overwhelming. But while it's tempting to stick around Vancouver, the rest of the province will always be calling your name.

Driving remains the most popular method of movement here and you can plan your routes via the handy **Drive BC** (www.drivebc.ca). There are also dozens of scenic BC Ferries (p394) services worth checking into – many of them take cars as well as walk-on passengers.

If you're traveling without a car, **Greyhound Canada** (www.greyhound.ca) operates many services throughout the region, with major routes to Whistler and across Vancouver Island – check regional sections throughout this chapter for information on these services. There are also many additional buses operated by smaller, private operators to Whistler, between the mainland and Vancouver Island and from Vancouver to the Sunshine Coast.

VIA Rail (p395) currently operates two picturesque train routes in BC; one weaves inland from Vancouver and one trundles across the north of the province. These services connect in Jasper, Alberta. There is also a popular scenic train, the Whistler Sea to Sky Climb (p399), operated by Rocky Mountaineer. It runs from May to October between North Vancouver and Whistler.

But if you really want to see the region at its best, consider a highly scenic floatplane hop from the city to the Southern Gulf Islands, Vancouver Island or beyond. See regional sections for information on local services.

What's New

➡ Robert Bateman Centre (p404)

➡ Townsite Brewing (p401)

➡ Hudson's on First (p412)

➡ Forbidden Vancouver (p382)

IT'S OFFICIAL

BC's provincial bird is the Steller's jay and its official mammal is the Kermode, a black bear with white fur.

For Kids

➡ Science World (p378)

➡ Ucluelet Aquarium (p418)

➡ Victoria Bug Zoo (p405)

➡ Ziptrek Ecotours (p396)

British Columbia Fast Facts

➡ **Population** 4.6 million

➡ **Area** 944,735 sq km

➡ **Capital** Victoria

Resources

➡ www.hellobc.com
Official Destination BC tourism site.

➡ www.bcbeer.ca
The BC beer guide.

➡ www.discover camping.ca BC Parks' campsite booking engine.

➡ www.surfing vancouverisland.com
Profiling BC's surf scene.

➡ www.cyclingbc.net
All things cycling in BC.

➡ www.winebc.com Guide to BC's tasty wine scene.

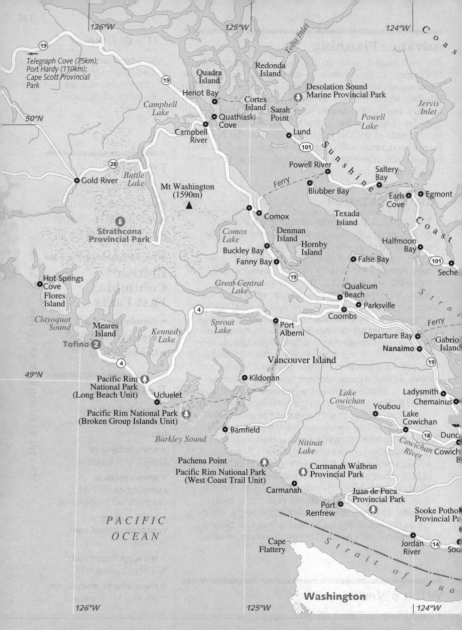

Vancouver, Whistler & Vancouver Island Highlights

❶ Stretching your legs on a breathtaking seawall stroll around Vancouver's **Stanley Park** (p375).

❷ Surfing up a storm (or just watching a storm) in **Tofino**

(p418) on Vancouver Island's wild west coast.

❸ Knocking back some lip-smacking BC craft beers at a chatty **Victoria** (p408) pub

❹ Skiing the Olympian slopes at **Whistler** (p395), then enjoying a warming après beverage in the village.

❺ Hugging the ancient trees in **Strathcona Provincial**

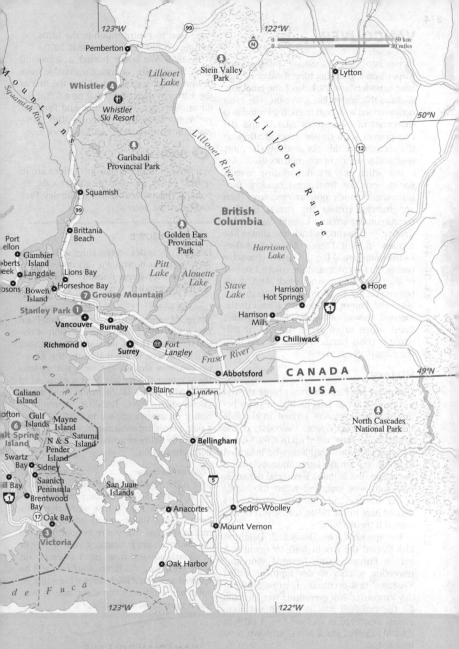

Park (p421) on a drive across Vancouver Island.

6 Puttering around Salt Spring Island's lively **Saturday Market** (p424) and scoffing

more than a few fruit and bakery treats.

7 Peering over the twinkling Vancouver cityscape from the top of **Grouse Mountain**

(p381), then hitting the Eye of the Wind tower for an even more dramatic view.

VANCOUVER

POP 666.500

Flying into YVR (Vancouver International Airport) on a glittering blue-sky day, it's not hard to understand the Lotus Land label that sticks to this region like a wetsuit. The calm ocean striped with boat trails, the crenulated shorelines of forest-green islands and the ever-present snow-dusted crags glinting on the horizon give this city arguably the most spectacular setting of any metropolis.

But while the grand backdrop means you're never far from great outdoor pursuits, there's much more to Vancouver than appearances. Hitting the streets on foot means coming across a kaleidoscope of distinctive neighborhoods, each one almost like a village in itself. There's bohemian, coffee-loving Commercial Dr; the hearty character bars of old Gastown; and the colorful streets of the West End 'gayborhood.' And that's before you get to the bustling artisan nest otherwise known as Granville Island or the forested seawall of Stanley Park, Canada's finest urban green space. In fact, if this really is Lotus Land, you'll be far too busy checking it all out to rest.

History

Historians say First Nations people thrived in this area for as long as 16,000 years before Spanish explorers arrived in the late 1500s. When Capt George Vancouver of the British Royal Navy sailed up in 1792, he met a couple of Spanish captains who informed him of their country's longstanding claim on the region. But Britain's territorial demands eventually won out, and when thousands of fur traders and gold-rush prospectors flocked here in the 1850s, the Brits officially named it their colony.

Entrepreneur John 'Gassy Jack' Deighton kick-started the city in 1867 by opening a bar on Burrard Inlet's forested shoreline, triggering a rash of development called 'Gastown' that eventually became modern-day Vancouver. Not everything went to plan for the fledgling city: it was almost completely destroyed in an 1886 fire. A prompt rebuild followed and a new downtown soon took shape.

Growing steadily throughout the 20th century, Vancouver added a National Hockey League (NHL) team and other accoutrements of a midsized North American city. Finally reflecting on its heritage, old-school Gastown was saved by gentrification in the 1970s, becoming a National Historic Site in 2010.

In 1986 Vancouver hosted a successful Expo World's Fair, sparking a massive wave of new development and adding the first of the mirrored skyscrapers that now define the downtown core. The Olympic and Paralympic Winter Games, staged here in 2010, showcased the city to a global audience once more.

◉ Sights

Vancouver's most popular attractions are in several easily walkable neighborhoods, especially Gastown, Chinatown, Stanley Park and Granville Island.

◉ Downtown

Bordered by water on two sides and Stanley Park on its tip, downtown Vancouver is centered on shop-lined Robson St, the city's main promenade.

Canada Place   LANDMARK
(Map p384; www.canadaplace.ca; 999 Canada Place Way; Ⓜ Waterfront) Vancouver's version of the Sydney Opera House, judging by the number of postcards on which it appears, this iconic landmark is shaped like sails jutting into the sky over the harbor. Now a cruise-ship terminal and convention center (next door's grass-roofed West Building convention-center expansion opened in 2010), it's also a pier, providing camera-triggering views of the North Shore mountains and some busy floatplane action.

FlyOver Canada   AMUSEMENT RIDE
(Map p384; www.flyovercanada.com; 999 Canada Pl; adult/child $20/15; ◷ 10am-9pm; Ⓜ Waterfront) Canada Place's new attraction, this breathtaking movie-screen simulator ride makes you feel like you're swooping across the entire country, waggling your legs over landmark scenery from coast to coast. En route your seat will lurch, your face will be sprayed and you'll likely have a big smile on your face. And once the short ride is over, you'll want to do it all again.

> ### CANADIAN DOLLARS
>
> Prices in this chapter are in Canadian dollars ($), except where US dollars (US$) are indicated.

**Bill Reid Gallery
of Northwest Coast Art**   GALLERY

(Map p384; www.billreidgallery.ca; 639 Hornby St;
adult/child $10/5; ⊙11am-5pm Wed-Sun; Ⓜ Bur-
rard) Showcasing carvings, paintings and
jewelry from Canada's most revered Haida
artist, this tranquil gallery is lined with fascinating and exquisite works – plus handy
touchscreens to tell you all about them. It's
centered on the Great Hall, where there's
often a carver at work, but also hit the mezzanine level: you'll be face to face with an
8.5m-long bronze of intertwined magical
creatures, complete with impressively long
tongues.

Vancouver Art Gallery   GALLERY

(Map p384; ☑ 604-662-4700; www.vanartgallery.
bc.ca; 750 Hornby St; adult/child $20/6; ⊙10am-
5pm Wed-Mon, to 9pm Tue; ☐5) The gallery has
dramatically transformed in recent years,
becoming a vital part of the city's cultural
scene. Contemporary exhibitions – often
showcasing Vancouver's renowned photo-
conceptualists – are now combined with
blockbuster international traveling shows.
Check out **Fuse** – staged every few months,
it's a quarterly late-night party where you
can hang out with the city's young arties
over wine and live music.

Vancouver Lookout   LOOKOUT

(Map p384; www.vancouverlookout.com; 555 W
Hastings St; adult/child $15.75/7.75; ⊙8:30am-
10:30pm; Ⓜ Waterfront) Expect your lurching
stomach to make a bid for freedom as the
glass elevator whisks you 169m to the apex
of this needle-like viewing tower. Once up
top, there's not much to do but check out
the awesome 360-degree vistas of city, sea
and mountains unfurling around you. For
context, peruse the historic photo panels
showing just how much the landscape has
changed.

BC Place Stadium   STADIUM

(Map p384; www.bcplacestadium.com; 777 Pacific
Blvd; Ⓜ Stadium-Chinatown) Recently renovated with a huge new crown-like retractable
roof, Vancouver's main sports arena is home
to two professional teams: the **BC Lions**
Canadian Football League (CFL) team and
the **Vancouver Whitecaps** soccer team.
Also used for major rock concerts and con-
sumer shows, it hosted the opening and
closing ceremonies for Vancouver's 2010
Winter Olympic Games. Head into the
Sports Hall of Fame and Museum to find out
more about the Games.

◉ Stanley Park

This magnificent 404-hectare park combines excellent attractions with a mystical
natural aura. Don't miss a stroll or cycle
(rentals near the W Georgia St entrance)
around the breathtaking 8.8km seawall.

Lost Lagoon   LAKE

(Map p384; www.stanleyparkecology.ca; ☐19) This
rustic area near the park's entrance was originally part of Coal Harbour. But after a cause-
way was built in 1916, the new body of water
transformed itself into a freshwater lake.
Today it's a nature sanctuary – keep your
eyes peeled for beady-eyed blue herons – and
its perimeter pathway is a favored stroll for
nature-huggers.

The excellent **Lost Lagoon Nature
House** provides exhibits and illumination
on the park's wildlife, history and ecology.

Miniature Railway   MINIATURE RAILWAY

(adult/child from $5; ⊙hours vary; ☐19) This
replica of the first passenger rail service
that rolled into Vancouver in 1887 is a firm
family favorite. It assumes three popular in-
carnations during the year: in summer, the
trundle through the trees has a First Nations
theme; it's dressed up for ghost fans at Hal-
loween; and from late November it becomes
a Christmas-decorated trundle.

Prices and hours vary depending on the
theme and time of year.

★**Vancouver Aquarium**   AQUARIUM

(☑ 604-659-3474; www.vanaqua.org; 845 Avison
Way; Jul & Aug adult/child $27/17; ⊙9:30am-6pm;
⊕; ☐19) Stanley Park's biggest draw, the
aquarium is home to 9000 water-loving
critters – including sharks, wolf eels, beluga
whales and a somewhat shy octopus. There's
also a small walk-through rainforest area of
birds, turtles and a statue-still sloth. Check
out the mesmerizing iridescent jellyfish
tanks as well as the schedule for feeding
times. The attraction's latest addition is its
4-D Experience: a 3-D movie theater with
added wind, mist and aromas.

If you're traveling with someone who
really loves marine animals, consider booking an Animal Encounter tour (from $60).

Second Beach & Third Beach   BEACH

(☐19) Second Beach is a family-friendly
area on the park's western side, with a
grassy playground, an ice-cream-serving
concession and the **Stanley Park
Pitch & Putt** course. It's also close to

Vancouver

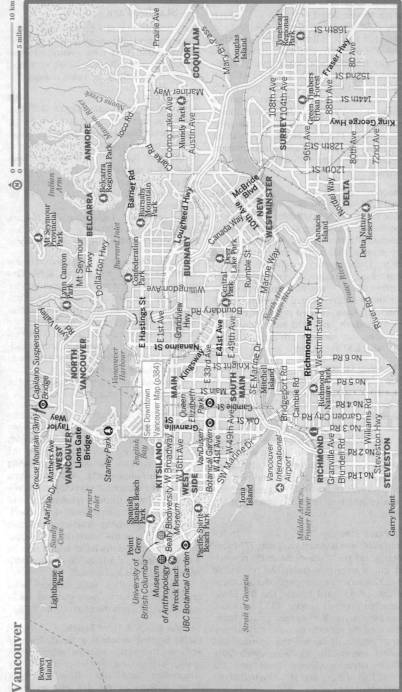

10 km
5 miles

Bowen Island

Lighthouse Park

Sandy Cove

WEST VANCOUVER

Marine Dr

Mathers Ave

Grouse Mountain (3km)

Capilano Suspension Bridge

Taylor Way

Lions Gate Bridge

NORTH VANCOUVER

Mt Seymour Provincial Park

Lynn Canyon Park

Mt Seymour Pkwy

Lynn Valley Rd

Dollarton Hwy

Indian Arm

BELCARRA

Belcarra Regional Park

Mossom Creek

Mission River

ANMORE

Ioco Rd

Noons Creek

PORT COQUITLAM

Prairie Ave

Mary Hill

Mariner Way

Douglas Island

Tynehead Regional Park

168th St

Fraser Hwy

80 Ave

152nd St

88th Ave

108th Ave

104th Ave

SURREY

144th St

Green Timbers Urban Forest

96th Ave

King George Hwy

128th St

120th St

80th Ave

72nd Ave

DELTA

Nordel Way

Delta Nature Reserve

Annacis Island

Stanley Park

Burrard Inlet

Spanish Banks Beach Park

English Bay

KITSILANO

Burrard Inlet

Clarke Rd

Barnet Rd

Burnaby Mountain Park

Confederation Park

Lougheed Hwy

BURNABY

Willingdon Ave

Canada Way

McBride Blvd

NEW WESTMINSTER

10th Ave

Deer Lake Park

Central Park

Rumble St

Marine Way

North Arm Fraser River

Fraser River

River Rd

River Rd

No 6 Rd

Richmond Fwy

Westminster Hwy

Como Lake Ave

Mundy Park

Austin Ave

E Hastings St

E 1st Ave

Grandview Hwy

Nanaimo St

Boundary Rd

E 33rd Ave

E 41st Ave

E 49th Ave

Knight St

Kingsway

Queen Elizabeth Park

MAIN

Main St

Cambie St

Oak St

SOUTH MAIN

SE Marine Dr

Mitchell Island

Bridgeport Rd

Cambie Rd

Garden City Rd

Richmond Nature Park

RICHMOND

Granville Ave

Blundell Rd

No 1 Rd

No 2 Rd

No 3 Rd

No 4 Rd

No 5 Rd

Williams Rd

Steveston Hwy

STEVESTON

Garry Point

Iona Island

Vancouver International Airport

Middle Arm Fraser River

W Broadway

W 16th Ave

WEST SIDE

Granville St

VanDusen Botanical Garden

W 41st Ave

SW Marine Dr

W 49th Ave

University of British Columbia

Point Grey

Museum of Anthropology

Wreck Beach

Beaty Biodiversity Museum

Pacific Spirit Beach Park

UBC Botanical Garden

Strait of Georgia

See Downtown Vancouver Map (p384)

Vancouver Harbour

Creperly Meadows, where free outdoor movie screenings take place in summer. Its main attraction, though, is its seasonal outdoor **swimming pool**. Alternatively, head to Third Beach for one of Vancouver's best sunset-watching spots.

West End

Dripping with wooden heritage homes and well-maintained older apartment blocks, this bustling residential neighborhood – home of Vancouver's gay community – combines seawall promenades and myriad midrange dining options.

Roedde House Museum   MUSEUM
(Map p384; www.roeddehouse.org; 1415 Barclay St; admission $5; ⊙1-4pm Tue-Fri & Sun; ☐5) For a glimpse of what the West End looked like before the apartment blocks, drop by this handsome 1893 Queen Anne–style mansion, now a lovingly preserved museum packed with antiques. Sunday entry – including tour, tea and cookies – is just $8. It's the centerpiece of Barclay Heritage Sq, a one-block site containing nine historic houses dating from 1890 to 1908.

English Bay Beach   BEACH
(cnr Denman St & Beach Ave; ☐5) Wandering south on Denman St, you'll spot a rustle of palm trees ahead announcing one of Canada's best urban beaches. Then, you'll see Vancouver's most popular public artwork: a series of oversized laughing figures that make everyone smile. There's a party atmosphere here in summer as locals catch rays and busker shows...or just ogle the volleyballers prancing around on the sand.

Yaletown

An old brick warehouse district transformed into swanky restaurants and boutiques, pedestrian-friendly Yaletown is where the city's beautiful people come to be seen.

Engine 374 Pavilion   MUSEUM
(Map p384; www.roundhouse.ca; Roundhouse Community Arts & Recreation Centre, 181 Roundhouse Mews; ⓂYaletown-Roundhouse) FREE On May 23, 1887 Engine 374 pulled Canada's first transcontinental passenger train into Vancouver, symbolically linking the country. Retired in 1945, the engine was (after many years of neglect) finally restored and placed in this lovely free-entry pavilion. Drop by for a chat with the friendly volunteers.

David Lam Park   PARK
(Map p384; www.vancouverparks.ca; cnr Drake St & Pacific Blvd; ⓂYaletown-Roundhouse) A crooked elbow of landscaped waterfront at the neck of False Creek, Yaletown's main green space is sometimes used for free alfresco summer movie screenings. It's an ideal launch point for a seawall walk along the north bank of False Creek to Science World; you'll pass intriguing public artworks and the glass condo towers that transformed the neighborhood in the 1990s.

Gastown & Chinatown

The city's oldest neighborhoods – both now National Historic Sites – are where Vancouver began. Many heritage buildings remain, most now housing cool bars, restaurants or trendy shops.

Steam Clock   LANDMARK
(Map p384; cnr Water & Cambie Sts; ⓂWaterfront) Halfway along Water St, this oddly popular tourist magnet lures the cameras with its tooting steam whistle. Built in 1977, the clock's mechanism is actually driven by electricity, while only the pipes on top are fueled by steam (this might cause a riot if you reveal it to the patiently waiting tourists). Sounding every 15 minutes, it marks each hour with little whistling symphonies.

Once you have the required photo, spend time exploring the rest of cobbled Water St – its well-preserved heritage buildings house shops, galleries and resto-bars.

Chinatown Millennium Gate   LANDMARK
(Map p384; cnr W Pender & Taylor Sts; ⓂStadium-Chinatown) Chinatown's towering entrance is the landmark most visitors look for here. Stand well back, since the decoration is mostly on its lofty upper reaches: an elaborately painted section topped with a terracotta-tiled roof. The characters inscribed on its eastern front implore you to 'Remember the past and look forward to the future.'

The gate sits on a historic site: a temporary wooden one was built here for a royal visit in 1912.

Dr Sun Yat-Sen
Classical Chinese Garden & Park   GARDENS
(Map p384; www.vancouverchinesegarden.com; 578 Carrall St; adult/child $12/9; ⊙9:30am-7pm; ⓂStadium-Chinatown) A tranquillity break from clamorous Chinatown, this intimate 'garden of ease' illustrates the Taoist symbolism behind the placing of gnarled pine trees,

winding covered pathways and ancient limestone formations. Entry includes a 45-minute guided tour – look out for the lazy turtles bobbing in the jade-colored water – where you'll learn that everything in the garden reflects balance and harmony.

If you're on a tight budget, check out the adjacent **Dr Sun Yat-Sen Park** instead. Not as elaborate as its sister, this free-entry spot is still a pleasant oasis of whispering grasses, a large fishpond and a small pagoda.

Chinatown Night Market MARKET

(Map p384; www.vancouverchinatownnightmarket. com; Keefer St, btwn Columbia & Main Sts; ⊘6-11pm Fri-Sun mid-May–early Sep; Ⓜ Stadium-Chinatown) Recently reinvented to compete with the success of larger night markets in Richmond, Chinatown's version is well worth a summer-evening visit. Cheap and cheerful trinkets still feature, but the highlight here is the food – it's like a walk-through buffet of fish balls, bubble tea and tornado potatoes. Check ahead: there's an eclectic roster of live entertainment including alfresco movie screenings.

Vancouver Police Museum MUSEUM

(Map p384; ☑ 604-665-3346; www.vancouver-policemuseum.ca; 240 E Cordova St; adult/child $12/8; ⊘9am-5pm Tue-Sat; ☐4) Illuminating the crime-and-vice-addled history of the region, this quirky museum is lined with confiscated weapons and counterfeit currency and has a former mortuary room where the walls are studded with preserved slivers of human tissue – spot the bullet-damaged brain slices. Consider a summertime Sins of the City walking tour to learn all about the area's old brothels and opium dens.

Science World MUSEUM

(Map p384; www.scienceworld.ca; 1455 Quebec St; adult/child $22.50/15.25; ⊘10am-5pm Mon-Fri, to 6pm Sat & Sun; ⑭; Ⓜ Main St-Science World) Under Vancouver's favorite geodesic dome (OK, its only one), the recently revamped science and nature showcase has added tons of new exhibition space and a cool outdoor park crammed with hands-on fun (yes, you *can* lift 2028kg). Inside there are two floors of educational play, from a walk-in hamster wheel to an air-driven ball maze and, of course, a karilloscope.

Alongside the permanent galleries, there are ever-changing visiting exhibitions and regular entertaining demonstrations of scientific principles for those who like to watch – the giant Omnimax Theatre takes that one step further.

⊙ Main Street & Commercial Drive

Home to Vancouver's hipster scene, Main St is lined with Vancouver's best indie stores and bars. There are also some cool-ass coffee shops – but you'll find even more of those further east on Commercial Dr, a funky, Bohemian strip famed for its Italian java haunts.

South False Creek Seawall WATERFRONT

(Map p384; cnr Quebec St & Terminal Ave; Ⓜ Main St-Science World) Starting a few steps from Science World, this popular waterfront trail

---

VANCOUVER FOR CHILDREN

Family-friendly Vancouver is stuffed with things to do with vacationing kids. Grab a copy of the free *Kids' Guide Vancouver* flyer from racks around town or visit www.kidsvancouver.com for tips and resources. If you're traveling without a car, hop on the SkyTrain or SeaBus transit services or the miniferry to Granville Island: kids love 'em – especially the newer SkyTrain cars, where they can sit up front and pretend they're driving. Under-fives travel free on all transit.

Stanley Park (p375) can easily keep most families occupied for a day. If it's hot, hit the water park at Lumberman's Arch or try the swimming pool at Second Beach; also consider the miniature railway. The park is a great place to bring a picnic, and its beaches – especially Third Beach – are highly kid-friendly. Save time for the Vancouver Aquarium (p375) and, if your kids have been good, consider a behind-the-scenes trainer tour. The city's other educational attractions include Science World (p378) and the HR MacMillan Space Centre (p379).

If you time your visit right, the city also has an array of family-friendly festivals, including the Pacific National Exhibition (p383), the Vancouver International Children's Festival (p382) and the fireworks fiesta known as the Celebration of Light (p383).

along False Creek's southern shoreline is about 3km long and takes you to Granville Island. You'll pass the giant **Olympic Village**, **Habitat Island** – a mini-sanctuary for passing bird life – and the dockside **Stamps Landing** area before reaching the back entrance to the island (it's actually a peninsula).

Hot Art Wet City   GALLERY

(www.hotartwetcity.com; 2206 Main St; ⊙noon-5pm Wed-Sat; ☐3) **FREE** Possibly the most fun you can have at a private gallery in Vancouver. Trip up the stairs at this funky little space and you're guaranteed some eye-popping art to look at. Mostly local artists are showcased and there's a new exhibition every month. Past themes have ranged from bizarre paintings of dolls' heads to art on beer bottles.

Grandview Park   PARK

(Commercial Dr, btwn Charles & William Sts; ☐20) The Drive's alfresco neighborhood hub is named after the smashing views peeking between its trees: to the north are the North Shore mountains, while to the west is a cityscape vista of twinkling towers. Teeming with buskers, dreadlocked drummers, impromptu sidewalk sales and and a waft or two of naughty-cigarette smoke, the park is a big summertime lure for locals.

⊙ Granville Island

Tucked under the looming Granville Bridge and studded with restaurants, bars, theaters and artisan studios, this gentrified former industrial peninsula – not actually an island – is one of Vancouver's best lazy-afternoon haunts.

★ Granville Island Public Market   MARKET

(Map p384; www.granvilleisland.com/public-market; Johnston St; ⊙9am-7pm; ☐50, ⚓miniferries) Vancouver's fave sunny-afternoon hangout, Granville Island's highlight is the Public Market, a multisensory smorgasbord of fish, cheese, fruit and bakery treats. Pick up some fixings for a picnic at nearby Vanier Park or hit the international food court (dine off-peak and you're more likely to snag a table).

Granville Island Brewing   BREWERY

(Map p384; ☏604-687-2739; www.gib.ca; 1441 Cartwright St; tours $9.75; ⊙tours noon, 1:30pm, 3pm, 4:30pm & 5:30pm; ☐50) One of Canada's oldest microbreweries offers half-hour tours where smiling guides walk you through the tiny brewing nook (production has mostly

shifted to larger premises), before depositing you in the Taproom for three 4oz samples. This will likely include the company's lager and cream ale, but if you're really lucky there'll be a small-batch seasonal made right here on the island.

⊙ Kitsilano

A former 1960s hippy haven, 'Kits' is now a pleasant neighborhood of heritage homes and browsable shops. Take a lazy afternoon stroll along store-lined W 4th Ave or hit the Vanier Park museums.

Museum of Vancouver   MUSEUM

(MOV; Map p384; www.museumofvancouver.ca; 1100 Chestnut St; adult/child $12/8; ⊙10am-5pm Fri-Wed, to 8pm Thu; ⊕; ☐22) One of the three well-established educational attractions clustered together in Vanier Park, the MOV has upped its game with cool new temporary exhibitions and regular late-opening parties aimed at an adult crowd. It hasn't changed everything, though. There are still colorful displays on local 1950s pop culture and 1960s hippie counterculture – a reminder that Kits was once the grass-smoking center of Vancouver's flower-power movement.

HR MacMillan Space Centre   MUSEUM

(Map p384; www.spacecentre.ca; 1100 Chestnut St; adult/child $15/11; ⊙10am-5pm; ⊕; ☐22) Popular with packs of marauding schoolkids – expect to have to elbow them out of the way to push the flashing buttons – this slightly dated science center illuminates the eye-opening world of space. There's plenty of fun to be had battling aliens, designing a spacecraft or strapping yourself in for a simulator ride to Mars, and there are movie presentations on all manner of spacey themes.

Drop by on Saturday evening for a date with a difference: a planetarium presentation, a mini-lecture on a hot space topic and a visit to the observatory to peek at the stars – all for $11.

Vancouver Maritime Museum   MUSEUM

(www.vancouvermaritimemuseum.com; 1905 Ogden Ave; adult/child $11/8.50; ⊙10am-5pm Tue-Sat, noon-5pm Sun; ☐22) The maritime museum combines dozens of intricate model ships, detailed re-created boat sections and some historic vessels, including the *St Roch*, a 1928 Royal Canadian Mounted Police Arctic patrol sailing ship that was the first vessel to navigate the legendary Northwest Passage in both directions.

University of British Columbia

West of Kits on a 400-hectare forested peninsula, UBC (www.ubc.ca) is the province's largest university and has a surprising number of visitor attractions.

★ Museum of Anthropology   MUSEUM
(www.moa.ubc.ca; 6393 NW Marine Dr; adult/child $16.75/14.50; ⊘10am-5pm Wed-Sun, to 9pm Tue; ⬚99B-Line) Vancouver's best museum is studded with spectacular First Nations totem poles and breathtaking carvings – but it's also teeming with artifacts from cultures around the world, from European ceramics to Cantonese opera costumes. Take one of the free daily tours for some context, but give yourself at least a couple of hours to explore on your own.

Beaty Biodiversity Museum   MUSEUM
(www.beatymuseum.ubc.ca; 2212 Main Mall; adult/child $12/8; ⊘10am-5pm; ⬚99B-Line) UBC's newest museum is also its most family-friendly. Start with the giant blue-whale skeleton in the entrance lobby, then descend to the main exhibition hall, which showcases more than two million natural-history exhibits. Check ahead for kid-friendly storytelling, puppet shows and hands-on events, and hit the on-site cafe if you need a rest from all that knowledge.

UBC Botanical Garden   GARDENS
(www.ubcbotanicalgarden.org; 6804 SW Marine Dr; adult/child $8/4; ⊘9:30am-5pm; ⬚99 B-Line, then C20) You'll find a giant collection of rhododendrons, a fascinating apothecary plot and a winter green space of off-season bloomers in this 28-hectare complex of themed gardens. Save time for the attraction's Greenheart Canopy Walkway (www.greenheartcanopywalkway.com; adult/child $20/6; ⊘9am-5pm), which lifts visitors 17m above the forest floor on a 308m guided eco tour. Walkway tickets are $20 but include garden entry.

West Side

From the heritage homes of Fairview and the strollable shops of South Granville, this area gives you several good reasons to visit.

VanDusen Botanical Garden   GARDENS
(www.vandusengarden.org; 5251 Oak St; adult/child $10.75/5.75; ⊘9am-9pm; ⬚17) The city's favorite ornamental green space, this 22-hectare, 255,000-plant idyll is a web of paths weaving through many small, specialized gardens: the Rhododendron Walk blazes with color in spring, while the Korean Pavilion is a focal point for a fascinating Asian collection. Great views of the Vancouver cityscape add photo-ready vistas. Free tours are offered daily at 2pm April to October.

Queen Elizabeth Park   PARK
(www.vancouverparks.ca; entrance cnr W 33rd Ave & Cambie St; ⬚15) The city's highest promontory – it's 167m above sea level and has panoramic views of the mountain-framed downtown skyscrapers – this 52-hectare park claims to house specimens of every tree native to Canada. Sports fields, manicured lawns and two formal gardens keep the locals happy, and you'll likely also see wide-eyed couples posing for their wedding photos.

If you want to be taken out to the ball game, the park's recently restored Nat Bailey Stadium is also a popular summer hangout for baseball fans.

Bloedel Conservatory   GARDENS
(☎604-257-8584; www.vancouverparks.ca; Queen Elizabeth Park; adult/child $6.50/3.25; ⊘9am-8pm Mon-Fri, 10am-8pm Sat & Sun; ⬚15) Cresting the hill in Queen Elizabeth Park, this lovely triodetic domed conservatory – an ideal indoor warm-up spot on a rainy day – is the area's green-fingered centerpiece. Its climate-controlled zones are home to 500 plant species, many koi carp and dozens of free-flying tropical birds, including parrots and macaws: ask for a free brochure to help you identify the exotic flora and fauna.

North Vancouver & West Vancouver

Accessed from downtown via SeaBus or the Lions Gate Bridge, the North Shore comprises the commuter community of North Vancouver plus posh 'West Van.'

Capilano Suspension Bridge   PARK
(www.capbridge.com; 3735 Capilano Rd; adult/child $34.95/12; ⊘8:30am-8pm; ⓐ; ⬚236 from Lonsdale Quay) As you walk gingerly onto one of the world's longest (140m) and highest (70m) suspension bridges, swaying gently over the roiling Capilano Canyon, remember that its thick steel cables are embedded in concrete. That should steady your feet – unless there are teenagers stamping across.

Added park attractions include a glass-bottomed cliffside walkway and an elevated canopy trail through the trees.

From May to September, Capilano makes it easy for you to get here from downtown by running a free shuttle from Canada Place and area hotels. Check the website for details.

🏃 Activities

With a reputation for outdoorsy locals who love a lip-smacking feast of rice cakes for breakfast, Vancouver is all about being active.

Grouse Mountain   SKIING
(www.grousemountain.com; 6400 Nancy Greene Way, North Vancouver; in winter adult/child $58/25; ☉9am-10pm mid-Nov–mid-Apr; 🚍236 from Lonsdale Quay) The North Shore's top outdoor hangout, family-friendly Grouse offers 26 ski and snowboard runs (including 14 night runs) in winter plus zip-lining, lumber-jack shows and grizzly-bear viewing in summer. A year-round highlight is the Eye of the Wind viewing tower. There are also a couple of dining options here, plus the infamous, ultra-steep Grouse Grind hiking route. Free shuttle from downtown in summer.

Cypress Provincial Park   HIKING
(www.bcparks.ca; Cypress Bowl Rd; ☉dawn-dusk) Around 8km north of West Van via Hwy 99, Cypress offers great summertime hikes, including the Baden-Powell, Yew Lake and Howe Sound Crest trails, which plunge through forests of cedar, yellow cypress and Douglas fir, and wind past little lakes and alpine meadows. It's also a popular area for mountain bikers, and Cypress becomes a snowy playground in winter.

Spokes Bicycle Rentals   BICYCLE RENTAL
(Map p384; www.vancouverbikerental.com; 1798 W Georgia St; adult per 1/7hr from $8.60/34.30; ☉8am-9pm; 🚍5) On the corner of W Georgia and Denman Sts, Spokes is the biggest of the bike shops crowding this stretch – these are the guys mostly responsible for all those tourists wobbling across the nearby road as though they've never ridden a bike in their lives. Spokes can also arrange guided bike tours of the city.

The park's 8.8km seawall trail is a great bike (or hiking) trail. And if you're inspired, you can follow the seawall beyond the park's perimeter and check out False Creek as well.

Ecomarine Paddlesport Centres   KAYAKING
(Map p384; ☑604-689-7575, 888-425-2925; www.ecomarine.com; 1668 Duranleau St; single kayak rental per 2/24hr $39/94; ☉9am-6pm Sun, Mon, Wed & Thu, to 9pm Tue, Fri & Sat; 🚍50) Headquartered on Granville Island, the friendly folks at Ecomarine offer guided tours (from $65) plus kayak and stand-up paddleboard (SUP) rentals. The center's **Jericho Beach branch** (☑604-222-3565; Jericho Sailing Centre, 1300 Discovery St, ☉9.30am-dusk late Apr-early Sep; 🚍4) organizes events and seminars where you can rub shoulders with local paddle nuts. And from June to September, you'll also find the outfit renting kayaks on English Bay Beach.

WHERE BRITISH COLUMBIA BEGAN

Little Fort Langley's tree-lined streets and 19th-century storefronts make it one of the Lower Mainland's most picturesque historic villages, ideal for an afternoon away from Vancouver. Its main historic highlight is the colorful **Fort Langley National Historic Site** (☑604-513-4777; www.pc.gc.ca/fortlangley; 23433 Mavis Ave; adult/child $7.80/3.90; ☉10am-4pm; 🚍501, then C62), perhaps the region's most important old-school landmark.

A fortified trading post since 1827, this is where James Douglas announced the creation of British Columbia (BC) in 1858, giving the site a legitimate claim to being the province's birthplace. With costumed re-enacters, re-created artisan workshops and a gold-panning area that's very popular with kids – who also enjoy charging around the wooden battlements – this is an ideal place for families who want to add a little education to their trip.

If you're driving from Vancouver, take Hwy 1 east for 40km, then take the 232nd St exit north. Follow the signs along 232nd St until you reach the stop sign at Glover Rd. Turn right here and continue into the village. Turn right again on Mavis Ave, just before the railway tracks. The fort's parking lot is at the end of the street.

Grouse Grind
RUNNING

If you really want a workout, try North Vancouver's Grouse Grind, a steep, sweat-triggering slog up the side of Grouse Mountain that's nicknamed 'Mother Nature's Stairmaster'. Reward yourself at the top with free access to the resort's facilities – although you'll have to pay $10 to get down via the Skyride gondola.

Windsure Adventure Watersports
WATER SPORTS

(☑604-224-0615; www.windsure.com; 1300 Discovery St; ☺9am-8:30pm Apr-Sep; ☐4) For those who want to be at one with the sea breeze, Windsure specializes in windsurfing, skimboarding and SUP for a variety of skill levels. Prices are reasonable (for example, one-day skimboard rental is under $25) and the venue is inside the Jericho Sailing Centre, home of the city's recreational aquatic community.

🖝 Tours

★ Forbidden Vancouver
WALKING TOUR

(www.forbiddenvancouver.ca; adult/concession $22/19; ☺Apr-Nov) This quirky company offers highly entertaining tours: a delve into Prohibition-era Vancouver and a poke around the seedy underbelly of historic Gastown. Not recommended for kids. Book ahead: tours fill up quickly. At the time of research, a third tour was planned to cover Granville St's colorful nightlife history.

Architectural Institute of British Columbia
WALKING TOUR

(☑604-683-8588; www.aibc.ca; tours $10; ☺Tue-Sun Jul & Aug) Local architecture students conduct these excellent one- to two-hour wanders, focusing on the buildings, history and heritage of several key Vancouver neighborhoods. There are six tours in all, and areas covered include Gastown, Strathcona, Yaletown, Chinatown, downtown and the West End.

Vancouver Foodie Tours
GUIDED TOUR

(Map p384; ☑877-804-9220; www.foodietours.ca; 1171 Alberni St; tours $69; ☺2-5pm Mon, Fri & Sat; ☐5) Of several culinary-themed strolls that have emerged in recent years, the Guilty Pleasures Gourmet Tour by Vancouver Foodie Tours is arguably the best. Your engaging host will lead you on a diverse sample-heavy stroll around downtown, taking in tastings at Chinese, Japanese and gourmet-sandwich joints, plus a wine tasting and a finale finish at the city's best gelato shop.

Harbour Cruises
BOAT TOUR

(Map p384; ☑800-663-1500, 604-688-7246; www.boatcruises.com; Denman St; adult/child $30/10; ☺May-Oct) View the city – and some unexpected wildlife – from the water on a 75-minute narrated harbor tour, weaving past Stanley Park, Lions Gate Bridge and the North Shore mountains. There's also a 2½-hour sunset dinner cruise (adult/child $79/69) with West Coast cuisine (ie salmon) and live music.

★ Festivals & Events

Chinese New Year
CULTURE

(www.vancouver-chinatown.com; ☺Jan or Feb) Festive kaleidoscope of dancing, parades and great food.

Vancouver International Wine Festival
WINE

(www.vanwinefest.ca; ☺late Mar) The city's oldest and best annual wine celebration.

Vancouver Craft Beer Week
BEER

(www.vancouvercraftbeerweek.com; ☺late May) A boozy roster of tastings, pairing dinners and tipple-fueled shenanigans.

Vancouver International Children's Festival
CHILDREN'S

(www.childrensfestival.ca; ☺late May) Storytelling, performance and activities on Granville Island.

ⓘ SAVE YOUR DOSH

The **Vanier Park Explore Pass** costs $30/24 per adult/child and covers entry to the Museum of Vancouver, the Vancouver Maritime Museum and the HR MacMillan Space Centre. It's available at each of the three attractions and can save you around $10 on individual adult entry. You can also save with the **UBC Museums and Gardens Pass**. It costs $33/28 per adult/child and includes entry to the Museum of Anthropology, the Botanical Garden, the Nitobe Memorial Garden and the Beaty Biodiversity Museum. Available at any of these attractions, it also includes discounts for the Greenheart Canopy Walkway, plus deals on campus parking, dining and shopping.

Bard on the Beach THEATER
(📞604-739-0559; www.bardonthebeach.org; ⊙ Jun-Sep) A season of four Shakespeare and Bard-related plays in Vanier Park tents.

**Vancouver International Jazz
Festival** MUSIC
(www.coastaljazz.ca; ⊙ Jun & Jul) **FREE** City-wide cornucopia of superstar shows and free outdoor events from mid-June.

Celebration of Light FIREWORKS
(www.hondacelebrationoflight.com; ⊙ late Jul) **FREE** International fireworks extravaganza in English Bay.

Pride Week CARNIVAL, PARADE
(www.vancouverpride.ca; ⊙ late Jul) Parties, concerts and fashion shows culminate in a giant pride parade.

**Pacific National
Exhibition** CULTURE, CHILDREN
(www.pne.bc.ca; ⊙ mid-Aug–Sep) Family-friendly shows, music concerts and a fairground in Hastings Park, East Vancouver.

**Vancouver International Fringe
Festival** PERFORMING ARTS
(www.vancouverfringe.com; ⊙ mid-Sep) Wild and wacky theatricals at mainstream and unconventional Granville Island venues.

Vancouver International Film Festival FILM
(www.viff.org; ⊙ late Sep-Oct) Popular two-week showcase of Canadian and international movies.

Eastside Culture Crawl CULTURE
(www.eastsideculturecrawl.com; ⊙ late Nov) East Vancouver artists open their studios for three days of wandering visitors.

🛏 Sleeping

Vancouver room rates peak in summer, but great deals abound in fall and early spring, when the weather can be almost as good. Tourism Vancouver (p394) and the province's **Hello BC** (📞800-435-5622; www.hellobc.com) provide listings and booking services.

🛏 Downtown

Samesun Backpackers Lodge HOSTEL $
(Map p384; 📞604-682-8226, 877-972-6378; www.samesun.com; 1018 Granville St; dm/r incl breakfast $35/95; @ ⚡; 🖵10) Vancouver's party hostel, the brightly painted Samesun is on the city's nightlife strip. Ask for a back room if you fancy a few hours of kip or just

head down to the on-site bar (provocatively called the Beaver) to join the beery throng. Dorms are comfortably small, and there's a large kitchen for your mystery-meat pasta dishes. Continental breakfast is included.

**Urban Hideaway
Guesthouse** GUESTHOUSE $$
(Map p384; 📞604-694-0600; www.urban-hideaway.com; 581 Richards St; d with shared bath $109, ste $159; @; 🅼Granville) This cozy but fiendishly well-hidden guesthouse is a word-of-mouth favorite in the heart of the city. Tuck yourself into one of the comfy rooms (the loft is recommended) or spend your time in the lounge areas downstairs. There are laundry facilities, a computer that's free to use and loaner bikes that are also gratis. Baths are mostly shared; the loft's bath is private.

Victorian Hotel HOTEL $$
(Map p384; 📞877-681-6369, 604-681-6369; www.victorianhotel.ca; 514 Homer St; r incl breakfast with shared/private bath $99/159; @ ⚡; 🅼Granville) The high-ceilinged rooms at this popular Euro-style heritage-building hotel combine glossy hardwood floors, a sprinkling of antiques, an occasional bay window and plenty of historical charm. The best rooms are in the renovated extension, where raindrop showers, marble bathroom floors and flat-screen TVs add a slice of luxe. Rates include continental breakfast, and rooms are provided with fans in summer.

⭐**St Regis Hotel** BOUTIQUE HOTEL $$$
(Map p384; 📞604-681-1135, 800-770-7929; www.stregishotel.com; 602 Dunsmuir St; d incl breakfast $220; ❄ @ ⚡; 🅼Granville) Transformed in recent years, the St Regis is now an art-lined boutique hotel in a 1913 heritage shell. Befitting its age, almost all the rooms seem to be a different size, and they exhibit a loungey élan with leather-look wallpaper, earth-toned bedspreads, flatscreen TVs and multimedia hubs. Rates include cooked breakfast, access to the nearby gym and free international phone calls.

Rosewood Hotel Georgia HOTEL $$$
(Map p384; 📞604-682-5566; www.rosewoodhotels.com; 801 W Georgia St; d $410; ❄ @ ⚡ ❄; 🅼Vancouver City Centre) Vancouver's current 'it' hotel underwent a recent stunning renovation that brought the 1927-built landmark back to its golden-age glory. Despite the abstract modern art lining its public areas, the hotel's rooms take a classic, elegant approach, with warming

Downtown Vancouver

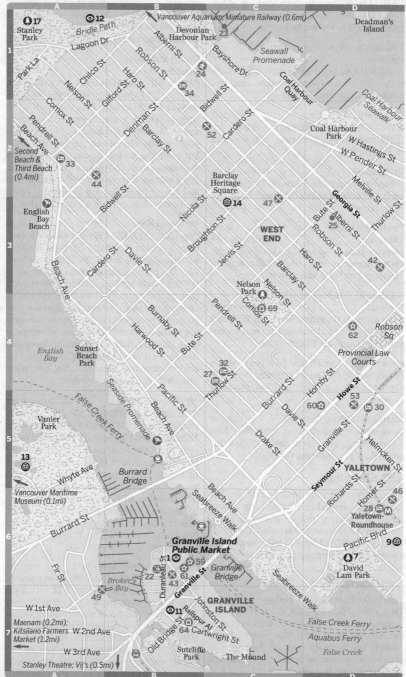

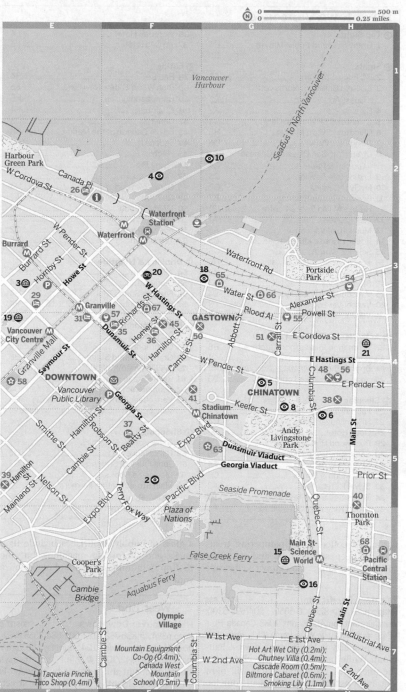

0 500 m
0 0.25 miles

Vancouver Harbour

Vancouver Harbour

SeaBus to North Vancouver

Harbour Green Park

Canada Pl

W Cordova St

26

Waterfront Station

Waterfront

Burrard

W Pender St

Burrard St

Hornby St

Howe St

3

29

19

31

Granville

Vancouver City Centre

Granville Mall

Seymour St

58

DOWNTOWN

Dunsmuir St

57

35

36

Richards St

Homer St

Hamilton St

20

W Hastings St

67

45

GASTOWN

50

Waterfront Rd

Water St

65

18

66

Blood Al

Abbott St

W Pender St

Cambie St

41

Smithe St

Hamilton St

Cambie St

Robson St

Beatty St

Nelson St

37

Georgia St

Vancouver Public Library

Portside Park

54

Alexander St

Powell St

55

E Cordova St

51

Carrall St

Columbia St

E Hastings St

48

56

E Pender St

38

6

21

5

CHINATOWN

Keefer St

8

Stadium-Chinatown

Andy Livingstone Park

Main St

Dunsmuir Viaduct

63

Georgia Viaduct

Expo Blvd

Prior St

40

Thornton Park

2

Pacific Blvd

Seaside Promenade

Plaza of Nations

Quebec St

Hamilton St

39

Mainland St

Expo Blvd

Terry Fox Way

Cooper's Park

Cambie Bridge

False Creek Ferry

Aquabus Ferry

Main St-Science World

15

Pacific Central Station

68

6

16

Olympic Village

Cambie St

W 1st Ave

W 2nd Ave

Columbia St

Quebec St

E 1st Ave

E 2nd Ave

Main St

Industrial Ave

Mountain Equipment Co-Op (0.4mi); Canada West Mountain School (0.5mi)

La Taqueria Pinche Taco Shop (0.4mi)

Hot Art Wet City (0.2mi); Chutney Villa (0.4mi); Cascade Room (0.5mi); Biltmore Cabaret (0.6mi); Smoking Lily (1.1mi)

earth and coffee tones, pampering treats such as deep soaker tubs and (in some rooms) sparkling downtown cityscape views.

Fairmont Pacific Rim   HOTEL $$$
(Map p384; ☎877-900-5350, 604-695-5300; www.fairmont.com/pacificrim; 1038 Canada Pl; d $249; ❋ ☞ ☎ ❋; Ⓜ Waterfront) This chic 377-room property is Vancouver's newest Fairmont. While many rooms have city views, the ones with waterfront vistas will blow you away, especially as you sit in your jetted tub or cube-shaped Japanese bath with

a glass of bubbly. Flourishes include iPod docks and Nespresso machines, but the rooftop swimming pool should monopolize your time.

🛏 West End

HI Vancouver Downtown   HOSTEL $
(Map p384; ☎866-762-4122, 604-684-4565; www.hihostels.ca/vancouver; 1114 Burnaby St; dm/r incl breakfast $42/108; @ ☞ ⓓ; ⌨6) It says 'downtown,' but this purpose-built hostel is on a quiet residential West End side street. Popular with older hostelers and families,

the dorms are all mercifully small. Private rooms are available. There's also bike storage, a full kitchen, and TV and games rooms, plus twice-weekly tours from April to November with legendary local guide Erik.

Sunset Inn & Suites HOTEL $$
(Map p384; ☎800-786-1997, 604-688-2474; www.sunsetinn.com; 1111 Burnaby St; ste incl breakfast $175; P ❄ @ 📶; 🚌6) A generous cut above most of the West End's self-catering suite hotels, the popular Sunset Inn offers larger-than-average rooms with full kitchenettes. Each has a balcony, and some – particularly those on south-facing higher floors – have partial views of English Bay. Rates include continental breakfast and, rare for Vancouver, free parking. The attentive staff is among the best in the city.

Sylvia Hotel HOTEL $$
(Map p384; ☎604-681-9321; www.sylviahotel.com; 1154 Gilford St; r $189; 🐾; 🚌5) Built in 1912, the ivy-covered Sylvia enjoys a prime location overlooking English Bay. Generations of guests keep coming back – many requesting the same room every year – for a dollop of old-world charm, plus a side order of first-name service. The rooms have a wide array of comfortable configurations, but best are the bedsit suites, which have kitchens and waterfront views.

Times Square Suites Hotel APARTMENT $$$
(Map p384; ☎877-684-2223, 604-684-2223; www.timessquaresuites.com; 1821 Robson St; ste $225; ❄ 📶 🐾; 🚌5) Superbly located a short walk from Stanley Park, this excellent West End hidden gem (even the entrance can be hard to spot) is the perfect apartment-style Vancouver option. Rooms are mostly one-bedroom suites and are spacious, with tubs, laundry facilities, full kitchens and superbly well-maintained (if slightly 1980s) decor. Rates include nearby gym access. There's a supermarket just across the street.

Yaletown

★YWCA Hotel HOSTEL $
(Map p384; ☎604-895-5830, 800-663-1424; www.ywcahotel.com; 733 Beatty St; s/d/tr with shared bath $73/90/117; ❄ @ 📶 👪; M Stadium-Chinatown) A good-value, well-located option offering nicely maintained (if spartan) rooms of the student-accommodations variety. There's a wide range of configurations here, from singles to five-bed rooms that are ideal for groups, and shared, semiprivate or private baths. Each room has a mini-refrigerator and guests can use the communal kitchens. Rates include access to the YWCA Health & Fitness Centre, a 10-minute walk away.

Opus Hotel BOUTIQUE HOTEL $$$
(Map p384; ☎604-642-6787, 866-642-6780; www.opushotel.com; 322 Davie St; r $299; ❄ @ 📶 🐾; M Yaletown-Roundhouse) The Opus kick-started Vancouver's boutique-hotel scene and, with its recent full-on revamp, it's still high on the city's most-stylish-sleepovers list. The spruced-up rooms have contemporary-chic interiors with bold colors, mod furnishings and feng-shui bed placements, while the luxe baths have clear windows overlooking the streets (visiting exhibitionists, take note).

Eating

Vancouver is arguably Canada's best dine-out city, combining rich ethnic dining with flourishing farm-to-table West Coast cuisine. Do not miss the seafood here.

Downtown

Finch's CAFE $
(Map p384; www.finchteahouse.com; 353 W Pender St; mains $5-10; ⏲9am-5pm Mon-Fri, 11am-4pm Sat; 🚌4) For a coveted seat at one of the dinged old tables, arrive off-peak at this sunny corner cafe that has a granny-chic look combining creaky wooden floors and junk-shop bric-a-brac. You'll be joining in-the-know hipsters and creative types who've been calling this their local for years. They come for the well-priced breakfasts (egg and soldiers: $2.95) plus freshly prepared gourmet baguette sandwiches and housemade soups.

Templeton DINER $$
(Map p384; www.thetempleton.ca; 1087 Granville St; mains $10-14; ⏲9am-11pm Mon-Wed, to 1am Thu-Sun; 👪; 🚌10) A chrome-and-vinyl '50s-look diner with a twist, Templeton chefs up plus-sized organic burgers, addictive fries, vegetarian quesadillas and perhaps the best hangover cure in town: the Big-Ass Breakfast. Sadly, the mini-jukeboxes on the tables don't work, but you can console yourself with a waistline-busting chocolate ice-cream float. Avoid weekend peak times or you'll be queuing for ages.

Chambar EUROPEAN $$$
(Map p384; ☎604-879-7119; www.chambar.com; 562 Beatty St; mains $23-33; ⏲5pm-midnight; M Stadium-Chinatown) This candlelit, brick-lined cave is a great place for a romantic

ⓘ FOOD-TRUCK FRENZY

Keen to emulate the legendary street-food scenes of Portland, OR, and Austin, TX, Vancouver jumped on the kitchen-equipped-truck bandwagon in 2010, launching a pilot scheme with 17 food carts. Now there are more than 100 and the number is growing. If you're wondering what to try and where to find them, consider favorites like TacoFino, Re-Up BBQ and Vij's Railway Express and look for vendors on downtown street corners – there are often several clustered around the Vancouver Art Gallery. For up-to-the-minute listings, opening hours and locations for street-food carts, go to www.streetfoodapp.com/vancouver.

night out. The sophisticated Belgian-esque menu includes perfectly delectable *moules et frites* (mussels and fries) and a braised lamb shank with figs that's a local dining legend. An impressive wine and cocktail list (try a blue-fig martini) is coupled with a great Belgian beer menu dripping with tripels and lambics.

Coast SEAFOOD $$$
(Map p384; ☑604-685-5010; www.coastrestaurant.ca; 1054 Alberni St; mains $18-42; ◷11:30am-1am Mon-Thu, to 2am Fri, 4pm-2am Sat, 4pm-1am Sun; ☐5) A buzzing seafood joint where Vancouver movers and shakers like to be seen scoffing a wide array of aquatic treats. Knowing reinventions of the classics include prawn or salmon flatbread pizzas, but it's the mighty seafood platter of salmon, cod, scallops and tiger prawns that sates true fish nuts. Lunchtime fish-and-chips to go costs $14, and there's also an excellent raw bar with oysters aplenty.

✕ West End

Sushi Mart JAPANESE $
(Map p384; www.sushimart.com; 1686 Robson St; sushi combos $7-18; ◷11:30am-3pm & 5-9pm Mon-Sat; ☐5) You'll be rubbing shoulders with chatty young Asians at the large communal dining table here, one of the best spots in town for a super-fresh sushi feast in a casual setting. Check the ever-changing blackboard showing what's available and then tuck into expertly prepared and well-priced shareable platters of all your fave *nigiri, maki* and sashimi treats. Udon dishes are also available.

Espana SPANISH $$
(Map p384; www.espanarestaurant.ca; 1118 Denman St; tapas plates $5-12; ◷5pm-1am Sun-Thu, to 2am Fri & Sat; ☐5) Reservations are not taken, but it's worth the line-up to get into Vancouver's best new Spanish tapas joint. The tables are crammed close and the atmosphere is warm and welcoming, triggering a hubbub of chat that's mostly centered on the great grub. The crispy squid and the cod and potato croquettes are delish, while the crispy chickpeas dish is a revelation.

★ Forage WEST COAST $$
(Map p384; ☑604-661-1400; www.foragevancouver.com; 1300 Robson St; mains $17-21; ◷6:30-10am & 5pm-midnight Mon-Fri, 7am-2pm & 5pm-midnight Sat & Sun; ☐5) ✿ A champion of the local farm-to-table scene, this sustainability-loving restaurant is the perfect way to sample the flavors of the region. Brunch has become a firm local favorite (turkey-sausage hash recommended), and for dinner the idea is to sample an array of tasting plates. The menu is innovative and highly seasonal, but look out for pork-tongue ravioli and roast bison bone marrow.

✕ Yaletown

★ Flying Pig WEST COAST $$
(Map p384; www.theflyingpigvan.com; 1168 Hamilton St; mains $18-24; ◷11:30am-midnight Mon-Fri, 10:30am-midnight Sat & Sun; Ⓜ Yaletown-Roundhouse) Yaletown's best midrange restaurant , a warm, woodsy bistro, has mastered the art of friendly service and excellent, savor-worthy dining. But since everyone else knows that, too, it's a good idea to dine off-peak to avoid the crowds. The dishes focus on seasonal local ingredients and are virtually guaranteed to make you smile: scallops and halibut are perfect, but the roast chicken is the city's best.

Blue Water Café + Raw Bar SEAFOOD $$$
(Map p384; ☑604-688-8078; www.bluewatercafe.net; 1095 Hamilton St; mains $25-44; ◷5pm-midnight; Ⓜ Yaletown-Roundhouse) Under expert chef Frank Pabst, this has become one of Vancouver's best high-concept seafood restaurants and is a highlight of Yaletown fine dining. Music gently percolates through the brick-lined, blue-hued interior, while seafood

towers, Arctic char and BC sablefish grace the tables inside and on the patio. Consider the semicircular raw bar and watch the whirling blades prepare delectable sushi and sashimi.

Gastown & Chinatown

★ **Rainier Provisions**   WEST COAST $
(Map p384; www.rainierprovisions.com; 2 W Cordova St; mains $8-12; ☺ 11am-8pm Mon-Fri, 9am-8pm Sat & Sun; ☐ 4) Revitalizing a former Gastown hotel building, this great-value cafe-bistro is a perfect fuel-up spot. Drop in for Stumptown coffee or dive into a hearty menu ranging from hot sandwich specials served with soup or salad to a heaping roast with all the extras. The sausage and roast potatoes is the winner, though – complete with local-made bangers.

Meat & Bread   SANDWICHES $
(Map p384; www.meatandbread.ca; 370 Cambie St; mains $7-9; ☺ 11am-5pm Mon-Sat; ☐ 14) Arrive early to avoid the lunchtime queue at Vancouver's favorite gourmet-sandwich shop and you might even snag one of the four tiny window perches. If not, you can hang with the hip locals at the chatty long-table, tucking into the daily-changing special, usually featuring slices of perfectly roasted local lamb, pork or chicken. The grilled-cheese sandwich is ace, too.

Campagnolo   ITALIAN $$
(Map p384; www.campagnolorestaurant.ca; 1020 Main St; mains $12-25; ☺ 11:30am-2:30pm & 5-10pm; ☐ 3) Eyebrows were raised when this contemporary Italian restaurant opened in a hitherto sketchy part of town. But intimate, minimalist Campagnolo has lured locals to make the effort to get here. And they've been rewarded with some of the city's best Italian cuisine: share some dishes, but don't miss the truffle-sausage rigatoni or the citrusy local octopus salad.

Gam Gok Yuen   CHINESE $$
(Map p384; 142 E Pender St; mains $7-14; ☺ 10:30am-8pm; ☐ 3) Try to block out the faded 1980s decor in this unassuming Chinatown dining room: the carnivorous, Hong Kong–style food is what keeps this place humming – especially the barbecued pork and duck dishes (the clammy front window of roasted meats probably gives the game away). Order at will, but make sure you include a hearty bowl of noodle soup.

★ **Bao Bei**   CHINESE $$
(Map p384; ☑ 604-688-0876; www.bao-bei.ca; 163 Keefer St; small plates $9-18; ☺ 5:30pm-midnight Mon-Sat; ☑; ☐ 3) Reinventing a Chinatown heritage building interior with funky flourishes, this hidden-gem Chinese brasserie is the area's most seductive dinner destination. Enjoying a local cult following, it brings a contemporary edge to Asian-eque, tapas-sized dishes like *shao bing*, octopus salad and crispy pork belly. There's also a tasty commitment to inventive cocktails, so don't despair if you have to wait at the bar for your table.

Main Street & Commercial Drive

Acorn   VEGETARIAN $$
(www.theacornrestaurant.ca; 3995 Main St; mains $17-19; ☺ 5:30pm-1am Tue-Thu, to 2am Fri & Sat, to midnight Sun; ☑; ☐ 3) Quickly becoming one of Vancouver's hottest vegetarian restaurants soon after its 2012 opening – hence the sometimes long wait for a table – the Acorn has since settled into being a dependable, dineresque joint for vegetarians looking for something more upscale than a mung-bean soup kitchen. Consider artfully presented dishes like beet ravioli and the excellent, crunch-tastic kale caesar salad.

Chutney Villa   INDIAN $$
(www.chutneyvilla.com; 147 E Broadway; mains $15-22; ☺ 11:30am-3pm & 5-10pm Mon-Fri, 11am-10pm Sat, 11am-9pm Sun; ☑; ☐ 9 or 99B) This warmly enveloping South Indian restaurant lures savvy Vancouverites with its lusciously spiced curries (the lamb poriyal is a favorite), best served with fluffy dosas to mop them up. There are some excellent vegetarian options, but make sure you end your meal with a hot Indian coffee, a house specialty.

Via Tevere   PIZZERIA $$
(www.viateverepizzeria.com; 1190 Victoria Dr; mains $12-19; ☺ 5-10pm Tue-Thu, to 11pm Fri & Sat, to 9pm Sun; ☐ 20) Just two blocks east from the Drive, it's worth the five-minute walk for what may well be East Van's best pizza – which is saying something, since the Drive is studded like an over-packed pepperoni pie with good pizza joints. It's run by a family with true Neapolitan roots. Check out the mosaic-tiled wood-fired oven, then launch yourself into a feast; capricciosa highly recommended.

Granville Island

★ Go Fish   SEAFOOD $
(Map p384; 1505 W 1st Ave; mains $8-14; ⊙11:30am-6:30pm Tue-Sun; ⊒50) A short stroll westwards along the seawall from the Granville Island entrance, this almost-too-popular seafood stand is one of the city's fave fish-and-chip joints, offering halibut, salmon or cod encased in crispy golden batter. The smashing (and lighter) fish tacos are also recommended, while ever-changing daily specials – brought in by the nearby fishing boats – often include scallop burgers or ahi tuna sandwiches.

★ Edible Canada at the Market   WEST COAST $$
(Map p384; ☑604-682-6681; www.ediblecanada. com/bistro; 1596 Johnston St; mains $18-29; ⊙11am-9pm Mon-Thu, to 10pm Fri-Sun; ⊒50) Granville Island's most popular bistro (book ahead) delivers a short but tempting menu of seasonal dishes from across Canada, often including perfectly prepared Alberta beef, Newfoundland fish and several BC treats (look out for slow-roasted pork belly). Consider sharing some small plates if you're feeling adventurous, perhaps topped with a naughty maple sugar pie dessert and a glass of ice wine.

Kitsilano & West Side

★ La Taqueria Pinche Taco Shop   MEXICAN $
(www.lataqueria.ca; 2549 Cambie St; 4 tacos $7-9.50; ⊙11am-8:30pm Mon-Sat; ☑; Ⓜ Broadway-City Hall) Vancouver's fave taco spot expanded from its tiny Hastings St location (which is still there) with this much larger storefront. It's just as crowded but, luckily, many of the visitors are going the take-out route. Snag a brightly painted table, then order at the counter from a dozen or so meat or veggie soft tacos (take your pick or ask for a selection), washed down with a cheap-ass beer. Service is warm and friendly here and the prices and quality ingredients are enough to keep you coming back: the tacos are $2.50 each or four for $9.50 (or just $7 if you take the vegetarian option).

Maenam   THAI $$
(☑604-730-5579; www.maenam.ca; 1938 W 4th Ave; mains $15-19; ⊙noon-2:30pm Tue-Sat & 5-10pm Mon-Sat; ☑; ⊒4) At this contemporary reinvention of the Thai-restaurant model, subtle and complex traditional and international influences flavor the menu, which invites exploration. You can start with the familiar (although even the pad Thai here is eye-poppingly different), but save room for something new: the *geng pa neua* beef curry is a sweet, salty and nutty treat.

Vij's   INDIAN $$$
(www.vijsrestaurant.ca; 1480 W 11th Ave; mains $24-30; ⊙5:30-10pm; ⊒10) Just off S Granville St, this Vancouver favorite is the high-water mark of contemporary East Indian cuisine, fusing regional ingredients, subtle global flourishes and classic ethnic flavors to produce an array of innovative dishes. The unique results range from signature wine-marinated 'lamb popsicles' to savorworthy meals like halibut, mussels and crab in a tomato-ginger curry. Reservations not accepted, which sometimes means a very long wait.

🍷 Drinking & Nightlife

Granville St, from Robson to Davie Sts, is a party district of mainstream haunts, but Gastown's brick-lined bars are far superior.

★ Alibi Room   PUB
(Map p384; www.alibi.ca; 157 Alexander St; ⊙5-11:30pm Mon-Fri, 10am-11:30pm Sat & Sun; ⊒4) Vancouver's best craft-beer tavern, this exposed-brick bar stocks an ever-changing roster of around 50 drafts from celebrated BC breweries like Phillips, Driftwood and Parallel 49. Adventurous taste-trippers – hipsters and old-lag beer fans alike – enjoy the 'frat bat' of four sample tipples: choose your own or ask to be surprised. And always check the board for ever-changing guest casks.

★ Railway Club   PUB
(Map p384; www.therailwayclub.com; 579 Dunsmuir St; ⊙4pm-2am Mon-Thu, noon-3am Fri, 3pm-3am Sat, 5pm-midnight Sun; Ⓜ Granville) A local-legend, pub-style music venue, the upstairs 'Rail' is accessed via an unobtrusive wooden door next to a 7-Eleven. Don't be put off: this is one of the city's friendliest bars and you'll fit right in as soon as you roll up to the bar – unusually for Vancouver, you have to order at the counter, since there's no table service. Live music nightly.

★ Storm Crow Tavern   PUB
(www.stormcrowtavern.com; 1305 Commercial Dr; ⊙4pm-1am Mon-Thu, 11am-1am Fri & Sat; ⊒20) Knowing the difference between Narnia and

Neverwhere is not a prerequisite for enjoying this smashing Commercial Dr nerd pub. But if you do, you'll certainly make new friends. With displays of Dr Who figures and steampunk rayguns – plus a TV that seems to be always screening *Game of Thrones* dive into the craft beer here and settle in for a fun evening.

★**Shameful Tiki Room**　　　　BAR
(www.shamefultikiroom.com; 4362 Main St; ⊙5pm-midnight Wed-Mon; ▣3) Slip through the curtains into this windowless snug and you'll be instantly transported to a Polynesian beach. The lighting – including glowing puffer-fish lampshades – is permanently set to dusk and the walls are lined with tiki masks and rattan coverings under a straw-shrouded ceiling. But it's the drinks that rock: seriously well-crafted classics from Zombies to Scorpion Bowls.

Cascade Room　　　　BAR
(www.thecascade.ca; 2616 Main St; ⊙5pm-1am Mon-Thu, to 2am Fri & Sat, to midnight Sun; ▣3) The perfect contemporary reinvention of a trad neighborhood bar, this is arguably Mt Pleasant's merriest watering hole. The top-drawer craft beer list runs from Fullers to Phillips and includes own-brand Main Street Pilsner, soon to be produced in a nearby new brewery building. Indulge in Main's best Sunday roast or hang with the locals at Monday's funtastic quiz or name-that-tune night.

Diamond　　　　COCKTAIL BAR
(Map p384; www.di6mond.com; 6 Powell St; ⊙5:30pm-1am Wed & Thu, to 2am Fri & Sat, to midnight Sun; ▣4) Head upstairs via the unassuming entrance and you'll find yourself in one of Vancouver's warmest little cocktail bars. A renovated heritage room studded with sash windows – try for a view seat – it's popular with local coolsters but rarely pretentious. A list of perfectly nailed cocktails helps (keep in mind that they're not cheap, though), coupled with a tasty tapas menu.

Fortune Sound Club　　　　CLUB
(Map p384; www.fortunesoundclub.com; 147 E Pender St; ⊙Wed-Sat; ▣3) The city's best club has transformed a tired Chinatown spot into a slick space with the kind of genuine staff and younger, hipster-cool crowd rarely seen in Vancouver venues. Slide inside and you'll find a giant dance floor bristling with party-loving locals just out for a good time. Expect weekend queues and check-out Happy End-

TOP FIVE BC BEERS

➡ Fat Tug IPA (Driftwood Brewery)

➡ Red Racer ESB (Central City Brewing)

➡ Old Jalopy Pale Ale (Powell Street Craft Brewery)

➡ Zunga Golde Blonde Ale (Townsite Brewing)

➡ Back Hand of God Stout (Crannog Ales)

ing Fridays, when you'll possibly dance your ass off. Reputedly home to one of the city's best sound systems. There's also a roster of regular bands to keep things interesting.

☆ Entertainment

Pick up Thursday's freebie *Georgia Straight* to tap into local happenings.

Live Music

★**Biltmore Cabaret**　　　　LIVE MUSIC
(www.biltmorecabaret.com; 2755 Prince Edward St; ▣9) One of Vancouver's best alt venues, the Biltmore is a firm favorite on the local indie scene. It's a low-ceilinged, vibe-tastic spot to mosh to local and touring musicians, and there are regular event nights: check the online calendar for upcoming happenings, or hit the eclectic monthly Talent Time, Wednesday's rave-like dance night or Sunday's ever-popular Kitty Nights burlesque show. If you want to socialize with the Main St locals in all their plaid-shirted glory, this is the place to be (and not just at the wildly popular monthly Ping Pong Club).

★**Commodore**　　　　LIVE MUSIC
(Map p384; www.commodoreballroom.ca; 868 Granville St; ▣10) Local bands know they've made it when they play Vancouver's best midsize venue, a restored art-deco ballroom that still has the city's bounciest dance floor – courtesy of tires placed under its floorboards. If you need a break from your moshing, collapse at one of the tables lining the perimeter, catch your breath with a bottled Stella and then plunge back in.

Cellar Jazz Club　　　　CABARET
(☎604-738-1959; www.cellarjazz.com; 3611 W Broadway; ⊙doors open 6:30pm; ▣9) A serious muso venue where you're required to keep the noise down and respect the performers

on the tiny corner stage, this subterranean 70-seat club is as close as you'll get in Vancouver to a classic jazz venue. Known for showcasing hot local performers and great touring acts, the atmospheric spot lures aficionados from across the region.

Theater & Cinemas

Scotiabank Theatre　　　　　　　CINEMA
(Map p384; www.cineplex.com; 900 Burrard St; tickets $12.50; 🚇2) Downtown's shiny multiplex was big enough to attract its own corporate sponsor when it opened in 2005 and it's the most likely theater to be screening the latest must-see *Avengers* sequel. In contrast, it also shows occasional live-broadcast performances from major cultural institutions like London's National Theatre and New York's Metropolitan Opera. Note: there are no matinee or Tuesday discounts.

Pacific Cinémathèque　　　　　　CINEMA
(Map p384; www.cinematheque.bc.ca; 1131 Howe St; tickets $11, double bills $14; 🚇10) This beloved repertory cinema operates like an ongoing film festival with a daily-changing program of movies. A $3 annual membership is required – pick it up at the door – before you can skulk in the dark with the chin-stroking movie buffs, who would name their children after Fellini and Bergman if they ever averted their gaze from the screen long enough to have relationships.

Arts Club Theatre Company　　　THEATER
(www.artsclub.com) Musicals, international classics and works by contemporary Canadian playwrights are part of the mix at this leading theater company. If you're curious about West Coast theatrics, look out for plays by Morris Panych, BC's favorite playwright son. The company's three performance spaces are the **Granville Island Stage** (Map p384; 1585 Johnston St; 🚇50), the nearby and more intimate **Revue Stage** (Map p384; 1601 Johnston St; 🚇50) and the refurbished 1930s **Stanley Theatre** (2750 Granville St; 🚇10).

★**Cultch**　　　　　　　　　　　　THEATER
(Vancouver East Cultural Centre; www.thecultch.com; 1895 Venables St; 🚇20) This once-abandoned 1909 church has been a gathering place for performers and audiences since being officially designated a cultural space in 1973. Following a comprehensive recent renovation, the beloved Cultch (as everyone calls it) is now one of Vancouver's entertainment jewels, with a busy roster of local, fringe and visiting theatrical shows from spoken word to touring Chekhov productions.

Sports

Vancouver Canucks　　　　　　　HOCKEY
(Map p384; www.canucks.com; Rogers Arena, 800 Griffiths Way; 🚇Stadium-Chinatown) The city's NHL team toyed with fans in 2011's Stanley Cup finals before losing Game 7 to the Boston Bruins, triggering riots and looting across Vancouver. But love runs deep and 'go, Canucks, go!' is still boomed out from a packed Rogers Arena at every game. Book your seat early or just head to a local bar for some raucous game-night atmosphere.

BC Lions　　　　　　　　　　　FOOTBALL
(Map p384; www.bclions.com; BC Place Stadium, 777 Pacific Blvd; tickets $32-112; ☺Jun-Nov; 🚇Stadium-Chinatown) The Lions is Vancouver's team in the CFL, a game that's arguably more exciting than its US NFL counterpart. It's had some decent showings over the past few years, winning the all-important Grey Cup championship most recently in 2011. Tickets are easy to come by – unless the boys are laying into their arch enemies, the Calgary Stampeders.

Vancouver Whitecaps　　　　　　SOCCER
(Map p384; www.whitecapsfc.com; BC Place Stadium, 777 Pacific Blvd; tickets $25-150; ☺Mar-Oct; 🚇Stadium-Chinatown) Now using BC Place Stadium as its home, Vancouver's leading soccer team plays in North America's top-tier Major League Soccer (MLS) arena. It's struggled a little since being promoted to the league in 2011, but has been finding its feet (useful for a soccer team) in recent seasons. It's a fun couple of hours – save time for a souvenir soccer-shirt purchase to impress everyone back home.

🔒 Shopping

While Robson St is fine for chain-store fashion, it's hard to beat Main St (south of 19th Ave) for indie boutiques. Gastown and Kitsilano's 4th Ave are also shopping hot spots.

★**Regional Assembly of Text**　　　　　　　　　ARTS & CRAFTS
(www.assemblyoftext.com; 3934 Main St; ☺11am-6pm Mon-Sat, noon-5pm Sun; 🚇3) This ironic antidote to the digital age lures ink-stained locals with its journals, handmade pencil boxes and T-shirts printed with typewriter motifs. Check out the tiny under-the-stairs gallery showcasing zines from around the

world, and don't miss the monthly letter-writing club (7pm, first Thursday of every month), where you can sip tea, scoff cookies and hammer away on vintage typewriters.

It's one of Vancouver's most original stores. Check out the little array of handmade self-published mini-books near the front window – where else can you read *One Shrew Too Few* and *Secret Thoughts of a Plain Yellow House*?

★ **Smoking Lily**   CLOTHING
(www.smokinglily.com; 3634 Main St; ⊙11am-6pm Mon-Sat, noon-5pm Sun; ▣3) Art-school cool rules here, with skirts, belts and halter tops whimsically accented with prints of ants, bicycles and the periodic table. Men's clothing is also (a smaller) part of the mix, with fish, skull and tractor T-shirts. It's hard to imagine a better souvenir than the silk tea cozy printed with a Pierre Trudeau likeness – ask the friendly staff for more recommendations.

John Fluevog Shoes   SHOES
(Map p384; www.fluevog.com; 65 Water St; ⊙10am-7pm Mon-Wed, to 8pm Thu & Fri, to 7pm Sat, noon-6pm Sun; Ⓜ Waterfront) Like an art gallery for shoes, this alluringly cavernous store showcases the famed footwear of local designer Fluevog, whose men's and women's boots and

---

TO MARKET, TO MARKET

A lip-smacking cornucopia of BC farm produce hits the stalls around Vancouver from June to October. Seasonal highlights include crunchy apples, lush peaches and juicy blueberries, while home-baked cakes and treats are frequent accompaniments. Don't be surprised to see zesty local cheese and a few arts and crafts added to the mix. To check out what's on offer hit the markets below and visit www.eatlocal.org for more listings.

Kitsilano Farmers Market (Kitsilano Community Centre, 2690 Larch St; ⊙10am-2pm Sun mid-May–mid-Oct; ▣4)

Main Street Station Farmers Market (Map p384; Thornton Park, 1100 Station St; ⊙3-7pm Wed Jun-Sep; Ⓜ Main St-Science World)

West End Farmers Market (Map p384; Nelson Park, btwn Bute & Thurlow Sts; ⊙9am-2pm Sat Jun–mid-Oct; ▣6)

---

brogues are what Doc Martens would have become if they'd stayed interesting and cutting edge. Pick up that pair of thigh-hugging dominatrix boots you've always wanted or settle on some designer-twisted loafers that would make anyone walk tall.

★ **Mountain Equipment Co-Op**   OUTDOOR EQUIPMENT
(www.mec.ca; 130 W Broadway; ⊙10am-7pm Mon-Wed, to 9pm Thu & Fri, 9am-6pm Sat, 11am-5pm Sun; ▣9) Grown hikers weep at the amazing selection of clothing, kayaks, sleeping bags and clever camping gadgets at this cavernous outdoors store: MEC has been encouraging fully-fledged outdoor enthusiasts for years. You'll have to be a member to buy, but that's easy to arrange for just $5. Equipment – canoes, kayaks, camping gear etc – can also be rented here.

Macleod's Books   BOOKS
(Map p384; 455 W Pender St; ⊙11am-6pm Mon-Sat, noon-5pm Sun; Ⓜ Granville) From its creaky floorboards to those skuzzy carpets and ever-teetering piles of books, this legendary locals' fave is the best place in town to peruse a cornucopia of used tomes. It's the ideal spot for a rainy-day browse through subjects from dance to the occult. Check the windows for posters of local readings and artsy happenings around the city.

Hill's Native Art   ARTS & CRAFTS
(Map p384; www.hills.ca; 165 Water St; ⊙9am-9pm; Ⓜ Waterfront) Launched in 1946 as a small trading post on Vancouver Island, the Hill's flagship store has many First Nations carvings, prints, ceremonial masks and cozy Cowichan sweaters, plus traditional music and books of historical interest. Artists are often found at work in the 3rd-floor gallery and this is a great spot to pick-up some authentic Aboriginal artworks for savoring at home.

★ **Gallery of BC Ceramics**   ARTS & CRAFTS
(Map p384; www.bcpotters.com; 1359 Cartwright St; ⊙10:30am-5:30pm; ▣50) The star of Granville Island's arts-and-crafts shops and the public face of the Potters Guild of BC, this excellent spot exhibits and sells the striking works of its member artists. You can pick up one-of-a-kind ceramic tankards or swirly-painted soup bowls – the hot items are the cool ramen-noodle cups, complete with holes for chopsticks. Well-priced art for everyone.

ℹ Information

INTERNET ACCESS

Vancouver Public Library (☏ 604-331-3603; 350 W Georgia St; ☺ 10am-9pm Mon-Thu, to 6pm Fri & Sat, noon-5pm Sun; Ⓜ Stadium-Chinatown) Free internet access on library computers as well as free wi-fi access with a wi-fi guest card from the information desk.

MEDIA & INTERNET RESOURCES

CKNW 980AM (www.cknw.com) News, traffic and talk radio station.

Georgia Straight (www.straight.com) Alternative weekly providing Vancouver's best entertainment listings. Free every Thursday.

Inside Vancouver (www.insidevancouver.ca) Stories on what to do in and around the city.

Vancouver Sun (www.vancouversun.com) Main city daily, with Thursday arts and entertainment listings pull-out.

MEDICAL SERVICES

Shoppers Drug Mart (☏ 604-669-2424; 1125 Davie St; ☺ 24hr; ☐ 6) Pharmacy chain.

St Paul's Hospital (☏ 604-682-2344; 1081 Burrard St; ☐ 22) Downtown accident-and-emergency hospital.

Ultima Medicentre (☏ 604-683-8138; www.ultimamedicentre.ca; Bentall Centre Plaza Level, 1055 Dunsmuir St; ☺ 8am-5pm Mon-Fri; Ⓜ Burrard) Appointments not necessary.

POST

Canada Post Main Outlet (Map p384; ☏ 604-662-5723; 349 W Georgia St; ☺ 8:30am-5:30pm Mon-Fri; Ⓜ Stadium-Chinatown)

TOURIST INFORMATION

Tourism Vancouver Visitors Centre (Map p384; ☏ 877-826-1717, 604-683-2000; www.tourismvancouver.com; 200 Burrard St; ☺ 8:30am-6pm; Ⓜ Waterfront) The visitor center is a large repository of resources, with a staff of helpful advisers ready to assist in planning your trip. Services and info available here include free maps, visitor guides, half-price theater tickets, accommodation and tour bookings, plus a host of glossy brochures on the city and the wider BC region.

ℹ Getting There & Away

AIR

Vancouver International Airport (YVR; www.yvr.ca) is the main West Coast hub for airlines from Canada, the US and international locales. It's in Richmond, a 13km, 30-minute drive from downtown.

Domestic flights arriving here include regular **Westjet** (☏ 888-937-8538; www.westjet.com) and **Air Canada** (www.aircanada.com) services. Linked to the main airport by free shuttle bus, the South Terminal receives BC-only flights from smaller airlines and floatplane operators.

Several handy floatplane services can also deliver you directly to the Vancouver waterfront's Seaplane Terminal. These include frequent **Harbour Air** (www.harbour-air.com) services from Victoria's Inner Harbour.

BOAT

BC Ferries (www.bcferries.com) services arrive at Tsawwassen – an hour south of downtown – from Vancouver Island's Swartz Bay (passenger/vehicle $15.50/51.25, 90 minutes) and Nanaimo's Duke Point (passenger/vehicle $15.50/51.25, two hours). Services also arrive here from the Southern Gulf Islands.

Ferries arrive at West Vancouver's Horseshoe Bay – 30 minutes from downtown – from Nanaimo's Departure Bay (passenger/vehicle $15.50/51.25, 90 minutes) and Langdale (passenger/vehicle $14.55/49.05, 40 minutes) on the Sunshine Coast.

BUS

Most out-of-town buses grind to a halt at Vancouver's **Pacific Central Station** (1150 Station St). **Greyhound Canada** (www.greyhound.ca) services arrive from Whistler (from $18, 2¾ hours), Kelowna (from $29, six hours) and beyond. Traveling via the BC Ferries Swartz Bay–Tsawwassen route, frequent **Pacific Coach Lines** (PCL; www.pacificcoach.com) services also trundle in from Victoria (from $44, 3½ hours). PCL also operates services from Whistler.

Snowbus (☏ 888-794-5511; www.snowbus.com) offers a winter-only ski-bus service to and from Whistler ($38, three hours).

Quick Coach Lines (www.quickcoach.com; ☎) runs an express shuttle between Seattle, WA, and Vancouver, departing from downtown Seattle (US$43.85, four hours) and Seattle's Sea-Tac International Airport (US$58.50, 3½ hours).

CAR & MOTORCYCLE

If you're coming from Washington state in the US, you'll be on the I-5 until you hit the border town of Blaine, then on Hwy 99 in Canada. It's about an hour's drive from here to downtown Vancouver. Hwy 99 continues through downtown, across the Lions Gate Bridge to Horseshoe Bay, Squamish and Whistler.

Coming from the east, you'll probably be on the Trans-Canada Hwy (Hwy 1), which snakes through the city's eastern end, eventually meeting with Hastings St. If you want to go downtown, turn left onto Hastings and follow it into the city center.

TRAIN

Trains trundle in from across Canada and the US at **Pacific Central Station** (1150 Station St). The Main St-Science World SkyTrain station is just across the street for connections to downtown and the suburbs.

VIA Rail (www.viarail.ca) Services arrive from Kamloops North (from $77, 10 hours), Jasper (from $167, 20 hours) and beyond.

Amtrak (www.amtrak.com; 🕿) US services arrive from Portland (from US$47, eight hours) and Seattle (from US$30, 3½ hours).

ⓘ Getting Around

TO/FROM THE AIRPORT

SkyTrain's Canada Line (adult one-way fare to downtown $7.75 to $10.50) is a transit train from the airport to downtown. Trains run every few minutes during the day and take around 25 minutes to reach downtown's Waterfront Station. If you prefer to cab it, budget $30 to $40 for the 30-minute taxi ride from the airport to your downtown hotel.

BICYCLE

With routes running across town, Vancouver is a relatively good cycling city. Cyclists can take bikes for free on SkyTrains, SeaBuses and rack-fitted transit buses. For maps and resources, see the **City of Vancouver** (www.vancouver.ca) website.

BOAT

Running mini-vessels (some big enough to carry bikes) between the foot of Hornby St and Granville Island, **Aquabus Ferries** (www.theaquabus.com; adult/child from $3/1.50) services spots along False Creek as far as Science World. Its cutthroat rival is **False Creek Ferries** (Map p384; www.granvilleislandferries.bc.ca; adult/child from $3/1.50), which operates a similar Granville Island service from the Aquatic Centre, plus additional ports of call around False Creek.

PUBLIC TRANSPORTATION

A ticket bought on any of the **TransLink** (www.translink.bc.ca) bus, SkyTrain and SeaBus services is valid for 90 minutes of travel on the entire network, depending on the zone you intend to travel in. The three zones become progressively more expensive the further you journey.

One-zone tickets are adult/child $2.75/1.75, two-zone tickets $4/2.75 and three-zone tickets $5.50/3.75. An all-day, all-zone pass costs $9.75/7.50. If you're traveling after 6:30pm or on weekends or holidays, all trips are classed as one-zone fares and cost $2.75/1.75. Children under five years travel free on all transit services.

At time of writing, a new swipeable farecard system called Compass was being installed – check the TransLink website for the latest information.

The aquatic SeaBus shuttle operates every 15 to 30 minutes throughout the day, taking 12 minutes to cross the Burrard Inlet between Waterfront Station and Lonsdale Quay. At Lonsdale there's a bus terminal servicing routes throughout North Vancouver and West Vancouver. Vessels are wheelchair accessible and bike friendly.

The SkyTrain rapid-transit network consists of three routes. The original Expo Line runs between downtown Vancouver and Surrey, via stops throughout Burnaby and New Westminster. The Millennium Line alights near shopping malls and suburban residential districts in Coquitlam and Burnaby. Opened in late 2009, the Canada Line links the city to the airport and Richmond. If you're heading for the airport from the city, make sure you board a YVR-bound train – some are heading to Richmond but not the airport.

Passengers departing on the Canada Line from the airport pay a $5 supplement on top of the regular transit fares; it's added to your fare when you buy your ticket from station vending machines. You don't have to pay the supplement when you're traveling to the airport.

TAXI

Flagging a downtown cab shouldn't take too long, but it's easiest to get your hotel to call you one. Operators include **Vancouver Taxi** (☑604-871-1111) and **Yellow Cab** (☑604-681-1111).

WHISTLER & THE SUNSHINE COAST

The winding Sea to Sky Hwy (Hwy 99) takes around 90 scenically impressive minutes to deliver you from Vancouver to Whistler. The celebrated ski resort has become equally popular as a summer destination in recent years, offering hiking, biking and adrenaline-rushing attractions.

Travelers who like to keep their tans topped up should also consider the Sunshine Coast. This 139km stretch of crenulated, mostly forested waterfront northwest of Vancouver is accessible via a 40-minute ferry ride from the outskirts of the city. Despite its proximity, it feels a million miles from Vancouver and is a popular outdoorsy destination.

Whistler

Host mountain for the 2010 Winter Olympics and nestled in the shade of the formidable Whistler and Blackcomb Mountains, this gabled village has a frosted, Christmas-card look from November to April. In summer, its outdoor expanses become an alpine treat for hikers and bikers, while zip-lining and rafting also lure the T-shirt crowd.

◉ Sights

Squamish Lil'wat Cultural Centre   MUSEUM

(www.slcc.ca; 4584 Blackcomb Way; adult/child $18/8; ⊙9:30am-5pm) ✎ This handsome, wood-beamed facility showcases two quite different First Nations groups – one coastal and one interior based. Take a tour for the vital context behind the museum-like exhibits – including four newly carved totem poles and a new upstairs gallery that includes a 1200-year-old ceremonial bowl. Ask about the summer barbecue dinners ($58) or nip to the downstairs cafe for delicious venison chili with traditional bannock.

Whistler Farmers Market   MARKET

(www.whistlerfarmersmarket.org; Upper Village; ⊙11am-4pm Sun Jun-Oct) If you're here in summer, head to the Upper Village and the plaza in front of the Fairmont Chateau Whistler for the lively Whistler Farmers Market, where you can peruse more than 50 tent-topped stands hawking everything from arts and crafts to stuff-your-face seasonal fruits and bakery treats. It's a Whistler summer highlight; arrive early for the best selection of goodies.

Whistler Museum   MUSEUM

(www.whistlermuseum.org; 4333 Main St; adult/child $7.50/4; ⊙11am-5pm) Tracing Whistler's development from wilderness outpost to Olympic resort, quirky exhibits here include a stuffed hoary marmot, a toilet-seat sailing trophy and a 2010 Games torch you can hold.

WIRED FOR FUN

Stepping out into thin air 70m above the forest floor might seem like a normal activity for a cartoon character, but Ziptrek Ecotours (www.ziptrek. com; adult/child from $99/79) zip-lining turns out to be one of the best ways to encounter the Whistler wilderness. Attached via a body harness to the cable you're about to slide down, you soon overcome your fear of flying solo. By the end of your time in the trees, you'll be turning midair somersaults, whooping like a banshee...and wanting to do it all again.

A new permanent exhibit on skiing history was also being developed on our visit. Check ahead for events (October's adult Lego party is a must) and consider the excellent by-donation village tours (1pm June to August).

🏃 Activities

With more than 40km of flower-and-forest alpine trails, most accessed via the Whistler Village Gondola, the region is ideal for those who like nature of the strollable variety. Favorite routes include the **High Note Trail**, which traverses pristine meadows and has stunning views of the blue-green waters of Cheakamus Lake. Route maps are available at the visitor center. The **Whistler Alpine Guides Bureau** (📞604-938-9242; www.whistler guides.com; 207B, 4368 Main St; adult/child from $79/59) offers guided hikes.

Whistler-Blackcomb   SKIING, SNOWBOARDING

(www.whistlerblackcomb.com; 1-day winter lift ticket adult/child $98/52) Comprising 37 lifts and crisscrossed with over 200 runs (more than half aimed at intermediate-level skiers), the Whistler-Blackcomb sister mountains were physically linked for the first time when the resort's mammoth 4.4km Peak 2 Peak Gondola opened in 2009 – it takes 11 minutes to shuttle wide-eyed powder hogs between the two high alpine areas, so you can hit the slopes on both mountains on the same day.

You can beat the crowds with an early-morning Fresh Tracks ticket ($18), which must be bought in advance at Whistler Village Gondola Guest Relations. With your regular lift ticket, it gets you an extra hour on the slopes and the ticket includes breakfast at the Roundhouse Lodge up top. Snowboard fans should also check out the freestyle terrain parks, mostly located on Blackcomb, including the Snow Cross and the Big Easy Terrain Garden.

Lost Lake   SKIING, SNOWBOARDING

(www.crosscountryconnection.bc.ca; day passes adult/child $17/8.50; ⊙8am-9pm) A pleasant stroll or free shuttle bus away from the village, Lost Lake is the hub for 22km of wooded cross-country ski trails, suitable for novices and experts alike. Around 4km of the trail is lit for additional nighttime skiing until 10pm and there's a handy 'warming hut' providing lessons and equipment rentals. Snowshoers are also well served in this area: you can stomp off on your own on 10km of trails or rent equipment and guides.

Whistler Mountain
Bike Park   MOUNTAIN BIKING

(http://bike.whistlerblackcomb.com; 1-day passes adult/child $53/31; ☺May-Oct) Colonizing the melted ski slopes in summer and accessed via the lift at the village's south end, Whistler Mountain Bike Park, at the base of Whistler Mountain, offers barreling downhill runs and an orgy of jumps, beams and bridges. You don't have to be a bike courier to stand the knee-buckling pace: easier routes are also available. But those with calves of steel should hit the spectacular **Top of the World Trail**. Outside the park area, winding trails around the region include the gentle **Valley Trail**, an easy 14km loop that encircles the village and its lake, meadow and mountain-chateau surroundings – recommended for first-timers.

🛏 Sleeping

Rates peak in winter here, but last-minute deals can still be had if you're planning an impromptu overnight from Vancouver – check the website of **Tourism Whistler** (www.whistler.com) for room sales and packages. Most hotels charge parking fees (up to $40 daily) and some also slap on resort fees (up to $25 daily) – confirm these before you book.

★HI Whistler Hostel   HOSTEL $

(☎866-762-4122, 604-962-0025; www.hihostels. ca; 1035 Legacy Way; dm/r $36/95; @🛜) Built as athlete accommodations for the 2010 Winter Olympics, this sparkling hostel is 7km south of the village near Function Junction (transit buses to/from town stop right outside). Book ahead for private rooms (with ensuites and TVs) or save by staying in a small dorm. Eschewing the sometimes institutionalized HI-hostel feel, this one has Ikea-esque furnishings, art-lined walls and a licensed cafe.

There's also a great TV room for rainy-day hunkering. But if it's fine, hit the nearby biking and hiking trails or barbecue on one of the two mountain-view decks. And when it's time to visit the village, the bus will have you there in around 15 minutes.

Riverside Resort   CAMPGROUND, CABIN $$

(☎604-905-5533;   www.riversidewhistler. com; 8018 Mons Rd; campsites/yurts/cabins $35/89/157; 🛜🏠) Beloved of in-the-know BC residents and just a few minutes past Whistler on Hwy 99, this facility-packed, family-friendly campground and RV park has elevated itself in recent years by adding

cozy cabin and yurt options. The yurts, with basic furnishings and electricity (bedding provided), are especially recommended. The resort's on-site Junction Café also serves great breakfasts.

Crystal Lodge & Suites   HOTEL $$

(☎800-667-3363,   604-932-2221;   www.crystal-lodge.com; 4154 Village Green; d/ste from $130/175; ❋🛜🏠) Not all rooms are created equal at the Crystal, forged from the fusion of two quite different hotel towers. Cheaper rooms in the South Tower are standard style – baths and refrigerators are the highlight – but those in the Lodge Wing match the handsome rock-and-beam lobby, complete with small balconies. Both share excellent proximity to restaurants and ski lifts.

Chalet Luise B&B Inn   B&B $$

(☎800-665-1998, 604-932-4187; www.chaletluise. com; 7461 Ambassador Cres; d from $125; 🕿) A five-minute trail walk from the village, this Bavarian-look pension has eight bright and sunny rooms – think pine furnishings and crisp white duvets – and a flower garden that's ideal for a spot of evening wine quaffing. Or you can just hop in the hot tub and dream about the large buffet breakfast coming your way in the morning. Free parking.

Whistler Village Inn & Suites   HOTEL $$

(☎800-663-6418, 604-932-4004; www.whistler-villageinnandsuites.com; 4429 Sundial Pl; d/ste $119/139; @🛜❋🏠) Superbly located in the heart of the village action (and a few steps from the Village Gondola), this comfy 1980s-stye hotel was renovated in recent years and now offers a wide range of sleep-over options. The studios and standard rooms are fine, but the loft suites are the way to go with their contemporary furnishings and handy kitchenettes.

Nita Lake Lodge   HOTEL $$$

(☎604-966-5700,   888-755-6482;   www.nita-lakelodge.com; 2135 Lake Placid Rd; d from $199; 🛜🏠) Adjoining Creekside railway station, and handy if you're coming up on the Rocky Mountaineer train, this swanky timber-framed lodge is perfect for a pampering retreat. Hugging the lakeside, the chic but cozy rooms feature individual patios, rock fireplaces and baths with heated floors and large tubs – some also have handy kitchens. Creekside lifts are a walkable few minutes away.

There's an excellent on-site West Coast restaurant, but a free shuttle can whisk you to the village if you want to dine further afield. Summer rates also include free-use bikes and fishing rods.

Eating

★ **Purebread** BAKERY $
(www.purebread.ca; 4338 Main St; baked goods $3-5; ☺8:30am-7pm) When this Function Junction legend finally opened a village branch, the locals came running. And they've been queuing ever since. They're here for the cornucopia of eye-rollingly-good bakery treats including salted-caramel bars, sour-cherry choc-chip cookies and the amazing Crack, a naughtily gooey shortbread cookie bar. There's savory here, too – go for the hearty homity pie.

Service is ever friendly and if you arrive just after the early-morning bake-a-thon, you can expect the aromas to lure you into tripling your purchase (at least). Wash it all down with a large coffee from Portland-based Stumptown.

Gone Village Eatery CAFE $
(www.gonevillageeatery.com; 4205 Village Sq; mains $6-12; ☺6:30am-9pm; @🤶) Aim for the only booth at this well-hidden locals' fave and tuck into a wide range of hearty, good-value comfort grub of the chili, chicken-curry and steak-and-potatoes variety – this is where many fuel up for a calorie-burning day on the slopes (have a Mars Bar coffee when you return). There are also internet computer terminals ($1 per 10 minutes).

Mexican Corner MEXICAN $$
(www.themexicancorner.ca; 4340 Lorimer Rd; mains $14-22; ☺11am-9:30pm) Bringing authentic Mexican dishes to Whistler for the first time, this chatty little corner spot (an additional larger location was being eyed during our visit) is the real deal for fans of perfect, freshly made taco, enchilada and quesadilla dishes. Go for the four-taco pastor plate (roast-pork tacos topped with a pineapple sliver), coupled with a pleasingly sour tamarind margarita.

Crêpe Montagne FRENCH $$
(www.crepemontagne.com; 4368 Main St; mains $8-24; ☺8am-10:30pm) This small, authentic and highly cozy creperie – hence the French accents percolating among the staff – offers a bewildering array of sweet and savory buckwheat crepes with fillings including ham, brie, asparagus, banana, strawberries and more (fondues are also available). Good

breakfast spot: go the waffle route and you'll be perfectly set up for an energetic day's skiing or snowboarding.

Christine's Mountain Top Dining WEST COAST $$
(☎604-938-7437; Rendezvous Lodge, Blackcomb Mountain; mains $12-22) The best of the handful of places to eat while you're enjoying a summertime summit stroll or winter ski day on the slopes at Blackcomb Mountain. Try for a view-tastic patio table and tuck into a seasonal seafood grill or a lovely applewood smoked cheddar grilled-cheese sandwich. Reservations recommended.

Araxi Restaurant & Bar WEST COAST $$$
(☎604-932-4540; www.araxi.com; 4222 Village Sq; mains $24-41; ☺5-11pm daily, plus brunch 10am-2pm Sat & Sun) Whistler's best splurge restaurant, Araxi chefs up an inventive and exquisite Pacific Northwest menu plus charming and courteous service. Try the BC halibut and drain the 15,000-bottle wine selection, but save room for dessert: a regional cheese plate or the amazing Okanagan apple cheesecake...or both.

Drinking & Nightlife

Merlin's Bar & Grill PUB
(4553 Blackcomb Way; ☺11am-1am) The best of Whistler's cavernous ski pubs, this Upper Village local also looks the part: log-lined walls, ceiling-mounted lift cars, bra-draped moose head and a large slope-facing patio. Menus (mounted on snowboard tips) cover the pub-grub classics and, although the beer is mostly of the generic Kokanee-like variety, there's usually some tasty Whistler Brewing ales available. Regular live music during peak season.

Dubh Linn Gate PUB
(☎604-905-4047; www.dubhlinngate.com; 4320 Sundial Cres; ☺8am-1am) Whistler's pubbiest pub, this dark, wood-lined joint would feel just like an authentic Ireland watering hole if not for the obligatory heated patio. Tuck yourself into a shady corner table and revive your inner leprechaun with a stout (Guinness as well as Murphys here). Even better is the (slightly pricey) BC craft brew menu and regular live music, often of the trad Irish variety.

Mount Currie Coffee Co CAFE
(www.mountcurriecoffee.com; 4369 Main St; ☺6:30am-5:30pm) A Pemberton fave that recently opened this toe-hold in the village,

FUNCTION JUNCTION

Take bus 1 southbound from Whistler village and within 20 minutes you'll be in the heart of the locals' fave neighborhood. **Function Junction** started life as a hidden-among-the-trees area where industrial businesses carried on without affecting the Christmas card-visuals of the village. But things have changed in recent years and it now resembles the early days of Vancouver's Granville Island, its industrial units slowly colonized by galleries and cafes. It's ideal for an afternoon of leisurely browsing, especially if you plan to dine. There are a couple of streets to explore here, but the best is **Millar Creek Rd**.

Start with a late breakfast at **Wild Wood Cafe** (www.wildwoodrestaurants.ca; 1085 Millar Creek Rd; mains $6-12; ☺6:30am-2pm Mon-Thu, to 3pm Fri & Sat, 9am-3pm Sun; ☎), a folky, ever-friendly neighborhood haunt where the eggs benny is recommended (it also serves up great burgers if it's lunchtime), then wander across – noticing the yarn-bombed trees en route – to **White Dog Whistler Studio Gallery** (www.white dogwhistler.com; 1074 Millar Creek Rd; ☺11am-6pm). Luna (the white dog in question) will be waiting to welcome you at the door of this smashing gallery where artist Penny Eder works. As well as displaying Penny's own work, the snob-free spot showcases the eclectic creations of dozens of local artists.

Finally, nip across to **Whistler Brewing Company** (www.whistlerbeer.com; 1045 Millar Creek Rd; tours $13.95; ☺1pm-8pm Mon-Thu, to 10pm Fri, noon-7pm Sat & Sun). The area's very own beer maker is responsible for challenging the chokehold of factory-made suds at bars in the village, and you can take a tour of the facilities here and try a few brews in the taproom – with any luck, the sought-after, winter-only Chestnut Ale will be available.

this off-the-beaten-path coffee nook (just follow Main St and you'll soon find it) is worth searching out for its perfectly prepped Intelligentsia java. Extras include hearty Pemberton beef wraps and – when you've reached your Americano limit – 'green machine smoothies.' And consider a mason-jar travel mug as a cool souvenir.

Moejoe's　　　　　　　　　　　　CLUB
(www.moejoes.com; 4155 Golfer's Approach; ☺9pm-2am Tue-Sun) Popular with the kind of under-30s who work in Whistler shops and coffeehouses, this is the best place in town if you like dancing yourself into a drooling heap. It's always crowded on Friday and Saturday nights, but if you want to mix it up with the locals, drop by on twice-a-month Wednesdays when Whistler workers roll in for free.

❶ Information

Northlands Medical Clinic (☎604-932-8362; www.northlandsclinic.com; 4359 Main St; ☺9am-5:30pm) Walk-in medical center.
Post Office (www.canadapost.ca; 4360 Lorimer Rd; ☺8am-5pm Mon-Fri, to noon Sat)
Public Library (☎604-935-8433; www. whistlerlibrary.ca; 4329 Main St; ☺11am-7pm Mon-Thu, to 5pm Fri-Sun; ☎) Free 24-hour wi-fi

(including around the building, outside opening hours). Internet-access computers are free for one hour per day.
Whistler Visitors Centre (☎800 944 7853, 604-935-3357; www.whistler.com; 4230 Gateway Dr; ☺8am-10pm) Flyer-lined visitor center with friendly staff.

❶ Getting There & Around

While most visitors arrive by car from Vancouver via Hwy 99, **Greyhound Canada** (www.greyhound.ca) buses also service the route, rolling into Creekside and Whistler village (from $14, 2¾ hours, six daily).

Pacific Coach Lines (www.pacificcoach.com) services arrive from Vancouver (from $49, two hours, five daily) and Vancouver International Airport, dropping off at Whistler hotels.

Snowbus (www.snowbus.com) operates a winter-only service from Vancouver ($38, three hours, two daily).

Trainspotters trundle into town on Rocky Mountaineer Vacations' **Whistler Sea to Sky Climb** (www.rockymountaineer.com), a picturesque coast and mountain weave from North Vancouver (from $169, three hours, daily May to mid-October).

Whistler's **WAVE** (www.busonline.ca) public buses (adult/child/one-day pass $2.50/2/7) are equipped with ski and bike racks.

Sunshine Coast

Stretching from Langdale to Lund along Hwy 101, the Sunshine Coast has an independent, island-like mentality that belies the fact that it's only a 40-minute ferry ride from West Vancouver's Horseshoe Bay. It's an easy region to explore, and there are plenty of activities to keep things lively, from kayaking to artists' studios. See **Sunshine Coast Tourism** (www.sunshinecoastcanada.com) for information.

❶ Getting There & Around

BC Ferries (www.bcferries.com) services arrive at Langdale, 6km northeast of Gibsons, from West Vancouver's Horseshoe Bay (passenger/vehicle $14.50/49, 40 minutes, eight daily).

Sunshine Coast Transit System (www.bus online.ca; adult/child $2.25/1.75) runs buses from the ferry terminal into Gibsons, Roberts Creek and Sechelt.

Malaspina Coach Lines (www.malaspina coach.com) buses arrive daily from Vancouver, via the ferry, in Gibsons ($35, two hours), Sechelt ($45, three hours) and Powell River ($66, five to six hours). Rates include ferry fares.

Gibsons

Your first port of call after docking in Langdale and driving on to town, Gibsons' pretty waterfront strip is named Gibsons Landing and it's a rainbow of painted wooden buildings perched over the marina. Drop by the **visitor center** (📞866-222-3806, 604-886-2374; www.gibsonschamber.com; 417 Marine Dr; ◷9am-5pm Jul & Aug, reduced hours low season) for information.

Putter around the rows of galleries and artisan stores here, especially along Marine Dr and Molly's Lane. Be sure to drop into the **Gibsons Public Art Gallery** (www.gib sonspublicartgallery.ca; 431 Marine Dr; ◷11am-4pm Thu-Mon), where monthly exhibitions showcase local artists – check the website for show openings.

Your best bet for a sleepover is the lovely **Bonniebrook Lodge** (📞604-886-2887; www. bonniebrook.com; 1532 Ocean Beach Esplanade; d from $200; 🐕🍽), a historic wood-built inn overlooking a quiet waterfront stretch.

Dining-wise, gourmet-seafood fans shouldn't miss **Smitty's Oyster House** (www.smittysoysterhouse.com; 643 School Rd; mains $9-23; ◷noon-late Tue-Sat, till 8pm Sun), which faces the boat-bobbing marina, for perfect fresh-catch treats. Alternatively,

amble along the pier at the nearby Government Dock for tasty tacos at the friendly, shack-like **Shed** (Government Dock; mains $6-12; ◷11am-4pm & 6-8pm).

Sechelt

The second-largest Sunshine Coast town, Sechelt isn't as funky as Gibsons and Powell River. But there are lots of outdoor-activity opportunities, plus good spots to fuel up. For information, drop by the **visitor center** (📞877-885-1036, 604-885-1036; www.sechelt visitorcentre.com; 5790 Teredo St; ◷9am-5pm).

With a good kayak launch site and a sandy, stroll-worthy beach, fir-and-cedar-forested **Porpoise Bay Provincial Park** (www.bcparks.ca) is 4km north of Sechelt via East Porpoise Bay Rd. There are trails throughout the park and an 84-site **campground** (www.discovercamping.ca; campsites $25) with handy hot showers.

If you didn't bring your kayak (or bike), **Pedals & Paddles** (📞604-885-6440; www. pedalspaddles.com; 7425 Sechelt Inlet Rd; rentals 2/24hr $32/80) organizes rentals and kayak tours of the inlet's tranquil waters.

If you like the idea of a secluded waterfront retreat, check out the two spacious suites and the cottage at **Beachside by the Bay** (📞604-741-0771; www.beachsidebythebay. com; 5005 Sunshine Coast Hwy; d $199-$239; 🛜). Facilities include full kitchens, covered outdoor hot tub and a huge private beach deck where you can spend the evening barbecuing and watching passing eagles.

And if it's time to eat, join the locals – and dive into a fresh-baked maple-cinnamon bun – at ever-buzzing **Wheatberries Bakery** (www.wheatberriesbakery.com; 5500 Wharf St; baked goods from $2; ◷7am-5pm; 🛜). Or hit the waterfront **Lighthouse Pub** (www.lighthouse pub.ca; 5764 Wharf Rd; mains $12-22), a quality neighborhood haunt where you can eavesdrop on Sunshine Coast gossip while feasting on hearty pub grub.

Powell River

A further ferry hop along Hwy 101 brings you to this funky spot, founded as a papermill town a century ago. Cooler than Sechelt and busier than Gibsons, it's well worth a sleepover.

Pick up a free heritage-buildings flyer from the **visitor center** (📞877-817-8669, 604-485-4701; www.discoverpowellriver.com; 4670 Joyce Ave; ◷9am-6pm) for a self-guided tour.

Highlights include the the the lovely **Patricia Theatre** (www.patriciatheatre.com; 5848 Ash Ave), Canada's oldest continuously operating cinema, and **Townsite Brewing** (www.townsitebrewing.com; 5824 Ash Ave; ⊘ 11am-7pm daily, tours 3pm Thu & Sat), where you can sample top tipples including Zunga Golden Blonde Ale.

It's a short stroll from the character-packed **Old Courthouse Inn** (⊅ 604-483-4000, 877-483-4777; www.oldcourthouseinn.ca; 6243 Walnut St; d from $89; ☎), occupying the town's former court chambers. Rooms are handsomely decorated with antiques.

And, at the end of the day, drop in for tacos (the 'meaty maverick' is recommended) at the tiny, bright-painted **Costa del Sol** (www.costadelsolcuisine.com; 4578 Marine Ave; mains $9.50-14; ⊘ 11:30am-9pm Sun, Mon, Wed & Thu, to 10pm Fri & Sat) – aim for a sunset-viewing spot on the patio.

VANCOUVER ISLAND

The largest populated landmass between here and New Zealand, Vancouver Island is laced with colorful, often quirky communities, many founded on logging or fishing and featuring the word 'Port' in their name.

Despite the general distaste among residents for the 'too busy' mainland, the locals are friendly and welcoming. But if you want to stay in their good books, don't refer to the place as 'Victoria Island,' a frequent mistake

BRITISH COLUMBIA'S OTHER WEST COAST TRAIL

Vancouver Island's West Coast Trail is so popular it's hard not to run into other hikers en route – that's if you can get one of the coveted daily access spots in the first place. But the Sunshine Coast offers its own under-the-radar version that many locals have only just started discovering. Running from Sarah Point to Saltery Bay, the 180km-long **Sunshine Coast Trail** is a wilderness paradise of ancient forests, stirring waterfronts and snow-capped vistas. Unlike the West Coast Trail, this one is free and reservations are not required – there are also free-use sleeping huts dotted along the route. See www.sunshinecoast-trail.com for information.

that can provoke an almost perceptible downgrading of your welcome.

While Victoria itself – the history-wrapped BC capital – is the first port of call for many, it should not be the only place you visit here. Food and wine fans will enjoy weaving through the Cowichan Valley; those craving a family-friendly enclave should hit seaside Parksville and Qualicum; outdoor-activity enthusiasts shouldn't miss surf-loving Tofino; and those who fancy an escape from the madding crowds should head for the North Island, one of BC's most rewarding wilderness areas.

For information, contact **Tourism Vancouver Island** (⊅ 250-754-3500; www.vancouverisland.travel).

Victoria

POP 84,000

With a population around 350,000 when you add in the suburbs, BC's picture-postcard capital was long touted as North America's most British city. Thankfully, its creaky attachment to Olde England has been superseded by a much more authentic local vibe in recent years.

Brightly painted Bohemian shops, wood-floored coffee bars and surprisingly innovative restaurants make this a destination well worth visiting on a short hop from Vancouver. You'll find BC's best museum, a park licked by a windswept seafront and a hefty doorstep of outdoor activities from whale-watching to kayaking and bike riding.

◉ Sights

Royal BC Museum MUSEUM
(www.royalbcmuseum.bc.ca; 675 Belleville St; adult/child from $16/10; ⊘ 10am-5pm Sun-Wed, to 10pm Thu-Sat) Start in the natural-history gallery on your visit to the province's best museum. Fronted by a beady-eyed woolly mammoth and lined with evocative dioramas – the elk peeking through trees is a favorite – next head up to the First Peoples exhibit with its fascinating mask gallery (look for a ferret-faced white man). But the highlight is the walk-through colonial street with its chatty Chinatown and detailed storefronts.

The museum hosts regular special exhibitions and also has a popular IMAX theater screening documentaries and Hollywood blockbusters.

Vancouver Island

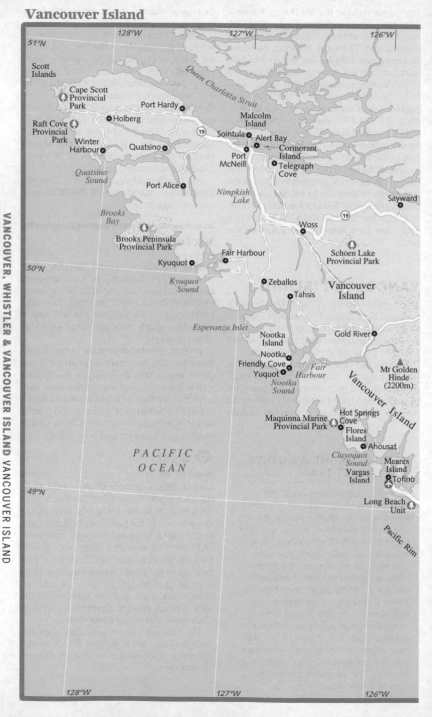

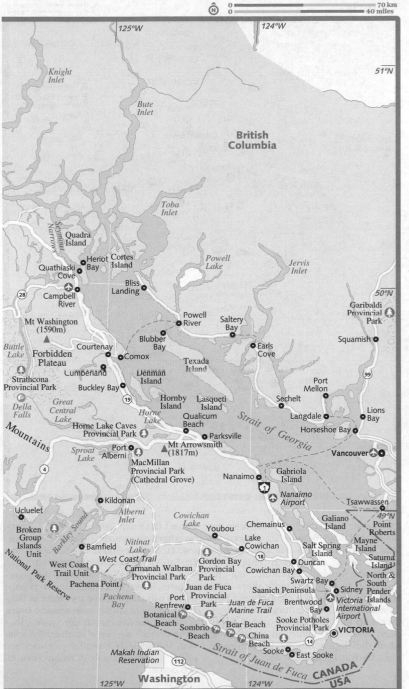

Victoria

Parliament Buildings   HISTORIC BUILDING
(www.leg.bc.ca; 501 Belleville St; ☺tours 9am-5pm) **FREE** This handsome confection of turrets, domes and stained glass is the province's working legislature, but it's also open to history-loving visitors. Peek behind the facade on a colorful (and free) 30-minute tour led by costumed Victorians, then stop for lunch at the 'secret' politicians' restaurant. Return in the evening, when the elegant exterior is illuminated like a Christmas tree.

Robert Bateman Centre   GALLERY
(www.batemancentre.org; 470 Belleville St; adult/child $12.50/8.50; ☺10am-6pm Sun-Wed, to 9pm Thu-Sat) Victoria's newest cultural attraction isn't just a gallery showcasing the photorealistic works of Canada's most popular nature painter, it's also a testament to Bateman's commitment to environmental issues. Start with the five-minute intro movie, then move through a series of small exhibit areas with 160 achingly beautiful paintings and prints showing animals in nature from BC and beyond.

Victoria

Victoria Bug Zoo ZOO
(www.bugzoo.com; 631 Courtney St; adult/child $10/7; ◉10:30am-5:30pm Mon-Sat, 11am-5pm Sun) The most fun any kid can have in Victoria without realizing it's educational. Step inside the brightly painted main room for a cornucopia of show-and-tell insect encounters. The excellent young guides talk about critters like frog beetles, dragon-headed crickets and the disturbingly large three-horned scarab beetles, and there are plenty of chances to snap shots of your kids handling the goods (under supervision).

Beacon Hill Park PARK
(www.beaconhillpark.ca; Douglas St) Fringed by crashing ocean, this waterfront park is ideal for feeling the wind in your hair – check out the windswept trees along the cliff top. You'll also find a gigantic totem pole, a Victorian cricket pitch and a marker for Mile 0 of Hwy 1, alongside a statue of Canadian legend Terry Fox. If you're here with kids, consider the popular children's farm as well (www.beaconhillchildrensfarm.ca).

Craigdarroch Castle MUSEUM
(www.thecastle.ca; 1050 Joan Cres; adult/child $13.75/5; ◉9am-7pm) An elegant turreted mansion built by a 19th-century coal baron with money to burn, this handsome 39-room landmark is dripping with period architecture and antique-packed rooms. Climb the tower's 87 steps (check out the stained glass en route) for views of the snowcapped Olympic Mountains.

Art Gallery of Greater Victoria GALLERY
(www.aggv.bc.ca; 1040 Moss St; adult/child $13/2.50; ◉10am-5pm Mon-Wed, Fri & Sat, to 9pm Thu, noon-5pm Sun) Head east of downtown on Fort St and follow the gallery street signs to one of Canada's best Emily Carr collections. Aside from Carr's swirling nature canvases, you'll find an ever-changing array of temporary exhibitions. Check online for events, including lectures, presentations and monthly late-night Urbanite socials when artsy coolsters roll in to mingle. Admission by donation on the first Tuesday of every month.

🏃 Activities

Whale-Watching
Raincoat-clad tourists head out by the boatload from Victoria throughout the May-to-October viewing season. The whales don't always show, so most excursions also visit the local haunts of lolling sea lions and portly elephant seals.

Prince of Whales
BOAT TOUR

(☎888-383-4884, 250-383-4884; www.prince
ofwhales.com; 812 Wharf St; adult/child from
$110/85) Long-established local operator.

Springtide Charters
BOAT TOUR

(☎800-470-3474, 250-384-4444; www.springtide
charters.com; 1119 Wharf St; adult/child from
$105/75) Popular local operator.

Kayaking

Paddling around the shoreline is the perfect
way to encounter this region, especially if
you spot soaring eagles and starfish-studded
beaches. You can rent equipment for your
own trek or join a tour of the area's watery
highlights.

Ocean River Adventures
KAYAKING

(☎800-909-4233, 250-381-4233; www.oceanriver.
com; 1824 Store St; rental per 2hr $40, tours from
$75; ⊙9:30am-6pm Mon-Wed & Sat, to 8pm Thu &
Fri, 10am-5pm Sun) Rentals and popular three-
hour harbor tours ($75).

Scuba Diving

The region's dive-friendly underwater ecosystem includes popular spots like Ogden
Point Breakwater and 10 Mile Point.

Ogden Point Dive Centre
DIVING

(☎250-380-9119; www.divevictoria.com; 199 Dallas
Rd; ⊙9am-6pm) Dive courses, rentals etc a
few minutes from the Inner Harbour.

VICTORIA'S STROLLABLE CHINATOWN

Start your exploration of Canada's oldest (and possibly smallest) Chinatown
at the handsome gate near the corner
of Government and Fisgard Sts. From
here, Fisgard is studded with neon
signs and traditional grocery stores,
while Fan Tan Alley – a narrow passage-
way between Fisgard St and Pandora
Ave – is a miniwarren of traditional
and trendy stores hawking cheap and
cheerful trinkets, cool used records
and funky artworks. If you crave company, consider a guided Chinatown
amble with **Discover the Past** (www.
discoverthepast.com; adult/child $15/13;
⊙10:30am Tue, Thu & Sat).

☞ Tours

Architectural Institute of BC
WALKING TOUR

(☎800-667-0753, ext 333, 604-683-8588; www.
aibc.ca; 1001 Douglas St; tours $10; ⊙10am & 1pm
Tue-Sun Jul & Aug) Six great-value, building-
themed walking tours covering angles from
art deco to ecclesiastical.

Pedaler
BICYCLE TOUR

(☎778-265-7433; www.thepedaler.ca; 719 Douglas
St; tours from $59; ⊙9am-6pm) Guided bike
tours weaving around local breweries, plus
history-themed and coffee-and-cake tour
alternatives.

CVS Cruise Victoria
BUS TOUR

(☎877-578-5552, 250-386-8652; www.cvscruise
victoria.com; 721 Government St; tours from
adult/child $30/16) With its fleet of biodiesel
coaches, CVS offers a hop-on, hop-off city
tour plus shuttles to Butchart Gardens.

☆ Festivals & Events

Victoria Tea Festival
TEA

(www.victoriateafestival.com; ⊙Feb) Huge showcase of tea and tea-making paraphenalia in
North America's cuppa-loving capital.

Victoria International JazzFest
JAZZ

(www.jazzvictoria.ca; ⊙late Jun) Ten days of toe-
tapping jazz shows.

Victoria International Buskers Festival
PERFORMING ARTS

(www.victoriabuskers.com; ⊙mid-Jul) Ten days
of street-performing action from local and
international artists.

Victoria Ska Fest
MUSIC

(www.victoriaskafest.ca; ⊙mid-Jul) Canada's
largest skank-tastic music festival.

Victoria Fringe Theater Festival
THEATER

(www.victoriafringe.com; ⊙late Aug) Two weeks
of quirky short plays and stand-ups throughout the city.

⊨ Sleeping

From heritage B&Bs to midrange motels and
swanky high-end hotels, Victoria is stuffed
with accommodations options for all budgets. Low season sees some great deals; Tourism Victoria's **room reservation service**
(☎800-663-3883, 250-953-2033; www.tourism-
victoria.com/hotels) can let you know what's
available.

HI Victoria Hostel
HOSTEL $

(☑888-883-0099, 250-385-4511; www.hihostels. ca; 516 Yates St; dm/d $30.80/88; @ 🛜) A quiet downtown hostel with two large single-sex dorms, three small co-eds and a couple of private rooms. Rates include free tea and coffee at breakfast, and there are movie nights, a large games room and a book-lined reading area to keep you occupied. Free city tours are also regularly scheduled.

Ocean Island Inn
HOSTEL $

(☑888-888-4180, 250-385-1788; www.oce-anisland.com; 791 Pandora Ave; dm/s/d from $28/40/46; @ 🛜) This funky, multicolored hostel is a labyrinth of small dorms and pri-vate rooms, some without windows. There's a large communal kitchen on the ground floor and a licensed lounge for breakfast, quiz nights and live music. There are also private, self-catering suites across town in a James Bay character house (from $121) – see www.oisuites.com for information.

Hotel Rialto
HOTEL $$

(☑250-383-4157; www.hotelrialto.ca; 653 Pandora Ave; d from $179; 🛜) Completely refurbished from the faded former budget hotel it once was, the Rialto is a well-located downtown option in an attractive century-old heritage building. Each of the mod-decorated rooms has refrigerator, microwave and flat-screen TV and some have tubs as well as showers. The lobby's popular tapas lounge is also open to non-guests. Highly solicitous staff.

Inn at Laurel Point
HOTEL $$

(☑800-663-7667, 250-386-8721; www.laurelpoint. com; 680 Montreal St; d from $169; ✻ @ 🛜 ✻ 🐾) Tucked along the Inner Harbour a short sea-side stroll from the downtown action, this friendly, art-lined and ever-comfortable ho-tel is all about the views across the water-front. Spacious rooms come with private balconies for drinking in the mesmerizing sunsets. Still owned by a local Victoria fam-ily, the inn offers a resort-like level of calm relaxation.

Swans Suite Hotel
HOTEL $$

(☑800-668-7926, 250-361-3310; www.swansho-tel.com; 506 Pandora Ave; d incl breakfast $185; 🛜🐾) This brick-built former warehouse has been transformed into an art-lined boutique hotel. Most rooms are spacious loft suites where you climb upstairs to bed in a gabled nook, and each is decorated with a comfy combination of wooden beams, rustic-chic furniture and deep leather sofas. The full kitchens are handy, but continental break-fast is included. There's also a brewpub downstairs.

Oswego Hotel
HOTEL $$$

(☑250-294-7500, 877-767-9346; www.oswegovic-toria.com; 500 Oswego St; d $205, 🛜🐾) Well hidden on a residential side street but only a short stroll from the Inner Harbour, this contemporary boutique hotel is an in-the-know favorite. Rooms come with granite floors, cedar beams and (in most units) small balconies. All have kitchens (think stainless steel) and deep bathtubs, making them more like apartments than hotel rooms. Cleverly, the smaller studio rooms have space-saving high-end Murphy beds.

Abbeymoore Manor B&B Inn
B&B $$$

(☑888-801-1811, 250-370-1470; www.abbeymoore. com; 1470 Rockland Ave; d from $199; 🛜) The handsome colonial exterior of this romantic 1912 arts-and-crafts mansion hides seven antique-lined rooms furnished with Victorian knickknacks. Some units also have kitchens and jetted tubs, and the hearty breakfast will fuel you up for a day of exploring: Craigdar-roch Castle and the Art Gallery of Greater Victoria are nearby.

Fairmont Empress Hotel
HOTEL $$$

(☑866-540-4429, 250-384-8111; www.fairmont. com/empress; 721 Government St; d $250; ✻ @ 🛜 ✻ 🐾) Rooms at this ivy-covered, century-old Inner Harbour landmark are elegant but conservative and some are quite small, yet the overall effect is grand and classy – from the Raj-style curry and cocktail restaurant to the sumptuous high tea sipped while over-looking the waterfront. Even if you don't stay, make sure you stroll through and soak up the old-world charm.

✖ Eating

Formerly dominated by tourist traps serv-ing nothing but poor-quality fish-and-chips, Victoria's dining scene has radically trans-formed in recent years. Pick up *Eat Maga-zine* (free) to see what's on the menu.

★ Red Fish Blue Fish
SEAFOOD $

(www.redfish-bluefish.com; 1006 Wharf St; mains $6-20; ⊙11:30am-7pm Mon-Thu, to 8pm Fri-Sun) On the waterfront boardwalk at the foot of Broughton St, this freight-container takeout shack serves a loyal clientele who just can't get enough of its fresh-made sustainable seafood. Highlights like scallop tacones, wild salmon sandwiches, tempura battered fish-and-chips and chunky Pacific Rim chowder all hit the spot. Find a waterfront perch to enjoy your nosh, but watch for hovering seagull mobsters.

Hernandéz
MEXICAN $

(www.hernandezcocina.com; 735 Yates St; mains $5-8; ⊙noon-8pm; ⯑) Fiendishly well hidden in an office-building lobby between Yates and View Sts, this Mexican hole-in-the-wall is a local favorite. Vegetarian options abound, but the *huarache de pollo* – thick tortilla with chicken – is legendary. Despite a recent expansion, there are never enough peak-time tables, so consider taking your butcher-paper parcel to Beacon Hill Park for a picnic. Cash only.

★ Jam Cafe
BREAKFAST $$

(www.jamcafevictoria.com; 542 Herald St; mains $8-16; ⊙8am-3pm) The locals won't tell you anything about this slightly off-the-beaten-path place. But that's not because they don't know about it; it's because they don't want you to add to the line-ups for the best breakfast in town. The delectable eggs-benny varieties are ever popular, but we also recommend the amazing (and very naughty) chicken French toast. Victorians are passionate about their brunches – it's their main social occasion – and this place is always humming. Arrive off-peak: there are no reservations and waiting for a table is common.

Legislative Dining Room
WEST COAST $$

(⯑250-387-3959; www.leg.bc.ca; room 606, Parliament Buildings, 501 Belleville St; mains $9-15; ⊙hours vary) One of Victoria's best-kept dining secrets, the Parliament Buildings has its own subsidized, old-school restaurant where MLAs (and the public) can drop by for a silver-service menu of regional dishes, ranging from salmon salads to velvety steaks and a BC-only wine list. Entry is via the security desk just inside the building's main entrance (photo ID required).

John's Place
DINER $$

(www.johnsplace.ca; 723 Pandora Ave; mains $7-16; ⊙7am-9pm Mon-Fri, 8am-4pm & 5-9pm Sat & Sun) This ever-friendly, wood-floored local hangout is lined with quirky memorabilia, and its menu is a cut above standard diner fare. They'll start you off with a basket of addictive housemade bread, but save room for heaping pasta dishes or an eggs-benny brunch. And don't leave without trying a

thick slab of pie from the case at the front. Perfect breakfast spot.

Pig BBQ Joint
BARBECUE $$

(www.pigbbqjoint.com; 1325 Blanshard St; mains $7.50-15; ⊙11am-10pm) Started as a hole-in-the-wall but now in larger new digs, this joint is all about the meat, starting with bulging, Texas-style pulled-pork sandwiches (beef-brisket and smoked-chicken variations are also offered). Go for the 'pig-size' serving if you're starving and make sure you add a side of crispy-fried mac 'n' cheese plus a draft of local Phillips Brewing beer.

Lotus Pond Vegetarian Restaurant
CHINESE $$

(www.lotuspond.webs.com; 617 Johnson St; mains $9-16; ⊙11am-3pm & 5-9pm Mon-Sat, noon-3pm & 5-8:30pm Sun; ⯑) This unassuming downtown spot was satisfying local vegetarians long before meat-free diets became fashionable. It's far superior to most Chinese eateries and has a menu that easily pleases carnivores as well as veggie types. The best time to come is lunchtime, when the busy buffet lures everyone in the vicinity. Don't miss the turnip cakes, a house specialty.

Ulla
WEST COAST $$$

(⯑250-590-8795; www.ulla.ca; 509 Fisgard St; mains $24-30; ⊙5:30-10pm Tue-Sat; ⯑) Hidden at the quiet end of Chinatown's Fisgard St, this is the best restaurant in the city to dive into perfectly prepared West Coast dining. In a wood-floored but contemporary room studded with local artworks (and cookbooks), you'll find a seasonal menu often including BC halibut or lamb plus a bounty of organic veggies – and if you're a vegetarian, the options for you are top notch.

Brasserie L'École
FRENCH $$$

(⯑250-475-6260; www.lecole.ca; 1715 Government St; mains $18-26; ⊙5:30-11pm Tue-Sat) Preparing West Coast ingredients with French bistro flare, this warm and ever-popular spot is perfect for an intimate night out. The dishes constantly change to reflect seasonal highlights like figs, salmonberries and heirloom tomatoes, but we recommend any seafood you find on the menu – plus the ever-available steak frites in a red wine and shallot sauce. Great cocktail spot, too.

🍷 Drinking & Nightlife

★ Garrick's Head
PUB

(www.bedfordregency.com; 1140 Government St; ⊙11am-11pm Mon-Thu, till midnight Fri & Sat, till

10pm Sun) A huge overhaul has transformed this once humdrum downtown pub into Victoria's best spot for trying locally made brews. Pull up a perch at the long bar and you'll be faced with 40-plus taps serving a comprehensive menu of beers from Driftwood, Phillips, Hoyne and beyond. Once or twice a month there are also guest casks to keep things lively. This is a good spot to fill up on pub grub before hitting the beer list (fish-and-chips recommended). You can also find the remnants of the old pub in the back room if you're feeling nostalgic.

Clive's Classic Lounge   LOUNGE
(www.clivesclassiclounge.com; 740 Burdett Ave; ⊙ 11am-midnight Mon-Wed, to 1am Thu & Fri, 5pm-1am Sat, to midnight Sun) Tucked into the lobby level of the Chateau Victoria Hotel, this has been the best spot in town for perfectly prepared cocktails as long as anyone can remember. Completely lacking the snobbishness of big-city cocktail haunts, this ever-cozy spot is totally dedicated to its mixed drinks menu – which means timeless classic cocktails as well as cool-ass fusion tipples that are a revelation.

★Spinnakers Gastro Brewpub   PUB
(www.spinnakers.com; 308 Catherine St; ⊙ 11am-10:30pm) One of Canada's first craft brewers, this wood-floored smasher is a short hop from downtown via Harbour Ferry. Sail in for copper-colored Nut Brown Ale and hoppy Blue Bridge Double IPA and check out the daily casks to see what's on special. Save room to eat: the menu here is true gourmet-gastropub grub.

☆ Entertainment

Check the freebie *Monday Magazine* weekly for local happenings.

Live Music
Logan's Pub   LIVE MUSIC
(www.loganspub.com; 1821 Cook St; ⊙ 3pm-1am Mon-Fri, 10am-1am Sat, 10am-midnight Sun) A 10-minute walk from downtown, this no-nonsense pub looks like nothing special from the outside, but its roster of shows is a fixture of the local indie scene. Friday and Saturday are your best bet for performances, but other nights are frequently also scheduled – check the online calendar to see what's coming up.

Theater & Cinemas
Victoria's main stages, **McPherson Playhouse** (☎ 250-386-6121; www.rmts.bc.ca; 3 Centennial Sq) and the rococo-interior **Royal Theatre** (www.rmts.bc.ca; 805 Broughton St), both offer mainstream visiting shows and performances. The latter is also the home of the **Victoria Symphony** (www.victoriasymphony.bc.ca) and **Pacific Opera Victoria** (www.pov.bc.ca).

Belfry Theatre   THEATER
(www.belfry.bc.ca; 1291 Gladstone Ave) Colonizing a restored church, this theater stages excellent contemporary productions by Canadian and international playwrights.

Cineplex Odeon   CINEMA
(www.cineplex.com; 780 Yates St) Downtown's movie-theater multiplex is within walking distance of all the action.

IMAX Theatre   CINEMA
(www.imaxvictoria.com) Screening large-format documentaries and Hollywood blockbusters, this theater is tucked into the Royal BC Museum.

🛍 Shopping

While Government St is a magnet for souvenir shoppers, those looking for more original purchases should head to the Johnson St stretch between Store and Government Sts, an old-town area lined with independent stores.

Regional Assembly of Text   STATIONERY
(www.assemblyoftext.com; 560 Johnson St; ⊙ 11am-6pm Mon-Sat, noon-5pm Sun) Vancouver's hipster stationery store has finally opened its much-anticipated Victoria branch, socked into a quirky space that resembles a hotel lobby from 1968. You'll find the same array of cool greeting cards and cool-ass journals plus the best Victoria postcards you'll ever find (postage available). Add the button-making table and typewriter stations ($2 for 20 minutes) and you'll be as happy as a shiny new paper clip.

Silk Road   TEA
(www.silkroadtea.com; 1624 Government St; ⊙ 10am-6pm Mon-Thu, to 8pm Fri & Sat, 11am-5pm Sun) A pilgrimage spot for regular and exotic tea fans, you can pick up all manner of leafy paraphernalia here. Alternatively, sidle up to the tasting bar to quaff some adventurous brews. There's also a small on-site spa where you can indulge in oil treatments and aromatherapy.

Milkman's Daughter   CLOTHING, ARTS & CRAFTS
(www.smokinglily.com; 1713 Government St; ⊙ 11am-6pm Tue-Sat, noon-5pm Sun & Mon) The

larger offshoot of Johnson St's tiny Smoking Lily, this enticing shop carries the full range of men's and women's togs and mixes in must-have arts and crafts from local and further-afield artisans (mostly also from the West Coast). It's an eclectic mix, from jewelry to pottery and buttons to notebooks, but it's easy to find something to fall in love with.

Munro's Books BOOKS
(www.munrobooks.com; 1108 Government St; ⏲9am-9pm Mon-Sat, 9:30am-6pm Sun) Like a cathedral to reading, this high-ceilinged local legend lures browsers who just like to hang out among the shelves. There's a good array of local-interest tomes as well as a fairly extensive travel section at the back on the left. Check out the piles of bargain books, too – they're not all copies of *How to Eat String* from 1972.

Ditch Records MUSIC
(www.ditchrecords.com; 784 Fort St; ⏲10am-6pm Mon-Sat, 11am-5pm Sun) In its larger new location for a couple of years now, Ditch is the locals' fave record store. Lined with tempting vinyl and furtive musos perusing releases by bands like the Meatmen and Nightmares on Wax, it's an ideal rainy-day hangout. And if it suddenly feels like time to socialize, you can book gig tickets here, too.

ℹ Information

Downtown Medical Centre (☑250-380-2210; 622 Courtney St; ⏲8:30am-5pm) Handy walk-in clinic.

Main Post Office (709 Yates St; ⏲9am-5pm Mon-Fri) Near the corner of Yates and Douglas Sts.

Victoria Visitors Centre (www.tourismvictoria. com; 812 Wharf St; ⏲8:30am-8:30pm) Busy, flyer-lined visitor center overlooking the Inner Harbour.

ℹ Getting There & Away

AIR

Victoria International Airport (www.victoria airport.com) is 26km north of the city via Hwy 17. **Air Canada** (www.aircanada.com) services arrive here from Vancouver (from $87, 25 minutes, up to 21 daily), while **Westjet** (www.westjet.com) flights arrive from Calgary (from $161, 90 minutes, four daily). Both airlines offer competing connections across Canada.

Harbour Air Seaplanes (www.harbour-air. com) arrive in the Inner Harbour from downtown Vancouver (from $129, 35 minutes) throughout

the day. Similar **Helijet** (www.helijet.com) helicopter services arrive from Vancouver (from $149, 35 minutes).

BOAT

BC Ferries (www.bcferries.com) arrive from mainland Tsawwassen (adult/child/vehicle $14/7/46.75, 90 minutes) at Swartz Bay, 27km north of Victoria via Hwy 17. Services arrive hourly throughout the day in summer but are reduced in the low season.

Victoria Clipper (www.clippervacations.com) services arrive in the Inner Harbour from Seattle (adult/child US$88/44, three hours, up to three a day).

Black Ball Transport (www.ferrytovictoria. com) boats also arrive from Port Angeles (adult/child/vehicle US$17/8.50/60.50, 90 minutes, up to four daily).

BUS

Services terminating at the city's main **bus station** (700 Douglas St) include **Greyhound Canada** (www.greyhound.ca) routes from Nanaimo ($13.50, 2½ hours, three daily) and across the island, along with frequent **Pacific Coach Lines** (www.pacificcoach.com) services from Vancouver (from $38, 3½ hours) and Vancouver International Airport ($44, four hours).

ℹ Getting Around

TO/FROM THE AIRPORT

AKAL Airporter (www.victoriaairporter.com) minibuses run between the airport and area hotels ($21, 30 minutes). In contrast, a taxi to downtown costs around $50, while transit buses 83, 86 and 88 take around 35 minutes and cost $2.50 – you may have to change buses at McTavish Exchange.

BICYCLE

Victoria is a great cycling capital with plenty of routes crisscrossing the city and beyond. Bike rentals are offered by **Cycle BC Rentals** (☑866-380-2453, 250-380-2453; www.cyclebc.ca; 685 Humboldt St; ⏲9am-5pm; 🖳).

BOAT

Victoria Harbour Ferry (www.victoria harbourferry.com; fares from $5) Covers the Inner Harbour, Songhees Park (for Spinnakers Brewpub) and other stops along the Gorge Waterway with its colorful armada of bath-size little boats.

PUBLIC TRANSPORTATION

Victoria Regional Transit (www.busonline.ca) Buses cover a wide area from Sidney to Sooke, with some routes served by modern double-deckers. Fares are $2.50/5 per adult/day pass. Children under five years travel free.

Saanich Peninsula & Around

Home of Vancouver Island's main airport and ferry terminal, this peninsula north of Victoria has more to offer than just a way to get from here to there. On a languid day out from Victoria, you'll find waterfront Sidney and BC's most popular garden attraction.

Sidney

At the peninsula's northern end, seafront Sidney is studded with 10 or so bookshops, enabling it to call itself BC's only 'Booktown.' It takes an hour to get here by transit bus from Victoria ($2.50, bus 70 or 72), and the heart of the town is Beacon Ave. Drop into the friendly chamber of commerce visitor center (☑ 250-665-7362; www.sidney.ca; 2281 Beacon Ave; ☺ 9am-5pm) when you arrive for tips.

You can spend a leisurely afternoon ducking into the likes of **Tanner's Books** (www.tannersbooks.com; 2436 Beacon Ave; ☺ 8am-9pm), with its massive magazine and large travel-book sections, and **Beacon Books** (2372 Beacon Ave; ☺ 10am-5:30pm Mon-Sat, noon-4pm Sun), where the used tomes are guarded by store cat Rosabelle. See www.sidneybooktown.ca for additional page-turning options.

The popular **Shaw Ocean Discovery Centre** (www.oceandiscovery.ca; 9811 Seaport Pl; adult/child $15/5; ☺ 10am-5pm) is Sidney's kid-luring highlight. Enter through a dramatic Disney-style entrance – it makes you think you're descending below the waves – then step into a gallery of aquatic exhibits, including alien-like jellyfish, a large touch tank with purple starfish and an octopus that likes to unscrew a glass jar to snag its fresh crab dinner.

If you're suddenly peckish, duck into **Carlos Cantina & Grill** (www.carloscantina.ca; 9816 4th St; mains $10-14; ☺ 11:30am-8:30pm) for authentic Mexican grub in a colorful, friendly setting (the fish tacos and $7.95 lunch special are recommended). Crank it up a notch with dinner at local fave **Sabhai Thai** (www.sabhai.ca; 2493 Beacon Ave; mains $12-18; ☺ 11:30am-2pm & 5-10pm), a cozy wood-floored room with a bonus patio and a good line in authentic curries. The lunch combos are especially good value.

Brentwood Bay

A 30-minute drive from Victoria via West Saanich Rd, the rolling farmlands here are chiefly known for **Butchart Gardens** (www.butchartgardens.com; 800 Benvenuto Ave; adult/child $30.20/10.30; ☺ 9am-10pm; 🚌 75), Vancouver Island's leading visitor attraction. The immaculate grounds are divided into separate gardens where there's always something in bloom. Summer is crowded, with tour buses rolling in relentlessly, but evening music performances and Saturday-night fireworks (July and August) make it all worthwhile. Tea fans, take note: the **Dining Room Restaurant** serves a smashing afternoon tea.

Also consider nearby **Victoria Butterfly Gardens** (www.butterflygardens.com; 1461 Benvenuto Ave; adult/child $15/5; ☺ 9am-7pm), which offers a kaleidoscope of thousands of fluttering critters (from around 75 species) in a free-flying environment. As well as watching them flit about and land on your head, you can eyeball exotic fish, plants and birds. Look out for Spike, the puna ibis bird that struts around as if he owns the place.

Sooke & Around

Rounding Vancouver Island's rustic southern tip towards Sooke (a 45-minute drive from Victoria), Hwy 14 is lined with twisted Garry oaks and unkempt hedgerows, while the houses – often artisan workshops or homely B&Bs – seem spookily hidden in the forest shadows.

Sharing the same building (and hours) as the visitor center, the fascinating **Sooke Region Museum** (www.sookeregionmuseum.com; 2070 Phillips Rd; ☺ 9am-5pm) **FREE** illuminates the area's rugged pioneer days. Check out Moss Cottage in the museum grounds: built in 1869, it's the oldest residence west of Victoria.

A 5km drive from Hwy 14 (the turnoff is east of Sooke), **Sooke Potholes Provincial Park** (www.bcparks.ca) is a favorite summer hangout among the locals. With rock pools and potholes carved into the river base during the last ice age, it's ideal for swimming and tube floating. Camping is available via the website of the **Land Conservancy** (www.conservancy.bc.ca; campsites $25; ☺ May-Sep).

You'll find B&Bs dotted along the route here, but for one of the province's most delightful and splurge-worthy sleepovers, head to Whiffen Spit's **Sooke Harbour House** (☑ 250-642-3421; www.sookeharbourhouse.com; 1528 Whiffen Spit Rd; d from $299; 🛜🦮). Paintings, sculptures and carved wood line its lovely rooms. The restaurant alone is worth a stop for its fine West Coast dining.

Cowichan Valley

A swift Hwy 1 drive northwest of Victoria, this farmland region is ripe for exploration. Check out what's available by contacting **Tourism Cowichan** (☑ 888-303-3337, 250-746-4636; www.tourismcowichan.com) for information.

Duncan

Developed as a logging-industry railroad stop – the gabled little station now houses a museum – Duncan is the valley's main community. A useful base for regional exploration, it's known for its totem poles, which dot downtown like sentinels.

If your First Nations curiosity is piqued, head to the **Quw'utsun' Cultural & Conference Centre** (www.quwutsun.ca; 200 Cowichan Way; adult/child $13/6; ⊘10am-4pm Mon-Sat Jun-Sep) to learn about carving and traditional salmon runs. Alternatively, drive 3km north of town to the **BC Forest Discovery Centre** (www.bcforestdiscoverycentre.com; 2892 Drinkwater Rd; adult/child $16/11; ⊘10am-4:30pm), complete with pioneer-era buildings, logging machinery and a working steam train.

The area's chatty hub, **Duncan Garage Cafe** (www.communityfarmstore.ca; 3330 Duncan St; mains $4-9; ⊘7:30am-6pm

Mon-Sat, 9am-5pm Sun) is in a refurbished heritage building that also houses a bookshop and an organic grocery store. But for a great meal, head to the delightful **Hudson's on First** (www.hudsonsonfirst.ca; 163 First St; mains $16-26; ⊘11am-2.30pm & 5-8.30pm Tue-Sun), which would be a top table option in far bigger cities. Farm-to-table local produce is the approach in an ever-changing seasonal menu that fuses West Coast ingredients with subtle European influences.

Cowichan Bay

'Cow Bay' to the locals, the region's most attractive pit stop is a colorful string of wooden buildings perched over a mountain-framed ocean inlet. It's worth an afternoon of your time, although it might take that long to find parking on a busy summer day.

Duck into the **Maritime Centre** (www.classicboats.org; 1761 Cowichan Bay Rd; admission by donation; ⊘dawn-dusk) to peruse some salty boat-building exhibits and intricate models.

If you're hungry, grab fish-and-chips from **Rock Cod Café** (www.rockcodcafe.com; 1759 Cowichan Bay Rd; mains $10-14; ⊘11am-9pm), or push out the boat – not literally – on the view-some patio deck of the charming **Masthead Restaurant** (☑ 250-748-3714; www.themastheadrestaurant.com; 1705 Cowichan Bay Rd; mains $24-37; ⊘5-10pm), where the three-course BC-sourced tasting menu is good value.

Alternatively, drop into **Hilary's Artisan Cheese** (www.hilaryscheese.com; 1737 Cowichan Bay Rd; ⊘9am-6pm) and **True Grain Bread** (www.truegrain.ca; 1725 Cowichan Bay Rd; ⊘8am-7pm Mon-Sat, to 5pm Sun) for the makings of a great picnic.

WORTH A TRIP

CANADA'S ONLY TEA FARM

Hidden in bucolic farmland 8km north of Duncan (it's not well signposted, so deploy your GPS), you'll find one of Canada's rarest agricultural operations. Tucked into the hillside, the oasis-like **Teafarm** (www.teafarm.ca; 8530 Richards Trail, North Cowichan; ⊘10am-5pm Wed-Sun) has been growing its own tea plants here for several years. The main harvest is coming soon, but until that time its contemporary, winery-like tasting room (or, better still, its flower-framed outdoor seating area) is the perfect spot to indulge in one of dozens of excellent tea blends – Sweet Morocco is recommended – along with some decadent sweet treats. The tea is served in lovely handmade pottery teapots made by owner Margit, while husband and tea guru Victor will be on hand to tell you about the operation. It's one of the most relaxing – and surprisingly good-value – ways to spend an hour or two in the region.

Chemainus

After the last sawmill shut down in 1983, tiny Chemainus became the model for BC communities dealing with declining resource jobs. Instead of submitting to a slow death, town officials commissioned a giant wall mural depicting local history. More than three dozen artworks were later added and a tourism industry was born. Stroll the Chemainus streets on a mural hunt and you'll pass artsy boutiques and tempting ice-cream shops.

The town's **Chemainus Inn** (☑877-246-4181, 250-246-4181; www.chemainushotel.com; 9573 Chemainus Rd; d from $169; [P][✷][✷][✷]) is like a midrange business hotel from a much larger community. Rooms are slick and comfortable and many include kitchens. Rates include breakfast.

Drop by the charming, heritage-building **Willow Street Cafe** (www.willowstreet cafe.com; 9749 Willow St; mains $5-12; ⊙8:30am-5pm) for a chat with the locals and a side order of hearty, housemade wraps, pizzas and sandwiches. In summer aim for a patio perch.

In the evening, the surprisingly large **Chemainus Theatre** (www.chemainus theatrefestival.ca; 9737 Chemainus Rd) stages professional productions – mostly popular plays and musicals – to keep you occupied.

Check in at the **visitor center** (☑250-246-3944; www.chemainus.bc.ca; 9796 Willow St; ⊙9am-5pm) for mural maps and further information.

Nanaimo

POP 87,000

Vancouver Island's 'second metropolis,' Nanaimo will never have the allure of tourist-magnet Victoria. But the Harbour City has undergone a quiet upgrade since the 1990s, with the emergence – especially on Commercial St and in the Old City Quarter – of cool shops and eateries, plus a slick new museum. With dedicated ferry services from the mainland, the city is also a handy hub for exploring the rest of the island. For more information, drop into the main **visitor center** (☑800-663-7337, 250-751-1556; www.tourismnanaimo.com; 2450 Northfield Rd; ⊙9am-6pm) or the summer-only satellite behind downtown's museum.

⊙ Sights & Activities

Nanaimo Museum   MUSEUM
(www.nanaimomuseum.ca; 100 Museum Way; adult/child $2/75¢; ⊙10am-5pm) Just off the Commercial St main drag, this excellent museum showcases the region's heritage, from First Nations to colonial, maritime, sporting and beyond. Highlights include a strong Coast Salish focus and a walk-through evocation of a coal mine that's popular with kids. Ask at the front desk about summer-only city walking tours plus entry to the nearby Bastion, an 1853 wooden tower fortification.

Newcastle Island Marine Provincial Park   PARK
(www.newcastleisland.ca) ✐ Nanaimo's rustic outdoor gem offers 22km of hiking and biking trails, plus beaches and wildlife-spotting. Traditional Coast Salish land, it was the site of shipyards and coal mines before becoming a popular summer excursion for locals in the 1930s when a tea pavilion was added. There's a seasonal eatery and regular First Nations dancing displays. The park is accessed by a 10-minute ferry hop from the harbor (adult/child return $9/5).

Old City Quarter   NEIGHBORHOOD
(www.oldcityquarter.com; cnr Fitzwilliam & Wesley Sts) A steep hike uphill from the waterfront on Bastion and Fitzwilliam Sts delivers you to a strollable heritage 'hood of independent stores, galleries and eateries in brightly painted old buildings. Highlights include McLeans Specialty Foods, A Wee Cupcakery and Fibber Magees, a large pub that has handsomely taken over the town's old train station. Look out for the heritage plaques on buildings in this area.

Wild Play Element Parks   AMUSEMENT PARK
(☑250-716-7874, 888-716-7374; www.wildplay.com; 35 Nanaimo River Rd; adult/child from $43/23; ⊙10am-6pm) The perfect spot to tire your kids out, this tree-lined adventure playground is packed with such adrenaline-pumping fun as bungee-jumping and scream-triggering zip-lining. But along with its fun obstacle courses, there's plenty of additional action to keep the family occupied, from woodsy walking trails to busy volleyball courts. Bring a picnic and come for at least half a day.

🛏 Sleeping

Painted Turtle Guesthouse
HOSTEL $

(📞 250-753-4432, 866-309-4432; www.painted
turtle.ca; 121 Bastion St; dm/r $27/80; @ 🛜) This
beautifully maintained budget property
in the heart of downtown combines small
dorms with very popular private rooms
(book ahead). A HI affiliate, its hardwood
floors and Ikea-esque furnishings line a
large and welcoming kitchen-lounge combo
and you can book tours from the front desk
if you've had enough of strumming the hostel's loaner guitar.

Coast Bastion Hotel
HOTEL $$

(📞 250-753-6601, 800-716-6199; www.coast
hotels.com; 11 Bastion St; d from $157; ❄ @ 🛜 ❄)
Downtown's best hotel has an unbeatable
location overlooking the harbor, with most
guests enjoying sparkling waterfront views
(if it's not foggy). Rooms have been well
refurbished with a lounge-modern élan in
recent years, adding flat-screen TVs and (in
most rooms) small refrigerators. The lobby
resto-bar is a popular hangout, but there's
also a spa if you want to relax. Excellent
front-desk staff.

Buccaneer Inn
MOTEL $$

(📞 250-753-1246, 877-282-6337; www.buc-
caneerinn.com; 1577 Stewart Ave; d/ste from
$80/140; 🛜) Handy for the Departure Bay
ferry terminal, this friendly, family-run
motel has a gleaming white exterior that
makes it hard to pass by. And it's worth
stopping: the neat and tidy approach is carried over into the maritime-themed rooms,
many of which have kitchenettes. Splurge
on a spacious suite and you'll have a fireplace, a full kitchen and a flat-screen TV.

🍴 Eating

★ Gabriel's Café
INTERNATIONAL $

(183 Commercial St; mains $6-9; ⊘ 8am-7pm
Mon-Fri, 9am-5pm Sat & Sun; 🖉) This perfectly
located downtown hole-in-the-wall is like a
static food truck. Chat with the man himself
behind the counter, then tuck into made-
from-scratch treats like pulled-pork breakfast wraps or the ever-popular Thai green
chili coconut curry rice bowl. Vegetarians
are also well looked after – try the black-
bean burger. There's not much room to sit
in this sunny little nook and it's best to arrive off-peak to avoid line-ups.

2 Chefs Affair
WEST COAST $$

(www.twochefsaffair.com; 123b Commercial St;
mains $8-15; ⊘ 8am-4:30pm Mon-Fri, to 3pm Sat
& Sun; 🛜) Focused on great comfort food
with a fresh, made-from-scratch approach,
this highly welcoming locals' haunt in the
heart of downtown is a great spot for break-
fast (go the French toast route). But lunch
is arguably even more enticing: ask for the
'menage a trois' and you won't be disap-
pointed – it comes with crab fishcake, can-
died salmon and garlic prawns.

Penny's Palapa
MEXICAN $$

(www.pennyspalapa.com; 10 Wharf St, Dock H;
mains $8-16; ⊘ 11am-8:30pm May-Sep; 🖉) This
tiny, flower-and-flag-decked floating hut
and patio in the harbor is a lovely spot for
an alfresco meal among the jostling boats.
An inventive, well-priced menu of Mexican
delights includes seasonal seafood specials
– the signature halibut tacos are recommended – plus some good vegetarian options. Arrive early: the dining area fills rapidly on balmy summer evenings. Drinks-
wise, it's all about the margaritas.

🍷 Drinking & Entertainment

Longwood Brewpub
BREWPUB

(www.longwoodbrewpub.com; 5775 Turner Rd;
⊘ 11am-midnight) Incongruously located in a
strip mall, this handsome stone and gabled
resto-pub combines a surprisingly good
menu with lip-smacking own-brewed beers.
Try for a deck table and decide between recommended mains like Cajun chicken que-
sadilla or halibut and prawn wraps – vegetarians should order the roast-vegetable
lasagna. For beer, hit the four-glass tasting
flight.

Dinghy Dock Pub
PUB

(www.dinghydockpub.com; 8 Pirates Lane; mains
$12-17; ⊘ 11:30am-11pm) Accessed via a mini-
ferry hop, this lively but old-school pub and
restaurant combo floating offshore from
Protection Island is a salty local legend
and a unique place to knock back a few
malty brews on the deck. The menu doesn't
stretch too far beyond fish-and-chips, but
there's live music on weekends to keep your
toes tapping. To get to the pub, take the
10-minute ferry ride ($9 return) from the
harbor.

Queen's Hotel   LIVE MUSIC
(☑ 250-754-6751; www.thequeens.ca; 34 Victoria Cres) The city's best live-music and dance spot, hosting an eclectic roster of performances and club nights, ranging from indie to jazz and country.

Port Theatre   THEATER
(☑ 250-754-8550; www.porttheatre.com; 125 Front St) Presenting local and touring live-theater shows.

❶ Getting There & Away

AIR

Nanaimo Airport (www.nanaimoairport.com) is 18km south of town via Hwy 1. **Air Canada** (www.aircanada.com) flights arrive here from Vancouver (from $77, 25 minutes) throughout the day.

Frequent **Harbour Air Seaplanes** (www.harbour-air.com) services arrive in the inner harbor from downtown Vancouver ($105, 25 minutes).

BOAT

BC Ferries (www.bcferries.com) from Tsawwassen (passenger/vehicle $14.50/49, two hours) arrive at Duke Point, 14km south of Nanaimo. Services from West Vancouver's Horseshoe Bay (passenger/vehicle $15.50/51.25, 95 minutes) arrive at Departure Bay, 3km north of the city center via Hwy 1.

BUS

Greyhound Canada (www.greyhound.ca) buses arrive from Victoria (from $13.50, two hours, three daily), Campbell River (from $18.50, three hours, three daily) and across the island.

❶ Getting Around

Downtown Nanaimo around the harbor is highly walkable, but after that the city spreads out and a car or strong bike legs are required. Be aware that taxis are expensive here.

Nanaimo Regional Transit (www.busonline.ca; single trip/day pass $2.50/6.25) Buses stop along Gordon St, west of Harbour Park Mall. Bus 2 goes to the Departure Bay ferry terminal. No city buses run to Duke Point.

Nanaimo Airporter (www.nanaimoairporter.com; from $26) Provides door-to-door service to downtown from both ferry terminals.

Parksville & Qualicum

This popular mid-island seaside region – which also includes rustic Coombs – has been a traditional destination for vacationing families for decades (hence the water parks and mini-golf attractions).

For more information on the area, visit www.parksvillequalicumbeach.com.

◉ Sights & Activities

Coombs Old Country Market   MARKET
(www.oldcountrymarket.com; 2326 Alberni Hwy, Coombs; ⊘9am-7pm) The mother of all pit stops, this sprawling food and crafts market is stuffed with bakery and produce delectables. It attracts huge numbers of visitors on balmy summer days, when cameras are pointed at the grassy roof where a herd of goats spends the season. Nip inside for giant ice-cream cones, heaping pizzas and the deli makings of a great picnic. Save time to explore the attendant store and attractions clustered around the site.

World Parrot Refuge   WILDLIFE RESERVE
(www.worldparrotrefuge.org; 2116 Alberni Hwy, Coombs; adult/child $14/10; ⊘10am-4pm) Rescuing exotic birds from captivity and nursing them back to health, this excellent educational facility has as its mantra that parrots are not pets. Pick up your earplugs at reception and stroll among the enclosures, each alive with recovering (and very noisy) birds. Don't be surprised when some screech a chirpy 'hello' as you stroll by.

Horne Lake Caves   PARK
(☑ 250-248-7829; www.hornelake.com; tours adult/child from $24/20; ⊘10am-5pm) Horne Lake Caves Provincial Park is a 45-minute drive from Parksville (take Hwy 19 towards Courtenay, then exit 75 and proceed for 12km on the gravel road), but it's worth it for BC's best spelunking. Some caves are open to the public for self-exploring, or the excellent guided tours are recommended – from family friendly to 'extreme.' Book ahead for these.

🍴 Sleeping & Eating

★ Free Spirit Spheres   CABIN $$
(☑ 250-757-9445; www.freespiritspheres.com; 420 Horne Lake Rd, Qualicum Beach; cabins from $145) These unique spherical treehouses enable guests to cocoon themselves in the forest canopy. Compact inside, Eve is small and basic, while Eryn and Melody are lined with built-in cabins. It's all about communing with nature (TVs are replaced with books), and guests receive a basket of tasty snacks on arrival. There's also a ground-level facilities block with sauna, BBQ and hotel-like showers. Book early for summer.

Crown Mansion BOUTIQUE HOTEL $$

(☑250-752-5776, 800-378-6811; www.crownmansion.com; 292 E Crescent Rd, Qualicum Beach; d from $160; ⊕) A sumptuous family home built in 1912, this handsome white-painted mansion was restored to its former glory and opened as a unique hotel in 2009. Recall past guests Bing Crosby and John Wayne as you check out the family crest in the library fireplace, then retire to your elegant room. Rates include continental breakfast – arrive early and snag the window table.

Fish Tales Café SEAFOOD $$

(336 W Island Hwy, Qualicum Beach; mains $8-24) This Qualicum fixture has the look of an old-school English teashop, but it's been reeling in visitors with its perfect fish-and-chips for years. It's worth exploring the non-deep-fried dishes – the two-person platter of scallops, shrimp, smoked salmon and mussels is recommended – and, if you arrive early enough, you can grab a table in the lovely garden.

JUAN DE FUCA PROVINCAL PARK

The 47km **Juan de Fuca Marine Trail** (www.juandefucamarinetrail.com) in **Juan de Fuca Provincial Park** (www.bcparks.ca) rivals the West Coast Trail as a must-do island trek. From east to west, its trailhead access points are China Beach, Sombrio Beach, Parkinson Creek and Botanical Beach.

It takes around four days to complete the route – the most difficult stretch is between Bear Beach and China Beach – but you don't have to go the whole hog. Be aware that some sections are often muddy and difficult to hike, while bear sightings and swift weather changes are not uncommon.

The route has several basic backcountry campsites and you can pay your camping fee ($10 per adult) at any of the trailheads. The most popular spot to pitch tents is the comparatively salubrious, family-friendly **China Beach Campground** (☑800-689-9025, 604-689-9025; www.discovercamping.ca; campsites $30; ⊕May-Sep), which has pit toilets and cold-water taps but no showers. There's a waterfall at the western end of the beach. Booking ahead in summer is essential.

ℹ Getting There & Away

Greyhound Canada (www.greyhound.ca) services arrive in Parksville from Victoria (from $18.50, three to four hours, five daily), Nanaimo (from $6.50, 40 minutes, five daily) and across the island. The same buses, with similar times and rates, serve Qualicum Beach.

Pacific Rim National Park Reserve

Dramatic, wave-whipped beaches and brooding, mist-licked forests make the **Pacific Rim National Park Reserve** (www.pc.gc.ca/pacificrim; park pass adult/child $7.80/6.80) a must-see for anyone interested in experiencing BC's raw West Coast wilderness. The 500-sq-km park comprises the northern Long Beach Unit, between Tofino and Ucluelet; the Broken Group Islands in Barkley Sound; and, to the south, the ever-popular West Coast Trail. First-timers should drop by the **Pacific Rim Visitor Centre** (☑250-726-4600; www.pacificrimvisitor.ca; 2791 Pacific Rim Hwy; ⊕10am-4:30pm) for maps and advice on exploring the region. If you're stopping in the park you'll need to pay for and display a pass, available at the visitor center or from the yellow dispensers dotted along the highway.

Long Beach Unit

Attracting the lion's share of visitors, Long Beach Unit is easily accessible by car along the Pacific Rim Hwy. Wide sandy beaches, untamed surf, lots of beachcombing nooks plus a living museum of old-growth rainforest are the main reasons for the summer tourist clamor. Cox Bay Beach alone is an ideal hangout for surfers and families – seabirds, sand dollars and purple or orange starfish abound.

For an introduction to the area's natural history and First Nations heritage, visit the **Kwisitis Centre** (Wick Rd; with park pass admission free; ⊕10am-4.30pm Mar-Aug) overlooking Wickaninnish Beach. And if you're suddenly inspired to plunge in for a stroll, try one of the following trails, keeping your eyes peeled for swooping bald eagles and giant banana slugs. Safety precautions apply: tread carefully over slippery surfaces and never turn your back on the mischievous surf.

➡ **Long Beach** Great scenery along the sandy shore (1.2km; easy).

→ **Rainforest Trail** Two interpretive loops through old-growth forest (1km; moderate).

→ **Schooner Trail** Through old- and second-growth forests with beach access (1km; moderate).

→ **Shorepine Bog** Loops around a moss-layered bog (800m; easy and wheelchair-accessible).

Broken Group Islands Unit

Comprising some 300 islands and rocks scattered across 80 sq km around the entrance to Barkley Sound, this serene natural wilderness is beloved of visiting kayakers – especially those who enjoy close-up views of whales, porpoises and multitudinous bird life. Compasses are required for navigating here, unless you fancy paddling to Hawaii.

If you're up for an advetnture, **Lady Rose Marine Services** (www.ladyrosemarine.com) will ship you and your kayak from Port Alberni to its Sechart Whaling Station Lodge (three hours away) in Barkley Sound on the MV *Francis Barkley*. The lodge rents kayaks ($40 to $60 per day) if you'd rather travel light, and it offers accommodation ($150/235 per single/double, including meals).

From there, popular paddle destinations include Gibraltar Island, one hour away, with its sheltered campground and explorable beaches and tidal pools. Willis Island (1½ hours from Sechart) is also popular. It has a campground and, at low tide, you can walk to the surrounding islands. Remote Benson Island (four hours from Sechart) has a campground, grazing deer and a blowhole.

Camping fees are $9.80 per night, payable at Sechart or to the boat-based staff who patrol the region – they can collect additional fees from you if you decide to stay longer. The campgrounds are predictably basic and have solar-composting toilets, but you must carry out all your garbage. Bring your own drinking water: island creeks are often dry in summer.

West Coast Trail Unit

The 75km West Coast Trail is BC's best-known hiking route. It's also one of the toughest. It's not for the uninitiated, and there are two things you'll need to know before tackling it: it will hurt and you'll want to do it again next year.

Winding along the wave-licked rainforest shoreline between trailhead information centers at Pachena Bay, 5km south of Bamfield on the north end, and Gordon River, 5km north of Port Renfrew on the southern tip, the entire stretch takes between six and seven days to complete. It's open May to September; access to the route during the mid-June to mid-September peak season is limited to 60 overnight backpackers each day and **reservations** (☑877-737-3783, 250-726-4453; www.reservation.pc.gc.ca; nonrefundable reservation fee $24.50) are required. All overnighters must pay a trail-user fee ($127.50) plus $30 to cover the two short ferry crossings on the route. All overnighters must attend a 1½-hour orientation session before departing. If you don't have a reservation, some permits are kept back for a daily wait-list system.

If you don't want to go the whole hog (you wimp), you can do a day hike or even hike half the trail from Pachena Bay, considered the easier end of the route. Overnight hikers who only hike this end of the trail can leave from Nitinat Lake. Day hikers are exempt from the large trail-user fee but need to get a free day-use permit at one of the trailheads.

West Coast Trailers must be able to manage rough, slippery terrain, stream crossings and adverse, suddenly changing weather. There are also more than 100 little (and some not-so-little) bridges and 70 ladders. Be prepared to treat or boil all water and cook on a lightweight camping stove (you'll be bringing in all your own food). Hikers can rest their weary muscles at any of the basic campsites along the route, most of which have solar-composting outhouses. It's recommended that you set out from a trailhead at least five hours before sundown to ensure you reach a campsite before nightfall – stumbling around in the dark is the prime cause of accidents on this route.

West Coast Trail Express (www.trailbus.com) runs a daily shuttle (May to September) to the trailheads. Book ahead in summer.

Ucluelet

POP 1600

Smaller and less touristy than Tofino to the north, Ucluelet (yew-klew-let) has more than a few charms of its own and is a good reminder of what Tofino was like before the resorts arrived. For some good reasons to stick around in 'Ukee' – including a dining scene that finally has some great options – make for the new visitor center (📋 250-726-2485; www. ucluelet.travel; 1604 Peninsula Rd; ☺ 9am-5pm).

👁 Sights & Activities

Ucluelet Aquarium AQUARIUM
(www.uclueletaquarium.org; Main St Waterfront Promenade; adult/child $12.50/6.25; ☺ 10am-6pm) 🐾 Replacing the tiny waterfront shack that stood nearby, the excellent Ucluelet Aquarium opened this much larger facility in 2012. It retains key approaches from the old place – marine critters are local and most are on a catch-and-release program – including the kid-luring touch tanks. But it's the enthusiasm of the young staff that sets this place apart, along with the ability to educate on issues of conservation without browbeating. In summer, look out for family-friendly lab workshops (free).

Wild Pacific Trail HIKING
(www.wildpacifictrail.com) Starting at the intersection of Peninsula and Coast Guard Rds, then winding around the wave-slapped cliffs past the lighthouse, the 8.5km Wild Pacific Trail offers smashing views of Barkley Sound and the Broken Group Islands. Seabirds are abundant and it's a good storm-watching spot – stick to the trail or the crashing waves might pluck you from the cliffs. Plans were in place on our visit to expand the route by another few kilometers – check the website for progress.

Majestic Ocean Kayaking KAYAKING
(www.oceankayaking.com; 1167 Helen Rd; tours from $67) Majestic Ocean Kayaking leads day trips around the area, plus multiday tours of the Broken Group Islands.

Relic Surf Shop SURFING
(www.relicsurfshop.com; 1998 Peninsula Rd; rentals from $30) If you want to practice the ways of surfing, check in with Relic Surf Shop.

🛏 Sleeping & Eating

Surfs Inn Guesthouse CABIN, HOSTEL $
(📋 250-726-4426; www.surfsinn.ca; 1874 Peninsula Rd; dm/cottages from $28/139; 🐾) It's hard to miss this blue-painted house near the center of town with its small, woodsy dorm rooms. But the real find is hidden out back: two cute cabins that are ideal for groups and families. One is larger and self-contained, while the other is divided into two suites with kitchenettes. Each has a BBQ. Ask about surf packages if you fancy hitting the waves.

Black Rock Oceanfront Resort HOTEL $$$
(📋 250-726-4800, 877-762-5011; www.blackrockresort.com; 596 Marine Dr; d from $269; 🐾🏊) Ucluelet's fanciest hotel feels like a transplant from Tofino. This dramatic waterfront resort offers kitchen-equipped suites, all wrapped in a contemporary wood and stone West Coast look. Many rooms have great views of the often dramatically stormy surf and there's also a vista-hugging restaurant specializing in regional nosh – plus a lobby-level bar shaped like a rolling wave.

★ Hank's WEST COAST $$
(www.hanksucluelet.com; 1576 Imperial Lane; mains $18-22; ☺ 5-11pm Wed-Mon) Closed every Tuesday so they can forage island farms for ingredients, this smashing addtion to Ukee's dining scene has quickly become a local fave. The fresh and local menu is divided between seafood and succulent barbecue (go for lamb), and there's a brilliant array of BC craft beers (plus 50-plus bottles from further afield) – look out for twice-monthly beer-cask nights.

ℹ Getting There & Around

Greyhound (www.greyhound.ca) Buses (operated by Tofino Bus) arrive from Port Alberni ($26, 90 minutes), Nanaimo ($46, three to four hours) and Victoria (from $34, five to seven hours), among others.

Tofino Bus (www.tofinobus.com) 'Beach Bus' services roll in along Hwy 4 from Tofino ($17, 40 minutes).

Tofino
POP 1900

Transformed from a sleepy hippie hangout into a popular eco-destination with high-end resorts, Tofino is like the Whistler of Vancouver Island.

👁 Sights

Inkwis Arts and Culture GALLERY
(www.inkwis-portal.com; 368 Main St; ☺ 11am-5pm Wed-Sun) The newest of several First Nations–focused galleries around Tofino's downtown drag, this spartan but friendly little space has a lively roster of ever-changing exhibitions – check the website for openings. And while the focus is contemporary First Nations, artists from other communities are also part of the mix, as well as workshops and a growing art-for-sale section.

Tofino Botanical Gardens GARDENS
(www.tbgf.org; 1084 Pacific Rim Hwy; 3-day pass adult/child $10/free; ☺9am-dusk) 🌿 Explore what coastal temperate rainforests are all about by checking out the frog pond, forest boardwalk, native plants and educational workshops at this smashing bird-packed rustic attraction. There's a seasonal cafe on-site for that essential glass of wine, while classical music is also piped through the gardens most evenings. There's also a $1 discount if you arrive car-free.

Maquinna Marine Provincial Park PARK
(www.bcparks.ca) 🌿 One of the most popular day trips from Tofino, the highlight here is **Hot Spring Cove.** Tranquillity-minded trekkers travel to the park by Zodiac boat or seaplane, watching for whales and other sea critters en route. From the boat landing, 2km of boardwalks lead to the natural hot pools.

Meares Island PARK
Visible through the mist and accessible via kayak or tour boat from the Tofino waterfront, Meares Island is home to the Big Tree Trail, a 400m boardwalk through old-growth forest that includes a stunning 1500-year-old red cedar. The island was the site of the key 1984 Clayoquot Sound antilogging protest that kicked off the region's latter-day environmental movement.

🏃 Activities

Pacific Surf School SURFING
(www.pacificsurfschool.com; 430 Campbell St; board rental 6/24hr $15/20) Offering rentals, camps and lessons for beginners.

Surf Sister SURFING
(www.surfsister.com; 625 Campbell St; lessons $79) Introductory lessons for boys and girls, plus women-only multiday courses.

Remote Passages KAYAKING
(www.remotepassages.com; 51 Wharf St; tours from $64) Short guided kayaking tours around Clayoquot Sound and the nearby islands.

Tofino Sea Kayaking KAYAKING
(www.tofino-kayaking.com; 320 Main St; tours from $60) Evocative guided paddles – one-day tour to the Freedom Cove floating gardens recommended.

STORMING TOFINO

Started as a clever marketing ploy to lure off-season visitors, storm-watching – viewing spectacularly crashing winter waves, then scampering back inside for hot chocolate with a face freckled by sea salt – has become a popular pastime on the island's west coast. There are usually good off-peak deals to be had in area accommodations during stormwatching season (typically November to March) and most hotels can supply you with loaner 'Tofino tuxedos' (otherwise known as waterproof gear). The best spots to catch a few crashing spectacles are Cox Bay, Chesterman Beach, Long Beach, Second Bay and Wickaninnish Beach. Don't get too close or turn your back on the waves: these gigantic swells will have you in the water within seconds given half the chance.

🞄 Tours

Jamie's Whaling Station BOAT TOUR
(www.jamies.com; 606 Campbell St; adult/child $99/69) Whale, bear and sea-lion spotting boat jaunts.

Ocean Outfitters BOAT TOUR
(www.oceanoutfitters.bc.ca; 368 Main St; adult/child $89/69) Popular whale-watching tours, with bear and hot-springs treks also offered.

🛏 Sleeping & Eating

Whalers on the Point Guesthouse HOSTEL $$
(☏250-725-3443, 855-725-3443; www.tofinohostel.com; 81 West St; dm/r from $37/93; @ 🛜) Close to the town center but with a secluded waterfront location (you'll spend plenty of time on the shoreline deck), this excellent HI hostel is a comfy wood-lined retreat. The dorms are mercifully small and some double-bed private rooms are also available. Facilities include a granite-countered kitchen, a BBQ patio, a games room and a wet sauna. Reservations essential in summer. Free parking.

Ocean Village Beach Resort CABIN $$$
(☏866-725-3755, 250-725-3755; www.oceanvillageresort.com; 555 Hellesen Dr; ste from $229; 🛜 🖼 🚼 🐕) Recently renovated and with a Scandinavian look, this immaculate beachside resort of 53 beehive-shaped cedar

cabins (hence the woodsy aroma when you step in the door) is a family favorite. Each unit faces a shoreline that's just a few steps away and all have handy kitchens. If your kids tire of the beach, there are surf lessons and a saltwater pool to keep them occupied. No in-room TVs.

Wickaninnish Inn HOTEL $$$
(☑800-333-4604, 250-725-3100; www.wickinn. com; Chesterman Beach; d from $399; ☎🐾) Cornering the market in luxury winter storm-watching packages, 'the Wick' is worth a stay any time of year. Embodying nature with its recycled wood furnishings, natural stone tiles and the ambience of a place grown rather than constructed, the sumptuous guest rooms have push-button gas fireplaces, two-person hot tubs and floor-to-ceiling windows. The region's most romantic accommodations.

Shelter WEST COAST $$
(www.shelterrestaurant.com; 601 Campbell St; mains $12-30; ☺11am-midnight) This woodsy, low-ceilinged haunt has kept expanding over the years but has never lost its welcoming local-hangout feel. The perfect spot to grab a chatty lunch (salmon surf bowls and a patio seat recommended), Shelter becomes an intimate dinner venue every evening, when the menu ratchets up to showcase finger-licking BC-sourced treats from seafood to gourmet burgers.

Sobo WEST COAST $$
(www.sobo.ca; 311 Neill St; mains $15-30; ☺11am-9pm) A local favorite that started out as a (still-remembered) purple food truck and is now a popular sit-down eatery. The focus at Sobo – meaning Sophisticated Bohemian – is seasonal West Coast ingredients prepared with international influences. It's a brilliant place to dive into fresh-catch seafood for dinner, but there's also a hearty lunch menu if you need an early fill-up (gourmet pizzas recommended).

❶ Information

Visitor Centre (☑250-725-3414; www.tourismtofino.com; 1426 Pacific Rim Hwy; ☺10am-6pm May-Sep, reduced hours low season) A short drive south of town, has detailed information on accommodations, hiking trails and surf spots.

❶ Getting There & Around

Orca Airways (www.flyorcaair.com) Flights arrive at Tofino Airport from Vancouver International Airport's South Terminal ($174, one hour, up to five daily).

Greyhound Canada (www.greyhound.ca) Services (operated by Tofino Bus) arrive from Port Alberni ($29, two hours), Nanaimo ($46, four hours) and Victoria ($69, six to seven hours), among others.

Tofino Bus (www.tofinobus.com) 'Beach Bus' services roll in along Hwy 4 from Ucluelet ($17, 40 minutes).

Comox Valley

Comprising the towns of Comox and Courtenay and the village of Cumberland, this is a region of rolling mountains, alpine meadows and colorful communities. A good outdoor-adventure base – this is a mountain-biking hotbed – its activity-triggering highlight is Mt Washington. Drop by the slick **Vancouver Island Visitor Centre** (☑885-400-2882; www.discovercomoxvalley.com; 3607 Small Rd, Cumberland; ☺9am-7pm) for area tips.

◉ Sights & Activities

The main reason for winter visits, **Mt Washington Alpine Resort** (www.mountwashington.ca; winter lift tickets adult/child $75/39) is the island's skiing mecca, with its 81 runs, snowshoeing park and popular night skiing. But there are also great summer activities here, including some of the region's best hiking trails.

With a life-size replica of an elasmosaur, a prehistoric marine reptile first discovered in the area, the excellent **Courtenay & District Museum & Palaeontology Centre** (www.courtenaymuseum.ca; 207 4th St, Courtenay; admission by donation; ☺10am-5pm Mon-Sat, noon-4pm Sun) also houses pioneer and First Nations exhibits.

Save time for a poke around charming Cumberland, a town built on mining that's now luring artsy young residents from across BC to its clapboard shops and houses. Get some historic context at the **Cumberland Museum** (www.cumberlandmuseum.ca; Dunsmuir Ave; admission by donation; ☺10am-5pm), with its little walk-through mine exhibit, then drop into **Dark Side Chocolates** (www.darksidechocolates. com; 2722 Dunsmuir Ave; choc selections from $5; ☺10am-4:30pm Tue-Sat) for treats (mint melties recommended).

🛏 Sleeping & Eating

★ **Riding Fool Hostel** ⠀⠀⠀⠀⠀⠀⠀HOSTEL $
(☑ 250-336-8250, 888-313-3665; www.riding fool.com; 2705 Dunsmuir Ave, Cumberland; dm/r $25/60; @ 🛜) One of BC's top hostels colonizes a restored Cumberland heritage building with rustic wooden interiors, a large kitchen and lounge area and – along with its small dorms – the kind of neat and tidy private rooms often found in midrange hotels. Bicycle rentals are available downstairs: this is a great hostel for hanging out with the mountain-biking crowd.

Kingfisher Oceanside Resort ⠀⠀⠀HOTEL $$
(☑ 250-338-1323, 800-663-7929; www.kingfisher spa.com; 4330 Island Hwy, Courtenay; r/ste from $145/220; @ 🛜 ☲ ☵) At this boutique waterfront lodge many of the rooms are oriented to focus on the waterfront, framed by islands and mountains. Rooms are generally large and comfortable, and many have full kitchens, so you can save on dining out – you'll likely blow it at the spa, though. A good spot to take a break from your road trip, there are some good off-season deals here.

Waverley Hotel Pub ⠀⠀⠀⠀⠀⠀BURGERS $$
(www.waverleyhotel.ca; 2692 Dunsmuir Ave, Cumberland; mains $9-15) If you're keen to meet the locals in Cumberland, hit this historic saloon for a pint of Blue Buck Ale. Food is of the hearty pub-grub variety – how many more reasons do you need to have a burger? – and there are often live bands on the kick-ass little stage.

Campbell River

POP 29,500

Southerners will tell you this marks the end of Vancouver Island civilization, but Campbell River is a handy drop-off point for wilderness tourism in Strathcona Provincial Park and is large enough to have attractions and services of its own. The **visitor center** (☑ 877-286-5705, 250-830-0411; www.campbellriver.travel; 1235 Shoppers Row; ⊙ 9am-6pm) can fill you in.

◎ Sights & Activities

Museum at Campbell River ⠀⠀⠀⠀MUSEUM
(www.crmuseum.ca; 470 Island Hwy; adult/child $8/5; ⊙ 10am-5pm) Showcasing aboriginal masks, an 1890s pioneer cabin and video footage of the world's largest artificial, nonnuclear blast (an underwater mountain in Seymour Narrows that caused dozens of shipwrecks before it was blown apart in a controlled explosion in 1958), this fascinating museum is worth an hour of anyone's time. In summer, ask about its popular history-themed boat cruises around the area.

Discovery Pier ⠀⠀⠀⠀⠀⠀⠀⠀LANDMARK
(rod rentals per half-day $6) Since locals claim the town as the 'Salmon Capital of the World' you should wet your line off the downtown Discovery Pier or just stroll along with the crowds and see what everyone else has caught. Much easier than catching your own lunch, you can also buy fish-and-chips (and ice cream) here. It's the perfect sunset spot to hang with the locals.

VAN ISLE'S ANCIENT WILDERNESS

Strathcona Provincial Park (www.bcparks.ca) 🏕, BC's oldest protected area and Vancouver Island's largest park, is inland from Campbell River on Hwy 28. Centered on Mt Golden Hinde (2200m), the island's highest point, Strathcona is a magnificent pristine wilderness crisscrossed with trail systems that deliver you to waterfalls, alpine meadows, glacial lakes and looming mountain crags.

On arrival at the main entrance, get your bearings at **Strathcona Park Lodge & Outdoor Education Centre** (www.strathcona.bc.ca). A one-stop shop for park activities, including kayaking, guided treks, yoga camps, zip-lining and rock climbing (all-in adventure packages are available, some aimed specifically at families), this is a great place to rub shoulders with other outdoorsy types. Head to the **Whale Dining Room** or **Canoe Club Café** eateries for a fuel up. The lodge also offers good accommodations: rooms and cabins that, in keeping with its low-impact approach to nature and commitment to eco-education, are sans telephones and TVs.

Notable park hiking trails include the **Paradise Meadows Loop** (2.2km), an easy amble in a delicate wildflower and evergreen ecosystem, and **Mt Becher** (5km), with its great views over the Comox Valley and mountain-lined Strait of Georgia. The 9km **Comox Glacier Trail** is quite an adventure: it's only recommended for advanced hikers.

🛏 Sleeping & Eating

Heron's Landing Hotel HOTEL $$
(☎250-923-2848, 888-923-2849; www.herons
landinghotel.com; 492 S Island Hwy; d incl breakfast
from $139; @ 🛜) Superior motel-style accom-
modation with renovated rooms, including
large loft suites ideal for families.

Shot in the Dark Cafe CAFE $$
(940 Island Hwy; mains $8-14; ◔8am-5pm Mon-
Sat; 🛜) Huge, freshly made sandwiches and
soups are the way to go at this pastel-hued
locals' fave. A good spot for cooked breakfast – especially if you haven't eaten for a
couple of days.

ⓘ Getting There & Around

Campbell River Airport (www.crairport.
ca) receives **Pacific Coastal Airlines** (www.
pacific-coastal.com) flights from Vancouver
International Airport (from $88, 45 minutes, up
to seven daily).

Greyhound Canada (www.greyhound.ca) services arrive from Port Hardy (from $35, three
hours, daily), Nanaimo (from $25, three hours,
two daily), Victoria (from $40, six to 10 hours,
four daily) and beyond.

Port Hardy

POP 3700

Settled by Europeans in the early 1800s, this
small north-island settlement is best known
as the arrival and departure point for BC
Ferries Inside Passage trips. It's also a handy
gear-up spot for the North Coast Trail. Head
to the **visitor center** (☎250-949-7622; www.
porthardy.travel; 7250 Market St; ◔9am-5pm)
for information, including comprehensive
North Coast Trail maps ($9.95).

🏃 Activities

The town is a great access point for exploring the north-island wilderness. Hikers can
book customized guided tours with the
friendly folk at **North Island Daytrippers**
(www.islanddaytrippers.com). For those who
prefer to paddle, **Odyssey Kayaking** (www.
odysseykayaking.com; from $50) can rent you
some gear and point you to local highlights
(Malei Island and Alder Bay recommended).
For dive fans, **Catala Charters** (www.catala-
charters.net; dive trips from $150) can have you
hanging out with local octopus and wolf eels.

🛏 Sleeping & Eating

**North Coast Trail
Backpackers Hostel** HOSTEL $
(☎250-949-9441, 866-448-6303; www.porthardy
hostel.webs.com; 8635 Granville St; dm/r from
$25/60; 🛜) Colonizing a former downtown
storefront, this labyrinthine hostel is a war-
ren of small and larger dorms, overseen by
friendly owners with plenty of tips on how
to encounter the region – they'll even pick
you up from the ferry if you call ahead. The
hostel's hub is a large rec room, and while
the kitchen is small, the adjoining cafe can
keep you well fueled. ·

Ecoscape Cabins CABIN $$
(☎250-949-8524; www.ecoscapecabins.com; 6305
Jensen Cove Rd; cabins $130-175; 🛜) A clutch of
immaculate cedar-wood cabins, divided be-
tween compact units – with flat-screen TVs,
microwaves and sunny porches (ideal for
couples) – and roomier hilltop units with
swankier furnishings, BBQs and expansive
views. There's a tranquil retreat feel to stay-
ing here and you should expect to see eagles
swooping around the nearby trees. Deer are
not uncommon, too.

Café Guido CAFE $
(7135 Market St; mains $5-8; ◔7am-6pm Mon-
Fri, 8am-6pm Sat, 8am-5pm Sun; 🛜) A friendly
locals' hangout where you'll easily end up
sticking around for an hour or two – es-
pecially if you hit the loungey sofas with a
tome purchased from the bookstore down-
stairs. Grilled panini are the way to go for
lunch (try the Nero), but there's always a
good soup special. Then nip upstairs to the
surprisingly large and diverse craft shop.

ⓘ Getting There & Around

Pacific Coastal Airlines (www.pacific-coastal.
com) services arrive in Port Hardy from Vancou-
ver (from $170, 75 minutes, up to four daily).

Greyhound Canada (☎800-661-8747; www.
greyhound.ca) buses roll into the northern
Vancouver Island region daily from Campbell
River, Nanaimo and beyond.

BC Ferries (☎888-223-3779; www.bcferries.
com) services arrive in Port Hardy from Prince
Rupert (passenger/vehicle $195/444, 15 hours,
schedules vary) via the spectacular Inside
Passage route.

North Island Transportation (nit@island.net)
operates a handy shuttle ($8) to and from the
Port Hardy ferry terminal via area hotels.

TELEGRAPH COVE

Built as a one-shack telegraph station, this charming wooden village has since expanded into one of northern Vancouver Island's main visitor lures. Its pioneer-outpost feel is enhanced by the dozens of brightly painted buildings perched around the marina on stilts. But be aware: it can get ultracrowded in summer.

Head first along the boardwalk to the smashing **Whale Interpretive Centre** (www.killerwhalecentre.org; suggested donation adult/child $3/1; ⊘ 9am-5pm), bristling with hands-on artifacts and artfully displayed skeletons of cougars, sea otters and a giant fin whale.

You can also see whales of the live variety just offshore: this is one of the island's top marine-life-viewing regions. **Stubbs Island Whale Watching** (www.stubbs-island.com; adult/child $99/84) will get you up close with the orcas on a boat trek – you might also see humpbacks, dolphins and sea lions. For a bear alternative, **Tide Rip Grizzly Tours** (www.tiderip.com; tours $299; ⊘ May-Sep) leads full-day trips to local beaches and inlets in search of the area's furry locals.

The well-established **Telegraph Cove Resorts** (☑ 250-928-3131, 800-200-4665; www.telegraphcoveresort.com; campsites/cabins from $28/120) provides accommodations in forested tent spaces and a string of rustic cabins on stilts overlooking the marina. The nearby and much newer **Dockside 29** (☑ 877-835-2683, 250-928-3163; www.telegraphcove.ca; d from $140) is a good, motel-style alternative. Its rooms have kitchenettes with hardwood floors and waterfront views.

The **Killer Whale Café** (mains $14-18; ⊘ May-Sep) is the cove's best eatery – the salmon, mussel and prawn linguini is recommended. The adjoining **Old Saltery Pub** is an atmospheric, wood-lined nook with a cozy central fireplace and tasty Killer Whale Pale Ale. It's a good spot to sit in a corner and pretend you're an old sea salt – eye patch optional.

Cape Scott Provincial Park

It's more than 550km from the comparatively metropolis-like streets of down-island Victoria to the nature-hugging trailhead of this remote **park** (www.bcparks.ca) on Vancouver Island's crenulated northern tip. But if you really want to experience the raw, ravishing beauty of BC – especially its unkempt shorelines, breeze-licked rainforests and stunning sandy bays animated with tumbling waves and beady-eyed seabirds – this should be your number-one destination.

Hike the well-maintained, relatively easy 1.6-mile San Josef Bay Trail and you'll stroll from the shady confines of the trees right onto one of the best beaches in BC; a breathtaking, windswept expanse of roiling water, forested crags and the kind of age-old caves that could easily harbor lost smugglers. You can camp right here on the beach or just admire the passing ospreys before plunging back into the trees.

With several wooded trails to tempt you – most are aimed at well-prepared hikers with plenty of gumption – the forest offers moss-covered yew trees, cedars that are centuries old and a soft carpet of sun-dappled ferns covering every square inch.

For further information on the park, and the northern Vancouver Island region, check in with **Vancouver Island North** (www.vancouverislandnorth.ca).

SOUTHERN GULF ISLANDS

Stressed Vancouverites often escape into the restorative arms of the rustic, ever-relaxed Southern Gulf Islands, strung like a necklace between the mainland and Vancouver Island. Formerly colonized by BC hippies and US draft dodgers, Salt Spring, Galiano, Mayne, Saturna and North and South Pender Islands deliver on their promise of idyllic, sigh-triggering getaways.

ⓘ Getting There & Around

BC Ferries (www.bcferries.com) Operates direct and non-direct services from Vancouver Island's Swartz Bay terminal to all the main Southern Gulf Islands. There are also direct and non-direct services from the mainland's Tsawwassen terminal.

Gulf Islands Water Taxi (http://saltspring.com/watertaxi) Runs myriad handy walk-on boat services between some of the islands.

Salt Spring Air (www.saltspringair.com) Floatplanes service the area with camera-hugging short hops from the mainland.

Salt Spring Island

POP 10,500

A former hippie enclave that's now the site of many rich vacation homes, pretty Salt Spring justifiably receives the majority of Gulf Island visitors. The heart of the community is Ganges, also the location of the **visitor center** (☑250-537-5252; www.saltspringtourism.com; 121 Lower Ganges Rd, Ganges; ☺9am-5pm).

◉ Sights & Activities

Saturday Market   MARKET
(☑250-537-4448;   www.saltspringmarket.com; Centennial Park; ☺8am-4pm Sat Apr-Oct) If you arrive on a summer weekend, the best way to dive into the community is at the thriving Saturday Market, where you can tuck into luscious island-grown fruit and piquant cheeses and peruse locally produced arts and crafts. There are small Tuesday and Wednesday options if you're keen to avoid the crowds.

Salt Spring Island Cheese   FARM
(www.saltspringcheese.com; 285 Reynolds Rd; ☺10am-5pm) Drop by this bucolic famstead for a wander around the idyllic facilties and a tasting or two in the winery-style shop – consider some Ruckles goat's cheese to go.

Ruckle Provincial Park   PARK
(www.bcparks.ca) Pack up your picnic and head over to Ruckle Provincial Park, a southeast gem with ragged shorelines, arbutus forests and sun-kissed farmlands. There are trails here for all skill levels, with Yeo Point making an ideal pit stop.

Salt Spring Adventure Co   KAYAKING
(☑250-537-2764, 877-537-2764; www.saltspringadventures.com; 124 Upper Ganges Rd, Ganges; tours from $50) When it's time to hit the water (not literally), touch base with this friendly operator. It can kit you out for a bobbling kayak tour around Ganges Harbour and beyond.

🛏 Sleeping & Eating

Harbour House Hotel   HOTEL $$
(☑888-799-5571,   250-537-5571;   www.saltspringharbourhouse.com; 121 Upper Ganges Rd, Ganges; d from $149; ☎) This smashing rustic-chic hotel with 17 rooms is just up the hill from the main Ganges action, but it feels like you're staying in a country cottage estate in England. The grounds are strewn with locally made artworks and the waterfront views will have your camera itching to be used. The restaurant is high-end gourmet (breakfast recommended).

★**Tree House Café**   CAFE $$
(www.treehousecafe.ca; 106 Purvis Lane, Ganges; mains $10-16) At this magical outdoor dining experience in the heart of Ganges you'll sit in the shade of a large plum tree as you choose from a menu of comfort pastas, Mexican specialties and gourmet burgers and sandwiches – the tuna melt is a local fave, perhaps washed down with a Salt Spring Ales porter. Live music every night in summer.

Gathering   FUSION $$
(115 Fulford Ganges Rd, Ganges; mains $8-16; ☺11am-midnight Tue-Sun) Lined with sci-fi artworks and a wall crammed with loaner board games, this new Ganges hangout is the perfect spot to spend a few hours. For food, there's tapas plus larger dishes combining local ingredients with international influences (think Moroccan spiced duck). Don't miss the crab-stuffed doughnuts, a menu standout perfect for fueling a leisurely evening of role-play gaming.

North & South Pender Islands

POP 2200

Once joined by a sandy isthmus, the North and South Penders are far quieter than Salt Spring and attract those looking for a low-key retreat. With pioneer farms, old-time orchards and almost 40 coves and beaches, the Penders – now linked by a single-lane bridge – are a good spot for cyclists and hikers. For visitor information check www.penderislandchamber.com.

◉ Sights & Activities

Enjoy the sand at **Medicine Beach** and **Clam Bay** on North Pender as well as **Gowlland Point** on the east coast of South Pender. Just over the bridge to South

Pender is Mt Norman, complete with a couple of hikes that promise grand views of the surrounding islands. The island also has a regular Saturday farmers market (www.pifi. ca; Pender Islands Recreation & Agriculture Hall, North Pender; ☺9:30am-1pm Sat Apr-Nov) in the community hall.

Many artists call Pender home and you can chat with them in their galleries and studios by downloading a pair of free maps from Pender Creatives (www.pendercreatives.com) that reveal exactly where they are (most are on North Pender). Alternatively, hit the water with a paddle (and hopefully a boat) via the friendly folks at Pender Island Kayak Adventures (www.kayakpenderisland.com; Otter Bay Marina; tours adult/child from $59/35).

🛏 Sleeping & Eating

Inn on Pender Island INN $$
(☑800-550-0172, 250-629-3353; www.innonpender.com; 4709 Canal Rd, North Pender; d/cabins from $79/159) At this rustic lodge with motel-style rooms and a couple of cozy, wood-lined cabins, you're surrounded by verdant woodland, which explains the frequent appearance of wandering deer. The lodge rooms are neat and clean and share an outdoor hot tub; the waterfront cabins have barrel-vaulted ceilings, full kitchens and little porches out front.

Poet's Cove Resort & Spa HOTEL $$$
(☑250-629-2100, 888-512-7638; www.poetscove.com; 9801 Spalding Rd, Bedwell Harbour, South Pender; d from $250; ☒) A luxurious harbor-front lodge with arts-and-crafts-accented rooms, most with great views across the glassy water. Extras include an activity center that books ecotours and fishing excursions, and there's also an elegant West Coast restaurant (Aurora), where you can dine in style. As well as this, the resort offers kayak treks plus a full-treatment spa, complete with that all-important steam cave.

Cafe at Hope Bay WEST COAST $$
(www.thecafeathopebay.com; 4301 Bedwell Harbour Rd, North Pender; mains $14-23; ☺11am-8:30pm Tue-Sun) West Coast ingredients with international influences rule at this bistro-style spot (closely followed by the sterling views across Plumper Sound). The fish-and-chips is predictably good, but dig deeper into the menu for less-expected treats such

as the lip-smacking coconut curried mussels and prawns. It's just a few minutes from the Otter Bay ferry dock.

Saturna Island
POP 325

Suffused with tranquillity, tiny Saturna is a natural retreat remote enough to deter casual visitors. Almost half the island, laced with curving bays, stunning rock bluffs and towering arbutus trees, is part of the Gulf Islands National Park Reserve and the only crowds you'll see are feral goats that have called this munchable area home. If you've had enough of civilization, this is the place to be. Visit the Saturna Island Tourism Association (www.saturnatourism.com) website for more information.

◎ Sights & Activities

On the north side of the island, Winter Cove has a white-sand beach that's popular for swimming, boating and fishing. If you're here for Canada Day (July 1), you should also partake in the island's main annual event in the adjoining Hunter Field. This communal Lamb Barbeque (www.saturnalambbarbeque.com; adult/child $20/10; ☺Jul 1), complete with live music, sack races, beer garden and a carnivorous feast, is centered on a fire pit surrounded by staked-out, slow-roasting sheep.

Walk off your meat belly the next day with a hike up Mt Warburton Pike (497m), where you'll spot wild goats, soaring eagles and restorative panoramic views of the surrounding islands: focus your binoculars and you might spy a whale or two sailing quietly along the coast.

Wine fans can enjoy tastings and tours at Saturna Island Winery (www.saturnavineyards.com; 8 Quarry Rd; ☺11:30am-5pm), which also has an on-site bistro.

🛏 Sleeping & Eating

Saturna Lodge HOTEL $$
(☑250-539-2254, 866-539-2254; www.saturna.ca; 130 Payne Rd; d from $129; ☺) A peaceful respite from the outside world, this friendly lodge property is surrounded by tree-fringed garden and offers six-room country-inn-style rooms (go for the spacious honeymoon suite). You're not far from the waterfront here and rates include a hearty breakfast to fuel you up for a day of exploring.

★ **Wild Thyme Coffee House** CAFE $
(www.wildthymecoffeehouse.com; 109 East Point Rd;
mains $6-10; ⊙6am-2pm Mon-Fri, 8am-4pm Sat &
Sun; 🛜) Located in and around a converted
and immaculately preserved antique double-
decker bus (named Lucy), this charming cafe
is a local landmark conveniently located not
far from the ferry dock. Diners can snag seats
inside the bus (tables have been added) and
tuck into wholesome breakfasts, soup and
sandwich lunches and baked treats all made
with foodie love. There's a focus on local ingredients and fair-trade coffee.

Mayne Island
POP 900

Once a stopover for gold-rush miners (who
nicknamed it 'Little Hell'), Mayne is the
region's most historic island. Long past its
importance as a commercial hub, it now
houses a colorful clutch of resident artists.
For visitor information, see www.mayne
islandchamber.ca.

The heritage **Agricultural Hall** in Miners
Bay hosts the lively **farmers market**
(⊙10am-1pm Sat Jul-Sep), with local crafts
and produce. Among the most visit-worthy
galleries and artisan studios on the island is
Mayne Island Glass Foundry (www.mayne
islandglass.com; 563 Aya Reach Rd), where recycled glass is used to fashion new jewelry
and ornaments – pick up a cool green-glass
slug for the road.

The south shore's **Dinner Bay Park** has
a lovely sandy beach, as well as an immacu-
late **Japanese Garden**, built by locals to
commemorate early 20th-century Japanese
residents.

For kayakers and stand-up paddle
boarders, **Bennett Bay Kayaking** (www.
bennettbaykayaking.com; kayak rentals/tours from
$33/65; ⊙Apr-Oct) can get you out on the wa-
ter here via rentals and tours.

If you're just too tired to head back to the
mainland, **Mayne Island Beach Resort**
(☎866-539-5399; www.mayneislandresort.com;
494 Arbutus Dr; d from $139; 🛜🍴🏊) combines
ocean-view rooms in a century-old inn with
swanky, luxe beach cottages. There's also a
spa and large resto-bar.

When it's time to eat, head for a patio
spot at the ever-friendly **Green House Bar
& Grill** (454 Village Bay Rd; mains $8-16; ⊙noon-
8pm Wed-Sun) and dive into freshly made
fries and heaping burgers.

Galiano Island
POP 1100

With the islands' widest ecological diversity,
this skinny landmass – named after a 1790s
Spanish explorer – offers activities for marine
enthusiasts and landlubbers alike.

The Sturdies Bay ferry end is markedly
busier than the rest of the island, which
becomes ever more forested and tranquil
as you continue your drive from the dock.
Drop into the **visitor info booth** (www.
galianoisland.com; 2590 Sturdies Bay Rd; ⊙Jul &
Aug) before you leave the ferry area – there's
also a garage, a post office and a bookstore
nearby.

Once you've got your bearings – ie driven
off the ferry – head for **Montague Harbour
Marine Provincial Park** for trails to beaches,
meadows and a cliff carved by glaciers. In
contrast, **Bodega Ridge Provincial Park** is
renowned for its eagle and cormorant bird
life and has spectacular drop-off viewpoints.

The protected waters of **Trincomali Channel** and the more chaotic waters of **Active
Pass** satisfy paddlers of all skill levels. **Galiano Kayaks** (☎250-539-2442; www.seakayak.
ca; 3451 Montague Rd; 2hr/day rental from $32/58,
tours from $55) can help with rentals and guid-
ed tours. And if you fancy exploring on land,
rent a moped from **Galiano Adventures**
(www.galianoadventures.com; Montague Harbour
Marina; rental per hour from $20; ⊙May-Sep).

Among the places to sleep on the island,
sophisticates will enjoy **Galiano Inn** (☎877-
530-3939, 250-539-3388; www.galianoinn.com; 134
Madrona Dr; d from $249; 🛜🏊), a Tuscan-style
villa with 10 elegant rooms, each with fireplace and romantic oceanfront terrace. And,
once you're done exploring, drop in for beer
and fish-and-chips at the venerable **Hum-
mingbird Pub** (www.hummingbirdpub.com;
47 Sturdies Bay Rd; mains $8-12), where you'll
likely run into everyone else on the island.

Understand the Pacific Northwest

Pacific Northwest Today

The Pacific Northwest is full of cutting-edge ideas and technology but it's also true to its eco-green roots. The region's cuisine has become famous, while its politics remain liberal, and though the economy has seen its ups and downs over the last few decades, new pioneers arrive every single day.

Best on Film

One Flew Over the Cuckoo's Nest (1975) Oscar-winning movie about a mental institution and its inhabitants, filmed in Salem, OR (the novel was based in Oregon).

Sleepless in Seattle (1993) Romantic comedy that highlighted Seattle's Space Needle, Pike Place Market and houseboat communities.

Twilight (2008) Highly popular vampire saga that catapulted sleepy Forks, WA (as well as other Pacific Northwest locations) onto the world's center stage.

Best in Print

The Good Rain: Across Time and Terrain in the Pacific Northwest (Timothy Egan). One man's narrative on the land he loves, with social, economic and political perspectives.

Faux Pas

Washington Flaunting that you moved here from California because real estate is cheaper.

Oregon Trying to pump your own gas at a service station.

British Columbia Mistaking a Canadian for an American.

Recent Times

Since the bursting of the high-tech bubble in 2000, the Pacific Northwest has had ups and downs trying to regain a foothold in this now-fickle field. And in recent years, many companies of all kinds have shut down, moved away or laid off workers. But, like the pioneers of so long ago, other companies continue to pop up or move to this popular region to fill in the empty spaces and help grow the population.

The real-estate market has also had its highs and lows, though in general the Pacific Northwest has done well, attracting those who seek to own a share of its bounty. Seattle, Portland and Vancouver had revitalized markets in mid-2013, with demand outstripping supply and causing a serious rise in values.

The Pacific Northwest keeps exerting a strong pull on the adventurous spirit. And though today's Northwest populations tend to be driven by espresso rather than the desire to chart new territory, there remains a culture founded on restless idealism and the sense that there's still more prospecting to do.

Small Talk

Mention the Northwest to folks outside this area and you'll start a conversation on the region's lush forests, snow-dusted volcanic mountains and amazing waterways and coastlines. Then you might move on to the region's high unemployment rates, its computer industry (aka 'Silicon Forest') and, last but not least, those drizzly skies and all that rain!

For the locals, politics is always a good topic (generally left-leaning on the west coast and right-leaning on the eastern side). How could anyone resist commenting on Washington's new laws legalizing both gay marriage and recreational marijuana use? Or voicing an opinion on whether fluoride is beneficial or malignant (after a 2013 vote, Portland remains the largest US city without fluoride in its water supply)? Or whether to allow coal shipments through Washington and Oregon's rail lines and down the Columbia River?

Sustainability is such a presence in this region that people at parties might be chatting about hot composting, keeping chickens and/or goats, city growth boundaries and – of course – the environment and what to do about it: paper or plastic? Local or organic? Hydroelectric power or salmon migration?

Sports talk is a no-brainer in this outdoor-loving region, even though Washington and Oregon only have a few major-league teams: the Seattle Seahawks (football) and Mariners (baseball), the Oregon Trail Blazers (basketball) and the Portland Timbers (soccer). Hockey-loving British Columbia, meanwhile, loves to gab about its Canucks.

Economic Biggies

Once covered in lush forests, it's no surprise that the Northwest, with its rich natural resources, invited colonization. Today Oregon and Washington continue to lead the USA in lumber production, while British Columbia contains most of Canada's marketable timber.

The Columbia and other Northwest rivers were once teeming with salmon, but overfishing, dam building and deforestation have nearly wiped out the species (conservation efforts are ongoing, however). Though much diminished, commercial and sport fishing still plays an important role in the regional economy.

The high-tech industry has redefined the region's personality by creating jobs and enriching support industries. The Seattle area continues to be headquarters for many big companies like Microsoft, Nintendo and Amazon.com, while Oregon's 'Silicon Forest' is supported by campuses of Intel, Tektronix and Google. British Columbia has its own high-tech niches, but Vancouver's vibrant film industry tends to steal the economic spotlight. Outdoor clothing and shoe companies like Nike, Columbia Sportswear and Adidas (North America office) are all based here, and – with the region's high precipitation – hydroelectric power is another big industry.

Agriculture flourishes along the moist valleys of the Rogue, Umpqua, Skagit and Fraser Rivers. The valleys along the Pacific Coast are famous for their dairy farms, and along the Columbia and Okanogan Rivers are vast orchards of apples, cherries, peaches and pears. And let's not forget the grape: Oregon's fertile Willamette Valley yields its famous pinot noir, while the irrigated vineyards of Washington's Columbia, Walla Walla and Yakima Valleys produce world-class chardonnays and merlots.

POPULATION: **15 MILLION**

AREA: **525,000 SQ MILES**

MINIMUM WAGE:
**WASHINGTON $9.32,
OREGON $9.10, BRITISH
COLUMBIA $10.25**

UNEMPLOYMENT RATES:
**WASHINGTON 7%,
OREGON 8.1%, BRITISH
COLUMBIA 6.6%**

**if Washington &
Oregon were 100 people**

78 would be white
11 would be Latino
6 would be Asian

3 would be
African American
2 would be
Native American

**if British Columbia
were 100 people**

74 would be white
20 would be Asian
3 would be
Native American

2 would be Latino
1 would be
African American

population per sq mile

WASHINGTON   OREGON   USA

≈ 40 people

History

The human history of the Pacific Northwest started about 20,000 years ago, when people first stepped into North America via a land bridge from Siberia to Alaska. This area, now underwater, is known as the Bering Strait. These early hunter-gatherers, the ancestors of Native Americans, spread down through the Americas over millennia, and a multitude of tribes, each with its own culture and language, flourished around the Pacific Northwest.

Today, Oregon has 10 federally recognized Native American tribes, while Washington has nearly 30 and British Columbia over a hundred.

In the mid-16th century, however, white people came knocking, which spelled the gradual demise of the First Nations. Explorers from Portugal, Spain, Britain and Russia all sought territorial claims, but it was the famed expedition of Lewis and Clark that first seriously mapped out the region and later nabbed an American foothold. A wealth of beavers and otters brought riches to many in the fur trade, and the principal British trading post of Fort Vancouver became an agricultural hub. Soon after, Oregon City was established, becoming the first incorporated city west of the Rockies.

The Northwest's population continued to thrive, with trading posts, farming and missionary work, and in 1843 the region's first government was voted into existence. There now existed opportunities for whole families to stake out new land and settle down. Thousands loaded up their possessions in covered wagons and headed west, following the sometimes treacherous Oregon and Applegate Trails, and often traveling up to eight months to reach their destinations.

By the 1880s the abundant land yielded fortunes in agriculture, fishing and logging. Railroads were built, making access and trading even easier. With the discovery of gold in the Canadian Klondike, Seattle flourished, and the two World Wars' demands on lumber and shipbuilding brought more industry to the area. Later in the 20th century the local economy shifted to high-tech and gave the area its 'Silicon Forest' nickname.

TIMELINE	20,000 BC	c 13,000 BC	c 5600 BC
	Nomadic people cross a land bridge connecting Asia and North America and disperse southward, becoming the ancestors of today's Native Americans.	Epic glacial floods carve out 4000ft cliffs along an 80-mile section of the Columbia River Gorge. Eventually the river will stretch to 1243 miles long.	Mt Mazama erupts in an explosion estimated to be over 40 times more powerful than Mt St Helens' in 1980. The subsequent caldera creates what is now Crater Lake.

Native Americans

Early coastal inhabitants – who tramped up and down the Pacific Coast, around Puget Sound and along river valleys – went out to sea in pursuit of whales or sea lions, or depended on catching salmon and cod and collecting shellfish. On land they hunted deer and elk while gathering berries and roots. Plenty of food was stored for the long winters, when free time could be spent on artistic, religious and cultural pursuits like putting on potlatches (ceremonial feasts), taking part in vision quests (spiritual trances) or carving dancing masks and totem poles. The construction of (ornately carved) cedar canoes led to extensive trading networks among the permanent settlements that stretched along the coast.

Inland, on the arid plateaus between the Cascades and the Rocky Mountains, a regional culture based on seasonal migration between rivers and temperate uplands developed among tribes including the Nez Perce, Cayuse, Spokane, Yakama and Kootenai. During salmon runs, the tribes gathered at rapids and waterfalls to net or harpoon fish, which they then dried or smoked. One such spot, highly significant to many native peoples as both fishing grounds and a community gathering place, was Celilo Falls, located 12 miles east of the present city of The Dalles on the Columbia River (unfortunately, construction of the Dalles Dam in 1957 submerged these falls).

In the harsh landscapes of Oregon's southern desert, yet another native culture evolved. Tribes such as the Shoshone, Paiute and Bannock were nomadic peoples who hunted and scavenged in the northern reaches of the Great Basin desert. Berries, roots and small game such as gophers and rabbits constituted their meager diet. Clusters of easily transported, woven-reed shelters made up migratory villages, while religious and cultural life focused on shamans, who could tap into the spirit world to heal sickness or bring success in hunting.

Europeans Take a Look

The first Europeans to clap eyes on the area were the crew of Portuguese explorer Juan Rodríguez Cabrillo. In 1542 his ships sailed from Mexico and, under the command of Bartolomé Ferrelo (Cabrillo died along the way), reached the mouth of the Rogue River in 1543; this is where the city of Gold Beach now stands. English explorer Sir Frances Drake checked out the region in 1579, but by the 18th century the Spanish had colonized the southern parts of California and begun to explore the northern Pacific Coast in earnest. They were looking for the Northwest Passage, a fabled direct water route from the Pacific Ocean to the Atlantic Ocean.

During the last ice age, so much water was trapped in huge glaciers that sea levels were up to 400ft lower than today. This created a land bridge between Alaska and Asia thought to have been over 1000 miles wide. Today the Bering Strait, at its narrowest, is 53 miles wide.

1543	1792	1793	1804
Juan Rodríguez Cabrillo's crew are the first Europeans to sight the Pacific Northwest coast. Cabrillo himself didn't see it, having died along the way.	American Robert Gray finds the elusive mouth of the Columbia River and sails upstream, becoming the first non–Native American to do so. He names the river after his ship, the *Columbia Rediviva*.	Scottish explorer Alexander Mackenzie becomes the first European to reach the Pacific Ocean (north of Mexico) via an overland route. He crosses the Canadian Rockies and reaches present-day Bella Coola, BC.	The Lewis and Clark Expedition – which consisted of 33 members, including Sacagawea – leaves St Louis, MO, on its journey toward the Pacific Ocean.

HISTORY LEWIS & CLARK

By 1774, Spanish frigates reached as far north as the Queen Charlotte Islands, claiming the Northwest coast for the Spanish crown.

The British, not to be outdone, were also looking for the Northwest Passage. In 1778, Captain James Cook explored the coast of present-day Oregon, Washington and British Columbia, landing at Nootka Sound on Vancouver Island. With him was George Vancouver, who in 1792 became the first European explorer to sail and chart the waters of Puget Sound (and left quite a legacy – Fort Vancouver, Vancouver, BC, Vancouver Island and Vancouver, WA, are all named after him). The Spanish attempted to build colonies along the Northwest coast; however, European politics forced Spain to give up its Northwest claim to Britain in 1792.

The Americans entered the scene in 1792 when Captain Robert Gray spotted the mouth of the Columbia River, where Astoria is today, through obscuring sandbars and hazardous currents. He sailed up the great waterway, traded with the Native Americans and named this great river the Columbia, in honor of his ship. The true importance of his discovery would be realized later, when it supported US territorial claims to the area.

Lewis & Clark

Like European explorers before them, Lewis and Clark came to the Pacific Northwest in search of adventure – and the fabled Northwest Passage. It started in 1801, when US president Thomas Jefferson enlisted his personal secretary, Meriwether Lewis, as leader of an expedition to chart North America's western regions. The goal was to find a waterway to the Pacific while exploring the newly acquired Louisiana Purchase and establishing a foothold for American interests. Lewis, then 27, had no training for exploration but couldn't resist this grand opportunity. He convinced his good friend, 33-year-old William Clark, an experienced frontiersman and army veteran, to tag along. In 1804 the party left St Louis, MO, heading west with an entourage of 40 adventurers.

The Corps of Discovery – the expedition's official name – fared relatively well, in part because of the presence of Sacagawea. This young Shoshone woman had been sold to, and become the wife of, Toussaint Charbonneau, a French-Canadian trapper who was part of the entourage. Sacagawea proved invaluable as a guide, translator and ambassador to the area's Native Americans. York, Clark's African American servant, also softened tensions between the group and the Native Americans.

The party traveled some 8000 miles in about two years, documenting everything they came across in their journals with such bad spelling that it must have taken historians a few extra years just to sort out what they wrote. Meticulous notes were made on 122 animals and 178 plants, with some new discoveries along the way. On November 15, 1805, the party

The Northwest Passage, a sea route connecting the Pacific and Atlantic Oceans through Canada's northern islands, is blocked by thick ice much of the year. However, climate change has now made it possible for ships to much more easily navigate this fabled waterway.

The daily logs of Lewis and Clark, as presented in Bernard DeVoto's carefully edited *Journals of Lewis and Clark*, are full of wild adventures, misspellings and wonderful candor.

1805	1811	1825	1829
Lewis and Clark finally reach the Pacific Ocean after 18 months of traveling. They lay groundwork that immensely aids future US expansion toward the West.	Pacific Fur Company mogul John Jacob Astor establishes Fort Astoria, the first permanent US settlement on the Pacific Coast. He later becomes the country's first millionaire.	Hudson's Bay Company establishes Fort Vancouver, which becomes the most prominent European presence in the Northwest. Today, Washington state's Vancouver is located here.	Oregon City becomes the first established city west of the Mississippi and the pot-of-gold destination for early pioneers traversing the Oregon Trail.

Historic Trails

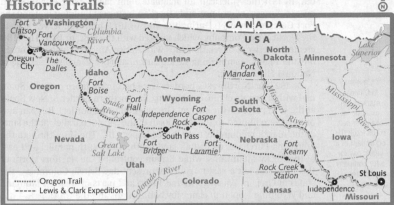

finally reached the mouth of the Columbia River and the Pacific Ocean at Cape Disappointment (now a state park in Washington). Needing to bed down for the winter, they established Fort Clatsop just south of Astoria, which today has been reconstructed in the Lewis & Clark National Historical Park.

Lewis and Clark returned to a heroes' welcome in St Louis in 1806. Lewis was later appointed governor of the Louisiana Territory, but he died a year later, possibly murdered, but more likely by suicide. Clark became governor of the Missouri Territory, living to be 68.

Otters & Beavers Lose Out

The British and Americans soon tapped into the Northwest's bounty of fur-bearing wildlife. While in the Northwest in 1778, Cook's crew traded with Native Americans for animal pelts, of which sea otter and beaver were the most valuable. This trade dominated British and US economic interests in the northern Pacific for the next 30 years, until the War of 1812 stuck a thorn in the side of relations between the two countries.

Trappers from two competing British fur-trading companies – the Hudson's Bay Company (HBC, still in operation today) and the North West Company – began to expand from their bases around Hudson's Bay and the Great Lakes, edging over the Rocky Mountains to establish fur-trading forts. These forts traded with local Native Americans for beaver, otter, fox, wolf or whatever other fur-bearing animal had yet to be wiped

Undaunted Courage, by Stephen Ambrose, is a compelling account of the Lewis and Clark expedition, following the footsteps of their extraordinary journey to the Pacific and back again.

1836

The Whitman Party (which includes the first two women to travel the Oregon Trail) establishes a mission near Walla Walla, WA. Their adventures would end in tragedy 11 years later.

1843

A slim-margin vote at Champoeg (30 miles south of current-day Portland) establishes Oregon's first independent government, weakening the British hold on the region.

➡ Covered wagon

out. In 1811 the American fur magnate John Jacob Astor established a post in Astoria (where presently there's a historical building housing the Fort George Brewery). During the War of 1812, however, it was sold to the North West Company, which merged with the HBC in 1821. The HBC created a network of relationships with Native American tribes throughout the region, establishing headquarters at Fort Vancouver – today a National Historic Site.

By 1827 the Northwest's borders were becoming more defined. Spain had withdrawn its claim, establishing the northern border of New Spain at the 47th parallel (the current Oregon–California border). Russian ambitions were limited to the land north of the 54° 40' parallel, at the start of the Alaska panhandle, near Prince Rupert, BC. The USA, through the Louisiana Purchase, owned all land south of the 49th parallel and east of the Rocky Mountains, while Britain controlled the territory north of this line. This left a vast territory of present-day British Columbia – the states of Oregon, Washington and Idaho and parts of western Montana and Wyoming – open to claims by both Britain and the USA.

The Treaty of Ghent, which ended the War of 1812, included an amendment that declared a joint custody (of sorts) of the Pacific Northwest: Britain and the USA could continue economic development in the area, but neither could establish an official government.

> In Chinese markets, an exceptional sea-otter pelt could fetch the equivalent of a year's pay for a fur-company laborer.

The Americans Settle In

Unlike most other early trading posts, which were basically repositories for goods, Fort Vancouver became a thriving, nearly self-sufficient agricultural community complete with mills, a dairy, gardens and fields.

Canadian-born Dr John McLoughlin, often called the 'father of Oregon,' was the capable steward of this post. He encouraged settlement beyond the precincts of the fort, and allowed retired HBC trappers to settle along the Willamette River in an area still called French Prairie. By 1828 these French Canadians, with their Native American wives, began to clear the land and build cabins. McLoughlin established a mill and incorporated the first town in the Northwest in 1829, at Oregon City. He later built a house there, which today is a museum.

> The oldest commercial corporation in North America is the Hudson's Bay Company, which once controlled the Pacific Northwest fur trade, conducted early exploration of the region and even functioned as a de facto government before the US took over.

The eventual decline of the fur trade, along with an influx of American farmers, traders and settlers from the east, all helped loosen the weakening British Empire's grip on the Pacific Northwest. But it was the missionaries who probably played the biggest role. In 1834, New England Methodists Daniel and Jason Lee founded a mission just north of present-day Salem. Other missionaries arrived in 1836, establishing missions near today's Walla Walla, WA, and Lewiston, ID.

Losing ground despite the Treaty of Ghent, the HBC hedged its bets and established another center of operations further north at Fort Vic-

1846	1847	1848	1850
The Oregon Treaty brings an end to land disputes between the US and Britain. Both countries had jointly occupied the region since the Treaty of 1818.	The Whitman Massacre starts the Cayuse War, resulting in the decimation of the Cayuse people and their forced relocation onto a reservation.	The Oregon territory officially becomes US land, with its capital at Oregon City. The territory's borders encompass today's Oregon, Washington and Idaho, plus parts of Wyoming and Montana.	Congress passes the Donation Land Act, which grants every white European settler and 'American half-breed Indian' 320 acres. Married couples can claim 640 acres.

toria, on Vancouver Island, BC. But the federal government did not offer military intervention to rid the area of British stragglers. If the settlers wanted an independent civil authority, they would have to do the dirty work themselves.

Rounding the Turn at Champoeg

By the early 1840s the Willamette Valley had become home to a rag-tag mix of 700 French-Canadian farmers, retired trappers, Protestant missionaries and general adventurers. Eager to establish some order to the region, the settlers created the framework for a budding government. Meetings led to an 1843 vote at Champoeg, along the Willamette River about 30 miles south of Portland (now Champoeg State Heritage Area). By a razor-thin 52-to-50 margin, a measure was passed to organize a provisional government independent of the HBC. The land north of the Columbia, however, would remain in control of the British – for a bit longer.

Meanwhile, the USA–Canada boundary dispute became a hotbed of contention. There was a fervent settler movement to occupy the Northwest all the way up to present-day Alaska. The 1844 presidential campaign slogan became '54/40 or fight' (referring to the geographical parallel). The bickering finally ended in 1846, when the British and Americans negotiated the Treaty of Oregon and agreed to today's present USA–Canada border, which runs along the 49th parallel.

Accepting its inevitable fate, the HBC gave up its headquarters at Fort Vancouver and hightailed it north to Fort Victoria on Vancouver Island (many British citizens followed, and Vancouver Island was designated a Crown colony in 1849). In 1848 Oregon officially became a US territory.

NORTHERN GOLD

Nothing draws fortune seekers more than the lure of riches. In 1851 gold was discovered in southern Oregon near the Rogue River valley. Prospectors and scoundrels flooded in, boomtowns popped up overnight and native populations were brushed aside. A year later gold was discovered near Scottsburg along the Umpqua River, while along the coast miners washed gold dust out of sands near Coos Bay and Gold Beach.

In 1861 the Blue Mountains of eastern Oregon became the next target for gold seekers, but violent clashes ensued between Native Americans and the newcomers. The result for most Native Americans was forced relocation to reservations, some as far away as Oklahoma. Meanwhile, the rush kept moving north into British Columbia's Fraser River and, over the next few decades, beyond into the Yukon Territory.

1851	1853	1858	1859
The first significant gold deposits are discovered near Jacksonville, starting a gold rush in Oregon. Thousands of fortune seekers pour into the state, creating new settlements and small towns.	The Washington Territory is created from the northernmost half of the Oregon Territory. Its borders later change, but they become permanent when Washington state is created in 1889.	Cascade Railroad Company is the region's first railroad and begins operations in the Columbia River Gorge. It will take 25 years for transcontinental rail lines to finally reach the Pacific Northwest.	On February 14, Oregon is admitted into the union and becomes the USA's 33rd state, about nine months after Minnesota achieves its own statehood.

Follow the Oregon Trail

In 1859 Oregon became the 33rd state of the union. It voted to outlaw slavery, but free blacks still couldn't settle here, and only white men over 21 were allowed to vote.

The party was now just getting started. In the Willamette Valley, nearly 900 new settlers arrived in one go, more than doubling the area's population. They were a trickle in what became a flood of migrants following the 2170-mile Oregon Trail, which edged south around the footsteps of the explorers before them – first Lewis and Clark, then adventurous fur trappers and intrepid missionaries (good interpretive centers exist today in Oregon's La Grande and Baker City). Between 1843 and 1860, over 50,000 fresh faces arrived to a brand-new future in the gorgeous Pacific Northwest.

Spanning six states, the Oregon Trail sorely tested the families who embarked on this perilous trip. Their belongings were squirreled away under canvas-topped wagons, which often trailed livestock. The journey could take up to eight months, and by the time the settlers reached eastern Oregon their food supplies were running on fumes. And there was one last challenge: when the weary parties arrived at the Columbia River in The Dalles, they had to choose between rafting themselves and all their belongings through the rapids in the Columbia River Gorge or struggling up the flanks of Mt Hood and descending via the precipitous Barlow Trail.

The journey ended at Oregon City, at the base of the falls of the Willamette River, which became the region's early seat of government. Above the falls, in the river's broad agricultural basin, small farming communities sprang up. Not far away, Portland, near the Willamette's confluence with the Columbia River, took on an early importance as a trade center.

Among the provisions recommended for those traveling the Oregon Trail were coffee (15lb per person), bacon (25lb per person), 1lb of castile soap, citric acid to prevent scurvy and a live cow for milk and emergency meat.

After Fort Vancouver fell to the Americans in 1846, explorers began to mosey up the Cowlitz River into the Puget Sound area, initially planting roots at Tumwater near Olympia. By 1851 a group of Oregon Trail pioneers, led by brothers Arthur and David Denny, set their sights on Elliott Bay and founded the port city of Seattle.

In 1846, seeking a route around the daunting Columbia River Gorge, a party of pioneers began to blaze a southern route into the Willamette Valley. This new Applegate Trail cut through the deserts of Nevada and California before turning north through the valleys of southern Oregon. Immigrants along this route established towns such as Eugene, and scouted the land in the Rogue, Umpqua and Klamath River valleys.

By the late 1850s settlers had staked claims to the best land in the western valleys. Some folks began looking east of the Cascades, particularly to the Grande Ronde River valley of present-day Oregon and the Walla Walla River valley of what would be Washington. Eastern Oregon didn't become a hot spot until the discovery of gold there in the 1860s.

1861
Gold is discovered in the Blue Mountains of eastern Oregon.

1871
British Columbia, Canada's third-largest province in area and population, becomes the country's sixth province to join into Confederation.

1889
On November 11, President Benjamin Harrison signs a bill making Washington the USA's 42nd state.

WITOLD SKRYPCZAK /GETTY IMAGES ©

➜ Gold-mining dredge, Oregon

CHIEF SEALTH

'How can you buy or sell the sky, the warmth of the land?' Chief Sealth of the Duwamish tribe reportedly stated in his famous 1854 speech. 'If we do not own the freshness of the air and the sparkle of the water, how can you buy them? Every shining pine needle, every sandy shore, every mist in the dark woods, every clearing and humming insect is holy in the memory and experience of my people...' Though it's unlikely Chief Sealth uttered these exact words, his thoughts are probably reflected in them.

The Seattle area was originally the homeland of the peaceful Duwamish tribe, who initially welcomed members of the Denny party (who founded Seattle) when they arrived in 1851. Chief Sealth (1786–1866) had urged peaceful coexistence between his tribe and the whites. Relations with other tribes in Puget Sound were not as good, however – in 1855 warfare erupted between the Native Americans and European settlers, and in the end the settlers prevailed.

The Duwamish were moved to the Port Madison Reservation in 1856 despite their peaceable history. In part to recognize Chief Sealth's aid and pacifist efforts, the settlers renamed their village 'Seattle', in the chief's honor. Today, his grave site lies in the cemetery behind St Peter's Church in Suquamish, just outside Seattle.

Decimation of Native Americans

By 1860 the Pacific Northwest's coast was strung with white settlements, and most major cities had been founded. The area's wildlife, especially the beaver and otter populations, had been nearly extinguished. European diseases had devastated whole Native American communities, while alcoholism took its own insidious toll on their cultures.

Missionaries eventually delivered the final blow. In 1847, near Walla Walla, the Whitman mission's attempts to bring Christianity to eastern Washington tribes ended in tragedy. The Cayuse Native Americans slew over a dozen missionaries in revenge for a measles epidemic. Settlers now felt justified in removing Native Americans from their land and incarcerating them on reservations. Coastal Native Americans were marched or shipped to reservations in 1855 and 1856, where increased illness, starvation and dislocation led to the complete extinction of many tribal groups. Even on Vancouver Island, where British policies were generally more enlightened, most arable land was given to European settlers. Missionaries worked to make illegal the traditional potlatches that formed the nucleus of coastal Native American religion and social life.

East of the Cascades, Native Americans were more resistant to the US military and settlers. Fierce battles were fought between the US Army and various tribes from 1855 to 1877. Especially bloody were the Rogue

1899	1937	1962	1980
Mt Rainier National Park is established on March 2, becoming the USA's fifth national park. It contains the highest point in the Cascade Range (over 14,000ft).	After three years and $88 million, Bonneville Dam is completed on the Columbia River. The construction provides 3000 crucial jobs during the Great Depression.	Seattle hosts the second major World's Fair since WWII; the Space Needle opens on the first day of the fair, April 21.	Mt St Helens blows her top, killing 57 people and destroying over 200 homes. Her elevation is cut from 9677ft to 8365ft, and where a peak once stood, a mile-wide crater is born.

River and Modoc Wars, in southern Oregon, and the Cayuse War, near Walla Walla. However, these Native American groups also ended up on reservations, dependent upon the federal government for subsistence.

More Recent Times

The incidents leading up to, during and after the tragic Whitman Massacre, which had wide-ranging repercussions in Oregon's history, are detailed at www.oregonpioneers.com/whitman.htm.

By the 1880s the Northwest's port cities boomed with the region's rich agricultural, fishing and logging resources. The Northern Pacific Railroad linked the Northwest to the eastern USA, making national markets more accessible and bringing in more settlers. Seattle became the area's most important seaport in 1897 when gold was discovered in the Canadian Klondike and prospectors poured into the city.

The World Wars brought further economic fortune to the Pacific Northwest, when the area became the nation's largest lumber producer and both Oregon's and Washington's naval yards bustled, along with William Boeing's airplane factory. The region continued to prosper through the second half of the 20th century, attracting new migrations of educated, progressively minded settlers from the nation's east and south. In the 1980s and '90s the economy shifted to the high-tech industry, embodied by Microsoft in Seattle and Intel in Portland.

But growth has not come without cost. The production of cheap hydroelectricity and massive irrigation projects along the Columbia have led to the near-irreversible destruction of the river's ecosystem. Dams have all but eliminated most runs of native salmon and have further disrupted the lives of remaining Native Americans who depend on the river. Logging of old-growth forests has left ugly scars, while 'Silicon Forest' had its own economic collapse at the turn of the 21st century. And Washington's Puget Sound area and Portland's extensive suburbs are groaning under the weight of rapidly growing population centers.

Still, the Pacific Northwest's inhabitants generally manage to find a reasonable balance between their natural resources and continued popularity. The region continues to be one of the USA's most beautiful places to visit...and settle down.

ECONOMIC GROWTH

1990	1995	2010	2012
The northern spotted owl is declared a threatened species, barring timber industries from clear-cutting certain old-growth forests. The controversy sparks debate across the Pacific Northwest.	Amazon, one of the first major companies to sell products online, is launched in Seattle. Originally started as a bookseller, it will not become profitable until 2001.	Vancouver hosts the Olympic winter games and wins 14 gold medals, including in men's and women's ice hockey. It is Canada's third time hosting, and Vancouver's first.	Washington votes to legalize gay marriage. It also legalizes the production, sale and possession of marijuana – becoming the first state (along with Colorado) to do so.

Life as a Pacific Northwesterner

People in the Pacific Northwest are some pretty cool cats, living a relatively laid-back lifestyle. But this doesn't mean Northwesterners don't care about what's going on around them. Quite the opposite: they're highly attuned to the economics and politics of the region, as well as to whatever might be going on outside it. And folks here aren't complacent: everyone is quick to voice their opinion, whether it's about the right to own guns, 'local' versus 'organic' produce or the wisdom of Washington's new marijuana law. Here in the Northwest, people are deeply concerned about their communities, the environment and what's happening in the world that might affect their valued and independent lives.

The People

A Texan, a Californian and an Oregonian were sitting around a campfire drinking. The Texan took a swig of whiskey, threw the bottle in the air and shot it with his pistol while yelling 'We have lots more whiskey where I come from!' The Californian sipped his zinfandel, grabbed the Texan's pistol, threw the wine bottle in the air, and shot it while yelling 'We have lots more wine where I come from!' The Oregonian guzzled his microbrew, grabbed the Texan's pistol, threw the empty in the air but caught the bottle and shot the Californian. He said 'We have lots of Californians where I come from, but I need to recycle this beer bottle'.

While not everyone in the Pacific Northwest is a tree-hugging hipster with activist tendencies and a penchant for latte, many locals are proud of their independent spirit, profess a love for nature and yes, will separate their plastics when it's time to recycle. They're a friendly lot and, despite the common tendency to denigrate Californians, most are transplants themselves. Why did they all come here, from all edges of the globe? Among other things, for the lush scenery, the good quality of life and the lack of pretension that often afflicts bigger, more popular places. Primping up and putting on airs is not a part of Northwestern everyday life, and wearing Gore-Tex outerwear to restaurants, concerts or social functions will rarely raise an eyebrow.

In a broad sense the Northwest shares the general cultures of the US and Canada but adds its own personal twist. In rural parts of eastern Oregon and Washington, the personality of the Old West is still very much alive. Fishing towns have a distinctive and often gritty sensibility that comes from making a living on the stormy Pacific Ocean. Urban centers have a reputation for progressive, somewhat maverick politics. Also, some folk do put emphasis on 'old family' legitimacy and connections, boasting of ancestors who came across the Oregon Trail or who were early Brits in Victoria. And while most urban Americans and Canadians are tolerant of individual eccentricities, rural Northwesterners tend to be conservative and perhaps a little skeptical of strangers.

There is indeed a wide mix of peoples in this great region, but they do tend to share several things in common: a do-it-yourself ethic, a respect

Oregon is home to Nike and Columbia Sportswear, while Washington is the birthplace of Starbucks and REI. Vancouver doesn't care – it scored the 2010 Winter Olympics.

BIG BRANDS

for the outdoors, and the desire to keep frills to a minimum. And a certain affableness – if you're friendly to a local, whether they're a city slicker or a country bumpkin, they often can't help but be friendly right back.

Livin' the Life

Washington and Oregon are the only US states with a 'death with dignity' act, by which some terminally ill patients are allowed to voluntarily end their lives.

The region's gorgeous waters, forests and mountains certainly help define the lifestyle of Northwesterners. Here, people can be close to nature without sacrificing the comforts of a sophisticated metropolis. During the week they'll work in city centers, dine at world-class restaurants and take in fine theatrical productions or cutting-edge live music. Then on weekends they'll head to the beach or ski slopes, or hike to the nearest mountaintop. And while they love their outdoors, Northwesterners can be just as happy inside their warm homes – especially when snow, drizzly rain and gray skies take over in winter. Reading, watching movies and drinking (both microbrew and coffee) are a few popular indoor pastimes, and the area is known for its bookstores, funky cinemas, breweries and cafes.

The Pacific Northwest lifestyle is generally relaxed, and a certain degree of eccentricity is even expected: that shabbily dressed, green-haired woman next to you at the coffee shop might be a tattoo artist – or a software developer at Microsoft. Portland's unofficial motto is 'Keep Portland

THE SPORTING LIFE

Outdoor-loving Pacific Northwesterners cherish their sports, whether they're players themselves or just watching their favorite teams go at it.

The Pacific Northwest's only National Football League (NFL) franchise is the Seattle Seahawks, owned by Microsoft cofounder Paul Allen (who also owns the Portland Trail Blazers and part of the Seattle Sounders). They played their first game in 1976 but have only made it to the Super Bowl once – in 2006. The American football regular season runs from September to December.

Generating nearly as much enthusiasm are contests between university teams, most notably the University of Washington Huskies, the Washington State University Cougars, the University of Oregon Ducks and the Oregon State University Beavers. The college football season runs from September to February.

Vancouver is home to the Canadian Football League's (CFL) BC Lions, who have won the Grey Cup six times, most recently in 2011 against the Winnipeg Blue Bombers. The season runs from June to November.

The Seattle Mariners are the region's only Major League Baseball (MLB) team. Minor league baseball has its fans as well, and is played by teams that include the Vancouver Canadians, Spokane Indians and Eugene Emeralds. Baseball season runs from April to October.

Portland's Trail Blazers are currently the region's only National Basketball Association (NBA) basketball team; the season runs from late October through mid-April. Seattle's professional women's basketball team is the WNBA's Seattle Storm; the city hasn't had a professional men's basketball team since the Supersonics moved to Oklahoma in 2008.

Visiting Vancouver during the October-to-April hockey season? Catch Canada's favorite sport, pastime and religion. The National Hockey League's (NHL) Vancouver Canucks have never won the Stanley Cup, but they came close a few times, most recently in 2011. Seattle's Thunderbirds and Portland's Winter Hawks are a couple of the region's other ice-hockey teams.

Soccer isn't a major spectator sport in the US, but the United Soccer League (USL) does have its fervent fans. The Seattle Sounders, the Portland Timbers and the Vancouver Whitecaps are the Pacific Northwest's teams, kicking it from March to October.

With its first season in 2013, the National Women's Soccer League (NWSL) was represented in the Pacific Northwest by the Seattle Reign FC and the Portland Thorns FC.

Weird,' while Seattle's popular Fremont neighborhood proclaims the 'freedom to be peculiar.' This spirit of independence is most extremely exemplified by the 'Republic of Cascadia' movement, which calls for Oregon, Washington and British Columbia to secede from the US and Canada. (Currently, however, there's no danger of this happening.) And let's not forget gays and lesbians, who are widely accepted and especially attracted to the Northwest's liberal cities. Girls, forget San Francisco – lesbians *love* Portland.

However, not everything is perfect in paradise; in big cities, urban sprawl and rising real-estate prices are a problem. And despite the large percentage of bicycle commuters, as well as great public-transportation systems, freeways get jammed during rush hour. Unemployment continues to be a big problem, as more and more people continue to be attracted to the region. Northwesterners are an adaptable lot, however. Like their ancestors who came over the Oregon Trail (or from California, the East Coast or Hong Kong), they've learned to change with the times – even as they voice their opinions and complain the whole way.

Multiculturalism

Combined, the current population of Oregon and Washington is 10.8 million, which amounts to about 3.5% of the total US population. By far the greatest concentrations of people huddle in Washington's Puget Sound area and Oregon's Willamette Valley. Oregon and Washington are among the fastest-growing states in the USA.

With a population of nearly 4.5 million, British Columbia is the third-most populous Canadian province, partly due to immigration largely from Hong Kong and to movement within Canada. The greater Vancouver area is home to over half those people.

Most US Northwesterners are Caucasian; minority groups include Latinos, Asians and African Americans. British Columbia, while largely founded by British settlers, has a much more racially mixed population. Over 40% of Vancouver's population is made up of minority groups, most with an Asian background.

The US government recognizes over three dozen Pacific Northwestern Native American tribes, for whom reservations or trust lands have been set aside. A number of other Native American groups in the region have no federally recognized status – without which they are ineligible for government assistance to support tribal schools and cultural centers. Moreover, without legal recognition, it is difficult for tribes to maintain cultural identity. The total Native American population of Oregon and Washington is around 194,000 (or 1.8% of the population).

In Canada, tribal bands control small tracts of land called reserves (though less than half of the country's native peoples actually inhabit these lands). First Nations inhabitants of British Columbia number roughly 196,000 (about 5% of BC's population).

Gay people living in the Pacific Northwest have more rights than in most other states and countries. In Washington and Canada same-sex marriage is legal, while Oregon recognizes same-sex domestic partnerships.

Music & the Arts

Blame it on the weather, or maybe it's all that natural beauty, but the Pacific Northwest is ground zero for right-brain thinkers and mind-blowing art. From music-makers to famous writers to glassblowers and cutting-edge architecture, you'll find creativity galore in this progressive and inspiring region.

The Seattle Sound: Then & Now

No other music genre is associated with the Pacific Northwest like grunge – that angst-driven, heavily riffed and distorted sound born in the late 1980s out of Seattle's garages and cherished by generation X. Evolved from music to a lifestyle (flannel shirt and ripped jeans, anyone?), grunge became a way to voice cynicism and disillusionment in a society of vanity and materialism.

Grunge was heavily influenced by a cult group called the Melvins, inspiring Seattle bands with their sludgy and aggressive mix of hardcore punk and heavy metal. Alternative-rock band Green River also had a heavy hand in the genre's beginnings – vocalist Mark Arm even coined the term 'grunge' (and its members later went on to start Mudhoney and Pearl Jam).

The real success didn't explode until record label Sub Pop – which signed many of the bigger grunge band names – put out Nirvana's *Nevermind* in 1991, skyrocketing the 'Seattle Sound' into mainstream music. Purists, however, shunned Nirvana for what they considered selling out to commercialism while overshadowing equally worthy bands like Soundgarden and Alice in Chains. In fact, some bands renounced their own fame and fortune, claiming it went against the spirit of the movement.

The general popularity of grunge continued through the early 1990s, but the very culture of the genre took part in its downfall. Bands lived hard and fast, never really taking themselves seriously: playing to friends for fun was more important than being successful in business. Many eventually succumbed to internal strife and drug abuse. The final blow was in 1994, when Kurt Cobain – the heart of Nirvana – commited suicide.

In the mid-1990s postgrunge was born. It was a commercially friendly, more accessible version of grunge, borrowing the sound and aesthetics of its predecessor but with an uplifting spirit. Popular bands showcasing this new genre were Foo Fighters (with ex-Nirvana drummer Dave Grohl), Creed, Bush, Candlebox and Matchbox Twenty.

Beyond Grunge

Rock wasn't born in the Pacific Northwest, but the region has certainly attracted more than its share of creative musicians. Jimi Hendrix, Anthony Ray (Sir Mix-a-Lot) and the Wilson sisters (of Heart) all grew up in the Seattle area. Bryan Adams, Sarah McLachlan and Nelly Furtado have British Columbia associations. Courtney Love (of Hole) was a teenage rockster in Portland, while Paul Revere and the Raiders put Oregon on the rock-music map in the mid-1960s.

GRUNGE

Powell's Books claims to be the largest independent new and used bookstore in the world. The main store takes up a whole city block, and it's been a part of Portland book culture since the early 1970s.

A few cities have especially connected with indie music. Seattle was the original stomping ground for Modest Mouse, Death Cab for Cutie and Band of Horses – and still has fantastic local bands and some legendary venues. Olympia, WA, has been a hotbed of indie rock and riot grrrls, and birthplace of the now-defunct groups Sleater-Kinney, Beat Happening and Bikini Kill. British Columbia can claim popular indie bands like The New Pornographers, Black Mountain and Hot Hot Heat, as well as the punksters Subhumans.

It's Portland, OR, however, which has really attracted indie bands: the city has boasted such diverse groups as folktronic hip-hop band Talkdemonic, alt-band The Decemberists and multigenre Pink Martini, not to mention The Shins, The Dandy Warhols, Blind Pilot, Blitzen Trapper and Elliot Smith.

Meanwhile, jazz and blues are alive and kicking, thanks to the region's early African American inhabitants. Seattle jazz was raging back in the 1930s and '40s, but today avant-garde artists like Bill Frisell and Wayne Horvitz hold their own. Portland's Grammy-winning jazz artist Esperanza Spalding has played in the White House twice, while blues musicians Robert Cray and Curtis Salgado got started in Eugene. Jazz performer Diana Krall lives (with hubby Elvis Costello) part-time in Vancouver, also home to blues musician Jim Byrnes. All three major cities host popular jazz and blues festivals, and are home to major operas and symphonies.

Pacific Northwest by the Book

Many great writers have either grown up in the Pacific Northwest or now call this region home. Washington's late Raymond Carver, known for his grim vision of working-class angst, has a collection of best stories in the volume *Where I'm Calling From* (1988). Novelist Mary McCarthy (1912–89) inspired the play *Imaginary Friends* by Nora Ephron and was known for her satirical, semi-autobiographical prose. David Guterson is famous for his award-winning *Snow Falling on Cedars* (1994), a vivid tale of prejudice in a San Juan Island fishing community. Popular author Tom Robbins, a La Conner resident, has won numerous devotees for his wacky, countercultural novels, including *Even Cowgirls Get the Blues* (1976).

Jon Krakauer is the award-winning author of *Into Thin Air* (1997) and *Under the Banner of Heaven* (2003), while Sherman Alexie is a Native American author who adapted his short story *This Is What It Means to Say Phoenix, Arizona* into the excellent movie *Smoke Signals* (1998). Timothy Egan, the Pulitzer Prize–winning novelist and journalist, lives in Seattle.

Oregon's biggest literary name is the late Ken Kesey, whose *One Flew Over the Cuckoo's Nest* (1962) became a textbook of 1960s nonconformity and inspired a movie that won five Oscars; Kesey also penned the brilliant *Sometimes a Great Notion* (1964). Novelist Chuck Palahniuk, best known for *Fight Club* (1996), lives part-time

MUSIC FESTIVALS

Early January

River City Bluegrass Festival
Highlights mostly bluegrass but also features country, folk, swing and even gospel; held in Portland.

February

Portland Jazz Festival Big-name national and international artists from American jazz saxophonist Pharoah Sanders to Brazilian singer-composer Luciana Souza.

Late May (Memorial Day Weekend)

Sasquatch Music Festival Held in a gorgeous location at the gorge amphitheater in George, WA, this festival has headlined some fine indie and alternative acts.

Late May

Northwest Folklife Festival Vibrant folk music, as well as dance, crafts, visual arts, workshops and films. One of the largest folk-oriented celebrations in North America. In Seattle.

June–July

Vancouver International Jazz Festival Showcasing regional and international artists like Miles Davis, Wynton Marsalis and Tito Puente.

Mid-late July

Vancouver Folk Music Festival Offers everything from Utah Phillips to hip-hop to Tuvan throat singers. This festival has a great location on the beachy sands of Jericho Beach Park.

in Portland and writes about it in *Fugitives and Refugees: A Walk in Portland, Oregon* (2003). Portland also boasts two novelists with a bent towards science fiction and fantasy: the prolific and multi-award-winning Ursula LeGuin is responsible for *The Left Hand of Darkness* (1969) and *The Farthest Shore* (1972), while Jean Auel is best known for her widely read *Clan of the Cave Bear* series.

British Columbia's ever-active literary scene has cultivated a wide range of talent. The English novelist and poet Malcolm Lowry, who's best known for his semi-autobiographical *Under the Volcano* (1947), lived in British Columbia for many years before his death in Sussex. British Columbia resident WP Kinsella's award-winning novel *Shoeless Joe* (1982) was adapted for the film *Field of Dreams* (1989). Douglas Coupland (*Generation X,* 1991) makes his home in Vancouver, as does science-fiction guru William Gibson, who coined the term 'cyberspace' in his 1984 novel *Neuromancer*.

Pacific Northwest in Cinema & Television

The Pacific Northwest has attracted the film and TV industries with low production costs, artistic talent and a range of gorgeous backdrops. However, many films produced in the region are set somewhere else: Oregon's Cascades doubled as the Colorado Rockies in *The Shining* (Mt Hood's Timberline Lodge had a cameo as the Overlook Hotel's front exterior); Roslyn, WA, stood in as Alaska in the TV series *Northern Exposure*; and the Vancouver area has represented everything from Tibet in Martin Scorsese's *Kundun* to New York City in Jackie Chan's *Rumble in the Bronx*.

But the Northwest often appears as itself in motion pictures, too. Seattle's skyline and quirky lifestyles are recognizable internationally, thanks to such productions as *Sleepless in Seattle* (1993) and the hit TV shows *Frasier* (1993–2004) and *Grey's Anatomy* (2005–). The cult TV series *Twin Peaks* (1990) was filmed in North Bend and Snoqualmie. Some of many movies filmed in Washington include *An Officer and a Gentleman* (1982), *The Hunt for Red October* (1990), *My Own Private Idaho* (1991)

Top Film Festivals

Portland International Film Festival, February

Seattle International Film Festival, May–June

Vancouver International Film Festival, September–October

Northwest Film & Video Festival (Portland), November

ROCKING OUT – ALBUMS FROM THE PACIFIC NORTHWEST

Black Mountain (Vancouver, BC) *Black Mountain* (2005)

The Dandy Warhols (Portland, OR) *Thirteen Tales From Urban Bohemia* (2000)

Death Cab for Cutie (Bellingham, WA) *Plans* (2005)

The Decemberists (Portland, OR) *The Crane Wife* (2006)

Foo Fighters (Seattle, WA) *One By One* (2002)

Hot Hot Heat (Victoria, BC) *Make Up The Breakdown* (2002)

Modest Mouse (Issaquah, WA) *Lonesome Crowded West* (1997)

The New Pornographers (Vancouver, BC) *Mass Romantic* (2000)

Pearl Jam (Seattle, WA) *Ten* (1991)

Pink Martini (Portland, OR) *Sympathique* (1997)

The Postal Service (Seattle, WA) *Give Up* (2003)

The Shins (Portland, OR) *Chutes Too Narrow* (2003)

Sleater-Kinney (Olympia, WA) *Call The Doctor* (1996)

Talkdemonic (Portland, OR) *Beat Romantic* (2006)

and *The Ring* (2002). The blockbuster *Twilight* movie series (2008–2012) was partly or mostly (depending on the movie) filmed in Washington, Oregon and Vancouver.

Oregon has an equally lively resume of movie credits that include *One Flew over the Cuckoo's Nest* (1975), *Animal House* (1978), *The Goonies* (1985), *Stand by Me* (1986), *Point Break* (1991) and *The Road* (2009). Portland often serves as a menacing backdrop for the brooding films of resident filmmaker Gus Van Sant, whose resumé includes *Drugstore Cowboy* (1989), *My Own Private Idaho* (1991) and *Elephant* (2003), all filmed in the Pacific Northwest. Portland-born Matt Groening created the hit cartoon show *The Simpsons* (1989–), which has many references to Portland's streets. TV series currently filming in Portland include *Portlandia* (2011–) and *Grimm* (2011–).

British Columbia is one of the centers of film in Canada, and Vancouver is a hot spot. Past movies and TV series shot in British Columbia include *The X-Files* (1993-2002), *Roxanne* (1987), *The Butterfly Effect* (2004) and *An Unfinished Life* (2005).

The Pacific Northwest's First Art

The first artists drawn to the Northwest's beauty were coastal Native Americans, whose tribes included the Haida, Salish, Tlingit and Tsimshian. The most well-known form of art in this region is the totem pole, clan symbols which denote wealth and prestige. Made of Western red cedar, these totems used stylized geometric shapes and the motifs of sacred animals (such as eagles, ravens and bears). They could reach 80ft in length and take up a year to complete.

Carved wooden masks are another popular form of Northwest coast art. These were originally used in dances, traditional ceremonies and even wars, often depicting supernatural beings or animal heads. They'd often be painted in red and black, and decorated with hair, feathers, fur and shells. Valued highly by private collectors, these Native American masks can go for tens of thousands of dollars today.

The fanciest Haida dugout canoes, which could be up to 60ft long, sometimes boasted carved prows and were decorated with beautiful animal images. Some other art forms practiced by the region's native peoples are basketry and blanket weaving.

Artists

Well-known Northwest coast artists include Bill Reid (1920–98), an outstanding Haida artist who acquired his skills from Mungo Martin, a Kwakiutl master carver of totem poles. He's a descendant of Charles Edenshaw, another legendary carver and silversmith. Robert Davidson, a contemporary British Columbia craftsman also of Haida descent, is a master mask and totem-pole carver who has been highly awarded for his interpretation of traditional Haida forms. Yet another British Columbia resident is Susan Point, who has combined personal style with traditional Salish art elements in a variety of artistic mediums; many of her works can be seen in public areas, such as at the Vancouver International Airport.

August

Blue Waters Bluegrass Festival Takes place at Medical Lake in eastern Washington; enjoy world-class lineups and fun workshops.

Early September

MusicfestNW Indie, hip-hop and punk bands play at this successful music fest in Portland.

October– November

Earshot Jazz Festival Seattle's three-week, eclectic jazz-concert series that highlights the work of innovative names who are redefining the genre.

Early September (Labor Day Weekend)

Bumbershoot Fun and famous Seattle music festival drawing up to 150,000 people; 15 stages showcase top-shelf music acts of all kinds.

Top Native American Art

Seattle Art Museum

University of Washington's Burke Museum

University of Oregon Museum of Natural & Cultural History

Bill Reid Gallery of Northwest Coast Art (Vancouver)

UBC Museum of Anthropology (Vancouver)

Royal British Columbia Museum (Victoria)

GLASSMASTER DALE CHIHULY

Dale Chihuly was born in Tacoma in 1941. After an education in design and fine arts, he apprenticed at Murano, the renowned glassmaking center near Venice. When Chihuly returned to the Seattle area in 1971, he helped found the Pilchuck Glass School, credited with transforming glass – previously used mostly for utilitarian or decorative purposes – into a medium of transcendent artistic expression. Chihuly's blown-glass sculptures are infused with lush color, sensual textures and a physicality that is both massive and delicate.

Chihuly's 25,000-sq-ft studio, called the Boathouse, is on Lake Union. In 1976 a car accident left him blind in one eye (he wears a trademark patch), and a few years later he dislocated a shoulder in a bodysurfing accident; ever since, he's hired others to do the glassblowing. He now oversees a team of artisans who perform the principal construction of his works.

The Seattle area boasts a number of Chihuly installations, including the beautiful Chihuly Garden & Glass. Tacoma has some huge pieces in the entrance of its Federal Courthouse, and the best feature at the nearby Museum of Glass is an outdoor pedestrian bridge with a glass ceiling. For smaller-scale work, don't miss Chihuly's permanent collection at the Tacoma Art Museum.

Architecture

Seattle's 605ft Space Needle is likely the Pacific Northwest's most famous structure. Completed in 1961 for the 1962 World's Fair, this landmark can withstand 200mph winds and has had several people jump off the top – with parachutes on. The Emerald City also boasts the Columbia Center, the region's tallest building at 937ft; head to the observation deck on the 73rd floor for an awe-inspiring view of the city. The Central Library and EMP Museum are other noteworthy buildings here.

Portland's controversial Portland Building, designed by Michael Graves, is a great example of the postmodern period. Out front is *Portlandia*, the second-largest hammered-copper statue in the world (after the Statue of Liberty). The glassy twin towers of the city's Oregon Convention Center are hard to miss from the freeway as you enter town; inside is the world's largest Foucault pendulum. And outside Salem is the Mount Angel Abbey, which boasts a modernist library designed by Finnish architect Alvar Aalto.

Vancouver's most notable structures include its huge, coliseumlike public library building and concrete-and-glass Museum of Anthropology, inspired by Native American dwellings. The Shangri-La building is the city's tallest glass tower, and a stunner.

With all those rivers, the region is famous for its bridges. Seattle's Spokane Street Bridge is a concrete, double-leaf swing bridge and has received awards for its innovative design – and it is claimed to be the only one of its kind in the world. The city's Elliot Avenue Helix (pedestrian) bridge is a stunner, with its DNA-ladder-like good looks.

Portland has 10 bridges spanning the Willamette River. The lovely St John's is the city's only suspension bridge, while the Hawthorne is the world's oldest vertical-lift bridge, and the Steel's lower and upper decks can move independently of each other – a unique trait among the world's bridges.

Meanwhile, Vancouver's landmark Lions Gate Bridge connects the city to the north shore, and is a lookalike to San Francisco's Golden Gate.

Possibly the area's most infamous bridge was the 1940 Tacoma Narrows Bridge (aka 'Galloping Gertie') in Puget Sound, which existed for only four months. It collapsed spectacularly in a windstorm due to structural flaws; its replacement was designed much more carefully.

Modern Art

Seattle Art Museum

Roq la Rue Gallery (Seattle)

Portland Art Museum

Schneider Museum of Art (Ashland)

Vancouver Art Gallery

Contemporary Art Gallery (Vancouver)

Beervana & Beyond

Pacific Northwesterners like to say that surviving the long, gray, rainy winters hinges on two things: beer and coffee. It's fitting then that American craft beer and artisan coffee, as we now know them, were born in these parts. But that's not all. There are also a booming wine industry, indie distilleries and a growing number of cider makers – businesses all born from the hardheaded Northwest drive to do things right.

Beer

While many West Coast breweries claim rights to the early roots of the craft-brewing movement, there's no doubt Northwest brewers greatly influenced the evolution of this country's craft-beer scene. In the early 1980s, a few intrepid brewers started selling their beer commercially in Portland, including Brian and Mike McMenamin, brothers who opened the first post-Prohibition brewpub in Oregon in 1985. The McMenamin chain now includes 57 locations in the Northwest – historic hotels, bars, restaurants, movie theaters and 24 brewpubs. Check them all out at www.mcmenamins.com.

Other still-operating pioneers include BridgePort Brewing and Widmer Brothers Brewery in Portland and Elysian Brewing, Pike Brewing and Hale's Ales in Seattle. All of these breweries started out making small-batch beers in a variety of styles, a strong deviation from the bland, mass-produced commercial beers that dominated the market at the time.

Craft brewing allowed brewers to get creative, and many of them started making beer inspired by traditional European styles before creating riffs of their own. Take the English-styled India Pale Ale (IPA), which once included hops as a preservative to keep beer fresh aboard long sea voyages between England and India. Northwest brewers added copious amounts of hops to create IPAs that taste and smell like everything from pine trees to grapefruit rinds.

Highly hopped beers have come to define the Northwest, which is appropriate considering 90% of the nation's hops are grown in Oregon and Washington. But it's not just the hops that local brewers say make their beers special, but pristine water, locally grown and malted barley, and a willingness to experiment with new styles and techniques.

Today, beer aficionados (otherwise known as beer geeks) sip and savor beer as they would wine, and some urban restaurants have beer 'programs', 'sommeliers' and cellars. Many brewpubs and restaurants host beer dinners, a chance to experience unique beers paired with multiple courses. But the heart of Northwest beer culture still rests inside the basic brewpub, a place where beers are brewed on site – which means you're drinking them straight from the source.

Stroll through a local grocery store to see the scope of what local brewers are producing, or ask locals where to go out for a craft beer. Chance are you're near a brewpub, even in tiny towns such as Twisp, WA, and Baker City, OR. When visiting larger craft breweries, ask about upcoming tours or tasting events.

Two of Portland's greatest passions meet in the guide *Hop in the Saddle: A Guide to Portland's Craft Beer Scene by Bike*. The slim title offers customized bike routes to the city's hottest beer spots.

BEER & BICYCLES

HOP TO IT

Every August, fragrant and sticky green hop cones – the flowers of the hop plant – reach maturity. During the hop harvest, which lasts just a few weeks, farmers strip the cones from the bines and dry almost all of them. The hops will eventually add bitterness and nuanced aromas and flavors to beers around the world.

Some farmers pull aside fresh undried hops for local brewers, who personally drive trucks to hop farms to pick up the crop, the defining ingredient in 'fresh-hop' beers. These beers are special: they can't be made in other parts of the country, as fresh hops must be added to a beer-in-progress within 24 hours of being picked. And they capture the bright and lively essence of a plant that defines Northwest beers.

Check out some of the region's best fresh-hop festivals in the fall to taste the range of beers made during harvest: Yakima's Fresh Hop Ale Festival, Hood River's Hops Fest and Portland's Fresh Hops Fest at Oaks Amusement Park.

Coffee

The Northwest's progressive coffee culture was born in 1971, when Starbucks opened its first location across from Pike Place Market in Seattle. The idea, to offer a variety of roasted beans from around the world in a comfortable cafe, helped start filling the American coffee mug with more refined, complicated (and expensive) drinks compared to the ubiquitous Folgers and diner cups of joe. Specialty coffeehouses started springing up in Seattle and Portland during the 1980s, the foundation of today's burgeoning coffee culture.

Today, you can find not only Starbucks on every corner in the Northwest (and USA, and abroad!), but also hundreds of independently owned coffeehouses. Coffeehouse culture in the Pacific Northwest encourages lingering; think free wi-fi, comfortable indoor and outdoor seating, and little pressure to buy more food and drink even after camping out at a table for hours. But the desire to caffeinate extends beyond the cafe; you'll be able to find drive-through coffee shacks in rural areas and on remote roads.

Locals take coffee just as seriously as beer, and for the most part, they prefer dark roasts. But ultimately the quality of the beans and the roast determines a coffee's popularity. As with most food and drink in these parts, consumers demand details about what they're consuming – the wheres, hows and whys of harvests and roastings.

That attention to detail has led to extensive coffee-sourcing programs at Northwest roasteries, and many coffee roasters personally travel around the globe to source beans. Only in this way can they describe how coffee farmers in Guatemala treat their workers and coffee trees. At the most high-level coffee cafes, experienced baristas will happily banter about the origins of any roast and will share their thoughts about bean grinds and more. Try a trendy 'pour-over' coffee if you get the chance.

Stumptown Coffee Roasters, which started in Portland with one roastery and cafe in 1999, helped small-batch roasting go mainstream (the company now has locations in Seattle, New York City and Los Angeles). These days, 'micro roasters,' who roast blends and single-origin coffees to precise specifications in garages, metal shops and basements, create some of the best coffee beans in the world. Many Northwest cafes now feature beans from multiple micro roasters, or they roast their own batches on site.

Left Coast Roast: A Guide to the Best Coffee and Roasters from San Francisco to Seattle, by Hanna Neuschwander, deconstructs the roasting process and reveals where to get some of the best coffee on this coast.

Wine

Many Northwesterners can remember a time when 'local wine' meant a varietal from northern California. That's because winegrowing in the Pacific Northwest is a relatively new phenomenon: most vines were planted in the past couple of decades. Recent successes have spurred a boom in grape planting and wine production.

For the visitor, the burgeoning wine industry can mean an odd mixture of hole-in-the-wall tasting rooms and sprawling new hotels with wine-themed spa treatments, and it's easy to find people who will tout the non-Napa nature of the local wine regions or reminisce about the simpler times of days gone by.

Oregon's modern wine movement began in the 1960s, most notably when a handful of Californians made their way north to Oregon's Willamette Valley and planted pinot noir grapes, a delicate and difficult-to-grow variety. Oregon's hot, dry summers, cool, wet winters and rich volcanic soils mimic conditions in Burgundy, one of the few places in the world where the grape thrives. Pioneers David Lett, Dick Erath and Charles Coury planted the first pinot grapes – along with pinot gris, chardonnay and riesling – and today the grape has come to signify Oregon wines. In 2011 the state boasted 463 wineries and more than 20,000 acres of planted grapes everywhere from the dry, eastern Snake River Valley American Viticulture Area (AVA) to the Rogue and Applegate Valleys in southern Oregon.

Washington, which shares the same latitude as the French Burgundy and Bordeaux regions, has become the second-most productive wine region in the country after California. Fans of the state's wines say it's all about the soil, which was enriched over 15,000 years ago when the Missoula floods deposited a thick layer of sediment around the Columbia River Gorge. The dry climate and long hours of daylight help produce Washington's eclectic mix of wines. The Columbia Valley AVA covers more than a third of the state and produces 99% of the state's wine. A small part of that area, the Walla Walla region, has become the state's 'Napa,' with a plethora of tasting rooms, wine shops and B&Bs. Other good bets include Yakima, Ellensburg and Spokane.

And don't forget British Columbia, which has over 200 wineries that straddle the Cascades: on Vancouver Island, the Gulf Islands and Fraser Valley and in the Okanagan Valley. These regions are known for crisp, fruity white and dessert wines, but reds, including cabernet sauvignon, cabernet franc, merlot and pinot noir, are just starting to catch up in number.

Biodynamics, one of the buzzwords in the wine world, focuses on the health of the soil by using organic and sustainable practices. For example, farmers deter pests by planting flowers or distributing bark chips rather than using pesticides.

Spirits

Ever pioneering when it comes to imbibing, small-batch distilleries are popping up all over the Pacific Northwest. There's Eau de Vie of Douglas fir and lava-filtered vodka from Clear Creek Distillery in Portland, which was founded by distilling pioneer Stephen McCarthy in 1986. Or a homegrown Wheat Whiskey from It's 5 Artisan Distillery in Cashmere, WA. Victoria Spirits in Victoria, BC, makes gin from wild-gathered botanicals.

In Portland, five east-side distillers make up Distillery Row, one of the only concentrations of artisan distillers in the country. These craft distillers have tasting-room hours, when visitors can sample everything from whiskey and absinthe to aquavit and fruit brandies. In the tradition of artisan craftsmanship, the owners are the distillers and they're frequently on hand to explain the distilling process and share their passion for the craft.

Buy a Distillery Row Passport (www.distilleryrowtours.com) for access to tastings and tours at seven participating locations in Portland, including an urban wine maker and a cider maker.

Pacific Northwest Cuisine

Try to think of a food that isn't grown, raised or harvested in the Pacific Northwest, and you'll realize why in-the-know gourmands have been putting down roots in the region for decades. Outsiders, who have been slower to discover the abundance, now flock here for the food, seeking a taste of Northwest cuisine prepared by talented chefs who cook local, seasonal foods with an alluring simplicity.

History

The late James Beard (1903–85), an American chef, food writer and Oregon native, believed that preparing foods simply, without too many ingredients or complicated cooking techniques, allowed their natural flavors to shine. This philosophy has greatly influenced modern Northwest cuisine.

In some of Beard's writings, he describes his first tastes of wild mushrooms, herbs, truffles, berries and seafood, both in his hometown of Portland and on the coast at Gearhart, where he spent his childhood summers. Those tastes of foods at their seasonal prime shaped his reverence for quality ingredients.

In the spirit of James Beard, Pacific Northwesterners don't like to think of their food as trendy or fussy, but at the same time they love to be considered innovative, especially when it comes to 'green', hyperconscious eating. Don't be surprised if, when sharing a meal with locals, the conversation turns to how the food was prepared, grown, harvested, slaughtered or caught, which inevitably leads to conversations about the

FUNGI FANATICS

Living in the Pacific Northwest means finding mushrooms growing everywhere from car trunks to manicured lawns, but the abundance can make for good eating. Edible wild mushrooms sprout year-round and include the fluted chanterelle, bolete (otherwise known as porcini), morel and matsutake.

While it's easy to walk into most woods and find mushrooms ripe for the picking, don't eat just anything. Always show an experienced mushroom picker the fruits of your foray – many toxic mushrooms look identical to edible ones. Mycological societies and foraging groups are scattered around the region and welcome visitors to meetings and 'field trips.'

Don't be surprised if you encounter some truffle enthusiasts along the way. While Europeans have been sniffing out the expensive underground fungi with pigs and dogs for hundreds of years, Americans are newer to the hunt – three new varieties of truffles were discovered in Oregon just 30 years ago. To go on a bona fide truffle hunt or learn more about the mysterious edibles, contact the Oregon-based **North American Truffling Society** (www.natruffling.org), or attend the annual **Truffle Festival** (www.oregontrufflefestival.com) in Eugene, OR, for dog-training workshops, elaborate truffle dinners and more.

morals and ethics of its consumption. These are people who love to show off their homegrown vegetables, neighborhood-picked fruit, eggs gathered from backyard chickens and honey from nearby hives.

Farmed & Wild

The diverse geography and climate – a mild, damp coastal region with sunny summers and arid farmland in the east – foster all types of farm-grown produce. Farmers in these parts grow plenty of fruit, from melons, grapes, apples and pears to strawberries, cherries and blueberries. Veggies thrive here too: potatoes, lentils, corn, asparagus and Walla Walla sweet onions, all of which feed local and overseas populations.

Other well-known farmed products include hazelnuts (also known as filbert nuts; Oregon produces 99.9% of the hazelnuts grown in the US) and herbs, especially lavender and spearmint. Hop farming is another regional specialty. The Northwest is the only region of the country with large-scale hop farms, which provide the sticky, fragrant cones that help add flavor, aroma and bitterness to many beers around the world.

Many wild foods thrive here as well, especially in the damper regions such as the Coast Range. Foragers there seek out year-round wild mushrooms, as well as summertime huckleberries and blackberries.

Seafood & Meat

With hundreds of miles of coastline and an impressive system of rivers, the Pacific Northwest offers seafood galore. Depending on the season, specialties include razor clams, mussels, prawns, albacore tuna, Dungeness crab and sturgeon. Salmon remains one of the region's most recognized foods, whether it's smoked, grilled, or in salads, quiches and sushi. On the coast you can always find good seafood and can buy directly from the boat if you're willing to take the time to ask around. Of course, the closer you are to the source the better the quality, so don't expect inland towns to have the freshest seafood.

While the Northwest has a reputation for vegetarian and vegan eating, the past few years have spawned a meat backlash, and in true Northwest style, the carnivore craze has involved sourcing top-quality meats locally (think pigs fed hazelnuts during their final days). Small-scale meat farmers who raise cattle, lambs, pigs, chickens and goats form relationships with urban chefs, who will sometimes visit farms to participate in slaughter. Also, some ranchers sell everything from grass-fed beef to pigs' feet and livers at farmers markets. Other evidence of meat mania? Butchering classes for the public as well as restaurants with their own 'house-cured' meats, such as pancetta, *sopressata* and sausage.

CULINARY CALENDAR & FOOD FESTIVALS

January
Oregon Truffle Festival
Eugene, OR.

February
Chinese New Year
Vancouver, BC.

March
Razor Clam Festival (www.oceanshores.org/clams.html)
Ocean Shores, WA.

April
Crab, Seafood & Wine Festival Astoria, OR.

May
Feast Tofino (www.feastbc.com), Tofino, BC.

June
Comox Valley Shellfish Festival (www.bcshellfishfestival.ca) Vancouver Island, BC.

Strawberry Festival (www.lebanonstrawberryfestival.com) Lebanon, OR.

Washington Brewers Festival (www.washingtonbeer.com) Redmond, WA.

July
Oregon Brewers Fest Portland, OR.

International Pinot Noir Celebration McMinnville, OR.

August
Garlic Fest (www.chehalisgarlicfest.com) Chehalis, WA.

September
Feast Portland (www.feastportland.com) Portland, OR.

Local Leanings

Finding local products has become a popular pursuit for an increasingly food-aware, eco-minded population (most of whom believe that shipping food long distances wastes precious resources). The year-round availability of fresh produce has spurred a fanaticism for seasonal eating. Many of those food fanatics prefer organic, sustainably produced edibles, and conventional farmers and vintners are working to meet the demand by undergoing the two- to three-year organic-certification process.

Farmers markets have become the best examples of this new hyper-awareness of food sourcing, and a handful operate year-round. Some of the most popular markets go beyond offering produce, with everything from pastries, artisan cheeses, honey and jams to prepared foods like wood-fired pizzas, roasted peppers, and biscuits and gravy.

Visit An Exploration of Portland Food & Drink (www.portlandfoodanddrink.com), the Chowhound board for the Pacific Northwest (www.chowhound.com/boards/4) and Food Carts Portland (www.foodcartsportland.com) for ideas.

If you miss the markets, don't worry. Many grocery stores and specialty food markets prominently label local foods. Large-scale brands like Tillamook Cheese, which makes cheese, yogurt and ice cream in the coastal town of Tillamook, OR, have a devoted customer base that enjoys supporting local economies. So does the fast-food chain Burgerville, which buys ingredients for its menus from local sources – it offers Walla Walla onion rings, blackberry or hazelnut milkshakes and Tillamook cheddar burgers.

Upscale restaurants also reflect the public's passion for local foods. Some menus name the farms and harvesters who supply specific ingredients. If you're curious, ask servers for details about a restaurant's sourcing practices – most likely they'll be used to such requests.

Regional Cuisines

The further you head inland, away from the region's biggest cities, the less you'll find things like pork finished on hazelnuts and discussions about organic produce. Expect more 'traditional' meat and potato dishes, pizzas and burgers, and fewer ethnic restaurants, with the exception of Mexican food. Thanks to a large immigrant population, you can find many excellent, authentic Mexican restaurants in unexpected places, like the Yakima Valley.

In the cities, you'll discover diverse ethnic cuisine, from Ethiopian to Ecuadorian, but it's Asian foods that really shine. Vancouver, in particular, offers a high concentration of Japanese, Thai, Chinese and Asian fusion

---

BEST COURSES

Portland Meat Collective (www.pdxmeat.com) Offers courses on butchery, sausage making, curing and cooking meat, and slaughtering. The school recently expanded to Olympia, WA, after a successful Kickstarter campaign.

Art of the Pie (www.artofthepie.com) Presents four-day Pie Camps and one-day workshops at various locations on the Olympic Peninsula, WA. Perfect your dough and learn secret baking techniques.

Diane's Market Kitchen (www.dianesmarketkitchen.com) Takes students to Pike Place Market in Seattle to shop for fresh ingredients for cooking classes that follow.

Wild Food Adventures (wildfoodadventures.com) Offers workshops that teach participants how to forage for edibles in nature, in various locations around the Pacific Northwest. Learn how to harvest wild berries, and make acorn pudding and cattail pancakes.

Modern Preserves (www.modernpreserves.com) Teaches classes on canning and cooking in the Portland area. Learn how to pickle, make jams and more.

restaurants, but it's easy to find all types of Asian food everywhere in the Northwest.

As for 'Northwest cuisine', the nebulous, all-encompassing term doesn't really mean much. Try asking a local, 'What exactly *is* Northwest cuisine?' and you might experience an uncomfortable pause followed by, 'local, seasonal and fresh', or 'organic and sustainable'. While those words won't conjure up an image of a specific dish or narrow to a section of the spice rack, they hint at what truly defines the regional fare: simplicity.

Vegetarians, Vegans & Special Diets

More than in any other part of the country, vegetarians and vegans will discover plenty of food made just for them. So many people practice animal-free eating that even the smallest cafes and restaurants will frequently carry vegan pastries or desserts. Even if you're not dining at a strictly vegan or vegetarian restaurant (of which there are a handful in larger cities), you'll discover vegetarian-friendly menus at most eateries in the metropolitan areas. Ethnic cuisine, such as Thai and Indian, usually includes many vegetarian items, and there's no shortage of delicious meat-free main dishes in cafes and restaurants and at food carts.

Outside the cities vegetarians have fewer choices, and vegans even fewer still. Avoid Mexican restaurants, which usually cook seemingly meat-free dishes in lard, and opt for pasta and pizza joints, although restaurants of every kind usually have at least one vegetarian main meal. Don't be surprised if small towns in the eastern parts of Washington and Oregon (prime cattle country) don't offer veggie burgers.

People with other types of dietary restrictions, including those who are gluten free or lactose intolerant, will find friendly foods everywhere from restaurants to grocery stores, especially in the cities. If you're looking to avoid specific ingredients, be sure to ask. Most restaurants are happy to accommodate you, and some already identify these types of foods on their menus.

Wenatchee River Salmon Festival (www.salmonfest. org), Leavenworth, WA.

October

Fresh Hop Ale Festival (www.freshhopalefestival.com) Yakima, WA.

Wild Mushroom Celebration (www.funbeach. com/mushroom) Long Beach Peninsula, WA.

November

Wine Country Thanksgiving (www.willamettewines.com) Willamette Valley, OR.

December

Holiday Ale Festival (www. holidayale.com) Portland, OR.

Wild Things

The Pacific Northwest is home, sweet home to a wide range of spectacular wildlife. The region's mix of ocean, forests, grasslands, deserts and mountains creates a great diversity of habitats for both national animals and plants, and many of these environments are protected within national wildlife refuges and parks. And while many animals can be relatively easily spotted from the shoreline or a vehicle, like grey whales or Roosevelt elk, others are much better at hiding in dense vegetation and rugged terrain. Be patient, and perhaps with a bit of luck you may be able to spot a bald eagle, a pronghorn antelope or even a killer whale. Just remember to bring your binoculars and a sense of discovery, and start seeking them out!

Animals

Elk & Land Mammals

Seasonal Guide to the Natural Year: A Month By Month Guide to Natural Events by James Luther Davis presents a seasonal breakdown and reveals the premier places to view wildlife in the Pacific Northwest.

Among the Pacific Northwest's signature animals is the Roosevelt elk, whose eerie bugling courtship calls can be heard each September and October in forested areas throughout the region. Full-grown males generally reach up to 1100lb and carry 5ft racks of antlers, so you won't soon forget catching sight of these creatures. During winter, large groups gather in lowland valleys and can be observed at a number of well-known sites such as Jewell Meadows Wildlife Area (about 65 miles northwest of Portland), Dean Creek Elk Viewing Area (along the Oregon coast near Reedsport) and along the Spirit Lake Memorial Hwy in Mt St Helens National Volcanic Monument. Also, Olympic National Park is home to the world's largest unmanaged herd of Roosevelt elk.

The open plains of eastern Oregon and Washington are the playing grounds of pronghorn antelope, curious-looking deerlike animals with two single black horns instead of antlers. Pronghorns belong to a unique antelope family and are only found in the American west, but they are more famous for being able to run up to 60mph for long stretches – they're the second-fastest land animal in the world. Boasting keen eyesight and an acute sense of smell, pronghorns keep their distance from humans, though they are sometimes spotted along highways, especially in the Hart Mountain National Antelope Refuge in southeast Oregon.

One of the elusive animals in Mt Rainier and other parks is the white mountain goat, which lives on high peaks and alpine meadows. Black bears and mountain lions also inhabit Mt Rainier and other Pacific Northwest forests, but their encounters with humans are rare. The beaver is another little-seen creature, but in the late 18th century they were so numerous that fur trading essentially started the exploration of the Pacific Northwest. It's also North America's largest rodent.

The marmot, another big rodent (which looks more like a fuzz ball), is often seen around mountain parking lots and campgrounds, especially in popular places such as Olympic National Park or Manning Provincial Park. Marmots are adorable and might beg for food scraps, but no matter how lovingly they gaze into your eyes, resist the temptation to feed them – or any other wild creature.

If you're very lucky, you might spot wild mustangs in southeast Oregon's Steens Mountain Range.

Fish

The rich ocean environment of the Pacific Northwest creates ideal conditions for a tremendous variety of fish and for the marine mammals that feed on them. Attesting to this fact are the many harbors and small fishing towns lining the coast.

Although salmon could be considered the lifeblood of the Pacific Northwest, even locals can be forgiven for having a hard time keeping the names of different species straight. Not only do scientists argue over how to name and separate the seven species of salmon that are currently recognized, but these important fish have been given dozens of confusing common names such as king, coho, chinook, sockeye and pink, to name but a few.

Salmon have a unique lifestyle of migrating out to sea as juveniles, then returning to the stream of their birth to breed and die as adults. The annual run of returning salmon used to be one of the greatest wildlife spectacles on the planet, with 11 to 16 million salmon in the Columbia River alone. Dams, habitat destruction, overfishing and hatcheries have reduced these majestic runs to mere shadows of their former selves, but conservation efforts – including the taking down of some dams – are being made to help bring back their numbers. You can easily view salmon in places such as the Bonneville Dam on the Columbia River, which has a fish-viewing window (October and November are the best months).

Close to the Bonneville Dam is the Bonneville Fish Hatchery, where you can glimpse the odd-looking white sturgeon (and say 'hi' to Herman the 10ft sturgeon, who has his own Facebook page). Historically, this monster fish can weigh up to 1800lb, grow to 20ft and reach 100 years old – and is a living fossil from the time of the dinosaurs. Unfortunately, in the Columbia River system the white sturgeon has been severely overfished and adversely impacted by other factors, including the river's many dams, poaching and sea-lion predation.

**Top Three
Geographic
Wonders**

Crater Lake

Columbia River
Gorge

Mt St Helens

FIRE & ICE: A GEOLOGIC HISTORY

From 16 to 13 million years ago, eastern Oregon and Washington witnessed one of the premier episodes of volcanic activity in earth's history. Due to shifting stresses in the earth's crust, much of interior western North America began cracking along thousands of lines and releasing enormous amounts of lava that flooded over the landscape. On multiple occasions, so much lava was produced that it filled the Columbia River channel and reached the Oregon coast, forming prominent headlands like Cape Lookout. Today, hardened lava flows can be seen at places such as Newberry National Volcanic Monument and the McKenzie Pass Area, in central Oregon; for a cool lava tube head to Mt St Helens' Ape Cave, in Washington.

The ice ages of the past two million years created a massive ice field from Washington to British Columbia – and virtually every mountain range in the rest of the region was blanketed by glaciers. Even more dramatically, tongues of ice extending southward out of Canada prevented the 3000-sq-mile glacial Lake Missoula in present-day Montana from draining. Consequently, on about 40 separate occasions, these massive ice dams burst, releasing more water than all the world's rivers combined and flooding much of eastern Washington up to 1000ft deep. Grand Coulee and Dry Falls of northeastern Washington are remnants of these spectacular floods, as are the crowd-pleasing waterfalls (such as Multnomah Falls) of the Columbia River Gorge that plummet over cliffs carved by the floods.

Orcas & Marine Mammals

The aptly named 'killer whale' or orca is one of the few animals capable of attacking adult seals. This fierce predator is the largest dolphin in the world and the undisputed spirit animal of Pacific Northwest waters. Spending their entire lives in pods led by dominant females, orcas have complex societies and large brains that rival those of humans. Several resident pods live around the San Juan Islands and prey on fish, while transient pods migrate along the outer coast and hunt seals, sea lions and sometimes whales. While on a ferry around Washington's Puget Sound, keep your eyes peeled – if you're lucky you may spot a dorsal fin or two. Vancouver's Telegraph Cove is another orca hot spot.

Anywhere on the Pacific Coast, it's hard to miss seals and sea lions. Most numerous are small, leopard-spotted harbor seals that drape themselves awkwardly over rocky headlands. From April to July harbor seal pups may be found resting on beaches while their mothers are hunting at sea. Well-intentioned people often take these pups to animal shelters without realizing that their mothers are nearby, so it's best to leave them alone.

The much larger and darker sea lions, with external ears and the ability to 'walk' on land by shuffling on their flippers, are renowned for the thick manes and roaring cries that give them their name. Sea lions easily adapt to human presence and can be common around docks and jetties, where they sometimes steal fish from fishermen.

Other famous marine mammals include gray and humpback whales, which make the longest migrations of any mammals in the world. The

Salmon conservation includes protecting populations around the entire Pacific Rim from the Russian Far East to northern California. Learn more at www. wildsalmoncenter. org.

TOP TIDE POOLS

Who doesn't like exploring tide pools? These miniature, fun-filled ecosystems are home to pretty starfish, colorful anemones, prickly sea urchins and secretive abalone. You can see hermit crabs scuttling about, small fishes darting around and mussels snapping shut. One or two hours before low tide is the best time for tide pooling; this gives you some time to explore before the tide comes back in.

Some words of warning, however: be aware of incoming tides and never get so absorbed in watching tide pools that you forget about the ocean. Sneaker waves are a serious danger and have swept away unwary beachgoers. Also, don't remove anything from a tide pool (it could be illegal!), and remember to watch where you step – hundreds of little lives will thank you.

Some exceptional places in the Pacific Northwest for exploring tide pools:

Haystack Rock, Cannon Beach, OR Lots of critters in the pools, and there are often docents to explain what you're seeing. Also, keep a lookout for puffins.

Yaquina Head Outstanding Nature Area, OR Fabulous pools, and rangers often guide tours to them. These tide pools are actually an old abandoned rock quarry.

Yachats, OR A couple miles of rocky shore to explore, all along the town. Also head south toward Florence and look for potential tide pools, as there are many in the area.

Rialto Beach, Olympic National Park, WA Head less than a mile north of the parking area, through 'Hole-in-the-Wall' (a hole in a rock) and seek out the tide pools. A beautiful, rugged beach, too.

Beach 4 near Kalaloch, Olympic National Park, WA Great tide pools, and large sandstone rocks with starfish and anemones clinging to their bases at low tide. Rangers here give nature talks, too.

Botanical Beach, Juan de Fuca Provincial Park, Vancouver Island, BC Host to one of the richest tidal zones on the West Coast. Granite and sandstone rocks shelter pools and their inhabitants.

best time to view them offshore is November to December and April to May; Depoe Bay in Oregon is an especially good place to spot them. Once hunted to near extinction, these majestic creatures have made a comeback and are a major reason for visiting the Pacific Northwest coast.

Birds

The Pacific Northwest is a stronghold for bald eagles, who feast on the annual salmon runs and nest in old-growth forests. With a 7.5ft wingspan, these impressive birds gather in huge numbers in places like Washington's Upper Skagit Bald Eagle Area and Oregon's Klamath Basin National Wildlife Refuges. Other raptors include ospreys, often seen along large bodies of water like the Columbia River; peregrine falcons, happy to nest along sheer cliffs or under urban bridges; and the northern spotted owl, which can only live in old-growth forests. Common coastal birds include pelicans, cormorants, sandpipers and puffins.

The region's two prominent jay species include the dark-blue, black-crested Steller's jay, which occupies conifer forests throughout the Pacific Northwest and is notable for its loud screeching calls as it swoops down on picnickers. Meanwhile, hikers and skiers in the high mountains may encounter the gray jay (or 'camp robber'), with its soft cooing whistles and gentle demeanor; these inquisitive jays are fearless in taking food from people's hands.

Clark's nutcracker, first observed by William Clark (of Lewis and Clark fame), is often found in high-altitude pine forests. Crows and ravens are other very commonly seen members of the corvid family; they're happy in both wild and more urban environments throughout the region. Sandhill cranes can sometimes be seen in fields, such as those on Sauvie Island near Portland.

In a more urban setting, Vaux's swifts put on an unforgettable show every September in northwest Portland, when up to 35,000 individuals (the largest congregation in the world) spiral down Chapman school's old chimney to roost for the night. The event has become a popular local attraction, and hundreds of people take blankets and snacks to watch the phenomenon occur at sunset. See http://audubonportland.org/local-birding/swiftwatch.

Plants & Trees

The west and east sides of the Cascade Range are like day and night when it comes to geographical differences. The wet and wild west side captures most rain clouds coming in from the ocean, relieving them of their moisture and creating humid forests full of green life jostling for space. Meanwhile, the dry, deserty east side – robbed of rains by the tall Cascades – is mostly the stomping grounds for sagebrush and other semi-arid-loving vegetation. However, there are still plenty of lush pockets here and there in this region, especially along the foothills of several beautiful mountain ranges.

West of the Cascades

This region supports the most impressive gathering of conifers anywhere in the world, with individual trees from six of the 30 or so species exceeding 500 years in age and reaching heights of over 195ft and diameters of 6ft to 10ft. This lofty and grand forest is not only home to many creatures but also the foundation for a vast logging economy that props up countless small rural towns throughout the region.

The most ecologically and significant conifers are the Douglas fir, western hemlock and western red cedar, with Sitka spruce being dominant in the coastal fog zone. Taken together, these four trees

---

Top Bird-Watching

Klamath Basin National Wildlife Refuges

Malheur National Wildlife Refuge

Sauvie Island Wildlife Area

Skagit River Bald Eagle Interpretive Center

WILD THINGS PLANTS & TREES

The adorable American pika is quickly becoming an endangered species. Pikas live mostly in alpine environments, and these are being lost to climate change. For your chance to spot one, keep your eyes peeled on Mt Rainier or at Crater Lake.

THE BANANA SLUG: DON'T TREAD ON ME

While walking down a forest path in one of the Pacific Northwest's many woodsy parks, you might come across a large, yellow slug sliming slowly along the trail and minding its own business. Don't panic and smash it underfoot; this isn't your typical garden pest but rather the Pacific banana slug – a native slug usually found in damp, coastal coniferous forests from California to Alaska. Banana slugs are part of healthy forest ecosystems, and their food sources include decaying plants, seeds, mushrooms and dead animals.

The official mascot of at least one university, the banana slug can come in several colors, from yellow to green to brown; many have black markings too. These gastropods can grow up to 10in long and are hermaphroditic (both male and female). Perhaps the most bizarre part of their mating ritual is that they often have to gnaw off each other's penises to separate after doing the deed. Then they keep crawling along their merry way – as newly formed females.

account for the majority of the forested landscapes from ocean edge to high Cascades peak.

On the west side of the Olympic Peninsula and in other coastal areas where rainfall may surpass 195in per year, these same trees reach incredible sizes and become engulfed in thick carpets of bright-green moss. These are the world-famous temperate rain forests of the Pacific Northwest.

Anyone hiking in these forests will soon come to recognize a common group of plants that form the typical understory. Included in this group are densely clumped sword ferns that cover entire hillsides, as well as taller thickets of small-leaved huckleberries bearing heavy loads of delicious fruit. The state flower of Washington, the pink-flowered rhododendron, and the state flower of Oregon, the holly-leaved Oregon grape, are abundant in these areas and add much color when in bloom.

The Great Bear Rainforest of coastal British Columbia is the largest intact temperate rain forest in the world and many environmental groups are working to keep it that way. See www.savethegreatbear.org.

East of the Cascades

Technically, the parched regions of eastern Oregon and Washington are semiarid grassland or sagebrush steppe. Forest cloaks some of the higher slopes and mountains, but the most common plant at lower elevations is the pungent sagebrush, the ubiquitous plant of the arid American west. Native grasses, cleared for crops or grazed out by cattle, are being replaced by an aggressive alien species called cheatgrass that leaves spiky seeds in your socks.

Common trees east of the Cascades include the stately ponderosa pine with its orange bark and sweet vanilla smell. A grove of ancient unlogged ponderosa pines is one of the most beautiful habitats in the Pacific Northwest; unfortunately, these are rare. In drier areas pines are replaced by densely foliaged western junipers, the scaly needles of which look like miniature lizard tails. Junipers produce crops of attractive blue-gray berries, which provide the major food for half a dozen types of bird.

A surprising sight east of the Cascades is the fall colors displayed by cottonwoods. These trees require a lot of water to survive, so look for patches of golden yellow and orange along rivers and streams – and enjoy a bit of color in this mostly dry region.

Sustainable Pacific Northwest

The Pacific Northwest is one of the most sustainable regions in the world. Seattle, Portland and Vancouver all lead US and Canadian cities in recycling, bike friendliness, public transportation, renewable-energy use and green architecture. In Seattle, eco-roofs adorn City Hall and the Ballard Library; in Portland, many street swales filter stormwater that would otherwise run off; and in Vancouver, electric-vehicle stalls are now required in all new condominium complexes. These are just a few examples of the region's culture of sustainability.

Of course, there's a flip side to every story. Urban sprawl is an issue in the suburbs of Seattle and Portland, and rush-hour traffic jams definitely exist. Clear-cut forests cause hillsides to erode and fill streams with silt, which, along with the hundreds of hydroelectric dams in the area, impact wild-salmon populations. And global climate change is occurring faster in the Pacific Northwest than in many other places in the world, affecting snow packs, melting glaciers and raising water levels in Puget Sound.

But most people living in this beautiful region realize that protecting what they have is a key to their future. They'll keep recycling, biking to work and doing whatever else they can to keep their environment as 'sustainable' as possible – and enjoy their glorious surroundings as reward.

Over 6% of Portlanders bike to work – the highest percentage in a large US city. Seattle's figure is about 3.5%, and Vancouver is at 4%. What's the national average? That would be 0.5%.

What's the Alternative?

Renewable energy is big – really big – in the Pacific Northwest. The region leads North America in green-power sales, and nuclear power is yesterday's news – in 2006 the Trojan nuclear power plant in Rainier, OR, was imploded to great fanfare.

Hydroelectric energy is huge in the Pacific Northwest, helped by all the rain feeding streams and rivers, which in turn power dams. In fact, the region gets up to 70% of its power needs from hydroelectric – more than any other region in the US. Some of the biggest systems here are the Grand Coulee Dam (itself the largest power generator in North America), the Bonneville Dam and the Bridge River Power Project. The Columbia River is North America's largest power-producing waterway.

The Columbia River system has over 400 dams – more than any other river system in the world.

Wind power is another huge player in the region, and in 2012 surpassed hydroelectric power for the first time in the Columbia River Gorge area. This area is the perfect home for wind farms: inland heat draws air from the coast through the narrow gorge, creating a tunnel that produces reliable and forceful winds. Oregon and Washington are two of the fastest-growing wind-energy producers in the country.

Solar energy is, surprisingly, alive and well in the drizzly Pacific Northwest. This ain't Arizona, but the region does get enough sun to make this alternative energy viable – and even popular. Solar panels are becoming

DON'T DAM THE SALMON

Salmon depend on cold, clear waters during the early stages of their development. Unfortunately, logging (which creates erosion above rivers and streams) and global warming are two strikes against them. A third is dams – and the Pacific Northwest has lots of them.

Dams hurt young salmon because they slow down water, which increases its temperature and the travel time for fish to get to the ocean. Many fish are also killed by hydroelectric turbines. And on the way back – going upstream – adult salmon have a hard time getting through dams, even with fish ladders to help them.

But things are slowly changing. Dams have been taken down on many rivers throughout the Pacific Northwest, and more are slated for removal. Even though some of these barriers aren't huge – at times they're only a few feet high – every dam bit (removed) helps when you're a fish fighting your way upstream.

more and more common on rooftops here, on both homes and businesses, and the region boasts multiple leading solar-energy manufacturing companies.

Wave, tide and geothermal energies are other potential sources of power in this geologically active area.

Eco-Cities of the Future

Seattle, Portland and Vancouver consistently top the 'Greenest Cities in the US' (or Canada) lists. With good public transportation, hundreds of miles of bike lanes and high-density population neighborhoods, these urban centers have made it a priority to live respectably within their natural surroundings.

And they're getting better. Vancouver wants to become the world's 'greenest city' by the year 2020; it already uses less energy and land per resident than its southerly big-city neighbors. Seattle is one of the top 'green building' cities in the country, and Portland has nudged its carbon emissions to 15% below its 2000 levels.

The 'New Urbanism' or 'Urban Village' concepts are also popular in the Pacific Northwest, and emphasize compact, walkable communities that cut down the need to drive everywhere for work, schools and shopping. These inner-city neighborhoods also facilitate a strong community feel to bring people together, a trait that has been lost in this era of modernism and urban sprawl.

Seattle, Portland and Vancouver are some of the top cities embracing the Leadership in Energy and Environmental Design (LEED) certification system for 'green' buildings. These buildings use safe, sustainable building materials and incorporate water- and energy-efficient systems. Local examples include Seattle's Justice Center and Hyatt Hotel at Olive 8, Portland's Ecotrust building and Avalon Hotel & Spa, and Vancouver's Port Authority. Also keep an eye out for eco-roofs, which are covered with soil and living plants. These green (literally!) roofs absorb and filter rainwater, provide insulation, create wildlife habitats and lower surrounding air temperatures – and look ubercool to boot.

Some people dislike wind power because of its association with bird and bat deaths. But when you take into account the wildlife killed by electric transmission lines and oil spills and the pollution created by dirty energy, the figures pale in comparison.

Survival Guide

Directory A–Z

Accommodations

Accommodations fall into one of three categories (prices are for a double room):

$ less than $100

$$ $100–$200

$$$ more than $200

Room prices listed are high-season rates, excluding local taxes.

We have marked exceptional picks with a ★ icon, but every property we recommend meets a certain baseline standard for quality within its class.

Prices vary widely depending on the season, festivals and holidays, whether it's a weekend and sometimes even vacancy rates. Prices are generally highest in summer (or in winter at ski-resort towns), and some places have two- or three-night minimum stays. Always ask about discounts, packages and promotional rates, especially in low seasons. Some places give better rates if you book online.

It's always a good idea to see a room before paying for it. Rooms can vary widely within an establishment. Reserve ahead during festivals and holidays, or in summer (especially on the coast). If you plan on arriving late, let your hotel know or it might give away your room.

Many lodgings have only nonsmoking rooms, but you can usually smoke outdoors. Air-conditioning is common in inland places but nearly nonexistent along the coast, which is much cooler. Many hotels take pets, but always ask beforehand (there's usually a fee). Wi-fi access is commonplace except in backcountry towns. Children (defined as anything from under six to under 18) can often stay free with their parents.

Except where noted below, rates listed in this guide do not include the applicable lodging tax:

Washington Outside Seattle, lodging-tax rates vary by county but are generally around 12% for hotels of about 50 rooms or more. Smaller hotels or B&Bs usually include taxes in their daily rates and this is what we quote. Seattle hotel rooms are subject to a tax of 15.6% (less for most B&Bs and historical properties).

Oregon Outside Portland, lodging tax is 6% to 10.5%. In Portland it's 11.5% to 14.5%, depending on the size of the hotel.

British Columbia Lodgings in British Columbia attract an 8% provincial sales tax (PST) plus a 5% goods and services tax (GST). Some British Columbia regions levy an additional tax on overnight accommodations of up to 2%.

B&Bs

If you want an intimate alternative to impersonal hotel rooms, stay at a B&B. They're typically in large homes (sometimes historical) with charming furnishings and just a few rooms – usually with private bathrooms. The owners tend to be friendly and are happy to offer advice on the area. Most B&Bs require reservations, though some will take the occasional drop-in. Nearly all prohibit smoking and many don't allow young children or pets. Substantial breakfasts are nearly always included in the price, which is usually between $90 and $200.

B&Bs abound throughout Oregon and Washington but are particularly concentrated on the islands of Puget Sound and along the Oregon coast. Countless B&B websites

---

BOOK YOUR STAY ONLINE

For more accommodations reviews by Lonely Planet authors, check out http://lonelyplanet.com/hotels. You'll find independent reviews, as well as recommendations on the best places to stay. Best of all, you can book online.

compile lists and photos, including the following:

Washington Bed & Breakfast Guild (www.wbbg.com)

Oregon Bed & Breakfast Guild (www.obbg.org)

BC Bed & Breakfast Innkeepers Guild (www.bcsbestbnbs.com)

Camping & Recreational Vehicles (RVs)

Camping is a wonderful, cheap way to appreciate the outdoors, especially in summer. The Pacific Northwest is strewn with campgrounds, both public and private, and pitching a tent usually costs $10 to $20. RV-site costs depend on hookups but generally run from $20 to $30.

Campground facilities vary widely. Basic or primitive campgrounds usually have vault toilets, fire pits and (sometimes) drinking water, and are most common in national forests and on Bureau of Land Management (BLM) land. The state- and national-park campgrounds tend to be the best equipped, featuring picnic benches, flush toilets, hot showers and RV hookups. Private campgrounds are usually close to town and tend to cater to RVers, with good services and facilities such as full hookups, showers, coin laundries, swimming pools, play areas, wi-fi and even small convenience stores.

Most campgrounds along the coast are open year-round, but inland where it snows they close in winter. Dispersed (or backcountry) camping is only permitted in national parks with a permit. It's a good idea to reserve campsites in summer.

Yurts, found mostly at state parks along the Oregon coast, are Mongolian-style round houses with a canvas shell. Reserve yurts as far in advance as you can in summer.

PRACTICALITIES

➡ **Time Zones** Pacific Standard Time: GMT minus eight (minus seven during daylight saving). A tiny sliver along the Oregon–Idaho border lies in the Mountain Standard Time zone – GMT minus seven (minus six during daylight saving).

➡ **Weights & Measures** In the US, for distance use feet, yards and miles; for weight use ounces, pounds and tons. Canada officially uses the metric system.

➡ **Radio** Tune into **NPR** (www.npr.org) for a progressive yet impartial approach to news and talk radio.

➡ **Post** The **US Postal Service** (www.usps.com) and **Canada Post** (www.canadapost.ca) provide dependable, timely service.

➡ **Laundry** Self-service, coin-operated laundries are widely available.

➡ **Smoking** Smoking is banned in all indoor public spaces throughout the Pacific Northwest, including bars and restaurants. Some bars have patios where smoking is allowed.

Hostels

The Pacific Northwest has just a handful of hostels, mostly in the big cities. Hostels are an excellent budget option; what they lack in amenities and privacy they make up for in savings and a ready-made travelers' community. Most have cooking facilities, common lounges, information boards, tour services and computer access. Dormitory beds (sometimes segregated by sex) average around $30, with private rooms priced similarly to rooms in a budget hotel. Some hostels have a small charge for sheet and towel rental.

Hostelling International (HI; www.hiusa.org) lists member hostels. Independent hostels have comparable rates and conditions to HI/ American Youth Hostel (AYH) hostels. During high seasons, reserve ahead.

Lodges

The word 'lodge' is used with great latitude in the Northwest. Places such as Timberline Lodge on Mt Hood and Paradise Inn on Mt Rainier

are magnificent old log structures boasting dozens of wood-infused, comfortable rooms with handcrafted details. Most other lodges are more modest. Those on the lakes of the Cascades have cabin accommodations, campsites, boat rentals and at least a small store if not a cafe. Some of these are just fine; others are quite unspectacular. If your standards are exacting, check websites and make careful inquiries before heading up long mountain roads to marginal accommodations best suited to hardened anglers.

Motels & Hotels

Motels are cheaper than hotels, with rooms that open to the outside and often surround a parking lot. Hotels have inside hallways, nicer lobbies and provide extra services.

As a rule, motels offer the best lodging value for money. Rooms are unmemorable but usually comfortably furnished and clean. Amenities vary, but expect a private bathroom, cable TV, wi-fi, a telephone with free local

RECREATION PASSES

If you plan on visiting many national or state parks, national forests or certain other recreation sites, consider getting a recreation pass to save money on admission or day-use fees (usually $5 or $10). There are several to choose from:

➔ General information: www.fs.usda.gov/detail/r6/passes-permits/recreation

➔ Washington: www.parks.wa.gov/permits

➔ Oregon: www.oregonstateparks.org/ckFiles/files/2012_pass_summary.pdf

➔ National parks: www.nps.gov/findapark/passes.htm

calls, heating and air-con. Many have small refrigerator, coffeemaker and microwave. Some have kitchenette, coin laundry and swimming pool.

Rental Accommodations

In many coastal areas and in central Oregon and Washington, owners of weekend or vacation homes depend on occasional rentals to help pay the mortgage. Most of these well-maintained, furnished homes have at least three bedrooms. For a family or group of friends these homes represent some of the best-value lodgings in the area.

Descriptions of rental properties can easily be found on the internet. Local visitor centers should also be able to supply information. Some restrictions apply: houses are often occupied by the owners on major holidays and summer weekends, there's usually a minimum stay of two nights and there may be a housekeeping fee.

Resorts

Certain parts of Oregon and Washington are home to huge resort communities offering diverse rental options such as condominiums, apartments, lodge rooms, cottages and houses. These are usually privately owned and rented out for supplemental income. More upscale versions boast amenities such as golf courses, tennis courts, swimming pools and guided outdoor activities.

Discount Cards

If you're a student, bring along your student ID, which can get you discounts on transportation and admission to sights and attractions. Many hostels in the Pacific Northwest are members of **HI-USA** (www.hiusa.org), which is affiliated with HI. You don't need a HI-USA card to stay at these hostels, but having one saves you a few bucks per night. You can buy one at the hostel when checking in.

For good lodging discounts, look for coupon books stacked outside highway rest stops.

People over the age of 65 (or sometimes younger) often qualify for the same discounts as students; any identification showing your date of birth should suffice. Folks 62 or older visiting national parks can get a **Senior Pass** (www.store.usgs.gov/pass/senior.html). For more information, contact the **American Association of Retired Persons** (AARP; www.aarp.org), an advocacy group for Americans 50 years and older and a good resource for travel discounts.

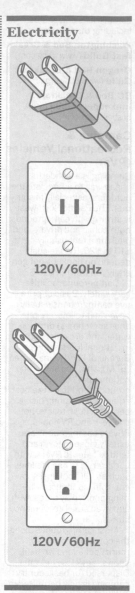

Electricity

120V/60Hz

120V/60Hz

Food

Restaurants in this book are broken down into three price categories. These prices represent the average cost of a main course.

$ less than $10

$$ $10–$20

$$$ more than $20

Gay & Lesbian Travelers

The Pacific Northwest is generally a very gay-friendly place. As elsewhere, gay life is most tolerated in urban centers while attitudes tend to be less accepting in the hinterlands. In the major cities of Seattle, Vancouver and Portland, and even some smaller towns, such as Eugene and Victoria, travelers will find everything from gay religious congregations to gay hiking clubs, while in the rural areas they may want to keep their orientation to themselves.

The Capitol Hill neighborhood is the center of gay life in Seattle. In Vancouver, the West End is gay-centric, while Commercial Dr is more lesbian-oriented. Queer-integrated Portland has no specific gay neighborhood (Sam Adams, Portland's mayor from 2008 to 2012, was the first openly gay mayor of a large US city).

Seattle Gay News (www. sgn.org) A weekly newspaper focusing on gay issues.

Just Out (www.justout.com) Free biweekly serving Portland's gay community.

Vancouver Pride Society (www.vancouverpride.ca) Check out the events link.

Tourist Vancouver (www. tourismvancouver.com/vancouver/gay-friendly-vancouver) Resources for gay-friendly Vancouver.

Health

Altitude Sickness

Acute Mountain Sickness (AMS), aka 'Altitude Sickness,' may develop in those who ascend rapidly to altitudes greater than 8000ft (2400m) but sometimes less. Being physically fit offers no protection. Those who have experienced AMS in the past are prone to future episodes. The risk increases with faster ascents, higher altitudes and greater exertion. Symptoms may include headache, nausea, vomiting, dizziness, malaise, insomnia and loss of appetite. Severe cases may be complicated by fluid in the lungs (high-altitude pulmonary edema) or swelling of the brain (high-altitude cerebral edema).

The best treatment for AMS is descent. If you are exhibiting symptoms, do not ascend. If symptoms are severe or persistent, descend immediately. When traveling to high altitudes, avoid overexertion, eat light meals and abstain from alcohol. If your symptoms are more than mild or don't resolve promptly, see a doctor. Altitude sickness should be taken seriously; it can be fatal when severe.

Heat Exhaustion or Heatstroke

Dehydration is the main contributor to heat exhaustion. Symptoms include weakness, headache, irritability, nausea or vomiting, sweaty skin, a fast but weak pulse and a normal or slightly elevated body temperature. Treatment involves getting the sufferer out of the heat, fanning the sufferer and applying cool wet cloths to the skin, laying the sufferer flat with their legs raised and rehydrating with water containing a quarter of a teaspoon of salt per liter. Recovery is usually rapid and it is common to feel weak for some days afterwards.

Heatstroke is a serious medical emergency. Symptoms come on suddenly and include weakness, nausea, a hot, dry body with a body temperature of over 106°F, dizziness, confusion, loss of coordination, fits and eventually collapse and loss of consciousness. Seek medical help and commence cooling by getting the person out of the heat, removing their clothes, fanning them and applying cool, wet cloths or ice to their body, especially to the groin and armpits.

Hypothermia

To prevent hypothermia, keep all body surfaces covered, including the head and neck. Synthetic materials such as fleece or Gore-Tex provide excellent insulation. The body loses heat faster when it is wet, so stay dry at all times. Change inner garments promptly when they become moist. Keep active, but get enough rest. Consume plenty of food and water. Be especially sure not to have any alcohol. Caffeine and tobacco should also be avoided.

Watch for the 'umbles' – stumbles, mumbles, fumbles and grumbles – which are important signs of impending hypothermia. If someone appears to be developing hypothermia, you should insulate them from the ground, protect them from the wind, remove wet clothing or cover them with a vapor barrier such as a plastic bag, and transport them immediately to a warm environment and a medical facility. Warm fluids (but not coffee or tea – noncaffeinated herbal teas are OK) may be given if the person is alert enough to swallow.

OCEAN WAVES & RIPTIDES

Never turn your back on the ocean when beachcombing or examining tide pools. Large 'sneaker waves' often catch the unwary and sweep them out to sea. If you're swimming and get caught in a riptide which pulls you away from shore, don't fight it – even expert swimmers can get exhausted and drown. Instead, swim parallel to the shoreline, and once the current stops pulling you out, swim back to shore.

INTERNATIONAL VISITORS

Entering the USA

Getting into the United States can be complicated, depending on your country of origin, as the rules keep changing. For up-to-date information about visas and immigration, check the website of the **US Department of State** (www.travel.state.gov) and the travel section of **US Customs & Border Protection** (www.cbp.gov).

For the most part, all foreign visitors need a visa to enter the US. Exceptions include most citizens from Canada and Bermuda, certain North American Free Trade Agreement (NAFTA) professional workers and those entering under the Visa Waiver Program (WVP). Visitors should carry their passport (valid for at least six months) and expect to be photographed and have their index fingers scanned.

Entering Canada

Visitors to Canada from major Western countries need no visa, but citizens of more than 150 nations do. Visa requirements change frequently, so check **Citizenship & Immigration Canada** (http://www.cic.gc.ca/english/visit/visas.asp) before you leave.

Officially, US citizens don't need a passport or visa to enter Canada by land; some proof of citizenship, such as a birth certificate along with state-issued photo identification, will ordinarily suffice. However, since the introduction of tighter border security, officials recommend that US citizens carry a passport to facilitate entry.

Customs

US customs allows each person over the age of 21 to bring 200 cigarettes or 100 cigars (non-Cuban unless from an authorized Cuba trip) duty free into the country, plus 1L of liquor. US citizens and permanent residents are allowed to import, duty free, $800 worth of gifts from abroad, while non-US citizens are allowed to bring in $100 worth. US law permits you to bring in, or take out, up to $10,000 (cash, travelers checks etc); greater amounts must be declared to customs.

Canadian Customs in British Columbia allows visitors 19 years and older to bring in 1.14L of liquor or 1.5L of wine or a case of beer (24 cans or bottles), plus 200 cigarettes and 50 cigars and 200g of loose tobacco, duty free. You can also bring in gifts up to $60 in value without being taxed.

Legal Matters

If you are stopped by the police for any reason in the USA, there is no system of paying fines on the spot. Attempting to pay the fine to the officer may lead to a charge of attempted bribery. Most matters can be handled by mail.

If you are arrested for more serious offenses, you have the right to remain silent and are presumed innocent until proven guilty. There is no legal reason to speak to a police officer if you don't wish to. All persons who are arrested are legally allowed the right to make one phone call. If you don't have a lawyer, friend or family member to help you, call your embassy. The police will give you the number upon request. If you don't have a lawyer, one will be appointed to you free of charge.

You must be at least 16 years old to drive in Oregon, Washington or British Columbia. Stiff fines, jail time and other penalties can be incurred for driving under the influence (DUI) of alcohol or drugs. It is also illegal to carry open containers of alcohol inside a vehicle. Containers that are full and sealed may be carried, but if they have been opened or are empty put them in the trunk.

Possessing illegal drugs is always a bad idea, and if you're caught expect fines, lengthy jail sentences and/ or deportation (if you're a foreigner). In late 2012, Washington state decriminalized marijuana use and possession for those over 21; look up details, however. Oregon is on the same path, so stay tuned.

Public Holidays

Holidays falling on a weekend are usually observed the following Monday.

New Year's Day January 1 (USA and Canada)

Martin Luther King Jr Day Third Monday in January (USA)

Family Day Second or third Monday in February (Canada)

Presidents' Day Third Monday in February (USA)

Good Friday Friday before Easter Sunday (Canada)

Easter Sunday in late March or early April (USA and Canada)

Easter Monday Monday after Easter (Canada)

Victoria Day Monday on or preceding May 24 (Canada)

Memorial Day Last Monday in May (USA)

Canada Day July 1, or July 2 if July 1 is Sunday (Canada)

Independence Day July 4 (USA)

Labor Day First Monday in September (USA and Canada)

Columbus Day Second Monday in October (USA)

Thanksgiving Day Second Monday in October (Canada); fourth Thursday in November (USA)

Veterans' Day November 11 (USA)

Remembrance Day November 11 (Canada)

Christmas Day December 25 (USA and Canada)

Boxing Day December 26 (Canada)

Safe Travel

The Pacific Northwest is generally a friendly and safe place to travel, though crime does exist – mostly in bigger cities. Take the usual precautions:

➡ Don't leave valuables visible in your vehicle, whether you're in a busy downtown street or at a remote hiking trailhead.

➡ Use ATMs in well-trafficked areas. In hotels, use safe-deposit boxes or place things in a locked bag.

➡ Ask around for neighborhoods to avoid. If you find yourself in a questionable place, act like you know where you're going, even if you don't.

LIQUOR LAWS

In bars throughout the Pacific Northwest, alcohol is generally served until 2am (Washington), 2:30am (Oregon) and 3am (Vancouver).

In Oregon and Washington, you can buy beer and wine at supermarkets, convenience stores or private outlets (ie gas stations, specialty wine shops). When buying liquor in these states, however, you'll have to seek out state-approved liquor stores. In British Columbia you can buy beer, wine and liquor from either private or government-sanctioned liquor stores; specialty wine shops also exist.

➡ Panhandlers are a problem in any city. Many suffer from psychiatric problems and drug abuse, but most are harmless. It's an individual judgment call whether to offer them anything – you might offer food if you have it. If you want to contribute toward a long-term solution, consider donating to a reputable charity that cares for the homeless.

➡ If you're accosted by a mugger, always hand over the goods fast – nothing is worth getting attacked. Some people keep a 'false' stash of cash to placate a possible mugger.

Here are some tips on local livestock or wildlife:

➡ Drivers should watch out for loose cattle and horses in remote countryside areas.

➡ When camping in bear country, use bear containers/boxes or hang food correctly. While hiking in bear country, wear bear bells or talk loudly to avoid surprising them. Bears will generally avoid people when they can. Never feed bears or other wildlife!

➡ It's unlikely you'll even glimpse a mountain lion (also called a cougar or puma). Adult travelers aren't much at risk of an attack, but unattended children and pets can be.

Loud noises and making yourself appear bigger (hold open your jacket) will usually scare them off.

➡ Rattlesnakes live in dry desert country and hikers can sometimes encounter them basking on trails. Give them a wide berth and they'll leave you alone. Wearing thick hiking boots offers some protection, as does staying out of thick underbrush.

Tipping

Tipping for certain services is the norm in the US and Canada. If service is truly appalling, however, don't tip. Customary tipping amounts:

SERVICE	USUAL TIP
bartenders	15% of the bill
bellhops, skycaps in airports	$1-2 per bag
housekeeping staff	$2 daily, left on the pillow each day
parking valets	$1-2
restaurant servers	15-20% of the pretax bill (no tax in Oregon)
taxi drivers	10-15% of metered fare

PACIFIC NORTHWEST WITH DOGS

The Pacific Northwest is a pretty friendly place to travel with your dog – though there are some rules. At national and state parks, check regulations: dogs are usually only allowed in certain areas, and must be leashed. Some city parks, however, have off-leash areas.

On long day trips, take breaks to let Fido stretch and do his business – highway rest stops often have pet areas. It's important to make sure your pet has a firmly attached collar ID or is chipped – losing your pet while on the road does not always result in *The Incredible Journey*. Bringing a familiar toy or blanket can be comforting.

Many Pacific Northwest hotels and motels have rooms set aside for well-behaved pooches, often requiring a small fee or deposit; weight limitations sometimes apply. Some places are especially pet friendly, like Kimpton hotels (www.kimptonhotels.com/services/pet-friendly.aspx). Avoid leaving dogs alone in a hotel room – it's a strange place and they might bark, disturbing other guests. Nearly all campgrounds allow dogs if they're leashed and picked up after. Smaller inns or B&Bs generally don't take pets, however. For a different take on boarding services in Portland and Seattle, see www.airpethotel.com.

Super-dog-friendly dining establishments in the big cities include Portland's **Lucky Labrador Brew Pub** (www.luckylab.com) and Seattle's **Norm's Eatery & Ale House** (460 N 36th St). Vancouver law doesn't allow dogs on patios, so things are more limited there.

For more details check out *The Dog Lover's Companion to the Pacific Northwest* or *Have Dog Will Travel–Northwest Edition*.

Tourist Information

Oregon, Washington and British Columbia have state and provincial tourist bureaus that offer glossy guides, maps and plenty of other pertinent travel information. Individual cities, towns and regions also maintain visitor centers, which are often run by the local chamber of commerce.

Washington State Tourism (www.experiencewa.com)

Oregon Tourism Commission (www.traveloregon.com)

Destination British Columbia (www.hellobc.com)

Travelers with Disabilities

If you have a physical disability, travel within the Pacific Northwest won't be too difficult. The Americans with Disabilities Act (ADA) requires all public buildings in the US – including most hotels, restaurants, theaters and museums – to be wheelchair accessible. Most sidewalks in the Pacific Northwest are wide and smooth and many intersections have curb cuts and sometimes audible crossing signals.

Lift-equipped buses are the norm in Washington, Oregon and British Columbia, and many taxi companies have wheelchair-accessible cabs. Some municipal bus networks provide door-to-door service for people with disabilities. Most car-rental franchises are able to provide hand-controlled models at no extra charge – but reserve well ahead. All major airlines, Greyhound buses and Amtrak trains allow service animals to accompany passengers (bring documentation for them). Airlines will also provide assistance for connecting, boarding and disembarking if requested with your reservation. Disabled travelers using Washington State Ferries should check www.wsdot.wa.gov/ferries/commuterupdates/ada for information on reduced fares and how to board.

Many state and national parks in the Northwest maintain a nature trail or two for use by travelers in wheelchairs. For a list of accessible trails in Washington state, see www.parks.wa.gov/ada%2Drec; for Oregon check www.traillink.com/stateactivity/or-wheelchair-accessible-trails.aspx. Meanwhile, British Columbia has a good general website at www.hellobc.com/british-columbia/about-bc/accessibility.aspx.

The America the Beautiful Access Pass (previously known as the Golden Access Passport; these are still honored) is available free to blind or permanently disabled US travelers with documentation. It gives free lifetime access to US national parks and wildlife refuges and 50% off campground use. For more information see www.nps.gov/findapark/passes.htm.

Rolling Rains Report (www.rollingrains.com) An advocate for inclusive travel. Interesting blog.

Emerging Horizons (www.emerginghorizons.com) An online magazine, with much information on accessible travel.

Mobility International USA (www.miusa.org) Runs educational exchange programs in the US and abroad.

Society for Accessible Travel & Hospitality (www.sath.org) Useful links and information specifically about travel.

Transportation

GETTING THERE & AWAY

Flights, tours and tickets can be booked online at lonelyplanet.com/bookings.

Air

Domestic airfares fluctuate significantly depending on the season, day of the week, and flexibility of the ticket for changes and refunds. Still, nothing determines fares more than demand, and when business is slow, airlines drop fares to fill seats. Airlines are competitive and at any given time any one of them could have the cheapest fare.

Most air travelers to the Pacific Northwest will arrive at one of three main airports:

Seattle-Tacoma International Airport (SEA; www.portseattle.org/Sea-Tac) Known locally as 'Sea-Tac'.

Portland International Airport (PDX; ☑503-460-4234; www.flypdx.com; 7000 NE Airport Way)

Vancouver International Airport (YVR; www.yvr.ca)

Land

Border Crossings

All crossings are open 24 hours except Lynden/Aldergrove, which is open 8am to midnight. During the week, expect to wait five to 20 minutes, an hour or more on weekends and during holidays. For up-to-date wait times, check www.cbsa-asfc.gc.ca/bwt-taf/menu-eng.html; it has links to other US–Canada border crossings. Tips and directions can be found at www.vancouver.hm/border.html.

Many travelers also cross the border by ferry, principally on journeys from Anacortes to Sidney (near Victoria), BC, and from Port Angeles to Victoria.

Blaine/Douglas (aka Peace Arch) crossing The main overland point of entry from Washington to Vancouver, BC. It's at the northern end of I-5, which continues as Hwy 99 on the Canadian side. This crossing has the longest lines.

Pacific Hwy crossing Commercial trucks (and regular vehicles) use this crossing, 3 miles east of Blaine/Douglas; from I-5, take exit 275 (the one before Blaine). If you're entering Canada with duty-free goods, you'll need to cross here.

Lynden/Aldergrove crossing A good choice during busy times is this little-known crossing about 30 miles east of Blaine/Douglas. Take exit 256 off I-5, just north of Bellingham, and follow Hwy 539.

Sumas/Huntingdon crossing Best for heading to British Columbia's interior is this crossing 62 miles east of Blaine/Douglas. Take exit 255 off I-5, just north of Bellingham, and follow Hwy 542 and then Hwy 9.

Bus

In car-oriented societies like the USA and Canada, bus travel takes second place. Service is infrequent or inconvenient, networks are sparse and fares can be rela-

---

CLIMATE CHANGE & TRAVEL

Every form of transport that relies on carbon-based fuel generates CO_2, the main cause of human-induced climate change. Modern travel is dependent on airplanes, which might use less fuel per kilometer per person than most cars but travel much greater distances. The altitude at which aircraft emit gases (including CO_2) and particles also contributes to their climate change impact. Many websites offer 'carbon calculators' that allow people to estimate the carbon emissions generated by their journey and, for those who wish to do so, to offset the impact of the greenhouse gases emitted with contributions to portfolios of climate-friendly initiatives throughout the world. Lonely Planet offsets the carbon footprint of all staff and author travel.

tively high. Air travel is often cheaper on long-distance routes, and it can even be cheaper to rent a car than take the bus, especially for shorter routes. However, very long-distance bus trips can be available at decent prices if you purchase or reserve tickets in advance.

The largest nationwide bus company in the USA and Canada, **Greyhound** (☑800-231-2222; www.greyhound.com) operates to major and minor cities throughout the Pacific Northwest; check its website for destinations and schedules. Tickets can be purchased by phone or online with a major credit card and mailed to you if purchased in advance, or picked up at the terminal with proper identification. Buying tickets in advance will save you money, as will traveling during weekdays and nonholiday times. Children, students, military personnel, veterans and seniors are eligible for discounts as well; check Greyhound's website for specifics.

Car & Motorcycle

Although the quickest way to get to the Pacific Northwest is usually by plane, the best way to get around is by car. If you have time, it can be less expensive to drive to the Pacific Northwest than to fly and rent a car. And the region is blessed with many scenic highways that make driving long distances a feasible alternative.

Note that driving regulations, such as speed limits and the permissibility of right turns on red lights or making U-turns, can vary somewhat from state to state.

Train

The Pacific Northwest is well served by **Amtrak** (☑800-872-7245; www.amtrak.com) in the USA and **VIA Rail** (☑888-842-7245; www.viarail.ca) in Canada. Trains are comfortable, if slow, and equipped with dining and lounge cars on long-distance routes.

Amtrak's *Coast Starlight* links Los Angeles to Portland and Seattle via Oakland and other West Coast cities. The *Empire Builder* runs from Chicago to the Pacific Northwest via Minneapolis and Spokane, where it separates to reach Portland and Seattle. VIA Rail's *Canadian* runs between Vancouver and Toronto. Schedules can be very fluid: arrival and departure times become less reliable the further you are from the starting point.

Amtrak fares vary greatly, depending on the season and current promotions. You can beat the rather stiff full-price fares by purchasing in advance – the earlier you buy, the better the fare. Round-trips are the best deal, but even these can be more expensive than airfares. Children, students, veterans, military personnel, seniors and American Automobile Association (AAA) members are eligible for discounts; check Amtrak's website for details, and for rail passes, which are a good option for longer travel periods.

GETTING AROUND

Air

Seattle, Portland and Vancouver are the principal hubs for flights to outlying Pacific Northwest cities, which include (but are not limited to) Klamath Falls, Eugene, Medford, Salem, Yakima, Walla Walla, Spokane, Bellingham and Wenatchee. Seattle also has air destinations in the San Juan Islands and Victoria.

Bicycle

Cycling is a very popular recreational activity in the Pacific Northwest, and an interesting, inexpensive and environmentally friendly way to travel. Roads are good, shoulders are usually wide, and there are many decent routes for bikes. Summer is best; during other seasons, changeable weather can be a drawback, especially at high altitudes where thunderstorms are frequent. In some areas, the wind can slow your progress to a crawl (traveling west to east and north to south is generally easier than the opposite), and water sources can be far apart. Spare parts are widely available and repair shops are numerous, but it's still important to know some basic mechanical things, such as fixing a flat tire.

Seattle, Portland and Vancouver all have great bike paths, and many streets have bike lanes. Some local buses in these cities provide bike racks, and you can also take your bike on light-rail systems, trains and ferries. On

---

NORTH TO ALASKA

Waaay at the northwest tip of North America lies the USA's 49th state, Alaska. It's the biggest state by far, and home to stupendous mountains, massive glaciers and amazing wildlife. Mt McKinley (the continent's highest peak) is here, as are huge numbers of humpback whales and bald eagles.

Thinking of stopping in? There are daily flights to Juneau, and you could always drive (and drive and drive) – but the best way to reach Alaska is probably by ferry. Think of it like taking a cruise ship through the inside passage, but cheaper and more interesting. The trip from Bellingham to Juneau takes nearly three days, but other routes are available. For more information see www.dot.state.ak.us/amhs.

BIKE PURCHASE, RENTALS & CO-OPS IN THE BIG CITIES

If you are thinking of buying a bicycle, consider patronizing bike cooperatives (co-ops) – worker-owned, nonprofit organizations that repair bikes and/or take in donated bikes and refurbish them for sale. They often encourage cycling by renting bikes, supporting community biking events and organizing work-for-trade programs.

Bike Kitchen (☑604-827-7333; www.thebikekitchen.com; 6138 Student Union Blvd, Vancouver) Student-run, full-service co-op that sells and rents refurbished bikes.

Wright Brothers Cycle Works (☑206-633-5132; www.wrightbrotherscycleworks.com; 219 N 36th St, Seattle) Offers co-op work space and bike-repair classes. Has programs helping children, such as earning helmets and locks in exchange for reading books.

BikeWorks (☑206-725-9408; www.bikeworks.org; 3709 S Ferdinand St, Seattle) Not really a co-op but a nonprofit organization with an 'earn-a-bike' youth program; offers maintenance classes and donates bikes to needy communities.

City Bikes (☑503-239-0553; www.citybikes.coop; 1914 SE Ankeny, Portland) Worker-run co-op that fixes bikes, and sells and rents them from its annex on 734 SE Ankeny.

Community Cycling Center (☑503-287-8786; www.communitycyclingcenter.org; 1700 NE Alberta St, Portland) Helps cyclists – especially youths – through educational bike programs and services.

the road, cyclists are generally treated courteously by motorists. Bicycles are prohibited on interstate highways if there is a frontage road; however, where a suitable frontage road or other alternative is lacking, cyclists are permitted on some interstates.

Seattle, Portland and Vancouver are all considering implementing bike-share programs. Stay tuned.

Bicycles can be transported by air, usually in a bike bag or box, although airlines often charge an additional fee. Check this with the airline in advance, preferably before you pay for your ticket. You can hire bikes in most cities for reasonable prices. Buying a bicycle is another option, and the Pacific Northwest has lots of bike shops with a wide range of choices. For used bikes check www.craigslist.com, but beware of stolen bikes.

In Oregon it's state law that children under 16 years old must wear helmets. In Washington mandatory helmet use varies, but most major cities or counties require helmets for all ages. In British Columbia all cyclists are required to wear a helmet. In any case, helmets are

easy to wear and reduce the risk of head injury.

Wearing highly reflective clothing makes you much more visible to cars, as do nightlights, which are required by law throughout most of the Pacific Northwest. Also, using the best lock you can get (usually a U-lock) is a must, as bike theft is fairly common; consider using two kinds of lock at the same time. Adding stickers and painting over expensive brand names to make your bike less desirable is another option.

Boat

Washington and British Columbia have two of the largest state-owned ferry systems in the world; these ferries access some of the most rewarding destinations in the Pacific Northwest. Some boats are passenger only, while others take both vehicles and passengers. Be aware that some summertime ferry routes can have long waits if you're in a car. Bring snacks, as ferry offerings are limited and expensive.

BC Ferries (☑888-223-3779; www.bcferries.com) Operates most of the ferries in British

Columbia. Primary links are between Tsawwassen (south of Vancouver) and Swartz Bay (on Vancouver Island), and to Nanaimo from Tsawwassen and Horseshoe Bay. BC Ferries services also link the Gulf Islands to Tsawwassen.

Black Ball's Coho Ferry (☑in British Columbia 250-386-2202, in Washington 360-457-4491; www.cohoferry.com) Privately operated; connects Victoria, BC, with Washington's Port Angeles (on the Olympic Peninsula).

Clipper Navigation (☑800-888-2535; www.clippervacations.com/clipper-ferry) Privately operated; operates the *Victoria Clipper*, a passenger ferry that connects Seattle with Victoria, BC. Stops at San Juan Islands mid-May through September, and also has whale-watching trips.

Washington State Ferries (WSF; ☑888-808-7977; www.wsdot.wa.gov/ferries) Operates most of the ferries in the Puget Sound area. Popular routes go to Bremerton and to Bainbridge and Vashon Islands from Seattle. WSF also operates the ferry system through the San Juan Islands and on to Sidney (near Victoria, on Vancouver Island, BC) from Anacortes.

Seattle Area Ferry Routes

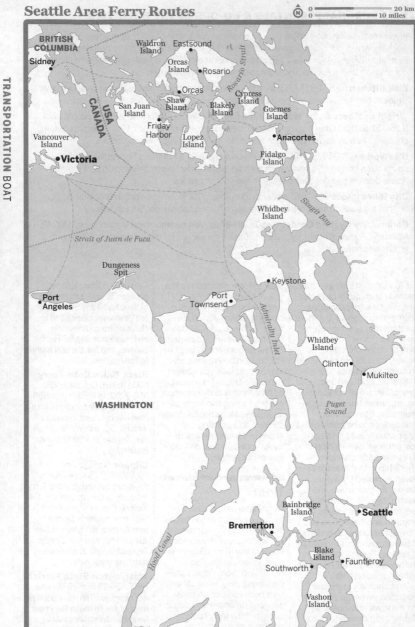

Bus

Greyhound ([☎]800-231-2222; www.greyhound.com) service is relatively good but infrequent, especially in more remote areas. Greyhound buses largely stick to the interstate-freeway system, while regional carriers provide service to outlying areas. In almost all cases, these smaller bus lines share depots and information services with Greyhound.

Generally, buses are clean, comfortable and reliable. Amenities include on-board lavatories, air-conditioning and slightly reclining seats. Smoking is not permitted. Buses break for meals every three to four hours, usually at fast-food restaurants or cafeteria-style truck stops. When you buy tickets a week in advance, discounts apply.

Bus stations are often dreary places. In small towns, where there is no station, buses stop in front of a specific business; in these cases, be prepared to pay the driver with exact change.

Car & Motorcycle

Unless you're traveling between major cities, car travel is practically a must in the Pacific Northwest. Getting to all those outdoor destinations is often impossible without your own wheels, especially if you're camping. Also, gasoline is relatively inexpensive. Use of seat belts is mandatory in the USA and Canada.

For tips and rules on driving in the USA, get an Oregon or Washington Driver Handbook at any Department of Motor Vehicles (DMV) office, or check online at www.dol. wa.gov/driverslicense/docs/driverguide-en.pdf (Washington) and www.odot.state. or.us/forms/dmv/37.pdf (Oregon). For tips on driving in Canada, see www.driving-in.com/canada.

Keep in mind that Oregon law prohibits you from pumping your own gasoline (except

on some Indian reservations); all stations are full service, so just sit back and enjoy it.

Automobile Associations

The **American Automobile Association** (AAA; [☎]800-222-4357, 800-444-8091; www.aaa.com) and **Canadian Automobile Association** (CAA; [☎]604-268-5500; www.caa.ca) provide useful information, free maps, travel discounts and routine road services such as tire repair and towing (free within a limited radius) for their members. Similar benefits or discounts are extended to the members of foreign affiliates, such as the Automobile Association in the UK; bring your membership card from your country of origin.

Driver's Licenses

It's highly recommended that foreigners driving in the Pacific Northwest get an International Driving Permit (IDP) to supplement their national or state driver's license. Note that the IDP is only valid if issued in the same country as your driver's license. Local traffic police are more likely to accept an IDP than an unfamiliar foreign license as valid identification. Your national automobile association can provide one for a small fee, and it's usually valid for a year.

Insurance

Auto insurance is obligatory for car owners in the Pacific Northwest. Rates fluctuate widely, depending on where the car is registered; it's usually cheaper if registered at an address in the suburbs or in a rural area, rather than in a central city. Male drivers under the age of 25 will pay astronomical rates. Collision coverage has become very expensive, with high deductibles, and is generally not worthwhile unless the car is somewhat valuable.

Obtaining insurance, however, is not as simple as walking into an agency, filling out a form and paying for it. Many

agencies refuse to insure drivers who have no car insurance – a classic catch-22. Those agencies that will do so often charge much higher rates because they presume a higher risk. The minimum policy term is usually six months, but some companies will refund the difference on a prorated basis if the car is sold and the policy voluntarily terminated. Shop around. If you're planning to drive in both the USA and Canada, make sure your insurance is valid in both countries.

Motorcycles & Scooters

With its beautiful coastline, national parks and backcountry deserts, there are some great opportunities for motorcycling in the Pacific Northwest. For foreigners, an IDP endorsed for motorcycles will simplify the rental process.

You can read motorcycle manuals at www.dol.wa.gov/driverslicense/docs/moto-manual.pdf (Washington) and www.odot.state.or.us/forms/dmv/6367.pdf (Oregon). For Vancouver, check out www.icbc.com/driver-licensing/getting-licensed/motorcycle-licence/road-sense-riders. Note that helmets are mandatory for both drivers and passengers.

Rentals are not cheap – motorcycles start at about $140 per day and scooters at about $75 per day. Insurance is mandatory and extra.

Cycle BC Rentals ([☎]866-380-2453; www.cyclebc.ca; Vancouver) Rents motorcycles and scooters; also in Victoria.

Mountain to Sound Motorcycle Adventures ([☎]425-222-5598; www.mtsma.com; Issaquah, near Seattle) Rentals and tours.

Northwest Motorcycle Adventures ([☎]360-241-6500; www.northwestmotorcycleadventures.com; Portland) Rentals and tours.

Scoot About ([☎]206-407-3362; www.scootabout.biz; Seattle) Scooter rentals.

Purchase

If you're spending a few months in the USA and Canada, a car may be a good investment. Keep in mind, however, that purchasing can be complicated and requires plenty of research.

It is possible to purchase a viable used car for less than $2000, but it might eventually need repair work that could cost several hundred dollars or more. It doesn't hurt to spend more to get a quality vehicle – you can sometimes sell it for close to what you paid. It's also worth having a mechanic check over the vehicle for problems; AAA has diagnostic centers that can do this for members.

Check the official value of a used car by looking it up in the **Kelley Blue Book** (www. kbb.com), which is a listing of cars by make, model and year that gives the average resale price. Local public libraries have copies.

Recreational Vehicles

You can drive, eat and sleep in a recreational vehicle (RV). It's easy to find campgrounds with hookups for electricity and water, but in big cities RVs are a nuisance, since there are few places to park or plug them in. They're cumbersome to navigate and they burn fuel at an alarming rate, but they solve transportation, accommodations and cooking needs in one fell swoop.

For RV rentals check www. rvra.org. For sales, service and supplies, try www.camp-ingworld.com. KOA (www. koa.com) offers generally excellent RV-oriented camp-grounds, while a good source for general RV-travel tips is www.rvtravel.com.

Rental

Major international rental agencies have offices throughout the Pacific Northwest. To rent a car, you must have a valid driver's license, (usually) be at least 21 years of age and present a major credit card or a large cash deposit. Drivers under 25 often pay a surcharge over the regular rental.

Agencies often have bargain rates for weekend or week-long rentals, especially outside the peak seasons or in conjunction with airline tickets. Prices vary greatly depending on the type or size of car, pick-up and drop-off locations, number of drivers etc. In general, expect to pay from $30 to $60 per day for a midsize car, more in peak seasons. Rates usually include unlimited mileage, but not taxes or insurance.

You may get better rates by prebooking from your home country. If you get a fly-drive package, local taxes may be an extra charge when you collect the car. Several online travel-reservation networks have up-to-the-minute information on car-rental rates at all the main airports. Compare their rates with any fly-drive package you're considering.

Basic liability insurance covers damage you may cause to another vehicle. Rental companies are required by law to provide the minimum level set by each state, but it usually isn't enough in the event of a serious accident. Many Americans already have enough insurance coverage under their personal car-insurance policies; check your own policy carefully. Foreign visitors should check their travel-insurance policies to see if they cover foreign rental cars. Rental companies charge about $15 per day for this extra coverage.

Insurance against damage or loss to the car itself, called Collision Damage Waiver (CDW) or Loss Damage Waiver (LDW), can cost $10 to $20 per day (and may have a deductible). The CDW may be voided if you cause an accident while breaking the law, however. Again, check your own coverage to see if you have comprehensive collision insurance.

Some credit cards cover CDW for rentals up to 15 days, provided you charge the entire cost of the rental to the card. Check with your credit-card company to determine the extent of coverage.

Most of the big international rental companies have desks at airports, in all major cities and in some smaller towns. For rates and reservations, check the internet or call toll-free:

Alamo (☑800-222-9075; www.alamo.com)

Avis (☑800-633-3469; www.avis.com)

Budget (☑800-218-7992; www.budget.com)

Dollar (☑800-800-4000; www.dollar.com)

Enterprise (☑800-261-7331; www.enterprise.com)

Hertz (☑800-654-3131; www.hertz.com)

National (☑800-227-7368; www.nationalcar.com)

Rent-A-Wreck (☑877-877-0700; www.rentawreck.com)

Thrifty (☑800-847-4389; www.thrifty.com)

Road Hazards

A few backcountry roads of the Pacific Northwest region are in open-range country where cattle forage along the

---

CAR SHARING

There are over two dozen car-sharing programs in the US. These programs usually require a membership fee (one-time and/or annual), plus a per-hour car-rental charge. Two of the biggest are Zipcar and Car2go, but there are many that operate only within a city or a few cities. They can be an economical way to rent (or share) a car if you only need wheels for an hour or two at a time.

ROAD DISTANCES (MILES)

	Ashland	Bend	Eugene	Medford	Mt Rainer	Olympic National Park	Portland	Seaside	Seattle	Spokane	Vancouver (BC)	Walla Walla
Bend	185											
Eugene	180	120										
Medford	15	175	165									
Mt Rainer	325	195	205	420								
Olympic National Park	425	305	265	505	175							
Portland	285	160	110	270	135	145						
Seaside	355	250	180	345	280	150	80					
Seattle	460	330	285	445	85	90	170	195				
Spokane	640	395	460	450	210	370	350	430	280			
Vancouver (BC)	600	470	425	585	180	130	315	335	140	410		
Walla Walla	470	285	350	450	175	350	245	320	270	160	410	
Whistler	675	640	500	??	300	305	390	410	215	495	70	485

highway. Deer and smaller wildlife are more of a road hazard on roads all around the region, however. Pay attention to the roadside, especially at night.

During winter months, especially at the higher elevations, there will be times when tire chains are required on snowy or icy roads. Sometimes such roads will be closed to cars without chains or 4WD, so it's a good idea to keep a set of chains in the trunk. Make sure they fit your tires, and practice putting them on *before* you're out there next to the busy highway in the cold. Also note that many car-rental companies specifically prohibit the use of chains on their vehicles. Roadside services might be available to attach chains to your tires for a fee.

Local Transportation

Though local bus networks are minimally developed in the hinterlands, the bigger cities have extensive services; with some planning, you can usually get wherever you want by bus. Because these systems are aimed at the commuting workforce rather than tourists, outside of peak commuting hours service may be sparse.

Portland boasts one of the country's best public-transportation systems, with a good light-rail system, bus service and downtown streetcars. Seattle also has an excellent transit system, with light rail, a monorail and ferries. And Vancouver's no slouch, either, with great bus, train and some ferry services. All three cities have direct public-transportation connections from their city centers to their airports.

Train

Amtrak (USA) and VIA Rail (Canada) trains provide an attractive, if costly, alternative to buses for travel between major points. Amtrak's *Cascades* train links Vancouver, BC, to Eugene, OR – via Seattle, Portland and Salem. This connects with Amtrak Thruway buses (a regional bus line under contract with Amtrak) to reach other destinations such as the Oregon coast.

A branch of Amtrak's daily *Empire Builder* leaves Portland and crosses to Vancouver, BC, before making its scenic run up the northern side of the Columbia River Gorge to meet the other eastbound half of the train in Spokane. The Seattle branch of the *Empire Builder* heads north to Everett before winding east to Spokane. Note that the westbound *Empire Builder* divides in Spokane for Portland and Seattle: make sure you're sitting in the correct portion of the train!

One thing to know about these trains: delays can be very frequent, so don't plan on getting anywhere exactly on time.

Behind the Scenes

SEND US YOUR FEEDBACK

We love to hear from travelers – your comments keep us on our toes and help make our books better. Our well-traveled team reads every word on what you loved or loathed about this book. Although we cannot reply individually to postal submissions, we always guarantee that your feedback goes straight to the appropriate authors, in time for the next edition. Each person who sends us information is thanked in the next edition – the most useful submissions are rewarded with a selection of digital PDF chapters.

Visit **lonelyplanet.com/contact** to submit your updates and suggestions or to ask for help. Our award-winning website also features inspirational travel stories, news and discussions.

Note: We may edit, reproduce and incorporate your comments in Lonely Planet products such as guidebooks, websites and digital products, so let us know if you don't want your comments reproduced or your name acknowledged. For a copy of our privacy policy visit lonelyplanet.com/privacy.

OUR READERS

Many thanks to the travelers who used the last edition and wrote to us with helpful hints, useful advice and interesting anecdotes: Alexa Talbot, Alina Gruppe, Armin Werner, Austin Riley, Chad Perry, Chris Newton, Jack Nuttall, Jim Couture, Josh James, Laura Paola, Laurence Erhat, Mai Winstrup, Matt Albee, Nicola Cutts, Rhonda Petty, Steen Ballegaard

AUTHOR THANKS

Sandra Bao

Thanks especially to my husband, Ben Greensfelder, who kept the house more or less in order (and the plants watered) while I was traipsing around Oregon. My co-authors have been patient and helpful with my many requests; a more experienced bunch I couldn't have asked for. Much appreciation to the staff of all the information centers I visited, of whom I asked endless questions, to those many hoteliers I interviewed for local information and to the friendly people of Oregon who were always ready to help me out.

Celeste Brash

Thanks to my family for helping me research beaches and mountains some days, and getting on at home without me on others. To old friends I found scattered across Washington: the Irwin family, Kati Halmos Jones, Dan Jones, the Forster family and Jackie Capalan-Auerbach. And to new friends I made: too many to mention! It was wonderful to work with Sandra Bao and Suki Gear, and from Brendan Sainsbury's excellent base text.

John Lee

Heartfelt thanks to my Dad for bringing me to Vancouver from the UK for my first visit back in 1986. I'll be over to see you soon, Dad!

Brendan Sainsbury

Thanks to all the untold bus drivers, tourist-info volunteers, restaurateurs, coffee baristas and indie punk rockers who helped me during my research. Special thanks to my wife, Liz, and seven-year-old son, Kieran, for their company on the road.

ACKNOWLEDGMENTS

Climate map data adapted from Peel MC, Finlayson BL & McMahon TA (2007) 'Updated World Map of the Köppen-Geiger Climate Classification', *Hydrology and Earth System Sciences*, 11, 1633–44.

Downtown Metro Service map courtesy of King County Metro Transit, February 2013.

Cover photograph: Mt Rainier and Eunice Lake, Philip Kramer/Getty Images.

THIS BOOK

This 6th edition of Lonely Planet's *Washington, Oregon & the Pacific Northwest* guidebook was researched and written by Sandra Bao, Celeste Brash, John Lee and Brendan Sainsbury. Sandra, John and Brendan wrote the last edition, along with Becky Ohlsen. This guidebook was commissioned in Lonely Planet's Oakland office, and produced by the following:

Commissioning Editors Suki Gear, Paula Hardy

Coordinating Editors Sarah Bailey, Anne Mason

Book Designer Lauren Egan

Managing Editors Sasha Baskett, Angela Tinson

Regional Senior Cartographer Alison Lyall

Assisting Editors Briohny Hooper, Kate Mathews, Anne Mulvaney, Charlotte Orr, Luna Soo, Gabrielle Stefanos, Amanda Williamson

Assisting Cartographers Jeff Cameron, Mick Garrett, Rachel Imeson, Jennifer Johnston

Cover Research Naomi Parker

Thanks to Anita Banh, Ryan Evans, Samantha Forge, Larissa Frost, Lorna Goodyer, Genesys India, Jouve India, Elizabeth Jones, Trent Paton, Dianne Schallmeiner, Gerard Walker, Juan Winata

Index

Map Legend

Sights

- Beach
- Bird Sanctuary
- Buddhist
- Castle/Palace
- Christian
- Confucian
- Hindu
- Islamic
- Jain
- Jewish
- Monument
- Museum/Gallery/Historic Building
- Ruin
- Sento Hot Baths/Onsen
- Shinto
- Sikh
- Taoist
- Winery/Vineyard
- Zoo/Wildlife Sanctuary
- Other Sight

Activities, Courses & Tours

- Bodysurfing
- Diving
- Canoeing/Kayaking
- Course/Tour
- Skiing
- Snorkeling
- Surfing
- Swimming/Pool
- Walking
- Windsurfing
- Other Activity

Sleeping

- Sleeping
- Camping

Eating

- Eating

Drinking & Nightlife

- Drinking & Nightlife
- Cafe

Entertainment

- Entertainment

Shopping

- Shopping

Information

- Bank
- Embassy/Consulate
- Hospital/Medical
- Internet
- Police
- Post Office
- Telephone
- Toilet
- Tourist Information
- Other Information

Geographic

- Beach
- Hut/Shelter
- Lighthouse
- Lookout
- Mountain/Volcano
- Oasis
- Park
- Pass
- Picnic Area
- Waterfall

Population

- Capital (National)
- Capital (State/Province)
- City/Large Town
- Town/Village

Transport

- Airport
- BART station
- Border crossing
- Boston T station
- Bus
- Cable car/Funicular
- Cycling
- Ferry
- Metro/Muni station
- Monorail
- Parking
- Petrol station
- Subway/SkyTrain station
- Taxi
- Train station/Railway
- Tram
- Underground station
- Other Transport

Note: Not all symbols displayed above appear on the maps in this book

Routes

- Tollway
- Freeway
- Primary
- Secondary
- Tertiary
- Lane
- Unsealed road
- Road under construction
- Plaza/Mall
- Steps
- Tunnel
- Pedestrian overpass
- Walking Tour
- Walking Tour detour
- Path/Walking Trail

Boundaries

- International
- State/Province
- Disputed
- Regional/Suburb
- Marine Park
- Cliff
- Wall

Hydrography

- River, Creek
- Intermittent River
- Canal
- Water
- Dry/Salt/Intermittent Lake
- Reef

Areas

- Airport/Runway
- Beach/Desert
- Cemetery (Christian)
- Cemetery (Other)
- Glacier
- Mudflat
- Park/Forest
- Sight (Building)
- Sportsground
- Swamp/Mangrove